C
3.

BATTLE REPORT

BATTLE REPORT

THE ATLANTIC WAR

Prepared from Official Sources by

Commander Walter Karig, USNR

with

Lieutenant Earl Burton, USNR

and

Lieutenant Stephen L. Freeland, USNR

PUBLISHED IN COOPERATION WITH
THE COUNCIL ON BOOKS IN WARTIME

FARRAR & RINEHART, INC. • 1946
New York • Toronto

This book has been manufactured in
accordance with paper conservation
orders of the War Production Board.

The illustrations for this book were selected and edited by Commander E. John Long, USNR, assisted by M. R. Smith, Chief Yeoman, USNR, and C. Earl Cooley, Sp(P) 1/c, USNR. Charts and
maps were drawn especially by George Sixta, Sp(P) 1/c, USNR.
All pictures are Official United States Navy Photographs unless
otherwise designated. Official Combat Art work is indicated by the
name of the artist.

Authors' Foreword

THIS is Volume II of the BATTLE REPORT series. It tells the story of the Navy's war in the Atlantic, the Arctic and the Mediterranean. Volume I[1] told of the first six months of war in the Pacific, and Volume III, now in preparation, will return to that theater of operations to describe the labors of the Navy in reversing the tide of defeat and retreat.

The late Secretary of the Navy, Frank Knox, initiated the series, which is carried on under authorization of his successor, Hon. James V. Forrestal, to provide the public with a narrative history of its Navy in this war. The series is issued through the Council on Books in Wartime, Inc., which designated Farrar & Rinehart as publishers. The books are issued at a price as close to cost as it is practicable to compute, and the authors receive no royalties; the preparation of these books is a part of their assigned duties. What margin of profit may accrue is returned to the public through the Secretary of the Navy by assignment to the Navy's public welfare agencies.

Much of the action herein related was performed without benefit of headlines; dictates of national security required that the War in the Atlantic be fought as a secret war. One illustration will serve to point the reasons: The war in the Atlantic was mainly an antisubmarine war and its principal effort had to be the safe transportation of troops and supplies to the far side of the ocean. Our problems in the Atlantic were Japan's problems in the Pacific. Rigid secrecy had to be maintained lest our accumulating successes in the war against Germany were learned and imitated by Japan in its war against the United States and the United Nations.

No apology is contained in the admission that this volume does not tell the whole story of the naval war against our European enemies. There are still some few details of techniques and equipment which remain secret to all, including the personnel of the Navy. As such, they are not deletions from the story of the Atlantic, but from the whole history of the war. Additionally, the scope of this book is not that of a definitive history but as a

[1] *Battle Report, Pearl Harbor to the Coral Sea,* by Comdr. Walter Karig and Lt. Welbourn Kelley, USNR. Farrar & Rinehart (Dec. 7, 1944), 499 pages, $3.50.

narrative tour of the battle areas of the Atlantic, the Caribbean, the Arctic and the Mediterranean. Instead of a minute chronicle of every action, with the earned citation of those who participated, this volume presents characteristic examples of that naval war on the sea, under it, in the air, and on the beaches and rivers of the Old World. It is not a story of battle alone. The theme ranges from prewar unpreparedness to the achievement of present-day power, comprehending not only the creation and use of the new Navy but the changes in the organization of the naval establishment.

Mainly the men speak for themselves in this book; the greatest task of the authors, who have each performed sea duty in the combat areas of the volume's setting, has been that of editorial selection and arrangement. Professional students of naval warfare will know at once that much technical information is not contained in the volume, but the authors submit that in screening their material they have been scrupulous in keeping the story whole.

Among the many responsible for making that material available to the writers, special acknowledgment is made to Captain Dudley W. Knox, USN (Ret.), in charge of the Office of Naval Records and Library, and to Captain Percy T. Wright, USN, and Lieutenant George Porter, USNR, of that office which contains, among other data priceless to the historian and to the national defense, film recordings in which the history of this war is related by those who made it. Thanks are also accorded to Captain Ellis Reed-Hill, USCG, to Brigadier General Robert L. Denig and Lieutenant Colonel Edward R. Hagenah of the Marine Corps, to Lieutenant Commander Malcolm M. Champlin, USNR, Lieutenant Craig Livingstone, USNR, and Lieutenant John King, USNR, of the Amphibious Training Command, to Lieutenant John Norris, USNR, of the Bureau of Aeronautics, to the Naval Attachés of the British and Netherlands Embassies and the Information Bureaus in Washington of those governments. Lieutenant Welbourn Kelley, USNR, co-author of BATTLE REPORT, Vol. I, gave generously of his time and advice in the preparation of this volume. Tedious research was performed in the files of the Bureau of Personnel by Lieutenant Harvey B. Matthews, USNR, Lieutenant Joseph Barber, USNR, and Lieutenant Hollis F. Peck, USNR, of the office of Commander Robert W. Wood, USNR. In both the present work and in Volume I, Lieutenant (jg) Roger W. Straus, Jr., USNR, served as liaison between authors and publishers, and Miss Julie Eidesheim was

responsible for the editorial styling. The Misses Estelle and Helene Philibert compiled the lists of awards and decorations. In the Office of Public
Information, from its recent Director, Rear Admiral A. S. Merrill, USN,
to Yeoman Elvina J. Sudol (W), USNR, thanks to all hands who from
time to time contributed to the making of this book.

WALTER KARIG
EARL BURTON
STEPHEN L. FREELAND

Table of Contents

Part I

Part II

Part III

Part IV

Part V

Part VI

Part VII

List of Illustrations

Photographs

Photographs appear in five sections. General classification headings are as follows:

Introduction

FROM Kittery to Key West the beaches were sodden with oil, and at night the horizon to seaward often glowed with smoky red where torpedoed merchantmen burned before the eyes of those on shore. Shipping was trapped for days on end in the nation's major Atlantic ports by submarine-laid mines. Every night, shore-hugging vessels were herded into pens, floating artificial harbors, to escape the U-boats. That was in 1942. And yet, in that year, the United States Navy safely convoyed across the Atlantic Ocean the armies and their supplies which drove the Axis forces out of northwestern Africa.

Two years later the enemy submarine was the hunted. Convoys of over 100 ships set forth across the Atlantic every five days. Fast troopships, the luxury liners of prewar days, crossed the ocean freely without escort. The brief supremacy of the U-boats was ended, and in Europe the "sacred soil of Germany" was quaking under the tramp of millions of men, was churned by millions of bombs, transported from the United States under protection of the United States Navy.

The transition from defeat to victory, from a losing defensive to complete conquest, is fundamentally the story of the growth and application of American sea power, in men-of-war, merchant ships and naval aviation.

This is not to minimize the tremendous labors of the Royal Navy, which the Nazis were afraid to challenge by invasion of the United Kingdom when the British Commonwealth stood alone against a triumphant Axis. The British fleet, the Royal Canadian Navy, and the fleet air arms of both, contributed in full share to the reconquest of the Atlantic. The parts played by the remnants of the Netherlands, Norwegian, Polish and Free French navies, employing British bases because their homelands were wholly occupied by the enemy, were vitally important to victory.

The British, by bottling up the German and Italian fleets and destroying those enemy elements which dared the blockade, served the United States fully as well as their homeland. The British Navy pioneered many of the implements and techniques which the United States Navy used to perfection in regaining control of the Atlantic—radar, the escort carrier, for example, and night flying, and many amphibious tactics and vessels.

But the war was won because the United States Navy was able, with such partnership, to escort 17,500 ships across the Atlantic; to put 3,500,000 troops ashore, and the more than 150,000,000 tons of fighting equipment and supplies needed to sustain them. The Navy delivered the bombs with which the RAF and the United States Army Air Forces wiped out German factories and communications. Naval aviation directed the gunfire from the ships of the fleet which covered the invasions of Africa, Italy and France. And the United States Navy was able to do all this because the people of the United States gave, without asking the cost, the men and women, the ships, the labor and the money to create the largest Navy ever to take to sea.

To achieve the victory dictated in Berlin, the enemy submarines had to be conquered. The mission of the U-boats was to blockade the United Kingdom and the Soviet Union, and to prevent troops and supplies from the Western Hemisphere reaching the Afro-European battlefields. The geographical position of the United States made it inevitable that that kind of war would penetrate its waters. Canada was a belligerent. Greenland and Iceland, subject to the crown of Denmark, were early targets of Nazi aggression. Off the eastern and southern coasts of the United States were island possessions of England, the Netherlands and France.

The Monroe Doctrine, fortified by several agreements with the other American republics, imposed a profound responsibility for the political status of European dependencies in the Western Hemishpere, where a lively Nazi propaganda conspired at the destruction of the democratic principle of government as well.

Geographically, politically and strategically, the United States policy of legislated neutrality was endangered from the outset of the war in Europe. With France fallen, the Netherlands overrun, Norway and Denmark captive, and the armies of Hitler and Mussolini standing in triumph on the seacoast of Europe from arctic to equator, the United States was in the fight, willy-nilly.

Shooting had begun in the Atlantic before the Japanese attack on Hawaii. December 8, 1941, date of the declaration of war on the United States by Germany and Italy, marks not a beginning but a date of transition. From a sniping war up to that time the Fascist powers moved into an all-out war, confident that their Oriental partner had so crippled American naval strength at Pearl Harbor that victory was certain.

As in the Pacific, early advantage lay with the enemy's use of the initiative in the Atlantic. As in the Pacific, the record of the first months of the Atlantic war is dark and discouraging, not even relieved by such highlights of satisfaction as Admiral Halsey's early raids with USS ENTERPRISE against the perimeter of Japanese conquest. Not until the United States had completed costly repairs to an inadequate national defense structure was control of the Atlantic regained by the great maritime powers.

Nor were these repairs simply tasks of refurbishing old ships, modernizing old equipment and building new fighting craft. Entirely new methods for defeating the enemy, then master of the ocean, had to be invented, and, once invented, to be produced and manned in the quantities, the overwhelming quantities, needed to make the inventions work.

The greatest of these inventions, of course, was radar (radio detection and ranging) in the development of which, it is fair to say, the Navy pioneered. As long ago as 1922, scientists of the Naval Research Laboratory, Dr. A. Hoyt Taylor and Leo C. Young, had discovered that objects passing through it distorted a directed radio wave. Upon this basis Army, Navy and civilian researchers elaborated, refined and experimented in the '30s. In 1935, Rear Admiral Harold G. Bowen, USN, then Chief of the Bureau of Engineering, at his own insistence secured $100,000 from the Naval Appropriations Committee of the House of Representatives specifically for radar research—the first appropriation of its kind.

Thereafter, the development of radar—it was given its name by a naval officer, Commander S. M. Tucker, USN—went forward at an accelerated pace as scientists of the armed services and civilians worked under the stimulus of an approaching war in Europe.

When that war came, the final element in the co-operative product, which radar had been from the first, was added. The British, who had also brought radio detection to a fine point, added their knowledge to ours. The result, in 1940, was a completely successful scientific alliance of American and British industry and ingenuity. It was an omen of future successful partnership in all the complicated enterprises of war, up to and including the atomic bomb, to the development of which the Navy contributed the services of such experts as Captain Parsons, USN, and other ordnance experts.

By 1941, when the Anglo-American partnership became unlimited with our entry into the war against the Axis, we had, in radar, a potentially deadly weapon against any attacking force the enemy might send against us. In the Atlantic, this attacking force was the U-boat, plus a few surface raiders. Early detection, possible through radar, could thwart them. Early detection, followed by aggressive action, could destroy them. And, ultimately, it did.

Meanwhile, however, there was the problem of building enough ships, equipping them and training the men who were to serve aboard them in the efficient use of not only radar, but all the other modern equipage of war. As if this problem were not enough in itself, Navy leadership had to look ahead to the time when actual freedom of the seas was ours again, to the time when that freedom could be used to hit the enemy at home. This meant not only the invention and construction of vast numbers of types of amphibious craft, and training their crews, but also perfecting the ways of using them by exhaustive tests under all conditions of battle and weather. Great as were these problems of material and methods for defense and attack, their solution would still have left the nation with only the inanimate part of a Navy. The hundreds of thousands of officers and men who would transform ships, planes, devices and plans into fighting units had to be recruited and trained. And all this we had to do while simultaneously meeting every necessity of ships, munitions and the standard implements of war not only for our own expanding forces but to supplement the war-shattered industry of the United Kingdom and the Soviet Union.

Contributing most to the U-boat's defeat was the combination of escort carriers (CVE), destroyers (DD), and destroyer escorts (DE), all radar-equipped. There were other factors—military, naval, aeronautical, even political and geographic—without which success would not have been readily achieved. They will be described. But the U-boats' obituary can be succinctly written in the abbreviations: CVE—DD—DE—radar.

Next to, and depending upon, the defeat of the submarines was the task of landing and supplying armies on the opposite coast of the Atlantic. Once ashore on the European continent, the Army itself would become an antisubmarine force, by capturing or sealing off the ports where once the U-boats were built, nourished and repaired. A new team, the Amphibious Force, to which Army, Navy, Marines and Coast Guard contributed men and skills, was formed to land on enemy shores. That required the creation, from inventor's dream to ultimate combat, of ships and craft the like of which had never traversed water.

And, backing up the amphibious and triphibious teams, were of course all the familiar elements of naval force—the big battleships, the swift hard-hitting cruisers, the fast giant carriers, minelayers, net-tenders, tugs, ponderous flying boats and lumbering armed merchantmen, all supported by an intricate shore establishment stemming from the Navy Department in Washington whose roots were civilian United States.

How victory in the Atlantic was won is a story that cannot be chronologically told. Too much had to be done at once, in two hemispheres, on both sides of the equator, to provide the narrative with plot and continuity. No one, not even the most farsighted of professional fighting men, anticipated the magnitude of labor and sacrifice the United States was shortly to shoulder when Adolf Hitler screamed the order that sent his fleet and his legions against Poland at five o'clock in the morning of September 1, 1939.

PART ONE

Neutrality Patrol — Defending the Hemisphere

Chapter One

TWO destroyers lay moored, bow and stern, to buoys in the harbor of Villefranche-sur-Mer. Nearby rode a light cruiser.

The Stars and Stripes slatted against the vividly blue Mediterranean sky in the brisk, offshore breeze. Across the water the sweet shrill of the bosun's pipe sang out clearly, as the crews mustered on station.

"Nothing to report" the logs of the American squadron read after muster and inspection. There was no warrant to include the tenseness of all hands, to record that the conversation in fo'c'sle and wardroom was not of home but of war.

It was the third day of September, 1939.

The destroyers were USS BADGER and JACOB JONES. The cruiser was USS TRENTON, the flagship of Rear Admiral Henry E. Lackey, USN.[1] Together the ships comprised Squadron 40-T, or "Forty-tare" in Navy parlance.

At 6 o'clock that morning the United Kingdom and France had declared war on Germany.

Two days before, the Nazis had invaded Poland, bombed Warsaw, blockaded and bombarded Gdynia. The French and British governments sent Hitler an ultimatum. The Fuehrer responded with a proclamation to the world that Germany had been wantonly attacked. Mr. John P. Hurley, United States Consul at Marseilles, had come aboard the TRENTON late that afternoon and was still conferring with Rear Admiral Lackey and Captain J. B. Barry, USN, skipper of the cruiser.

Forty-tare had reached Villefranche the week before after visits to Rotterdam, Le Havre and Saint-Nazaire. At every port the talk had been of war, or of its avoidance. Now war had come. Those green shores belonged to a country at war. The men aboard any one of the ships felt comfort, somehow, in looking across to the flags of the United States on

[1] All ranks given in this book are those held at the time of the events described.

3

the others. Since yesterday an ensign had been hoisted at the fore in addition to the colors aft.

At 11:30, September 3, 1939, the official word was passed from Washington: "ENGLAND and FRANCE are at WAR with GERMANY"
was the way it was inscribed in the TRENTON's log.

On September 6, Rear Admiral C. E. Courtney, USN, took command
of the squadron. That same day, in Washington, the President of the
United States ordered a patrol "extending several hundred miles to sea"
to be maintained of the country's Atlantic coast by destroyers, Coast
Guard vessels and aircraft; it was directed further that the 110 destroyers
laid up since the last war be rehabilitated.

Forty-tare, blacked out by night now, and holding antiaircraft drills,
weighed anchor and passed through the Strait of Gibraltar on September
20 to pause awhile at Lisbon. It had been the United States naval unit
nearest the war at its fiery birth, although not close enough to see it. But,
on the very day of war, other Americans had been brought into forcible
and fatal contact with the war when the British liner ATHENIA was
torpedoed without warning off the Scottish coast. A United States Maritime Commission cargo ship, CITY OF FLINT, rescued more than two
hundred survivors.

Master of that freighter (itself overcrowded with twenty-nine Americans fleeing Europe and happy for any accommodations) was Joseph
Aloysius Gainard, holder of an inactive lieutenant commander's commission in the United States Naval Reserve. As an ensign, USNR, Gainard
had been torpedoed himself aboard the naval transport PRESIDENT
LINCOLN in 1918.

Gainard brought his shipload of survivors to the United States, took
on a general cargo for Liverpool and Glasgow, and sailed on October 3
into adventure that was to bring him the Navy Cross, and his countrymen
closer to the realities of the war.

For, while the United States was not to declare war on the Axis until
December 8, 1941, after hostilities had been opened by the enemy, the
inevitability of conflict was plain to anyone who knew the nature of war
and its symptoms. Even if the United States could remain at peace, it was
clear that that position could be maintained only by armed resistance to
war's encroachment.

So the government's precautions employed two broad policies: the
first was to attempt to keep belligerents out of American waters, and

Americans out of belligerent areas by Act of Congress; the other and more realistic policy was to prepare adequate armed resistance against any belligerent intrusion. Preparations for both had been attempted fully two years before the Germans crossed Poland's frontiers. Neutrality by legislation was implemented by Congressional acceptance of President Franklin D. Roosevelt's recommendation in January, 1938, for rearmament and an increase in naval strength above the replacements permitted by the Vinson-Trammel Act of 1934.

On September 6, 1938, Chief of Naval Operations Admiral William D. Leahy had announced the formation of the Atlantic Squadron. The United States had inherent rights to the sea lanes; it had merchantmen plying those lanes; it had persons and properties abroad. To protect our rights, our ships, our citizens and property men-o'-war were needed, hence the Atlantic Squadron. Rear Admiral Ford A. Todd, USN, was placed in command of the seven cruisers and seven destroyers which comprised the force.

A few weeks later the Munich Conference, instead of buying "peace in our time" brought war even closer. Quietly, the Atlantic Squadron was strengthened. By 1939 it encompassed Battleship Division 5: USS NEW YORK, ARKANSAS, TEXAS and WYOMING; Cruiser Division 7 with the SAN FRANCISCO as flagship and the QUINCY, TUSCALOOSA and VINCENNES; Cruiser Division 8 with the PHILADELPHIA as flagship and the BROOKLYN, SAVANNAH and NASHVILLE. Operating with Cruiser Divisions 7 and 8 was the HONOLULU, flagship of Cruiser Battle Force.

Destroyer strength in the Atlantic Squadron consisted of Destroyer Divisions 10, 21, 25, 30, 31 and 32. On July 1, 1939, a carrier, USS RANGER, joined the squadron, and in addition the special squadron 40-T was formed for patrol duty in European waters.

Between that time and the attack on Pearl Harbor the Atlantic was to become an area of insidious, grueling struggle where an undeclared war was being fought by Nazi Germany for domination of the Western seas.

Within that interval, too, both the legal and military barriers for the protection of the United States were to be modified and expanded to meet the pressure of overt events. On September 8, 1939, the President issued a proclamation of limited emergency which declared ". . . *that a national emergency exists in connection with and to the extent necessary for proper observance, safeguarding and enforcing of the neutrality of the United States, and the strengthening of our national defense within the limits of peacetime authorization."* It continued with " . . . *the Navy and the Marine Corps will be charged with additional and important duties in connection with such national emergency requiring increases in their present enlisted strength within the limits of these authorizations."*

This order authorized an increase in enlisted strength from the peacetime limit of 131,485 to 145,000 men for the Navy, and brought the Marine Corps up to 25,000 men.

The limited national emergency, which increased naval personnel, also demanded the use of every available naval ship. On September 14, 1939, after almost two years of work, the USS MUSTIN, 60th destroyer to be built since 1934, was placed in active service.

On the same day MUSTIN was commissioned, the Navy Department announced that forty of the 110 decommissioned destroyers were to be recommissioned for duty on the neutrality patrol.

Eight of these forty, AARON WARD, BUCHANAN, WICKES, HALE, TWIGGS, YARNALL, CROWNINSHIELD, and PHILIP, were later to be included in the fifty over-age destroyer deal with Great Britain for Atlantic base leases.

Another, the REUBEN JAMES, was to be the first American warship sunk by enemy action on October 31, 1941, and the BERNADOU and COLE were to earn Presidential Unit Citations as converted craft of the amphibious fleet that invaded North Africa on November 8, 1942.

With these recommissioned destroyers, the Atlantic Squadron was more nearly prepared to enforce the neutrality of the United States. But neutrality embraced considerably more than simply fending belligerents from the shores of the nation's seaboard. The United States was historically committed to hemispheric defense by the Monroe Doctrine. The collaboration of its sister American republics was essential in drawing a line of demarcation, within which no belligerent raider or submarine might operate. On October 2, 1939, a Congress of American Republics met in Panama to consider the mutuality of problems and interests posed by the war. It proclaimed a neutral zone some 300 miles in depth surrounding the Americas, with the exception of Canada. The resolution forbade belligerent raiders and submarines to operate within this zone; a belligerent act within the area might be considered by American republics sufficient to incur war.

Since the United States Navy was the only armed force equal to maintaining a patrol in this vast area, it was obvious on whom must fall the responsibility for effectively enforcing the proclamation.

Navy Day that year, October 26, brought a terse message from the White House to the Secretary of the Navy, Charles Edison.

> My dear Mr. Secretary,
> . . . At one of the most tragic periods in human history, the United States is blessed in that we are at peace with all the world. That peace we shall strive to maintain by all honorable and just means. With a world in arms, this country is compelled as never before to maintain an adequate and positive defense. The most promising way to preserve our peace lies in the ability to defend our sea frontiers.

"Positive defense," mentioned in the President's Navy Day note to Secretary Edison, was further enhanced on November 4 when the Neutrality Act of 1939 became law, replacing the Arms Embargo Act. This was frankly a device to keep the United States out of war by keeping the aspects of war distant and by minimizing provocation or excuse for attack.

Arming of merchant vessels was prohibited, loans to belligerents were outlawed. A "cash and carry" policy was outlined under which belligerents were required to transport their own materials purchased in the United States and pay for them before being granted clearance. American ships and citizens were prohibited from entering combat zones.

Under the Neutrality Act, the President was empowered to define combat zones into which American ships and aircraft could not go. Such a forbidden zone was immediately proclaimed, fencing off the North Sea, the British Isles, the Bay of Biscay, and the adjacent portion of the Atlantic to a line about 350 miles west of Ireland. In addition, the act authorized the President to restrict use of United States ports and territorial waters by foreign submarines and merchant vessels.

All unaware, Captain Joseph Aloysius Gainard contributed to that experiment in averting war by passive resistance. The CITY OF FLINT was in the headlines again.

Gainard had discharged his passenger list of American refugees and ATHENIA survivors, and sailed for the United Kingdom on October 3, 1939. Six days and 1,250 miles out of New York, the merchantman was overtaken by the German "pocket battleship" DEUTSCHLAND. Despite Gainard's protests, a prize crew was put aboard, and the master found himself a prisoner on his own ship. The Stars and Stripes came down, and up went the Swastika.

Then began one of the most fantastic voyages ever to be successfully completed. The freighter was taken into Tromsö Harbor, Norway, on October 21. The Norwegian government refused to permit the Germans to remain with their prize. Three days later the cables hummed. The CITY OF FLINT was in Murmansk, with the prize crew claiming the ancient privilege of "havarie," or respite from damage at sea. Soviet inspectors were sent to the ship and permission was granted the Germans to remain long enough to effect emergency repairs, but the Americans aboard could not be regarded as prisoners. Then the waif vessel and its unhappy and antagonistic crew was thrust out in the open seas again, with the British Home Fleet hot on the trail. Dodging along the Norwegian coast, paced by Royal Navy units, the Nazi kidnapers put into Haugesund. Again the Norwegian authorities refused to grant anchorage, but the Nazis had had enough of trying to bring home their prize through the blockade. They dropped anchor, regardless. Promptly the Norwegians put the German prize crew under arrest and internment, and the FLINT was ceremoniously returned to her master. Captain Gainard put his cargo ashore at Bergen and, with the American flag flying proudly once more, brought his vessel back to her home port in ample time for Thanksgiving.

(For "distinguished service in the line of his profession—His skill, fine judgment and devotion to duty . . . of the highest order and in accordance with the best traditions of the Naval service," Joseph A. Gainard was awarded the Navy Cross, the first to be conferred in this war. He was called back to active duty, promoted to commander and ultimately captain, USNR, and died while commanding a naval transport on December 23, 1943. A destroyer has been named for him.)

But the saga of the CITY OF FLINT convinced Congress, probably a majority of the country concurring, that the American flag must not venture into areas where it was in danger of being torn down. Emboldened, the Nazis were soon to be following in pursuit of that flag in waters reserved to it.

By January, 1940, America's role in a warring world was still not clear, but even for barely adequate defense more ships and bases were needed.

The Tenth Naval District, which included all the Caribbean territories of the United States, was established with headquarters in San Juan, Puerto Rico, and Rear Admiral Raymond A. Spruance, USN, placed in command—COMTEN.

Congress was again asked for more ships, and on June 14, 1940, the day after USS NORTH CAROLINA was launched in the New York Navy Yard, the President signed a bill authorizing an 11 per cent expansion in combatant ship strength.

Germany invaded Denmark and Norway on April 9, 1940. On May 10, the Luftwaffe bombed airfields in the Low Countries and the invasion of the Netherlands began. The mocked "sitzkrieg" was over. The wind had shifted, driving the conflagration westward.

On May 21, the Acting Secretary of the Navy, Lewis Compton, sent a message to all naval establishments ordering them to expedite the naval shipbuilding program and all other work relating to national defense. Orders were given to increase working forces to a two-shift basis and to add at least 15,000 civilian employees to shipyards within three months.

One week later the United States was shocked by the sudden capitulation of King Leopold and the Belgian Army, and elated by the dramatic rescue of the British Army from the bomb-shaken beach of Dunkerque in a hastily mustered fleet of tugs, yachts, fishing smacks and launches.

On the day of the evacuation, May 28, 1940, three more United States naval vessels had been ordered to European waters. They were the heavy cruiser USS VINCENNES and the destroyers TRUXTUN and SIMPSON. It was made quite clear that these ships were not to convoy merchant vessels, but were proceeding to Lisbon, Portugal, for the purpose of protecting American interests. (Later, the cruiser VINCENNES was to go down fighting a Jap fleet one dark night off Savo Bay, and her escort the destroyer TRUXTUN was destined for a tragic end on the morning of February 18, 1942, when she was swept aground in a winter storm off the St. Lawrence Harbor, Newfoundland.)

But this was to be a quick trip to Lisbon and back for the VINCENNES, which was under special orders. She was the cruiser that brought back the cargo of gold purchased by this country from France, a purchase that gave the desperate French government credit in the United States for munitions never to be delivered. Three weeks later, France was beaten.

The USS WASHINGTON, a 35,000-ton battleship, was launched in the Philadelphia Navy Yard on June 1, 1940, followed twelve days later by the launching in New York of the USS NORTH CAROLINA. They were the first battleships built since the WEST VIRGINIA, which left the ways in Newport News, Virginia, on November 19, 1921. A capitulation of our naval strength at the time the WASHINGTON was launched showed that 130 naval vessels, both auxiliary and combatant, had been placed in com-

mission since 1933. Sixty-six additional ships were on the building ways
and the naval appropriation bill for the next fiscal year provided for
24 additional craft.

In the light of former treaty limitations the Navy was growing, but
even the figure of 220 new ships, 90 of which were not yet built, was
lamentably inadequate for the job already on hand. Ships have to be
rotated in patrol duty, brought in for overhaul and provided with relief.
No navy's fleet on paper is ever its full strength at sea. In July USS OMAHA,
BARRY and GOFF, for example, relieved Squadron Forty-Tare, now the
TRENTON, DICKERSON, and HERBERT, which had been operating out of
Lisbon since September 21, 1939.

Italy entered the war on June 19, 1940. Three days later France
capitulated. The world waited for the invasion of England.

On June 19, too, President Franklin D. Roosevelt signed what was
popularly called the Two-Ocean Navy Bill. This act authorized the greatest expansion in our naval history—1,325,000 tons of combatant ships.
Congress did not vote the funds until September 9, but the Navy was
getting strength, on paper at least, commensurate with its responsibility.

In midyear, the Navy had a new chief. Frank Knox, publisher of
the Chicago *Daily News* and Republican vice-presidential candidate in
1936, accepted appointment as secretary to succeed Charles Edison.
Knox's accession, with that of Henry L. Stimson as secretary of war,
showed to the world the unity of the United States in the face of mounting foreign menace. Edison, under whose administration the groundwork
(literally groundwork) for the expanded Navy had been laid, wished to
seek the governorship of New Jersey, and succeeded at the next election.

The Navy at this time began to buy ships for conversion. Among them
were two 15,000-ton Grace liners bought for $1,300,000 apiece—the
SANTA BARBARA and the SANTA MARIA. Renamed the MCCAWLEY and the
BARNETT, these former luxury liners that had given bon voyage to so
many vacationers were to be converted to transports. In the yet uncon-
ceived amphibious service they were to land troops on far shores where
no vacations awaited them—and the MCCAWLEY'S last port of call was
the coral bottom of Blanche Channel between New Georgia and Rendova.

Money for the Two-Ocean Navy was provided in the Second Sup-
plemental National Defense Appropriation Act, signed by the President
on September 9. This authorized the Navy to award contracts and allo-
cate the building of 200 combat naval vessels. So urgent was the need

for these ships, and so well laid were the plans for procuring them, that within two hours after the President signed the act, Acting Secretary of the Navy Lewis Compton had allocated to Navy Yards and signed contracts for the building of those 200 ships, as well as 2,400 new planes.[1]

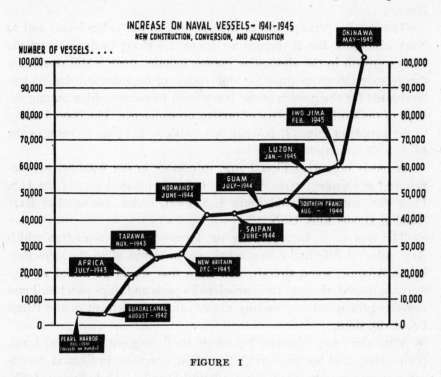

FIGURE I

Together with previous Congressional defense appropriations, the Navy was now within realization of its authorized goal of 689 fighting ships and 15,000 aircraft.

[1] The status of the shipbuilding program at the time the 200 contracts were awarded was:

Type	Built	Building	Total
Battleships	15	17	32
Carriers	6	12	18
Cruisers	37	48	85
Destroyers	247*	171	418*
Submarines	103	82	185
	408*	330	738*

* Includes the 50 over-age destroyers later traded to Great Britain and 46 ex-destroyers converted into other types.

Expansion was not a simple matter of adding more ships and men to the established naval pattern. For efficient functional purposes alone, new dispositions had to be made of the nation's first line of defense, and so began a series of alterations in the organization of the Navy.

The details, perhaps, are of interest only to the professionals and to Navy historians. But if there is no drama, no glory, in the story of the Navy's growth in the all-too-few prewar months, there is still reason for the average citizen to trace the dull course of organization that had to be charted for the growth of the Navy from its sorry position among the fleets of the world to its place of present pre-eminence. The Navy belongs to the people at large. It is what they make it, in ships, in men, in the efficient co-ordination of those two.

A newly organized Fleet Force, to operate in the Atlantic, was announced in October, 1940. This was to be an integral part of the U.S. Fleet, designated as Patrol Force U.S. Fleet, under command of Rear Admiral Hayne Ellis, USN.

The new force, incorporating the former Atlantic Squadron which Rear Admiral Ellis had commanded, was to consist of all the ships then in the Atlantic, some aircraft, new ships that would be added as they were completed, recently recommissioned vessels and ships purchased and converted for naval use, making the eventual complement of the Patrol Force 125 ships.

With this reorganization, Squadron 40-T, assigned to neutral European waters, and Special Service Squadron, operating in Central American waters, were abolished. Rear Admiral David McD. LeBreton, USN, who had been commanding Squadron 40-T, was given command of Battleship Division 5, and Rear Admiral Henry K. Hewitt, USN, left the command of Special Service Squadron to take over the command of Cruiser Division 8.

Rear Admiral Arthur B. Cook, USN, commanding what was formerly Aircraft Scouting Force, was given the command of the newly formed Aircraft Patrol Force U.S. Fleet, with additional duty as Commander Carrier Division 3; and Captain Richard S. Edwards was detached from duty as commanding officer of USS COLORADO and assigned duty commanding Submarines Patrol Force, U.S. Fleet.

The Navy in the Atlantic was getting organized for war, although even at this time "war" meant only the policing of our neutral zones. The

United States at large seemed optimistic that such would be the limit of the fleet's operations.

The former Grace liners, USS MC CAWLEY and BARNETT, converted into transports, with 2,900 officers and men of the First Marine Brigade commanded by Brigadier General Holland M. Smith, sailed on October 12 for Guantanamo, Cuba. Eight destroyers and six patrol planes of Patrol Force went along. Together, ships and planes and men were to practice "amphibious" landings. Use of the word "amphibious" is a deliberate anachronism. That welding of land, sea and air forces which the Marines had pioneered was yet without definition or title.

But Patrol Force, United States Fleet, as such, was to be short-lived. On February 1, 1941, the organization of the United States Fleet was changed.

Patrol Force, United States Fleet, now became the Atlantic Fleet, and Rear Admiral Ernest J. King, USN, who had succeeded Rear Admiral Ellis as Patrol Force Commander in December, was promoted to full Admiral and Commander in Chief of that Fleet. Rear Admiral Husband E. Kimmel, USN, was likewise raised to four-star rank and made Commander in Chief United States Fleet (CINCUS) as well as Commander in Chief Pacific Fleet. Admiral Thomas C. Hart, USN, continued as CinC Asiatic Fleet. CINCUS, later changed to COMINCH because of the unhappy connotation of the first abbreviation, was charged with the additional duty of originating standard methods of operation and training for the seagoing forces of the Navy, and placed in charge of any joint operations of the fleets, responsible to the Chief of Naval Operations. (In March, 1942, Admiral King—who succeeded Admiral Kimmel as COMINCH upon the latter's removal after the Pearl Harbor attack December 7, 1941—also became Chief of Naval Operations.)

The organization of the United States Fleet was now a framework into which new ships and new officers and men could grow and be fitted. It still lacked ships and men, but both were being added as fast as shipyards and training centers could turn them out, and the Navy could assign them.

Now it is necessary to go back five months and to follow another thread in the fabric of the national defense. So much happened at once, as the nation labored mightily to repair its twenty-year neglect, that it is impossible to establish a chronology that does not make confusion out of what was essentially an orderly process.

.The United States could train defenders from its huge reservoirs of manpower. It could build ships in its great yards, from raw materials out of its inexhaustible resources. But the United States could not change geography. If the purpose of all the defense preparations was to keep a real or potential enemy as remote from American shores as could be managed, then the islands east of those shores had to be utilized. If not converted to the continental and hemispheric defense, the islands were not a neutral factor but a potential menace, vulnerable to unfriendly seizure, each a utility in any scheme of attack on this country.

Fortunately the islands, while not independent members of the American family of nations, were (with the exception of French Martinique and Guadeloupe) under the friendliest of sovereignty. If the geography of North America could not be changed, it could be integrated for the hemisphere's safety. The process was to revive that ancient and forgotten art of America's youth, the "swap," and a piece of horse trading on a scale beyond the first Yankee's imagination was consequently negotiated.

Chapter Two

THE planned exchange of fifty over-age American destroyers to Great Britain for rent-free naval and air base leasehold in the Atlantic was announced by Acting Secretary of the Navy James Forrestal on September 3, 1940.

President Roosevelt said that it was the most important event in the defense of the United States since Thomas Jefferson's Louisiana Purchase.

Chief of Naval Operations Admiral Harold R. Stark had certified that the exchange of fifty over-age destroyers for offshore Atlantic bases would strengthen the total defense of the United States, and that by this standard these destroyers were not essential to our defense. We needed the destroyers; we needed the bases more.

Acquisition of the base sites under 99-year lease linked a protective net around the northern hemisphere of the utmost strategical importance in our defense plans.

The exchange was equally important to Great Britain and her Royal Navy.

What was not known to the British or American public at that time—and presumed not to be known in Germany—was that in rescuing the British Army at Dunkerque the Royal Navy had lost 85 destroyers. Ten were sunk outright and 75 were so severely damaged that they had to be written off the books for the long time needed for suitable repair. British naval strength was already stretched thin in vital escort and convoy duty, with the coast of Europe from Norway's tip to the southern end of France in German hands.

So, on the evening of the second day following the announced exchange, the USS AARON WARD eased away from her pier in Boston harbor and headed into the Atlantic. Following in column came USS HALE and ABEL P. UPSHUR. Three of the fifty destroyers were off to Canada and World War II. Aboard each was a crew of sixty, officers and men, about half the normal complement.

Behind, in the harbor, were five more destroyers poised and waiting to leave. Men were painting the hulls, blotting out the old names, loading oil for an Atlantic crossing, racking full stores of torpedoes and stocking up on shells.

Then the five left, WOOD, WELLES, CROWNINSHIELD, BUCHANAN, and HERNDON. They still flew the United States flag, but not the commission pennants that mark a ship in active United States service.

The eight destroyers, looking slightly top-heavy with their flat decks and four tall funnels, steamed up the Harbor of Halifax, Nova Scotia. They dropped anchor long enough for British crews to come aboard, then set their course for sea again.

This was the first training run, the introduction of the British sailors to the American ships. These ships were designed during the first World War. They were small, 314 feet and 1,190 tons, with a draft of nine and a quarter feet and a normal complement of 122. They were lightly armed with four 4-inch guns, one 3-inch antiaircraft gun, and twelve 21-inch torpedo tubes. They had a top speed of 35 knots.

On September 9 the British were sufficiently familiar with the destroyers to take over. The exchange ceremonies were simple. Rear Admiral Ferdinand L. Reichmuth, representing the United States Navy, Rear Admiral Stewart Bonham-Carter of the Royal Navy, and Rear Admiral Percy W. Nelles, Royal Canadian Navy, were present. An American bugler sounded colors for the last time. The American ensign came down and the American crews came ashore. British sailors took their stations and the British ensign with the captains' pennants were hoisted, indicating that these vessels were now in formal commission as part of the Royal Navy.

The Atlantic crossing was an ordeal. British crews had had only a short shakedown on the destroyers before they took over. Many things about the ships were new and different, and it would be long before that familiarity was established which would enable the British ratings really to call the ships their own. The men, for one thing, were used to sleeping in hammocks instead of bunks. A well-slung hammock can take a terrific ship roll without disturbing the occupant. Not so a bunk. The ships ran into a full Atlantic gale on the way over and the tiny, 30-foot beam destroyers began a 40-degree roll. The men had difficulty staying in their bunks. Even in calm weather the hammock addicts complained about sleeping on a mattress.

"It's like lying on a bloody sack of jelly," one man said.

On September 27 the ships reached Belfast after a test of both men and machinery. The complicated American electrical appliances, the ship's telephone system, and all the devices new to the British were mastered by trial and error which blew fuses and heated refrigerators. Even the showers, which took a delicate touch to get a comfortable mixture of scalding steam and ice water, were a source of temper loss. But what the crews hadn't learned about the American ships on their first Atlantic crossing they were to have ample time to learn in the future. The ships were now to start convoy and coastal patrol with scarcely a break for eighteen continuous months.

The last of the fifty ships was delivered to the Royal Navy within four months.

To the English, who have something of a flair for naming ships, one of the immediate problems that came to mind in the destroyer exchange was that of rechristening them. American destroyers are named for men of the United States Navy who have died in the service. Someone in the Admiralty suggested giving the fifty names of towns common to both England and the United States.[1]

With few exceptions the fifty old destroyers settled down to the undramatic, dogged duty of guarding the convoys across the North Atlantic and over the top of the world to Russia.

In July, 1943, the British Admiralty announced that HMS WELLS had traveled more than a quarter of a million convoy miles without once breaking down. Another, HMS LINCOLN, was turned over to the Nor-

---

[1] British names in parentheses; C.M.—Canadian manned.
D.D. 70 CONWAY (LEWES); 72 CONNER (LEEDS); 73 STOCKTON (LUDLOW); 75 WICKES (MONTGOMERY); 76 PHILIP (LANCASTER); 78 EVANS (MANSFIELD); 81 SIGOURNEY (NEWPORT); 88 ROBINSON (NEWMARKET); 89 RINGGOLD (NEWARK); 93 FAIRFAX (RICHMOND); 108 WILLIAMS (ST. CLAIR C.M.); 127 TWIGGS (LEAMINGTON); 131 BUCHANAN (CAMPBELTOWN); 132 AARON WARD (CASTLETON); 133 HALE (CALDWELL); 134 CROWNINSHIELD (CHELSEA); 135 TILLMAN (WELLS); 140 CLAXTON (SALISBURY); 143 YARNALL (LINCOLN); 162 THATCHER (NIAGARA C.M.); 167 COWELL (BRIGHTON); 168 MADDOX (GEORGETOWN); 169 FOOTE (ROXBOROUGH); 170 KALK (HAMILTON); 175 MACKENSIE (ANNAPOLIS C.M.); 181 HOPEWELL (BATH); 182 THOMAS (ST. ALBANS); 183 HARADEN (COLUMBIA C.M.); 184 ABBOT (CHARLESTON); 185 DORAN (ST. MARYS); 190 SATTERLEE (BELMONT); 191 MASON (BROADWATER); 193 A. P. UPSHUR (CLARE); 194 HUNT (BROADWAY); 195 W. C. WOOD (CHESTERFIELD); 197 BRANCH (BEVERLEY); 198 HERNDON (CHURCHILL); 252 MCCOOK (ST. CROIX); 253 MCCALLA (STANLEY); 254 RODGERS (SHERWOOD); 256 BANCROFT (ST. FRANCIS C.M.); 257 WELLES (CAMERON); 258 AULICK (BURNHAM); 263 LAUB (BURWELL); 264 MCLANAHAN (BRADFORD); 265 EDWARDS (BUXTON); 268 SHUBRICK (RIPLEY); 269 BAILEY (READING); 273 SWASEY (ROCKINGHAM); 274 MEADE (RAMSEY).

wegian government by the Royal Navy as a result of a military agreement
between the British and the Norwegians. His Norwegian Majesty's ship
LINCOLN set a record of 40,000 sea miles traveled in 190 continuous days.
The LINCOLN's commander was a 30-year-old Norwegian, who had been
captured and held as a prisoner of war when the Germans invaded
Norway. He escaped across the Swedish border, made his way to England
and re-entered the war in command of the old American destroyer.

Another of the fifty destroyers later transferred by the British to the
Norwegian Navy was USS THOMAS, renamed HMS ST. ALBANS. In one
year, flying the flag of the Royal Norwegian Navy, the ST. ALBANS logged
a 90,000-mile odyssey which included carrying Commando troops to
Norway, running battles with Nazi bombers in the icy Murmansk convoy
run, and her fair share of submarine and weather trouble in the North
Atlantic convoy lanes. She was commanded by a Norwegian with a crew
of Canadians, Danes, Britons and Norwegians. To the Norwegians in the
crew she was home, the only home they had known since their escape
from Norway. On one Murmansk convoy run she lived through a five-
day bombing attack by German planes and shot down one. Safe in Murmansk harbor; while the cargo ships were unloading, five torpedoes suddenly passed less than 20 feet from her bow and exploded in the side of a
tanker lying nearby.

With the ST. ALBANS on one "Beef Run" to Iceland was HMS ST.
MARYS. For thirty-six hours the ST. MARYS steamed head-on into a North
Atlantic howler, only to find herself, when the gale subsided, 30 miles
astern of her former position.

Another time, the ST. MARYS was shepherding a convoy through a
black winter night when a submarine contact warning sounded. During
the attack on the underwater enemy, a merchant ship collided with the
destroyer.

The ST. MARYS' thin bows gave way to the heavier merchant ship.
Water poured in the jagged hole of twisted bow, but the bulkhead held.
Fuel oil was pumped from the forward tank to an empty tank aft, lifting
the damaged bow. In this condition the destroyer again took up the
attack, laid a fatal pattern of depth charges around the lingering submarine and later caught up with the convoy. They were rugged ships,
those ancients, and their alien crews learned to love them.

Dubious victor in the "Battle" of LaSola Island was HMS CHURCHILL,
named not for the Prime Minister but for a Wessex village and Churchill

Downs, Kentucky. The urge for battle had its inspiration in a visit the Hon. Winston Churchill paid to his destroyer-nonnamesake, following the Atlantic conference with President Roosevelt aboard the cruiser AUGUSTA in August, 1941. When the Prime Minister took his leave of HMS CHURCHILL he promised another visit as soon as he had been notified that the ship had sunk a U-boat.

Mindful of this, one dark night off the coast of Venezuela, a lookout shouted warning of a conning tower just visible in the night light. The crews jumped to station. Depth charges forked out and fell, pushing up great geysers of water. The forward guns blazed at the conning tower.

A clipped order was given and CHURCHILL turned for a run in, a ram to kill. Vision being what it was, the destroyer missed by about six yards. A rebuff for poor piloting was strangled in its utterance as the ship passed the object and the crew had a rail-eye view of the "submarine." It was an islet reef, about 10 feet high and some 200 feet long!

But they were not all comic battles that the CHURCHILL fought. During one of her troop convoy escort trips she was suddenly diverted and ordered to join a certain patrol. Thus she found herself in the company that encircled the doomed German battleship BISMARCK.

Two of the destroyers were to be rechristened a third time after the British crews took over. The first was HMS WELLS, once USS TILLMAN. This ship soon became popularly and better known as HMS TOWER OF BABEL because the officers aboard were more fluent in Dutch, French, Italian, Spanish, Swedish and Danish than in English. Later she took aboard fourteen Free French sailors, which clinched the view of the crew that the ship was a floating island of the United Nations.

The other destroyer was USS RODGERS, which had officially become HMS SHERWOOD. This ship probably kept an even closer link with America than did its sister destroyers. In the wardroom hung two pictures of an American family that was acting as "godparents" for the ship and crew, supplying stores that varied from cigarettes and candy to leather jackets and razors.

On Christmas Day, 1942, the ship's radio was tuned in on shore stations. Clear and inviting came announcers' voices, describing Christmas dinners of turkey and mince pie, while the mess tables of HMS SHERWOOD faced a lean and meager diet of sea biscuit and cold tinned corned beef. That morning heavy seas had broached the galley fuel tanks. But before the storm put the galley out of commission, the cook had baked a tremendous cake. As the last of the crackers and wisps of brick-red corned beef disappeared, the cook came in with the cake. He placed it on the captain's table. As expectant eyes watched the knife poised, ready to cut, the ship shuddered and rolled on a mountain of a wave. The next few minutes were spent in scraping cake from the overhead. The memory of that loss was still poignant when the destroyer's skipper, climbing down the ladder from the bridge, suddenly found himself hanging by his hands straight out over the sea, 20 feet below. He regained his feet on the second roll, but the third one caught him just as he entered his cabin, washed him inside and left him floating. Then and there HMS SHERWOOD became HMS HORIZONTAL.

One of the most exotic paint jobs in the four-stacker fleet was on HMS BROADWAY, a pair of great staring eyes on her bows. Lieutenant Commander Thomas Taylor, RN, skipper of the BROADWAY, had made his first kill and had the DSO to show for it, when (being an old China hand) he decided that HMS BROADWAY should be embellished. And so a pair of great staring eyes was painted on her bows, in the manner of the Chinese junks which are so provided in order to see and avoid sea-devils.

What more sensible decoration could there be for a ship that hunted submarines, what better definition of a U-boat? So, even after the ship changed commands and through several refittings and repaintings, the eyes remained.

At this writing, seven of the old destroyers have been lost in line of duty. The first to go down was HMS BROADWATER. She was torpedoed in October, 1941, during a running battle with a Nazi submarine on the North Atlantic convoy route. The seventh, HMS ROCKINGHAM, was lost in October, 1944.

Second to go was the old USS MC CALLA, also torpedoed in Atlantic convoy duty but not before destroying one of the pack of submarines that had attacked the merchant fleet.

Two were lost in 1942, HMS BURNHAM and HMS CAMPBELTOWN. HMS BATH was lost under Norwegian command in 1943, as was HMS BEVERLEY. The men of the BEVERLEY relate two stories in particular about their ship: a victorious battle against a superior German force on the bloody Murmansk Run and a no less desperate victory over an Atlantic storm.

The Murmansk trip began in the spring of 1942, the year when a voyage to that port was the toughest assignment in any Navy. The Germans had planes, subs and surface ships based in Norway. Their morale was high, and they got plenty of practice in bombing, torpedoing and shelling Allied shipping.

On one voyage the BEVERLEY, with three other British destroyers, was attacked. Five times superior enemy forces, destroyers of the HANS LODY or NARVIK class, struck. And five times, through heavy snow squalls and thick ice drifts, the BEVERLEY fought back. The German ships were larger and more modern; their guns bigger, their armor thicker, their speed better. Attack followed attack as the convoy fought on through thick ice drifts. Then gradually the enemy fire lost its accuracy, fell off. At last it ceased completely. The guns of BEVERLEY and the other destroyers had found their mark. The old American destroyer, in stouthearted British command, had beaten the best the Germans could put up against her.

The other story of the BEVERLEY is a battle with the weather and it was almost the last one of her career. In mid-December, 1942, she was caught in one of the worst Atlantic storms in history. For fourteen days the ship fought wind and water. One funnel was blown away completely. The lifeboats went next, crushed like soda crackers and swept clear of the deck by wind and waves. Guard rails were bent flat on the deck by force of the weather.

On the fourteenth day she arrived at a port in Newfoundland. She had barely enough fuel left for another five hours' run. But her sister ship HMS CHESTERFIELD made port with no fuel at all, coasting the last few yards to the fuel ship under residual way with tanks dry.

Of the seven ships destroyed, the death of CAMPBELTOWN was the most spectacular and costly to the enemy. Built in 1919, the ship was christened USS BUCHANAN in honor of Captain Franklin Buchanan of Baltimore, organizer and first superintendent of the United States Naval Academy at Annapolis. For eighteen months before her magnificent suicide she was on constant convoy and coastal patrol. Although rechristened HMS CAMPBELTOWN, she was always affectionately known to her British crew as "Old Buck."

She was the ship, packed with five tons of high explosives behind a bow reinforced with concrete, that ran the gantlet of German shore batteries and blew up the main lock gates of the great drydock at Saint-Nazaire.

The CAMPBELTOWN was scheduled to ram the gates at 0130 Saturday morning. A delayed-action fuse had been fitted to give the Commando forces sufficient time to complete other demolition assignments and withdraw before the main explosion, which was set for 0400.

The British naval forces approached Saint-Nazaire under an RAF bombing cover. German flak aimed at the English planes made a white-hot umbrella over the ships of the Royal Navy as they entered the estuary of the river. Suddenly the shore defenses realized there was a force at sea as well as in the air threatening their security. Two powerful searchlights fingered the darkness and swept out over the ships. The light caught the CAMPBELTOWN for a moment; then it shifted to focus on the MTBs and MLs carrying the Commandos. The destroyer headed immediately for the last dock it would ever approach, the one near the lock gates, the only dock on the Atlantic east coast capable of berthing the Nazi battleship TIRPITZ.

The noise of battle was such that gun crews on the CAMPBELTOWN were unable to hear orders from the bridge. The destroyer pushed past her last barrier before the entrance to the drydock, a German flak ship which she left in flames. The cook shut down the cooking ranges in the galley for the last time and went up to his gun position.

A speed of 20 knots was ordered for the final charge into the dock gates. And, as one man said, "She piled herself up on them with the sureness of a ferret diving into a hole," at 0134, only four minutes behind schedule.

Their ship tight against the gates, like a cork jammed in a bottle, the destroyer's gun crews continued to fire their guns even after the bow was ablaze. Only when the flames spread to the guns did the crew abandon ship and run to the adjacent landing stages, now swept with German bullets. The engine-room gang had carried on until the CAMPBELTOWN had crashed into the dock gates, keeping up till the end the steam for 20 knots.

The majority of the crew was evacuated by motor launches and three and a half hours later the delayed-action explosive went off, bottling up the channel and rendering the dock useless for many months.

The Coast Guard, which was incorporated in the Navy on November 1, 1941, also turned over 10 LAKE class cutters [1] to be manned by

---

[1] The cutters, with their new British names in parentheses: SARANAC (BANFF); TAHOE (FISHGUARD); PONTCHARTRAIN (HARTLAND); MENDOTA (CULVER); CHELAN (LULWORTH); SEBAGO (WALNEY); CAYUGA (TOTLAND); CHAMPLAIN (SENNEN); SHOSHONE (LANDGUARD); ITASCA (GORLESTON).

DIRECTING THE COAST GUARD TO OPERATE AS
A PART OF THE NAVY

By virtue of the authority vested in me by section 1 of the act of Congress approved January 28, 1915, 38 Stat. 800 (U.S.C., title 14, sec. 1), as amended by sections 5 and 6 of the act of July 11, 1941, Public Law 166, 77th Congress, 1st Session; it is hereby directed that the Coast Guard shall from this date, until further orders, operate as a part of the Navy, subject to the orders of the Secretary of the Navy.

All Coast Guard personnel operating as a part of the Navy, subject to the orders of the Secretary of the Navy, pursuant to this order, shall, while so serving, be subject to the laws enacted for the government of the Navy: Provided, That in the initiation, prosecution, and completion of disciplinary action, including remission or mitigation of punishments for any offense committed by any officer or enlisted man of the Coast Guard, the jurisdiction shall depend upon and be in accordance with the laws and regulations of the Department having jurisdiction of the person of such offender at the various stages of such action: Provided further, That any punishment imposed and executed in accordance with the provisions of this paragraph shall not exceed that to which the offender was liable at the time of the commission of the offense.

Franklin D Roosevelt

THE WHITE HOUSE,

November / , 1941.

23

British and Canadians. Their histories represented every phase of Coast Guard activity.

The CHELAN was the cutter credited with discovering the vast submarine mountain range lying off Kiska; she was the cutter that rushed aid to the city of Nome, Alaska, during the fire of 1934. In 1936, when the Spanish Civil War threatened our interests, it was the CAYUGA (in the harbor of Le Havre on a cadet cruise) that received orders to proceed immediately to San Sebastian for the protection of the American Embassy and other United States citizens in Spain. The ITASCA made the last recorded radio contact with Amelia Earhart on her last flight in 1937, and for two weeks searched for the lost plane.

The war record of the ten cutters with the British was to be equally noteworthy. The CULVER was sunk in a fight with a German submarine. The LULWORTH rammed and sank the Italian submarine PIETRO CALVI. The WALNEY and the HARTLAND were the team that crashed the harbor boom at Oran in the invasion of North Africa, an act of flaming heroism to rank with that of the CAMPBELTOWN at Saint-Nazaire.

Chapter Three

THE bases that we acquired, leased for 99 years, in exchange for the fifty destroyers, came at a time when the fleet organization was under study.

The Navy's Atlantic forces had gradually been building up from the original Patrol Force until it had reached fleet dimensions. The new bases now gave the Atlantic Fleet an operating theater that extended the sea frontier hundreds of miles in the direction of our potential enemies. Our defensive outposts extended in a great arc from the Grand Banks to the mouths of the Amazon—Newfoundland, Bermuda,[1] The Bahamas, Jamaica, St. Lucia, Trinidad, Antigua, British Guiana.

By June, 1941, the British government had leased such crown land as was included in the selected sites and set in motion the necessary steps to acquire, at a price mutually satisfactory, the privately owned land included in the areas desired by the United States. The leases gave the United States exclusive right to govern the land occupied and, in time of war, to take *any* action in *any* part of the colony or possession necessary to defend the American area.

Bermuda, 600 miles east of Cape Hatteras and midway between Newfoundland and Puerto Rico in the Atlantic, was an outpost of inestimable value for the defense of continental United States. And it was there that our most extensive base installations were made. Its reefbound Great Sound afforded a base for destroyers and seaplanes of the antisubmarine patrol, which extended their scope well beyond mid-Atlantic.

In September a United States Army-Navy Survey Board, led by Rear Admiral John W. Greenslade, USN, left Washington to survey sites for the bases there.[2]

---

[1] Technically sites in Newfoundland and Bermuda were negotiated separately.

[2] Accompanying the Admiral were: Capt. R. S. Crenshaw, USN, the Navy's Director of War Plans; Capt. Duette W. Rose, USN, of the Supply Corps; Comdr. Calvin T. Durgin, USN, of the Bureau of Aeronautics; Comdr. Kendal B. Bragg, USN, of the Civil Engineer Corps; Comdr. Harold Biesemeier, USN, of the Judge Advocate General's Office; Lt. Col. Omar T. Pfeiffer, USMC; and Brig. Gen. Jacob L. Devers, Col. A. J. Maloney and Maj. T. Griffiss, of the Army.

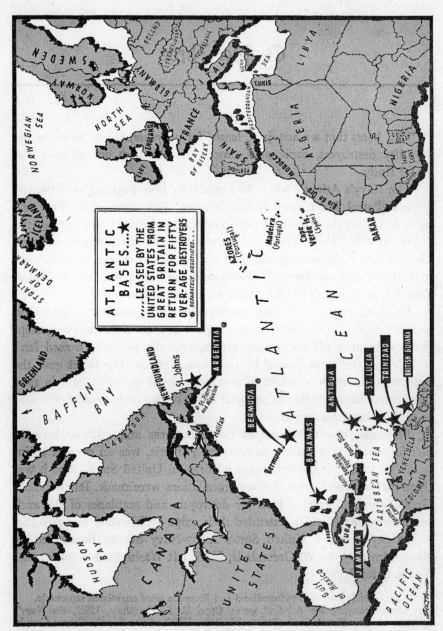

ATLANTIC BASES....
....LEASED BY THE
UNITED STATES FROM
GREAT BRITAIN IN
RETURN FOR FIFTY
OVER-AGE DESTROYERS....
❋ SEPARATELY NEGOTIATED ❋

FIGURE 2

26

The Navy selected a site opposite Hamilton Island, including two islands and adjacent bays, of approximately 50 acres in area. Dredging and filling the area between the islands and the shore linked all together in a naval air station site. Alterations to the entrance to Castle Harbour, such as relocating a highway and a railroad and building a drawbridge, made it usable for ships and seaplanes. Explosive dumps were located on the small islands between St. David's and Hamilton Island along the eastern entrance to Castle Harbour. Construction costs were put at $11,250,000.

The Bahamas were planned for use as a secondary patrol-plane base, forming a chain that would give the United States absolute command of the two Caribbean entrances, Florida Strait and the Windward Passage. The lease here gave us the use of Abraham Bay and a small area of adjacent land on Mayaguana Island. A site was selected for a seaplane base on the island in position to command the Windward Passage between Cuba and Haiti. The cost was placed at $2,550,000.

Jamaica, already a minor British naval fueling station, with a fine harbor at Kingston, was developed as a secondary base for United States patrol planes, submarines, destroyers and cruisers. Leases here covered a fleet anchorage at Portland Bight and a land area, including Goat Island with the adjacent bays, of approximately 33 square miles in and east of Galleon Harbour, for a seaplane base to cost $2,750,000.

An area on Portland Bight and Portland Island was set aside for the location of defense batteries and approximately 100 acres in the vicinity of Williams Field station was planned for recreation grounds and a hospital mess. There was one mile square, about five miles south of Maypen along Bakers Canal, to be used as an emergency and auxiliary landing field.

In addition to these areas, we were given the right to develop resources and facilities of the Port Royal Dockyard, under British control, for the joint use of United States and British forces. Reciprocal rights were also to be granted both United States and British military aircraft in the use of airfields built by the joint effort of both countries.

Antigua, in the Leeward Islands, and St. Lucia, in the Windward Islands, guarding the Anegada Passage and the Windward Islands approaches to the Caribbean, were in good position for intermediate patrol-plane and submarine bases. On Antigua was leased an area on Parham Sound, opposite Long Island, about two and three-quarters miles north of Parham and measuring about two and three-quarters by one mile. The lease included the narrow peninsula on the east side of Parham harbor about a mile long and a quarter of a mile wide, known as Crabs. On St. Lucia, the lease included 120 acres on Gros Islet Bay. The development for these islands provided for seaplane operating bases, repairs and facilities, at a cost of $2,920,000 and $1,625,000 respectively.

The bases acquired at Trinidad closed the hitherto open southern gateway to the Caribbean and made more secure the protection of the tankers carrying oil from the great Netherlands West Indies refineries. The harbor at Port-of-Spain afforded a secondary fortified fleet base and other areas were excellent for major long-range land- and sea-based patrol planes. Plans for Trinidad provided for a seaplane base, berthing for ships, a fleet anchorage, and a limited amount of repair facilities and housing for the station complement, to cost $17,855,000.

The bases in British Guiana were suitable for servicing aircraft and lighter naval vessels and safeguarding at that time the vital shipments of bauxite ore sorely needed in the manufacture of aluminum. The lease in this area included a patrol squadron base with hangars, 25 miles from the mouth of the Demerara River, and a second air base near Suddie on the west bank of the mouth of the Essequibo River, with a construction cost of $1,800,000.

At the northern end of the chain of bases was Newfoundland, whose ice-free harbors left year-round navigation open to destroyers, submarines and patrol planes. Land for an air base and Army training force was leased on Argentia peninsula, as well as two square miles south of Little Placentia harbor. The Navy acquired a site on Placentia Bay, a splendid body of water, for seaplane operation, which was bordered by slowly rising land, roughly leveled by glacial action. The naval base site of approximately 22 acres on the south side of St. John's harbor, included 1,250 feet of wharfage for handling supplies and equipment. A site for an Army defensive force of approximately 160 acres north of Quidi Vidi Lake completed the lease.

Newfoundland is a bleak place with continual damp weather and fog, but it is an outpost of immense strategical importance. Contractors arrived at Argentia in January, 1941, and began work at once in clearing, grading, and building wharves. By June, 2,500 men were up there and work was nearing completion on the $17,050,000 project of constructing barracks, messhalls, hangars, shops, runways and all the components of a naval air base.

Construction requirements and problems varied with each base. The climates between Newfoundland and British Guiana ranged from subarctic to tropical. In Bermuda, especial care was taken to adopt an architecture that would blend with the buildings already there.

Fighting physical handicaps that ranged from ice-covered lava badlands and frozen peat to tropical jungle, these bases were built and operating by the time the Navy was called upon to meet its first big order of the Atlantic war.

Chapter Four

EVEN while misguided persons were proving to the satisfaction of some of their countrymen that the Western Hemisphere was safe from invasion, Hitler's vanguards were invading it and establishing themselves in Greenland.

That bleak subcontinent, jutting into the aerial and oceanic traffic lanes between North America and Northern Europe, is under the Danish crown. It is not only a sentinel port and way station on the intercontinental routes, but it lies in the area where northern Europe's weather is brewed.

Greenland was important to the Germans. Shortly after the Nazi occupation of Denmark on April 9, 1940, German observers were in Greenland preparing the establishment of meteorological stations from which Berlin could be accurately informed what the weather would be over the North Atlantic, the British Isles and France days in advance—data priceless to the German land, air and submarine forces. They could, too, scout the eastbound convoys, estimate their size and their escort strength, and inform the German Admiralty when a fat target was due off the Irish coast.

German invasion of Greenland was in defiance of the Monroe Doctrine and in contempt of the Congress of American Foreign Ministers held in July, 1940, at Havana. But with the enactment of Lend-Lease the presence of German military units in Greenland became an issue of more realistic moment to this government.

Lend-Lease became law on March 11, 1941. The act meant that the industrial resources of the United States would flow to the British Commonwealth in volume limited only by the Allied ability to transport and convoy the cargoes. There was a natural unwillingness to see this material, costly in time, labor and substance, lost in transit. The only recourse was to guard the cargo ships within the prescribed limits of hemispheric waters. That decision gave Greenland greater prominence in the Navy's scheme of operations. A survey party under Coast Guard auspices was dispatched to the island on March 17, and on April 9—a year to the day from the German invasion of Denmark—United States Marines were landed in Greenland.

The landing was announced by the State Department. An agreement had been signed that day between the Secretary of State, acting on behalf of the United States government, and the Danish Minister, Henrik de Kauffman, acting on behalf of the King of Denmark, sovereign of Greenland. The agreement, after explicitly recognizing the Danish sovereignty over Greenland, granted the United States the right to locate and construct airfields and facilities for the defense of Greenland and for the defense of the American continent.

There had been many circumstances leading up to the agreement and to the landing of Marines.

On May 3, 1940, the Greenland Councils, meeting at Godhavn, less than a month after Denmark's capitulation, adopted a resolution in the name of the people of Greenland reaffirming their allegiance to King Christian X of Denmark. During this same month the Coast Guard cutter COMANCHE sailed for Godthaab, via Ivigtut. On board as passenger was the first American Consul en route to Greenland. Shortly thereafter Canada established a Consulate. There was considerable concern at this time for the cryolite mine at Ivigtut, a mine that furnished practically the entire world's supply of that mineral essential to the smelting of aluminum. The United States had agreed to sell armament to the autonomous Greenland government for the defense of this mine. Guns were supplied and a few Coast Guardsmen, experienced gunners, were allowed to resign their ratings and to be employed as guards at the mine. The men arrived in August, 1940.

Meanwhile, at the consultation of American Foreign Ministers at Havana in July, it was declared that any attempt on the part of a non-American power against the territory or political independence of an American state would be considered an act of aggression. And during the summer of 1940 German activity on the eastern coast of Greenland became apparent.

Three Nazi ships proceeding from Norwegian territory under German occupation arrived off the coast of Greenland ostensibly for commercial or scientific purposes. At least one of these ships landed parties whose mission was to set up meteorological stations to furnish weather forecasts to Nazi Europe, and flash North Atlantic ship movements to Nazi submarines at sea. These parties were cleaned out, when, in mid-September, the Norwegian gunboat FRIDTJOF NANSEN, under British control, arrived at Torgilsbu. Landing parties destroyed the German radio equipment found there and captured the personnel. However, late in the fall, German air reconnaissance appeared over east Greenland under circumstances indicating that there was continued activity somewhere in that region.

In August the Coast Guard cutter NORTHLAND made a survey of various Greenland harbors. While in Ivigtut, the NORTHLAND's crew installed the armament, brought up earlier by another Coast Guard cutter, the CAMPBELL, to guard the cryolite mine.

Returning to home port in December, the men of the NORTHLAND began an immediate assembly and organization of all information obtained on the Greenland cruise. They wrote a *Greenland Pilot* and prepared a great many new charts of the remote area they had just left, while the paralyzing arctic winter locked Greenland behind an almost impenetrable barricade of ice, snow and hurricane winds. On the earliest date that could be risked, March 17, 1941, the Coast Guard cutter CAYUGA left Boston Harbor with the South Greenland Survey Expedition aboard. This group, operating under State, War, Treasury and Navy Department orders, had instructions to locate and recommend non-military airfields, seaplane bases, radio stations, meteorological stations, aids to navigation, and furnish hydrographic information.

Word of this expedition, apparently, was not slow in reaching Germany. On March 26 the Nazi government gave warning that ships operating in the North Atlantic laid themselves open "to the danger of destruction," candid enough manifestation of Germany's intent to tolerate no neutral nonsense about freedom of the seas.

Twenty-four hours later, and ten days after the CAYUGA's departure, a German bomber was reported flying over the eastern coast of Greenland, and on March 28 another German plane was seen in reconnaissance over the same territory.

The Coast Guard cutter MODOC, searching the area between Greenland's southern tip and Iceland for survivors of a torpedoed merchantman, the SS MARCONI, found herself squarely in the middle of battle on May 24, which subsequently proved to be the opening phases of the duel between the German battleship BISMARCK and HMS HOOD, in which the British battle cruiser was wiped out by one lucky salvo which touched off her magazines.

The MODOC had been informed that BISMARCK was on the rampage in the North Atlantic and suspected what was going on when "a large man-of-war" was seen on the horizon off the cutter's port bow, shooting at airplanes which swept overhead from the opposite point of the compass. Then, far off, three other unidentified warships emerged from the haze, with MODOC unhappily in the middle of the developing fight. The cutter sent out a signal that she was "leaving this hot area," and headed northwest at full speed for Cape Farewell, under an arc of combat as the British and Germans engaged.

The rest is history. HMS HOOD was sunk, and the BISMARCK and PRINZ EUGEN were lost to the British pursuit for two days, when it again fell to an American to have a front-row seat at the battle's resumption. But Ensign L. B. Smith had no ship with which to make a discreet withdrawal from a war in which the United States Navy had no legal part. Ensign Smith was on duty as a military observer, and instructor in the techniques of the PBY, with Squadron 209 of the RAF. The big amphibious plane was flying only 500 feet above the sea, through broken scudding clouds, when Smith saw something on the ocean below.

"What the devil is that?" he asked Flying Officer Briggs, the pilot. "Looks like a battleship."

"It's the BISMARCK," bawled Briggs, shouting to the radioman to broadcast the location of the Nazi's pride.

The BISMARCK, sighting the PBY in the same instant, let loose with all her impressive assortment of antiaircraft guns, and to Smith she was "all one big winking flame" of gunfire. A shell whizzed through the plane's deck between the pilot and copilot, and the heavy aircraft was rocked and buffeted by bursts as it maneuvered out of range.

Down upon the scene, then, hurtled Swordfish torpedo planes from HMS ARK ROYAL, to harry the Nazi warship until the Home Fleet's cruisers and destroyers could catch up and hammer the BISMARCK into wreckage.

Under the circumstances it appeared that further steps for the defense of Greenland were necessary to bring that land within the system of hemispheric defense outlined at the Havana meeting, and so the negotiations were begun that produced the "Agreement Relating to the Defense of Greenland" and the departure of the Marines, to the prophetic words of the Corps' hymn: ". . . to the snow of far-off northern lands."

The first organized United States patrol of Greenland waters for hemispheric defense—the South Greenland Patrol—began on June 1, 1941, under Coast Guard command with Coast Guard ships; the COMANCHE, RARITAN and MODOC together with USS BOWDOIN. The patrol, commanded by Lieutenant Commander H. G. Belford, USCG, took station in the area where Axis interference with convoys seemed most likely to occur, the sea lanes from Cape Brewster to Cape Farewell to Upernivik.

On June 7, the President approved the "Basic Joint Army and Navy Plan for Defense of Greenland." This plan provided for a second patrol, the Northeast Greenland Patrol, which was organized July 1, with the cutters NORTHLAND, NORTH STAR, and USS BEAR. In charge of this patrol was Commander Edward H. Smith of the Coast Guard, whose previous duty on the Ice Patrol and vast knowledge of the arctic and northern regions had earned him the nickname of "Iceberg Smith." Both patrols were incorporated, in October, 1941, as the Greenland Patrol.

The ships assigned to this work needed no introduction either to cold waters or to patrol work. They had cruised the region and still farther north in peacetime with the Ice Patrol, and the rigors of convoy patrol differed only slightly from the old days when the Coast Guard had kept a watch on Rum Row, marking down and chasing "rummies."

Thus was joined a battle that has had little mention in the headlines, a long elemental battle during which it was a positive relief to see a mortal foeman, a fight in which the field of battle itself was far more deadly than the enemy. In summer the fog shifted in and out over the ice fields, closing in so thick sometimes you couldn't see the wheelhouse from the wing of the bridge. In autumn the gales began. In winter the darkness came to stay as the cold rode on the wings of the blizzard and every step out of doors was an act of heroism; it took almost six months and the lives of three men to rescue the crew of a wounded B-17 from the spot where they'd crashed on the icecap. Spring brought more fog than sun, more icebergs than open water. And through all this our men still fought Germans, but this last was a comparative picnic, a pleasant intermission, although, ultimately, it is what they were there for. Someday their story may be told in full as it deserves to be.

The first cruise of the NORTHLAND and the BEAR forming the Northeast Greenland Patrol began in July, 1941. Both ships were veterans. The BEAR was built in Scotland in 1874 for work in the Newfoundland seal grounds originally. But in the same year she was turned over to the Navy to lead the Greely Relief Expedition. Two years later she was transferred again, this time to the Revenue Marine and carried the Treasury Department's ensign around Cape Horn to San Francisco. From there she went north on arctic duty, averaging 16,000 cruising miles a year. Forty-two times the BEAR crossed the Arctic Circle on the Bering Sea Patrol before she was condemned and decommissioned in 1926. The faithful old steam-barkentine, less than 200 feet long and not quite 30 feet wide at the beam, had earned a rest. It looked for a while as though she might get it. She was sent to the city of Oakland, California, as a marine museum. Then, in 1933, Admiral Byrd made his antarctic trip and he needed a good ship for ice sailing. The BEAR was broken out of her museum moorings, made shipshape, and off she sailed. In 1941 she was again returned to active duty and sent to the top of the world on the Greenland Patrol.

The NORTHLAND had been built to replace the BEAR when the latter was first decommissioned in 1926. This was the affinity between these two ships that befitted their sailing off together on patrol.

By September, NORTHLAND, NORTH STAR and BEAR were patrolling the northeast Greenland area around the mammoth glacial deposit known the The Ice Pack. Inland, the Sledge Patrol, a group of reliable experienced Danish hunters organized by Commander Smith during the summer, covered the trackless wasteland miles of Greenland by dog sledge and reported to the Army and the Coast Guard any unusual or suspicious activity they might encounter.

One September day they flashed such a report to the NORTH STAR. They had seen a Norwegian ship put in to a small cove. Investigating further in the guise of trappers, men of the Patrol talked to crew members of the ship and learned that she had carried passengers to Greenland who were now ashore, somewhere inland.

The NORTH STAR relayed this information to NORTHLAND, who was closer to the position of the Norwegian ship. The NORTHLAND acknowledged and got underway immediately. On September 12 a lookout shouted the word that the ship was sighted. She was small, about 60 tons, outside the three-mile limit off Hold-with-Hope and heading for Mackenzie Bay, Greenland.

Captain Carl Christian von Paulsen, Coast Guard flier and former commanding officer of Coast Guard Base No. 7 at East Gloucester, was skipper of the NORTHLAND. He gave the order to follow the Norwegian ship at full speed. The cutter was armed, and the crew was at battle stations as she drew alongside the foreign ship inside Mackenzie Bay. The name on the little Norwegian ship was plainly visible, BUSKOE. Captain von Paulsen gave Lieutenant (jg) Leroy McCluskey, USCGR, boarding orders: "Find out what she's doing here, and whether the Sledge Patrol report about landing someone on the coast is true."

The crew of the NORTHLAND waited while McCluskey disappeared in the cabin of the BUSKOE.

He returned some time later with a grim look on his face and made his report to the captain. The BUSKOE's captain was Hallvard Devold, a Norwegian arctic explorer of some note. With him was a crew of nine. So far, so good. Then McCluskey reported more interesting news. The BUSKOE was loaded with the latest expensive radio equipment. For a dingy little sealer this was unusual to say the least. After lengthy grueling of captain and crew McCluskey got this story: The radio equipment had been put aboard in the Lofoten Islands by the German Gestapo. Next a party of Norwegian "hunters and trappers" had been taken aboard to be set down somewhere in Greenland. The hunters had taken a considerable amount of radio equipment ashore with them, near one of the many trapping stations in northeast Greenland.

The evidence was incriminating. Captain von Paulsen put a prize crew from the NORTHLAND aboard the BUSKOE, whose crew offered no resistance. The BEAR arrived as the Norwegian ship was taken in custody and the BUSKOE, with Coast Guard prize crew aboard, was turned over to be escorted to Boston. The NORTHLAND then headed for the hunting station where the "trappers" had carried their radio equipment.

Two days later NORTHLAND anchored in the icy blue water five miles out from the hunting station. Preparations had been made for a landing. McCluskey, with Lieutenant (jg) Carlton Skinner, USCGR, a former Washington newspaperman, selected a small group of men from the crew, armed them and outlined the plan for surrounding the trapping station.

It was two o'clock in the morning when the motorboat eased down from the davits on NORTHLAND and started to shore with the landing party. Some forty minutes later the group of fur-wrapped, armed men stepped ashore and silently dispersed in a fan-shaped movement toward the small cabin that was the trapping station. It was three o'clock when McCluskey, backed by half the landing party, cautiously walked up the snowy path to the door. Quiet reconnaissance showed that no one was standing a watch. The cabin's occupants, confident that they were securely hidden in the arctic desert, were tranquilly sleeping.

McCluskey pounded on the cabin door with the butt of his gun. There was a shuffling sound inside the cabin, and movement toward the door. The latch lifted, the door squeaked open on its frost-rimed hinges and a sleepy, disheveled figure in long underwear stood gaping into the barrels of ready guns.

Once inside the cabin, McCluskey saw that there were two other occupants of the tiny building, both staring from their bunks as if in the grip of nightmare. The entry of the Coast Guard party had been so sudden and so quietly accomplished that there was no resistance. There had been no time for the men to destroy any papers, and the radio equipment, although not set up, was there in evidence for transmitting meteorological information.

With persistent questioning, McCluskey managed to get the story of the man who greeted them in underwear. His name was Jacob Bradley, a member of the Norwegian Quisling party who had proved inefficient and untrustworthy, however, to the Germans, who demanded exactness in such people. He was dismissed from his first political job. Ostracized by loyal Norwegians, blackballed from other means of employment because of a bad Gestapo dossier, he had floundered about for months before the Germans gave him another chance. He was told that he had scant choice in the matter; take the job now offered or starve. He took it. It was to be radio operator of a weather station planned for Greenland.

The other two members of his party discovered in the cabin turned out to be more or less camouflage. They were bona fide trappers. Although Norwegian, they had no strong feeling either toward the Germans or toward America.

"In fact," said Lieutenant Skinner, "it was quite possible that they were responsible for preventing the radio station from getting into operation before the NORTHLAND arrived."

The radio equipment, which was all new and made in Germany, was destroyed, and the three men were taken aboard the NORTHLAND to be turned over to immigration authorities at a United States port.

The Patrol had two more encounters with the Nazis, who are nothing if not persistent. As in the case of the BUSKOE, it was the Sledge Patrol that first discovered the presence of the enemy.

Early in 1943 they stumbled onto another German radio and weather station hidden away in a remote part of the country. This time the Germans were alert and attacked the Patrol, taking two of its members prisoners and killing a third. Following this, the Nazis sent a raiding party to the small hunting and weather station above the Arctic Circle manned by a handful of Danes armed only with hunting rifles and a few pistols. The Germans made their attack at night, armed with machine guns. In the darkness most of the Danes escaped, but some were taken prisoner.

Later, the lieutenant in command of the German Greenland Expedition, as the Nazi force was known, made the mistake of soliciting one of his Danish prisoners to act as his guide in further exploration of the east Greenland coast. At the first opportunity the Danish guide overpowered his German captor. After a 40-day trip by dog sled he brought the shackled German into an Army post and turned him over to custody.

With the information thus received about the German military weather base, the location was bombed and strafed by U.S. Army Air Force planes under the command of Colonel Bernt Balchen in May. As soon as ice conditions permitted, Rear Admiral Smith ordered Captain von Paulsen to set out with NORTHLAND and NORTH STAR to clean up and destroy any installations left undamaged by the bombing.

Shortly after striking the ice area, NORTH STAR jammed and stuck, and there she remained held solidly in the ice pack for nearly a month. The NORTHLAND was favored when a westerly wind opened a lead in the ice which she followed to clear water, while her crew gave the razzberry to the NORTH STAR. Later, when a German patrol bomber spotted and attacked them, they were doubly glad to have open water for maneuvering. They fought off the Nazi, and continued until close to the estimated position of the German station. Here the NORTHLAND launched her scout plane to reconnoiter. It returned with the exact location of the station, and the landing parties made ready to disembark. There were two groups, the Coast Guard party, under the command of Captain von Paulsen, and Army demolition experts under the command of Captain Melvin M. Jensen.

When the parties landed, some seven miles from their goal, they stepped ashore in mud so thick the men sank to their knees at every step.

Topping a rise, after hours of plodding, they saw that the Army bombing raid in May had destroyed all the main buildings except a small generator shack. A supply ship lay in the harbor, gutted and abandoned. There were no Germans in sight.

"We had gone ashore prepared for anything," said Captain von Paulsen. "What we found was slightly anticlimactical."

The weather station had been small, but solidly constructed, with outpost buildings connected by telephone. There were a short-wave radio, a transmitter, and an emergency generator, all evidence of having been laid out for permanent occupation. There were defensive machine-gun emplacements and large caches of food, drifted over by snow.

The Coast Guard and Army men spent two days in careful, scientific destruction. Toward the end they were startled by a hoarse hail. A lone and dejected German approached, hands high in surrender. He was Dr. Rolf Senssen, the sole survivor, and he brokenly told a grim story until, thawed with American food, he reverted to the Nazi, arrogant and unco-operative. Around his middle was slung a cluster of "potato masher" grenades. Senssen admitted that he had hidden when the landing party approached, hoping to catch a large group of the party together at one time, to destroy them with the grenades.

The German was put aboard the NORTHLAND, along with his sled dogs, all the food, arms and ammunition left of his station. The NORTH-LAND was running low on food supplies. No small part of her triumph, therefore, was the capture of the German stores of Norwegian sardines packed in rich Italian olive oil, and a quantity of good Danish butter.

As late as the autumn of 1944, long after the liberation of Paris, the Coast Guard fought and won its toughest campaign against the Nazi invaders, a campaign that lasted nearly three months and was waged for the most part only 700 miles from the North Pole. Again the NORTHLAND was in the thick of it.

First intimations of another German establishment were supplied early in July by Captain Nils Jensen of the Sledge Patrol. Then, heading a party of eight men, he went out to make a closer reconnaissance, and, in sight of an apparently well-defended group of buildings, Jensen left his party to make the closest possible examination alone. As he watched the changing of the guard, noting the sentries' beat and the location of gun mounts, the Dane was surprised from the rear by a bearded Nazi officer.

Jensen was quicker on the draw. Hurdling the body of the German, he rejoined his squad and the Danes escaped in a running battle with pursuing Nazis armed with submachine guns.

The NORTHLAND, accompanied by the new cutter STORIS, reached the area on July 30: Cape Sussi, northernmost tip of Shannon Island. Land-ing parties were sent ashore from three directions, only to find that the Germans had fled inland. The installation was destroyed, including powerful shortwave radio equipment and extensive stores of fuel, food and ammunition. Four miles distant an abandoned Nazi armed trawler was locked in the ice, partially dismantled. It, too, was demolished by the Coast Guard.

The area was searched for a month, without reward until September 1, when another armed trawler was hailed by NORTHLAND. The German ship began agile evasive tactics, a prelude to a 70-mile chase during which NORTHLAND's skipper, Lieutenant Commander R. W. Butcher, USCG, managed to outmaneuver the faster Nazi craft and bring it under his guns. But the Germans had no stomach for battle. They scuttled their craft, rowed over to the NORTHLAND, the commander of the crew of twenty-eight dramatically surrendering his sword to Commander Butcher. The sword now hangs in the cutter's wardroom and on Lieutenant Commander Butcher's breast is the red-and-white ribbon of the Legion of Merit.

While the NORTHLAND was pursuing the Nazi ship (the COBURG), her companion vessel STORIS (Lieutenant Commander R. W. Thresher, USCG) was delayed by the necessity of fighting off a Focke-Wulf bomber.

During the chase, NORTHLAND's company had been puzzled by two great explosions in the water, which, they concluded, had been from mines inexpertly dropped in the cutter's path. But from the prisoners it was learned that they had been torpedoes from a submarine, aimed at the NORTHLAND but detonated against the ice floes.

There was nothing to do, then, but to go after the submarine.

The sea was full of ice, from iceberg size to slushy floes, and there was no such thing as a straight course to set when, some hours later, the submarine was sighted on the surface 9,000 yards distant. The NORTHLAND opened with her deck guns and strove against the ice fields to reach the submarine. It disappeared. Next day the cutter's seaplane was sent aloft, and after a two-hour search it located the U-boat. Lieutenant (jg) Kenneth N. Bilderback, USCGR, dropped his two light demolition bombs on the ship's reinforced shell, without effect of course. He radioed the NORTHLAND and received the mournful news that the cutter had smashed her rudder in the ice and could not proceed. For two days, while the STORIS kept watch, the NORTHLAND's crew labored in the icy water to contrive a jury rig by which the hand steering was contrived, but Commodore Earl G. Rose, USCG, commander of the Greenland Patrol, asked Rear Admiral Smith to order the two new icebreaking cutters, EASTWIND and SOUTHWIND, to relieve the damaged ship and her partner.

The submarine was seen once again, before the relieving vessels arrived, but it dived to safety miles out of range. Bilderback received the Air Medal for his work against the submarine.

On October 2, the EASTWIND's patrol plane, flown by Ensign Joseph T. McCormick, USCG, spotted something more interesting than a submarine—a cluster of huts on Little Koldewey Island. Captain C. W. Thomas, USCG, skipper of the cutter, pushed his ship as close as safety allowed, and sent two platoons ashore to storm the obviously Nazi installation. They returned to the cutter with three officers and nine enlisted men of the German Army, all wearing uniforms, a dog of questionable parentage and a large quantity of meteorological and radio equipment, besides a collection of phonograph records which included some choice American jazz. The captured materiel was turned over to the Greenland government for military use. The prisoners were quartered on the cutter, and the German books, games and pinochle cards captured with the more important booty were returned to them. However, they were soon to have company from home.

On October 15 an unidentified vessel, an armed trawler by her rig, was sighted 15 miles off Cape Borgen, Greenland. Late that night the cutters EASTWIND and SOUTHWIND (Captain R. M. Hoyle, USCG) closed in on the Nazi. The trawler dodged around icebergs, the air crackling with code from its powerful radio. Then the German skipper picked a wrong path through the ice and found himself in a cul-de-sac. In plain language he sent his farewell message to the Reich: *"Heil Heimat—alles gutes—danke schön"—Hail to the homeland—all of the best—thanks.* Twenty prisoners filed across the ice to the cutters, four Coast Guard officers and thirty men boarded the surrendered ship, the EXTERNSTEINE. The EASTWIND's prize crew solemnly renamed the trawler EAST BREEZE, backed her out of the ice and took her to port, intact.

In addition to weather patrol, icebreaking and rescue details, the Greenland Patrol, which by March 1, 1943, consisted of 34 ships, 27 of them Coast Guard vessels, acted as escort for convoys running between Newfoundland and various bases on Greenland. Prior to the United States' Declaration of War on December 8, 1941, the Coast Guard ships had often been utilized by the Navy on national defense missions such as the Greenland Patrol. Thereafter integrated with the Navy, the Coast Guard's larger cutters and patrol boats, capable of offshore operations, had been assigned to the Fleet, to Naval Sea Frontiers, and to Navy Task Forces, for convoy, antisubmarine and patrol duty. Some of those cutters sank submarines, and some were sunk by submarines, in their role of protecting the merchant convoys.

These brushes with human enemies were, as has been suggested, actually treats for the Coast Guard. The Coast Guard's ships had an assortment of jobs in addition to patrolling: supplying facilities for weather forecasts for Army bases, making hydrographic surveys of many uncharted areas, clearing harbors of ice, locating and surveying possible airfield sites, bringing in supplies, mail, arms and ammunition to the military and Sledge Patrol bases, ferrying small boats and personnel between Greenland stations. They proved their motto—"Semper Paratus."

The greatest hazards these small ships faced in their work were gales and fog and ice. The ships were veterans of ice fighting, if their crews, in the main, were not. But the personnel soon learned that when an ice pack closes tight around the ship it is useless to attempt to batter through. The only thing to do is to wait until the pack shifts, a lead opens, and then follow the break in the ice in the general direction the navigator has set until the pack closes in again.

A ship meets many kinds of ice in Greenland waters. Probably the most dangerous is the "storis," the Danish term for large ice, for which the United States Coast Guard cutter was named. Such ice breaks off from the arctic pack in great bergs and floats down with the Greenland currents in the spring and summer into Atlantic shipping lines. Least dangerous is slush ice, which consists largely of tailings, drifting chunks broken from the ice pack. Ice of this variety is not too dangerous of itself but a field of it may conceal a large growler, which can be fatal to a ship's bottom.

Within the ice pack itself, or within the area in which the ice pack is found, there is a great deal of fog. Such fog is the navigator's nightmare, since it often hides the horizon for days and prevents him from ascertaining position and drift.

The steadiest job that fell to the ships on the Greenland Patrol was icebreaking in the fjords, a chore which only its importance lifted above the status of sheer drudgery. But the fjords had to be cleared; the Army had to get fuel and stores landed to create and supply projected airfields, airfields later vital in ferrying planes to Europe once the United States entered the war.

With the United States in the war, Greenland became a shuttle stop on the aerial routes to Europe and a good many ships were assigned to clear the fjords. The NORTHLAND proved to be the most efficient ice-breaker (and it took her almost six weeks to break the ice in Senderstrom Fjord alone in the spring of 1942). Icebreaking in a fjord is very different from the same job in a river where the current, constantly flowing downstream, carries away the broken ice. In a fjord, with no steady current, the ebb tide carries the broken ice out only to have it come washing back again on the flood. The only way ice is eliminated naturally from a fjord is when a favorable wind works with the outgoing tide.

There are two accepted methods of icebreaking: ramming and paring. The NORTHLAND with her long sloping keel forward was particularly effective in ramming; she could run a large part of her length right up on the ice and break through floes up to 20 inches thick. Above that thickness she had to ram, back off and ram again. The sharp-bowed COMANCHE class cutters, designed for icebreaking in rivers, were limited to that slow, unsatisfactory but better-than-nothing technique. The paring method of icebreaking is just what the name implies: the ship, rudder hard over, simply gouges a path for herself, traveling an elliptical course.

Constantly changing weather proved another obstacle for the ships on the Greenland Patrol. There would be a week or ten days when the average temperature was between 50 and 60 degrees, under a bright sun with the sea calm.

Then, suddenly, the barometer would plummet. The wind would rise as the mercury dropped until it was blowing a hurricane, with gusts over 100 miles an hour. On one occasion the patrol was caught in such a weather change when they were 17 miles off the shore. The wind started from the northeast. At the end of two and a half days of running head-on into the wind, often at full speed, and never less than one-third speed, the NORTHLAND was able to get a position. The navigator found that she was approximately 10 miles from the beach now—she had made seven miles in two and a half days!

The long hours of battling weather and ice on the Greenland Patrol were sometimes livened by that short, danger-packed message that electrifies all ships at sea that receive it—an SOS. Such a message came into the radio shack of the NORTHLAND in November, 1942, as she was sailing along the east coast of Greenland.

Three Canadian fliers had crashed on the icecap about halfway between Cape Farewell and Amasalik. Commander Francis C. Pollard,

USCG, who was in command of NORTHLAND at the time, headed immediately for the area where the plane had crashed. The cutter was pushing her way through the ice in record time, when a thick fog immobilized her for four days. As soon as the fog lifted enough for a position to be taken, the ship was forced in again through the ice toward an uncharted bay on the coast, near which the aviators had fallen. The area surrounding the bay was carefully searched. A reconnaissance by NORTHLAND's airplane found no sight of the three lost men. It was wholly unreasonable to believe the fliers had survived after eighteen days, but when it was dark, the captain ordered star shells and flares fired in hope that the pilots could thus locate the ship, and somehow make their presence known to the rescuers. There was no response. Next day the search was resumed, again fruitlessly.

Flares were lighted again on the second night. Then, off in the distance, an answering light blinked, faded, then glowed in a steady blaze. A small boat was sent hurrying across the ice-choked bay in the direction of the answering light. Three huddled figures were silhouetted against a waning fire on the edge of a glacier. The beacon they had lit in answer to the ship's flares was made from their overcoats.

In the final desperate effort to signal their location they had sacrificed their warm clothing, the last protection against the cold in case their signal went unseen. Rations were down to one biscuit a day, and their hands and feet were badly frozen. The choice was whether their coats would serve as a signal or as shrouds, for they could not have survived many hours more.

Commander Pollard was later presented with a silver plate by Air Vice-Marshal MacNeece Foster, deputy head of the Canadian Royal Air Force delegation in the United States, for the rescue.

A few days later another plane crashed on the icecap. It was a Flying Fortress, Britain-bound. When the plane dropped to the ice its body snapped, and broke. One man was seriously injured, Sergeant Paul J. Spina, who was thrown clear. His arm was broken above the wrist and he lost his gloves. His hands froze before he could be carried back into the plane.

The crew rigged sheltered quarters in the tail section of the broken fuselage. The radio was broken by the crash, and in the freezing, cramped and unlighted wreck Corporal Loren H. Haworth toiled to repair it. High winds and driving snow forced the men to stay within the crumpled section of the wrecked plane for ten days. Then the weight of the metal plus the men, caused a fissure to open in the ice under the tail section. It was lashed to the forward part of the plane, and the men prayed that it would hold.

Two weeks after the B-17 crashed, Haworth was able to tap out a message on the patched-up radio. It was picked up and rebroadcast, and somewhere in the icepack a vessel heard and turned for shore. It was the NORTHLAND again.

She anchored off the coast, as near as she could get to the scene of the crash. Meantime Colonel Bernt Balchen, AUS, had flown over and dropped supplies to the B-17 crew, and there was word that a dog-team rescue crew was on its way overland.

The pilot of the NORTHLAND's Grumman amphibian reconnaissance plane was Lieutenant John A. Pritchard, 29-year-old Coast Guard aviator who had been flying the treacherous North Atlantic air patrol for the past nine months.

He requested permission from his skipper to take his amphibian plane into the scene of the crash and attempt to land and take off.

That simple request covered an incalculably dangerous operation. No one had ever attempted landing and taking off from the Greenland icecap. It would have been an impossible undertaking for a land plane. With the amphibian plane, Pritchard reasoned, there was the chance that the float would act as a sled. If he was right, there was a chance for the wrecked soldiers; if not—

Permission was granted. Selecting Benjamin A. Bottoms, RM 1/c, to accompany him, Pritchard took off. The assembled crew of the NORTHLAND manned the rail, cheering.

After circling the desolate ice waste for thirty minutes, Pritchard sighted the wrecked B-17. As he swooped low over the shipwrecked men, Bottoms tapped out a message asking what the chances appeared to be of making a landing. The men of the wrecked plane, with delivery almost within their grasp, returned a despairing negative. A landing was impossible. But Pritchard had already made his own decision.

Seasoned arctic flier that he was, he knew the unpredictable dangers the snow might conceal. He started down in a shallow glide to a long slope where the ice was covered with a blanket of heavy snow. A great crystal wake was thrown high as the float struck the snow. Slowly the plane lost speed, and finally stopped as if against a soft cushion.

Radioman Bottoms was ordered to stay with the plane, keep in radio contact with the NORTHLAND, and also keep the Grumman's engines turning over. Pritchard had landed in a spot about four miles from the B-17. It took him an hour and a quarter of careful walking, using a pole to test for crevasses, to get to the Fortress crew.

When he arrived he found the men weakened from lack of food and intense cold. One had a broken arm, two others were suffering from frostbite gangrene. The amphibian had space for only two passengers. The choice as to who would be first was easily determined; those worst hurt—Sergeant Alexander F. Tucciarone and Staff Sergeant Lloyd Puryear. With the help of one of the sturdier survivors Pritchard managed to get the men over the four snow-drifted miles to the Grumman.

For the take-off the plane was turned, nose downhill. Pritchard gunned the motor and shouted that he would be back the next day. He did not add: "If I can get away from *here*."

Setting the plane down on the snow had been smooth, if dangerous. Getting it aloft would be the real test. There was no smooth water here to taxi and try again if the first attempt failed. There could be only a first attempt. As the propellers bit the thin cold air the snow squealed under the float. The plane was moving. It gathered speed and the snow swirled up like talcum. The Grumman rose, then settled again. Another bump, and another, and with each one the plane rose a little higher before reluctantly settling down. On the fourth bounce she lifted free and high. The plane was airborne. The first landing and take-off in history had been made from the Greenland icecap, and in a seaplane!

Long after sunset Pritchard taxied up to the NORTHLAND and his waiting shipmates. There was joy, and there was argument. To try a second rescue was pushing good luck too far. No, if it had been done once, the second attempt should be less risky—

The next day, November 29, the Army men saw the Grumman coming in again. But, as if in jealous pursuit, Greenland weather was riding close behind: fog, oozing down like grease-thick gravy along the bay and the coast. Pritchard landed, and saw he must take off immediately, and that with a light load. One man was to go out this time, Corporal Haworth, the man who had fixed the wrecked radio. Again Lieutenant Pritchard bounced his plane from the icecap, and disappeared into the fog.

Disappeared: No one ever saw Pritchard, Bottoms or Haworth again.

PLATE I—(*upper*) President Franklin D. Roosevelt just before (*left*) and just after (*right*) sign-
ing the Lend-Lease Bill to give aid to Britain, China, and Greece, March 11, 1941. One of
the six pens he used was presented to the Navy and is now in the Naval Academy Museum,
Annapolis, Maryland. (*Associated Press Photos.*) (*lower*) Secretary of the Navy Frank Knox
and Admiral Ernest J. King, USN, discuss Atlantic defenses aboard the USS AUGUSTA off
Bermuda in September, 1941. Admiral King, at the time Commander in Chief of the U. S.
Atlantic Fleet, was later (December 20, 1941) made Commander in Chief United States Fleet.

PLATE II—With war clouds spreading rapidly over the Atlantic in September, 1940, England and America do mammoth scale "horse trading." For 50 over-age U. S. Navy destroyers, Great Britain leased rent-free naval and air base sites in eight of its possessions off the American coasts. (*upper left*) U. S. Jack Tars at Halifax, Nova Scotia, show the limeys how our "cans" work. On September 9, 1940, Rear Admiral F. L. Reichmuth (*above*) turned eight ships (USS WOOD, WELLES, CROWINSHIELD, BUCHANAN, HERNDON, AARON WARD, HALE, and ABEL P. UPSHUR) over to the Royal Navy. (*Wide World Photo.*) (*center left*) A year after England leased bases to us on a 99-year basis, Frank Knox, Secretary of the Navy, arrived in Bermuda for an inspection of the most important of our eight new outposts. (*Wide World Photo.*) (*lower*) Lonely and desolate was the Bahama base on Abraham Bay and Mayaguara Island, but this patrol plane site helped to guard the Windward Passage against marauding German submarines.

PLATE III—(*above*) Rear Admiral John W. Greenslade, USN, Chairman of the U. S. Army-Navy Survey Board, which selected sites for the bases. (*upper right*) Argentia, northern anchor of the chain of new bases, is a bleak place with continual damp weather and fog, belying the shining silver for which it was named. Quonset huts are quarters for men, hospital wards, storage sheds, and even club and bar. (*center*) An old rock fort marks the eastern end of Kingston harbor, Jamaica, but it is the modern U. S. base for patrol planes, submarine destroyers and cruisers nearby that makes the island a real stronghold of American defense. (*lower left*) The USS INDEPENDENCE, carrier, on a shakedown cruise, approaches Dragon's Mouth, north entrance to the Gulf of Paria, Trinidad, B.W.I. One of the world's largest torpedo nets protects this vital base. (*lower right*) Marines in St. Lucia, a seaplane operating base, strategically located in the Windward Islands of the West Indies. (*Marine Corps Photo.*)

PLATE IV—(*left*) History was in the
making when the USS SOUTH DA-
KOTA, first of a mighty new class of
battleships, slid down the ways at
Camden, New Jersey, June 7, 1941.
The SOUTH DAKOTA, later to win re-
nown in the Pacific as "Battleship
X" or "The Big Bastard," proved at
the Battle of Santa Cruz that the
modern battleship can stand up
against sustained aerial attack. Note
the keel of the USS SANTA FE,
cruiser, being lowered onto the smoking ways—symbolic of the feverish
race to arm us for the war that had
become inevitable. (*Philadelphia In-
quirer Photo.*) (*lower*) USS TREN-
TON, cruiser, was flagship of Squadron 40-T, or "Forty Tare" in Navy
parlance, at Villefranche-sur-mer on
September 3, 1939—the day the
United Kingdom and France declared war on Germany. *Insets:* Rear
Admiral Henry E. Lackey, USN
(*right*), and Rear Admiral C. D.
Courtney, USN (*left*), commanding
officers of "Forty Tare" which established the first U. S. Navy neutrality
patrol "extending several hundred
miles to sea."

PLATE V—(*right*) The first of many similar scenes which angered the American public. Seamen survivors from the clearly identified American freighter ROBIN MOOR, sunk by a German submarine in the South Atlantic, May 21, 1941 —many months before Pearl Harbor. These men floated for 13 days before being picked up by a British ship. On May 27, 1941, an unlimited national emergency was proclaimed by President Roosevelt. (*Associated Press Photo.*)

(*left*) Another step that led to war. The steamship ZAMZAM under the neutral flag of Egypt, with 120 Americans aboard, was sunk by Germans on May 19, 1941, in the South Atlantic. Many lives were lost. (*Associated Press Photo.*)

(*right*) After war was declared by the United States on Germany, sinkings by U-boats were greatly accelerated. Most of the victims were slow merchant ships. Here 16 survivors of the torpedoed troop transport HENRY R. MALLORY are rescued by the Coast Guard. More than 300 Americans lost their lives in this disaster alone. (*Coast Guard Photo.*)

PLATE VI—(*above*) Vice Admiral Russell R. Waesche, USCG, Commandant of the U. S. Coast Guard. (*Coast Guard Photo.*) (*left*) All part of the day's work in bleak Greenland. Hunting for Nazi weather stations, Coast Guardsmen often overcame obstacles that might have discouraged Arctic explorers. Repeated German attempts to set up bases in Greenland were frustrated. Coast Guardsmen first landed in Greenland March 17, 1941 to be followed on April 9, 1941, by U. S. Marines. (*Coast Guard Photo.*) (*lower*) German trawler EXTERNSTEIN, one of several enemy ships captured by the alert action of Coast Guard cutters of the Greenland patrol. The ship carried radio-weather equipment. Twenty Nazi prisoners were taken. Renamed EAST BREEZE, she was taken to the U. S. intact. (*Coast Guard Photo.*)

PLATE VII—(*above*) Rear Admiral Edward H. "Iceberg" Smith, USCG, Commander of the Northeast Greenland patrol. Organized July 1, 1941, the patrol consisted of the cutters NORTHLAND, NORTH STAR, and BEAR. (*right*) A crude shack, but for a short time it broadcast weather information of invaluable aid to Nazi air, land, sea, and undersea forces. Coast Guardsmen found it abandoned on Shannon Island. It was burned. (*Coast Guard Photo.*) (*lower*) Like figures in a fantastic Arctic ballet, a file of bewildered Germans surrenders to Coast Guardsmen who discovered their radio-weather station on the Greenland coast. Coast Guardsmen and U. S. Marines also safeguarded the cryolite mine at Ivigtut, important source of the mineral essential to the smelting of aluminum. (*Coast Guard Photo.*)

PLATE VIII—In June, 1941, the number of ships torpedoed in the Atlantic rose to such an alarming number that the British Admiralty stopped publishing the figures. Early in July, 1941, Task Force 19 was organized by Admiral Ernest J. King, USN, as CINCLANT (Commander in Chief, Atlantic) and was our first naval foreign expeditionary force of the still undeclared war. Above are some of the ships of the Force. *Left row, top to bottom:* USS NEW YORK, battleship; USS NASHVILLE, cruiser; USS FULLER, attack transport, and USS GLEAVES, destroyer. *Right row, top to bottom:* USS ARKANSAS, battleship; USS BROOKLYN, cruiser; USS HEYWOOD, transport, and USS BENSON, destroyer.

PLATE IX—It was a mixed lot of vessels that made up Task Force 19 to Iceland, but their names are written large in the annals of World War II. Many ships in the pioneer force were later to see much action in the Mediterranean and in the Pacific. Typical of the craft of "Nineteen" were: *Left row, top to bottom:* USS MAYO, USS LANSDALE, and USS CHARLES F. HUGHES, destroyers; and USS CHEROKEE, fleet tug. *Right row, top to bottom:* USS HILARY P. JONES and USS MADISON, destroyers; USS SALAMONIE, oiler; and USS GEORGE E. BADGER, seaplane tender.

PLATE x—On July 7, 1941, exactly five months before Pearl Harbor, an American naval task force of 23 ships landed U. S. Marines at Reykjavik, Iceland, at the invitation of the Icelandic government. Here Prime Minister Winston Churchill reviews the Marines, who released British troops badly needed in Africa on August 16, 1941. *Insets:* (*left*) Rear Admiral David McD. Lebreton, USN, Commanding Officer of the U. S. Naval Task Force 19 to Iceland, and (*right*) Major General John Marston, USMC, leader of the First Provisional Brigade in Iceland. (*Marine Corps Photo.*) (*lower*) Iceland did not chill the famous American sense of humor, as is evidenced by the name U. S. Navy airmen gave their fleet air base there.

PLATE XI—(*upper*) The "Witch" rides out an Arctic gale. USS WICHITA, flagship of Vice Admiral Robert C. Giffen, USN, (*inset right*) led a second task force to Iceland, bringing in Army troops and Air Force units to supplement and later replace the Marine garrison. (*inset left*) Rear Admiral Forde A. Todd, USN, Commanding Officer of the U. S. Atlantic Squadron that preceded the Atlantic Fleet. (*lower*) The dawn patrol over Iceland. U. S. Navy planes constantly patrolled the convoy lanes off the new naval operating base, formally announced by Secretary of the Navy Frank Knox on November 8, 1941. *Inset:* Rear Admiral James L. Kauffman, USN, Commandant of N.O.B., Iceland.

PLATE XII—The cruisers above all have long and glorious battle records. *Left row, top to bottom:* USS QUINCY, USS AUGUSTA, and USS HONOLULU. *Right row, top to bottom:* USS VINCENNES, USS TUSCALOOSA, and USS SAN FRANCISCO. The QUINCY and VINCENNES were later lost in the Pacific. First American naval warship to be attacked by a German U-boat was the old destroyer GREER (*lower left*), September 4, 1941. Fortunately, the Nazis missed. The oiler SALINAS (*lower right*) on October 30, 1941, was not so lucky. She was hit thrice, but by super-human effort and amazing damage control she was able to make port under her own power.

PLATE XIII—(*upper*) One of the most incredible rescues of the war. When an Army B-17 (Flying Fortress) en route to Europe was forced down on the desolate Greenland icecap, Navy flyers came to their aid with a PBY flying boat. This photograph, taken from the Navy plane, shows the B-17 resting on the snow, August 6, 1942. (*lower*) Lieutenant A. Y. Parunak, Captain of the Navy PBY which rescued the stranded crew of the B-17, stands at the edge of a little lake formed by melting snow on the icecap. The lake, less than two miles across, was just long enough for a take-off at the 4,200-foot altitude. In another PBY rescue of B-17 flyers, April 5, 1943, a Navy flying boat was able to land and take off on the snow itself.

PLATE XIV—(*upper*) President Roose
velt boards HMS PRINCE O
WALES in Placentia Bay for on
of the historic Atlantic Charte
meetings with Prime Ministe
Winston Churchill, August 1c
1942. At his side is his son an
aide, Captain Elliott Roosevel
USAAF. In the background ca
be seen the hills of Newfound
land, drab setting for one of th
most momentous conferences i
history. The destroyer alongsid
is the USS McDougal. (*left*) Un
consciously President Roosevelt
fingers form a "V" for Victor
symbol during a conversation wit
Prime Minister Churchill. Direc
ly behind the two leaders stan
Admiral Ernest J. King, USN
General George C. Marshal
USA, and General Sir John Dil

PLATE XV—(*upper*) Monday evening, August 11, 1941, was "guest night" aboard HMS PRINCE OF WALES. *Seated, left to right:* Sir Alexander Cadogan, Permanent Under Secretary of State for Foreign Affairs; Air Chief Marshall Wilfred Freeman; Prime Minister Churchill; President Roosevelt; Admiral Sir Dudley Pound; Field Marshall Sir John Dill; Lord Cherwell. *Back row, left to right:* Averill Harriman; Harry Hopkins; Admiral E. J. King, USN; Admiral Ross McIntire, USN; Sumner Welles; Major General E. M. Watson; John Roosevelt; Admiral H. S. Stark, USN; Rear Admiral J. R. Beardall, USN, Naval Aide to the President; General G. C. Marshall, USA; and Franklin D. Roosevelt, Jr. (*lower*) Following church services aboard the PRINCE OF WALES conference leaders pose for an informal photograph—later autographed for and by President Roosevelt.

PLATE XVI—(*upper*) First prize of the neutrality patrol—November 6, 1941. A boarding crew from the USS OMAHA cautiously approaches a strange looking ship flying the U. S. flag with the name "SS WILLMOTO, of Philadelphia" on the stern. It proved to be the German motorship ODENWALD, en route from Japan to Germany. The Germans tried to scuttle her, but the OMAHA put a prize crew aboard (*lower*) which patched up the ship and brought her valuable cargo of rubber, copper, and chemicals to the United States.

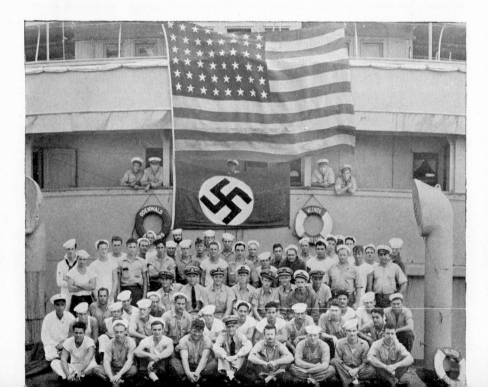

Only the plane's wreckage was later discovered. There was no sign of the three men. They had, therefore, not been killed in the crash.

(Lieutenant Pritchard and Radioman Benjamin A. Bottoms were awarded the Distinguished Flying Cross posthumously by Admiral Royal E. Ingersoll, Commander in Chief United States Atlantic Fleet, for saving the lives of two Army men, and the attempt to save the life of another which cost them their own.)

A searching party of five men was put ashore from the NORTHLAND on December 3, 1942. Ensign Richard L. Fuller, USCGR, was in command; with him were Pharmacist's Mate Gerard A. Hearn; Boatswain's Mate Harold A. Green; Coxswain Stanley Preble, and Aviation Machinist's Mate Donald A. Drisko. They were optimistic. The plane's last signal had given Pritchard's position only five miles away. Five miles only—but the fruitless search was to last five bitter winter months.

Drisko had a special interest in this search for Pritchard and Bottoms. Bottoms had gone on the first flight and returned a hero. Donald Drisko wanted to go with Pritchard on the second rescue. Bottoms agreed to toss for it. A nickel spun in the arctic sunlight. Bottoms called it—and won. And lost his life.

The men landed, fully equipped for a rescue expedition, facing the icecap which they had to scale before they could start on the trek across the snow field.

Each man was armed, carried a compass, a knife, a small pack and a section of tent. Behind them they dragged a short sled known as a "mooserunner." Their food supplies consisted of raisins, oatmeal and tea. They had a tiny kerosene stove with a limited supply of fuel. There were two sleeping bags, and each man had snowshoes. The men were roped together at 50-foot intervals. To distribute their weight on the ice, and to diminish the chances of falling into a crevasse, each man wore 7½-foot skis.

The lost plane had last been heard from only five miles inland. But one mile on an active glacier can be an eternity, and this glacier was active, full of crevasses, shifting and constantly forming anew. They were hidden and covered by a film of drifting, powdered snow about three feet deep, impossible to walk on without snowshoes. Even then, it was like walking knee-deep in talcum powder.

The wind began to blow. It was slow and snow-filled at first, whipping over the ice at about 40 miles an hour. Then it increased until it seemed that all the snow blanket was in the air, whistling crystal pellets. It was foolhardy and impossible to walk under such conditions where the first misstep would mean a sudden drop into a yawning crack.

Storm and exhaustion kept the party tent-bound for thirty days. Hearn had to perform impromptu dentisting when teeth of two of the men loosened and ached. Most of the time the party merely lay wrapped in sleeping bags. The gasoline supply for the lamp ran out, and they lived by candlelight.

The rescue attempts of the Army and the Navy to get the B-17 crew members off the icecap had been going on. A motor sled with three men sent out by the Army broke down, and made that many more to rescue.

Taking inspiration from Lieutenant Pritchard's successful pontoon landing on the snow, naval aviation authorities at Newfoundland decided to risk an all-out rescue attempt in a PBY-5A, one of the big flying ships of the North Atlantic antisubmarine patrol.

Lieutenant Bernard W. Dunlop, USNR, piloted the PBY to the ice-cap for the first try on February 5, and succeeded in getting off the stranded motor-sled party and one member of the B-17 crew whose feet were badly frozen. Bad weather prevented another attempt until March 17, and by then the area around the wrecked bomber had become so checkered with crevasses and drifts that the nearest possible landing area was six miles distant. The Army aviators were too weak to make the trek, so Dunlop carried a dog team, sled and three men to the chosen landing place. The three Army aviators were carried back over the six miles in two days, but foul weather again prevented Dunlop from making the final rescue try.

On April 5 the PBY belly-whoppered to a landing 100 yards from the camp of rescued and rescuers. The six men and nine dogs were taken aboard, but in the take-off the overloaded plane's starboard engine caught fire and Dunlop had to land again. The flames were extinguished, and after hours of repeated effort the big flying boat was airborne at last— and then the fire-crippled engine cut out. Dunlop brought the plane safely to base, with so little fuel in his tanks that he was unable to circle the field.

The NORTHLAND's party returned on foot, and regained the cutter on May 8—five months after they'd set out.

Chapter Five

B Y MAY of 1941 Lend-Lease material was piling up in some ports faster than ships could carry it way. The long arm of Germany's underwater weapon was reaching out to drag down this flow of munitions to Great Britain. On the Admiralty charts the locations of ship sinkings strewed both North and South Atlantic like a map of the Milky Way. Ships were being sunk faster than the yards of Scotland, England and the United States could launch them. The heaviest attacks were delivered at the northern route, against convoys skirting Greenland and Iceland in waters of the Western Hemisphere.

On May 21, an American merchant ship, the ROBIN MOOR, was torpedoed and sunk by a German submarine in the South Atlantic, her passengers and crew left in lifeboats hundreds of miles from land. There was no explanation or apology from the German government. Six days later an unlimited national emergency was proclaimed by President Roosevelt. He explained the necessity and the meaning of "unlimited national emergency" in a radio address to the nation, and said it would entail expansion of the naval patrol in the Atlantic by more ships, planes and personnel.

"Our patrols are helping now," the statement read, "to insure delivery of the needed supplies to Britain. All additional measures necessary to deliver the goods will be taken."

The need for "additional measures" was rapidly becoming apparent. In the next month, June of 1941, the number of ships torpedoed rose to such an alarming number that the British Admiralty stopped publishing the figures. And Germany's conviction in total victory was displayed by Hitler's Baltic-to-Black Sea invasion of the Soviet Union.

On July 7, an American naval task force landed United States Marines at Reykjavik, Iceland, the consent of the Icelanders being couched in terms of invitation.

49

The garrisoning of Iceland by American forces was announced this day on the floor of Congress by a message from the President, which read, in part:

> In accordance with the understanding so reached, forces of the United States Navy have today arrived in Iceland in order to supplement, and eventually to replace the British forces which have until now been stationed in Iceland in order to insure the adequate defense of that country. . . .
>
> As Commander in Chief I have consequently issued orders to the Navy that all necessary steps be taken to insure the safety of communications in the approaches between Iceland and the United States, as well as on the seas between the United States and all other strategic outposts.

Iceland, whence Leifur Heppni, "Leif the Lucky," had sailed with his Viking crew to discover the North American continent 941 years before, was an independent kingdom whose ruler was Christian X of Denmark. Its climate is tempered by the eastward-reaching Gulf Stream and ameliorated by many hot springs, but it is bleak at best. Its rugged, proud inhabitants are the world's most literate people. More books are published in Icelandic, in proportion to population, than in any other language. The 120,000 Icelanders are governed by the oldest popularly-elected Parliament on earth, the Althing, which was established in A.D. 930. They are a race unto themselves, predominantly Scandinavian in origin with some small admixture of Celt; there are no Eskimos in their family tree, nor yet in their community.

Like Switzerland, Iceland is traditionally neutral, but Iceland's neutrality, unlike Switzerland's, is assailed by geography in an interhemispheric conflict. The island, not quite as large as the state of Pennsylvania, fits like a loose cork between the land masses of the hemispheres, in the neck of the North Atlantic. Who dominates Iceland dominates the aerial and oceanic highways between the Old World and the New.

The Axis realized that, before embarking upon world conquest. In 1933 Italy's Air Marshal Balbo flew the route, and in ensuing years the Germans experimented with gliders there and made extensive geographic and meteorological surveys of the inland. In 1939 Germany's Lufthansa sought to exercise an eight-year-old option for developing airdrome sites in Iceland, but the Althing, fully alert to the crisis approaching in Europe, refused.

In April, 1940, the Germans invaded Denmark and thereby made a prisoner of Iceland's king. Launching forthwith on their submarine campaign, the Nazis gave clear implication that Iceland, like Greenland, was important to their scheme of conquest. Britain, whose respect for the neutrality of Norway and Denmark had aided the German invasion of both, sent a mixed force to Iceland on May 10, 1940, a few strides in advance of a German invasion. Britain could not negotiate admission of her garrisoning forces in advance; there was no time, and there was graver risk that the Germans would learn of the negotiations and seize Iceland as they had pounced upon its sister kingdom.

Assured that the British forces would respect Iceland's neutrality, would in no way interfere with the domestic government or economy of its 120,000 inhabitants, and would be evacuated as soon as the common menace of Nazi invasion was defeated, the Iceland parliament accepted the situation co-operatively. A year later, after the establishment of United States forces in Greenland, President Roosevelt negotiated the replacement of British protection over Iceland. The 15,000 Empire troops who were providing the tiny kingdom's defenses were urgently needed in Africa. Iceland realized that the British protective force would be replaced by a Nazi army of conquest if not by the friendly Americans, and again in a spirit of choice between evil and inconvenience the Althing invited the United States to mount guard, 530 nautical miles from Nazi-infested Norway, 450 miles from the nearest United Kingdom landfall, half the lesser distance to Greenland.

There were 23 American ships in the task force under Rear Admiral David McD. LeBreton, USN, that entered Reykjavik harbor on July 7, 1941, including two battleships, two cruisers and nine destroyers. Transports, loaded with Marines, supply ships and seaplane tenders for the escorting patrol planes of VP-2 made up the rest.[1]

---

[1] Task Force 19, Rear Admiral David McD. LeBreton, USN, commanding, was ordered assembled by Admiral Ernest J. King as CINCLANT and was the first naval foreign expeditionary force of the still-undeclared war. It consisted of Battle Division 5, less USS TEXAS and WYOMING: USS NEW YORK (Capt. James G. Ware, USN); USS ARKANSAS (Capt. Carleton E. Bryant, USN); two light cruisers of Cruiser Division 8, USS BROOKLYN (Capt. Ellis S. Stone, USN) and USS NASHVILLE (Capt. Francis S. Craven, USN); nine destroyers of Desron 7, USS PLUNKETT (Lt. Comdr. William A. Graham, USN), NIBLACK (Lt. Comdr Edward R. Durgin, USN), BENSON (Lt. Comdr. Arthur L. Pleasants, Jr., USN), GLEAVES (Lt. Comdr. Edward H. Pierce, USN), MADISON (Lt. Comdr. Thomas E. Boyce, USN), LANSDALE (Lt. Comdr. John Connor, USN), MAYO (Lt. Comdr. Campbell D. Emory, USN), HILARY P. JONES (Lt. Comdr. Sherman R. Clark, USN), and CHARLES F. HUGHES (Lt. Comdr. George

The convoy was intact except for one ship, a destroyer that had dropped out of formation on July 5 to go to the signal of a foundering lifeboat. This destroyer reached Reykjavik a day late, on July 8, and aboard were four American women.

The story of how four American women happened to be carried into Reykjavik in a Navy destroyer the day after the Marines landed has its beginning in New Orleans, where ten women took passage to England as part of the Harvard Unit of Red Cross nurses.

They sailed June 5, aboard the Norwegian motorship VIGRID in a British convoy. About noon on the 23rd, the passengers aboard the VIGRID felt a gradual change in the familiar vibration of their ship. One of the motors had stopped and she was losing speed. The VIGRID, unable to keep up, dropped out of formation, and the people standing at her rails watched the convoy disappear over the horizon with the sickening realization of their helplessness.

Around midnight Captain Harold Holst, skipper of the VIGRID, sent his officers through the wallowing ship with the warning that there were submarines in the area. At 7 : 15 in the morning, well past the dangerous hour of dawn, the passengers' speculations on their safety were abruptly ended as two torpedoes crashed into the vessel without warning. Within ten minutes the thirty-seven crew members and the ten American nurses were in the four lifeboats, and the VIGRID had sunk.

One of the women was Miss Marion Blissett, a native of Kalkaska, Michigan, and a graduate of the Henry Ford Hospital in Detroit, later commissioned in the Navy Nurse Corps.

"The lifeboat I was in was terribly crowded so I was transferred to the captain's boat," said Miss Blissett. "The boat I left is one of the two that were never found."

A few moments after that, Miss Blissett recalls, the dark hull of the submarine broke the surface of the water and an officer stepped out of the conning tower. He shouted questions to Captain Holst: What was the ship's name, what cargo was carried, from whence and to where? He

---

L. Menocal, USN) ; the seaplane tender USS GOLDSBOROUGH (Lt. Comdr. Stanley J. Michael, USN) and the tender GEORGE E. BADGER (Lt. Comdr. Robert S. Purvis, USN) servicing VP-52, commanded by Lt. Comdr. Charles C. McDonald, USN; Transport Division 2, USS HEYWOOD (Capt. Rivers J. Carstarphen, USN), FULLER (Capt. Paul S. Theiss, USN), W. P. BIDDLE (Capt. Campbell D. Edgar, USN) ; supply ships ARCTURUS (Comdr. Henry Hartley, USN), HAMUL (Comdr. Elwood M. Tilson, USN), ORIZABA (Capt. Clarence Gulbranson, USN) ; the oiler SALAMONIE (Comdr. Theodore M. Waldschmidt, USN), the fleet tug CHEROKEE (Lt. Comdr. L. F. Weaver, USN).

noted the answers, and, bellowing the promise that a ship would be sent to pick up the survivors, the submarine officer re-entered the hatch and the U-boat submerged.

"Around noon the next day," said Miss Blissett, "we had a terrible disappointment. We saw another convoy quite close and signaled to them. They seemed to see us and one ship headed toward us, then suddenly turned back into the convoy. We were left behind! Three hours later the sub surfaced again near us. We knew then why we had been abandoned by the convoy."

After this the group of four lifeboats divided, two of them setting a course for the Irish coast. One of these boats, with Nurses Margaret I. Somerville and Helen Jurewicz aboard, was picked up a few days later by a British warship. The other two headed for Greenland, 400 miles northwest, led by the captain's lifeboat containing Miss Blissett and three other Red Cross nurses—Lillian N. Pesnicak, Rachel M. St. Pierre and Victoria M. Pelc.

For days, the little boats pitched and tossed in the stormy North Atlantic without an hour's calm. After one especially stormy night Miss Blissett's lifeboat found itself alone. The other boat was lost—or foundered.

Strict rationing was imposed, and even with the rain each person was allowed only four ounces of water every twelve hours. Food consisted of three small tinned Swedish meat balls at noon, and for the first six days, one piece of hardtack to each person. For the last six days a half biscuit was the day's ration.

Over and over Captain Holst expressed his amazement and admiration at the manner in which the American girls in his boat withstood the lifeboat ordeal. But once when Captain Holst evidenced gloom he uttered a wish that Miss Blissett thinks now was prophetic:

"I wish your President would tell your Navy to get the hell out of those Navy Yards and go look for you girls!"

On the evening of July 5, Captain Holst's wish (which at the time seemed as remote as a wish for magic carpet) came true, as Miss Blissett recalls. One man on watch thought he saw a ship. Others stood up to look; they had gone through a like performance almost daily, but this time there really was a ship—and another, and another. The horizon seemed filled with ships!

The sailors waved shirts, caps, jackets, oars. A destroyer sliced away from the convoy and came leaping to investigate.

"Captain Holst shouted, 'Blissett, that's *your* flag—*your* Navy—wave to them!' " the nurse relates. "Even then Captain Holst's meaning impressed me. I realized how he longed to have a Navy and a flag to which he could have waved for rescue."

The destroyer was USS CHARLES F. HUGHES. She came smartly about to place the lifeboat in her lee, lines were passed, and a cargo net unrolled over the side. The women went first, clinging with swollen, frostbitten fingers to the net and the reaching hands of the bluejackets.

The destroyer dropped out of the convoy for a day in fruitless search for the other lifeboat, which had become separated during a night storm.

Miss Blissett and her three nurse companions were sent to the English hospital in Reykjavik where they spent five days resting. Then they boarded the ORIZABA and were returned to the United States. Lost at sea were Nurses Phyllis Lou Evans, Dorothea L. Koehn, Dorothy C. Morse and Nancie M. Pett.

Few men in the Iceland Task Force that steamed into Reykjavik harbor on July 7, 1941, knew what they were going to see when they set foot on land. On the side of the harbor was a group of camouflaged British merchant ships. Ahead of them, tied up at jetties, were rows of small needle-masted fishing smacks and behind these the cobbled shore was lined with rows of fish-drying sheds. The all-pervading odor was to provide the American men, never hesitant or deliberately delicate in selecting one, with a nickname for these new people with whom they were to associate. It was "Codhead."

The American transports and supply ships docked near the jetties and the Marines of the 1st Provisional Brigade, led by Brigadier General John Marston, USMC, walked down the gangplanks carrying light war packs.[1] They could see the signs of war here, the spirals of barbed-wire entanglements placed by the British troops, and the sandbagged gun emplacements at every intersection of the narrow streets. As to the citizens of Iceland, the troops might reasonably have been excused if they had expected to meet Eskimos. To most of the men, Iceland was a relatively small island hanging from the Arctic Circle like an icicle, about whose inhabitants

---

[1] The units of the brigade were: 6th Marines (Col. Leo D. Hermle, USMC); 5th Defense Battalion (Col. Lloyd L. Leech, USMC); 2nd Battalion, 10th Marines (Lt. Col. John B. Wilson); 3rd Platoon, 1st Scout Company; Company C, 1st Engineer Battalion; Company A, 2nd Medical Battalion; 1st Platoon, Company A, 2nd Service Battalion; Company A, 2nd Tank Battalion. Tarawa, Saipan and Guam were battle honors later to be inscribed on their standards.

the school geographies had little to say. It was with respect, as well as surprise, that they inspected the sturdy blond Vikings impassively watching the disembarkation.

Before work on the Iceland base was a month old, another 21-ship task force had arrived bringing in Army troops and Army Air Force units to supplement, and later replace, the Marine garrison. Rear Admiral Robert C. Giffen, USN, was the commander of this task force. His flagship was the cruiser WICHITA (Captain James T. Alexander, USN), and there followed in train a fleet of fighting ships which were, like the "Witch," to make naval history: The battleship MISSISSIPPI (Captain Theodore S. Wilkinson, USN), for example, which, under succeeding skippers, played a mighty part in the Battle of the Pacific from the Aleutians to the equator; and the battered little obsolete destroyer REUBEN JAMES (Lieutenant Commander Heywood L. Edwards, USN) which was to make history of another, and tragic sort, when torpedoed without warning a few weeks later. And there was the carrier WASP (Captain John W. Reeves, Jr., USN) which was later to be the first American carrier into the Mediterranean when she ferried planes into besieged Malta. On this cruise she carried the Army Air Force's 33rd Pursuit Squadron. There were the two cruisers VINCENNES (Captain Frederick Louis Riefkohl, USN), and QUINCY (Captain Charlton E. Battle, USN) which were to be sunk fighting the Japs off Savo Island, and the cruiser TUSCALOOSA (Captain Lee P. Johnson, USN), one of the American naval ships to bombard the coast of Normandy on the distant dawn of the invasion of Europe.

The Army transport, USS AMERICAN LEGION, was the cause of the only incident that occurred on the second convoy to Iceland. The flagship received a signal from the transport one afternoon saying that she had run aground. This seemed unlikely since the charts of the area showed a depth of 700 fathoms, so the flagship swung over to investigate. It was remotely possible that the ship had struck a reef. But the AMERICAN LEGION had struck a large whale, not a reef. The sharp bow of the transport had sliced into the huge mammal and it stuck there like a pickle on a fork prong. With a little effort the whale was separated from the bow and the ship joined the convoy, which proceeded through seas foul with flotsam from torpedoed ships and iridescent with oil slicks from the bilges of submarines.

When work on the base first started the men lived in tents and then progressed to Quonset huts until the regular facilities of a naval base, including comfortable quarters for officers and men, wardroom, clubs, recreation halls, and even a dry-cleaning establishment, were completed. In addition, a naval air station about five miles from Reykjavik, adjacent to RAF and Royal Norwegian Air Force stations, was built for patrol planes and to be used as an antisubmarine operations base. Commissioned in September of 1942 was another naval base, Camp Knox, with housing facilities for five to six hundred men. This was laid out as a section base, port director's headquarters, a receiving unit, and a depot for tanklighter crews. Hvalfjordor, a large anchorage about 40 miles northwest of Reykjavik, was selected as the convoy forming ground and anchorage for large warships.

By November 8, the job was far enough along for Secretary of the Navy Knox to announce the establishment of Naval Operating Base, Iceland. NOB Iceland became a part of the command of Commander in Chief Atlantic Fleet Admiral Ernest J. King, for both administration and task purposes. Rear Admiral James L. Kauffman, USN, was named Commandant of the Base.

The men on Iceland had another job to do as well as constructing a naval base. There was a little public relations work necessary. Some have attributed the native suspicion of Americans to that major American commodity, the motion picture. Movies were intensely popular with the people of Iceland, but unfortunately the cinematic diet provided for them by Hollywood's exporters was the worse half of the average double-feature bill. The Icelanders were not to be blamed if they accepted the evidence that when an American was not a gun-totin' cowboy, he was bound to be a sinister, slang-slinging gangster.

But Icelanders love to dance. So do Americans. It takes a boy and a girl to make a dance, hence an entree to the social life of Iceland. The Stork Club of Reykjavik is the Borg Hotel, a modern establishment that holds a public dance every night of the week, including Sundays, to the music of a creditable jazz orchestra. It wasn't long before this word spread. At first the Iceland girls puzzled the Americans. Always ready to accept an invitation to dance, they would never return to the man's table or invite him to sit at theirs. When the dance was over they bowed, exchanged pleasantries and returned to their own table for a drink of "apple sin," a local soft drink much like orange squash, or the near beer that was as close to liquor as local law permitted.

Once the Navy base was established, so was normal social intercourse. The weekly dance at the base ended always with a buffet supper which helped thaw the Icelanders' chill. For one thing, ham and highballs were standard items; the Icelanders love ham, which they have to import. With all European commerce cut off, the meat diet was either mutton or pony steak, alternating with fish, augmented by potatoes, turnips, rhubarb and bilberries. What the Icelanders lack in variety for the main courses, however, they make up in pastries, and even the most particular of Navy CPOs has no criticism of the strong, black coffee always available in every Iceland kitchen. Thus a fair exchange, ham and highballs for coffee and cakes, was worked out. It wasn't long before the young ladies and their families found the Americans socially acceptable and some even matrimonially so.

But if Icelandic grilled pony with bilberry jam seemed strange to Americans, some of our food was equally strange to them; watermelon, for instance. One Navy man learned from the young woman he was squiring that neither she nor her family had ever seen, tasted or heard of a watermelon. A friend on the supply ship was given a most particular commission to execute, and on the next trip to Iceland he delivered a beautiful, plump watermelon.

The Navy man sent his prized gift to the house at noon and the messenger returned with an invitation for the donor to share the treat that evening. He arrived to find the family in despair and chagrin. Dinner was not ready, and in sorrowing proof they led him into the gleaming kitchen where the rotund, green watermelon was seething in the largest copper caldron. "It had been boiling since noon and it is still tough," the apologetic hostess explained.

Except for scrub birch and shoulder-high willow, Iceland is treeless, another deficiency which one American set himself to correct. Aviation Chief Metalsmith Robert Bryant of Salt Lake City arrived there from duty in the Pacific. The barren, rocky land was strange contrast to lush Pacific vegetation. Bryant decided to do something about it, even if nature refused to co-operate.

His inspiration was contained in the piles of empty five-gallon jam and tomato juice cans. Bryant flattened them into sheets—from which he snipped palm leaves. Discarded iron pipes were salvaged and wrapped with burlap to make the tree trunks. Smaller steel rods were bolted to the trunk to make branches to which the tin leaves were then soldered. A film of green paint was applied and the tree was finished!

The first two of these assembly-line trees were "planted" at the entrance to the base. Two more were placed at the entrance of the Officers' Club. Then other men began to get ideas. Throughout the camp there appeared other concomitants to give Iceland a touch of home. Street signs were staked up proclaiming a cinder path to be Broadway or Michigan Avenue, and dummy wooden fire plugs began to dot the company streets. There were even a few red fire-alarm boxes, and a dummy subway kiosk was being planned by one Marine unit when it received sailing orders.

By September, 1941, additional Army troops had landed in Iceland and Major General Charles H. Bonesteel, USA, relieved Brigadier General John Marston, USMC, as Commanding General of the United States forces in Iceland. In the first issue of the Marine newspaper in Iceland, *The Arctic Marine*, dated September 25, General Marston wrote the following editorial:

> Upon the occasion of being relieved as commanding general of the United States forces in Iceland by Major General Charles H. Bonesteel, U.S. Army, I wish to express to the First Marine Brigade my appreciation for the unstinted effort they have made to complete the Army housing program. It has been particularly gratifying to observe the friendly cooperation among the Army, Navy and Marine Corps, and the uncomplaining manner in which many disagreeable and backbreaking tasks have been performed. This fine demonstration of wholehearted team work is an exhibition of which any commanding officer would be proud, and I am proud of every officer and man in this Brigade.

As in Greenland, continued German nuisance raids and reconnaissance runs occurred over Iceland. German bombs fell in the northern part of the island and trawlers and fishing boats were strafed in the outlying waters. The first German plane was shot down in the summer of 1942. It was a four-motored Focke Wulf on patrol from Norway. An Army pilot in a P-38, also on patrol, surprised the German bomber and shot it down within sight of land. The enemy plane exploded when it struck the water. Crash boats were sent out immediately to gather up possible remains of the wreckage to study. The only thing they could find were the pilot's lungs, in perfect condition, lying on the water as if a surgeon had laid them out for inspection. They were picked up by the doctors aboard and taken back as an example of the peculiar effects of blast.

The occupation of Iceland was a double stride forward in naval strategy. It meant that under the neutrality laws Lend-Lease shipping could be protected to within 450 nautical miles of its British destination. It meant that an elaborate program for guarding the sea lanes could now be carried out. In a broad sense it meant a gigantic patrol of the wide North Atlantic lane by shore-based, long-range United States and Canadian Patrol planes that could now fan out from Iceland as well as from Greenland and Newfoundland. It provided a more than mid-point base for aircraft carriers, destroyers and cruisers which could be assigned vital lanes to protect. Within this area faster merchant ships could with reasonable safety travel alone and the slower ones in convoys through the most dangerous area.

And, for the second part, it meant that none of these uses could be employed by the Germans against American shipping, or otherwise to combat the United States' doctrine of hemispheric solidarity and freedom of the seas.

Chapter Six

T HE pride of the English Navy, HMS PRINCE OF WALES (Captain
John Catterell Leach, RN, DSO), had been discharged from a shipyard and pronounced well and ready for action after her encounter with
the Nazi battleship BISMARCK. On the 4th day of August she put to sea.

On the same day the presidential yacht, USS POTOMAC (ex-USCG
ELECTRA), stood out from the Virginia capes on the other side of the
Atlantic, and headed northeast.

Aboard the battleship was Prime Minister Churchill and his Chiefs
of Staff, who had boarded a destroyer in the harbor of the obscure Scottish fishing village of Thurso the day before, that took them to where the
massive PRINCE OF WALES lay at anchor.

Mr. Harry Hopkins, who had been conferring on Lend-Lease with
Mr. Churchill a fortnight earlier and who had gone on to Moscow from
London, flew back in time to board the battleship off Scapa Flow.
The PRINCE OF WALES had been fitted out as a flagship. What would
be the Admiral's quarters were given over to the Prime Minister. These
were in the stern of the ship, more like a hotel suite than a cabin.
There was one large saloon or lounge with chintz-covered couches
and armchairs. There was a dining saloon, bathroom, a stateroom and a
pantry. The stateroom was the least-used of the suite; the lounge became
a teeming office, the seat of government of the United Kingdom. But that
was a secret.

It shortly became no secret that President Roosevelt was aboard the
POTOMAC. The Navy Department so announced on August 5:

> After a night of restful sleep President continuing cruise North-
> ern waters to undisclosed destination. Attired in sport shirt and
> slacks President enjoying air from fantail. . . . President some
> time discussing affairs with Commander-in-Chief Atlantic Fleet
> (Admiral Ernest J. King). All on board well.

The next day, with disarming levity, the Navy announced:

> Cruise ship proceeding slowly along coast with party fishing from stern. Weather fair, sea smooth. Potomac River sailors responding to New England air after Washington summer.
>
> (August 7) All members of party showing effects of sunning. Fishing luck good. No destination announced. President being kept in close touch international situation by Navy radio. All aboard well and weather excellent.
>
> (August 8) Cruise uneventful and weather continues fair. President spent most day working on official papers. POTOMAC and CALYPSO (auxiliary; tender to POTOMAC) moved close inshore today and received fuel, water and provision.
>
> (August 9) Ship anchored in fog. Prospects for fishing appear very poor today. Everything quiet on board. No especial news.

This August 9 sentence "No especial news" was no understatement on the part of POTOMAC's communique writer, for the President was not aboard that day. Off the coast of Massachusetts he and his party had left the POTOMAC and gone aboard the cruiser AUGUSTA, the flagship of Admiral E. J. King, CINCLANT, and commanded by Captain G. A. Wright, USN. Had there been a communique writer aboard the AUGUSTA, and had he been allowed to break security, there would have been very special news, the biggest news story of the year, for it was this August 9, 1941, that President Roosevelt and Prime Minister Churchill met for the first time.

The rendezvous was in Placentia Bay, Newfoundland, at nine o'clock in the morning. On the stroke of two bells, by the PRINCE OF WALES's clocks, the battleship and her escort of three Royal Canadian Navy destroyers, HMCS RIPLEY, RESTIGOUCHE and ASSINIBOINE approached the entrance to the bay. Two American destroyers were cutting through the water with their signal flags blowing. The battleship slowed down as one destroyer, USS MCDOUGAL (Commander William W. Warlick, USN), drew alongside with a boarding officer. The two ships snuggled together and the American naval officer stepped across to the British ship. Berthing arrangements were made, he explained, but the Prime Minister was not expected until nine o'clock, not for an hour and a half.

Captain Leach of the PRINCE OF WALES, thinking he was on time since his clocks had read 0900, was puzzled until watches were checked and the discrepancy discovered. The American Navy was not keeping local Newfoundland summer time and the PRINCE OF WALES was, which created a 90-minute difference.

The somewhat awkward situation was resolved when Captain Leach promptly decided to turn about and make a second arrival at the Placentia berthing area. So the big battleship steamed off on an unscheduled 90-minute round trip up the coast. Upon returning, she was met by the two American destroyers which escorted her through the broad entrance of Placentia Bay, one of the largest anchorages in the Western Hemisphere which cuts into the southeastern corner of Newfoundland for 90 miles.

Inside the bay, in the lee of a rocky promontory, were the waiting American ships. In the center of the group was the cruiser AUGUSTA with the President aboard. Flanking the AUGUSTA was the cruiser TUSCALOOSA and the battleship ARKANSAS. And dotting the wide anchorage like vicious little water-bulldogs were destroyers of Desdiv 17. Overhead patrol planes circled.

The schedule for the first day called for a meeting of the President and the Prime Minister aboard the AUGUSTA at eleven o'clock. Beneath an awning on the AUGUSTA's deck, the Americans waited.

The Prime Minister came first; as he stepped on the gangplank to walk over to the deck of the AUGUSTA all hands stood at attention. The President stood in the center of his group of staff officers. Following directly behind Mr. Churchill came his First Sea Lord, Admiral Sir Dudley Pound, and Mr. Hopkins. The bosun's pipe shrilled and as the Prime Minister's feet touched the deck of the American cruiser, the Navy Band began "God Save the King." The Prime Minister stood in salute. Then from a pocket he took a letter, written by King George. The letter was handed to the President and the two men shook hands.

August 9 was a Saturday. Most of the afternoon was spent in discussing the three-day schedule of conferences to follow. That afternoon a gig full of cartons was sent from the AUGUSTA to the PRINCE OF WALES. There were over 1,500 of these boxes; one for every man on the British battleship. Each box contained 200 cigarettes, a half pound of cheese, two apples and an orange, and a card reading: "The President of the United States of America sends his compliments and best wishes."

That evening the Prime Minister dined with President Roosevelt. As evening came and the daylight grew dim, the lights of the ships began to blink and shine. To the men of the PRINCE OF WALES this sight of lighted ships was almost as novel as the sight of the President himself. Having lived in a blacked-out ship for two years it was almost fearsome to see their home, the great battleship, a lighted target. It was decided to light the PRINCE OF WALES, however, since the American ships were all lighted. It was remotely possible that an enemy plane might come over on a bombing run or in reconnaissance and a blacked-out ship in the middle of lighted ships would arouse suspicions. (When the lights were turned off, the last night of the conference, they were never to go on again for the PRINCE OF WALES. She was torpedoed off the Malay coast by the Japanese four months later almost to the day.)

The following day, Sunday, joint church services were held aboard the PRINCE OF WALES. The President and his staff boarded the USS MC DOUGAL which had been tied alongside the AUGUSTA. With the President on the destroyer's bridge, the ship eased away from the cruiser and nudged her way alongside the British battleship until she was in a position where the decks were level. The procedure of the day before was repeated in reverse. Prime Minister Churchill waited at the gangplank with his chiefs of staff, Admiral Sir Dudley Pound; General Sir John D. Dill, Chief of the Imperial General Staff; Air Chief Marshal W. R. Freeman and Sir Humphrey Wellwyn.

Beside Mr. Churchill and his staff stood a guard of honor and a Royal Marine band. The President, on the arm of his son Captain Elliott Roosevelt, came aboard the PRINCE OF WALES first. As they stepped on deck, the guard presented arms and the Royal Marine band played "The Star-Spangled Banner." Behind the President came Admiral Harold R. Stark, Chief of Naval Operations; Admiral Ernest J. King, Commander in Chief United States Atlantic Fleet; General George C. Marshall, Chief of Staff United States Army; General H. H. Arnold, Chief of the Army Air Forces; Brigadier General George Watson, Military Aide to the President; Mr. Sumner Welles, Under Secretary of State; Mr. Averell Harriman and Mr. Harry Hopkins.

The staff moved to where seats had been arranged and the Sunday Service began by singing "O God, Our Help in Ages Past," and "Onward, Christian Soldiers."

The President and his staff were entertained at Sunday luncheon by Mr. Churchill in the wardroom of the PRINCE OF WALES. There was one item on the menu of special interest: turtle soup. The Prime Minister explained that it had been the custom of Lords of the Admiralty when visiting abroad to take with them a turtle, a custom that had its origin when the British Navy, in order to watch Napoleon at St. Helena, occupied Ascension Island. The first warship to return to England from Ascension Island carried with it a turtle for the Admiralty. Others followed the example until it became a ritual not only for the Lords of the Admiralty to be tendered a turtle, but to make gifts of them to the larders of important guests and hosts-of-state.

When Mr. Churchill had left wartime London, no turtle was to be found, but one of his enterprising officers did unearth, in a West End grocery, a forgotten store of ration-free tinned turtle soup which he bought as the most acceptable substitute for the living reptile. It was this turtle soup that was served for Sunday luncheon.

Monday, August 11, was spent in almost continuous conference aboard the AUGUSTA. The evening was lightened by declaring a "guest night" aboard the PRINCE OF WALES. The guests relaxed around the ship's bar and the party began with a Royal Navy commander proposing the health of the President, followed by the band playing "The Star-Spangled Banner." This courtesy was returned when an American officer proposed the health of the King, and the ship's band played the British national anthem.

At five o'clock the next morning, August 12, Lord Beaverbrook, the British Minister of Supply, came aboard the PRINCE OF WALES, having been flown from England to Newfoundland. This was the last day of conferences. Mr. Churchill and Lord Beaverbrook made their last trip to the AUGUSTA for a final meeting with the President. Launches made continual round trips between the cruiser and the battleship. About four-thirty in the afternoon the last member of the Prime Minister's staff left the AUGUSTA and boarded the British battleship.

The meeting was over. The American destroyers spread and began to take their places in escort formation. At exactly five o'clock the PRINCE OF WALES swung past the AUGUSTA, rendering a salute, and started out of Placentia Bay, bound for Iceland. Aboard one of the destroyers was Ensign Franklin Roosevelt, Jr., assigned by the President to be Mr. Churchill's aide during the Prime Minister's visit to Iceland.

A little later the AUGUSTA got underway and on August 14, off the coast of Maine, the President and his staff transferred to USS POTOMAC for the return trip to Washington.

By this time the news of the Atlantic meeting had been released to the world and the first attempt at defining "war aims" was made public in the form of the Atlantic Charter.

PART TWO

Arctic Operations — Greenland and Iceland

Chapter Seven

FOR some months after the passage of the Lend-Lease Act, United States naval ships patrolled the convoy lanes, broadcasting the presence of any raiders discovered. Existing orders allowed American naval ships to issue such information as a warning to American merchantmen, but permitted no attack on unfriendly vessels.

On the morning of September 4, 1941, a German submarine made the first attack of the war on an American naval warship.

The ship was USS GREER, an old World War flush-deck type destroyer, one of those ordered recommissioned for Atlantic Patrol on September 14, 1939. The captain of the destroyer, Lieutenant Commander Laurence Hugh Frost, USN, had been in command exactly a month to the day. His ship was small in comparison to modern destroyers: 1,200 tons, 314 feet long, with a 30-foot beam. She was armed with four 4-inch guns, three antiaircraft guns and twelve 21-inch torpedo tubes.

On that September morning the GREER was about 175 miles southwest of Iceland with a load of mail and freight for the new American base. Her position was squarely in the well-traveled lane of shipping between Iceland and American ports. It was an area also marked off by the German government six months before as a zone within which vessels exposed themselves "to the danger of destruction." She might, in fact, have served as the entrance buoy for what was even then known to all merchant seamen as "Torpedo Junction."

At 8:40 a British patrol plane approached and circled the GREER, flashing the signal that a submarine had submerged about ten miles directly ahead of the destroyer. The message was acknowledged and the patrol plane returned to the position where the submarine had disappeared.

The GREER increased speed and started to zigzag. Forty minutes later a soundman on the destroyer reported contact with the submarine. Care-

67

fully plotting the sub's course, the GREER followed the sound wake and broadcast the sub's position.

At 10:32 the British patrol plane dropped four depth charges on the submarine's position, circled the spot for twenty minutes and made off. The bombs did not damage the submarine, whose motors were soon registering on the GREER's detectors again.

At 12:40 the sound indicator showed that the submarine was closing in on the GREER. The lookouts sung out that they could see a disturbance and a change of color on the water's surface a few hundred yards off the destroyer's starboard bow, visual evidence of the submarine's proximity. At no time was the periscope of the U-boat seen.

"Torpedo!"

The attack was opened at 12:48. First the telltale impulse bubble, marked the discharge of a torpedo by the submarine. A minute later the seething track of the torpedo passed a hundred yards astern of the GREER.

For all that it was a miss, a wide miss, the intent was deadly clear. Germany had fired the first shot against the United States Navy. The GREER had either to counterattack or remain a target for further torpedoes that might next time find their mark. That was no choice—she attacked. A pattern of eight depth charges was hurled at the submarine's location; the time of the GREER's answer to the challenge was logged at 1256.

Two minutes later the submarine attacked again. The wake of the second torpedo was sighted 500 yards away on the starboard how. The GREER made a hard turn to port and the torpedo passed 300 yards clear of the ship.

Now the destroyer lost contact with the U-boat. But with the avowed killer hiding near, Lieutenant Commander Frost's duty to his ship and his men was clear. He continued the search—at twelve minutes past three the soundman reported certain contact again. This time the GREER took action without waiting for a third torpedo. Eleven depth charges fanned out in a pattern over the contact area.

No debris, not even a bubble of oil, rose to the surface. Contact with the submarine was again lost. Almost certainly undamaged, the U-boat dove deep, to conserve its torpedoes in all probability for prey more usefully attacked than an over-age American destroyer. The GREER continued searching until 6:40 that evening without making further contact. She then continued to Iceland.

But the GREER incident brought to sharp focus a situation that was inexorably reaching serious proportions. What was to be the nation's policy and the Navy's part in this undeclared war within our territorial waters and against ships clearly marked as American? To be sure, international law is habitually more honored in the breach than in the observance, but so far the United States had scrupulously remained within the letter of the law, whereas torpedoing ships without warning was its cynical repudiation.

The attack on the GREER was one more in a growing list of neutrality violations. In July an American battleship had been shadowed for hours by a submarine maneuvering itself into attack position. Since it was known with absolute certainty that no British or American submarine was or had been operating in this area at the time, the inference was obvious. At one time the submarine was close enough to the battleship for lookouts to report sighting the periscope.

An American ship, the ROBIN MOOR, had been sunk late in May, 1941. In August another American owned ship, the SS SESSA, flying the Panamanian flag, was first torpedoed without warning and then shelled in the vicinity of Greenland. Had the German followed the civilized procedure of "visit and search" he would have found no contraband. The neutral ship's cargo was civilian supplies for Greenland.

Three days after the GREER attack, another United States merchant ship, the STEEL SEAFARER, was sunk without warning by German aircraft in the Red Sea, 220 miles south of Suez. Without formality, Germany was making war on the American flag.

On the evening of September 11, seven days after the GREER attack, the President sat before a microphone in the White House, and announced to the world a policy for which the Navy had been waiting.

> Upon our naval and air patrol—now operating in large numbers over a vast expanse of the Atlantic Ocean—falls the duty of maintaining the American policy of freedom of the seas. That means . . . our patrolling vessels and planes will protect all merchant ships, not only American ships, but ships of any flag, engaged in commerce in our defense waters.
>
> From now on, if German or Italian vessels of war enter the waters, the protection of which is necessary for American defense, they do so at their own peril.
>
> The orders which I have given as Commander-in-Chief of the United States Army and Navy are to carry out that policy at once.

This was the "shoot on sight" order. The Navy was ready to carry out that order.

But what of the merchant ships, the unarmed prime targets of the U-boats? The Axis had forbidden the seas to American shipping. Congress, faced with the reality of a European war, had amended the Neutrality Act of 1936 to permit belligerents to purchase munitions "cash and carry," although Lend-Lease had canceled the "cash" provision. United States merchant vessels were forbidden to enter "combat zones," defined by the President to include the area enclosing the North Sea, British waters extending 350 miles west of Ireland, and the Bay of Biscay. That is, the United States had voluntarily cut off its own traffic with Belgium, Holland, Denmark, Sweden, Finland and the all-season ports in Norway despite which the Axis was attacking our ships wherever found.

The men who manned these ships, and sank with them when the ships went down, wanted guns for self-protection. To get the guns on merchant ships required Congressional action, the repeal of section 6 of the 1939 Neutrality Act. By October 13, the House Foreign Affairs Committee had drafted a Joint Resolution for this repeal and Secretary of Navy Knox, with Chief of Naval Operations Admiral Harold R. Stark, appeared before the committee to urge the passage of the resolution.

Before the Neutrality Act was repealed, however, more ships of the United States Navy were attacked, and one sunk.

Chapter Eight

THE first naval vessel attacked after the President's "shoot on sight" orders, and the second to be the target of Nazi torpedoes, was one of the new 1,630-ton destroyers built in 1940, USS KEARNY. She was torpedoed in the glare of a burning tanker in the early morning of October 17, 1941.

Less than twenty months earlier Miss Mary Kearny of Richmond, Virginia, had shattered a bunting-wrapped bottle of American champagne over the stem of the new $5,000,000 destroyer in the shipyards at Kearny, New Jersey. A few weeks later Lieutenant Commander Anthony L. Danis, USN, who had survived the crash of the Navy dirigible MACON on February 12, 1935, took command of the slim, 40-knot ship that mounted five of the new 5-inch dual-purpose guns.

The KEARNY was a new ship of a new class that had caused considerable controversy, and had been dubbed the "top-heavies." There was a question in the minds of the doubtful as to whether they could stand up in action. But they were highly compartmented, to localize damage, and had strong double bottoms to minimize mine or torpedo explosions. And the men who built the KEARNY had faith in her, a faith that was not misplaced.

It was almost midnight. In a few minutes the calendar day of October 16 would be over. The men on watch were thinking of hot coffee and the warm "sack." Below, the oncoming watch was reluctantly astir. Ahead of the KEARNY in a silent pattern, whose form was lost in the black night, were merchant ships in convoy bound for Iceland 350 miles away.

One submarine alarm had broken that pattern of the ships and spread them like frightened water bugs, earlier in the day. But now the dread hour after sunset, when the water is all confusing shadow and every object on the surface stands in sharp silhouette against the sky, was securely past.

71

Off in the dark distance the black calm of night was suddenly ripped apart by distress signals from merchant ships under attack.

The sleep-shattering sound of General Quarters squawked its urgent summons through the ship as the KEARNY headed full speed toward the scene of attack.

The glow from the rockets over the convoy seemed to linger and then flare violently. A tanker was suddenly blazing, her burning oil spreading out on the water as the hulk began to sink. Against the glare the KEARNY's men could see a corvette idling in circles, trying to pick up survivors. The destroyer sprayed a pattern of depth charges from the fantail in an effort to disperse submarines which were likely to be lying deck-awash to avoid detection.

Somehow, one of the submarine pack either managed to maneuver to a position between the convoy and the KEARNY, or else caught the destroyer bearing down upon it in point-blank range. A lookout shouted his warning of a torpedo track—two—three—a fan of torpedoes!

Lieutenant Commander Danis ordered the wheel hard over to port. The ship heeled to the rudder. A foaming streak shot across her bow, and then the destroyer lurched farther to port as a torpedo crashed into her starboard side, piercing a great hole just below the water line. The force of the explosion was forward and upward. Four men who were on the deck were hurled over the side as the fire-room overhead—the ceiling in naval parlance—was blown open with such force that wreckage was thrown onto the bridge.

The detonation not only tore open the starboard side of the ship and ripped out the deck plates, but it blew away the starboard wing of the bridge and crumpled the deck house. The forward stack was broken and thrown back. The roar of the explosion was succeeded by a demoniacal screeching that drowned out cries of pain and bellowed orders; the steam siren had jammed wide open.

Down below, the forward bulkhead of the boiler room was broken through and the compartment where seven scalded men were trapped was flooding. But the after bulkhead, although deflected, held firm, leaving the forward engine room intact. Lieutenant Robert J. Esslinger, USN, the engineering and damage-control officer, and Chief Machinist's Mate Aucie McDaniel, were credited with saving the engine room. Seeing the last remaining bulkhead, bulged by the explosion, giving way under pressure of the inrushing sea, they shored up the danger point and saved the vital engines in the face of immediate annihilation. Another man, Harold Charles Barnard, S 1/c, although stunned by the explosion, groped through the forward compartments checking all watertight fittings, realizing that at any moment the ship might sink.

Engine-room controls, compass and steering gear had been smashed on the bridge, and, to make things worse, the men on the bridge could hear nothing nor make themselves heard above the scream of the open siren. For long minutes the wounded ship seemed to be without movement; then the bridge saw a feeble wake. The engines were still running and the shattered ship was still underway!

When he saw that the explosion had cut off control of the ship from the bridge, Chief Quartermaster Harold McDougal knew what to do, and did it. By the time the engines were again pushing the destroyer through the water, he was able to steer by hand from the second conning station aft. Also responsible for the ship's remaining in control was another quartermaster, John Booth, whose battle station was in the after steering engine room. Alone, and trapped if the ship went down, he went to work to make the shift to hand-steering. A third quartermaster, Muscoe Holland, saw that Booth was alone and would be unable to get out of the compartment if the ship were abandoned. He ran to the escape hatch which opened from the outside, unbolted it, tossed Booth a life jacket, and then stood by to lend what assistance he could in bringing the ship under control.

Without a compass, McDougal steered by the flag, using it as windsock to determine direction by the way the breeze was blowing.

The signal rockets were wet and misfired. The only signaling device that could get word to the KEARNY's sister ships in the convoy of her situation was a Very pistol. In a few moments another destroyer came steaming over to the KEARNY's side in response to the flares. It was the old four-stacker GREER, which had escaped the first attack of German torpedoes on an American warship. The word passed that the KEARNY would be able to make port under her own power but the GREER was asked to search the area for the four men blown over the side when the torpedo struck. That dangerous mission was destined to be without success.

So the KEARNY began the long, limping voyage into port. All hands remained at General Quarters from midnight until six o'clock in the morning following the attack. Their ship had been cut almost completely through from the turn of the bilge on the starboard side. Only the heavy deck edge and side plating on the starboard side remained intact. Despite the fact that the forward boiler room was flooded, the ship remained upright with very little change in trim, and although the forward engine room was just abaft the shattered compartment, the machinery was so well built that the engine continued to run even though its foundation was twisted off center.

"In so far as I have been able to discover," said Under Secretary of the Navy James Forrestal, at the time the KEARNY reached port, "there is no record of any destroyer sustaining a direct torpedo hit in so vital a part of the ship being able to proceed to port."

But mark that the company and crew held together as well as the ship. Eleven men were dead or missing, and fully as many more wounded. Every man not rendered helpless turned to in the terrible emergency, and many had to do the work of two. So well had Lieutenant Commander Danis organized his team that every member knew his job and the job of the man next to him, and did it without being told.

Danis won the Navy Cross for that. Two other men received the Navy Cross: Chief Machinist's Mate Aucie McDaniel, and the engineering officer, Lieutenant Robert J. Esslinger, who had prevented the engine room from flooding at risk of their lives. Letters of commendation from the Secretary of the Navy and an advancement in rating came to Paddock, Booth, Holland, Barnard and a third-class shipfitter, Samuel Kurtz.

Letters of commendation were sent from the Commander in Chief Atlantic Fleet to McDougal, Blake, Chief Yeoman Henry Leenknecht and Chief Torpedoman Clarence Mann. Lieutenant Eugene Sarsfield, USN, the executive officer, and Ensign Reuben Perley, Jr., assistant engineering officer, were also commended by the Secretary of the Navy. It was Sarsfield's after-battle report that told the story of Kurtz and Leenknecht.

"Kurtz was at his station on the depth charge release when the explosion occurred, and was critically wounded. In spite of the loss of blood that nearly cost his life and terrible pain from compound fractures of both legs, he remained quiet and calm and the display of courage made by him as he lay waiting for medical aid was of invaluable aid to the morale of all those on the bridge. His attention to duty and exceptional courage when wounded was a splendid display of naval discipline which had its effect on the crew."

Yeoman Leenknecht rescued Kurtz, who was on the verge of falling overboard from the shattered bridge as the wounded destroyer struggled against the sea. Leenknecht, without regard for personal safety, crawled out on the swaying starboard wing of the bridge, which had been almost completely shot away, gave his shipmate rough-and-ready first aid and carried him to safety.

The wounded men were turned over to the attention of a first-class pharmacist's mate, Robert Paddock, who was commended and promoted to a chief's rating with the following citation:

"By his untiring efforts, constant vigilance, cheerful giving of himself without rest, and knowledge of his duties he was able to keep alive the wounded and aid the mentally shocked so that all were kept alive and comfortable until the ship's arrival in port and transfer of the patients to the hospital. The doctors who later took charge of the patients highly praised his work."

One of the men whose life was saved was Chief Boatswain's Mate Leonard Frontakowski, of Norfolk, Virginia. Frontakowski was not injured in the explosion of the torpedo attack, but later, when he was struck by a lifeboat that was torn from its moorings and swept across the deck of the ship as the damaged destroyer rolled in the rough North Atlantic seas. He was carried to a temporary dressing station and given first aid, but he had lost so much blood a transfusion was needed as quickly as possible if "Boats" was to live.

Another destroyer which hove in sight eighteen hours after the attack was signaled with a request for blood plasma and a doctor. The doctor was on board, but not the blood plasma. An urgent request was radioed for a patrol plane to bring out plasma, and the surgeon, Lieutenant (jg) R. W. Rommell (MC), USNR, was lowered over the side of the destroyer in a whaleboat into pitching high seas to reach the KEARNY.

The passage between the two destroyers was rough, slow and dangerous, but successful. Dr. Rommell had scarcely completed his examination of Frontakowski, when the patrol plane was sighted. It circled and banked low over the injured ship. Then a package dropped. It missed the deck of the destroyer and landed in the waves far astern. Men sprang to a boat while others strained their eyes to keep in sight the bobbing parcel that meant a shipmate's life. Fortunately, the package had been wrapped in a watertight oilskin and the precious plasma was safe, when it was retrieved.

But Frontakowski was certainly dying. The first transfusion showed no effect, the second likewise. But by the time the third vial of plasma was in his veins the patient began to rally. When the ship reached Iceland, he was rushed to a service hospital where he received the final care that placed him back on active service a few months later. It took all the efforts of two ships, and an airplane, besides the blood of three anonymous civilians back home, to do it. The Navy thinks a man's life is worth it.

The KEARNY herself likewise had an amazing recovery. Her hospital was the Navy repair ship USS VULCAN, commanded by Captain Leon S. Fiske, USN.

In a few short months, working under extremely hard and unsatisfactory conditions for the type of repair work needed, KEARNY too rejoined her Atlantic Destroyer Squadron.

A glimpse of the difficulties involved in returning the destroyer to active duty is contained in a letter from Admiral E. J. King to Captain Fiske:

> Appreciating that the temporary repairs were rapidly accomplished in an open, notoriously rough harbor in icy water at a latitude and season where the available hours of daylight must have been very few and when the dangers and difficulties of working within an improvised caisson under such conditions were great, the successful accomplishment of this feat of repairs merits the sincere admiration of all, and is an inspiration to those in the Naval service ashore who are building and repairing units of the fleet.

Chapter Nine

THE next American ship attacked by German submarines was USS SALINAS, a 16,000-ton naval oil tanker launched in 1921. Early in the morning of October 30, 1941, the ship was southwest of Iceland on the first leg of a return trip in ballast to the United States. The night was starless, and it was still dark when, without warning, two torpedoes crashed through the plates of the old tanker.

The ship lurched to a dead stop and began to list while lookouts scanned the darkness to identify the attackers. Gun crews raced to their battle stations, while damage-control teams pelted below to ascertain the damage. The rest of the men were ordered to stand by the abandon-ship stations. It was impossible to tell whether the torpedoes had been launched from a submarine or a surface raider. Then, seventeen minutes after the attack, lookouts sighted a submarine circling to starboard. They shouted the warning: "Submarine broad on the sta'b'd—" and then gulped. "Torpedo track—three torpedoes—!"

Down below the engineering officer, Lieutenant (jg) Theodore L. Jermann, USNR, with two machinist's mates, Francis McIntyre and Rual Wilson, were struggling to secure overboard valves and lines ruptured by the first explosion. Icy salt water was pouring in, threatening to flood the engine room. The repair crew was just making headway against the inrushing sea when its members were hurled to the deck as one of the three torpedoes of the second attack tore into the oiler aft, between engine room and stern. Without stopping to rub their bruises the men went furiously to work, the sound of gunfire from the topside telling them that the SALINAS had located her assailant and was joining battle.

Lieutenant (jg) Jermann climbed to the bridge and saluted the skipper, Commander Harley F. Cope, USN, who was directing the fight with a cigar clenched between his teeth. Rapidly Jermann appraised the damage: If he could muster a detail from the men at abandon-ship stations, he said, he could restore the SALINAS to operating condition.

"Make it so," ordered Commander Cope, above the cheers of a gun crew which believed it had scored a hit on the diving submarine.

An amazing amount of makeshift connections and repairs was necessary. When the ship was first struck she began to list. Ballast had to be shifted to correct the list. All the electrical appliances and lines had to be spliced. The ship's organization began its efficient functioning. A quick check found all hands present and accounted for. Repair crews were quickly organized, and went to work comforted by the arrival of the destroyer USS DUPONT, which came charging up out of the dawn to stand by for rescue or combat.

A third submarine alarm only made the crew work harder. Above the clamor of their work they heard the cr-r-rump of depth charges. The DUPONT had taken external affairs in hand.

Although the ship was not fatally injured, most of the torpedo holes being above waterline, the structural damages were considerable. Even before the largest, 30-foot-square hole was plugged, the ship got underway on her course toward home. Deck and engineering forces labored to prevent the damaged parts of the ship from failing under the stress of heavy seas and the motion of the vessel.

In a later report on this period, the captain said of Electrician's Mate Albert Brown: "He was called upon to perform so many jobs and repair so many parts of the equipment that it seemed to me incredible that one man could work so continuously for twenty-four hours a day for over four days. Simple praise and commendation hardly appear adequate in his case."

By the time the destroyer returned, the men working on the SALINAS reported that she was ready to get underway. Escorted by the destroyer, which made periodic circles astern to break up the wide, telltale track of oil seeping from the broached tanks, the SALINAS started home.

For their work in repairing the ship and getting her into home port, four men won the Navy Cross: the captain of the ship, Commander Cope; the engineering officer, Lieutenant (jg) Jermann; Lieutenant Commander Ashton B. Smith, the executive officer; and Chief Machinist's Mate Francis McIntyre. Nineteen members of the crew were given promotions in rate in recognition of their services.

Back in port, after the excitement had subsided, someone thought it would be nice to compliment Commander Cope on the manner in which he maintained his calmness during the attack, when he strode the bridge with a cigar clenched in his teeth.

Commander Cope answered, "Hell, I had that cigar in my mouth to keep my teeth from chattering."

Chapter Ten

SO FAR luck was with the fleet in its encounters with the German submarines. Ships had been damaged but not sunk. Lives had been lost, but not in disastrous proportions.

Then, in the early morning of October 31, 1941, it happened.

The USS REUBEN JAMES, broken in two by a single well-placed torpedo, sank in a matter of seconds with a loss of 197 lives, the first American naval ship to be sunk by enemy action since 1918.

The REUBEN JAMES was another of the old four-stacker destroyers finished too late to enter the last war, too old to withstand the blows of the new one. She was a ship that carried a proud name: the name of a boatswain's mate in the Navy's war against the Barbary Coast pirates, the man who had saved the life of Captain Stephen Decatur by taking the blow of a pirate's scimitar intended for his commander.

It was a proud crew that sailed on the old, thin-skinned REUBEN JAMES. On the forward bulkhead of the tiny wardroom hung one of the Navy's oldest trophies, the curved, polished, steel-bladed scimitar that the bosun had wrested from the Barbary Coast pirate. Over it was an old steel engraving of Stephen Decatur's hand-to-hand fight with the pirates showing James rushing in to catch the deadly blow. The commanding officer was Lieutenant Commander Heywood L. Edwards—"Tex" Edwards—USN, who had been a familiar figure on the canvas mats of the Naval Academy and a star member of the Olympic wrestling team, renowned as well for his adroit seamanship and for having the smartest yet happiest destroyer on the Iceland run.

The "Rube," as her men called the ship, had made innumerable trips without mishap or excitement to Iceland. When she was in Iceland, the crew knew they could look forward to a series of shuttle trips between the barren fleet anchorage of Hvalfjordur and the city lights—such as they are—of Reykjavik. The REUBEN JAMES and Tex Edwards was a favorite combination of Rear Admiral R. C. Griffin, Commander Cruiser Division 7. So frequently was the destroyer called upon by the Admiral that the Rube earned the additional sobriquet of "Admiral Ike's Taxi."

The last trip of the REUBEN JAMES began as all those preceding it. She left a busy United States port one day late in October. A few miles out she picked up her convoy bound for Iceland. As the ships worked their way north through colder waters, the monotony of another voyage in escort duty set in. Watch succeeded watch and nothing happened. The tricky half-light of dawn gave way to daylight and the safety of visibility; the dangerous half-light of dusk gave way to the safety of invisibility. And nothing happened.

The torpedo struck in the dark hours of the early morning, hitting somewhere amidship on the port side, in approximately the same place as the KEARNY's wound, and the REUBEN JAMES was torn in two. The forward part sank immediately. The stern section remained afloat for a few minutes. Then there was a terrific explosion and the last of the REUBEN JAMES vanished.

Of the 145 men and officers of the destroyer, only 37 uninjured and 8 wounded were recovered. One hundred men were lost, including Tex Edwards.

Some who survived the initial torpedo strike were killed a few minutes later when the after section blew up. One of the men who survived both explosions was a fireman, Robert Carr of Buffalo, New York.

Carr was clinging to one of the three rafts that had not been destroyed; 70 feet away the thirty men on the balsa floats saw the half-ship weirdly afloat.

"Then there was a blinding flash," reports Carr. "It felt like I was swimming. Then I realized I couldn't feel any water under me. I turned head-down. I was about 25 feet above the water.

"Then I landed smack on my back in the waves. Parts of the ship, steel and jagged sections were flying through the air, and hitting the water all around me."

Carr managed to get back to the rafts. Where there had been thirty men before, there were now only about fifteen still clinging dazedly to the sides.

The men were covered with heavy black fuel oil, and the night was so dark that when a man lost his grip on the raft he was gone. The explosion had twisted the rafts and tossed them like spinning plates on the oil slick. Half had been unable to hold on.

The experience of Seaman Daniel J. Del Grosso, who had worked in the National Park Service in Arizona before joining the Navy, was typical of many.

He was asleep in his bunk when the torpedo struck. Knocked to the deck by the explosion he tugged at his life jacket. It was pinned beneath a twisted beam. Del Grosso ran up to the open deck without waiting to grab for clothes, after that.

"The oil was thick, but it sort of kept the water warm," he said later in an interview. But it was not warmth Del Grosso felt. He was numb with cold. He floundered to a raft and hauled himself aboard, only to slide off as a wave tilted it. Somebody grabbed him and held on. Eight men, vomiting oil, clung to the raft for three hours. They had not enough clothes between them to attire one.

Something loomed close.

"It's the goddam sub surfacing."

"Lay low, everybody."

The men cowered on the raft as the shape passed. Then they saw it was one of the convoy's destroyers. They shouted, and tried to draw themselves erect on the raft that tilted and spun in the ship's wake. The destroyer passed out of sight.

Hours later the destroyer returned with others, sighted the raft in the dirty dawn and took the men aboard. The ships joining in the intensive search for survivors were the destroyers USS BENSON (Lieutenant Commander Arthur L. Pleasants, USN), HILARY P. JONES (Lieutenant Commander Sherman R. Clark, USN), NIBLACK (Lieutenant Commander Edward R. Durgin, USN), and TARBELL (Lieutenant Commander Solomon D. Willingham, USN). A total of forty-six men were rescued before the search was abandoned. One of them died two days later.

On Sunday, December 14, a memorial service was held for the hundred men of the REUBEN JAMES. Families of the lost men were invited to attend.

At ten o'clock they assembled under a covered area of the quarterdeck on the U.S. frigate CONSTITUTION in the Boston Navy Yard. A light rain was falling as the Yard chaplain lifted his hands in prayer:

"Let Thy benediction rest upon their graves. May the solemn surge of the ocean, music they loved in life, be their never-ceasing requiem."

After the prayer six women dropped floral wreaths on the ebbing tide that carried the flowers out to sea.

Chapter Eleven

TWO weeks after the sinking of the REUBEN JAMES, and one month after Secretary of Navy Knox and Chief of Naval Operations Admiral Harold R. Stark had appeared before the House Foreign Affairs Committee to urge repeal of the 1939 Neutrality Act, the restrictive clauses of that law were expunged by Congress. Merchantmen were to be armed, and permitted to enter the harbors of belligerent nations.

There was bitter controversy over the repeal, but within that month the KEARNY and the SALINAS were torpedoed and the REUBEN JAMES was sunk. There was more at stake than academic debate, and the Germans themselves had, by their attacks, supplied a powerful argument for repeal.

Secretary Knox had promised that merchant ships could be armed: guns and the men to use them would be ready as soon as the law allowed and ships were ready. Without going into too much detail, the merchant ships would be armed with 3-inch to 5-inch guns and heavy-caliber machine guns; some with antiaircraft guns. Trained Navy gun crews, ten men to sixteen men in each, depending on the ship's size and armament, would be ready, the Secretary said.

The Neutrality Law was amended November 13. On November 15 the first quota of 24 officers and 192 men was ready to board ship. Among the questions debated in the press as well as in Congress was the real effectiveness of arming merchant ships. This was partly answered by a news dispatch from London which appeared in the New York *Times* for October 10, 1941, relating that since the beginning of the war, armed British merchant vessels had engaged in seventy successful engagements with U-boats, and had shot down more than eighty German planes.

Then there was the story of the JERVIS BAY, one of the brightest acts of heroism in the entire war: The armed British merchantman, fighting until its guns were awash, held off a German pocket battleship and enabled the escape of a large convoy to England with cargoes intact.

Yes, the lowly beef-boats could fight indeed. But there was more to the guns than their firepower. Against unarmed ships the submarine could lie in wait until the vessel came within gun range, and with a few shots from its deck gun send the helpless merchantman to the bottom. No submarine would dark risk such an attack if the merchant ship were able to shoot back. A submarine is a delicate and vulnerable ship. It cannot risk direct hits, even by a 3-incher. Against armed ships, the submarine must fight submerged, sometimes with not even the periscope showing. Handicapped in this way, the U-boat's aim is, of course, less effective. The submarine might have to fire several torpedoes and still not score a direct hit. When the torpedoes are expended, the subs must then return to home port, and next to a submarine sunk, a submarine in its pen was best so far as American ships at sea were concerned.

A priority system for arming merchantmen was announced by Secretary Knox: Ships plying to and from the British Isles and Northern Europe would be armed first. Ships to and from the Red Sea area would receive second consideration, and ships sailing the South American run would be third on the list.

What the Secretary had in mind when he promised earlier that the men and guns would be ready for the ships as soon as the ships were ready had its basis in the fact that the Navy had been training gun crews for fleet use since April 15, 1941. Although they were not designated for service on merchant vessels, the men were available for duty wherever guns were mounted.

In October, with repeal of the Neutrality Act's essential clauses predictable, the Navy organized a school at the Little Creek, Virginia, Section Base, to train gun crew teams of officers and men specifically for merchant ships. A monthly graduate quota of thirty officers and three hundred men was set; enough to man 30 ships. This was the beginning of the Navy's Armed Guard.

The magnitude of the job of arming our fleet of 1,375 merchant ships, plus the possibility that the authority to do it might come at any moment, precluded any lengthy training program. A basic course in gunnery, surface, antiaircraft and rapid-fire guns, was outlined. The Bureau of Supplies and Accounts organized a flexible system for paying men who would be scattered throughout the world, with the same regularity as if they were on a Navy ship. They could be paid by the master of the ship, any Navy disbursing officer, by naval attachés and consuls.

Plans were projected for two Armed Guard Centers, or pools, that would act as a central location for receiving, quartering, equipping and assigning men who finished their training. One was to be located in the old Naval Receiving Station in South Brooklyn, New York, and the other was to be in San Francisco. The West Coast was later to get an Armed Guard training school in San Diego.

Lack of trained personnel was only one big problem in a mass of lesser ones. Most of the ships had to undergo alterations before they could receive the guns. Merchant masters, in some instances, were reluctant to see the Navy guns swung over the side and secured on their ships. Even though the gun crews had orders to fire in defense only, they felt that those guns were inviting attack they had so far avoided. Personnel problems also developed. The civilian sailors were sea-wise and salty and at first looked askance at bluejackets who had never, in many cases, been to sea at all. The bluejackets, in turn, had uncomplimentary ideas about the merchant seamen who collected bonuses for dangerous cruises and wore mufti. It is to the credit of both services that the ultimate result soon proved to be a mutual respect and complete understanding.

Before half a dozen ships could put to sea with deck guns mounted and manned, the undeclared war that Germany had waged against Maritime America became formalized. On December 7 the Oriental arm of the Axis delivered a declaration of war on the United States in the carrier-plane and submarine attack on Pearl Harbor. Next day Germany and Italy, by formal declaration, confirmed the war that Hitler had actually begun with the attack on USS GREER.

PART THREE

Antisubmarine War — The Armed Guard,

Escorts and Carriers

FIGURE

CONVOY ROUTES

Chapter Twelve

———————————————————————————

I T IS apparent that the Navy was committed to two desperately difficult tasks in combating the submarines.

The most urgent labor was to ensure delivery to the United Kingdom and the Soviet Union of the munitions upon which the security of us all depended. To that task was soon added the protection of our armies transported to North Africa, Italy and, eventually, France.

The second labor was to protect the coastal seaways of the United States against the submarines which boldly attacked ships within sight of shore, ships carrying petroleum from Texas, rubber and coffee from Brazil, bananas and hemp and tin from Central and South America; ships laden with the products of our own industry proceeding to a convoy rendezvous.

Nor was protection enough, in either task. A defensive war against the submarine could not be afforded. Ultimately it had to be an aggressive war, a war not to fight off the submarines but to carry the fight to them. But that had to come later. Now there were not means enough for adequate defense alone.

Every fighting ship that could apply itself to the first task was assigned to escort the convoys. On the transatlantic convoy routes the United Nations came into actual being, as the men-o'-war of the United States, Great Britain, Canada, Poland, Norway and the Netherlands shepherded merchantmen flying the flags of those and half a dozen other countries. Destroyers, corvettes, armed trawlers, and not enough at that.

On the Atlantic coast the beaches were foul with oil from torpedoed tankers whose sultry red flames were reflected in the windows of seaside cities and towns. Our harbors from Jacksonville north to New York, the entire Chesapeake and Delaware Bay areas, were effectively blocked for days at a time by enemy submarine-laid mines in 1942 and 1943. No ship could move safely in those mighty ports until German mines had been swept from them.

In January the system of Sea Frontiers was established on the framework of the old (1929) Coastal Frontier Forces with Admiral Adolphus Andrews in command of the Eastern Sea Frontier—ESF in the Navy's everyday lexicon thereafter. It extended in a broad belt from Canadian waters to northern Florida, and under its command were unified all military forces—Army, Navy, Air Force and Coast Guard.

That was Admiral Andrews's bailiwick, and no man was better equipped to understand how tough the assignment was, or how to make a success of it. He had been commander of the Scouting Force and head of the submarine school at New London. He was—and is—an authority on submarine warfare and antisubmarine warfare, but the country had not provided the tools with which to put his knowledge to use.

Against an average of thirty modern, long-range Nazi submarines, Admiral Andrews mustered less than a dozen each of old 110-foot subchasers and all-weather Coast Guard craft, five World War I wooden-hulled Eagle boats, three seagoing yachts and four blimps. This motley and somewhat tatterdemalion fleet had to uphold the majesty and might of the United States in the nation's own coastal water. It had to oppose at least an equal number of double-hulled, 20-knot submarines equipped with the latest electronic ears and eyes, armed with 4-inch guns, capable of diving 100 fathoms deep. It had to guard hundreds of ships upon which the industrial East depended for much of its fuel, food and raw materials.

In January, 1942, the submarines sank better than a ship a day in the Atlantic. In February, they nearly doubled their score and improved upon that in March. From Kittery to Miami the sands were sodden with petroleum that killed fish, destroyed water fowl and made hazards where there had been recreation and beauty. It was oil from tankers and from the bunkers of merchantmen, and mixed with it were human bodies, shattered lifeboats, sodden lifebuoys, and all the ugly, tragic debris of marine disaster. And it washed on our own shores, the shores that "Hitler would never invade."

Coastal convoys were, of course, the remedy; but there were no escort ships. Those afloat were inadequate enough for the transatlantic task. Until they could be replaced by faster, more lethal ships upon which the yards were toiling night and day, they were needed where they were. The Army First Bomber Command added its strength to the naval aircraft that patrolled the sea lanes. The Civil Air Patrol donated its volunteer surveillance from unarmed sporting planes, and blimps, including some that lately had been taking up sightseers, joined the grim game of hide-and-seek.

It was during these early days in 1942, of groping for the enemy with insufficient weapons or trained personnel, that an enlisted pilot, Donald Francis Mason, AMM 1/c, lightened the gloom with his terse, alliterative message from the air: "Sighted sub; sank same." Mason, flying on off-shore patrol, "dove to low altitude, and dropped two depth bombs which straddled the periscope" of the submarine he had detected. "The conning tower ran clear of the water for a short period and then sank again. A large patch of oil soon covered the area. This attack was adjudged successful."

Mason wired his now-famous and endlessly parodied message, and found himself famous, promoted to chief, and decorated with the Distinguished Flying Cross. A few weeks later Chief Mason again "sighted" an Axis craft on the surface, swooped down and released his depth charges. All the charges scored hits on the underwater vessel and it blew up, scattering wreckage over a large area. For his second kill, Mason was promoted to ensign and awarded a Gold Star in equivalent to a second Distinguished Flying Cross.

Submarines soon found daylight hunting to be dangerous. They lay submerged in the sea lanes during the sunlight hours, and picked off their prey by night, aided by the glow of the coastal communities against which the lumbering cargo ships were silhouetted.

War was very, very close to the inviolate American earth, while Civilian Defense teams drilled against the arrival of Hitler's bombers, Hitler's submarines.

A black-out was ordered the length of the coast. Eastern Sea Frontier studied charts and statistics. From Maine to Virginia the coast was indented by harbors. A ship leaving Bath, in Maine, in the morning, could be sheltered in Boston before evening. From Boston to New York was a daylight run, and from New York to Delaware Bay another. Between sunrise and sunset a ship could steam from the shelter of the Delaware Capes to the security of the Chesapeake's broad mouth, with relative safety from torpedoes. Merchant ships were ordered to leapfrog down the coast. Submarine captains watched the ships steam past while they lay at periscope depth, but at night the sea lanes were empty. The Germans prowled, scouted, calculated, and then congregated around

Hatteras for easy pickings again, south of the deep-water night havens. The U-boat captains settled back in their aluminum chairs like Prussian deer hunters waiting in their carpeted blinds for the game to be driven in front of their guns.

But ESF had anticipated the Germans' solution and was at work with another makeshift. Where nature had provided no harbors, the Navy was making its own, even as it was to build an artificial bay on the French coast two years later. With submarine nets and mines and great booms, pens were built at intervals of 125 miles from North Carolina to Florida, into which ships put at night like sheep behind an electrified fence. To Admiral Andrews's hodgepodge fleet four 1918 class destroyers, veterans of the Iceland run, were added in April. Sinkings declined.

In May coastwise convoying became practicable, with Coast Guard craft the backbone of the system that was further implemented by the expanded Coast Guard Reserve in the two months following. Although the submarines' bag for the entire Atlantic showed an abrupt rise in May, only four ships were lost that month in the 1,200-mile beat of ESF's watchmen.

But again the Nazi captains were thwarted only as long as it took them to analyze the situation. The submarines suddenly shifted to the Caribbean and the Gulf of Mexico, and as the overworked escort ships turned their convoys loose in those virtually inland seas, the day came when they found the Nazis waiting for the fat merchantmen. Again the Navy Department's graph of sinkings crept upward. The Germans were trying hard to cut the United Nations' life line to the Mediterranean as General Rommel's drive on Egypt and the Near East rumbled into high.

By June, 1942, despite accelerated production of merchant shipping, there were 12 per cent fewer vessels plying the United States Atlantic Strategic Area than in January. But by that time half the ships in that area were afforded at least some degree of convoy protection. On June 17, Admiral King notified the commands of the Eastern and Gulf Sea Frontiers (Admirals Andrews and Kauffman) that all civilian craft capable of remaining at sea at cruising speeds for forty-eight hours, and preferably of carrying four 300-pound depth charges and a 50-caliber machine gun were to be acquired. The response from civilian owners was immediate, and frequently crews went with the boats, all incorporated into the Coast Guard Reserve together. Owners may have winced as they watched hand-rubbed mahogany, scoured teak and gleaming bright-work disappear under thick gray paint, but they themselves as often as not put on the uniform of a chief boatswain's mate and traded a luxurious office for the heaving deck of a YP. This splinter-fleet was organized as a picket line spaced along the 50-fathom curve of the Atlantic and Gulf coast, particularly in those areas where submarines were found to be concentrated, and there they served as floating sentries until the converted fleet was given its honorable discharge in December, 1944.

Makeshift and patchwork measures, all of these, pitted against a powerful and determined fleet of modern submarines as superior to the 1918 U-boat as the 1942 airplanes were to the wire-strutted crates of World War I. Antisubmarine methods had not kept pace with the development of the fast, heavily armed and armored, deep-diving submarine; they were the same that had been employed against von Tirpitz's pig-boats twenty-four years before, except for the mounting use of the airplane. Land-based planes of the Army and the Navy, the LTA force of blimps, and the Navy's big "flying whales" were steadily driving the submarine to sea, where the patrols and pickets were forcing them to remain hidden by day.

What was needed, obviously, was an air cover for our shipping wherever it might be: airplanes to spot submarines before the convoys came into torpedo range, anywhere at sea.

Needed, too, were new weapons with which to combat the new underwater cruisers.

Both needs had been anticipated, and were being met, although before the remedies could be applied sinkings mounted to a million tons a month and the war came perilously close to victory for the submarines.

The German answer to the convoy was the wolf-pack, a name so descriptive it needs no elaborating explanation. The countermeasure to the wolf-pack was the radar-guided CVE-DD-DE combination, the team of small carriers, destroyers and destroyer escorts—baby flat-tops and tin cans.

By October, 1942, antisubmarine technique plus shipyard production had restored the average number of merchant ships in daily operation to the January level; by December, despite the vastly increased demand for full cargoes for our troops in Africa and the Solomons and Great Britain, the average number was 5 per cent higher than January's. In March, 1943, the average was 15 per cent greater.

The "umbrella" of air patrol had spread over the Western Atlantic

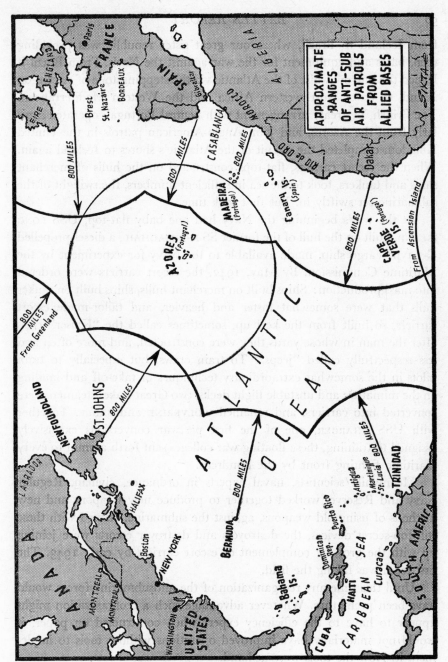

APPROXIMATE RANGES OF ANTI-SUB AIR PATROLS FROM ALLIED BASES

FIGURE 4

95

from Iceland to Brazil, where our great sister republic was providing men, bases and equipment for the war against the Nazis. From Brazil it leaped the narrow waist of the Atlantic via the steppingstone of Ascension Island, to cover Northwestern Africa and the Western Mediterranean. The British, by treaty arrangement with neutral Portugal, operated similarly from the Azores, and joint Anglo-American patrols in the United Kingdom completed the circuit of the Atlantic's shores to Iceland again. When the escort carriers, flat-tops constructed on the hulls of merchant ships and tankers, took to the sea in sufficient numbers, the twilight of the submarine set swiftly in. But that took time.

At the war's beginning the Navy had one baby flat-top, USS LONG ISLAND, built on the hull of the former SS MORMACMAIL, a diesel-propelled C-3 type cargo ship, made available to the Navy for experiment by the Maritime Commission. By May, 1942, the escort carriers were ordered into mass production: Ships built on merchant hulls, ships built on tanker hulls that were somewhat faster and heavier, and tailor-made escort carriers, so built from the keel up, sometimes called the "Kaiser" class after the man in whose yards they were constructed, and more often and less respectfully called "jeeps." To train crews, but especially to train pilots in the somewhat extraordinary techniques of take-off and landing on the miniature and unstable flight decks, two Great Lakes steamers were converted into carriers, and renamed WOLVERINE and SABLE. Together with USS CHARGER, one of the first postwar conversions exclusively assigned to training, these floating war colleges sent forth alumni to every maritime fighting front by the hundreds.

Meanwhile scientists, naval experts in ordnance, civilian, Regular Navy and Reserve, worked together to produce new weapons and new methods of using old weapons, against the submarine. Armed with these still top-secret devices, the destroyers and destroyer escorts were joining up with the growing complement of escort carriers by early 1943. The first team was taking the field.

Until this time any reorganization of the antisubmarine forces would have been premature. Whatever advantage such a reorganization might appear to have to the efficiency expert when constructed on paper, it would not materially have improved operations without tools to implement it. Now the tools were at hand.

Hitler, too, found need for reorganization in the face of his submarines' dwindling successes. He appointed Admiral Karl Doenitz as Chief of

Submarine Warfare, and Doenitz talked a very good war indeed. The United States Navy, not influenced by Doenitz's appointment or dire predictions, announced the formation in May of the Tenth Fleet.

Now the whole grim business of fighting the submarine was concentrated in one organization. In that fight the Germans were still ahead on points.

Admiral King, Commander in Chief United States Fleet, and Chief of Naval Operations, assumed command of the Tenth Fleet, and his assistant chief of staff in charge of antisubmarine warfare became Chief of Staff. As such, Admiral Francis S. Low, USN, "Froggy" to his classmates of '15, exercised administrative command of the organization subject to Admiral King's direct orders.

Tenth Fleet had no ships or planes directly attached to it. It operated, and still does at this writing, through the Fleet and Sea Frontier commands, exercising over-all co-ordination. Its duties were categorically stated to be: destruction of enemy submarines and protection of Allied shipping in the United States Atlantic area, support of "other" antisubmarine forces in the Atlantic, control over all shipping in the areas of command, and correlation of antisubmarine research, development and training. ("Support of 'other' antisubmarine forces" covered the close liaison between the United States Navy and the Royal Navy.)

One of the units of the naval establishment thus co-ordinated with the Tenth Fleet's antisubmarine program was COMAIRLANT, the all-over aviation command under CINCLANT. COMAIRLANT, the abbreviation for Commander Air Force Atlantic Fleet, was organized as such in January, 1943, under command of Rear Admiral Alva D. Bernhard, USN, who had been Commander Fleet Air Wings Atlantic Fleet. An outgrowth of the original 1941 Naval Air Commands, the organization had passed through several metamorphoses until, in its final form, it was charged with the maintenance, allocation, distribution and supervision of aviation personnel and materiel in the area. Rear Admiral Patrick N. L. Bellinger, USN, succeeded Admiral Cook in March; he became vice-admiral in October, 1943.

Less than a year after the formation of the Tenth Fleet, Admiral Low told the American Society of Newspaper Editors (Washington, D.C., April 22, 1944) that "The German U-boat today is sinking considerably less than one half of one per cent of the ships being convoyed across the Atlantic" and that "we believe that it takes the Germans two or three times as long to *build* a submarine as that vessel may expect to *endure* on combat patrol."

The 1943 Allied losses to the submarine were announced by the United States and British governments as 40 per cent under 1942; the greatest part of that radically reduced loss was suffered in the first quarter of the year. In the second half of 1943, more enemy submarines were sunk than Allied ships were torpedoed, and in 1944 and 1945, despite brief, desperate rallies by picked U-boat squadrons, the discrepancy steadily widened.

The Germans fought hard against the reversing tide of success. Every new antisubmarine technique was met by some effort at countermeasure: Torpedoes that left no wake to be spotted by alert lookouts; magnetic torpedoes that converted near misses to bull's-eyes; sonic torpedoes, equipped with electric "ears," that altered their course to follow and overtake the most agile of zigzagging ships. When the baby flat-tops finally spread the air umbrella over the middle Atlantic, and no submarine could surface anywhere between the arctic and the antarctic without fear of aerial bombing, the Germans installed antiaircraft batteries on the U-boats. The ships remained on the surface to fight it out with the bombers and blimps, tactics which soon erased the lighter-than-air crafts' particularly useful ability to hover over a surfaced submarine and drop bombs on it with the nonchalance of a chief carpenter's mate dropping lumps of sugar into his mug of tar-strong coffee.

Germany's newest submarines possessed an amazing ruggedness. In 1944 it took six Navy planes, a Navy blimp and an Army bomber ten hours to sink one in the Caribbean. Bigger ships have been sunk faster by fewer aircraft. The American answer to submarine antiaircraft batteries was the rocket gun. In the first encounter between the new weapon and a new submarine, two Navy planes using rockets took fewer minutes to destroy the U-boat than it had taken hours to sink the one in the Caribbean.

By 1944 the prophecy made by Secretary Knox in 1943, that "each time they [the U-boats] go out, there will be a sharply increasing likelihood that they will not come back," was confirmed. The German submarine service, the elite of Hitler's naval combat forces, so deteriorated that the Germans were forced to draft men to go to sea. Reports of mutinies were heard in 1944 and grew in numbers and authenticity in early 1945.

A tremendous factor in reducing the submarine from a grisly menace to an intermittent nuisance was the work performed by the British Royal Air Force, the British Naval Air Arm, and the Royal Navy. CHAOP was the code name for that team which guarded the Western Sea Approaches. Surviving submarines returning from the Western Atlantic were harried as they approached the European coast, and their concrete pens at Lorient and other ports of occupied France were under constant bombardment.

It was teamwork that finally beat the submarines; teamwork implemented with ships, aircraft, weapons and techniques that had only been ideas when the emergency broke. It was teamwork of the United States with the United Kingdom, the Soviet Union, Canada, Brazil, France, the Netherlands, Norway and Poland; it was teamwork of the United States Navy with the Army. (The Army Air Force was relieved of antisubmarine routine in November, 1943.)

But, especially, it was teamwork between the Navy's elements in the air, on the surface, in the shabby, wallboard offices in Washington and the headquarters of the Sea Frontiers. In the van of the fight were the Armed Guard crews, the destroyer and destroyer-escort men, the pilots, crews and companies of the carriers.

It is impossible to give credit to all the persons, men and women both, who contributed to the mastery of the U-boat. It would take volumes of encyclopedic size to record the heroisms performed in the Battle of the Atlantic. Here, then, it is only possible to sketch a few illustrations to serve as memoranda for the citizens of the United States whose security was preserved by thousands of anonymous men in the dungarees of the working Navy.

There should be special and reiterated mention of the men who flew the monotonous patrols that drove the submarines from Atlantic shores. They rarely saw a submarine, and more rarely sank one, because the U-boats feared to show themselves to the sky sentries who maintained the ceaseless, monotonous patrol of the coastal sea lanes.

Here follow a few characteristic examples of combat against the underwater marauders with which Hitler hoped to starve Great Britain and make impotent the industrial and military manpower of the United States. Each story could be duplicated over and over to fill a shelf of sturdy books. The authors' effort is not to present the extraordinary, but the average experience of the men in the several echelons of the antisubmarine war. Here are episodes to illustrate what it meant to be a member of the Armed Guard, or part of a ship's company on a bronco-shaming destroyer, in the crew of a torpedo-bomber or aboard a baby flat-top from which the torpedo bombers swarmed in that strangest of combats, undersea vs. oversea. Each narrative is, in its way, a salute to the unnamed thousands who served as well (and, maybe, sometimes better) and to the thousands of others who could record no triumphs, for the conclusive reason that the enemy refused to give battle.

Chapter Thirteen

AT first, Armed Guard duty was the least coveted assignment in the Navy. A normal greeting extended to a shipmate who received orders to the Armed Guard was "Well, so-long, fish-bait. It was nice knowing you." An exclusive society was projected, "The Bitter Enders," whose membership was limited to Armed Guard personnel surviving a torpedoing. Someone originated a paraphrase that the Armed Guard ironically adopted as its war-cry: "Stand by. Prepare to Fire. Abandon ship!"

Or, even more to the point, after "Sighted sub; sank same" became famous, was the Armed Guard version—"Sighted sub. Glub! Glub!"

Men—and boys—who had never seen salt spray in their lives returned from one Armed Guard cruise veterans of both the sea and the war.

There was one run that became wardroom and liberty legend. It was told and retold by those that lived through to tell it. And the men who had been on it were forever considered a little higher in the echelon of Armed Guard veterans. It was the "Murmansk run."

The German armies were at the very gates of Moscow by the end of 1941. Relief, in the form of American war supplies, had to get through to the Soviet forces. The shortest practicable route for this material was over the Arctic Circle and around the North Cape of Norway down to the port of Murmansk or into the White Sea to Archangel. Bitter weather and a ruthless enemy combined to make that the most dangerous of voyages.

Not only was there danger from enemy submarines, based all along the Norwegian coast; German airfields were close at hand, and—a more serious potential menace than either—the heavy units of the German fleet, the VON TIRPITZ, the HIPPER, the SCHEER and LUTZOW together with squadrons of destroyers lurked in the deep rugged Alten Fjord, a constant murderous threat against anything smaller than a battleship daring to pass near their lair.

To combat these heavy craft, the British Home Fleet had to maintain a constant patrol of the waters with ships of similar armor and armament. More than this, the Home Fleet had to protect each Russia-bound convoy. It was a heavy duty for a navy that had already taken serious losses. Help was needed, and help was forthcoming.

On March 26, 1942, Task Force 99, under the command of Rear Admiral Robert C. Giffen, Jr., USN, sailed from Casco Bay, Maine, for Scapa Flow, to operate with the Home Fleet. The Admiral flew his flag from the battleship USS WASHINGTON (Captain Howard H. J. Benson, USN, commanding) and his force comprised the carrier WASP (Captain John W. Reeves, Jr., USN), the cruisers WICHITA (Captain Harry W. Hill, USN) and TUSCALOOSA (Captain Norman C. Gillette, USN), and the destroyers of Desron 8 (Captain Don P. Moon, USN).[1]

The WASP was detached from the Task Force for a special mission upon her arrival, and the remaining ships took up their share of the burden of keeping the big German vessels bottled up out of harm's way.

Late in June a special job came up, one which promised vital action and, possibly, a chance to end the threat of the German "fleet-in-being." Reconnaissance and intelligence agreed that the TIRPITZ and the Nazi cruisers were being readied for sea. At the same time one of the largest and most important convoys was heading for Murmansk.

The TUSCALOOSA and WICHITA were assigned to the Cruiser Covering Force to escort the convoy from Iceland around the North Cape under the command of Admiral Hamilton, RN. The WASHINGTON joined the heavy units of the Home Fleet under the command of Admiral Tooey, RN.

The prime mission of the Cruiser Covering Force was to get the convoy through, with the secondary mission of luring or delaying any heavy units of the Nazis into range of the big boys of the Allied force. German air and submarine attacks were expected in great strength; a previous Murmansk convoy had got through with little damage, which made Hitler angry. The particular convoy, PQ 17, being covered represented some seven hundred million dollars' worth of arms for hard-

---

[1] USS WAINWRIGHT (Lt. Comdr. H. R. Gibbs, USN), LANG (Lt. Comdr. Erskine A. Seay, USN), STERRETT (Comdr. Jesse G. Coward, USN), WILSON (Lt. Comdr. Russell G. Sturges, USN), PLUNKETT (Lt. Comdr. William H. Standley, Jr., USN), MADISON (Comdr. William B. Ammon, USN).

pressed Russia, which made the Nazis anxious. An added prize for the Germans was convoy PQ 13, outward bound from Murmansk, scheduled to pass PQ 17 to northward of North Cape.

The TIRPITZ was lured out together with one or two cruisers (reports do not agree), a large screen of destroyers and a whole fleet of covering aircraft. She eluded the heavy ships of the Home Fleet, and, while she never struck at either convoy, her presence in the area caused the Cruiser Covering Force to be withdrawn. The convoy scattered and found its way to Murmansk as best it could under continued heavy air and undersea attack.

"Heavy air and undersea attack" could well have been a standard daily entry in any log of an Armed Guard officer. It would have fitted naturally and normally after that other standard entry "Steaming as before."

One of the veterans of the Murmansk run is Lieutenant Robert B. Ricks, USNR, of Gainesville, Georgia, now skipper of a destroyer escort, who was awarded the first Silver Star Medal presented to an Armed Guard officer.

Lieutenant Ricks was assigned to SS EXPOSITOR in February, 1942. Even by this time there were not enough men to give every officer a full gun crew. To man his one 4-inch 50-caliber gun and four 30-caliber machine guns, Ricks had only four seamen and a signalman striker— "striker" in Navy language meaning an enlisted man studying for noncommissioned promotion.

At nine o'clock in the morning of March 4, 1942, the EXPOSITOR left Pier 98 in Philadelphia and headed for New York. Here, a cargo was taken aboard which caused the Armed Guard crew to feel a few shivers against which their pea jackets were no protection.

The cargo was 5,000 rounds of 75-mm. shells, 5,000 rounds of 37-mm. shells and 5,000 cases of TNT. With this lethal load aboard, the ammunition ship was incorporated in a convoy bound for the Clyde Anchorage in Loch Long off Gourock, Scotland. At 2:30 in the morning of March 27, the ships dropped anchor in that great convoy berthing spot. But the EXPOSITOR was not unloaded. On April 1, they were on the move again, in company with three other American merchant ships, SS LANCASTER, ALCOA RAMBLER and PAUL LUCKENBACH. The morning was clear and the weather was fine. The water of Loch Long lapped gently on the gray stone seawalls of Gourock. The gun crew watched the brown hills of Scotland fade in and they swapped wise cracks about April Fools' Day. Their destination was certainly the Soviet Union, and on whom would the joke be if they didn't make it?

At four o'clock that afternoon the lead ship in the convoy began to turn. A message had been received from the British Admiralty ordering the convoy to return to Gourock. Anchored again in Loch Long, the reason for the return was made known. The DEMS Office (Defensive Equipment for Merchant Ships, the counterpart of the Navy's Armed Guard) had decided the ships were insufficiently armed. To the men of the EXPOSITOR, this was another certain proof that they were embarking on the hazardous Murmansk run.

Next day additional guns arrived on board, two 20-mm. Oerlikon AA machine guns and one twin-mount Hotchkiss machine gun. It was an embarrassment of riches. The battle bill for the gun crew had been complicated before with only five men to man five guns. Now, with additional guns, volunteers from the merchant crew had to be drilled in their use.

On April 7, the quartet, under Admiralty orders, left for the Lynn of Lorn, off Lismore Island, Scotland. Three days later, a convoy which now consisted of twenty-five ships, American, British and Russian, steamed out of the Lynn of Lorn bound for Reykjavik, Iceland, its last stop on the way to North Russia. On the 15th the ships arrived off Reykjavik harbor and were ordered to Iceland's convoy anchorage area, Hvalfjordur Bay. Their only excitement en route had been watching the destroyer-escort explode sixteen floating mines by gunfire.

There the ships remained for ten days, surrounded by grim, brown lava cliffs from whose tops bristled antiaircraft artillery. It was remote from Reykjavik's few urban attractions, and the crew heard with relief that they were to be on the move again, even though it was now officially announced: "Destination, Murmansk."

Then at 0800, April 26, the convoy began to move. On the second day out of Iceland, lookouts reported what was to be a continuous hazard all the way to Murmansk—floating mines.

The third day was stormy. The sky was low and goosefeather-gray and occasional snow flurries blotted out ships ahead. It was still morning when a plane was heard, flying very high. By the sound, it seemed to be circling.

"One of those God-damned vultures," a veteran merchant seaman growled.

The plane kept circling. "He's radioing our position, speed and course," the seaman added knowingly. "And he's smart. The bastard knows enough to keep out of range. He's just a spotter. We'll be in for it in a little while."

"What do you mean?" a novice asked.

"Bombers, that's what."

The EXPOSITOR plodded along with the convoy. All hands grew as fond of snow as a small boy with a new sled. Sunshine, alternating with the flurries, was reviled. Thus for four hours, and then—

"I don't remember how many planes there were," Lieutenant Ricks says. "We had just passed through a snow squall and were in the clear when we saw them coming in on our starboard bow."

The signal to commence firing was hoisted. The entire convoy seemed to open fire at the same time. The planes roared over the fire-belching ships, their bombs falling off to the starboard side of the convoy. The bombers climbed higher and disappeared into the clouds.

Nobody had a chance to say "scared 'em off, hey?" before one of the planes screamed down through the clouds on a dive-bombing run aimed at the lead ship in the port column. The antiaircraft cruiser guarding the convoy opened fire with every gun on her deck. Guns from the merchantmen in the first three columns joined on the instant. It was a blanket of fire such as no German pilot had ever expected to face. The bomber never came out of its dive. It crashed about 150 yards off the port side of the number one column without dropping its bomb load.

That was all.

The EXPOSITOR's Armed Guard crew had had its indoctrinating baptism of fire. Not very exciting at that. *Buzz—whoosh—bang—bang!* But the old-timers muttered something about "luck" and wondered aloud what the next time would be like, and how soon.

"We felt pretty good about it," Lieutenant Ricks recalls. "We had shot down one of the planes, there was no damage done to us and we had driven off the others. Spirits were pretty high."

The convoy wallowed along resolutely, and without molestation. Then at 3:30 the following afternoon, two more "vultures" were sighted. Again the spotters carefully avoided flying over the convoy in gun range. They circled far out of firing range. They were still there five hours later, when the last man came up from evening mess blinking at the bright arctic sun. Then, as if the pilot had spent all that time building up courage, one of the planes suddenly streaked toward the port wing of the convoy. As the antiaircraft fire began to find the range, the bomber tilted off on a wide tack and climbed high into screening clouds. A moment later it flashed over the convoy for a second try and again the antiaircraft fire forced the plane to seek cloud refuge. The pilot seemed determined to have at least one shot at the ships. The third time he came out of the clouds in a steep dive at the port wing of the convoy. It was his last. Streams of tracers poured into the plane and followed it as it crashed into the ocean. The companion bomber made no attempt to attack. It straightened out and disappeared over the horizon.

Gun crews remained at their stations on watch. It was still snowing in flurries and there was the feeling that something else was going to happen.

It lacked about an hour for sunset, which is to say it was one o'clock in the morning when the Commodore hoisted a signal.

"Expect attack!"

Three planes were slanted in toward the starboard and the ships opened fire.

"This was our first glimpse of torpedo bombers," said Ricks. "The three planes continued their approach in formation toward us. It looked like an attempt to pick off the leading line of ships. They came in low, flying about fifty or seventy-five feet above the water."

Then the torpedoes began to drop. The men at the guns kept their eyes on the planes. Above the ear-splitting chatter of the ordnance they heard the hollow, reverberating explosion that even the novices knew meant torpedoes had found targets against hulls.

The starboard plane of the trio crashed in flames, as its companions sheered off into the clouds. Then the gunners could look around.

They saw the SS BOTHAVEN, the Commodore's ship, plunging bow first into the water while men spilled from the decks and swam toward the three lifeboats that had been launched. Where SS CAPE CORSO had been was a flame-shot column of smoke.

"The explosion of that ship sent flames five hundred feet in the air," said Lieutenant Ricks. "The entire mid-section seemed to blow up. The ship was a flaming mass. It sank in about thirty seconds, and there were no survivors."

SS JUTLAND, steam pouring from her vents, was dead in the water and its crew taking to the boats from decks that inched closer and closer to the sea.

"Three ships sunk by two torpedoes?" somebody demanded. "A submarine must have got one of them."

And, as if in confirmation, the EXPOSITOR's lookout shouted: "Submarine!"

"Where away?" The sea beyond the convoy's perimeter was empty. The lookout was correct—fantastically correct. A conning tower was rising in the very center of the convoy and just a few yards from the EXPOSITOR's starboard quarter!

"The periscope was only about ten or fifteen feet away from the ship," reminisces Lieutenant Ricks, "and the submarine was surfacing. It was so close aboard that none of our guns could be brought to bear, no machine guns, no broadside guns, no nothing. And nobody else in the convoy could shoot at it without hitting us—loaded with TNT. It was kind of embarrassing to say the least."

One of the cooks aboard the EXPOSITOR was standing on the fantail by the stern gun when the sub's conning tower bubbled up under his bulging eyes. The man stood there, unable to believe what he saw. Then he turned to the mute gun, which had been depressed to its lowest trajectory. The mess hand rushed over to the piece, grabbed it by the barrel and tried to tug it into position to fire, grunting and groaning as he pulled.

The submarine continued to surface until the conning tower was awash, while the EXPOSITOR widened the distance from it.

By the time the submarine was 25 yards away, the 4-inch gun could be brought to bear on the German craft. The first shot missed. The gun was still too high. The second was a direct hit on the conning tower, at 30 or 40 yards. It was blown completely off.

After the second shot, the submarine appeared to be sinking. Water boiled up in a great froth of air and bubbles. As the man watched the oil spreading over the submarine's grave the lookout yelled: "Torpedo track off port bow!"

The ship jolted as her screws went into reverse. A few feet in front of her bow the torpedo hissed its way to nowhere.

"I think the submarines and aircraft worked in very close co-operation on a job like this," Lieutenant Ricks calculates. "The reconnaissance planes did nothing but circle the convoy, evidently radioing to the subs, or to where the message could be relayed to them, our position, course and speed. Then the subs would lie ahead of the convoy and as we came by would let us have it. This particular submarine that came up in the center of the convoy was evidently hurt by some of the heavy depth charges that had been dropped by the DEs and corvettes after the CAPE CORSO was hit."

This marked the end of enemy action for that day. But as the ships fell into their convoy position, filling up the gaps left by the torpedoed, a fourth casualty was discovered. A British corvette had disappeared in the melee, wiped out by a torpedo.

The only casualty aboard the EXPOSITOR was a seaman's dungarees. The deck hand, his arms full of 40-mm. ammunition, was on a ladder in the path of the 4-inch gun's blast.

"The concussion ripped his pants off, and I literally mean off," Lieutenant Ricks recalls. "He didn't have a stitch on him. He stood there in a daze for a moment, and then dropped his shells and tumbled to the deck after them. Somebody ran to pick him up. There wasn't any more of a scratch or bruise on him than there was pants. He was just dazed, and he couldn't quite figure out why he was mother-naked."

May 3 was almost logged as an uneventful day, but a few minutes before midnight the attack signal was again jerked up the halyards. This time the Germans changed tactics. Two torpedo bombers appeared, one on each wing of the convoy. They launched their tin fish simultaneously against both flanks of the flotilla. It was a clean miss all the way around. No torpedo found its mark, nor did a shot from the antiaircraft guns.

Although evidences of submarine activity continued for the remaining week of the voyage, there were no further engagements with the Germans. The Armed Guard crew could not loaf the time away, however. Watches had to be maintained at any cost and the men worked with little rest and less sleep.

On May 6 the convoy anchored in the harbor of Murmansk. The port could accommodate only about ten ships at the docks, which had been bombed and rebuilt many times with timber.

As the EXPOSITOR berthed, a sailor standing near Ricks made inquiry about liberty ashore.

"I've dated all kinds of women in the world except Russians," he observed. "I'd like to get me a date with a Russian."

He leaned over the rail to watch a Russian woman stevedore walking along the pier below. She stopped to pick up a length of piling obstructing the path and nonchalantly tossed the 120-pound log out of the way. The sailor spat reflectively into the water.

"On second thought," he said, "I don't believe I care to meet these women."

Now the weather sided against the Germans. It snowed. It snowed so hard for two days that the vessel's stern was invisible from the bridge. The blizzard hampered the unloading considerably but it grounded the Luftwaffe until the third day. Then the sun came out, and with it the bombers, skimming close over the ridge of low hills that curved around the harbor.

Twelve of the big multi-motored aircraft headed for the sitting ducks. The gun crews went into action; everybody else scattered for shelter.

It seemed impossible that the Germans could miss. They did; the gunners didn't. Only nine of the bombers flew back toward Finland, two brought down by gunfire and one by a Russian fighter plane that buzzed up to meet them.

After the EXPOSITOR unloaded she traded places with an ammunition ship.

"I don't know whether that ammunition ship had been spotted or not," said Lieutenant Ricks, "but that afternoon when we had taken her anchorage out in the stream we were the target for a direct attack by six dive bombers.

"Bombs dropped fore and aft and to both sides of us, but they all missed by about a hundred yards. We were completely circled by bombs, but we weren't hit."

The next day, about the same time in the early afternoon, the bombers came again. This time the misses were nearer.

"In fact," Ricks recalls, "the spray from the first bomb completely obscured the ship. The British destroyer that was sitting on our starboard quarter signaled to ask 'What damage?' Just as our signalman prepared to answer 'No damage' a second flight of dive bombers came heading for us.

"The bombs fell so near that the concussion lifted the ship and shook her like a dog shakes a rat."

The twenty-two ships were unloaded in twenty days, despite bombings, blizzards and inadequate wharfing. The men were anxious to leave.

Murmansk was a pile of rubble. New buildings were all made of wood so that they could be reconstructed quickly. There was the International Club, open to everyone, for hot tea, chess and tattered old magazines in six languages, but the ship was the most comfortable place to stay when off duty.

On May 21 the convoy left for Iceland. Twice in the first three days submarine contacts were made.

Late in the afternoon of the third day—late by the clocks, not by the sun—a reconnaissance plane began its vulturelike circling beyond firing range. Presently a torpedo bomber joined in the circular vigil above the ships. For three hours the tantalizing surveillance continued. Then each dropped two green flares. Ten minutes later red flares were dropped, signals to lurking submarines.

But, as if in response to the flares, a Hurricane fighter plane was catapulted from a British ship. It started in pursuit of the torpedo bomber. Both planes disappeared in a cloud bank, where the fighter evidently lost its prey, because ten minutes later the Hurricane returned and started to close in on the second German plane. Seconds later the torpedo bomber popped out of the cloud and turned to join the fight. But it was too late to save the reconnaissance plane. A savage burst of fire from the Hurricane sent the first Nazi crashing into the sea. The bomber fled, and the Hurricane streaked after it. The pursuit vanished over the horizon.

The convoy churned on, the empty ships riding high. Then a shout went up from the decks of the watching ships. The Hurricane was returning—alone. It pancaked on the water near its mother ship and a boat put out to it. The men crowding the rails of the other ships saw the pilot taken aboard, his plane abandoned. A little while later a flutter of flags broke out on the Englishman. The pilot had died of wounds. For the remainder of the day all flags were flown at half mast in honor of the fighter who had given his life to save the ships.

Next day the now familiar shores of Iceland were sighted. The voyage was almost over. There was the sub-infested water between Reykjavik and New York to cover, but after what the men had already been through that seemed almost a humdrum chore. The ships remained in Iceland for two dreary, chafing weeks. Only the master of the ship and the Armed Guard officer were permitted to go ashore, and then for the transaction of official business only.

PLATE XVII—(*upper*) The USS KEARNY (*left*), lashed to a sister destroyer to keep from capsizing, limps into Iceland. The KEARNY, first U. S. combat ship to be hit by a Nazi submarine in World War II (October 17, 1941), took the full force of a torpedo amidships on her starboard side. Her crew, despite 22 casualties, brought her into port under her own power. (*Signal Corps Photo.*) *Inset:* Commander Anthony L. Danis, USN, Commanding Officer. (*lower*) Despite the lack of drydock and other facilities in Iceland, the USS VULCAN, repair ship, welded a caisson to the torpedo hole in the KEARNY. In a few weeks the KEARNY was able to sail back to the U. S. for complete repairs. She later saw much action in the Mediterranean campaigns. *Inset:* Captain Leon S. Fiske, USN, Commanding Officer of USS VULCAN.

PLATE XVIII—First U. S. combat ship sunk by the Nazis was the USS REUBEN JAMES. It broke in two from one well-placed torpedo in the early dawn of October 31, 1941, sinking almost instantly with a loss of 100 lives. Oil-covered survivors, like shiny seals, are fished out of the icy water by men of the USS NIBLACK, while another destroyer (the USS BENSON or the USS HILARY P. JONES) stands guard in the background. (*Painting by Lieut. Comdr. Griffith Baily Coale, USNR.*)

(*left*) Lieutenant Commander H. L. "Tex" Edwards, USN, Commanding Officer, who was lost. (*right*) Lieutenant Commander Griffith Baily Coale, USNR, Combat Artist aboard the USS NIBLACK, made the only pictorial record of the historic but tragic event.

PLATE XIX—Flames from her own oil tanks rise like a funeral pyre as the ill-fated REUBEN JAMES plunges to the bottom. Only 46 survivors were picked up, many men being killed by the ship's own depth charges. Lieutenant Commander Coale, who painted this and the graphic scene on the opposite page, was the first of the Navy's combat artists to see action. Operating under the sponsorship of the Office of Public Relations of the Navy, official combat artists have taken part in every major naval operation in the Atlantic and the Pacific. In depicting night action, activity in foul weather or over vast expanses of sea, artists have a considerable advantage over official photographers. Together the two groups, artists and photographers, are obtaining the most complete pictorial record ever made by any armed service, allied or enemy, in any war.

chant tanker refused to "give up the ship." Incredible as it may seem from these pictures, the terrific fire was brought under control and the vessel was salvaged. (*above*) Admiral Royal E. Ingersoll, USN, Commander in Chief, U. S. Atlantic Fleet.

(*right*) It takes real courage to battle against odds like these. In schools at Norfolk, Pearl Harbor, and other naval centers both Navy and merchant seamen were taught the latest means of fire fighting and damage control. Here, aboard the PENNSYLVANIA SUN, a seaman uses a special foam developed for tanker fires.

(*left*) After the flames had been extinguished, the charred skeleton of a victim of the Battle of the Atlantic was found where he had fallen in the attempt to save his ship.

PLATE XXI—(*right*) Under the original Neutrality Act our merchant ships, unarmed, were sitting ducks for enemy submarines. On November 13, 1941, the act was amended by Congress and guns were soon swung aboard ships. The Navy also supplied gun crews of 10 to 16 men each. Here, in Hoboken, N. J., the first gun is mounted on a U. S. merchant ship, November 26, 1941. (*above*) Vice Admiral Adolphus Andrews, USN, Commander, Eastern Sea Frontier.

(*left*) Navy Armed Guard gun crews on merchant ships had a hard, lonely, and thankless task. There was little time for training; much had to be learned by doing. With bitter humor the Armed Guard coined for itself the motto: "Sighted sub! Glub, glub!"

(*right*) The magnetic mine, one of Hitler's secret weapons, sank many ships until degaussing equipment could be installed. Here degaussing cables are being strung, preparatory to installation on an Allied merchant ship.

PLATE XXII—Nerve center. Here, behind guarded and locked doors at Eastern Sea Frontier Headquarters, New York, scattered reports on Nazi underseas raiders, listings of convoys, and other air and sea intelligence data became an ever-changing battle plan on the main situation board (*upper right*). The latter was magnetized to retain "pips," or plastic symbols, indicating ships, convoys, and subs; and "hamburgers," or cloth-covered strips, giving technical data. Colored lights showed weather conditions. (*lower*) The control platform faced the main situation board. Officers here assembled and translated reports of movements of ship and aircraft along the entire Atlantic seaboard. These two photographs give but a hint of the infinite pains with which anti-sub warfare was waged ashore as well as afloat.

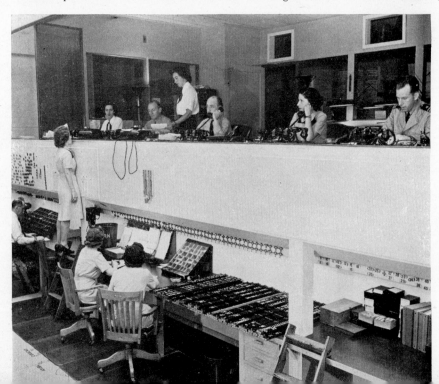

PLATE XXIII—(*right*) Ten-minute sub-killer! Even the little PCs shared in running up the toll of Nazi U-boats. Although depth charges actually sank the German raider, the forward gun crew of the PC-565 scored several hits when the sub briefly broached surface, September 7, 1943.

(*left*) The BURZA, a Polish destroyer, joins the security patrol. It was on the trans-Atlantic convoy routes that the idea of a United Nations was put into practical operation. Men-o'-war of the United States, Great Britain, Canada, Norway, Poland and the Netherlands shepherded merchantmen flying the flags of a dozen or more Allied or neutral countries. (*Coast Guard Photo.*)

(*right*) The AA gun crew of a carrier watches a converted yacht of the Coast Guard YP (or "Yippee") patrol slip by with sails set. From June, 1942, until their honorable discharge in December, 1944, the floating sentries of the "splinter fleet" helped to push the U-boat ever farther from our shores. For them it was risky work. The deck gun of a sub could blast most YP boats out of the water.

PLATE XXIV—(*left*) One of the outstanding photo series of the war is this group of six pictures taken from the Coast Guard cutter SPENCER, in mid-Atlantic, April 17, 1943. Here a pattern of depth charges blasts the submarine, forcing it to surface. (*Coast Guard Photo.*)

(*right*) The SPENCER opens fire. As soon as the U-boat surfaced, the Coast Guard cutter trained its guns on the raider, scoring direct hits on the conning tower and preventing the Nazis from manning their guns. (*Coast Guard Photo.*)

(*left*) Like a terrier and a rat: bearing down on the U-boat, the cutter's guns forced most of the crew to jump overboard to escape a hail of machine-gun bullets. Note the terror-stricken Nazi clinging to the conning tower, and another swimming away at the right. (*Coast Guard Photo.*)

PLATE XXV—(*right*) Closing in on its prey, the SPENCER keeps up a steady fire. Note the effect of the cutter's marksmanship on all parts of the submarine. The Nazi holding the stanchion amidships disappeared a moment later. (*Coast Guard Photo*.)

(*left*) Cease firing—pick up survivors! Men from the SPENCER board the U-boat a few minutes before it made its final dive. Several Nazi crew members were fished from the icy water. Meanwhile the rest of the convoy steamed safely on. (*Coast Guard Photo*.)

(*right*) "Scratch one U-boat!" Last sight of the doomed German raider was the bow disappearing beneath the waters of the North Atlantic. In the distance (*right*) can be seen the USCGS DUANE, which screened her sister ship, the SPENCER, from attack by another U-boat during the battle. (*Coast Guard Photo*.)

PLATE XXVI—(*left*) Panicky Nazis pour from the conning tower of a German submarine raider, forced to the surface by depth charges. Twelve survivors were picked up. (*Coast Guard Photo.*)

(*right*) Atlantic version of the Nazi salute! When a Coast Guard convoy cutter sank his submarine this German survivor threw both arms into the air and shouted "Kamerad!" because he feared that he would be left to die in the icy water. He was taken prisoner. (*Coast Guard Photo.*)

(*left*) Charleston, S. C., Navy Yard is "host" to 33 survivors of a German submarine sunk off the Carolina coast by the U. S. Coast Guard patrol craft ICARUS (background). The sub's commanding officer, Kapitan Leutnant Hellmut Rathke, stands at the right, front row.

PLATE XXVII—(*right*) A second
enemy to fight—the weather.
"Oh, for the South Pacific!"
mutter these bluejackets as
they shovel snow and ice from
the flight deck of a Navy carrier, at anchor in a North
Atlantic port. The planes are
Grumman Avenger torpedo
bombers.

(*left*) Transferring a wounded
Nazi submarine captain from
the destroyer, which picked
him up, to the baby flat-top
whose Grumman Avenger torpedo bombers sank his vessel
with a loss of all but 33 of his
crew. This same escort carrier
depth-bombed and sank three
German subs in four days.

(*right*) The Great Lakes played
a vital role in winning the Battle of the Atlantic. Not only
did this region train thousands
of men and launch scores of
ships, but it even converted
old sidewheel steamers into
carriers. Chicago rubbed its
eyes as smoking coal burners,
such as the USS WOLVER-
INE (*above*) and USS SABLE,
launched and took on planes,
in final training of flyers destined for CVE duty on the
Atlantic.

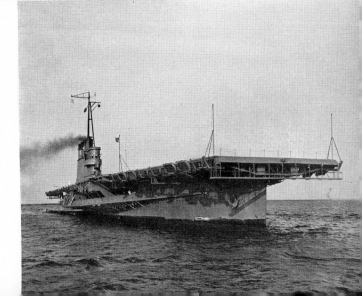

PLATE XXVIII—How to sink a German U-boat from the air. (*left*) On July 12, 1943, two TBF-1 and two F4F-4 planes from the USS BOGUE proved that the wolf-pack had met its master in a hard-hitting combination of escort carriers and destroyers. The raider, sunk in only 23 minutes, is sighted and the attack begins.

(*right*) In the fourth run against the desperately dodging Nazi submarine two depth bombs are dropped by a plane piloted by Lieutenant (jg) W. F. Chamberlain, USNR. Continuous strafing support by F4Fs prevented the Germans from using their anti-aircraft.

(*left*) A few minutes later spattered foam marks where aerial bombs straddled the U-boat, slowing its speed and crippling its controls. The submarine is a big one, capable of many weeks of patrol without returning to base.

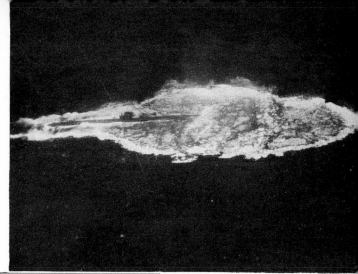

PLATE XXIX—(*right*) Continuing the attack, a plane piloted by Lieutenant W. S. Fowler, USNR, moves in for the kill. The big submarine swings in tight circles—perhaps its steering gear is jammed—as the crew begins to jump into the sea. Not a ship was lost from the convoy the U-boat intended to raid.

(*left*) The knock-out punch. As more depth charges straddle her hull, the Nazi raider breaks in two and finally blows up, sending a geyser of water and debris high in the air. These scenes are typical of many enacted in 1943 and 1944 as a result of attacks by planes from the BOGUE, CARD, CORE, BLOCK ISLAND, GUADALCANAL and other baby flat-tops of the antisubmarine patrols.

(*right*) Circling planes hover over the smoke and curving oil slick that marks the end of the trail for another German U-boat. Seventeen survivors were picked up by the USS OSMOND INGRAM, one of the accompanying destroyers of the task force.

PLATE XXX—(*upper*) Escort carrier and planes guard the life line of supply. The German answer to the protected convoy was the wolf-pack of many submarines. The Allied reply to that was a combination of small carriers, destroyers, and destroyer escorts—"baby flat-tops and tin cans." The planes are Douglas Dauntless, an early convoy type. *Insets:* (*left*) Rear Admiral Alva D. Bernhard, USN, Commander, Air Force, Atlantic Fleet. (*right*) Rear Admiral Francis S. Low, USN, first administrative officer, Tenth Fleet. (*lower*) One of the war's rarest sights—the torpedo room of a modern German submarine (U-505). Because the Nazi crew had opened the seacocks and expected their craft to sink, no effort was made to alter or destroy equipment. A U. S. Navy salvage crew from USS GUADALCANAL, despite danger of booby traps, succeeded in closing valves and saving the craft for study by our antisubmarine experts. The action took place June 4, 1944.

PLATE XXXI—(*right*) For the first time since 1815 a foreign enemy man-o'-war is boarded and captured on the high seas. With her stern already settling as the Nazis attempted to scuttle her, the U-505 is salvaged by U. S. seamen from a task group headed by escort carrier USS GUADALCANAL, June 4, 1944. Here a tow line is secured to the bow, as fellow salvagers close valves below.

(*left*) A strange place for a U. S. Navy carrier skipper! Captain Daniel V. Gallery, USN, commanding officer of the USS GUADALCANAL, in the conning tower of his prize—U-505. He personally went below in the sub and searched for booby traps.

(*right*) An ignominious predicament for a Nazi submarine: the U-505 is towed to Bermuda by the USS GUADALCANAL, which meantime carries on routine flight patrols.

PLATE XXXII—Back to the days of hand-to-hand fighting. On November 11, 1943, the USS BORIE, an old flush-deck destroyer, rammed a U-boat and found itself stuck fast. Then followed one of the strangest episodes of the war, with everything from shell cases to knives being used as weapons. The sub finally sank, but the BORIE was so badly damaged she had to be destroyed also. (*Drawing by Official Coast Guard Combat Artist, Warrant Boatswain Hunter Wood.*)

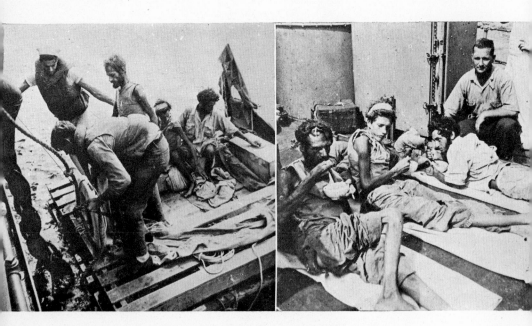

On January 24, 1943, a U. S. Navy patrol boat picked up, off the Brazilian coast, a raft with three emaciated merchant seamen who had been adrift 83 days. The survivor at the right (*right photograph*) is Basil Dominic Izzi, of South Barry, Massachusetts, who later took part in bond and industrial incentive drives.

On June 10 the confinement was broken. The ships left under escort. Eight days later the men were reminded that they still were a long way from home. A steamer on the edge of the convoy was torpedoed. Four men were killed in the explosion, the rest taken aboard other ships. Two days later another was torpedoed and sunk. Both time the attackers escaped, undetected.

At one o'clock on June 28, the EXPOSITOR dropped anchor just off the Statue of Liberty in New York harbor. One Armed Guard crew had returned with all hands intact from the Murmansk run—12,000 miles, 116 days, the ship safe, and the metaphorical scalp of one submarine nailed to the mainmast. It was—just another voyage; tougher than most, easier than some.

Ricks's adventures were probably duplicated scores of times. They are related here not because they are exceptional, but because they are illustrative. And not all gun crews survived the German-Finnish gantlet to tell their stories.

The route to Archangel was, if anything, worse than the Murmansk run for being longer. Consider the experiences of Lieutenant Albert Maynard, USNR, Armed Guard officer on SS SCHOHARIE, which brought a shipload of tanks, ammunition and food to Murmansk in a convoy that numbered forty ships at sailing, and twenty-seven upon arrival at the subarctic port.

The convoy was one of the more important, in the constant line of supply to the Soviet Union. Stalingrad and Leningrad were in what seemed to be the last stages of siege and destruction. To make delivery of the desperately needed supplies as secure as possible, the British provided the convoy with an escort of a converted aircraft carrier, a light cruiser, two antiaircraft cruisers, twenty-one destroyers and a small fleet of corvettes, minesweepers and trawlers—a task force in itself. And yet, a third of the convoy was lost.

It was on Sunday, September 13, 1942, on the seventh day out of Iceland, that Lieutenant Maynard looked over the side in the course of gun inspection to see a British merchantman instantly blotted out in steam and smoke. Before the signal to scatter could be raised, a second ship was torpedoed.

The superstitious in that convoy had reason to confirm their distaste for the number 13. Before that September day was done, a wolf-pack of submarines ran riot inside the convoy's columns, a swarm of thirty-seven Heinkel torpedo planes made an attack at 25 feet above the water, and a half dozen Ju-88s subjected the ships to a dive-bombing attack. A total of ten merchantmen was sunk, some outright, others left crippled with corvette protection only to be sent down later by the Nazis' aerial rear guard.

Lieutenant Maynard, with desperate sincerity, described the lulls in the battle as the unforgettable parts of the daylong fight with an enemy who alternately dropped from the sky or rose from the ocean depths. The business of fighting off dive bombers above, torpedo planes at deck level, and submarines, is too wholly occupying to permit mental note-taking.

"During the attacks our reaction was not fright," Maynard remembers. "But in the letdown periods of quiet, it would be silly to say one of us was not downright scared."

The view over the side was not cheering. Cargo ships in convoy may not pause or break the established pattern to rescue the shipwrecked. That job is left for the escorting warships. But it does not boost the morale of the Armed Guardsman to see men struggling in the icy brine as their own ship passes through the flotsam of battle; they are humanly prone to wonder when it will be their turn to cling with numbing fingers to a shattered spar and see the ships go by.

"There were men in the water, and men in lifeboats," Maynard recalls. "Some of them swearing, some praying, and some mockingly sticking out their thumbs and calling 'Going my way, mister?' as we slid by not a hundred feet from them."

Monday was inaugurated by the torpedoing of a tanker early in the morning. At noon thirteen torpedo planes came out of the clouds and concentrated on the carrier, whose own fighters shot down six of the enemy without loss. Half an hour later twenty Heinkels swarmed over the horizon. One of them torpedoed an ammunition ship which disintegrated just as the plane skimmed over the stricken vessel's masts; the explosion blasted the Nazi plane and its crew to atoms.

Day in, day out, the Heinkels and Junkers plagued the convoy. The thirteenth ship was lost to Finnish dive bombers just as the battered flotilla stood in for the straits of the White Sea, but the convoy had to fight off attacks every day at sea of the four remaining, and for the four moonlit nights of unloading at Archangel.

"And that," Lieutenant Maynard concludes, "is about all that happened on our trip to Archangel," a trip during which he himself once had to grab a fifty-caliber gun and train it against a Voss-Ha 140 boring in on the SCHOHARIE. The plane disappeared in a blur of flame and smoke, and tumbled "just like a ball of fire" into the sea.

"I think that was the most fun I had on the entire voyage," Maynard muses.

pered on our trip to Archangel," . . . trip during which he himself once tried to grab a Nazi machine gun and turn it against a Nazi. He lay boring in on the periscope sight. The ghost of the pool of flame and smoke . . . and rumbled, just that.

"I think that was the most fun I had on the entire voyage," Maynard mused.

Chapter Fourteen

LIEUTENANT RICKS, Lieutenant Maynard: Their stories could be duplicated and elaborated by the hundreds of Armed Guard officers and men who commuted from Atlantic ports of the United States to Iceland, the United Kingdom ("Yookay," eventually), the Soviet Union, Africa, the Near East, South America, and wherever ships ply salt water. Many did not return to tell their stories of submarine torpedoing and the Nazi captains' favorite target practice on lifeboats and rafts.

One other convoy assignment matched the northern gantlet; the desperately maintained line of supply to the long-besieged island of Malta, that bit of rock south of Sicily whose inhabitants and defenders withstood everything that the Germans and Italians could bring to bear against them.

Supplies for Malta were vital, and embraced not only guns and ammunition but food, medicine, clothing. Malta was the one last Allied base in the Mediterranean. Generals Montgomery and Rommel were rumbling in seesaw drives across North Africa. Tobruk fell, was recaptured and fell again. Even when Rommel backed the British Eighth Army almost to the streets of Alexandria, Malta still stood, an unsinkable carrier athwart the Axis supply lines to Africa.

But under the strain of constant combat against overwhelming odds, Malta was becoming an unsinkable carrier without aircraft. The winter of 1941–42 saw this shortage reach its most acute phase. Axis raids were becoming more frequent and heavier, the defending planes fewer. Nearest Allied air bases were beyond fighter range, as Rommel pushed the British back to the gates of Cairo.

To get planes to the island-fortress by cargo ship meant risking them to air, undersea and surface attack. There was one long chance of helping Malta; fly the planes in, ready to fight as soon as they got there. This meant just one thing—steaming a carrier through the Strait of Gibraltar, past all the Axis agents in Spain and Spanish Morocco into the Mediterranean, which was virtually a Fascist lake. It was a long, long chance—and the United States Navy took it to relieve a sorely pressed ally.

On April 15, the USS WASP, commanded by Captain John Walter Reeves, Jr., USN, left Scotland carrying more than forty Spitfires and RAF pilots for Malta. On the night of the 20–21st she slipped through the Strait and at dawn on the 22nd flew off her planes.

Berlin Betty in her throaty, sexy voice announced the WASP's presence in the Mediterranean and cooed commiseration for the "poor American boys and their fine ship" certain to be sunk. She could have saved herself the trouble; the WASP, her British planes safely launched, and safely arrived at Malta, was steaming back to Scotland unmolested.

On May 3 she was at sea again on the same errand. Once again she darted deep into enemy waters, launched her planes and retired without interference (except from Herr Goebbels's radio warriors, who claimed her sinking).

The take-off of the planes was not without incident, however. One Spitfire failed to become airborne and plummeted directly in front of the carrier's onrushing bow; another, finding its auxiliary fuel tanks inoperative, returned to the WASP and made incidental history by accomplishing a successful landing on her flight deck, the first time a high-speed land fighter had succeeded in such a maneuver.

The value of these daring missions is demonstrated by the messages the WASP received as she headed once more for Scotland:

(May 9th) First 3 flights landed at 1010 while a raid was on . . .
(May 9th, later) All groups of Spitfires have now arrived Malta. They have been refueled and were in action within thirty-five minutes of landing. First count not yet possible but casualties believed to be few . . . (signed) Commanding Officer, Malta.
(May 10th) Almost continuous air battle has been in progress since 0830 and the delivery of the aircraft. After refueling they have been in the air many times—We have lost three Spitfires and the enemy has had thirty of his aircraft destroyed or damaged. We are most grateful to you all. (signed) Commanding Officer, Malta.
(May 11th) To the Captain and Ship's Company of the USS WASP: Many thanks to you all for the timely help. Who said a wasp couldn't sting twice? (signed) Winston Churchill.

The planes helped Malta, but they did not relieve the siege. Only cargo ships could do that, bringing in the essential food, fuel and ammunition to the beleaguered island through enemy-dominated waters, under enemy-dominated skies.

American ships protected by Navy Armed Guard units swelled the Malta supply line; swelled, too, the casualty lists of a sea for whose control men have fought since the Phoenicians sent their galleys from Asia Minor to the Atlantic.

In April, 1942, two American merchant ships were lying at anchor in New York harbor—SS CHANT and SS TANIMBAR. On each was an Armed Guard crew. On the CHANT, Ensign Regis J. Schaefer, USNR, was the officer in charge of the gunners and on the TANIMBAR it was Ensign Clarence S. Lagerlof, another Reserve officer.

The SS CHANT sailed purposefully up the East River from the Army Transport Base, South Brooklyn, New York, on April 21, after having taken on ammunition near the Statue of Liberty, and arrived in Halifax on April 23. On Sunday, April 26, one of a convoy of twenty-six ships shepherded by six escort vessels, the CHANT headed across the Atlantic. Ensign Schaefer had tested the 4-inch gun and found it satisfactory, but one 50-caliber and one 30-caliber gun jammed on the first firing test. These guns were repaired and a battle bill was drawn up, augmenting the naval gunners with gunners from the troops on board.

Convoy formation was good. There were no stragglers. Zigzag plans were followed whenever visibility allowed and emergency turns were practiced twice a day. As the convoy approached the Irish coast it divided, one section going to Liverpool and the other to Belfast. The CHANT was in the latter group. On May 5 this section anchored in Belfast and began unloading. British officers from DEMS came aboard to check the armament, replenish supplies and make repairs where necessary.

Then the Armed Guard crew of the CHANT had the first hint that Belfast was not their ultimate destination. New armament started coming aboard, much of it unfamiliar, all of it designed for repelling aircraft. The gun crews were ordered ashore for two days' schooling in the new weapons. Their Alma Mater was the "Dome," where simulated air attacks were projected by cinema on a simulated sky, similar to that of a planetarium. A dummy gun was mounted in the center of the hemispherical room. The student gunners aimed at shadow planes on the dome's sky, firing a beam of light, while a sound track imitated the noise of motors, diving planes and gunfire. Under such realistic conditions the gunner learned to "lead" his target, to squeeze the trigger instead of jerking it, and, most difficult of all, to conserve his fire.

On May 16 the CHANT left Belfast for Glasgow, Scotland, with a small and incongruous cargo of steel rails and canned milk. The ship was berthed near a familiar-looking vessel, soon identified as SS TANIMBAR, which had left New York on April 30, lost her convoy off Halifax May 5, and had completed the hazardous crossing alone. And now the two Armed Guard officers were informed that the ships were transferred to orders of the British Admiralty and were to be even more heavily armed. "Something," they agreed, "is up."

The best gun positions were selected and what structural work was necessary began immediately. Two Browning 30-caliber guns were added port and starboard; 40-mm. Bofors Army mobile mounts and 20-mm. Oerlikons were substituted for the 50-caliber gun nests; a 3-inch 12-pounder mounted above and forward of the existing 4-inch guns, and two 30-caliber rifles were supplied each crew for sinking floating mines.

"What are they trying to do, make cruisers out of us?" the men wondered.

Thirty of the merchant seamen, volunteers, were given instruction ashore in gunnery, and paid 10 shillings—$2—a day for learning. Just before the ships were declared ready for sailing, additional British Navy personnel reported aboard: two officers, two petty officers and twelve seamen, three signalmen and one radioman who reported to the ship's regular company and six British Army men to operate the two mounted Bofors.

Even yet the destination of the ships was secret. At the final convoy conference only the masters of the ships attended, even though the usual procedure was to include Armed Guard officers as well. At this conference, the merchant skippers were told that Freetown, West Africa, was the convoy destination.

But the secret was out when an overlooked bill of lading on a crate of medical supplies was seen to read "For Malta," and bets were paid off to the knowing who had, days before, wagered from the nature of the cargo that the Mediterranean citadel was to be the port of call.

The convoy left Scotland on June 4 with a British escort of ten destroyers and two cruisers, sailing from the Clyde to the Irish Channel, around the northern coast of Ireland and south until a 90-degree turn to port set the course for the Strait of Gibraltar.

On the night of June 11, the ships streamed their paravanes to protect themselves against enemy mines as the convoy entered the strait. Off to starboard the lights of Tangier gleamed like tiny clusters of electric fruit.

The Mediterranean dawn was turning to blue when the last brown Spanish hills disappeared, and over the horizon streamed a double column of warships. They were the convoy's Mediterranean escort, and they came up fast. There was the battleship MALAYA, that had been repaired in the Brooklyn Navy Yard in September, 1941; there were two carriers, EAGLE and ARGUS, and, in support, there were five cruisers and twenty-one destroyers.

At 10:15 that morning, June 12, with everyone still hugely impressed by the escort strength around them and entertaining a sneaking hope that the enemy would dare try to challenge it, General Quarters sounded. An Italian reconnaissance plane soared over the convoy, circled and dropped three bombs (which missed), and then streaked northward as the escort screen opened a heavy antiaircraft barrage.

On the CHANT every possible preparation was made to make the gun batteries ready for important action and the ship safe. Magazines for the Oerlikons were taken out of ready boxes and placed in position around the perimeter of the gun nest. Ammunition for the 12-pounder was brought up from the magazine and stowed below the gun base. General Quarters was maintained throughout the convoy all the day and night of June 13. The Italian bomber's bold approach and easy escape had sobered all hands. When the Axis planes came over in numbers, somebody was bound to get hit.

The TANIMBAR was the first.

Five minutes after another Italian reconnaissance bomber had surveyed the convoy at 10:15 on the morning of June 14, the hose crew on the TANIMBAR was busy wetting down the wooden decks to minimize the danger of fire should a bomb strike. At ten minutes past, eleven aircraft were reported heading toward the convoy on the port bow. Five minutes more, and fifty planes swept in from the direction of Sardinia in a grand assault. It was a combined attack by high- and medium-level bombers and torpedo planes. The guns of the outer escort greeted the attackers and as the planes broke through the outer screen fire, the merchantmen began to spout steel. Torpedo bombers, flying deck-high, twisted through the screen of destroyers to head down the center of the convoy. One cut across the bow of the CHANT into a cone of fire. It flared a comet's tail of fiery smoke, and as it shot across the bow of the TANIMBAR, a scant 150 feet to port, Ensign Lagerlof's men on the bridge 20-mm. gun ripped the bomber with bullets which sent it crashing in flames to the water. Three enemy planes were shot down in this initial attack.

The crews of the two American ships were waving mutual congratulations when, at 11 : 25, the planes wheeled in again. A single torpedo plane bored in toward the TANIMBAR's starboard beam. Every gun on the ship opened fire, but at 1,000 yards the pilot launched his torpedo and escaped in a turning climb. As the gunners raised their sights the torpedo smashed into the TANIMBAR and just as the ship lurched under that impact two bombs dropped on its decks from a medium-level bomber. Before the men's eyes could recover from the flash of the explosion the entire midship section was aflame. The ship sagged into a 20-degree list to starboard, and the order to abandon ship was passed. In five minutes all that remained of the TANIMBAR was a film of wreckage on the sea, and dazed men struggling to reach the life rafts.

Thirty men were killed. Among the Armed Guard the casualties were limited to burns suffered by three men, who were in the water almost an hour before the British minesweeper HYTHE picked them up.

The men on the CHANT had little hope for their friends on the TANIMBAR and less time to express it, for their guns had to be kept going until their attackers were fought off, and by that time the survivors were left far astern. They saw the cruiser HMS LIVERPOOL, smoking and listing to starboard, drop out of line and turn back to Gibraltar as they labored to prepare for the next onslaught. One Oerlikon gun, which had jammed, was cleaned. Empty cartridges were jettisoned and magazines reloaded. All hands now knew the destructive force of a combined bomber- and torpedo-plane attack. They also knew the worth of their guns. A signal from the flagship counted twelve of the attacking aircraft shot down.

The men ate at their gun stations but the afternoon was quiet except for alerts. Then at ten minutes after six that evening dive bombers gave the convoy a light once-over that caused no damage and cost the attackers one plane, shot down by carrier-based fighters.

Two hours later forty enemy aircraft came in to attack. Two of them were shot down and the others left without scoring a hit. At 9 : 30 the major part of the escort left the convoy to return to Gibraltar, having reached the narrows of the Mediterranean and the limit of their effectiveness and calculated risk. There were left: one antiaircraft cruiser, eight

British and Polish destroyers, four minesweepers and six motor launches. The men on the merchant ships felt almost nakedly alone.

At ten o'clock came the first night attack. One four-motored bomber passed too close to the CHANT, and every starboard gun on the ship scored. The bomber banked steeply and pinwheeled wing over flaming wing into the sea. No ships were struck. No other plane shot down.

Shortly after midnight the convoy slid by the huge rock, formed like some gigantic prehistoric saurian basking, that is Zemboa Island. Then Zembretta Island. And at two o'clock in the morning of June 15, the lighthouse of Cape Bon was sighted. The convoy was now deep in the Tunis War Channel. Malta was still twenty-four long hazardous hours away, but the CHANT was not to make it, although all but four of the men aboard were to land there.

At 2: 30 the coastal batteries on the Island of Pantelleria, far astern, woke up and opened fire on the convoy, just passing out of range. Aircraft could be seen in the light of the gun flashes, but there was no damage. What remained of the night was quiet. At 6: 20 in the morning the convoy was attacked by an Italian force of two cruisers and three destroyers, which sent over a salvo that splashed some of the merchantmen, but fled when the British cruiser and destroyers opened fire.

The Italian ships were hardly out of sight when the convoy was attacked again, this time by Nazi Ju-88s. Two of the bombers circled high over the CHANT, out of range of her guns. Then one plane peeled off in a 70-degree dive for the motorship. Ensign Schaefer bade his impatient gunners hold their fire until the bomber was certainly in range. Down, down, down the bomber hurtled. At the officer's command all guns on the ship began to fire. The plane swung upward and outward; a tiny string of innocuous-looking specks separated from the bomber and continued on the bee line for the merchantman's deck.

That stick of bombs struck the CHANT amidships on the starboard side. The mainmast crashed to port. Shattered concrete from the bridge and the deck cargo of coal filled the air with flying grit and dust, through which the ship's superstructure could be seen twisted and torn. A 15-foot square section of the hull was ripped off, smashing the starboard lifeboats.

From start of the dive to the finish of the CHANT, four seconds had passed.

After a short swim through the acrid, choking fumes of the smoke screen, the survivors were picked up by the British minesweeper RYE, from whose deck the oil-smeared men of the CHANT watched their ship go down. They did not see the bomber that sank the CHANT; it had already hurtled flaming into the sea.

One other ship, a tanker, was so damaged in this attack that she had to be sunk by the convoy's escort guns.

The curtain of fire maintained around Malta by the enemy had not yet been penetrated by the men from the sunken American merchant ships. Intermittent air attacks and one heavy bombing by Ju-88s, and a second foray by Italian destroyers, harried the convoy that day. British Spitfires from Malta helped keep the enemy from scoring, and the Americans on HMS RYE helped haul one British fighter pilot out of the water into which he parachuted from his crippled plane after shooting down a Junker.

Half an hour before midnight the convoy stood in for Valletta harbor, the sweepers in the van streaming their paravanes to bring up mines. The final casualty to the mixed fleet came at 1:15 in the morning: a Polish destroyer struck a mine the sweepers missed, and sank.

At three o'clock on the morning of June 16 the convoy anchored in Valletta under the lee of Malta's bombpocked, honeycombed hills. The trip was over. One more convoy had arrived to sustain the garrison and the people of the besieged island, with a loss of only three ships and thirty-four men after five days of almost continuous battle.

Shortly after dawn the Armed Guard crews of TANIMBAR and CHANT met, deep in the rock shelters behind the British submarine base. Except for the three of the TANIMBAR who were burned and three from the CHANT with sprains and cuts, there were no casualties among them. First aid, food and beds were provided, and word was flashed to the Navy Department in Washington that all hands were safe.

Two weeks later the United States naval contingent filed aboard a British submarine and were returned to Gibraltar. There they were put on a British merchantman for Scotland, transshipped to the transport USS WEST POINT, and on September 5 arrived in New York to report for further duty.

Ensigns Regis J. Schaefer and Clarence S. Lagerlof were awarded the Silver Star.

There was no monotony for the men who fought their way back and forth, and up and down the sea lanes to where desperate troops converted the precious cargoes into the tools of victory. Only when survivors of a sunken ship climbed aboard a raft was monotony the lot of the Navy's guardsmen and their colleagues of the Merchant Marine—the monotony of hunger, thirst, sunburn and drenchings, until death or rescue ended suffering.

There was Seaman Basil D. Izzi, who spent eighty-three days on a raft, sixty-seven of them on a diet of raw fish, raw seagull and rainwater, during which his officer, Ensign James Maddox, USNR, and a fellow Armed Guardsman, Seaman George Beezley, died. Surviving with Izzi were two merchant seamen, Cornelius van der Slot and Nicko Hoogendam.

John Jefferson Waller, S 2/c, was aboard a raft for only a week after SS MERRIMACK, a lake-type steamer serving as an Army transport, was torpedoed in the well-traveled ship lane between Mobile, Alabama, and Cristobal, Canal Zone. He was one of an Armed Guard crew of eight under command of Ensign Hunter Marshall III, USNR, and the only one to survive. There is a destroyer escort named for Marshall, who was never seen again after he gave the order to abandon ship, an order not issued until the MERRIMACK spun in a half circle preparatory to her final dive. It is bad to be on a raft in the open sea; it can be worse to wait for rescue, as Waller did, where one sees ships pass, unseeing, almost every day.

These are random stories out of hundreds, most of which will never be told. Waller was picked up, with seven other survivors, by the destroyer USS BORIE, later to make a name for herself in the winning of the Battle of the Atlantic. The Caribbean, which looks so safely encompassed by friendly land on the maps of home atlases, so far from Germany, was no safer from submarine forays than the open ocean. The SS NATHANIEL HAWTHORNE found it less so. On November 6, 1942, on the homeward leg of a cruise that had taken her to the Persian Gulf, the steamer was torpedoed just out of Trinidad, and sank in less than a minute. Lieutenant (jg) Kenneth Muir, USNR, badly wounded, would not leave the ship until he was sure all the men of his Armed Guard crew had escaped. Seven of the ten did not, so swiftly did the HAWTHORNE sink, and Muir went down with the ship. A posthumous Navy Cross was sent to his parents in Pelham, New York.

Many of the Navy's newest destroyers and destroyer escorts bear names to commemorate Armed Guard officers who, like Muir, lost their lives in battle. There is, for example, the USS BORUM. The story of how that DE came to bear the name of a young Reserve Armed Guard officer has all the bitter irony of a Greek tragedy.

Lieutenant (jg) John R. Borum, USNR, commanded the Armed Guard on a merchant tanker, SS BRILLIANT, which was torpedoed before dawn east of Newfoundland on November 18, 1942. The torpedo tore a 40-foot hole in the ship's starboard side and ignited the gushing oil. The ship's master and eight men on the bridge looked down on what appeared to be a flaming deck; the master sounded the "Abandon ship" signal, and the nine men ran to a lifeboat which capsized as it was launched. A British corvette, HMS BURY, escorting the convoy, picked up the men who were half dead from exposure.

They were the only ones to leave the BRILLIANT.

Fighting his way through the smoke, Third Officer J. C. Cameron collided with Borum, who coolly suggested: "Why don't you shut off that abandon ship whistle and try to put out the fire?" Cameron said that the youngster's sang-froid perversely struck him as extraordinarily funny, and he stood laughing, "and this in itself gave me a feeling of confidence." He rang the engine room, and through the tube came the third engineer's bellow: "What in hell's wrong up there?"

Everything was under control below-decks. Cameron, with the help of others, managed to smother the fires with the steam extinguishers. The ship, which had been listing and settling, returned to even keel and, although the mechanical steering gear was jammed, the ship was found to respond to the hand wheel. The engines were intact. In response to the corvette's query Cameron signaled that the BRILLIANT was able to carry on, at 3 knots. He was given his position and a course for St. John's, Newfoundland, and the corvette crowded on steam to overtake the convoy.

So there was the BRILLIANT, crippled and gaping, alone in the submarine wolf-pack's favored hunting grounds. Cameron took counsel with Borum. Their combined knowledge of navigation was sketchy, but they agreed to stand watch and watch in an attempt to get the ship to port.

Slogging through heavy seas that caused the strained deck plates to buckle and the pump-room bulkheads to warp, the ship reached St. John's on the evening of November 22, with the last-minute aid of a pilot put aboard by a schooner within sight of land. At St. John's temporary repairs to the BRILLIANT were undertaken, and a cable dispatched to

Halifax, Nova Scotia, requesting a tow to that port, where the ship could again be made seaworthy.

In mid-January the BRILLIANT was towed out of St. John's. Out of the harbor a quartering gale began to belabor the ships. During the night of January 20 the towline parted and the patched and helpless BRILLIANT broke in two and sank. With her went Lieutenant Borum, who had stuck by his ship when the captain fled, had helped bring her to port although by no stretch of his orders was that expected of him.

Another story, that, out of the crowded files.

Not all the merchantmen lost in that long battle of endurance for control of the Atlantic were submarines' prey. Some fell to raiders, ships disguised as friendly cargo carriers which revealed their true colors (to use correctly a metaphor long used by landsmen), when they brought a wayfaring steamer under their hidden guns.

At high noon on September 7, 1942, en route from Capetown to Paramaribo, the United States cargo ship SS STEPHEN HOPKINS sighted two strange motorships. The vessels identified themselves forthwith by a salvo of shell fire that raked the ship's decks. The story of the engagement is tersely told in the citation accompanying a posthumous Navy Cross for the STEPHEN HOPKINS's Armed Guard officer, Lieutenant (jg) Kenneth M. Willett, USNR:

> In an attack launched by the enemy, and with no friendly ship in sight, Lt. (jg) Willett promptly manned his station on the 4-inch gun as the first shell struck and opened fire on the most heavily armed of the two enemy raiders. Although seriously wounded in the stomach almost immediately, he kept up a sustained and rapid fire at close range, hitting his target along the water line with most of the 35 shells fired. Because of his great personal valor and gallant spirit of self-sacrifice, he was able to maintain a determined and heroic defense of his ship until forced by a magazine explosion to cease his fire. Still refusing to give up, Lt. (jg) Willett, obviously weakened and suffering, went down on deck and was last seen helping to cast loose the life rafts in a desperate effort to save the lives of others. His vessel was shelled repeatedly from stem to stern but before she plunged stern first, wrecked and blazing into the sea, her guns had inflicted serious damage on both enemy raiders and caused the probable destruction of one of them.

Twenty-one men manned a lifeboat when the abandon-ship order was given by the STEPHEN HOPKINS's master, Captain Paul Buck of Merrimacport, Massachusetts. As the boat touched water, a shell burst against the ship's side, fragments killing two of the occupants and wounding four.

Twenty-eight days later, the lifeboat beached at the tiny Brazilian coastal village of Barra da Stabapoana. Fifteen half-starved, sun-blistered men had survived: half the Armed Guard's crew of ten, and ten of the ship's complement of forty-one, including Second Engineer George Cronk, who as the only surviving officer commanded the lifeboat and brought it safely to land.

These are but an illustrative few of the stories of heroism and courage that the Armed Guard has accumulated. Its grim, unlovely and unsung job of getting merchant cargoes safely through the zone of war has not been exceeded in danger or importance by any Navy duty in the Atlantic. The Armed Guard had to be expanded in personnel so rapidly that it became known almost as a Navy within the Navy. Training progressed from a bare outline of gunnery to intensive courses in complicated weapons, and armament increased until it took twenty-four men instead of ten to work the guns. Between the time the first merchant ship was equipped with an Armed Guard crew and the June 6 D-day for Normandy in 1944, a daily average of 5.4 merchant ships was armed and supplied with Armed Guard crews.

There have been awards commensurate with the duties of this job. From the Russian government, for the Murmansk run, came two awards of the Order of Patriots War, First Degree, and two of the Second Degree, to Armed Guard officers. Six officers were presented with the Order of the Red Star. There have been, between the Armed Guard's inception and July, 1944, five Navy Crosses awarded Armed Guard officers; 70 Silver Stars; 5,367 letters of commendation to both officers and men; 19 Navy and Marine Corps Medals; and 13 Bronze Star Medals. Five destroyer escorts bear the names of Armed Guardsmen who lost their lives in carrying out their duties.

In thinking of the Armed Guard as they fought it out with the enemy in all the oceans of the world, it is easy to lose sight of the fact that other Americans were there too, fighting right alongside of them; the Merchant seamen, officers and crew, who manned the ships the Armed Guard defended.

The prewar Merchant Marine of the United States employed about fifty to seventy thousand men. When the conflict became general, it was immediately apparent that our cargo fleet needed to be greatly expanded if we were to supply ourselves and our allies. This meant a vast ship-building program, which has received its meed of notice, and a vast training program, which has not.

Under the direction of the War Shipping Administration, headed by Vice-Admiral Emory S. Land, USN (Ret.), and including as deputy administrators, Rear Admiral Howard S. Vickery, USN, and Captain Edward Macauley, USN (Ret.), the training and procurement program built the Merchant Service into a force 200,000 strong. Much, if not all, of the officer training under this program, and a large portion of the crew training, was done by Navy and Coast Guard personnel.

Trained and ready, these officers and men of our Merchant Marine shared the war at sea with their uniformed countrymen in the Navy. They fought their way, and took their losses—5,579 dead and missing, 487 prisoners of war, 984 vessels sunk—in every sea. They battled through the convoy routes, they anchored off the beachheads, they eased their way through the minefields. No account of the United States' war at sea could be complete without testimony to the great deeds of the American Merchant Marine. As General of the Armies Dwight D. Eisenhower, Supreme Commander Allied Expeditionary Forces, said in summing up their service, "With the Navy was always the Merchant Marine, in which Americans have served with a devotion to duty and a disregard for danger and hardship that defies any attempt to describe."

Particularly during the early days of American fighting the Merchant Marine and the Armed Guard seemed to be tackling the German U-boats and surface raiders alone. Actually, even then, the Navy's air arm was on the job.

Chapter Fifteen

PATROL WING—later Fleet Air Wing—7 could have adopted as its mascot Cerberus, the three-headed dog that guards the gates of Hades. It was hell, all right, flying neutrality and, later, combat patrol in Catalinas, Hudsons and Venturas through the gales and fogs of the Iceland-Greenland-Newfoundland apex of the Atlantic, guarding convoys past Torpedo Junction, and with that mission accomplished, splitting up to hunt U-boats in the Bay of Biscay, the English Channel and African waters. Its VP-73 (Patrol Squadron 73), jockeying PBY-5As on instruments through subarctic fogs "only a little less solid than Greenland's icy mountains," scored the first proved kill of a submarine by American naval air forces.

Probably that record will be vigorously challenged, but there it is on the books. Other submarines were sunk earlier, at least to the pilots' satisfaction, but so many whales, reefs and hulks drifting awash were bombed, too, that the Navy early ruled that to claim a fox the hunter had to bring home the brush.

It was in the spring of 1942 that Captain "Dan" Gallery, USN, commander of the Fleet Air Base in Iceland, was lecturing the pilots on the Department's new rules for crediting a kill. Positive and irrefutable evidence—such as prisoners—was necessary before the Navy would credit a plane or a ship with a victory.

"What it amounts to is this," Captain Gallery said. "You have to bring the skipper's pants."

There was a reason, and an important one, for the rigid rule. The Navy could not be optimistic over the number of submarines sunk. It had to lean backward in estimating the size and disposition of the enemy fleet, and the canny Germans had already learned to fool novice opponents by releasing oil and floating junk after submerging under attack to give ocular evidence of destruction. If the antisubmarine force command accepted an oil slick and fragments of wood and paper as proof of a "kill," let alone bombs dropped on a basking whale, all calculations of enemy power would be thrown out of balance—to the enemy's advantage.

"You have to bring back the skipper's pants" was the ironic slogan of Air Wing 7. How could an airplane stop to pick up souvenirs? the crews asked each other, a little bitterly.

VP-73 had several brushes with submarines after that dictum, in some of which, the crews swore by all the Norse gods, the U-boats had no chance of escape.

Then Lieutenant Robert Hopgood, USNR, was ordered out to pick up a convoy heading eastward for Torpedo Junction. "Hoppy" had Lieutenant (jg) Bradford ("Tex") Dyer, USNR, along as second pilot, and Tex tells the story:

"We were flying about five hundred feet off the water, with a forty-knot gale bumping us around, and rain squalls making visibility spotty. I sighted a ship on the surface. 'Lead destroyer of the convoy,' I told myself, and took another look. It was a submarine.

"I told Hoppy, and he dove in. As we came in we noticed there were two or three men on the conning tower. We dropped all our bombs and got a nice straddle, hitting the sub. Then we came back and made three strafing runs. The U-boat fired back. We could see her begin to blow compressed air and oil, and men running around the deck. She appeared to be badly damaged."

Then rain enveloped the Catalina and her antagonist. The men in the plane tried to count the holes torn in their craft by the submarine's flak, and made it an even two dozen. A radio message to the convoy described the inconclusive battle as the flying boat circled, hoping for a break in the weather.

It came two hours later, and revealed a startling sight, Dyer relates.

"The sub's crew had come upon an Icelandic vessel and had boarded it, and then had tried to run the bow of the submarine up over the ship's deck to keep it afloat. The gun crew still on the U-boat's deck fired at us."

Hopgood circled the crippled submarine out of gun range while its crew toiled to make repairs. Then out of the rain squalls charged a British destroyer to take the situation in hand. The submarine was scuttled.

"How many prisoners?" the Catalina blinker-signaled.

"Fifty-two. Nice work," the destroyer signaled in reply. "Now find one for us."

Hopgood and his crew received credit—the first recorded credit under the new rules, so far as can be determined now—for the Navy plane's elimination of the U-boat. But Hopgood was not satisfied. The rules as laid down by Captain Gallery had not been strictly met. Certain negotiations of a most irregular but highly stimulating nature were initiated with the Royal Navy. Some weeks later a lumpy bundle was delivered to the VP-73 headquarters.

Its contents were nailed to the wall of a Nissen hut where the fliers messed, and Captain Gallery was summoned to view the prize.

It was the U-boat skipper's pants!

VP-73 was the one unit most consistently with Fleet Air Wing 7— Patrol Wing, or Patwing, 7 prior to the change in organizational nomenclature in November, 1942. It was with Patwing 7 in the Caribbean, with VPs 71, 72 and 74, 1939 through 1941. Pearl Harbor found Patwing 7 split between Iceland, Newfoundland and Fleet Air Base Quonset Point, Rhode Island. In February it consisted of VPs 73 and 74, and 82; 82 and, later, 84 and 87 of Patwing 8 were with the group for a while, as was VP-93. VP, for the remaining few who have not yet mastered the unpronounceable combinations of consonants which aviation has forced upon our vocabularies, means a squadron of heavier-than-air patrol planes.

Captain Henry W. Mullinix, USN, later to be made rear admiral and to lose his life in the Pacific, led Patwing 7 into war. In the summer of 1942 the command passed to Commander L. T. Hundt, USN, and then to Captain Felix L. Baker, USN. Captain William H. Hamilton, USN, took command in May, 1943, when the Wing's operations came under the all-embracing direction of the Tenth Fleet, and he led it to Europe in August of that year, although VP-73 had blazed the way across the Atlantic to participate in the 1942 invasion of Africa.

But Patwing 7 went to war on both sides of the world, for part of it was hurried to the Pacific soon after Japan's blow at Pearl Harbor.

It was VP-73, under command first of Lieutenant Commander James E. Leeper, USN, that the reader anonymously met in the Iceland chapter of this volume. The Greenland patrol was inaugurated by VP-93 under Commander Claude W. Hamam, USN. Working closely with the Coast Guard and the Army Air Force, these units spent more time in grindingly monotonous patrols than in shaking U-boat skippers out of their trousers. Medals and publicity are not granted for endless hours of empty patrolling, and the occasional fights with submarines were holiday interludes in the inglorious and incessant battle against fog, rain and gales.

But the twin war against enemy and elements was interrupted also by calls for rescue. Lieutenant (jg) A. Y. Parunak, USN, was sent out to rescue some Army aviators who had crashed on the Greenland icecap. He put his lumbering big PBY down in a shallow pool of melted snow, took the Army men aboard, and put his overloaded plane back into the air again from the big puddle—which providentially provided pond, incidentally, disappeared next day. For that, Parunak was awarded the Distinguished Flying Cross.

The Army made it all even when Colonel Bernt Balchen organized a dog-sledge party and rescued one PBY crew that had crashed on the icecap when caught in a storm that continued so many days that aerial rescue was out of the question, and, except for Colonel Balchen's string of malemutes, any rescue seemed impossible.

VP-73, under Lieutenant Commander A. S. ("Sandy") Hayward, USN, was relieved in October, 1942, when Lieutenant Commander J. J. Underhill, USN, led VP-84 to Reykjavik from Argentia, Newfoundland, to take over its chilly duties. Half the unit was in the air on the first leg of the long hop home to Quonset, and the other half was packing up and exchanging wild hopes for duty near Broadway or Coral Gables, when countermanding orders were flashed from Washington. The half that were awing returned, and before its engines were cold the entire unit took off for North Ireland. There and in England they waited for more than a week, when the occupation of Morocco by the United Nations forces gave them an idea where their next duty might be.

It was.

It was, too, a quick transition from the arctic to the torrid zone of Africa. Based first at Port Lyautey and later at Agadir, VP-73 shared in the same old monotonous grind of searching the convoy lanes for submarines. The relatively calmer weather might have accentuated the monotony, but for the spice given the job by the knowledge that German aircraft might be encountered at any time. And although the pilots had become practiced in making a dive bomber out of a PBY—something neither its makers nor the Navy had ever contemplated—there was no human ingenuity that could make the big, slow flying boats agile enough to engage in a dogfight.

Or so they thought, until Lieutenant John ("Count") Drew, USNR, was interrupted by a Focke-Wulf 200 while providing air cover for a small convoy.

Lieutenant (jg) Edward ("Frenchy") Bourgeault, USNR, the second pilot, tells the story:

"As the F-W approached to make a run on the convoy, we kept climbing, making tight turns between it and the ships. The Heinie leveled off to make his run, and we set a collision course for him. Both planes were shooting. He had a cannon as well as machine guns.

"At the last minute he turned off to avoid getting rammed. He kept trying, climbing and then leveling off for a pass at the ships. But we kept climbing with him, always inside, and we'd get in the way every time he made his run. Then we'd chase him away. Imagine a PBY chasing a Focke-Wulf!

"Once he got through when we lost him in the clouds, and he got in a hit. It was good bombing, but he didn't try again. We chased him away, but couldn't catch him, of course."

A Catalina had outfought a 4-engine German F-W! The boys were congratulating themselves when another Focke swooped down on the convoy, and Drew repeated his tactics of tight turns and collision courses.

"We'd got nearly to 13,000 feet when the Nazi started a really determined run. We got squarely in his way. Both airplanes were shooting at pretty close range. The Heinie fire was whipping through our plane, and Lieutenant Lee Kennedy, USNR, our navigator, had a narrow escape. He was heading back to after station and stopped to look back for a moment just as a burst of machine-gun fire whipped right through the plane where he would have been, if he hadn't stopped. Then our nose-gunner, Aviation Ordnanceman 1/c Carl Adams, got home with some good bursts. They said afterward he worked his guns up and down like a pump handle. The Focke-Wulf started trailing smoke and then turned for home. We tried to chase him but he pulled away."

The entire crew of that PBY was awarded the Distinguished Flying Cross for that, but no decoration, some of them say, is equal to the honor of having put a Catalina through a dogfight—*two* dogfights—against superior speed, maneuverability and firing-power.

VP-84 inherited from the boys of 73 the worst arctic winter in the annals of meteorology. Despite incredible gales, fought over water and over uncharted Greenland searching out Nazi weather stations, 84 hung up "a really magnificent record" in the words of the RAF Coastal Command. Five credited submarine kills were the biggest chapter in its eleven months' history of war in the arctic, before the squadron shoved off to England, under command of Lieutenant Commander P. C. Staley, USN, who succeeded Lieutenant Commander Underhill in March, 1943.

Squadrons VP-93 and VP-92, partially equipped with fast new Venturas, chalked up at least two victories, too, before the area was turned over to the Royal Canadian Air Force and Patwing 7 headed across the Atlantic, in the summer of 1943.

The entire antisubmarine picture was changing, shifting, and gradually crystallizing into the pattern that was to conquer the U-boat and render the German helpless to interrupt the flood of men and machines pouring across the ocean.

Biggest factor in that altered picture was, in the final analysis, the CVE-DD-DE-radar team earlier mentioned, but that sub-busting combination could not have fulfilled its destiny without the ship-and-plane combination that drove the Germans from the coastal waters first.

Doenitz's merry pirates invented the wolf-pack, claimed the middle wastes of the Atlantic as their own, and apparently the stupid British and Americans were forced to acknowledge that proprietorship. "Milk-cow" submarines brought the U-boats fuel, mail and fresh rations; crews sunned themselves on the decks until an approaching convoy was detected. The pack deployed for the kill, and, when the ships came in range, made the water boil with torpedoes from the flanks and astern. Then the pack dove deep, rocked and strained by depth charges, the laggards and the wounded sprayed with shellfire from the Armed Guard. It was dangerous sport, to be sure, and often fatal, but the odds were with the submarine and so was the score.

Then, early in 1943, the sun-bathing Nazis happily playing skat on deck in safe mid-ocean, looked up to see airplanes where no airplanes should be. It was incredible, *unverständlich!* Next, a submarine skipper caught sight of a weird and horrid craft through his periscope—a squat, sawed-off carrier from whose plunging decks airplanes took off to scour the lairs of the wolf-packs. The CVE had arrived.

Chapter Sixteen

C FOR CARRIER, V for heavier-than-air, E for escort; the first one in the Atlantic was USS BOGUE (Captain Giles E. Short, USN), closely followed by USS CARD (Captain A. J. ("Buster") Isbell, USN)— first CVE to win a Presidential Unit Citation; sixteen subs positively destroyed—later to be joined by CORE, BLOCK ISLAND, CROATAN and others. All were hybrids, built on merchant hulls, and by that token as slow as the cargo ships they escorted. They did not need speed. That was furnished by the Grumman Wildcats and Avengers that sped from the decks in all weather, not only to defend the convoys from submarines but to track down and attack the U-boats scores of miles from the plodding ships, with the destroyers knifing up to make certain of the kill. Presidential unit citations are worn by the company and crew of both BOGUE and CARD to testify that they broke the back of the submarines, and the heart of the Nazi navy.

The BOGUE left her Puget Sound birthplace in November, 1942, with the CARD only a week behind in the long trek through the Panama Canal to the North Atlantic.

The BOGUE's first assignment was with the British command to escort convoys from the vicinity of Newfoundland to the Western Sea Approaches, this side of Iceland. It was rough, monotonous work, never quite crossing the Atlantic, turning over the intact herd of cargo ships to the escort ships that came out from Scotland and England's Irish Sea ports to complete the shepherding job. The BOGUE went to work on St. Valentine's Day, 1943. There were contacts but no combats on the first two voyages. First bombs were dropped on an enemy submarine by Lieutenant Roger C. ("Stomp") Santee, USN, on April 28, with undetermined results. That was during the carrier's third eastward voyage, and the skirmish was like the first storm-heralding breeze that breaks the calm.

On the return westward Lieutenant Commander William McClure Drane, USN, squadron skipper, spotted a fully surfaced submarine scouting the convoy. It was standard wolf-pack practice. The submarine was just out of line of visibility from the ships, counting their composition and protection, and summoning its mates to the attack.

It was 2000 Navy time—8 P.M. of a calm, end-of-May spring evening, but the calm ended abruptly for the U-boat when Drane charged down-sun upon the spying submarine and dropped a full load of bombs that obscured the U-boat in a hydra-headed geyser. In the few seconds it took Drane to bank his plane and reverse course, the submarine had vanished. It happened so quickly that neither turret nor tail gunner was able to catch the target in the plane's machine-gun cameras.

But there were no "skipper's pants" to prove a kill, and on the BOGUE's virgin scoreboard was chalked only a "possible."

Long before dawn the next day, May 22, BOGUE's planes were aloft again, searching for the pack mates of Bill Drane's victim. At 0530 in the morning the interphone gabbled the code words that meant Lieutenant (jg) Roger ("Bud") Kuhn, USN, was announcing an attack.

The mechanical voice-box clicked and snored, and then bellowed forth in plain language, code forgotten: "She's down by the stern and fighting back." Captain Short ordered immediate support to be flown to Kuhn but they met him coming back.

Over the coffee cups the pilot related that the submarine opened up with her deck guns as he started his run, far out of range.

"By the time I got my bombs aimed the tracers were coming pretty close. Then I got within range and opened up with my forward machine gun. My tracers seemed to disappear right into the conning tower. I don't know whether I hit the gun crew but at any rate they stopped firing a couple of seconds before I released my load. When I looked back the sub was completely enveloped in spray. When she came out, her stern was down and she was slowly spinning in a circle, at about two knots, I'd say.

"While she was settling in the water another gun crew came up and started firing at me. Then there was blinding flash, a sheet of spray, and she slid under, with her bow up at about a thirty-degree angle . . ."

The proof was in a set of damp photographic prints taken by Kuhn's crew, Mitchell S. Gos, ARM 2/c, and David A. Smith, AMM 3/c. The scoreboard registered it as another "probable (very)." At 0800 came another contact, reported by one of the destroyers. From decks and cockpits, the convoy saw the iridescent plumes of white water as the depth bombs hurled their crushing explosive force in every direction. Oil spread over the sea. This was graded as a "possible" kill.

At 10 : 00 the voice-box squawked again, Ensign Stewart Doty, USNR, reporting that he was attacking the third submarine of the day, and lunchtime still two hours off. Before he turned off his radio transmitter, Doty could be heard yelling to his tail gunner, R. E. Pollock, S 1/c: "Hey, get a picture of her while she's straight up and down."

Pollock did, and so did Turret Gunner Arthur N. Cox, AMM 2/c; a sequence of pictures showing the four bombs bursting close aboard, and then the U-boat sliding stern first, bow angled high, into the sea. Another "probable."

Now, this was good hunting! Two "possibles" and two "probables" in fourteen hours, and not a single torpedo loosed against the convoy. Even if there was no *positive* proof that the submarine had been destroyed, the argument ran around the wardroom lunch tables, they were certainly not being done any good by the kind of bombing that sent them tail-first in an involuntary dive.

The squawk-box interrupted the discussion : Lieutenant (jg) Robert Stearns, USNR, announcing that he was attacking a submarine with bombs and gunfire, reporting the visibly hit U-boat going down. Frank Dittmer, AOM 3/c, and E. L. Myers, S 1/c, Stearns' crewman, brought back pictures of a battered submarine, sure enough, but going down by the bow. It could have been under control. Up went another "possible" on the board.

The rest of the day provided nothing but the healthy exercise—and sheer boredom—of routine work. Dinnertime was approaching; the 5 : 30 shift of enlisted diners was annihilating steak and mashed potatoes, when the bull-horn roared :

"Now hear this!"

You listen to that, on shipboard. All hands.

"Now hear this! Our planes have bombed a German submarine to the surface and it is now waving a white flag of surrender."

Lieutenant Charles H. Roberts, USNR, gunnery officer of the BOGUE, relates that "if they had sounded General Quarters or Abandon Ship, or passed the word that Hedy Lamarr was giving away hundred-dollar bills on the flight deck, the lower decks could not have been evacuated more quickly.

"After a quick look-around, first from the walkways and then the flight deck, we realized this attack, like the others, had been made at submarine shadowing-distance—just over the horizon. So there was nothing for us off watch to do but wait for the word."

Two planes had shared the victory.

Lieutenant (jg) W. F. Chamberlain, USNR, caught the submarine napping—perhaps not aware that airplanes now had the run of the mid-Atlantic—and literally lifted it out of the water with a thousand pounds of TNT dropped in a stern-on run. The U-boat rolled over on its beam, righted itself, and crash-dived. Chamberlain was sure he had mortally wounded the submarine, and the gun photographs turned in by James O. Stine, ARM 2/c, and Donald L. Clark, AMM 2/c, later showed a perfect bomb straddle. He cruised over the spot where the submarine went down, hoping for conclusive evidence to come to the surface.

Just then Lieutenant H. S. Roberts, USNR, came up in another Avenger, carrying a bellyful of bombs. Just as he came upon the scene the submarine popped to the surface under him, like a cork released underwater. Startled, Roberts put his plane over in a steep dive and let go his charge. Men boiled up out of the hatches, waving a white flag.

The two planes circled the wallowing, sinking submarine until an escort ship, HMCS ST. LAURENT, arrived. As the ship came about, the Germans leaped into the sea and the submarine settled out of sight. Twenty-one life-jacketed Nazis were fished out of the water. The "skipper's pants" had been captured, with the skipper inside.

So ended May 23, 1943, for USS BOGUE and company. It is a date to remember, a date to stand by itself in all the chronologies from now on, for it marks the day that the U-boat's doom was sounded in the Battle of the Atlantic. The wolf-pack had met its masters.

The BOGUE went on to new battles, with new squadrons aboard, to win them all, and to come back with prisoners or with less active evidence of submarines destroyed.

On December 12, a classic example of CVE-DD teamwork was provided for the textbooks when the destroyer USS CLEMSON (Lieutenant W. F. Moran, USNR) picked up the sound of a submerged submarine and laid a pattern of depth bombs over the area. The BOGUE's plane took aerial station to watch for the U-boat or, more to be desired, debris to prove its destruction.

The three other destroyers of the convoy, USS DUPONT (Commander J. G. Marshall, USN), OSMOND INGRAM (Lieutenant Commander R. F.

Miller, USN), and GEORGE E. BADGER (Lieutenant T. H. Byrd, USNR) lent a hand. All the rest of the day and during the night the destroyers' sound gear registered intermittent contact. Once, during the night, the submarine surfaced, evidently hoping to recharge its batteries, only to be driven down by gunfire from the destroyers.

At 0400 next morning the planes were in the air again, and at 0810 Lieutenant (jg) Harold G. Bradshaw, USN, picked up a snaking oil track, and notified the destroyers of his find. The CLEMSON and INGRAM charged up to the designated area and began a judicious sowing of depth bombs; their supply was running short.

Three hours of this. Three hours and five minutes—and six minutes. Suddenly the water boiled, and the submarine surfaced, a big fellow, one of the Nazis' newest.

Lieutenant James E. Ogle III, USNR, piloting a TBF, saw the U-boat came up and shouted the view halloo over his radio. Two Wildcat fighters, piloted by Lieutenant (jg) Marshall Burstad, USNR, and Ensign Thomas E. Jenkins, USNR, streaked over from the BOGUE, guns chattering as Ogle banked for a bombing run. The three planes ceased firing, however, when Germans poured from the hatches and leaped into the sea, abandoning ship.

It was not so much surrender as mutiny, however. The submarine's officers and some of her crew manned the deck guns and let go against the destroyers. One of the shells hit the INGRAM, killing one man and wounding eight. It was a desperate hit of last-stand defiance. In six minutes the submarine began to turn tight circles, her decks more nearly awash at each turn. The last man on deck jumped into the sea.

The commander, executive officer and forty-four enlisted men were taken prisoners.

The BOGUE task force in that fight was commanded by Captain Joseph B. Dunn, USN. Lieutenant Commander C. W. Stewart, USN, was in command of the BOGUE's airmen, and Commander E. W. Yancey, USN, was commander of the escorts. The BADGER, incidentally, carried as evidence of one submarine kill not the skipper's pants, but a German translation of *The Murders in the Rue Morgue* which came to the surface together with grislier and less durable evidence of destruction underwater by depth bombs.

To the reader one story is much like another, in these annals, as has been remarked before. This is no chronology, no diary, of the war in the

Atlantic. The minute record, the just award of all credit where due, the roll call of all who won or died to help the winning, these important details must be left for the historians.

The CVE-DD-DE teams herded their convoys back and forth across the Atlantic, aircraft scouting far ahead and wide on the flanks, in the joint labors of offense and defense. And ton upon ton of equipment crossed the Atlantic, later to cross the English Channel—safely. It was a record not achieved without tragic losses, and at least once produced a battle more reminiscent of the ancient sea fights when men fought hand to hand on sinking hulks.

It was the destroyer BORIE (Lieutenant Charles H. Hutchins, USNR) that went off over the horizon one night to investigate at first hand the long-range evidence of submarines and came upon two of them, a few fathoms apart, on the surface. With gunfire and depth bombs the BORIE accounted for the nearest, and sent back the report: "Scratch one pig-boat—am searching for more."

The second submarine made a run for a rain squall that was trailing its enveloping water curtain nearby. Hutchins turned in pursuit. The U-boat was one of the big ones; whether from disability or arrant braggadocio, it did not submerge but elected to fight it out with the old World War four-stacker on the surface.

The BORIE closed with the U-boat and turned to ram. The destroyer's sharp bow knifed through the sub's outer skin, and then crumpled and bent as all the power of the ship's engines drove her crushingly upon the submarine. The Germans came up fighting, the destroyer's crew jammed on the foc's'le fighting back. Rifles, pistols, empty shell cases, everything and anything that came to hand was used in that brief, savage foray at close quarters, and then, its back broken, the submarine went suddenly down and the BORIE lurched free, drove forward under the impulse of her straining engines, to find herself mortally wounded, too.

Next morning the CARD's airplanes directed to the spot by radar located the battered destroyer, rolling in a heavy sea, barely able to keep her stern to the wind. Her sister escorts, destroyers of like vintage, USS GOFF (Lieutenant Commander Hinton I. Smith, USNR) and BARRY (Lieutenant Commander Herbert D. Hill, USNR) stood by all day while the crew of the BORIE struggled to repair leaking hull and crippled engines. It was a gallant but useless labor. Shortly after nightfall Hutchins signaled that he would be forced to abandon ship. Twenty-foot waves whose tops were whipped into spray by the gale made the prospects grim indeed for the men on the sinking destroyer, but to the everlasting credit of all hands, rescuers and rescued, all but twenty-one men of the BORIE's complement of almost ten times that number were taken from the boiling sea alive.

Once, when he led his force into a concentration of thirty submarines and the destroyer LEARY (Commander John B. Pye, USN) was torpedoed in the act of ramming one of the U-boats, Captain Isbell ordered his escorts to turn from battle to rescue work. All night the CARD, self-detached from the protection of her destroyers, circled and zigzagged until every survivor that could be located was fished out of the 46-degree brine of the North Atlantic.

A young officer reporting to the bridge for the morning watch found Captain Isbell, unshaved, red-eyed, gulping a cup of coffee.

"Good morning, sir," the watch officer said.

"Beautiful morning," the Captain replied over the rim of his cup. "For a while there, I thought we wouldn't see it."

(Someday an entire book should be written on the Navy's rescue work. No American bluejacket, officer or pilot has ever been left to his own fate anywhere that the Navy has fought in this war. The labor may be impromptu, as in the instance just recorded, or accomplished by the elaborately integrated rescue missions organized for constant duty with the fleet. And in this humanitarian work, the accomplishments of the lighter-than-air craft, the Navy's big blimps, is almost a volume in itself. If the airships had served no other function in this war—and they con-voyed thousands of ships on the nation's three seacoasts without loss in the first two years of combat—their record of locating and rescuing ship-wrecked and airwrecked men merits them national gratitude.)

It was aboard the CARD, too, that a drama was enacted one night to shame Hollywood's script writers.

Lieutenant (jg) Roger C. Kuhn, USNR, veteran sub-buster of the BOGUE's first battle and now aboard the sister ship, was next to last man to set his TBF down on the dark, wallowing flight deck of the carrier. Still aloft, and dangerously late, was his close friend and roommate, Lieutenant (jg) Harry E. Fryatt, USNR, but Fryatt's plane was slow in returning because it had taken a 40-mm. shell into its frame from a battling U-boat.

Fryatt arrived at last, circled the CARD and was waved in, but as he put his landing wheels down only one unfolded. The mechanism of the other had been crippled by the shell.

There was only one thing to do: retract the free wheel and make a belly landing on the deck.

Then the free wheel jammed. Fryatt could not get it back into its slot in the wing. If he tried to land on one "leg," the chances were 100 to 1 that the plane would pivot and go over the side, with what damage to the ship none could estimate. If the plane went over the side, the odds were even longer against its pilot or crew surviving. By the same token, Fryatt could not make a crash landing in the tumultuous sea with darkness fast closing in.

Captain Isbell calculated all the chances, and ordered Fryatt to crash-land on deck. He directed that Kuhn's plane be parked at the carrier's stern, broadside to the axis of the deck, to act as a barrier against Fryatt's skidding over the edge.

Kuhn knew the odds as well as did the Captain. At first he thought he could not bear to see his roommate come in to all but certain death, and he ran down the ladder to his cabin. There he changed his mind. He picked up Fryatt's flashlight where it lay on the berth, and climbed to the flight deck with the mad idea of diving over the side, should Fryatt skid into the sea. Kuhn was a champion swimmer, too good a swimmer to have believed, in calmer thought, that his plan was feasible. He stood beside his own plane, to watch Fryatt make his approach, coast in over the edge of the deck, and stall his engine for the crash landing.

The big TBF pirouetted on its one wheel, crashed into the super-structure, bounced back to the far edge of the deck and then in a final flip it sideswiped Kuhn's parked plane. That craft veered under the impact, and Kuhn was catapulted over the stern.

He hit the life rail on the deck below, and hung there, bruised and breathless, clawing for a hold, when suddenly the teetering plane above slid over the edge as the ship lurched, and Kuhn twisted himself out of its path to drop into the screw-churned icy ocean.

The dazed pilot kicked his way to the surface, and when he struck out to swim he found the electric torch still in his grip. Mechanically, he turned it on.

No one on deck knew Kuhn had stationed himself at the ship's stern, but Aviation Chief Ordnanceman R. L. Goodwin, USNR, thought he saw a body go into the sea. "Man overboard!" he shouted, and threw a life preserver at the target made by the flashlight's small ray.

"Man overboard!" The signal flew through the convoy. In response the destroyer BARRY backed water, picked up the wavering torchlight, and closed in for the rescue. Another life preserver, with rope attached, was accurately tossed to Kuhn, so accurately that it struck him in the head and nearly stunned him. As the battered pilot fitted the canvas-covered circlet around him, a submarine poked into the convoy to make a pass at the easy mark of a sitting destroyer, and the BARRY lurched forward to escape attack, towing Kuhn like a living surfboard skittering atop the water until he was pulled hand-over-hand to the deck.

That's all there is to the story. It is just an incident out of routine.

A few pages back, the story was told of the BORIE's last fight. One of the escort destroyers attached to the baby flat-top USS BLOCK ISLAND (Captain Logan C. Ramsey, USN) also rammed a submarine, and was rammed in return, with a hand-to-hand battle between, in the Stephen Decatur tradition.

She was USS BUCKLEY, and her captain was Lieutenant Commander B. M. Abel, USNR. The BLOCK ISLAND's TBFs had made fleeting contact with a submarine at nightfall, and the BUCKLEY was ordered to investigate. Not until a quarter past two in the morning was contact reestablished by a night-flying plane, which reported the submarine on the surface nearly thirty miles from the destroyer. The BUCKLEY raced in.

A mile and a half from the submarine the destroyer escort's lookouts sighted the U-boat in the broad silver track of the full May moon. The submarine neither submerged nor took evasive action. Instead, it baffled the escort's crew by firing three red flares. Whatever the signal was intended to be, the BUCKLEY accepted it as a challenge to battle and opened fire at 2,200 yards, the submarine answering with its deck guns.

The first salvo from the DE scored a hit, and the submarine maneuvered to open the range while the BUCKLEY crowded on steam to close the gap. They overtook the U-boat and closed in, running parallel to the Nazi with scarce 20 yards of open water between them, before turning to ram.

The DE's bow slid over the sub's deck and hung poised. Neither vessel could bring guns to bear, but the Nazis swarmed up on deck with rifles and small arms and, to the momentary consternation of BUCKLEY's crew, showed every intention of boarding their ship. The amazing effrontery of the Germans galvanized the DE men. As the first Nazi's head appeared over the ship's bow, a fist smashed into the face. Fighting with only bare hands and whatever missile came to hand—spitkits, coffee mugs, empty shell cases—the DE boys beat back the well-armed Nazis with no greater casualties than knuckles barked on Teutonic bone. Then the destroyer escort's bow slid off the submarine's deck, just as hand grenades and rifles reached the men battling there. Torpedomen tossed grenades into the submarine's hatch, from which flames set by the shell fire were plainly seen. Momentarily the ships were side by side. Then the submarine swerved sharply to port and struck the BUCKLEY a glancing blow. A grenade was tossed into the control room through its still-open hatch, and with that the submarine—hatches still open and ruddy from internal fires—slid, rolling, under the surface.

Just another condensed chapter from the histories still to be written. Not since the Tripolitan Wars, though, had American seamen thus stood by to repel boarders. Maybe history actually does repeat itself. But it was not to hand-to-hand fighting that the submarine succumbed. It was the air-and-surface teamwork, the integrated, interdependent, mutually supporting teamwork of naval aviation and the ships of the fleet.

One time the ancient command "Away boarders!" was sounded on the Atlantic, on June 4, 1944, when a task force commanded by Captain Dan V. Gallery, USN, captured a German submarine and brought it home in triumph at the end of a towline.

Captain Gallery had planned that capture. He conceived the idea back on April 9, 1944, when his team of baby carrier-destroyers won a running fight with the U-515, commanded by Kapitan Werner Henke who wore the Knight's Cross of the Iron Cross, with oak leaves no less. After the Nazi crew abandoned ship, the task force poured armor-piercing shells into the submarine for five minutes before sinking it.

"Next time," Captain Gallery mused on the bridge of his carrier, USS GUADALCANAL, "why sink her?"

A return to home port intervened before Captain Gallery's team had another submarine under their guns, and in his conferences ashore the Captain obtained enthusiastic permission to attempt his capture.

The first sound contact was made by the destroyer USS CHATELAIN, commanded by Lieutenant Commander Dudley S. Knox, Jr., USNR, son of the Navy's historian, Captain Dudley S. Knox, USN (Ret.). Captain Gallery ordered the GUADALCANAL to head into the wind and began to launch his planes, even as Knox reported "am starting to attack." Ensign J. W. Cadle, USNR, flying a Grumman Wildcat, sighted the submerged submarine, and his vision was immediately confirmed by another Wildcat pilot, Lieutenant W. W. Roberts, USNR. The two fliers fired their machine guns into the sea, to direct the destroyers, as the submarine maneuvered for escape.

After twelve minutes of depth-charging the submarine was licked. It blundered to the surface not 700 yards from the CHATELAIN, which opened up with small-caliber guns, as previously planned. The USS PILLSBURY (Lieutenant Commander George W. Casselman, USNR) and JENKS (Lieutenant Commander J. F. Way, USN) joined in peppering the sub with resounding, but not too lethal, gunfire as the Nazis scrambled through the hatch and dived overboard. When, by rough count, the estimated complement of the submarine was in the water, the order was given by the division commander, Commander F. S. Hall, USN:

"CHATELAIN and JENKS pick up survivors. PILLSBURY is going to board. Away, boarding parties—lower away whaleboats!"

The surfaced submarine was moving in a tight circle at 7 knots, and the boarding party (commanded by Lieutenant (jg) A. L. David, USNR) had difficulty in climbing aboard. It is to be doubted that they heard Captain Gallery's broadcast encouragement "Ride 'im, cowboys" as they strove to get a line on the wallowing submarine.

David, with S. E. Wdowiak, RM2/c, and A. W. Knispel, TM3/c, plunged down below-decks through the open conning tower hatch to make a highly precarious search for time bombs and to close the sea cocks. They found the submarine filling rapidly, and strove successfully to stop the inrushing sea. The towline was then passed to the GUADALCANAL, and Captain Gallery himself boarded the submarine to adjust her steering mechanism, which had been jammed.

The captured Nazis, herded on the decks of the CHATELAIN, watched open-mouthed as the Stars and Stripes were run up on the submarine's stubby radio mast, and their ship responded like a led ox to the tug of the towline. Dubbed the "Junior" by the GUADALCANAL crew, the submarine was successfully pulled into Bermuda, where her crew of fifty-seven men—only one had been killed—were also turned over to the United States naval authorities. Oberleutnant zur See Harald Lange, skipper of the submarine U-505, was the only man wounded.

Also part of the task force that uniquely revived the cutlass-in-hand tactics of 1815 were USS POPE (Lieutenant Commander E. H. Headland, USN) and FLAHERTY (Lieutenant Commander M. Johnston. USNR). Lieutenant Norman D. Hodson, USNR, was the aircraft squadron commander.

Early in 1944 Grumman TBF Avengers of the BLOCK ISLAND's squadron initiated the Nazi submarines in a new form of warfare—rockets. The only trouble the pilots find with rockets is that they have been too deadly effective.

It was harder than ever, now, to bring back "the skipper's pants" or acceptable substitute therefor.

A few weeks later USS BLOCK ISLAND, whose command had passed to Captain F. Massie Hughes, USN, was sunk by three underwater hits. Under Captain Hughes, the little carrier's toll of submarines had risen to the second highest of all the CVEs, and the crew had renamed the ship "USS FBI"—Fighting Block Island.

All but six men, killed in the explosion, were rescued by two of the four supporting destroyer escorts, USS AHRENS (Commander Morgan H. Harris, USNR) and ROBERT I. PAINE (Lieutenant Commander Drayton Cochran, USNR), the AHRENS taking 674 of the survivors aboard, the PAINE 277. The two other escort vessels of the task force, USS ELMORE (Lieutenant Commander George L. Conkey, USN) and BARR (Lieutenant Commander Henry H. Love, USNR), stood guard over the rescue and report having successfully attacked a submarine.

One of the crew who lost his life was pinned by one crushed leg under a mass of twisted steel between the catwalk and the buckled overhang of the flight deck. Although the man was obviously mortally wounded, desperate attempts at rescue were made by Lieutenant Commander Fred A. Ballard, USNR, and Chief Carpenter's Mate Clarence M. Bailey, USN. With a blowtorch and by main strength they tried to clear away the debris that pinned the dying man to the sinking ship. Thwarted in those efforts, they guided Commander Joseph L. Custer, (MC) USNR, senior medical officer, to where the bluejacket lay trapped. The surgeon, working on the tilting deck of the dying BLOCK ISLAND, surrounded by shattered, buckled steel that shifted with every lurch of the ship, administered a local anesthetic and amputated the sailor's crushed leg, but the man died as he was hauled free.

His defeated rescuers swam to safety.

Captain Hughes received from First Sea Lord Alexander of the British Admiralty a message expressing "regrets at the loss of such a gallant and splendid ship," but before this obituary is published another USS BLOCK ISLAND will be in operation.

Chapter Seventeen

THE Navy's war in the Atlantic was not fought in sections, a bit at a time, although that is the only way its story can be told. During the period of the great battles to break through the U-boats' control of the North Atlantic, while Patwing 78 was making history, while the Armed Guard was taking its beating and doing its grim job, while the escort carriers were just beginning to confound the Nazi's navyless conquest of the sea, and the Coast Guard was driving the Wehrmacht's advance guard from Greenland—all this time an almost anonymous United States Fleet was waging a full-scale war on the farther side of the equator.

There, where Africa thrusts a huge shoulder belligerently at Brazil's easternmost bulge, the enemy made his nearest approach of military menace to the Western Hemisphere. The Atlantic narrows to easy jumping distance—a geographical situation of which, however, the United States and its allies took first and complete advantage. We not only bridged the Atlantic straits, but plugged its sea lanes against convoy-hunting submarines and enemy blockade runners.

It was an area not only of geographic peculiarity and naval challenge; it was, simultaneously and in direct consequence, an area of nice political balance. The international situation on our southern flank was extremely delicate; when Rear Admiral Jonas H. Ingram, USN, led his task force across the equator on neutrality patrol in the spring of 1941, he was carrying out the provisions of the 1939 Pan-American conference under particularly strained circumstances.

Vichy-controlled Casablanca and Dakar in Africa were fine bases for Nazi submarines on the east coast of the Atlantic; on our own side of the ocean the French islands of Martinique and Guadeloupe were, in possibility at least, U-boat supply, refueling and information centers. Whether so used or not, these western outposts of Naziphile Vichy France were a disturbing element in the American scene.

The situation was further complicated by the entrenchment of Axis nationals, with their inevitable company of agents, propagandists and general troublemakers, in South America. In Brazil alone were two million Italians and eight hundred thousand Germans, and they had plenty of propaganda material to work with. The Allies were taking a licking; France, to which South America had always looked for cultural leadership, had fallen and, worse, its new government was collaborating with the Germans; Russia was hated in the overwhelmingly Catholic countries as being anticlerical; Spain was neutral, but made no secret of her sympathies; Britain had never attempted to exert much influence; and the United States was still suspect of entertaining ambitions of "el imperialismo Yanqui."

Even Pearl Harbor and our entry into the war against the Axis didn't change matters much at first. Axis propaganda was still rolling in high in South America. Movie houses showed Japanese newsreels (processed and distributed by Germany) of the "total destruction" of the United States Fleet at Pearl Harbor. And the Navy Department, plotting an unpleasant surprise for the Nipponese, did not care to refute the fiction of the Rome-Berlin-Tokyo propaganda. It was "reasoned," wherever the Axis had a mouthpiece, that if Hitler, Hirohito & Co. had not known they were a cinch to win they would not have attacked the United States.

One country in which the Axis ideological pressures were particularly and strongly applied was Brazil. But Brazil, territorially the largest republic in the two Americas, nearest of them all to the Old World, resisted the Fascist leverage. Without much prospect of material reward, Brazil gave all necessary co-operation to Admiral Ingram's naval police force, and when the disaster of Pearl Harbor appeared to have weakened the ability of the United States to defend itself and to aid its neighbor, Brazil extended its assistance to ever-widening limits until finally the republic was itself mobilized for war against the Axis.

Brazil's part in the war transcends its use of arms against the enemy. The European victory might have been much delayed had not the sister nation to the south contributed so generously to the turning of the tide of war.

Secretary of State Cordell Hull said so. The story of the North African campaign that started the Nazis on the long and bloody road of retreat "might have been different," Mr. Hull said in characteristic understatement, except for Brazil's aid.

Early in the summer of 1941 Admiral Ingram, then commanding Cruiser Division 2 based on San Juan, Puerto Rico, and Guantanamo, Cuba, was assigned to neutrality patrol of the waters between the West Indies, the Cape Verde Islands, and the "hump" of Brazil. Recife and Bahia, in Brazil, were to be his southern ports of replenishment. The diplomatic arrangements were made in Washington; the material arrangements he would have to conclude for himself on the spot.

USS MEMPHIS (Captain C. J. Parrish, USN) was the Admiral's flagship, and with it cruised the CINCINNATI (Captain H. W. Graf, USN) and the destroyers DAVIS (Commander C. C. Hartman, USN) and WARRINGTON (Commander F. G. Fahrion, USN). Shortly after the patrol's inception its strength was doubled by the inclusion of the cruisers OMAHA (Captain Theodore E. Chandler, USN) and MILWAUKEE (Captain A. McGlasson, USN) and the destroyers SOMERS (Commander J. C. Metzel, USN) and JOUETT (Commander G. W. Clark, USN) as Task Force 2 under command of Captain Archibald McGlasson, USN.

The OMAHA and her attendant destroyer, SOMERS, had the fortune to draw first blood for the patrol when, on November 6, 1941, they encountered a darkened ship with the United States flag painted on her sides, and flying from her signal halyards the code for the SS WILLMOTO of Philadelphia—the name also painted on her stern. But, except for such superficialities, the ship presented a decidedly un-American appearance. She was hailed, and made no answer. A signal was sent directing the merchantman to lie to and receive a boarding party, and as the OMAHA's launch headed for the ship with Lieutenant G. K. Carmichael, USN, a new set of signals fluttered from the signal bridge: "Am sinking. Send boats."

Although Carmichael's arrival on the steamship's deck was signaled by two explosions in the hold, the false WILLMOTO did not sink, and the German crew that rowed to the cruiser for rescue watched in chagrin as men of the OMAHA's engineering department patched up the damage done by the demolition charges and got the disguised vessel underway. She was revealed to be the SS ODENWALD, en route from Japan with 3,857 tons of rubber, besides a mixed cargo of tires, copper, brass and chemicals, all of which was swiftly put to use against its former owners when the prize reached the United States.

Admiral Ingram was on the eastern leg of his triangular patrol area, aboard his flagship, when word of the attack on Pearl Harbor crackled on the MEMPHIS's radio. When next he put into Recife, a few days later, his status had changed. He was now commanding a belligerent force in neutral waters.

Brazil was prompt, but not precipitate, in accommodating itself to the change. As a fighting force the United States Fleet had greater needs, to enable it to perform its grimmer responsibilities. Marines, Army units, Army Air Force and naval aviation squadrons were required at once to secure the southernmost flank of the anti-Axis American arc. When three provisional companies of Marines were flown in seven planes to guard American naval property in Belem, Natal and Recife, the Brazilian government refused to allow them to bear arms—until the citizenry became accustomed to having foreign fighting men in their midst. As soon as Marines were no novelty to the Brazilians, permission was given for them to uncrate their rifles, which had been stowed away on the fleet oiler, USS PATOKA (Commander W. N. Thornton, USN).

The PATOKA, incidentally, became Admiral Ingram's flagship in August, 1942, just before the task force's designation was changed to South Atlantic Force (Fourth Fleet) and when its operational area was altered to include all of the Atlantic below 10° N and west of 20° W. The fleet's forces had far to range, and the Admiral's business was to stay at the hub of operations—for which no warship could be spared.

Early in December, 1941, the Brazilian government waived its strict neutrality laws to permit regular air ferry service over its territory on the Washington-to-Cairo route across the waist of the Atlantic. Three provisional companies of United States Marines were permitted to land, and by early 1942 hundreds of United States naval and military personnel were in Brazil, at Belem, Natal and Recife, supervising the construction by Brazilian labor of bulk storage facilities for millions of gallons of gasoline and fuel oil, building airstrips, barracks, roads, and base facilities. The United States was accorded unrestricted use of a corridor on the north coast of the republic as far south as Recife for the movement of military aircraft, and Brazil waived custom duties and visa requirements to expedite the movements of men and materiel.

President Getulio Vargas also turned over to Admiral Ingram for the United States Navy the spacious, modern federal tuberculosis sanatorium at Tejipio, which, under command and direction of Captain Walter G. Roper, USN (Ret.), was conducted as a rest and rehabilitation center for American naval personnel. Axis ships which had taken shelter from British—and now United States—warships, were interned, then expropriated and the best of them sold to the United States. The United States was also given virtual military possession of Fernando de Noronha Island, a penal colony 300 miles off the coast on the route to Africa, as a refueling center and seaplane base.

Perhaps some of the co-operation thus freely accorded was in return for the amiable relationship maintained between the navies of the two republics since 1922, when a United States naval mission was set up under jurisdiction of the Brazilian Ministry of Marine. Meanwhile, Brazil was a powerful aid to the Allied cause as a source of supply for coffee, quartz crystal, rubber, tantalite, mica, beryl and other rare natural products essential to the arms and comfort of fighting men.

When German agents, in an effort to discredit the United States and drive down the exchange, offered American currency confiscated in Europe at 20 cents for the dollar, Brazil promptly made it a penal offense to traffic in the money. The Brazilian government also divested itself of avowed Axis sympathizers, and rounded up German, Italian and Japanese aliens suspected of espionage.

Angered by Brazil's refusal to bow to the wishes of the Master Race, enraged by Brazil's adherence to her Pan-American pledges, the Germans took reprisals. During the week of August 15, U-boats sank five Brazilian ships.

That was all that was needed. On August 22, Brazil declared war on Germany.

The republic's efficient, if small, Navy had been on antisubmarine neutrality patrol for over a year, as had its Army and Navy Air Forces. Now Brazil had units of every armed service in the European Theater, thus wiping out with vengeance Hitler's boast that he would make Brazil the nucleus of Germany's empire in the Western Hemisphere.

Brazilian co-operation also enabled the British and the United States Navy and Army Air Forces to make full use of Ascension Island, a cindery atom of British Empire halfway between South America and Africa in the straits of the Atlantic. Thirty-four square miles of extinct volcano, Ascension did not discourage Army engineers who built airstrips (moving 380,000 cubic yards to build one 7,000-foot runway) to enable short-range airplanes to cross the Atlantic under their own power. The Navy's PB4Ys flew out of Ascension in both directions to keep the Atlantic narrows under constant surveillance, and more submarines were sunk in that barrier patrol than in any comparable area of the ocean.

"Miss Ascension and your wife gets a pension" was the motto of the fliers of Fleet Air Wing 16 based on the waterless cinder pile.

Fleet Air Wing 16 was organized in February, 1943, under command of Captain Rosmore D. Lyon, USN, former commandant of the Naval Air Station at Corpus Christi, Texas, where so many South American pilots were trained. The first units of FAW 16 were taken from Air Wing 11 of the Caribbean patrol, based on Puerto Rico. Its main base was established at Natal, Brazil, in April, 1943, but elements of the air wing were spotted at other strategic points including Ascension, where units of Headquarters Squadron—Hedron, in the telescoped nomenclature of the Navy—and VB-107 brought great grief to the Axis forces afloat. They had some grief of their own, too. Units based on Fernando de Noronha, Brazil's equivalent of Czarist Siberia, were changed every four months; so dreary was life on the tiny penal-colony island that the chief amusement available was beard-growing contests.

Captain Lyon also numbered two squadrons of blimps in his command, the first nonrigid lighter-than-air ships to cross the equator. Captain W. E. Zimmerman, USN, was in direct command of the sixteen LTAs, which did notable convoy work but again distinguished themselves as no heavier-than-air craft can by their rescue work.

The K-106, piloted by Lieutenant R. A. Powers, USNR, was especially adept at picking wrecked fliers out of jungles. On December 1, 1943, Powers not only rescued the crew and passengers of an Army transport plane that had crashed in a forest impenetrable from any direction except the air, but hovered over the treetops while an especially valuable cargo was hoisted aboard. Less than three months later the E-106 joined with K-11 (Ensign W. T. Raleigh, USNR) to rescue the crews of two Army bombers from the jungle, Boatswain J. F. Desmond, USN, proving himself particularly adept at sliding down a rope from the blimps to organize the Army men into woodsmen, chopping a clearing into which the airship could be delicately maneuvered so that the rescued men could climb aboard.

From the Brazilian coast 1,240 miles eastward to Ascension, surface ships of the Fourth Fleet in destroyer or cruiser-destroyer task groups maintained a constant patrol, linked by air with units of FAW 16 from the island and the mainland. Westward from the African coast British and Free French naval forces maintained the air-and-sea barrier on their half of the Atlantic's narrow waist.

On New Year's Day, 1944, a Liberator from VB-107 on Ascension, piloted by Lieutenant S. K. Taylor, USNR, picked up a fast merchantman, unescorted, and dropped down to investigate. The ship was challenged, and identified itself as the British SS GLENBANK. Taylor circled the vessel, to satisfy himself that all was as should be, when the blockade runner showed itself for what it was by opening fire at the bomber, knocking out the No. 2 engine and wounding a member of the airplane's crew. Taylor headed for Ascension, broadcasting the merchantman's description, course and location.

From somewhere over the horizon the destroyer USS SOMERS turned in the direction reported by Taylor and put on all steam. The message was also picked up by Taylor's teammate, Lieutenant R. T. Johnson, USNR, who headed his bomber for the pursuit. He picked up the Nazi's trail but had to drop it when a combination of low visibility and lower gasoline supply made further chase fruitless. The next morning Johnson was back in the air before daylight, hot on the scent again. He flashed over the racing SOMERS and then, conspicuous for the long wake kicked up by its desperately churning screws, the blockade runner was sighted again. It began to zigzag sharply.

Johnson prepared for a bombing run on the racing ship. There must have been crack gunners aboard the Nazi, for, with the same accuracy that had put Taylor out of combat the day before, the first salvo from the ship scored.

His crippled plane rocked by ack-ack, Johnson reported the ship's position to the avenging destroyer, still over the horizon, and then headed for base. At Ascension the radio tower maintained constant contact with the wounded plane. Men and officers stood by, tense and helpless, "sweating it out" for Johnson. He reported one engine cutting out; flying on two, now. A hundred miles to go; ninety.

"Number three engine dead."

Eighty miles left; now only seventy. From Ascension, rescue planes had taken off.

Seventy miles—and silence from the bomber. The operator on Ascension worked his key desperately. There was no answer from Johnson.

When the rescue planes reached the area there was not even an oil slick or a handful of debris to show where VB-107—B-12 had gone down, although the search was maintained at wave-top level until dark.

The SOMERS caught up with the blockade runner and pumped the Nazi full of shells a few hours later. The sixty survivors picked up by the destroyer identified their ship as the WESSERLAND.

Two days later an observation plane launched by the USS OMAHA spotted another suspicious-looking ship which the cruiser and its accompanying destroyer, USS JOUETT, polished off in short order. Survivors said it was the Nazi merchantman RIO GRANDE. The prisoners were still being questioned the next day when the cruiser picked up a message from one of the Mariner bombers of the Natal wing of the barrier patrol. It was another lone ship of doubtful identity.

As the warships bore down, the merchantman spouted smoke and steam. The Germans had scuttled their vessel with time bombs. The destroyer USS DAVIS was detailed to pick up the Nazis on rafts and in lifeboats; the other ships were too crowded with prisoners to accommodate more.

Thus was the Nazi SS BURGENLAND added to the bag of the WESSERLAND and RIO GRANDE: three ships totaling more than 21,000 tons lost to Germany. More serious to the Nazi war machine was the loss of cargo, rubber and tin and other essential materials looted from the Netherlands East Indies and contributed to the Reich by its Japanese ally.

The rubber floated. United States Navy tugs salvaged enough natural rubber from the sea above the graves of the blockade runners "to make tires for 5,000 bombers," Lieutenant John H. Cutler, USNR, reports.

Another catch of consequence was a submarine commanded by one of Germany's national heroes, Kapitanleutnant Fritz Guggenberger, who sank HMS ARK ROYAL and 50,000 tons of United Nations shipping and who had the Knight's Order of the Iron Cross pinned on him by Adolf Hitler himself, at a great public ceremony.

Guggenberger's status from cocky, lethal Nazi hero to prisoner of war was brought about when William Stotts, AR 2/c, USNR, looked through a port in a Martin Mariner on patrol and saw the submarine cruising on the surface. He shouted his discovery to the pilot, Lieutenant (jg) Roy S. Whitcomb, USN. Whitcomb screened his approach with some providentially provided clouds, and came roaring down on the Nazi. As he flashed over the submarine, only 50 feet above her decks, copilot Donald T. Ward, NAP 1/c, USN, dropped the bombs that jarred the Iron Cross off Guggenberger's chest. Whitcomb threw a rubber raft to the men abandoning the shattered U-boat. The survivors, including Guggenberger, were picked up by the seaplane tender USS BARNEGAT.

Such was the routine of United States naval forces in the South Atlantic. Working intimately with the United States Army and Navy Air Forces, and the Brazilian armed forces, synchronized with the workings of the British and Fighting French on the opposite side of the Atlantic, they plugged up Germany's only access to Asia. By keeping the transatlantic route between the Americas and North Africa open, and starting convoys bearing South American raw materials (coffee went off rationing, thanks to the United States Navy) safely on their way to the United States, our naval forces ensured delivery of vital supplies to Allied ports. The Fourth Fleet earned a hearty "Well done" for its part in the Battle of the Atlantic. The contraband it destroyed, the submarines sunk or harried into impotence, can be presumed to have shortened the war against Germany, Italy and the Axis's European satellites by an incalculable margin.

Had, for example, a certain convoy—AS4 on the code lists of Washington and London—not crossed safely to Africa in July, 1942, the British armies might have been driven east of the Suez. Ten ships, bearing 500 tanks with full technical equipment and crews, raced at urgent British request to the Red Sea, where their death-dealing cargoes rolled into action against Rommel at El Alamein. Prime Minister Churchill publicly credited the United States Army's tanks with throwing the decisive punch into the battle. It was the cruisers and destroyers of Admiral Ingram's forces that escorted the ships through submarine concentrations to British waters with the loss of only one freighter (immediately replaced).

Before leaving this résumé of war as it was waged from the eastern shores of the American continents, it is necessary again to depart from chronology to mention the role played by the French and Netherlands West Indies.

"Curaçao" is the inclusive term for the Netherlands' constituent territories in the Caribbean, which are neither possessions nor colonies but an overseas commonwealth of that nation, a detached province of five islands—Curaçao, Aruba, Saba, St. Eustatius and St. Martin, the last-named shared with France. Curaçao and Aruba, close to the Venezuelan coast, are of vast strategic importance because there the bulk of

Venezuela's crude petroleum is refined—as much as 500,000 barrels a day. The Germans were not unaware of the importance of Curaçao and Aruba to the United Nations' air and surface fleets and their submarines lurked thickly to intercept tankers leaving the islands, which the Nazis even shelled from the sea. United States Army forces were landed on those two islands to protect them shortly after the Netherlands had been overrun, and the United States Navy helped the Royal Netherlands Navy to patrol adjacent waters.

Not much help was needed, however. The tiny but grimly efficient Netherlands fleet gave as much aid to the defense of the Caribbean as it received. One gunboat alone, the training ship VAN KINSBERGEN, destroyed twelve German or German-controlled vessels totaling 66,000 tons in the intra-American sea.

There were difficulties though with Vichy France's West Indian outposts.

When France fell, a number of French warships, merchantmen and tankers took refuge in the ports of the island-colonies of Martinique and Guadeloupe. There was the carrier BÉARN, with 105 lend-lease American airplanes; the light cruiser EMIL BERTIN, the training cruiser JEANNE D'ARC, the merchant cruiser BARFLEUR, three armed merchantmen, six tankers and armed harbor craft; a sizable fleet and, what with France's anomalous position in the international scene, one that would have to be watched. But the United States Navy had urgent use for its fighting ships elsewhere, on neutrality patrol and, later, in the Battle of the Atlantic.

The United States could not afford to detach a battleship or two, several cruisers and squadrons of destroyers to guard against a foray of the French ships. Nor could the British, who had to keep the known German naval strength bottled up in the North Sea. Therefore, negotiations were opened with the French military governor of the islands, Admiral Georges Robert. Vice-Admiral John H. Hoover, USN, commandant of the Tenth Naval District, negotiated an agreement, under State Department auspices, with Admiral Robert in May, 1942, whereby the sting of the French ships would be drawn through the removal of mechanical units and certain armament.

The agreement had been partially consummated, and was in process of enlargement when the Allied invasion of North Africa was carried out against initial Vichy French resistance. Admiral Robert thereupon broke off the negotiations, maintaining that he took his orders from the Pétain-Laval government. The United States government retaliated by declaring an embargo against the French islands, which are incapable of supporting their population of 600,000 without outside help.

That was in November, 1942. By spring of 1943 Guadeloupe and Martinique were on short rations, and more than a thousand white male inhabitants had deserted the islands to enlist with Major Jean Victor Sarrat, formerly of the Guadeloupe garrison, who was organizing a Fighting French regiment at Fort Dix, New Jersey. Sporadic insurrections were breaking out, but Admiral Robert steadfastly refused to reopen negotiations with the United States without permission of Marshal Pétain. On April 30, Secretary of State Cordell Hull broke off relations with the French West Indies, recalled the United States Consul, Marcel E. Maligne, and turned the whole situation over to the Navy for disposition.

Diplomatically, Admiral Hoover told American newspaper correspondents that there was no danger of hostilities or any impairment of United States security to fear. When, on June 30, Admiral Robert requested the State Department to send a plenipotentiary to discuss "a change of authority" with him, the response was left to the Navy and Admiral Hoover went to Martinique on July 3. A few days before, Robert had refused to receive Admiral Robert Battet, chief of the French Naval Mission in the United States and commander of the French naval forces co-operating in the occupation of North Africa.

Whatever amicable disposition of a rapidly deteriorating situation might have been achieved by the American and French admirals in conference, the exiled French government interrupted to bring about a wholly satisfactory settlement. General Henri Giraud, copresident of the French Committee of National Liberation, flew to the United States from Algiers, by way of Africa, to confer with United States diplomatic and naval officials. He named Henri Etienne Hoppenot, who was accepted by Admiral Robert, as governor of the French West Indies. M. Hoppenot, who had been director of Civil Services with the French mission in Washington, left at once for consultations with Admirals Hoover and Robert. The latter relinquished his command on July 14, Bastille Day, and under the terms agreed upon the French naval and cargo vessels were at once rehabilitated for service against the Axis. Two relief ships, with some 6,500 tons of food and fuel, were dispatched from the United

States to the islands, and the only gap in the solid front of American Atlantic states was closed, as far south as the Argentine.

Islands played almost as big a part in this war as ships, being comparable to unsinkable and immovable ships in their military purposes. In the early autumn of 1943 Great Britain invoked a five-and-a-half centuries old treaty with Portugal to obtain base rights in the Azores, that group of islands in mid-Atlantic which are nearer Massachusetts than Hawaii is to California, and closer still to the portals of Europe.

The treaty, signed by Edward III of Great Britain and King Ferdinand and Queen Eleanor of Portugal in 1373, read that "In the first place we settle and covenant that they shall be from this day forward . . . true and faithful friends . . . friends to friends . . . enemies to enemies . . . and shall assist and maintain each other mutually by sea and by land."

In a deal much like the destroyers-for-bases negotiated by the United States and Great Britain, the United Kingdom gave two corvettes to Portugal in exchange for base rights in the Azores, and on October 13, 1943, the British Navy and the Royal Air Force moved in "for the duration." On the same day President Roosevelt publicly announced that the United States would share the new British facilities, and on November 25 the formal request was made of the Portuguese government. The limited facilities, however, made American use of the islands suitable chiefly for emergencies.

But by that time the Battle of the Atlantic had passed from a desperate stand-off fight to a steady progress along the road to victory. Not only was the submarine harried from the sea; its pens and bases were destroyed from the air. The factories that built it, the oil refineries that fueled it, all were targets for a drenching rain of bombs from the RAF and the USAAF. And as our armies moved forward they too became antisubmarine attackers, capturing the ports and harbors, first in the Mediterranean and then in France and the Lowlands, where the U-boats, driven from the sea, holed up.

Chapter Eighteen

ON May 16, 1945, Admiral Jonas H. Ingram gave an informal report on the antisubmarine campaign in the office of Secretary of the Navy Forrestal. Thus it was revealed that out of about five hundred German submarines destroyed in the Atlantic Ocean and adjacent European waters from 1939 to the war's end, the United States Navy had accounted for a verified 126; 15 more were sunk by Allied forces under United States control.

In its ruthless search for the U-boats, the Atlantic Fleet steamed 30,000,000 miles in pursuit of submarines and raiders. That fleet also escorted 16,760 troop and cargo vessels to the African-European Theater with a loss of only 15 to the enemy. In the final year of the war only two ships were torpedoed in convoy, and one of those made Gibraltar successfully, and this when convoys of more than a hundred ships each were leaving the United States every five days.

Admiral Ingram revealed also that the Germans were on the verge of starting a new phase of submarine warfare, one that could have done much damage before countermeasures could be effected, when the Wehrmacht's collapse left the U-boats homeless.

"We knew they had put a lot of fancy gadgets on them," Admiral Ingram said. "Increased them in size, increased their radius, increased their effectiveness, and made it much more difficult to get them. But they were pressed for time. The Russian offensive drove them out of the Baltic, and the heavy bombings in their shipbuilding places put their program back."

Enough of the new submarines put to sea—and were bagged—for the Atlantic Fleet to learn what the threatening improvements were. For one thing, the new U-boats could stay wholly submerged for weeks at a time.

"I know from the captive submarine crews," Admiral Ingram said, "that one ship that started out submerged on March 21 did not take air until April 9. Another captive reported that they had a submarine that could stay submerged seven weeks. In the early days of the war those fellows had to come up so many hours a day and our planes would spot them, and we'd go get them. In the last stages of this campaign, those babies spent most of their time submerged, and if we ever got them any place where the water was shallow enough—less than 600 feet—they'd just go down and stay on the bottom, and I am positive in my mind of instances where they have stayed on the bottom for two weeks. We thought they had gone, and would leave, and up they would come."

Four carriers and 75 destroyers and destroyer escorts put Doenitz's new submarines to the test, however. They hounded the first flotilla of supersubs from mid-Atlantic to within sight of the continental United States, sinking eight of them before they could get a shot at any ship themselves.

"Two or three got through to the coast," Admiral Ingram confesses. "They torpedoed five ships and sank two, and we got them close to the coast, one right off Newport Harbor two weeks ago, the last one of the bunch."

Admiral Ingram also revealed that one Japanese submarine had been sunk in the North Atlantic, identified as such by the debris.

Most of the work of the Atlantic Fleet—which included training men and shaking down the ships for the Pacific Theater—had to be kept secret until the war neared its end, Admiral Ingram said.

"My boys in blue in the Atlantic Fleet have been down in what I sort of call the 'Well of secrecy,' " the Admiral said. "There in the Atlantic are over 125,000 officers and more than a million men who have manned and trained and reconditioned everything that is going to the Pacific—that is, reinforce the forces there.

"The mission of the Atlantic Fleet was to keep the sea lanes open, to make an effective blockade of the Axis powers in the Atlantic, and also protect neutral shipping and Allied shipping. The Battle of the Atlantic is going to go down as one of the decisive battles of the war, because if the Battle of the Atlantic had not been won, war in Europe would not have gone on. In early 1943, when the Germans had as many as 450 submarines available, it was just nip and tuck, and if they had kept on at the rate of sinkings of early '43 for the remainder of that year, I doubt if there would have been any invasions in the Mediterranean or Normandy, or any Great Britain."

PART FOUR

African Invasion — The Start of Amphibious War

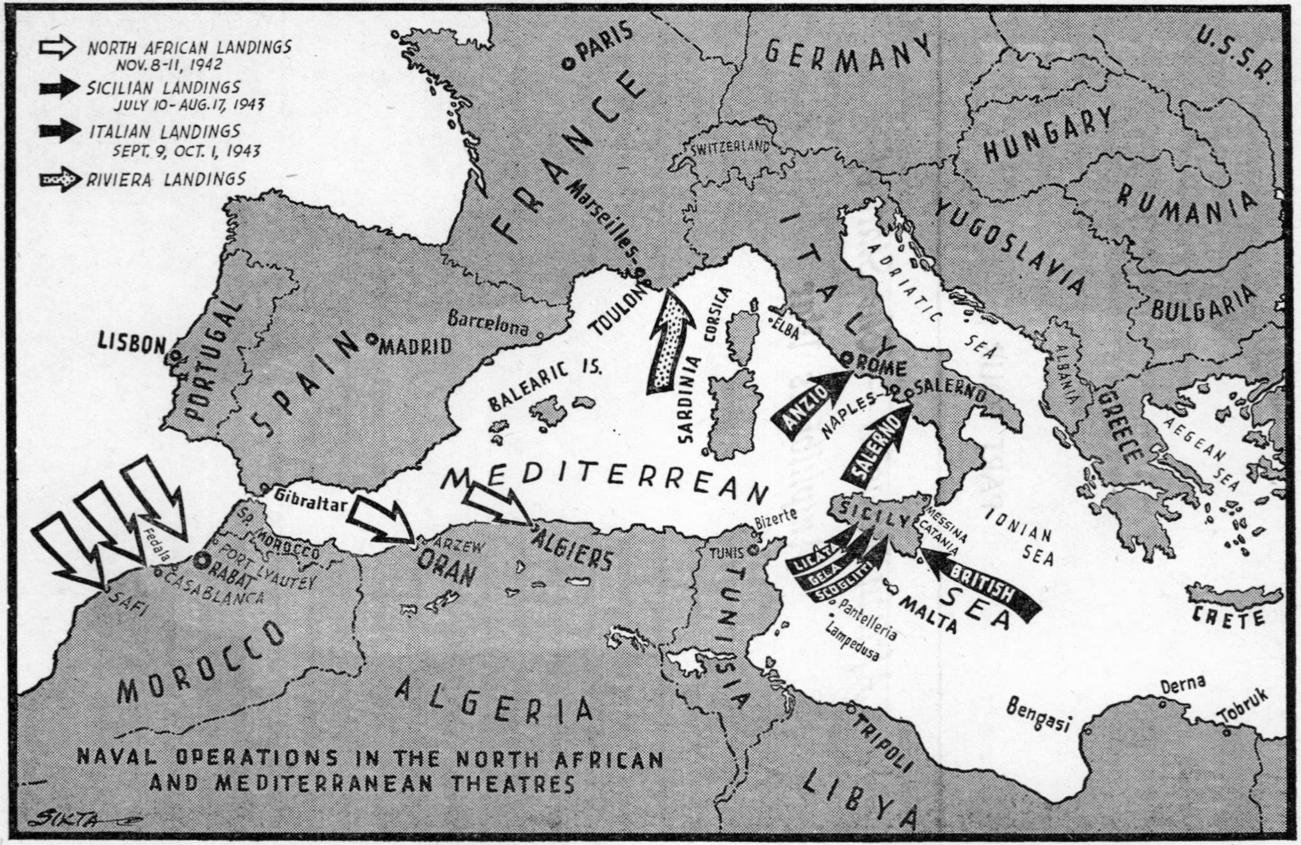
NORTH AFRICAN LANDINGS NOV. 8-11, 1942
SICILIAN LANDINGS JULY 10-AUG. 17, 1943
ITALIAN LANDINGS SEPT. 9, OCT. 1, 1943
RIVIERA LANDINGS
PARIS
GERMANY
U.S.S.R.
FRANCE
SWITZERLAND
HUNGARY
RUMANIA
YUGOSLAVIA
BULGARIA
Marseilles
TOULON
ITALY
ADRIATIC SEA
ALBANIA
GREECE
AEGEAN SEA
LISBON
PORTUGAL
SPAIN
MADRID
Barcelona
BALEARIC IS.
CORSICA
ELBA
SARDINIA
ROME
ANZIO
NAPLES
SALERNO
MEDITERRANEAN
Gibraltar
Sp. MOROCCO
Fedala
PORT LYAUTEY
RABAT
CASABLANCA
SAFI
ARZEW
ORAN
ALGIERS
Bizerte
TUNIS
SICILY
MESSINA
CATANIA
IONIAN SEA
LICATA
GELA
SCOGLITTI
BRITISH
SEA
MALTA
Pantelleria
Lampedusa
CRETE
MOROCCO
ALGERIA
TUNISIA
TRIPOLI
Bengasi
Derna
Tobruk
LIBYA
NAVAL OPERATIONS IN THE NORTH AFRICAN AND MEDITERRANEAN THEATRES
SIKTA

FIGURE 5

Chapter Nineteen

THE transition from defensive to aggressive warfare, from makeshift to superiority in men and equipment, was achieved of course by a mobilized United States, a nation that sent its sons from the farm and the desert to the oceans, a nation that built seagoing vessels 2,000 miles from salt water.

It was that teamwork of the whole republic, not just the courage and canniness of the armed forces, that enabled Admiral Ernest J. King, Commander in Chief United States Fleet, to report to Secretary of the Navy James Forrestal on March 1, 1944: "Submarines have not been driven from the seas, but they have changed status from menace to problem."

The preceding chapters of this narrative have tried to show how that change was effected by the forces at sea and in the air. Having won the ocean, the Navy proceeded to utilize it to blast at enemy-held shores and to convoy to them the armies General Eisenhower was to lead to victories in Africa, Italy, France and Germany. That is the story about to begin in the next chapter.

But this was a war, afloat or ashore or in the sky, that could not be fought by Minutemen forsaking the plow, grabbing the family musket, and faring forth into battle with the barnyard muck not dry on their boots. Behind each fighting man's combat experience was a long, arduous period of training to equip him with the strange new skills he had to master in order to be the survivor when he came to grips with the enemy. And, for every fighting man, half a dozen had to be trained in the science of providing those in actual combat with everything they needed, from food, weapons and ships to religious and physical comfort.

It was an Homeric task, that building of a Navy from a skeleton of 126,418 in 1939, when Hitler sent his hordes into Poland, to a body of close to three and a half million. How that was done is a story richer in achievement than in drama. Behind every person in the Navy who has performed an act of heroism, or has done a hard job well, there is the system that selected him and trained him and imbued him with the know-how, spirit and confidence to do just what he did.[1]

Of all the training and procurement problems faced—and solved— in the first year of the war, none was more difficult than those presented by the need for an Amphibious Force—although the need was not then known by that or any other name.

The need was for fighting ships and lesser craft that could go where no ship or boat had gone before, right up on the enemy's beaches, to carry trained troops who could step from ship into battle with guns blazing, confident in the knowledge that ordnance and ample supplies were immediately behind them: a fighting team of keels and wheels and men that could come in from the sea without pause and drive inland. Amphibious—as an alligator is—a deadly fighting organism in the water or out of it, or halfway between.

But how would it be manned, how implemented? Who would command it? How would it operate? Those were mysteries, but mysteries that would have to be solved swiftly, boldly, expensively. With Lend-Leased bases in the Atlantic, and outposts in the Caribbean, Brazil, Newfoundland, Greenland and Iceland, the Navy was moderately well equipped to fight a defensive war in the Atlantic; in the Pacific, Japanese amphibious operations were making it increasingly difficult to do even that. And everywhere was the growing evidence that a defensive war was a losing war. But how was the transition to be effected?

There was very little to go on: The Marines had worked out a basic doctrine, formulated in *The Landing Force Manual,* in the years between 1935 and 1939, during which they had held maneuvers with the Fleet a few times. The Army had given one division of engineers some training, largely simulated, in assault landings. There had been two joint Army-Navy-Marine exercises in 1941, which taught all branches of the service much, and no lesson more valuable than that there was an appalling lot to learn.

Even the first step had still to be taken, to decide just who was to run the show. Army, Navy, Coast Guard and Marine Corps each had a right to be considered, for amphibious operations entailed something of the specialties of each. Army engineers were experienced small-boat men,

[1] See Appendix A for a more detailed account of the training program of the Navy.

and furthermore, in any large-scale landing operations it would be the Army that would do the land fighting. But up to the moment the soldiers hit the beach, the primary pattern of ship operation and protection, of wind and weather, were Navy concerns. Furthermore, the Marines were a part of the Navy and after all they had actually had more practice making landings than anyone else. Then, too, all the original Army units of the Amphibious Corps were Marine trained. Coast Guardsmen probably knew more than anyone in either armed service about the business of handling small boats in surf. It was a problem for the very highest levels of command, and from those levels came the decision: The Amphibious Force was to operate as part of the Navy—in joint operation all responsibility for getting the Army ashore was to be the Navy's. The Army had to say when and where and in what order they wanted to be landed.

On March 14, 1942, Rear Admiral Noland M. Brainard, USN, was appointed to organize and command the Amphibious Force, with Captain Lee P. Johnson, USN, as Chief of Staff. He hoisted his flag without ceremony aboard the USS BIDDLE. The orders were, in effect, to make bricks without straw, without clay, without kilns, without an instruction book on how to make bricks and without any exact specifications on how the bricks were to be used. Admiral Brainard had no staff, no headquarters, no personnel to train, no place to train them, no craft to train them with, no modern precedents (except the Japanese) that could be called successful. And, on March 14, 1942, when Amphibious Force, Atlantic Fleet, as an autonomous command under CINCLANT, came into being he had no idea of where it would be fighting.

The Force had transports—on paper—transferred to it from the Service Force, Atlantic Fleet, but most of them were in the process of conversion from peacetime use. This meant, in some cases, a virtual rebuilding of the vessels; installation of booms and davits strong enough to handle landing craft and tanks, building of troop compartments, the mounting of guns, the creation of ammunition lockers, and a hundred and one other major and minor changes. These ships were incorporated into the Amphibious Force as one of its three principal divisions—the Transport Group. The other two were the Landing Craft Group and the Landing Force Group (the latter under Army command since, obviously, it is the Army that does the landing).

In the Landing Craft Group, the Amphibious Force had boats of two types on hand: LCPs (Landing Craft, Personnel) and LCMs (Landing Craft, Mechanized,[1] and three more, LCIs, LCTs and LSTs, in the drawing-board stage.

The first two types, products of the study that followed the Marine landing maneuvers of the previous decade, were designed to be carried aboard transports. Therefore, it was possible to begin training crews for these small boats right aboard the few available transports. It was a

[1] *Type*	*Capacity*	*Length*	*Beam*	*Crew*
LCP, LCP(R), LCVP (landing craft personnel [ramp], landing craft vehicle or personnel)	36 men, 7500 lbs. cargo, one jeep, or one 105-mm. gun	36' 8"	10' 10"	3, 1 officer per 3 craft
LCM—landing craft mechanized	one 30-ton tank, or 60,000 lbs. cargo	50'	14' 1"	4, 1 officer per 3 craft
LCS(S)—landing craft support (small)—rocket craft	crew and ammunition	36' 8"	10' 10"	6, 1 officer

These craft were developed as a result of the Marine maneuvers with the Fleet in 1936–1939. The LCVP has superseded the other personnel carriers.
These craft and the LCS(S) are designed to be slung in davits. The LCMs are carried on deck and handled by cargo booms.

LCT—Mark V Landing craft tanks	Five 30-ton, four 40-ton or three 50-ton tanks or 9 trucks, or 150 tons of cargo	117' 6"	32'	13, 1 officer
LCT—Mark VI	As above	120' 4"	32'	12, 1 officer
LCI (L) Type 1	Army personnel—6 officers, 182 men or 75 tons cargo	158' 6"	23' 3"	24, 3 officers
Landing craft infantry Type 2	9 officers, 196 men, 32 tons cargo	As above	As above	28, 3 officers
LST—Landing ship tanks	4 or 6, LCVPs on davits; 1 LCT on deck, twenty-seven 25-ton tanks, or fifteen 40-ton tanks or equivalent on tank deck. 168 troops	345' 10"	54'	7–9 officers 204–220 men

These craft were developed in co-operation with the British Admiralty who began planning the invasion of Europe, while their troops were still being evacuated from Dunkerque. The LCTs were an outgrowth of the Continental river barges (the British version is considerably longer than the American). The LST, product of joint Anglo-American planning and study, evolved from the shallow-draft Lake Maracaibo tankers. The six types of landing craft described here composed the original Landing Craft Group of the Amphibious Force, and represent all the main types used in the Atlantic and Mediterranean Amphibious Operations.

makeshift, but at least it got the training started, which was what Rear
Admiral Brainard had been ordered to do.

His staff—when it was assigned—squeezed itself somehow into
cramped quarters in NOB (Naval Operating Base) Norfolk; quarters
so cramped that, as one officer recalls it, "The only way you could tell
rank was by where an officer was sitting in relation to the one desk; if
he sat behind it he was a flag officer; if he sat on it, he was a senior
officer; under it, a junior officer. Ensigns and yeomen worked standing up."

This, naturally, led to a sense of impermanence, which was enhanced
by the secrecy surrounding the whole Amphibious Force. Making a virtue
of necessity, it was decided that the enemy should know nothing of the
force the United States didn't yet have. The address of the command was
a New York Fleet Post Office number, and many an officer seeking to
report to Amphibious Headquarters spent a full day trying to find out
where to go.

Early in June of 1942, when the Navy's amphibious program swung
into high under the forceful guidance of Rear Admiral Henry K. Hewitt,
USN, who had succeeded Rear Admiral Brainard in April. Drafts
began to pour into Norfolk at the rate of a thousand men every two
weeks. Quartering trainees aboard the transports was out of the question,
not only because there were not enough transports to quarter the small-
boat men, but also because crews for the larger landing craft, the LCIs,
LCTs and LSTs, were streaming in, and they had to be housed and
schooled ashore until these vessels were built. Amphibious Training Bases
(ATBs) had to be built, and quickly.

The first of these to come into being was the ATB at Solomons Island,
Maryland, followed in a few months by the ATB at Little Creek, Virginia. These bases had much in common—overcrowding, lack of facilities, shortage of base personnel. They differed in one important respect:
at Solomons, where it seemed to rain all the time, standard equipment
for every barrack was a shovel to scoop out the mud; but at Little Creek,
where it also seemed to rain all the time, the standard equipment for
every barrack was a broom to sweep out the sand. Those were the conditions that welcomed newcomers to the Amphibious Force in the summer
of 1942. Chow lines were long; water, at Little Creek at least, was
rationed; recreation facilities were nonexistent (but there was no time
for recreation anyhow). Over all was the constant thought that here was

a new and untried method of waging war the success of which (and the life of every man in it) depended on themselves and only themselves.

The officers and men who arrived by the thousands to make up the Amphibious Force were no veterans. They were ensigns right out of fresh-water colleges by way of indoctrination school; men right out of the farms and factories via boot camp. Untried craft and untried crews met for the first time on the Chesapeake, and the groans of maltreated engines mingled with the groans of bewildered officers and men as they settled down to the unremitting toil of producing a new combat force full-grown. There were some exceptions; now and then a tough egg who had made himself completely unpopular in the Fleet would wake up to find he was bound for Norfolk and Amphibs. For a while it was the Navy man's version of the fate worse than death. One young ensign will never forget his indoctrination to the Amphibious Force. He was riding down to Norfolk behind two enlisted men, one of whom was reciting a list of crimes against Navy discipline that had all the impressiveness of Homer's catalogue of the ships. Said the other, admiring, but dazed, "You mean to tell me they didn't give you a BCD [Bad Conduct Discharge] for that?"

"Hell no!" said the hard guy. "I got fifteen days in the brig and orders to Amphibious."

"Geez!" gasped the first. "That's a lousy break."

The ensign's bright gold stripe probably made a pretty contrast to the green of his face, and his frame of mind wasn't helped when another ensign joined him and asked genially, "You going to the Ensign Disposal School?"

"The wha—what?"

"The Ensign Disposal School—the Amphibious Force?"

When these greenhorns, and the sprinkling of nuts too tough for any other branch of the Navy to crack, arrived at Norfolk during the early months of the command, what they found to greet them was not reassuring. Training had started from transports on the Chesapeake near Solomons, the ships themselves housing the trainees.

Training went on, in almost every kind of condition but one—actual surf and open sea. In the summer of 1942 it wasn't exactly healthy for ships to lie to in open water, even three miles from our own shore. And there were not enough ships to risk.

But, though training was lacking in actual surf and ocean swell—a lack that was felt severely a little later—much was learned. Crews of the transports learned, the hard way, all the cantankerous characteristics of the LCM as it swung from a cargo boom in a high wind. By trial and error and constant work they improved their debarkation and unloading times. Convoy station keeping and maneuvering, even with ships completely darkened, became routine. If learning by doing is proper pedagogy, the small-boat men had the best of training. They kept at it night and day, fair weather and foul; getting fed when and if they came alongside a transport for a handout, which usually consisted of coffee and bologna (it had another brisk name, descriptive but unprintable) sandwiches. And they made mistakes. On one dark nasty night, for example, after milling around for what seemed like hours, first in their assembly circles off the starboard quarters of their transports and later, after loading, in their rendezvous circles, the small boats started out for the beach. It was, as has been said, a miserable night, but the small-boat men kept good formation and landed well just at dawn. The only trouble was they had landed on the wrong side of Chesapeake bay.

And as the small-boat men and officers learned, so did the transport officers and crews, and so did the higher echelons.

The difficulties the small boats had in finding their way in the dark led to the adoption of the Control Boat and the Line-of-Departure method of finding position, and the Scout and Raider technique of beach-marking familiar now to all who view the newsreels. Problems of fire support were particularly bothersome, since the very ships which should have been practicing it were away on the more immediately vital duty of guarding convoys. This very lack, though, was responsible for the first use of what has come to be one of this war's most potent weapons —the rocket. It was plain to everyone that the waves of small craft stood in greatest need of protection as they neared the beach and drew within range of light machine-gun, mortar and small-arms fire. But this was just the time the heavy ships furnishing the preliminary neutralizing bombardment would have to lift their fire for fear of hitting their own men. To bridge the gap the little LCSS (Landing Craft Support, Small) with its banks of twelve rocket-launching racks on each gunwale was devised. It had shallow draft, easy maneuverability, and its rockets packed a devastating punch. It seemed just the answer. The Amphibious Force was an outfit willing to try anything. The rocket craft worked well in maneuvers. It worked even better when ultimately brought to bear against the enemy.

Other experiments were under way at the same time, some of them as prosaic as learning new and effective ways of carrying cargo, human or freight. The principles of combat loading were jointly devised by Army and Navy, whereby a transport would carry everything needed in the first battle by the troops embarked on that transport, and all stowed to come out in order of need and use. Divisions, regiments and companies were fitted into a wholly new table of organization, into teams to coincide exactly with the number of boats in a wave, the number of waves in an assault.

And then, in May, one element of the team was removed. The Marine Divisions, which had been training with the Army and the Navy and at their own base at New River, North Carolina, suddenly got their orders. They weren't going to tackle the Wehrmacht, after all. Another task had been found for them. No one knew what it was, or where, until the Leathernecks turned up in the news of victory in the Pacific; a place called Guadalcanal. They shipped out on the six transports that were best prepared for operations.

Late in the summer, just about the time the Amphibious trainees learned what their late colleagues of the Marine Corps were doing, the training program was considerably complicated by still another new problem. In addition to the regular training it was conducting, the Amphibious Force Command was told to prepare and train for a specific operation. This was like asking a coach in the midst of spring practice with a bunch of freshmen to put a team on the field next Saturday to beat the national champions; only in the case of Rear Admiral Hewitt, he couldn't refuse the game.

It was going to be something big. Rear Admiral Hewitt looked over his squad, and on August 28 made a report to CINCLANT on the state of readiness of the Amphibious Force. It was glum reading then; it serves now, however, to show a small fraction of the endeavor that went into organizing an amphibious force.

It stated in effect:

That the 3rd and 9th Infantry Divisions, USA, had had good training thus far, but that the 2nd and 3rd Armored Divisions had had no training at all. Furthermore, the two infantry divisions had had no training in night landings and subsequent movement ashore, nor had they been trained in open sea surf landings of large units from transports. They were not sufficiently well trained in combat loading. One division further had reported a critical need for basic ground training and a shortage of trained officers and technicians.

The report proposed to put the troops in camps to complete training while transport quartermasters (the Army officers in charge of loading transports), shore parties, communications sections and naval gunfire support personnel went to school. After that entire units would be trained in tactical night maneuvers, movement inland, landing of supplies, movement to distribution points and evacuation.

Naval units were not a great deal better off than the Army (the report continued); combatant ships which would be used to cover an amphibious operation had little training because they had been off on other duties, necessarily. Submarines should have trained in reconnaissance of enemy harbors and beaches. Minesweepers and minelayers should have had training with amphibious forces. It was recommended that all vessels which might take part in an amphibious operation should be made available to joint training with the transports of the Amphibious Force.

At the time of the report, there were twelve APs (transports) and four AKs (cargo ships) attached to the Force. Eight of the APs, which had reported to the command prior to August 1, were considered to have had a reasonably sufficient amount of training in ship-to-shore movement and convoy maneuver for the coming operation. Three of the remainder were still in shakedown, and the twelfth was not due to report until September 4. Three of the four AKs had had some training. Boat crews and beach parties (the latter being the Navy personnel on the beach who act as traffic cops for incoming craft) were in training and promised to be ready when the ships were.

Three vessels were under consideration as possible headquarters ships for control of a joint operation, but it would take several months to ready any one of them. A headquarters ship of some sort "is to be desired" (said the report with appealing mildness), a battleship or a cruiser, fitted as a flagship, available to the Command for training and actual operations.

The status of equipment for communications, support craft, and navigational aids was not satisfactory. LCS(L) (Landing Craft Support [Large]) had been ordered but they would not be ready for some time, so support ships would have to be improvised. Machine guns for small landing craft had been ordered, but not received. None of the navigational aids for landing craft had appeared for trial, let alone for installation. Quantities and types of bombardment ammunition were not satisfactory; delivery must be stepped up.

Landing craft were too noisy and lacked protection for men embarked.

The Force had had no experience in operating with aircraft; however, naval aviators were just being attached to the staff to acquaint fliers with the needs of amphibious operations. The same vital training for Army fliers would be undertaken as soon as practicable.

Army communications training had been only fair but it promised to improve since personnel of the Ninth Division had been "frozen." The 2nd Armored Division had had no amphibious communications work. The same thing was true of most of the Navy transport personnel. Control craft with special equipment had been requested but not received. No joint communications training had been accomplished, though a school was about to get under way. And the lack in training was matched by the lack in equipment. Communications equipment was mostly of ordinary commercial standard and did not meet minimum Navy requirements.

And so went the report, hardly an inspiring picture for the high command on August 28, 1942, less than two months from the determined sailing date for the first major amphibious operation in the Atlantic.

There was only one way to meet that date: to work harder, faster, to work longer hours. It was done.

There is not space enough here even to mention, let alone give just credit to, all the men in positions of important command who at once directed and shared that work. They were the base personnel from CO to cook at all the ATBs, to whom planning, organization, operation and training were not problems to be taken in order, but emergencies to be met concurrently and immediately. The admiral and his staff had to order and plan for operations they had never tried in combat or seen tried, involving techniques they were still learning, craft they did not possess, equipment they'd never seen, and personnel almost entirely new to the Navy. They had to do all this at the same time that older, better established, better known branches of the Navy also were seeking desperately for men, equipment and labor in the same ways and from the same fluctuating sources.

And the Chesapeake Bay country, once the center of a special kind of American civilization, easygoing, gourmet, self-centered, was transformed by all this. It became the "Cradle of Invasions." From the inception of the Amphibious Training Command, more than 500,000 men were graduated with 60,000 ships as teams for 37 successful invasions of enemy beaches in Europe, Asia and Africa.

When Rear Admiral Hewitt left to assume command of the Eighth Fleet and the Navy in North African waters, amphibious training fell to the command of his former chief of staff, Captain Lee P. Johnson, USN. Early in 1944, Captain Johnson was promoted to commodore and given a Pacific command. He was followed by Rear Admiral Francis W. Rockwell, USN, who brought to the command not only the experience that had engineered successful amphibious operations in the Aleutians but also firsthand information, acquired in the Philippines, of how the enemy did it. Under him the command attained its greatest size.

But the first major invasion, the one which was to set in motion the forces eventually to smash Fascism in its own citadels, was reared in a very rough-and-ready cradle, and on very scant rations. It was toughened by adversity and its collective wits sharpened by the necessity of making its own way in an uncharted world of desperate conflict.

There was confusion, out of which came order, order and a great strength. It was a strength soon to receive its first test, and to prove itself abundantly in the greatest amphibious operation the world had yet seen —the invasion of the distant threatening shores of Africa.

Chapter Twenty

GREAT BRITAIN, standing alone against the Axis and wondering when the church bells would toll to warn of an invasion, was laying plans to land an army in northwest Africa. With the United States in the war, those plans were delayed to broaden the invasion front by inclusion of American naval and military forces.

The original decision had been to land some 55,000 men in the vicinity of Casablanca. The new plans included landings at Mehdia, Port Lyautey and Safi, and the potential invasion theater was then extended along the Mediterranean coastline of Africa to include Algeria.

For this joint operation (known as *Operation Torch*) the United States was to furnish the Commander in Chief Allied Forces. Lieutenant General Dwight D. Eisenhower, then Commanding General European Theater of Operations, was given this command. Major General Mark W. Clark was later appointed Deputy Commander in Chief. General Eisenhower had already established a headquarters in London. For *Torch* he was supplied with a combined United States-British staff. Vice-Admiral Sir Bertram Ramsay, RN, was nominated to be General Eisenhower's principal naval subordinate, but was relieved in mid-October by Admiral Sir Andrew Browne Cunningham, RN, who assumed the title "Naval Commander Expeditionary Force." The United States Navy was represented by Rear Admiral Bernhard H. Bieri, USN, Deputy Chief of Staff United States Atlantic Fleet.

The final agreement for the invasion of French Morocco and Algiers gave the United States charge of the military and naval operations on the Atlantic coast of Morocco, with Casablanca the major objective. The cities of Oran and Algiers would be objectives of joint British-American forces, with the British supplying all naval units with the exception of a few transports.

The expedition against Morocco was organized as the Western Task Force. The naval component was under the command of Rear Admiral

PLATE XXXIII—(*upper*) Two Nazi U-boats caught on the surface! One (left) is apparently a "milk cow" submarine, about to refuel the other. So swift was the approach of a Grumman Avenger torpedo bomber, from one of the Navy's escort carriers, that both subs were heavily attacked with depth charges (plume of spray, right) before they could submerge. (*lower*) Last moments of a Nazi raider. German sailors cringe as a U. S. Navy plane rakes their U-boat with machine-gun fire. Shortly afterward the submarine went down under a hail of depth bombs from Navy Liberators (PB4YS) and Army Mitchells (B-25s) of the anti-sub patrol.

PLATE XXXIV—(*upper*) Mrs. Eleanor Roosevelt is guest of honor at a luncheon at Tejipio, Brazilian recreation center for U. S. Navy men. At her left is Captain Walter C. Roper, USN (Retired), commanding officer. To her right is O. C. Campaynome, CM2c, USN. Tejipio, a former tuberculosis sanitarium, was given to the U. S. Navy by President Getulio Vargas, of Brazil. Renamed Atlanta, it served as a rest and recreation center for officers and men, nerve-strained after weeks at sea. (*lower*) "Sailors on horseback" offer thrills and spills at Peachtree Downs, the race track.

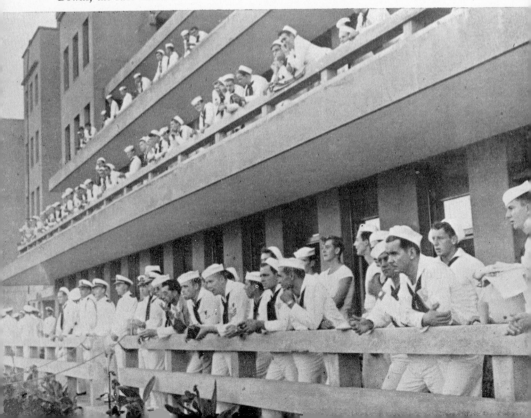

PLATE XXXV—Familiarly and affectionately known as the "banana fleet," these ships maintained the tedious neutrality patrol of sub-infested waters between the West Indies, the Cape Verde Islands, and the "hump" of Brazil during the summer and fall of 1941. *Left row, top to bottom:* USS MILWAUKEE and USS OMAHA, cruisers; USS WARRINGTON and USS JOUETT, destroyers. *Right row, top to bottom:* USS CINCINNATI and USS MEMPHIS (flagship), cruisers; and USS DAVIS and USS SOMERS, destroyers. Vice Admiral Jonas H. Ingram, USN, commanded the task force.

PLATE XXXVI—(*upper*) Brazil, who declared war on the Axis, August 22, 1942, received five U. S. Navy Vega Ventura bombers in a special ceremony at Ibura Field, Recife, on March 30, 1944. The planes became a part of Brazil's antisubmarine patrol. (*lower*) Following the presentation of the five bombers, Vice Admiral Jonas H. Ingram, USN, Commander of the Fourth Fleet, received a surprise award of FAB (Brazilian Air Force) wing insignia. Lieutenant Colonel Castro Lima, FAB, shakes hands with the delighted Vice Admiral as Brazil's Minister of Air, Joaquim Pedro Salgado, looks on. Genuine "Good Neighbor" feeling between the two commands smoothed over many problems and eliminated much red tape. Net result: the Nazi submarine menace was quickly driven from the South Atlantic.

PLATE XXXVII—(*left*) In addition to planes, the U. S. Navy also made available to Brazil several PCs, or submarine chasers, to assist in patroling one of the longest coastlines in the Western World. (*right*) The USS BUCKLEY, in drydock, shows a bow slightly the worse for wear after ramming a Nazi submarine in southern Atlantic waters. The BUCKLEY was escorting the escort carrier USS BLOCK ISLAND at the time. The sub sank.

(*left*) Quartz, used in radio, was one reason Brazil was such a valuable partner of the Allies. Other products of our most important South American neighbor are: coffee, rubber, tantalite, mica, beryl, tropical fruits and medicines. (*right*) So great was radio's need for Brazil's quartz that the mineral was rushed north in Naval Air Transport planes.

PLATE XXXVIII—(*upper left*) Brazil honors the captain of the U. S. Navy transport which carried the first Brazilian Expeditionary Force to Europe. General Enrico Gaspar Dutra, Minister of War, presents the Brazilian Order of Military Merit to Commander Paul S. Maguire, USNR, as Rear Admiral José Maria Neiva, of the Brazilian Navy, and Brigadier General Oswaldo Cordeiro de Farias, of the Brazilian Army (right), looks on. (*upper right*) The first Brazilian force ever to fight overseas boards a U. S. Navy transport, bound for Europe. Brazilians helped to push the Nazis out of Italy. (*lower*) Not content with sending one expeditionary force to Europe, Brazil organized a second. Here a few of the thousands of troops who made up the second force mass on the deck of a U. S. Navy transport to witness a King Neptune ceremony.

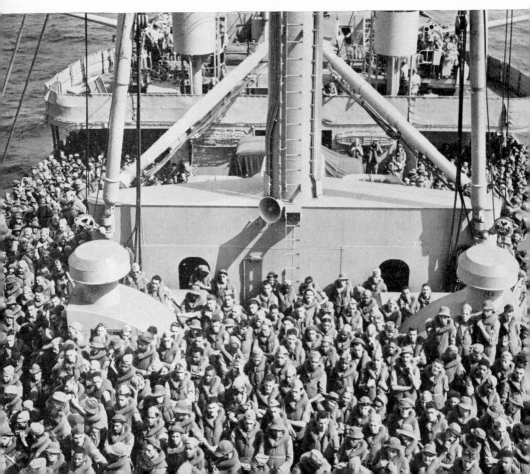

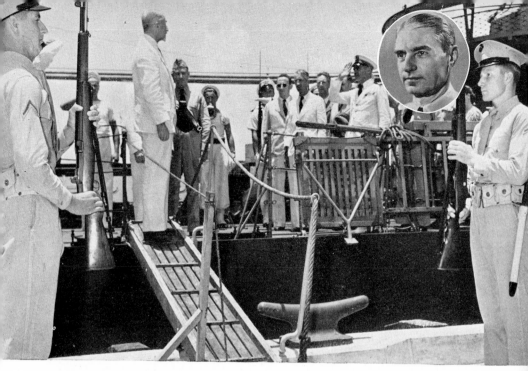

PLATE XXXIX—End of an incident. In civilian clothes, Admiral Georges Robert, former high commissioner of Martinique, disembarks in Puerto Rico to confer with Rear Admiral John H. Hoover, USN (*inset*), Commandant of the Tenth Naval District. Admiral Robert for seven months defied a U. S. Government embargo against the French West Indies. (*lower*) "Miss Ascension and your wife gets a pension," was the motto of Fleet Air Wing 16, based on the lonely South Atlantic island. Here Vice Admiral Jonas H. Ingram, USN, and an Army aide inspect the site of the future air base and stepping stone to Africa. *Inset:* Captain R. D. Lyon, USN, organizer of FAW 16, February, 1943.

PLATE XL—(*upper*) They work as well as fight. Seabees, whose name was derived from the initials of "Construction Battalions," were organized early in the war by Rear Admiral Ben Moreell, USN, when it was found that civilians could not be used satisfactorily for work on advanced bases. Here Seabees take the commando course at Camp Endicott, R. I. (*lower*) Rear Admiral Randall Jacobs, USN, Chief of the Bureau of Naval Personnel, reviews the nucleus of women's organizations in the Navy, which eventually numbered 110,000 Waves, Spars, and Marines. Lieutenant Commander Mildred McAfee, USNR, Director of the Waves, presents her staff (*left to right*): Lieutenant Elizabeth Reynard, USNR; Lieutenant Jean T. Palmer, USNR; Lieutenant (jg) Virginia Carlin, USNR; Lieutenant (jg) Marian Enright, USNR; and Ensign Dorothy Foster, USNR.

PLATE XLI—(*upper*) Sisters of the Navy in Miami. Splendid examples of the women who released "men to fight" are: Katherine Roberts, of Lake Worth, Fla., a Marine; Phylis James, of New Castle, Pa., a Wave; and June Crawford, of Denver, Col., a Coast Guard Spar. (*lower*) She served the Navy in two wars: a study in contrasts is afforded by the Yeomanette garb of Miss Joy Bright, taken in 1918, and the officer's uniform of Mrs. Joy Bright Hancock, of the Waves. Mrs. Hancock, now a Commander, has been on duty in Hawaii.

PLATE XLII—The U. S. Navy of World War II may be divided, like Gaul, into three parts: Big Ship Navy, Little Ship Navy and Flat Bottom Navy. Greatest of these is the Flat Bottom, or Amphibious. Of 100,000 units comprising the U. S. Navy in May, 1945, 82,266 were landing ships or craft. Here are shown eight principal types. *Left row, top to bottom:* LSD (Landing Ship, Dock); LCS (Landing Craft, Support); LCM (Landing Craft, Medium); LCR (Landing Craft, Rubber); Alligator (amphibious tractor). *Right row, top to bottom:* LST (Landing Ship, Tank); LCT (Landing Craft, Tank); LCVP (Landing Craft, Vehicles, Personnel); LSM (Landing Ship, Medium); and LCI (Landing Craft, Infantry).

PLATE XLIII—Grandad of all Attack Transports. The USS WILLIAM P. BIDDLE became the first of many APAs (Auxiliary Personnel, Assault) on March 14, 1942, when Rear Admiral R. M. Brainard, USN (*inset*) hoisted his flag aboard her without ceremony. Previously the "Billy B" was with the first U. S. Navy task force to Iceland, and later took part in the African, Sicilian, Marshall Islands, Guam, Leyte, Lingayen, and Mindoro operations. She was built in 1919, as the SS CITY OF SAN FRANCISCO.

Landing Ship, Horse (LSH), or "Shipping in the Reign of King Henry III" (A.D. 1269). It has not been determined whether this drawing is a clever hoax or not, but, if true, the open bow door on the vessel (lower right) illustrates the old adage "there is nothing new under the sun."

PLATE XLIV—(*left*) Wonder ship of World War II, the LST is ungainly, slow, in fact a real ugly duckling. But it nevertheless has done everything expected of it, and more. Here, with rails laid inside and down the ramp, it

becomes a car ferry. (*above*) Rear Admiral R. L. Conolly, USN, who directed the LST "Cub Carriers" experiment.

(*right*) Even its creators at the Bureau of Ships were amazed when word came back from Italy that LSTs were being used as carriers! From a special deck, tiny Piper Cubs were launched for observation purposes during the Nettuno Bay operation. The planes, however, could not be landed aboard.

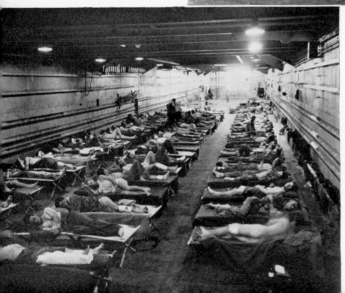

(*left*) On landing operations, after all cargo had been put ashore, the LST became a convenient means of transporting wounded back to base hospitals or hospital ships. Many lives were saved because the injured could be sheltered from the elements. (*Marine Corps Photo.*)

PLATE XLV—(*right*) Enormous firepower can be concentrated in even an LCI (Landing Craft, Infantry) by the use of rockets arranged in racks and fired singly or in salvo. Although such rockets do not have much range, they have the destructive force of five-inch shells. Thus amphibious craft can provide part of their own bombardment support.

(*left*)—LBK (Landing Boat, Kitchen), diner of the "Elsie" (LC) fleet. Scores of small craft, which become separated from their transports on D-days, created an eating problem until this strange auxiliary was added to the amphibious fleet. The white LBK looks weird among more martial boats, but it never lacks enthusiastic callers.

(*right*) Rubber landing boats are generally used in conjunction with other craft, such as the LCI (as shown here), APD (Fast Transport), LSM (Landing Ship, Medium), etc. The LCR requires little shipping space and is an excellent means of moving troops and supplies through coral reefs and over offshore shoals.

PLATE XLVI—(*left*) An old sailing ship, the MARSALA, anchored off Little Creek, Virginia, became the mother of amphibious training. Up and down her wooden sides daily swarmed waves of soldiers and sailors in dress rehearsals for the ship-to-shore maneuvers that spelled success for our forces in Sicily, Salerno, Anzio, Normandy, and the Riviera. By a strange coincidence the MARSALA bore the name of a Sicilian town that would become familiar as a landing place to many who trained aboard her. (*lower*) There were no veterans in the Amphibious Force—everybody started from scratch! Here early recruits shove off from Norfolk Training Base, using the first small boats of a still highly unorganized service. (*Water colors by Ensign Mitchell Jamieson, USNR.*)

PLATE XLVII—The battle for a continent began when the French battleship JEAN BART and French Moroccan shore batteries fired at our forces off Casablanca. Twin geysers of water mark exploding shells which missed U. S. ships during D-day of *Operation Torch,* November 8, 1942. *(lower)* For the first time since the war with Spain in 1898, a battleship of the U. S. Navy engages an enemy. Guns of the USS MASSACHUSETTS support the landing forces and, with the aid of Navy planes, finally silence the mighty JEAN BART in Casablanca harbor.

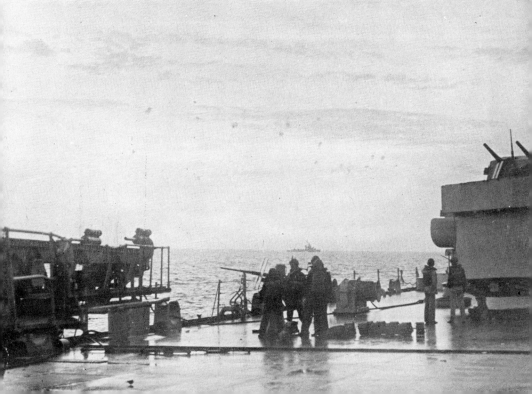

PLATE XLVIII—(*above*) Captain Jerauld Wright, USN, one of the group who made preliminary plans for the African landings, three weeks before D-day. (*left*) Over the side at Fedala, French Morocco. Fedala, 14 miles northwest of Casablanca, was one of the major objectives of the French Moroccan landings, known as *Operation Torch*. (*lower*) U. S. landing barges speed shoreward off Fedala. Note the tense expressions on the faces of the two men in the foreground. This was the first real baptism of fire for America's growing amphibious forces.

Henry K. Hewitt, USN, and the Army forces were commanded by Major General George S. Patton, USA.

The mission of the Western Task Force was stated simply: To establish the Army on beachheads near Safi, Fedala, Mehdia and Port Lyautey, and to support the ensuing military operations on land in order to capture Casablanca as a base for further military and naval operations.

Although there were to be three landings on the coast of French Morocco, the major objective was Casablanca harbor, a modern seaport. The strategy for occupying Casablanca involved the simultaneous capture of the other three harbors, the most important of which was Fedala, 14 miles northwest of Casablanca. The landings at Mehdia, 65 miles north of Casablanca, and at Safi, 125 miles south of the port, were designed to get troops ashore and approach the city of Casablanca from the rear by land.

Although the mission of the Western Task Force might appear simple on paper, it involved a multitude of problems. In the first place, amphibious warfare had never been attempted on a scale called for in the plans for *Torch*.

The first difficulty was geography itself. The coast of Morocco is rocky, with long sloping beaches. This meant transports would have to lie a considerable distance from shore to discharge troops. The jagged, rocky beaches were a hazard to the small assault boats. The problem was to locate the few beach areas where landing craft could come ashore with reasonable safety. Through intelligence reports and photographic reconnaissance enough were found in strategic areas to ensure making the landings feasible.

But there was another and constant problem, that of Africa's heavy ground swells, high surf and great tides, all factors of vital importance in planning an amphibious landing. And those conditions were highly unpredictable. Swells towering 16 to 20 feet were not uncommon along the Moroccan coast. High surf from these swells was found too frequently in fair weather. Such things as a low atmospheric pressure moving from the Azores toward Spain would cause a heavy surf off Morocco in the space of a day. On the other hand, a similar atmospheric condition moving south from Iceland would not be felt for two or three days.

It was discovered that the worst surf condition along the Moroccan coast was caused by an atmospheric depression between Bermuda and Newfoundland. After a lapse of about thirty-six hours high surf and gale winds could be expected on Morocco. It was, all in all, a nasty problem for a force that had had its training—all ten weeks, or less, of it—in the comparatively calm coziness of the Chesapeake.

A continuous watch of meteorological conditions over the entire Atlantic area was kept and plotted as the planning for *Torch* progressed. Nothing could be overlooked. Bad coastal weather naturally increased as winter approached. In view of the date chosen for D-day, November 8, 1942, weather predictions and meteorological information had to be absolutely accurate. Submarines were ordered to the Moroccan coast two days in advance of the main convoys to act as weather stations. So accurate and closely timed were the meteorologists' data that the troops of the Western Task Force had been ashore only a few hours when the surf along the Moroccan coast built up so high that landing on the exposed beaches would have been disastrous had the operation been delayed or the weather miscalculated.

It may have been because of these beach and weather conditions that the landings on the Moroccan beaches were met with such light opposition. The defenders did not believe a landing through the surf was possible and were expecting attacks on more sheltered spots.

Of course, in addition to the weather, there were military defenses to be taken into account. The fixed defenses along the Moroccan coast were supplemented by mobile strength drawn from the French Army. The number of units usually maintained in Morocco was 13 infantry regiments, 8 cavalry regiments with 4 artillery regiments and 3 batteries. (A French infantry regiment normally consists of 3,120 men, a cavalry regiment of 1,140 men, an artillery regiment of 1,683 men.) The artillery consisted of two regiments of African artillery, two regiments of Colonial artillery and three batteries of the Foreign Legion. Most of the fieldpieces were 75s with some 65s. There was also one regiment of antiaircraft artillery. The air strength in Morocco was not sufficient cause for worry. The total number of Vichy planes, both Army and Navy, was estimated to be 168, and the airfields from which they could operate were scattered and weakly defended by antiaircraft units.

Anglo-American hopes were that the French would accept the offer of amity that would precede the landings, or put up only a token resistance. Fighting against Frenchmen, so many of whom were battling on the Allied side, was an unpalatable prospect.

The toughest opposition, should the Vichy command elect to resist, was the fleet strength at Casablanca—one battleship, two light cruisers, three flotilla leaders, six destroyers, twelve submarines, and one sloop.[1] In other words, a lot of firepower.

Such, roughly, was the opposing strength that would contest the landings of the Western Task Force in Morocco.

The Army strength of the Western Task Force was built around the United States Army's 6th and 9th Divisions. The amphibious training of these divisions was modeled on the 1st Division's 1939 experimental landing maneuvers at Culebra Island, Puerto Rico; the amphibious experiments of the 3rd Division at Fort Washington, Puget Sound, and Marine landing doctrines perfected by Major General Holland M. Smith, USMC.

Army and Navy were then brought together for joint training in the Chesapeake Bay area, at Camp Bradford, Virginia, and Solomons Island, Maryland.

The problem of transport for this amphibious operation was an acute one. The Navy was to furnish transportation for 1,920 officers and 35,385 men with full battle equipment and material. Space had to be provided on the transport for 250 tanks, plus the bulky landing craft.

On June 1, 1942, there were only eight ships assigned to and operating with the Amphibious Force, United States Atlantic Fleet. As training progressed and time moved nearer to D-day, more ships were acquired. Some were new construction, some were transferred from other commands. Five transports were transferred to Admiral Hewitt's force from the West Coast. Eleven other ships were converted to assault transports during August and September. By October 1, there were twenty-six transports and seven cargo ships standing by at Hampton Roads, Virginia. Three weeks later they were combat loaded with all the ugly paraphernalia of war, and so crowded with soldiers that the men had to sleep in shifts.

The task force organization was in three parts: the Assault Force of transports and landing craft to make the landings at Mehdia, Fedala and Safi; the Covering Group of warships, which would protect the landing forces against the defending fleet at Casablanca, and the Air Group.

To avoid congestion, just before the main convoy sailed, the Covering Group was sent to Casco Bay, Maine, and the Air Group, which included

---

[1] Battleship: JEAN BART; light cruisers: GLOIRE and PRIMAGUET; flotilla leaders: ALBATROS, LE MALIN, and MILAN; destroyers: ALCYON, BRESTOIS, FOUGEUX, FRONDEUR, SIMOUN, TEMPÈTE; submarines: ACTÉON, ARCHIMÈDE, AURORE, CÉRÈS, CONQUÉRANT, IRIS, MÉDUSE, ORPHÉE, PALIAS, PSYCHE, TONNANT and VÉNUS; sloop: BOUDEUSE.

five carriers,[1] to Bermuda. The departure of the convoy itself from the United States was to be made in two groups, which would leave on successive days.

The first convoy group, consisting of ships assigned to the Mehdia and Safi landings, started out of the Hampton Roads channel at ten o'clock on the morning of October 23. The second group, the ships for the Fedala landing, left twenty-four hours later. On the same day, the Covering Group put out to sea from Casco Bay, Maine, and on October 25 the Air Group left Bermuda for a rendezvous of the entire Western Task Force on October 26.

Two ships were left behind. One was USS HARRY LEE, an old converted passenger ship that had been giving her commanding officer, Captain James W. Whitfield, USN, severe headaches for several weeks. She was afflicted with an unpredictable list. She was known, not too affectionately by the crew, as the "Listing Lee." The LEE was part of the Safi group. On the night before that group was scheduled to leave Hampton Roads, the LEE was lying anchored, combat loaded and ready to sail, in her berthing space. At one minute past midnight a watch officer reported to Captain Whitfield that one of the turbines had burned out. Orders were sent for a tug to haul the transport back into the Norfolk Navy Base for repairs.

The tug came and began towing the LEE into base. By ten o'clock the next morning, as her convoy got underway and left her, the engineers notified Captain Whitfield that the damaged turbine had been by-passed and his ship could now run at a 5-knot clip on a low pressure turbine. In other words, she could not sail as she was.

The problem now confronting Captain Whitfield was either to repair the LEE or shift to another transport and catch up with convoy. The latter course was decided upon. There was a new transport available, USS CALVERT, commissioned about ten days earlier. But owing to priority given the ships assigned to *Torch* the CALVERT was without amphibious equipment. She hadn't even had a shakedown cruise. This meant that not only did the cargo have to be shifted, but there had to be an exchange of about 250 officers and men. All the LEE's assault boats and gear and all the other assault equipment which the CALVERT did not possess had to be switched.

---

[1] USS RANGER (Capt. Calvin T. Durgin, USN), SUWANEE (Capt. Joseph J. Clark, USN), SANGAMON (Capt. Carlos W. Wieber, USN), SANTEE (Capt. William D. Sample, USN), and CHENANGO (Capt. Ben H. Wyatt, USN).

The previous combat loading of the LEE had taken eight days. The work of unloading and reloading the cargo onto the CALVERT was started at 1 P.M. on Friday. Most of the cargo had to be handled by hand. Care had to be taken to avoid damage and at the same time work at top speed. And the CALVERT could not be loaded as fast as the LEE was unloaded, because the gear had to be stowed in order of its use—the top layer of one had to be the top layer of the other.

By midnight Saturday the shift was completed and CALVERT, combat loaded and fit to fight, sailed the next morning. Escorted by two destroyers, USS BOYLE (Lieutenant Commander Eugene S. Karpe, USN) and EBERLE (Lieutenant Commander Karl F. Poehlmann, USN), the CALVERT joined her convoy group in mid-Atlantic on October 30; she was getting her shakedown, after all.

The second ship left behind, which raced at a futile, stumbling 9 knots to join the invasion convoy, was SS CONTESSA. The CONTESSA was the result of a long search to find a shallow-draft ship that could steam up the 12-mile passage of the Sebou River to Port Lyautey with fuel, bombs and supplies for our planes that would be using the airfield there as soon as it was taken.

A check of all available transports was made and none found with draft shallow enough to go up the 17-foot channel of the Sebou. Then someone remembered the CONTESSA, an old 5,500-ton British-built fruit ship. She was, at the time, somewhere in the Atlantic bound for New York. She was reached by radio and diverted to Newport News, Virginia. Although operated by the United States Maritime Commission, she flew the Honduran flag. Her captain, William H. John, was British; the first mate, Italian-American; the second mate, Norwegian; the third mate, American. The first engineer was British; the second, German-American; the third, Honduran. In the crew were Filipinos, Swedes, Danes, Estonians, Spaniards, Portuguese, Mexicans, Peruvians, Belgians, Brazilians, Finns, Arabs and Australians.

The CONTESSA received her orders and reached Newport News, but once there her league-of-nations crew scattered. In order to round up a new crew, the Norfolk jails were canvassed and the doors thrown open to men who would sign on the CONTESSA. Captain John had traded one motley crew for another, but he volunteered to sail the ship, unescorted, across the Atlantic to the Navy's destination.

Commodore Lee P. Johnson, USN, called a Reserve Officer, Lieutenant A. V. Leslie, into his office in the old Nansemond Hotel at Ocean View, which had become headquarters of the Amphibious Force, for a conference. Leslie was to sail on the CONTESSA as a "liaison officer" with authority to assume control should the crew get out of hand. Only he was to know the destination of the ship. Commodore Johnson handed him charts, maps and navigation instructions. He was told that no papers could be carried on the CONTESSA since she was to be unescorted, and if she carried charts they might fall into enemy hands, thus endangering the entire operations of *Torch*. Leslie spent a day in the Commodore's office. When he left he had memorized the details.

On October 26, the CONTESSA left Hampton Roads on her long lonely voyage into battle.

When the Task Force met in mid-Atlantic it formed a nine-column convoy headed by Rear Admiral Hewitt's flagship, the cruiser AUGUSTA (Captain Edward H. Jones, USN) and the battleships NEW YORK (Captain Kemp C. Christian, USN) and TEXAS (Captain Charles A. Baker, USN). The routing of the invasion convoy had been carefully planned so that even if the ships were sighted their destination would not be obvious. The initial course of the first group, the Mehdia and Safi units, was south after leaving Hampton Roads on a course for the West Indies, apparently. When well out of sight of the coast, the course was changed to north.

The second group, the Fedala units, steered a northeasterly course from Hampton Roads, as if heading for the British Isles. The two groups met on the afternoon of October 26 and again the course was changed, this time sharply to the southeast, as if the ultimate destination were Dakar. This general course was held until south of the Azores and west of the Canary Islands. Here the course was changed again, the ships turning to the east in the general direction of Gibraltar.

Every precaution for secrecy was taken. Orders went out to all ships that nothing was to be thrown overboard during daylight. Bilges were not to be pumped until after twilight, and all cans were to be well punctured before disposal, to ensure their sinking.

As the convoy drew closer to North Africa, coastwise shipping appeared. On November 6 air contact was established with Gibraltar. Several fishing craft and coastal steamers were sighted, rounded up and held until after D-day.

On the night of November 6–7, weather reports were secured from

the War and Navy Departments in Washington and from the five submarines [1] anchored off the Moroccan coast.

From the weather reports of the submarines and from Washington,
the fleet meteorologist of the Western Task Force was able to predict that
favorable wind, swell and weather conditions would prevail for the next
forty-eight hours. This was November 7, 1942. All was in readiness for
a fight, but the order had been given that under no circumstances were
Americans to fire the first shot.

There was reason for this caution. Contact had already been established with key French military figures in North Africa. Indeed, one
general had been brought out of France in a cinematic rescue and established in the area. If negotiations with the anti-Vichy elements proved
satisfactory to them (and their first concern was the honor of France), if
they were then able to convince their colleagues in all levels of command,
there might very well be no opposition to our landing.

The story of these secret negotiations and the rescue of General
Giraud is more like a scenario for a spy story than a segment of military
history. But it actually happened.

Three weeks before D-day for *Operation Torch* there landed secretly
in Africa, from a British submarine, Major General Mark Clark, then
Deputy Commander to General Eisenhower, and four other members of
Eisenhower's staff; Captain Jerauld Wright, USN, Colonel Julius Holmes,
Brigadier Lyman Lemnitzer and Colonel Arch Hamblem, plus two British
Commando officers. They paddled in kayaks, following a guarded signal
flashed to them from a lonely house on a grim Algerian cliff.

On the shore they were met by two Americans, Robert Murphy,
United States Consul General in North Africa, and Vice-Consul Ridgeway Knight. The group retired to the lonely house, where it waited tensely
all night for the arrival of the French Army representatives. Not till seven
o'clock, and daylight, did the French officers arrive. The parleys lasted
all that day. From them the members of General Eisenhower's staff
learned of the disposition of French military and naval forces, and their
defense plans against any invasion. They learned, too, that, while the
great bulk of the French Army in Africa loathed the thought of collabora-

[1] The submarines were well spotted. There was Lt. Comdr. John R. Waterman,
USN, in the BARB, off Safi; the BLACKFISH, with Lt. Comdr. John F. Davidson, USN,
off Dakar; the HERRING, with Lt. Comdr. Raymond W. Johnson, USN, off Casablanca;
the SHAD, with Lt. Comdr. Edgar J. MacGregor, III, USN, off Mehdia; and Lt. Comdr.
John S. McCain, Jr., USN, in the GUNNEL, lying off Fedala.

tion with the Boche, they would not act in concert with the Allies unless they were ordered to do so by a French military leader whom they could trust and respect implicitly. Who was such an officer? The Frenchmen were unanimous: General Henri Honoré Giraud. The Americans promised to deliver General Giraud from his virtual imprisonment behind the German lines in France.

They may themselves have been aghast at the size of the contract they had signed, but more immediate peril suddenly occupied their attention. Just as the conference was drawing to a natural close, the meeting was tipped off that the Vichy police were on their way to the lonely house. The French officers departed hastily to their posts; the American officers departed hastily to the cellar. There they hid while the two diplomatic representatives talked the police out of an extensive search. Then, when the coast was clear, they made for the beach to return to their submarine—one of the Royal Navy's smaller ships, commanded by Lieutenant N. L. A. Jewell, RN. But the surf was too high to launch their kayaks, and it stayed too high until four o'clock the next morning. Then a momentary shift in the wind coupled with the imminence of daylight afforded light and calmer seas, the opportunity and the incentive for a try.

Captain Wright, as Senior Naval Officer Present, had command of the flotilla—perhaps the lightest in tonnage and the heaviest in gold braid in the history of war—and got it back to the submarine safely. Two days later General Clark and his staff were back in London. A week later Captain Wright was at sea again in the same submarine on the worse half of his secret mission. He was going to aid General Giraud to escape from the Germans.

For a week the little sub played hide-and-seek with German surface and air patrols off the French coast. Then, one night, it sneaked into a tiny bay and surfaced a bare thousand yards from shore. Once again there was an exchange of furtive signals, once again the period of breath-held waiting. Then there was a light grating sound, and a tiny rowboat rubbed against the submarine's side. In it was General Giraud. The promise made in secret a week earlier was kept. Instead of a stanch foe, the invaders could now count on a sincere ally.

It was in consequence of the two missions that the Anglo-American fleet (which included Netherlands, Norwegian and Polish units) had the order not to fire first. It might be that the friends in Africa would have the situation completely under control when the United Nations forces

hove within range. On the other hand, while it was certain there would
be no bitterly prolonged resistance from the French, once Giraud had
spoken, it was still likely that not all French garrisons would get the word
in time or believe it, once it had been passed.

There were plenty of German and Vichy agents, and agents provoca-
teurs, to intercept, to confuse, to threaten.

We could not shoot first, but we had to be ready to shoot fast and
plentifully if it came to shooting. When this occurred, a code word had
been devised that would flash throughout the Western Task Force that
our landings would be opposed. That signal was a good American game
starter—"Play Ball."

Chapter Twenty-one

AT 0600 on November 7, the ships that were to land at Safi left the main convoy of the Western Task Force and steamed south. This was the Southern Attack Group, commanded by Rear Admiral Lyal A. Davidson, USN, with his flagship the PHILADELPHIA (Captain Paul Hendren, USN), which would be part of the Fire Support Group consisting of a battleship and six destroyers.[1]

These transports were carrying the Army's Sub-Task Force 1, under the command of Major General Ernest N. Harmon, and consisting of one Regimental Combat Team, reinforced: The 47th Infantry of the 9th Division; one light armored battalion team, and one medium armored battalion cambat team, a total of 327 officers, 6,096 men, 54 light tanks and 54 medium tanks.

The destroyer screen of the Attack Group comprised six destroyers, a minesweeper, a minelayer, a tug and an oiler.[2] In this flotilla the COLE and BERNADOU looked like interlopers, or masqueraders, because most of their superstructure had been cut down for purposes unknown to most of the men in the task force who pondered the weird appearance of the "sawed-off and hammered-down" ships.

At 2345—a quarter before midnight—all the ships of the Southern Attack Group were in their prearranged positions, eight miles out in the water from Safi. The little port city sparkled with lights. The troops on the transports had been briefed again and again on maps, models and

---

[1] Battleship: NEW YORK (Capt. Kemp C. Christian, USN); destroyers: MERVINE (Lt. Comdr. Solomon A. Willingham, USN), KNIGHT (Lt. Richard B. Levin, USN), and BEATTY (Lt. Comdr. Frederick C. Stelter, Jr., USN). The transports were the CALVERT, DOROTHEA L. DIX, HARRIS, LAKEHURST, LYON and TITANIA.

[2] Destroyers: USS BERNADOU (Lt. Comdr. Robert E. Braddy, Jr., USN), COLE (Lt. Comdr. George G. Palmer, USN), COWIE (Lt. Comdr. Charles J. Whiting, USN), DORAN (Lt. Comdr. Howard W. Gordon, Jr., USN), HAMILTON (Lt. Comdr. Robert R. Sampson, USN), QUICK, (Lt. Comdr. Roger B. Nickerson, USN); the minesweeper HOWARD (Lt. Comdr. Charles J. Zondorak, USN), the minelayer MONADNOCK (Comdr. Frederick O. Goldsmith, USN), the tug CHEROKEE (Lt. Jacob F. Lawson, USN) and the oiler MERRIMACK (Capt. William E. Hilbert, USN).

charts until, as one man said, "We could have found our way into Safi blindfolded." Across the water from the ships were the landing beaches. Their code designations were Red, Blue, Green and Yellow. What their real names were, nobody cared. Now they were just black against black. Above and beyond the beaches waited the guns the landing forces would face. There were two Navy coast defense batteries, the Batterie Railleuse and the Batterie des Passes. The former was located on the Pointe de la Tour, which jutted out into the Atlantic 2¾ miles northwest of Safi. Here, there were four 130-mm. guns on circular concrete emplacements, with a range of 19,000 yards. There was a fire control station with four 50-caliber antiaircraft machine guns.

The Batterie des Passes was about 2,000 yards north of Safi with two 75-mm. guns. Two miles south of the city was an Army battery of three 155-mm. guns.

In the garrison at Safi were 35 officers and 1,000 troops of the Foreign Legion and the Moroccan tirailleurs. Back of Safi, at Marrakech, within a five-hour march, was another garrison of between three and four hundred troops. And there were small forces at Mazagan to the north and at Mogador to the south of Safi.

Protection against the gun batteries at Safi would come from the Fire Support Group, which had taken its position around the transport area. The NEW YORK was in a position to fire on the Batterie Railleuse from the northwest while the PHILADELPHIA was on station both to support the fire of the NEW YORK and to get the range of the battery south of Safi. The destroyers MERVINE, BEATTY and KNIGHT had jockeyed into position for close-in fire on the beaches to support the landing troops.

The long, broad sea wall, or mole, jutting at right angles to Safi harbor with its cranes and unloading facilities made that port an important objective. The tanks on the transport LAKEHURST were too heavy to be unloaded through the surf. The ship would have to be laid against the sea wall so that the tanks could be hoisted ashore by the cranes.

So, of course, the sea wall and the port area immediately behind it had to be captured first, before the real landings could begin. And that was the job assigned to BERNADOU and COLE. They had been DDs at one time, old four-piper destroyers. Now with masts, stacks, and most of the superstructure cut off, riding low in the water, they were called APDs, assault personnel destroyers. Every man aboard had volunteered for this assignment without knowing what it was to be. All they had been told when they left Norfolk was that they were probably going on a "suicide lash-up." They were to come back with Presidential Unit Citations, and very few casualties.

The two ships were to enter the harbor thirty minutes before H-hour, to seize the sea wall and adjacent port facilities. Aboard BERNADOU were K and L Companies of the 47th Infantry, two hundred specially trained assault troops; on COLE was a contingent of naval personnel. Troops of BERNADOU were to occupy strategic points in the port, and the men on COLE were to seize the mole with its important cranes and unloading facilities, and to operate the machinery when the ships came alongside.

H-hour was 0400. A little before midnight the landing craft were swung over the sides of the transports, and the troops climbed down the nets into them. By 0345 the black water was filled with slowly circling, soldier-laden boats. Then, at a signal, the aquatic merry-go-round ceased. The landing craft fell into a long, narrow V formation and, following the wake and dumpy silhouette of the COLE, headed in toward the harbor. Ahead of COLE was BERNADOU, and the whole procession was led by a tiny scout boat in which rode Ensign John J. Bell, USNR, whose task it was to locate the traffic control point off the end of the mole, where BERNADOU and COLE would turn to enter the harbor, and from which the waves of landing craft would be directed to the two beaches north of the sea wall.

Back on the transports men gripped night glasses and watched. And on the fire-support ships men stood by their guns and waited. The first wave of invasion craft neared the end of the sea wall still undiscovered. Then at 0410, as the BERNADOU came cautiously around the mole, she was challenged by a flashing light. Her captain, Lieutenant Commander Braddy, replied with the same signal and the light died. There were a few minutes more of peace, and then the guns of Safi shattered any remaining hope of an invasion without resistance.

"As soon as they opened fire," said Lieutenant William R. Brewster, USN, the BERNADOU's gunnery officer, "Captain Braddy picked up the TBS and gave the signal 'Play Ball!' We started shooting; we opened up with everything we had, six 3-inch guns and five 20-mm. guns. The ship must have looked like the Fourth of July."

The metaphor is no exaggeration. Someone, back in the United States, had conceived a spectacularly graphic appeal to the French, an elaborate skyrocket that was supposed to burst into an aerial representation of the Stars and Stripes. Whether the dampness was to blame or the pyrotechnician had set himself too complicated a task, all that the rocket did when a chief petty officer touch it off was to make a polychrome glare which illuminated the ships and landing craft for the batteries. Probably this was the first use of the rocket in this war, even though its intent was not lethal. The incident is related here to end whatever doubt and confusion may still linger in the minds of those who were there, and wondered just what on earth (or in sky) the fireworks meant.

Within two minutes, the guns of the destroyer MERVINE were pumping salvos at the Batterie des Passes, but it so happened that one gun on the BERNADOU was trained almost directly on the battery when it opened fire. Taking a range on the gun flashes, 1,500 yards away, only a slight adjustment was necessary for the BERNADOU to register a direct hit. Within six minutes the battery was silenced.

The MERVINE then opened on the Batterie Railleuse, just as it revealed its position by shelling BERNADOU and COLE, now within the inner harbor. The NEW YORK and the PHILADELPHIA received the "Play Ball" signal and sent a smothering arch of salvos on the Batterie Railleuse. It was still dark. Aim could be taken only at the gun flashes that came from the crest of the 460-foot cliff. A lucky shell in the second salvo did the trick. It struck the ground on the crest of the cliff, about 50 feet in front of the battery control tower, ricocheted through the observation slot in the tower and completely demolished the range finder.

This temporarily silenced the battery and undoubtedly saved BERNADOU and COLE from severe damage. In the meantime, the landings were going according to plan. Firing as she went, BERNADOU continued to head for her target, Green Beach, at the land end of the mole. Machine-gun and rifle bullets splattered and ricocheted with shrill whines against her steel plates as she pushed toward the jetty. Two soldiers, expert grenadiers, were stationed on the fire-control platform, hurling their "pineapples" at every flash of gunfire along the pier. At 0445 the BERNADOU's bottom scraped sand. As she jolted to a stop, the assault troops of L and K Companies were over the side, swimming and wading to shore where they fanned out through the area.

Behind, the COLE with her naval landing party, had experienced some difficulty in finding her objective in the darkness, but Ensign Bell, in the scout boat, guided her in. She landed her force on Mercantile Dock shortly after BERNADOU's troops had gone over the side, capturing three small moored vessels and the giant cranes with little difficulty.

By 0640 ten waves of assault troops had landed on their beaches, and then, surprisingly, the guns of Batterie Railleuse suddenly opened fire again. The aim was bad. Six or eight shells fell far short of the NEW YORK, and those aimed at the PHILADELPHIA fell wide by a mile. Planes from the carrier SANTEE were overhead by 0700, to direct the cruiser fire, and the battery was permanently silenced in a few minutes by PHILADELPHIA's guns.

By 0920 troops had landed on Yahudi Beach, south of the tower, and by ten o'clock in the morning the Army, with the COLE's guns providing a barrage, captured the radio station at Safi. Troops were still coming ashore from the landing craft when shell splashes began to stipple the harbor. The source of this fire was found to be the French Army's 155s two miles south of Safi. The PHILADELPHIA moved into firing position and, with the aid of airplanes spotting, wiped out the well-camouflaged battery in three salvos. At 1130 the battery was in the possession of our Army troops. Thirty minutes later, Batterie Railleuse surrendered after destroying its guns. The last of the gun positions around Safi was silenced. The transports could now unload.

At two o'clock in the afternoon, LAKEHURST moved into the harbor and tied up along the sea wall, where the captured cranes unloaded the heavy tanks. An hour and a half later, TITANIA moored beside her and all the other transports edged in closer to the port. Behind the transports a double antisubmarine screen was established and planes from the SANTEE were patrolling as far as 60 miles off shore. Scout planes from the PHILADELPHIA had made reconnaissance flights inland as far as 25 miles, and reported 25 aircraft at Marrakech airfield.

By the end of D-day, Major General Harmon reported that the town of Safi had been taken, except for a few snipers, and that a beachhead of 5,000 yards was now safely in our hands.

Amphibious warfare had emerged from the Atlantic, certainly not yet full grown, but by its potency showing the Axis bitter promise of what the young giant would do as it grew in strength and experience.

On the morning of D-plus-one, November 9, warning was received from the Army of a possible 40-plane raid. All aircraft on the antisubmarine patrol were immediately launched for reconnaissance. Then a heavy fog bank settled in, covering Safi and the surrounding area. One attacking plane came through the overcast for a run on the LAKEHURST, still tied up at the dock. One bomb struck the pier, killing five men and wounding ten, and destroying two trucks and a light antiaircraft gun. The plane was shot down by the transport gunners.

Meantime a reconnaissance plane from the SANTEE dropped two bombs on the Marrakech airfield after having been fired on by the ground defenses. A flight of bombers and fighters was ordered launched from SANTEE to investigate a report that four two-motored bombers were on the Marrakech airfield with their engines turning, and to take appropriate action. The Army forces were getting ready to move north toward Casablanca. Those bombers could not be left to attack from the rear.

The carrier planes were scarcely airborne when the expected counterattack from the Marrakech garrison developed. A relief column of fourteen trucks was sighted on the road east of Bou Ghedra, 15 miles from Safi. At the urgent request of the Army three planes, already bound for Marrakech combat patrol, were diverted, located the truck column, and destroyed twelve of the troop-laden vehicles.

When the day's work was over, the SANTEE planes (all of which returned safely) reported the destruction or damage of forty vehicles between Safi and Marrakech, the destruction of twenty planes at Marrakech, and one hangar wrecked. The NEW YORK, with a destroyer screen of HOWARD and HAMILTON, and the tug CHEROKEE, then proceeded north to assist in the Fedala landings.

By November 10, the post-invasion let-down had begun. The last transports were finishing their unloading. The MERRIMACK had arrived and was refueling the destroyers. The PHILADELPHIA had gone out to the SANTEE, about 60 miles offshore, to refuel, which necessary and time-taking chore was enlivened by a submarine firing two torpedoes at extreme long range, which passed between the cruiser and her escort, the DORAN.

The planes from SANTEE were circling in patrol over the green and gray Moroccan land, keeping opposing truck trains and troop concentrations pinned down and the air free of enemy planes. One pilot reported downing a twin-engined bomber over Bou Ghedra, while another was shot down a few miles from Safi. One plane from the PHILADELPHIA reported dropping a bomb on a beached submarine at Cape Blanco. The DORAN, sent to investigate, returned to Safi with word that the submarine had been taken. It was the French MÉDUSE.

The PHILADELPHIA, escorted by COWIE and KNIGHT, steamed off to act as artillery for the Army in its advance on Mazagan, while the COLE, with six landing craft, sailed with fuel and supplies for the military column of tanks and trucks. The Navy's ships provided artillery support 10 miles deep, besides victuals and supplies for the advancing Army, in a combined land-sea operation unique in modern warfare at the time. Very early the next morning, November 11, the BERNADOU, loaded with more troops and supplies, left Safi for Mazagan.

At 0300 a dispatch had come in for Major General Harmon ordering him to be in a position to attack Casablanca by noon. Three hours later another signal was received that "Casablanca may capitulate within the next few hours." Fifteen minutes after this message arrived, Rear Admiral Hewitt sent the word "Cease Firing" to the forces surrounding that city. Then, a few minutes before nine o'clock, the Army radioed the naval Fire Support Group, "Stop bombing over Mazagan. No fight if no bombs."

As it proved, reconnaissance planes from SANTEE and PHILADELPHIA flying over Mazagan inspired the garrison to surrender without a shot. One of the Army's air liaison officers at Mazagan said, "Your airplanes arrived at the psychological moment and caused hasty precipitation of enemy resistance, which was threatening to become ugly. They gave up immediately. The credit for the surrender of Mazagan should be given to the SANTEE and her squadrons."

An hour later Major General Harmon received the surrender of Azimur and the forces posted at the bridges over the Oued Rebia to the tanks and mechanized force that had by-passed Mazagan and were on the open road that led to Casablanca.

Because the harbor at Safi was taken so quickly, the loss of small boats was extraordinarily light. Out of 121 landing craft used, only 9 were damaged. Eight of these were subsequently salvaged.

At 2348 that night the ships in the water off Safi received the message: "Hostilities in French Morocco have ceased. Be especially vigilant against Axis submarines."

Chapter Twenty-two

SIXTY-FIVE miles above Casablanca the Northern Attack Group had attacked Mehdia and Port Lyautey to form the other prong of the great pincer movement.

This group was commanded by Rear Admiral Monroe Kelly, USN, aboard his flagship USS TEXAS, which was part of the Fire Support Group consisting of the cruiser SAVANNAH (Captain Leon S. Fiske, USN) and destroyers.[1]

The Army Sub-Task Force [2] for this area was under the command of Brigadier General Lucian K. Truscott, Jr.

The destroyer DALLAS (Lieutenant Commander Robert Brodie, Jr., USN) had the special assignment to run up the Sebou River with the Ranger Detachment to Port Lyautey and its airfield. Also part of the flotilla were the oiler KENNEBEC (Commander Stewart S. Reynolds, USN), carrying two small fire-support craft equipped with rockets for shore bombardment, and the seaplane tender BARNEGAT, commanded by Commander Felix L. Baker, USN.

For the Northern Attack Group H-hour was also 0400 on November 8.

By midnight of November 7, all the ships of the group were in position off Mehdia. From their decks could be seen the twinkling chain of lights linking Rabat to Mehdia along the unsuspecting shore. At least four

[1] The destroyers were ROE (Lt. Comdr. Rathel L. Nolan, Jr., USN), KEARNY (Comdr. Adolph H. Oswold, USN), and ERICSSON (Lt. Comdr. William R. Headden, USN). The supporting screen was the destroyers LIVERMORE (Comdr. Vernon Huber, USN), EBERLE (Lt. Comdr. Karl F. Poehlman, USN), and PARKER (Lt. Comdr. John W. Bays, USN), and the minesweepers RAVEN (Lt. Comdr. Colby G. Rucker, USN) and OSPREY (Lt. Comdr. Cecil L. Blackwell, USN).

[2] This consisted of a Regimental Combat Team Reinforced, the 60th Infantry, 9th Division; a Ranger Detachment; one light armored battalion combat team, 2nd Armored Division. The total was 526 officers, 8,573 enlisted men and 65 light tanks.

The transports carrying these troops, equipment and supplies were USS ALGORAB, HENRY T. ALLEN, SUSAN B. ANTHONY, ANNE ARUNDEL, GEORGE CLYMER, ELECTRA, FLORENCE NIGHTINGALE, and JOHN PENN.

ships innocently passed the convoy, turning and disappearing in the direction of the Sebou River and Port Lyautey.

Port Lyautey airfield was nine miles up the shallow river. The city itself was two miles farther up the sluggish stream. The defense there would be slight, only some mobile artillery and antiaircraft guns. Stiffer resistance, if there was to be any, would come at the mouth of the river, at Mehdia, and from the stone fort on the heights commanding the river approaches. Mehdia lay nestled on the south bank of the river, her sea approach guarded by the Batterie Ponsot, with two 138.6-mm. guns overlooking all the sea approaches to the Sebou River within a range of 18,000 yards, and the Batterie des Passes, with two 75-mm. guns. South of the river's mouth, and behind the beach, stretched a long, marshy lagoon, a natural obstacle to infantry or tank operations.

Three landing points had been selected, one three miles below the mouth of the Sebou River and beyond the south tip of the lagoon, one four miles to the north of the river's mouth, and one close to the south side of the jetty at the mouth of the Sebou.

Shortly after midnight the troops began to leave the transports for landing craft. The sea was smooth under a cloudy sky. From the SUSAN B. ANTHONY the dark figures of the Army Ranger unit climbed into boats and were ferried to the DALLAS. With them was a member of the Free French Forces, René Malavergne, who was to steer the destroyer up the dark Sebou River. Before the war he had been a chief pilot on that river and knew every curve and channel.

The fire-support destroyers took their stations. The ROE went to the south of the river mouth, the KEARNY to the north, and the ERICSSON stood back in reserve. Somewhat behind schedule came the signal for the troops to go ashore.

Eighteen assault waves were crowding the beaches before the defenders of Mehdia realized all was not well. Discovery came when a searchlight stabbed out from the top of the fort back of Mehdia to illuminate the beach. A brief, brisk crackle of small-arms fire followed from the fort, Keeping in mind his instructions to avoid conflict if at all possible, Rear Admiral Kelly ordered the ROE to ignore this firing. Then, a few minutes later, EBERLE reported that a shore battery had flung one salvo at the landing boats. The destroyer was ordered to return the fire immediately.

It was six o'clock in the morning now. The beaches north and south of the river mouth had been taken by surprise and with practically no opposition. At the middle beach, just south of the jetty at the mouth of the Sebou, the reception was hotter, and some of the sharpest fighting of the entire campaign of occupation occurred in that African dawn.

Both SAVANNAH and TEXAS had planes in the air when the shore batteries opened on the ROE. The first salvo was short. The destroyer returned the fire from a range of 5,000 yards. In reply, three more salvos came from the shore, after which the battery was silent for ten minutes. Hopes were high in the American forces that the French troops had rebelled, but then firing recommenced, with the shells falling much closer. Once the ROE barely managed to reverse its course in time to avoid a hit.

While this ship-to-shore duel was under way, at about 0630, the TEXAS broadcast the first American Army communique in North Africa, separate proclamations by General Eisenhower, addressed to the French authorities and the French citizens in North Africa. The message to the Vichy-controlled authorities read:

> Here is a communication from the American General, Eisenhower, Commander in Chief of the forces now disembarking in French North Africa. This is one of the general staff officers who speaks to you. This communication, of the highest importance, is addressed to the French Armies on land, sea and air in North Africa:
>
> "Frenchmen of North Africa, the forces which I have the honor of commanding come to you as friends to make war against your enemies.
>
> "This is a military operation directed against the Italian-German military forces in North Africa. Our only objective is to defeat the enemy and to free France. I need not tell you that we have no designs either on North Africa or on any part of the French Empire. We count on your friendship, and we ask your aid.
>
> "I have given formal orders that no offensive action be undertaken against you on condition that you for your part take the same attitude.
>
> "To avoid any possible misunderstanding, make the following signals:
>
> "By day, fly the French tricolor and the American flag, one above the other. I repeat, by day, fly the French tricolor and the American flag, one above the other, or two, I repeat, two, tricolors, one above the other.
>
> "By night, turn on a searchlight and direct it vertically toward the sky. I repeat, by night, turn on a searchlight and direct it vertically toward the sky.

"Moreover, for reasons of military security, we are obliged to give you the following orders. Any refusal to follow them will be interpreted as proof of hostile intention on your part. Here are the orders:

" 'To all naval and merchant marine units: First, stay where you are. Secondly, make no attempt to scuttle your vessels.

" 'To Coast Guard Units: Withdraw from the neighborhood of your cannon and your stations.

" 'To Aviation Units: Do not take off. All airplanes must remain in their usual places.

" 'General Orders: In general you must obey all orders given to you by my officers.'

"We come, I repeat, as friends, not as enemies. We shall not be the first to fire. Follow exactly the orders which I have just given you. Thus you will avoid any possibility of a conflict, which could only be useful to our enemies. We summon you as comrades to the common fight against the invaders of France. The war has entered the phase of liberation."

The second proclamation was addressed to the people of North Africa. It read:

The President of the United States has asked me as commanding officer of the American Expeditionary Forces to convey to all the people in Morocco and in North Africa the following message:

"No nation is more closely bound by historic ties and deep affection to the people of France and their friends than the United States of America.

"Americans are striving not only for their own safe future, but also for the restoration of the ideals, the liberties, and the democracy of all those who have lived under the Tricolor.

"We come among you to save you from conquerors who would remove forever your rights of self-government, your rights to religious freedom, and your rights to live your own lives in peace.

"We come among you solely to destroy your enemies and not to harm you.

"We come among you with the assurance that we will leave just as soon as the menace of Germany and Italy is removed from you.

"I am appealing to your sense of realism, self-interest and ideals. Do not obstruct this great purpose.

"Help us and the day of a world peace will be hastened."

Despite this explanation, resistance continued. The Frenchmen manning guns and airplanes were probably not aware that the broadcast appeal had been made. They had their orders to resist, and, until those orders were rescinded, resist they would.

At 0710 the order "Play Ball" went to the ships of the Northern Attack Group, and a general offensive was on. Ten minutes later, landing craft were strafed by two planes. The KEARNY, ERICSSON and OSPREY opened fire. Eight more planes appeared, and Rear Admiral Kelly requested air support from our own forces. It came in a few minutes, twenty F4Fs from nearby carriers.

By ten o'clock in the morning the Army was holding the beachhead south of the river. The next objective of the troops here was the fort, in the Kasba, or native section, of Mehdia, which was keeping the river entrance and the ships under fire. By noon, troops had reached the lighthouse, south of the fort. They had taken advantage of a ridge that crossed the lagoon, charging over it and up to the base of the lighthouse with very few casualties.

The DALLAS, carrying the unit of Army Rangers destined for Port Lyautey, had been unable to get up the river because of the guns on the fort. The SAVANNAH would pump round after round of shells into the stone fortress and apparently silence its guns, but as soon as the DALLAS would approach the river mouth, the fort began firing again and the destroyer had to turn and head out. Sooner or later the trip would have to be made. The airfield at Port Lyautey had to be taken, and it was the task of DALLAS to get the Rangers close enough to do the job.

For four hours SAVANNAH continued to pump shells into the fort whose guns were sealing the river entrance; 892 rounds of 6-inch explosives and 236 rounds of 5-inch ammunition went into the walled stronghold before its guns were battered into silence. At the same time, the ancient TEXAS was doing what she could to hasten the fall of Port Lyautey by shelling its ammunition dumps, nine miles inland, with 14-inch bombardment shells.

Late in the afternoon, a group of about sixty Army troops succeeded in creeping from the lighthouse to the base of the fort. At sundown the ships took up their night positions and the unloading of the transports continued. The Navy awaited news from the Army ashore.

The news, when it came, was bad. November 9 opened with a strong counterattack by the defenders of Mehdia. The troops that had infiltrated to the base of the fort were captured, and the Army was back where it had started from. Then, a few minutes before 0800, news came from Navy spotters ashore that enemy tanks were approaching on the road from Rabat. Naval gunfire was ordered and the SAVANNAH started firing from the directions given by the spotter. Three tanks were struck, and the others scattered in retreat, and this first, most dangerous threat was turned back.

This incident marked the beginning of the citation-strewn saga of the naval gunfire liaison officers, whose specialty rapidly became recognized as saving the day. Sooner or later, in every invasion in the African-European Theater naval gunfire was called on to deliver the critical blows the Army needed to reduce tough prepared positions, break up troop concentrations, turn back tank thrusts. And it was the gunfire liaison officers—the "gun lazy boys"—working with the Army in advanced, exposed observation posts, who called the shots for the ships' big guns.

These ground-hugging sailors form one corner of the triangular Shore Fire Control Party, the other corners being an Army artillery spotter and the ships that do the shooting, the fire-support ships. In addition to spotting for naval fire, the "gun lazy" had to know Army artillery procedure and terminology; a forward observation post is not the safest place to be during an action, and if the Army spotter was incapacitated a Navy man had to take over his job, too.

In organization the fire-support arrangements usually call for an ensign to work with a combat team (a reduced battalion), a lieutenant (junior grade) with a regimental combat team (two or three cambat teams), and a lieutenant with a combat division. Training for these officers included a great deal of work in Army camps, where sailors are a novelty, to say the least. When the first officers showed up for training with paratroop divisions, their new colleagues in khaki happily invented the rumor that the Navy was training men to be dropped on enemy submarines.

Fifteen naval gunfire liaison officers were employed in the Moroccan landings; three landed at Safi, three at Mehdia, nine at Fedala. The trio at Mehdia and Port Lyautey was kept busiest. It was they who discovered the tanks crawling in to the attack from Rabat and called for bombardment from SAVANNAH, but the most effective teamwork was demonstrated later when a concentration of heavy French tanks attacked Brigadier General Truscott's lighter force.

The tank battle was fought a considerable distance from the Navy shore observation post, and what visibility existed at first was soon erased by dust and smoke. It was impossible to distinguish the outnumbered American tanks from the attackers. The Navy liaison officers radioed the situation to one of the fleet planes overhead and passed the ball to the pilot. The plane dived low over the tank concentration, identified the disposition of the vehicles and informed its cruiser of the position the attacking tanks occupied. The SAVANNAH's guns trained on the spot, and, as much to the surprise of the American forces as to the consternation of the Vichyites, a concentrated fire from an unknown source smashed the attack.

The surviving tanks wheeled and raced for cover. The accuracy of the cruiser's gunfire and the airplane's quick calculation are illustrated by the reports that show the opposing tank forces only 500 yards apart.

Sometime during the day, November 9, it was discovered that a net across the mouth of the Sebou River would keep the Ranger-bearing DALLAS from entering even with the guns from the fort silenced. The net had to be cut and the river entrance opened, for on this night the destroyer had to force the river for the attack on the airfield.

To a Navy crew from the transport GEORGE CLYMER was assigned the mission of going in after dark and cutting the cables that held the net. Guiding the small boat in through the darkness, with no light and with as little noise as possible, the coxswain eased up to the jetty. The crew started to work. The first cable was cut, and the net sagged. Then rifle and machine-gun fire from the south bank of the river told the men they had been discovered. While some of the crew answered the fire with carbines, others worked desperately on the remaining cables. Bullets whipped through the thin walls of the boat. The cable cutting went on. They could not leave until the net was down, even if they went down first. At last the final cable was cut and the net released. The coxswain shoved the leaking boat off, men took inventory. Not a man had been hit, although every man had missed death by inches. But the river was now ready for the DALLAS.

By this time everyone including the Ranger unit and the pilot, René Malavergne, who was now being referred to as the "Mark Twain of Morocco," was anxious to have a go at the river and get on with their part of the operation at Port Lyautey.

Pilot Malavergne soon had the chance to prove his skill and earn the admiration of everyone on the destroyer. He did both. The DALLAS nosed around the river jetties and into the passage. Not only was the water shallow, but the channel was narrow. Every inch of the way up the river, DALLAS was scraping bottom like a Mississippi catfish.

There was some excitement down in the engine room as the bridge called for more steam, more power and more speed. The instruments down there showed that the destroyer was then going 25 knots! The propellers were turning a 25-knot speed, but the actual progress up stream was only 5 knots. The ship was pushing through as much soft black mud as she was water. But the ship and the pilot were fighting that mud, and they won. The airfield of Port Lyautey, spread out beyond marshland, was almost in sight, but here at the turn of the river was an obstacle no one had counted on. Two river steamers lay scuttled on either side of the banks.

But the pilot made it. Her bottom scraping the mud and her flanks scraping paint, DALLAS passed between the scuttled ships, made the turn, and ran up to the airfield's landing dock. Over the side went the Rangers, but before the last man was on the dock, two 75-mm. guns, around the next bend of the river, opened fire. Shells fell within 30 feet of the DALLAS, and the destroyer whirled her 3-inch battery for return fire, when a plane from the SAVANNAH located the source of danger exactly and dropped two bombs with complete accuracy. Direct hits were scored on the guns and on their ammunition dump adjacent.

In a short time the Rangers signaled that they had occupied the Port Lyautey airfield.

Shortly after this airfield was occupied, the TEXAS received an Army request to bombard the road leading east from the city to Meknes, over which trucks and other military vehicles were moving out of the city. From 17,000 yards away, the TEXAS opened fire with her 14-inch guns; 214 rounds of bombardment ammunition into the road and surrounding country halted the exodus.

Then Rear Admiral Kelly substituted words for shells and directed them from TEXAS in a broadcast to the people of Port Lyautey.

He said:

> We have had to capture the fort at Mehdia. We have had to take your airfield at Port Lyautey. We have been forced to bombard the roads east of your city. We have had to bomb your trucks marching to reinforce you.
>
> These measures have been taken for only one reason: because your officials continue to oppose our purpose which is to assist in

restoring France to Frenchmen and to Frenchmen alone. Such was the promise of the President of the United States. This promise will be kept.

Why continue this unfortunate and useless resistance? You know that the United States because of its great power will not cease until it has broken the resistance of your chiefs.

Join with us. Stop this useless waste of lives and use them later in the fight against your real enemy—Germany.

The broadcast brought no response except continued gunfire. While the message was being sent, the first United States Army fighter planes were coming in to land at the Port Lyautey airfield, some of the seventy-seven P-40-Fs, ferried across the Atlantic on the Navy carrier CHENANGO. It was to supply these planes with fuel and parts, and to bring material for the early maintenance of the airfield, that the old steamer CONTESSA, with her jailbird crew, her tired boilers, her worn, rusty hull and her tough old fighting skipper had been pressed into service.

She lost her way, turned up at Safi, instead of Mehdia, a few hours before the southern landings were made. She was sent north, under escort of the destroyer COWIE to report to Admiral Kelly. The admiral ordered the CONTESSA to take her cargo of aviation gasoline and supplies up the Sebou River to the Port Lyautey airfield as soon as possible after its capture. When that word came, up she started, through the winding, narrow, mud-choked channel. She wasn't as hardy a ship as DALLAS. Her seams began to leak, and her plates dented from pushing against the bottom. But she crawled, butted and wormed her way within two miles of the airfield dock before she was stopped. There the ebb tide caught her, and swung the old tramp around until her bow was pointing downstream. Lighters were rushed down the river. The precious cargo was unloaded and towed to the airfield. Riding high, now, the old CONTESSA went downstream to deep water, her mission accomplished.

The last point of resistance was the thick-walled stone fort in the Kasba of Mehdia. By noon, troops had successfully surrounded it, and isolated it from the rest of the city, but there was still no surrender. A concentrated naval bombardment directed against this "Beau Geste" citadel was requested by Brigadier General Truscott. Between one and two o'clock in the afternoon of November 10, the SAVANNAH bombarded the gray stone walls.

A Naval gunfire liaison officer, Ensign John Perry, USNR, had landed with the assault troops on the beach just south of the river mouth. For two days he had made a foxhole-to-foxhole advance with the troops against the fort, fighting as an infantryman and, as a naval officer directing ship fire at the fort. The thick-walled fort was still absorbing the bombardment from sea and from the ground troops' 75-mm. howitzers. Then the liaison officer cocked an eye skyward, picked up his radiophone and said, "Can you help?"

He was talking to a patrol of dive bombers flying somewhere in the vicinity.

The answer was prompt. "Can do!"

Four minutes later they had dropped their 500-pound bombs. Troops waiting in the trenches around the gates charged the main gate with machine guns and grenades as the last bomb exploded, while Ensign Perry, with another group, went in to force a side portal. The gates opened and the defenders came out, Senegalese and Legionnaires. They tossed their side arms and weapons aside with one hand and reached for the offered American cigarettes with the other.

With the fall of the fort, Mehdia and Port Lyautey were secure. It had been a hard day of fighting for Army and Navy.

Ashore and on shipboard men rested and waited for what the next day would bring. It was the most hoped-for order that was issued at dawn by Brigadier General Truscott: "Cease Firing." Armistice negotiations had begun.

Word spread through the land. Throughout the day, pilots on patrol over the Meknes road reported that the French troops, when sighting an American plane, would wave in salute as the plane flew over.

A few minutes after ten o'clock that night the ships off Mehdia shared the instructions broadcast to the liberating forces: "Hostilities in French Morocco have ceased. Be especially vigilant against Axis submarines."

Chapter Twenty-three

WHILE landing forces were going ashore at Safi, to the south, and at Mehdia, in the north, the Center Attack Group,[1] larger than the other two combined forces, was striking at Fedala, a fortified seaside resort twelve miles north of Casablanca.

The Army's Sub-Task Force of the Center Attack Group was under the command of Major General Jonathan W. Anderson.[2] Its objective was to capture Fedala and then advance on Casablanca from the rear, joining with the converging forces coming up from the south and down from the north.

There were four defense batteries in the Fedala area, starting with the Batterie Fort Blondin, located at Chergui on the mouth of the Neffifkh River about three miles north of Fedala harbor, and mounting four 138.6-mm. guns. There was a second fortification called the Batterie du Port, located at the base of Cape Fedala, with two 100-mm. guns that had a clear sweep of the harbor area. Another, the Batterie des Passes, with two 75-mm. guns, guarded the tip of Cape Fedala, and there was an Army antiaircraft battery of four 75-mm. guns along the railroad tracks just south of the Fedala settlement.

As the transports swung into their anchorage area off Fedala a few hours before H-hour, the lookouts could see a light flashing in the distance.

---

[1] This group, commanded by Captain Robert M. Emmet, USN, consisted of transports LEONARD WOOD, ANCON, ARCTURUS, WILLIAM P. BIDDLE, TASKER H. BLISS, CHARLES CARROLL, JOSEPH T. DICKMAN, JOSEPH HEWES, THOMAS JEFFERSON, OBERON, PROCYON, EDWARD RUTLEDGE, HUGH L. SCOTT, ELIZABETH C. STANTON, and THURSTON, with a screen of destroyers and minesweepers: The USS WOOLSEY (Comdr. Bernard L. Austin, USN), EDISON (Lt. Comdr. William R. Headden, USN), BRISTOL (Lt. Comdr. John A. Glick, USN), BOYLE (Lt. Comdr. Eugene S. Karpe, USN), MURPHY (Lt. Comdr. Leonard W. Bailey, USN), TILLMAN (Capt. Francis D. McCorkle, USN), MIANTONOMAH (Comdr. Raymond D. Edwards, USN), HOGAN (Lt. Comdr. Ulysses S. G. Sharp, Jr., USN), PALMER (Lt. Comdr. Joshua W. Cooper, USN), STANSBURY (Lt. Comdr. Joseph B. Maher, USN) and USS AUK (Lt. Comdr. William D. Ryan, USNR).

[2] It comprised the 3rd Division (7th, 15th, and 30th Infantry Regiments reinforced); 3rd Armored Reconnaissance Battalion; 1st Battalion, 67th Armored Regiment; totaling 1,067 officers, 18,716 men and 77 light tanks.

It was the lighthouse on El Hank, a point of rocky land jutting out into the sea south of Casablanca. Across the water from the ships stretched six designated landing beaches, from the bathing cabanas of Fedala to the village of Mansuria.

Besides the light flashing at El Hank, navigation lights were curiously blinking through the night off Cape Fedala. No particular importance was placed on the lights. Perhaps nothing much could have been done about them, anyhow. Before H-hour, however, their reason for being was made very clear.

The LEONARD WOOD, the Transport Group flagship, led the other ships into the anchorage area and commenced unloading troops. Her scout boat joined those of the CHARLES CARROLL and JOSEPH T. DICKMAN and left for the shore to set up markers, and signals that would guide each landing craft coxswain to his particular beach.

And then, in the middle of this blacked-out activity, the reason for the navigation lights on Cape Fedala was suddenly revealed. Around the cape, heading straight for the transports and circling landing craft, steamed a French corvette escorting a small convoy of coastal steamers, lights shining like showboats, and seeming the brighter for the blackness in which the invasion forces labored.

This was a problem the book hadn't included. It might give the entire show away: H-hour was still distant. A blacked-out United States destroyer raced in to intercept the corvette, to divert the little convoy from the path of the assembling landing craft.

Unfortunately, the captain of the escort ship was a zealous young officer, a lieutenant who had his orders and was taking them with utmost seriousness. He refused to deviate from those orders, and ordered his corvette full speed ahead. As the ship surged forward a burst of machine-gun fire cut across the corvette's bow. The destroyer pulled up alongside and a boarding crew went over the side to the French ship. The burst of fire had killed the lieutenant and nine of his men, but the convoy had been stopped. The prize crew took over control of the corvette, rounded up the steamers and led the procession down the coast to an anchorage between Casablanca and Fedala to wait out H-hour.

Just before daylight the waves of landing craft started in. As the first wave came within sight of the dim African coastline, searchlights at Fort Blondin shot out over the slit of the Neffifkh River and settled their

beams on the incoming pattern of blunt-nosed landing craft. The support
vessels immediately opened fire on the searchlights. The leading assault
boats charged ahead and, churning into the mud and sand, dropped their
ramps on the beaches.

The invasion was under way.

Thirty minutes later the guns around the searchlights at Chergui and
from the batteries at Fedala opened a cross fire at the control boats and
the beaches. The challenge was picked up immediately, the destroyers
WILKES (Lieutenant Commander John B. McLean, USN) and SWANSON
(Lieutenant Commander Lewis M. Markham, Jr., USN) firing on
Fedala, and the MURPHY and LUDLOW (Lieutenant Commander Liles W.
Creighton, USN) training their guns on the battery at Chergui.

At 6020 the signal flashed out from Admiral Hewitt to "Play Ball"—
the general offensive was on. Five minutes after this message, the
BROOKLYN (Captain Francis C. Denebrink, USN), which was part of the
Fire Support Group, opened fire on Chergui as the MURPHY, struck by a
shell which penetrated to the engine room and started a fire, retired to
take her place in the outer screen to repair the damage. Rocket boats were
in close to shore now, adding the screaming, eerie fire of their new
ammunition.

By ten o'clock the shelling from the shore batteries stopped, and the
LEONARD WOOD, followed by the other transports, began moving in closer
to shore. Supplies and equipment from the transports moved smoothly to
the shore as the BROOKLYN stood guard to answer any fire that might be
directed against this traffic. There was no report of Army progress behind
the beaches, but it was assumed to be moving according to schedule
because there were only faint, sporadic bursts of machine-gun and
flurries of rifle fire from the defending positions.

Part of the unloading on the beaches was speeded up by an idea of
Ensign Stephen L. R. McNichols, USNR, whose boat crews, dead tired
after hours of driving their landing craft through gunfire and around
hidden reefs, were now tackling the job of ferrying tons of supplies from
transport to shore. McNichols had noticed that the most active people on
the beaches were the scores of Arabs who had appeared from nowhere
to beg cigarettes. A smoke, and an American one at that, was a superb
luxury. Moroccans had been rationed to thirty packs of cigarettes a year.
After some bargaining, McNichols organized a labor battalion from the
Arabs to unload the supplies from the landing craft at a fixed wage of one

cigarette an hour. The weary small-boat crews had a well-earned rest and the supplies were quickly unloaded.

At another beach, a chief boatswain's mate, Lloyd M. Morris, was acting as Beachmaster, the man who directs the traffic of supply boats coming from transport to shore. Two landing craft had been unloaded and were washed high and dry on the beach by the surf. The problem was how to get them off the beach, get them floating and back to the transports. This problem was still unsolved when planes came over on a bombing run. Morris shouted an order for his men to disperse and get clear of the landing craft, which offered a nice target for a bombardier. The men ran and a shower of bombs came hurtling down at the boats. After they passed, the men returned to count the damage. Not a man was injured. They turned to inspect the boats. Not only were they not damaged, but one bomb had fallen between the two craft, exploding a large crater in the sand that was quickly filling with water and floating the boats. In a few minutes, both landing craft were afloat. The coxswains jumped in, maneuvered easily out of the crater-lake and into the surf to return for more supplies.

During the bombardment the Army command called upon the French garrisons for surrender. The French commandant refused to receive an American emissary, evidently relying on the resistance of the French fleet in nearby Casablanca, which, without his knowledge, was then being slowly shelled and bombed into surrender. As a result, the commander of the Fedala garrison continued to press a delaying action.

But at 2:30 in the afternoon Fedala surrendered, being the most swiftly taken objective of the Moroccan campaign. Ashore, the troops were moving inland and south to Casablanca's rear, one infantry patrol cutting across the local golf course. At the end of the long, level fairway they saw an airplane, toward which a group of men were running desperately. Ordered to halt, the men made a show of resistance, and then, as the American rifles snapped into firing position, they started to resist, reconsidered and surrendered.

The ten men proved to be a catch worth bagging, the guard of the Nazi Military Armistice Commission in Fedala, four officers and six enlisted Wehrmacht men. War had come to their cozy quarters in Fedala so quickly that morning that their first warning was when one of the men looked pop-eyed out of a window and saw grim-faced American assault troops marching by.

The opposition offered by the fleet units at Casablanca had been anticipated and a battle plan was laid out accordingly with definite targets assigned to ships of the Covering Group [1] while the landings were taking place north at Fedala.

The MASSACHUSETTS was given the prime target of the area, the Point El Hank battery and the battleship JEAN BART, which, although not in commission, had 15-inch gun turrets that were in firing condition. The plan was to place MASSACHUSETTS in a position where she could fire at the JEAN BART, if it became necessary, from her forward turrets, and use the after turrets to bombard the guns at Point El Hank.

The TUSCALOOSA was given the job of riding herd on the submarines that nested in Casablanca harbor with the additional task of watching for cruisers and other craft that might attempt to leave the harbor after the Fedala landings began. The cruisers PHOENIX and WICHITA, the "Old Witch" who was veteran of Iceland and the North Atlantic, were to concentrate on the Point El Hank guns first, then shift to other targets as they became known.

The destroyers of the Covering Group were the watchdogs of the big ships, guarding against submarines, offering antiaircraft protection against bombers and torpedo planes, and ready to bombard shore batteries or any light vessel that offered opposition.

After the landing at Safi started, messages were intercepted indicating that the Southern Attack Group was meeting with fight. It seemed likely that Casablanca also would offer resistance. Scout planes were sent in on reconnaissance, and ran into antiaircraft fire and attack by enemy fighters. Then six hostile fighter planes flew into vision of the Fleet, coming in at about 1,200 feet. Flashing the order to fire, the MASSACHUSETTS turned her 5-inch forward battery on the planes, with every ship in the group training its antiaircraft guns in concert.

A few salvos were sufficient. One plane was shot down, another disappeared flying out of control; the others turned and streaked inland. But they had obtained what they wanted—firing data for Casablanca's big guns.

[1] This Covering Group, Rear Admiral Robert C. ("Ike") Giffen, USN, commanding, consisting of the battleship USS MASSACHUSETTS (Capt. Francis E. M. Whiting, USN), the cruisers TUSCALOOSA (Capt. Norman C. Gillette, USN) and WICHITA (Capt. Francis S. Low, USN), and the destroyers WAINWRIGHT (Lt. Comdr. Robert H. Gibbs, USN), MAYRANT (Lt. Comdr. Edward K. Walker, USN), RHIND (Comdr. Henry T. Read, USN), and JENKINS (Lt. Comdr. Harry F. Miller, USN) with the oiler CHEMUNG (Comdr. John L. Twomey, USN).

Before the smoke puffs from the last shrapnel burst melted, the long-range batteries on El Hank opened up. The first salvo straddled the MASSACHUSETTS. Then came bigger splashes. Ten miles away, a turret of 15-inch guns from the JEAN BART was canceling hope of peaceful landings. The answer was colorful, if not close. The JEAN BART was using dye-loaded shells, shells that would explode and color the splash a brilliant yellow, green or red. Some were close. One shell with a yellow splash landed so close to the AUGUSTA, aboard which Rear Admiral Hewitt and Major General Patton were, that a dye-filled geyser broke over the cruiser and deluged the chartroom, staining maps and papers ocher.

It was a strange, impersonal fight between the American ships and the JEAN BART and its landlocked supporters. A soft wind from the southwest furrowed the sea. Ten miles away shells were being hurled at the American ships, which were returning salvo for salvo, not through hate, but because duty demanded that the harbor had to be defended by the one side and entered by the other. Entry couldn't be made while guns protested. As the hot sun rose over the Atlas Mountains, beat down on the Moroccan desert, and its light reflected from the white walls of Casablanca and the sea before it, the attack became more difficult. All the advantages of sighting, aiming, and spotting were with the French, while the sun's glare and shimmering haze confused the spotters on the American ships.

From four minutes after 7 o'clock in the morning till twenty minutes of eight MASSACHUSETTS fired her main batteries at the JEAN BART from ranges of 14 to 17 miles, turning one turret to shoot at the El Hank battery. After the third salvo, spotting by air became difficult because of the smoke, antiaircraft fire and enemy fighters over the target. A system of indirect firing was started, using the El Hank lighthouse as a bearing. Before the spotting planes were driven from the area, however, they reported that the JEAN BART had received one hit, and two shells had struck the Môle du Commerce, the pier at which she was anchored. Fifteen minutes later, the JEAN BART's main battery ceased firing, although a smaller turret kept up an intermittent shelling.

In the meantime, the TUSCALOOSA had begun to send shells into the submarine berthing area of Casablanca harbor, pausing after a few rounds to shell the battery at Table d'Aukasha, up the coast from the harbor, for twenty minutes and silencing it.

The WICHITA fired first on El Hank, then joined TUSCALOOSA in shelling the submarine pens. Firing continued at these targets; orders were flashed to the two cruisers to concentrate on the harbor entrance. The planes had reported that the submarines were preparing to leave.

Instead, a group of destroyers moved slowly out of Casablanca harbor. Rear Admiral Hewitt ordered Rear Admiral Giffen of the Covering Group, and Rear Admiral Ernest D. McWhorter, USN, Commander of the Carrier Group, to intercept the destroyers.

The AUGUSTA and the BROOKLYN, with four destroyers, WILKES, SWANSON, LUDLOW and ROWAN (Lieutenant Commander Robert S. Ford, USN), steamed across the path of the approaching French ships. First fire came from the French destroyer MILAN which selected the WILKES as target. The shells fell short, and AUGUSTA and BROOKLYN opened up. The French destroyers reversed course in evasive action, then returned to attack. After a ten-minute duel the destroyers turned and headed back for Casablanca. On the way they were attacked by planes from the RANGER and by MASSACHUSETTS, WICHITA and TUSCALOOSA. The French destroyers gallantly returned all fire, and with excellent shooting. The MASSACHUSETTS was hit twice, with slight damage, and another shell passed through the ship's colors. The BROOKLYN was hit by a dud, which wounded six men.

But American aim and fire-power were superior. The MILAN, with three shell holes at the waterline, beached near Roches Noires. The destroyer FOUGUEUX took three salvos from the MASSACHUSETTS and sank. The destroyer BOULONNAIS's steering gear was crippled.

As the destroyer circled out of control the light cruiser PRIMAGUET was sighted leaving the harbor and heading out to aid the BOULONNAIS.

The French ships began to accumulate hits. The BOULONNAIS was engaged by AUGUSTA, and sank. The others turned back toward their harbor. The destroyer BRESTOIS, hit several times, began to list and was just able to make port where she turned and capsized off the Jetée Delure at midnight. The crippled FRONDEUR also was able to make port, down by the stern, but sank at her berth during the night. The PRIMAGUET and the destroyers ALBATROS and ALCYON managed to gain the harbor, from which they continued to fire.

It was still only eleven o'clock in the morning of D-day. The TUSCALOOSA, WICHITA and RHIND were ordered in at close quarters to engage the survivors. For forty minutes the opposing ships dueled at short range, during which time WICHITA was struck by a shell, injuring fourteen men.

But PRIMAGUET was badly damaged by five shells striking her below the waterline and an 8-inch shell bursting her number 3 turret. Her fight was finished. She crept into sheltered water of Roches Noires, where an airplane found her and demolished her decks forward of the stacks with bombs.

Soon after PRIMAGUET ran for cover, ALBATROS was hit by two shells, one below the waterline, and by two bombs amidships. Completely helpless, she was beached at Roches Noires. The only vessel to return to port intact was ALCYON.

Intermittent fire continued to be exchanged with the battery at El Hank. In the early afternoon, when news was received that Fedala had been captured, Major General Patton and his staff went ashore in a small boat to continue the operation from a land command post. Once established ashore, Major General Patton sent a demand, under flag of truce, for the surrender of Admiral Michelier, French commander of the Casablanca area. To make the trip from Fedala to Casablanca Admiralty Grounds, an American car that had belonged to the German Armistice Commission was "borrowed." The car was driven by Major Francis M. Rogers, USMCR, Rear Admiral Hewitt's representative, and the party included Colonel Hobart R. Gay, Chief of Staff to Major General Patton, Colonel William H. Wilbur, and a French lieutenant colonel of the 11th Algerian Tirailleurs. Although they flew a flag of truce, the party made part of their journey in darkness and drew considerable fire on their dash to Casablanca. Colonel Wilbur, who had landed with the first assault waves at Fedala, was awarded the Medal of Honor for his part in the general operation, and Major Rogers received the Silver Star. Their mission to Casablanca, however, was not a success.

Admiral Michelier refused the American delegation an audience, sending his aide to talk with the American party through the closed gates of Admiralty Grounds. As they were talking of surrender, the guns in the harbor behind them started to fire again. The aide made a broad Gallic gesture.

"That is your answer," he said. He saluted, turned smartly, and left.

So, Casablanca was to get more bombs, more shells, and troops at her back door before the capitulation came.

It was felt that the psychological effect of seeing their proud battleship pounded to scrap iron would hasten capitulation and convince Admiral Michelier of the futility of further resistance, so on the afternoon of November 10 nine dive bombers, armed with 1,000-pound bombs, took off from USS RANGER to destroy the JEAN BART. The attack was successful. When the planes finished there were two great craters of twisted steel fore and aft, spiraling coils of wire, cables and grotesque shapes of jagged iron, in the battleship below. Despite this damage, the ship's 15-inch gun turret and fire-control station were still serviceable.

The knockout blow, a combined land, sea and air attack on Casablanca, was planned for November 11. There was no significance in the anniversary of 1918. The ships of the bombardment units were on their way, and the planes of the Air Group were nearly over their objectives at Casablanca when Admiral Michelier requested a cessation of hostilities.

It took quick work to halt the attack. Frantic counterorders went out by radio, phone and visual signals to hold fire, that the operation was canceled. To the planes in the air went the message, "Urgent, urgent, urgent . . . cease firing in Casablanca area," and the bombers came back in formation, their bombs still in the racks. The patrols went up as usual, but the fighting was over.

That afternoon Admiral Michelier and Rear Admiral Hewitt met over a truce table to arrange the terms of an armistice. The terms imposed were not a conqueror's. The ships at Casablanca would continue to fly the French flag, would continue to be manned by French sailors, and would retain their guns and ammunition. The shore batteries would remain in French hands.

Capitulation of the French did not end hostilities in Morocco. Rear Admiral Hewitt's announcement of the end of French resistance closed with the warning: "Be especially vigilant against Axis submarines."

If the warning needed any emphasis, the Nazis soon supplied it. In two days submarines sank seven ships,[1] four off Fedala, the "easy" beach.

By November 17 most of the remaining transports had gathered under the command of Captain Robert M. Emmet, USN, for the return voyage to Hampton Roads, Virginia. Two days later, November 19, a naval operating base was established at Casablanca to be incorporated into the Moroccan Sea Frontier Forces.

The mission of the Western Task Force in Morocco was finished.

[1] The ships sunk were the transports JOSEPH HUGHES, HUGH L. SCOTT, EDWARD RUTLEDGE and TASKER H. BLISS. The oiler USS WINOOSKI (Comdr. John E. Murphy, USN), USS ELECTRA (AK 21) and the destroyer USS HAMBLETON (Comdr. Forrest Close, USN) were torpedoed but not sunk.

Chapter Twenty-four

THREE hours before the Western Task Force began sending its assault troops ashore at Safi, Mehdia and Fedala, the Inside Task Force was landing along the Mediterranean at Arzeu, Oran and Algiers.

These were the British and American First Army troops that had sailed from England with the Royal Navy, slipping through the Strait of Gibraltar under the very eyes of the German spotters in Spain's Tangier, on to their invasion rendezvous at 0100 on the morning of November 8, 1942.

The objective of the Inside Task Force was to occupy the major ports of Algeria, landing troops to join with the Army strength coming east from the Morocco landings for the overland campaign into Tunisia. There a junction with the British Eighth Army moving westward over Tripolitania would drive the last German and Italian soldier from North Africa.

This juncture was to be accomplished by a combined thrust at two points, one at Oran-Arzeu, the other at the city of Algiers. Rear Admiral Sir Harold M. Burroughs, RN, had naval command of the operation at Algiers, while Commodore Thomas Troubridge, RN, commanded for the Oran area. Their Army counterparts were Major General Charles W. Ryder, USA, and Major General Lloyd B. Fredendall, USA.

Well fortified and strongly defended, Oran, with a population of 200,000, was second in size only to Algiers of all the ports on the Barbary coast. Lying only 245 miles east of Gibraltar, it overlooks a narrow stretch of the Mediterranean where the nearest European headland is a slight hundred miles away. Possession of Oran by the Axis would have given them a strangle hold on Allied communications through the sea.

The main harbor of Oran was modern and well equipped, protected by a jetty extending parallel to the shore and divided into several basins formed by projecting wharves. Its entrance is from the northeast, through a narrow channel.

Three miles away, on the western horn of the crescent of which Oran is the center, is the small Arab town, Mers-el-Kebir. This western horn of the crescent is divided into a pronglike shape that forms a second harbor, the harbor of Mers-el-Kebir, a potentially excellent military anchorage which the French had been working for years in a desultory fashion to perfect.

Both harbors were well defended. The coast was laced with guns. East of Oran harbor entrance were two batteries. The first had two 75-mm. guns and the second was studded with four 120-mm. guns. Facing the harbor entrance itself at Cape Blanc was a battery of four 75-mm. guns plus several dual-purpose guns. And to the west of the town of Oran were four other batteries. There were four 75-mm. guns on the fort of Saint Gregario, 577 feet above the western water of the harbor, and two 95-mm. guns at Fort Lamoune on Point Mona. Still farther to the west of the harbor is Fort Santa Cruz, standing on the highest of the sea-washed cliffs that overlook the harbors. The dual-purpose guns on this thick stone fortress swung out over the shrine of "Notre Dame de Santa Cruz en Reconnaissance" below. Her statue, weatherpocked and head bowed, her hand held in benediction over the spreading city of Oran and the harbor beyond, stands gray against the light-blue African sky. To the west of the fort runs a flume-shaped valley where clouds blow down and swirl through the trees to melt against the hot rocks below the shrine. It was down this valley that the British planes had come on July 4, 1940, to bomb the French fleet in the harbor out of usefulness to the Germans.

Still farther around the harbor's edge 1,404 feet above the water is the Djebel Marabout where four 90-mms. plus a battery of dual-purpose guns dominated the bay. Around the horn at Mers-el-Kebir was a battery of two 75-mm. guns and four 75-mm. dual-purpose guns that faced south toward the anchorage. Only a few feet lower were the guns on Djebel Santo, a battery of four 194-mms. that could sweep the sea approaches with a wide range.

To contest this strength, Commodore Troubridge had a task force that consisted of:

    1 battleship—HMS RODNEY
    1 aircraft carrier—HMS FURIOUS
    2 auxiliary aircraft carriers—HMS BITER and DASHER
    1 antiaircraft ship—HMS DELHI

  1 auxiliary antiaircraft ship—HMS ALYNBANK
13 destroyers
  8 minesweepers
  2 sloops
  6 corvettes
  2 cutters (ex-U.S. Coast Guard)—HMS WALNEY and HARTLAND
  8 trawlers
15 landing ships, infantry
  5 personnel ships
23 motor transport ships
(These were in addition to the supporting units of the British Mediterranean Fleet.)

Major General Fredendall's Army units consisted of:

    1st Division
        16th Infantry Regimental Combat Team
        18th Infantry Regimental Combat Team
        26th Infantry Regimental Combat Team
      Combat Command B, 1st Armored Division
      2nd Battalion, 503rd Parachute Regiment
      1st Ranger Battalion

In all, there was a total of 39,000 officers and men poised for the assault on Oran and Arzeu.

From the ports, they would spread out to seize the nearby red-roofed buildings and hangars at La Senia airfield and push on through the flat acres of grapevines and wheatfields and beyond the salt marsh to the airfield at Tarafoui. Others would strike down the railroad that led from Oran to Algiers to occupy Orleansville, an important inland communications town 40 miles from the sea.

The landings were certain to be contested. In making the plans, therefore, a strategy was used similar to that employed in the Casablanca area where a landing in force was made at Fedala, the small port north of Casablanca, for an approach to the rear of the city.

For the approach by land to the rear of Oran, landings were planned for the small port of Arzeu, a small snug harbor on the eastern side of the Cape Ferrat promontory, 25 miles around the coast to the east of Oran. It lies just south of Djebel Sicioum, the mountain backbone of Cape Ferrat. On the east slope of Djebel Sicioum nestled Fort Supérieur with a battery of four guns. Down at Fort de la Pointe, where the harbor breakwater starts, was another battery of two 75-mm. guns.

Plans called for the assault on Arzeu to start with the landing of two companies of American Rangers near the breakwater battery on Fort de la Pointe at H-hour (0100), to seize the fort and beaches. Another advance party was to follow on signal into the harbor proper. In charge of the latter party was Captain Walter Ansel, USN. With him would be three other officers: Lieutenant Colonel Louis C. Plain, USMC; Lieutenant Commander Curtis B. Munson, USN, and Ensign Frank Olender, USN, with eleven Marine enlisted men.

The Ranger unit left first, moving silently through the darkness in their small boats toward the breakwater. At twenty-five minutes before H-hour, Captain Ansel's group left their transport, the ROYAL ULSTER-MAN, and started in toward the harbor in an LCA (Landing Craft Assault, a British landing craft), followed by the destroyer HMS CALPE which was to act as a support ship.

At the harbor entrance the LCA and the destroyer stopped. H-hour had passed, and Fort de la Pointe and the shore along the harbor south of that battery should be in the Rangers' hands. But no gunfire had been heard, no signal of success had been fired by the Ranger landing unit.

Captain Ansel decided to enter the harbor regardless. The little LCA nosed into Arzeu harbor and headed for the docks at the far end.

Somewhere between the third mole and the Grand Quai, the Rangers were heard in action. A burst of machine-gun fire echoed across the water. The helmsman of Captain Ansel's craft changed course sharply to avoid running into the line of fire and started back toward Mole 3. As he did so, a lookout reported that two ships could be seen, one next to Mole 3 and the other alongside the Grand Quai.

As Captain Ansel pondered the tactics, four brilliant rockets trailed up into the night sky. It was the success signal from the Rangers, indicating the raiders had finished their mission.

Captain Ansel at once gave the order to board the ships. The first was RICHEBOURG, the second PARME. Both ships were about 3,000 tons and their captains, when told the object of the boarding parties, and assured that the ships were now under protection of the United States, accepted the situation philosophically.

A third ship boarded was MEONIA, a Danish vessel that the French had only recently acquired. The Ranger units were informed that three ships were now available to confine prisoners, and presently the first lot arrived, scar-faced, eye-rolling Senegalese troops to be held until hostilities ended.

By daylight all ships in the harbor had been seized. But with daylight, French fire from the shore flared violently forth. Large-caliber rifle and machine-gun fire was especially heavy from the southern breakwater across the harbor and from the seaplane base back of the Jetée du Sud, reinforced by sniping from the high ground above the harbor. Two armed LCAs were unable to silence the fire from the jetty, so they laid down a smoke screen behind which the troops landed. Before the acrid smoke blanket drifted ashore, the soldiers had silenced the guns on the jetty and occupied the seaplane base. By 0745, the Rangers signaled they had consolidated all the Fort de la Pointe area and that all French naval personnel including the crew of a small patrol vessel were prisoner. With this news, all of Arzeu was promptly occupied in force by the 1st Division, which set up headquarters in the town as a base for the attack on Oran.

That was to be an infinitely more difficult operation.

Regardless of the progress of the Army troops approaching Oran from the rear from Arzeu, and without benefit of preliminary bombardment, two ships were to enter the harbor, all guns firing, sometime between H-hour and H-plus-two, to break the boom blocking the harbor and to knock out the guns on Cape Blanc and Point Mona.

It would not have been a small job for the largest of warships. It was a superhuman task for the two ships selected and, like most superhuman tasks, it failed. They were two small cutters, HMS WALNEY and HMS HARTLAND, which only the spring before had been the SEBAGO and the PONTCHARTRAIN, Lake class cutters of the United States Coast Guard, before being transferred to Great Britain under Lend-Lease.

At H-hour the small ships stood off Cape Ferrat's sandy tip. From the mast of each British cutter streamed the American flag, and from the signal hoists the British naval ensign. It was truly a combined-operations thrust, a British-American, Army-Navy jab into a harbor that had overwhelming ordnance.

Aboard the ships were five hundred United States combat troops. They were seasoned with a group of forty specially trained British sailors and twelve men who had perfected the fine art of demolition, plus thirty United States Navy engine-room men who had gone through the toughest kind of training in the cold, rocky harbors of Northern Scotland.

These ships and men were going into the harbor to capture the guns and men of Fort Lamoune and the battery on Cape Blanc, to capture and hold the wharves, and to board and hold the merchant ships in the harbor to prevent scuttling. That last was the particular job of the thirty United States Navy engine-room men, for one ship sunk in the right position would, for weeks, seal the harbor to the invasion ships waiting outside.

And these two ships were to go in alone, without support. There would be no cruisers and destroyers to back them up as there had been for BERNADOU and COLE at Safi. And, before either ship could enter the harbor, the boom at the entrance had to be broken. The old ex-Coast Guard cutter WALNEY drew this assignment, only instead of ice, this time she would be cutting the long, iron underwater gate placed there to keep ships out.

When they left Cape Ferrat for the approach to Oran harbor, the WALNEY was in the lead, followed by HARTLAND and two motor launches.

But before WALNEY was close enough to the harbor entrance to order steam for the full-speed charge against the boom, an alarm had been sounded in the city and a searchlight mounted high on the rocks struck through the darkness. Both ships turned and released a smoke trail to hide them from the light, and as they turned, the guns on the shore opened fire.

The firing stopped as the smoke screen settled down, and the little cutters turned again to enter the harbor, this time all hope of surprise gone. Full speed ahead was ordered. The WALNEY was on her way. Again the lights clamped talons of brilliance on the little ship while the guns from the shore sent round after round of hot steel at the vessel, which had been designed to withstand nothing tougher than Lake Erie ice. This time there was no turning back. Her bow was pointed straight at the harbor entrance. She struck the boom. There was a soft jar as the sharp prow touched the cables, a moment of labor against the steel's resistance. Then she was through. The cables parted. The boom was down, and WALNEY went in. She steamed the length of the harbor, past destroyers and a cruiser firing at her from almost point-blank range. Streams of tracer bullets from four destroyers and two surfaced submarines poured into her bridge and machine-gun fire sprayed the open decks like water from a garden hose.

Of eighteen men on WALNEY's bridge, only one survived. None was left alive on the quarter-deck. Yet the WALNEY reached her position. With her captain dead and decks ablaze she went ahead, and then, at her goal, she exploded, at a point close to where the French destroyer ÉPERVIER was moored.

The HARTLAND followed the WALNEY through the broken boom about 600 yards astern, but just as she passed through her main steampipe was cut by a shell. The French destroyer TYPHON had opened fire on her, but had stopped after a few salvos to avoid damaging the other French ships in line of fire. The shell that had cut the HARTLAND's steampipe had been a mortal hit.

The engine room was a caldron of cordite fumes mixed with live high-pressure steam. But HARTLAND's stokers, most of them boys in their teens, managed to keep a head of steam sufficient to drive the ship to a position west of the Môle de Ravin Blanc. Then she drifted, burning and out of control. Driven from below-decks by the fire that was rapidly gutting the ship, the troops and sailors stepped into the sweeping machine-gun fire from ships in the harbor and emplacements ashore. At 0410 the order was given to abandon ship. She burned for four more hours, then exploded and sank. Forty per cent of the men on HARTLAND were killed. Only two managed to get ashore with weapons. The survivors, about two hundred, almost every man wounded, were taken prisoner and released only when the city of Oran was captured on November 10.

The mission of keeping the ships in the harbor from being sabotaged and scuttled had failed. Three floating drydocks, three submarines and twenty-five other ships were put out of commission, before the British naval forces occupied the harbor. But it was one of those magnificent failures, like the fabulous charge of the Light Brigade, that outlives some victories. Meanwhile men, supplies and equipment were rolling up through the sandy beaches on the overland drive to Oran, as the transports discharged their human and mechanical freight at Les Andalouses, 12 miles west.

At 0328 HMS AURORA, patrolling in a 5-mile sweep out from Oran, shot out the searchlight that was betraying the movements of the task force. With that, the French destroyer TRAMONTANE sortied and, after a short engagement with AURORA, burst into flames and began to sink. Two other destroyers, TORNADE and TYPHON, and an escort ship, SUR-PRISE, steamed out to the burning TRAMONTANE on a rescue mission. The British warships held their fire, but suddenly the French destroyers opened fire on HMS CALPE and BOADICEA and fired a torpedo at AURORA. The BOADICEA was struck well forward by the shell, and a running fight began. The SURPRISE was hit, and sank. The TORNADE was struck by a broadside and headed blazing for the shore. The third ship, TYPHON, was struck by a shell on the stern and turned back to Oran harbor, breaking off the engagement at 0727, one minute shy of four hours after AURORA's guns first spoke.

For the rest of D-day, the support ships, including the battleship RODNEY, were busy with intermittent duels with the shore batteries at Mers-el-Kebir and Djebel Santo, but by dusk Oran was gripped in the pincers of troops and tanks from the landings at Arzeu and Les Andalouses. The airfields at Tarafoui and La Senia were in Allied hands.

Next day, November 9, an increasingly heavy surf added its opposition to the landings. The loss of the small boats became a serious element of attrition besides delaying the debarkation of troops, tanks and munitions. The French destroyers ÉPERVIER and TYPHON made another dash from the harbor. HMS AURORA, which had driven them into hiding the previous day, closed in for the engagement, joined by HMS JAMAICA, but the TYPHON was successfully beached near the harbor, blocking the entrance. The breaking of the boom was nullified. The burning ÉPERVIER drifted ashore south of Pointe de l'Aiguille.

As the troops neared the city, resistance stiffened but by nightfall of D-plus-one, troops were seven miles east and three miles west of their objective, Oran.

The final assault was planned for November 10. The morning started with heavy shore bombardment by HMS RODNEY. At a few minutes past two o'clock in the afternoon word was flashed that armistice negotiations were under way, and all firing ceased.

In a few short hours American tanks were rumbling down the dusty streets of Oran and plans had been started to clear the harbor below of the black-bottomed ships lying on their sides.

Chapter Twenty-five

THE harbor-city of Algiers was the most important objective of the entire North African campaign. It was important politically as well as militarily. Its occupation by Allied forces would inevitably affect the feeling in Europe and its position on the Mediterranean was of great strategic value.

The city itself lies white and sprawling on hillsides that run down to the half-moon harbor and bay that arches from Pointe Pescade on the west to Cape Matifou on the east. The hills of the city had been well fortified and in the face of strong resistance its capture would be a major operation.

The plan for the landings here was to put troops ashore on both sides of the city. To the west, they would land at Sidi Ferruch, a favorite bathing beach for Algerians and a smooth invasion shore. To the east, they would land on beaches around the tip of Cape Matifou.

The American troops who would make the landings were under the command of Major General Charles W. Ryder, USA. The Naval Task Force [1] for the Algiers landings was under the command of Rear Admiral Sir Harold M. Burroughs, RN.

[1] It consisted of the following strength:
   4 cruisers—HMS SHEFFIELD, BERMUDA, SCYLLA and CHARYBDIS
   1 aircraft carrier—HMS ARGUS
   3 auxiliary aircraft carriers—HMS POLOMARES, POZARICA and TYNWALD
   1 monitor—HMS ROBERTS
  13 destroyers
   7 minesweepers
   3 sloops
   7 corvettes
   8 trawlers
   6 LSIs
   5 personnel ships
  16 motor transport ships
   In addition there was a transport division of five American ships in command of Capt. Campbell D. Edgar, USN. Three were troop transports, which started out from the Clyde and passed through the Pillars of Hercules into the Mediterranean. Com. Roger C. Heimer, USCG, had command of the SAMUEL CHASE; Capt. Olton R. Bennehoff, USN, had the THOMAS STONE, and Lt. Comdr. Duncan Cook, USNR, was captain of the LEEDSTOWN, and there were two cargo ships.

On the morning of the day before D-day a torpedo explosion tore out the stern of the transport THOMAS STONE, wrecking her rudder and propeller. She was left behind while the rest of the convoy sailed on for Algiers.

The American transports were to unload on the four beaches lying east of Algiers, around Cape Matifou. They reached their anchorage off these beaches shortly aften ten o'clock on the night of November 7. In an hour the small assault boats were loaded, waiting for the signal to go in. The first wave left the SAMUEL CHASE and was on the beach fifteen minutes after H-hour. On the way in, a searchlight from the shore began to sweep seaward and the guns of Algiers began to fire. This was answered by the screen of destroyers, and intermittent firing continued well on through the early hours of the morning.

After the first wave landed, the transports moved to within a mile of shore in preparation for the unloading of equipment.

The fighting in Algiers at no time reached the intensity that it had in the other areas. The airfield at Sidi Ferruch was occupied by American troops at three o'clock in the morning, two hours after H-hour, and the large airfield at Maison Blanche, west of Algiers, was taken at 8:30 on the same morning. Within twelve hours the Army had occupied the high ground two miles west of Algiers and had also taken Blida airfield that nestled against the mountains to the south.

Two shore batteries, one at Cape Matifou and the other at Fort d'Estrées, offered stubborn resistance. But after a severe bombardment by the cruiser HMS BERMUDA their shelling of the beaches stopped.

The only serious resistance met by the Algiers task force came from German planes at 5:30 in the afternoon, just when the weather also had seemed to turn against the landing operations with a strong wind and high surf. The LEEDSTOWN was the only vessel hit. Already French artillery on the shore was silent and the Allied troops were standing by their guns as the opposing forces parleyed under a white flag. By seven o'clock in the evening the armistice was arranged and the occupation of Algiers had begun.

German air attacks continued through November 9 and 10.

The German attack against the transport LEEDSTOWN was well planned and successful. The formation of planes that came over the transport anchorage were Heinkel bombers and torpedo-carrying Ju-88's. One Ju-88 came over from LEEDSTOWN's starboard quarter to port quarter flying 50 feet high. While this plane was being shot down, another came at low altitude directly astern and launched two torpedoes. One struck the transport in the steering engine room, flooding number 6 hold. Nevertheless, unloading was continued.

During the night the weather grew worse. It was impossible to continue the unloading under these combined obstacles of wind and damage. Then at 12:55 bombs from two enemy planes straddled the transport. Fifteen minutes later two torpedoes smashed with terrific force into LEEDSTOWN's midships, and she began settling by the bow with a sharp starboard list. It was then that her captain, Lieutenant Commander Duncan Cook, gave the order to abandon ship. HMS SAMPHIRE stood by to take off casualties, while the rest of the crew launched rafts.

The men in the rafts were lucky on two counts: first, that the wind was blowing from the LEEDSTOWN straight to the beach that led up to Ain Taya; second, in the fact that on the beach was a member of the United States Navy Shore Party, Chief Boatswain's Mate Hunter Wood, whose job it was to direct the traffic of incoming jeeps, ammunition, food and medical equipment. He had seen the LEEDSTOWN shudder under the impact of the last two torpedoes and had watched the men go overboard on the rafts, and he saw that the wind was blowing them toward his beach. He also saw, what the men in the boats couldn't see, how rough and pounding the surf was where they were going to land.

"I saw the rafts drifting toward my beach," Hunter Wood recalls, "and the sea by this time was very heavy, and there was a very, very strong undertow from the beach. I sent what men I had with me out along the beach over into the rocky section at both ends. There were very few sandy stretches there where a raft could come in. However, it seemed more or less good luck, or the fates, that brought the sailors from the LEEDSTOWN in there. The majority of those rafts managed to get right in the sandy area. The wind blew them on a straight line from the stern of the LEEDSTOWN to the town of Ain Taya where we were. As they came in on the rafts, the sailors were singing, trying to keep up their morale, I guess. But they didn't realize how treacherous the surf was. It never looks as large from the seaward as it really is.

"As they came near, we took off our clothes and went out in the surf with small lines as far as we dared to go. We sang out to the sailors to get out of their rafts and hang on to the sides. Some of them heard, some of them didn't. Then the rafts came in and capsized in the surf. The terrific look of shock and strain on the faces of the sailors as they came in after having been bombed and torpedoed and then taking that additional abuse . . . !

"They were floating around in the water, face down, in their kapok jackets, more or less unconscious. Some of the rafts, when they capsized, came down on top of the men. Others were struck by the rafts that were being carried back out to sea by the undertow.

"Everyone worked until nearly exhausted. Even the Arabs from Ain Taya helped. They would cut large reeds, about fifteen feet long, and wade out into the surf, holding them for the men to grab and then pull them ashore.

"And the soldiers were helping, too. The beach was quite a scene of activity, I should say, for two and a half or three hours."

When the men from the LEEDSTOWN were taken from the water, they were carried back to an old theater in Ain Taya, where the floor had been covered with a thick mattress of straw. They lay shivering and cold while the French people of the village rushed brandy and wine down and brought shoes and warm clothes.

That night the men heard a loud explosion. It was the LEEDSTOWN blowing up just before she sank.

It was on the morning of November 9 that the troops of the wounded THOMAS STONE saw the white buildings of Algiers for the first time. They were too late to invade, but they brought with them an adventure story that has become an Amphibious Force legend by this time.

When their ship was torpedoed on the morning of November 7, they were a good 160 miles from Algiers, with H-hour less than twenty-four hours away and their convoy disappearing in the distance. Of all the troops on the three transports, the men on the THOMAS STONE had received the most training for an amphibious landing.

Because of this, Captain Olton R. Bennehoff made his decision. He talked with the Army officer commanding the troops, Major Walter M. Oates, who added his approval—approval of a daring plan: to launch the ship's boats there, 160 miles from their beaches, so that the troops could participate in the capture of Algiers. There would be eight hundred men in a tiny armada of twenty-eight landing craft, escorted by the British corvette HMS SPEY.

It was seven o'clock that evening when they left, with Lieutenant (jg)

Ralph C. Marler, USNR, in charge of the small boats. No stranger
armada had been seen in those seas since the Phoenicians' time.

The little boats started out at a speed of better than 8 knots, which
soon proved too stiff for them, and was reduced to 6 knots. Two hours
later an engine in one of the boats broke down. Twenty-seven craft and
HMS SPEY went slowly on their way while repairs were made. The engine was fixed and the boat caught up with the others an hour and a half
later. By this time two more boats had stopped with engine trouble and
it was then 9:30 in the evening, three hours and thirty minutes until
H-hour would be signaled 145 miles away.

From this time on, there was never a period of thirty minutes in
which all boats were able to move at the same time. And every time a
boat stopped, it had to be towed until repaired.

Then the captain of the SPEY told Lieutenant Marler that he had
just received orders to return to the THOMAS STONE. Marler and Major
Oates held a hurried conference on whether to take their small boats the
rest of the way without escort, and reluctantly decided that with the
trouble they had been having, it was doubtful if the little fleet could make
shore safely. The SPEY's captain received another set of orders an hour
later, this time giving him a choice, take the little fleet back to the
transport or on to Algiers. The decision was to be theirs. Lieutenant
Marler promptly chose the road to Algiers.

The boats had left the crippled transport in calm seas in a quartering
wind. Toward midnight the wind was blowing half a gale and heavy seas
were running head-on. Two of the craft collided. Marler ordered the
occupants of the damaged boat shifted to the SPEY and the craft scuttled.

Still hard luck dogged the brave little flotilla, although all hope of
being on the Algerian beach at H-hour had vanished. Now the only concern was to get the eight hundred troops and the boats' crews to safety.
One by one, as the boats broke down, they were scuttled and their occupants transferred to the corvette. At last the amphibious fleet was reduced
to seven, all shipping water, none with a compass in working order, and
every man aboard drenched, shivering and seasick.

It was decided in a conference aboard the SPEY, which was rendered
more gloomy by radio reports that the landings at Algiers had been accomplished, to scuttle all but two support boats, which would be towed, and
transfer all troops to the corvette. During the morning one of the two boats
broke loose, and an hour was lost in recovering the craft and repairing

the lines. The SPEY's commander told Marler that, if a similar break happened again, he would not stop for recovery. By now the whole world knew that the invasion was under way, and submarines were undoubtedly heading in for Algiers. Marler and Oates agreed without argument.

A few minutes later one towline snapped. An hour afterward the other boat went adrift. This left Major Oates with just the one lifeboat of the SPEY to put his eight hundred troops ashore, and no facilities for rescue should the storm-slowed corvette be torpedoed.

But at 10:30 that night the lights of Algiers were sighted ahead, and at eleven o'clock the SPEY received orders to anchor until morning. Algiers had surrendered and the harbor would be free to enter at daylight. At seven in the morning of November 9, the SPEY berthed alongside the long concrete quay that had accommodated so many tourists on peacetime cruises, and the troops and sailormen walked ingloriously down the gangplank, all their suffering and hardship in vain.

Many of the men wondered what had become of the THOMAS STONE. Two days later she was hauled into harbor by HMS WISHART and a Royal Navy tug, ST. DAY, which had put out from Gibraltar to rescue the transport and its cargo of machines and munitions.

Her propeller shaft was broken, her steering gear knocked loose from its foundation, and all her electrical equipment, diesel engines and pumps were dead and corroded by a 4-day salt-water bath. The fact that she was still afloat was due only to the superb seamanship of her captain and crew and the skillful aid of the British ships which had brought her to port.

When the news that the THOMAS STONE had reached Algiers came to Admiral Burroughs, he sent the following message:

"My warmest congratulations on the splendid effort put up by the USS THOMAS STONE. The determination to take part in this operation, whatever the obstacle, is an example to us all."

The congratulations took all the sting out of the anticlimax.

After the armistice of Algiers was signed, facilities for unloading the transports were plentiful. Friendly relations were soon established with the French authorities and the occupation of the surrounding country was started. At dawn on the morning of November 11, the 36th Infantry Brigade landed at Bougie without opposition.

The advance on Tunis was under way.

And plans for the invasion of Sicily were already on paper.

And so the Amphibious Force had met its first test successfully;

landed troops in the face of enemy fire, landed enough supplies to keep them going. But neither Army nor Navy was wholly satisfied, and the battle reports on the operation indicate that dissatisfaction plainly enough; combat loading was still not properly understood, communications still weren't operating smoothly, small boats weren't able to handle freight in the high surf. More training, more planning, newer techniques were called for by all levels of command. For the success in North Africa made two things clear: the job could be done, and with that fact established, it had to be done better, if Germany was to be driven inland in Europe.

The battle reports went back to Washington, to the Army and Navy commands concerned. The transports returned to the United States to resume routine ferry work to England and now to Africa. Most of the small boats and their crews came back to Little Creek for further training. But some remained in Africa to serve in unloading Liberty ships, to carry Guard Mail, to transport Army engineering and Navy salvage parties in the ruined harbors; in short, to do the hundred and one arduous tasks that remain after a successful assault. This is a point to remember: while the assault phase of an operation may be completed in a day or two, the mopping-up process requires that men and craft remain on the job for months after the fighting has passed into other theaters, clearing harbors, landing cargoes and troops.

After *Operation Torch,* the Amphibious Force in North Africa actually expanded, despite the return of the transports and most of the small boats. The larger landing craft, the LSTs, LCIs and LCTs, which had still been building when the African task force sailed under Rear Admiral Hewitt, were ready to leave the States late in January, 1943.

The LSTs, each bearing an LCT on her deck, shoved off for Oran and Algiers at the rate of one convoy a fortnight beginning in late February. It was not a good time for making an Atlantic passage; enemy submarines were active, and winter was the weather for them. However, all the ships got through safely.

LCI Flotilla 1, under command of Captain Lorenzo S. Sabin, USN, cleared Cape Henry, bound for Bermuda on February 15 in a convoy that also included a group of British LCIs and a flotilla of LSTs.

The voyage demonstrated that the new and untried ships would be able to stand up against the roughest kind of weather in Neptune's bag of tricks. The "spitkits," as they soon were called (after the tin can ash trays secured to ships' life rails), sailed through snow, rain, sleet and fog in high seas and calm, in temperatures that shifted from 6 below zero to 75 above, Fahrenheit, in thirty-six hours.

They broke down, did the spitkits, but never for long or for serious defects. It was not a pleasure cruise. It took twenty days for the convoy to reach Gibraltar, and eighteen of them were conspicuous for foul weather. All hands were seasick, but the logs show that not a watch was missed. Perhaps the men realized that the only way the voyage could be concluded in minimum time was for all hands to work zealously. It was not only tortured and rebellious stomachs for which surcease was sought, but relief from worry about submarines. The rumor had spread, too, that from anything above 1,000 feet in the air, an LCI looked to an aviator exactly like a submarine.

The layover at Gibraltar was pleasantly uneventful. The Rock apes were dutifully observed, as were the cinemas, souvenir shops and taverns of Main Street, and then the flotilla headed for Arzeu on the African coast of the Mediterranean, east of Oran. There the crews spent weeks in joint maneuvers with Army troops, forging a fighting team truly amphibious, before moving closer to the front. Flotilla 1 arrived at Bizerte the day in May that stronghold surrendered. The craft anchored off the jetty, happily unaware they were in mined waters until made grimly conscious of their peril when an aviation crash boat blew up in their midst.

In less than forty-eight hours the men had their first opportunity to "fire their guns in anger." Enemy planes appeared overhead, and the boys of Flotilla 1 fired with an enthusiasm that considerably exceeded their accuracy. Long after the order to cease firing had been given, some of the gun crews were still prone to fire bursts at seagulls and sometimes nothing more substantial than imagination.

No enemy planes were shot down, but it is also certain that none lingered in the vicinity.

The first successful antiaircraft work by the new amphibious vessels was done by LCT 33. This craft, commanded by Ensign J. A. Anderson, USNR, was returning one morning to her base at Arzeu after a routine ferrying mission to Tenez on April 20, when she was attacked in broad daylight by a German bomber. It's a question which of the combatants was the more surprised; Anderson, on the con of his craft first noticed the German when she came out of the morning haze about a thousand yards off his starboard quarter. He wasn't even sure it was an enemy plane until it flashed over him and he saw the bomb bay doors swing open. A moment later two geysers sprung out of the sea off his port bow. The enemy plane made a sweeping turn, almost majestic in its deliberation, and started its second run. By this time the 33 had her guns manned. They had never been fired before, because the 33 had been in commission only eleven days and working hard at routine chores all the time. The Nazi, who probably had never seen or heard of an LCT before, took his time getting set for his second run on this new, fat, and apparently unprotected target. Then he came roaring in, from almost dead astern this time. The novice gunners held the fire of their 20-mms. like veterans, until the big Junkers was a scant 500 yards away. Then they opened up.

That was the Nazi's first and last view of an LCT. The gunners pumped 105 rounds in his immediate vicinity ("At least half of them hits," said Ensign Anderson proudly) and the big bomber cartwheeled into the sea.

This victory did a lot for the morale of the Amphibious Force in Africa. The men had become part of the fighting Navy. They packed a punch. Their main punch, of course, would always be the men and equipment they carried for the Army, but none the less it did everyone good to know they could slug it out with the enemy when they had to. They were soon to have more chances for *Operation Husky,* the invasion of Sicily, was set for sixty days after the fall of the Germans in North Africa. And Rommel's army was crumbling fast.

The Amphibious Force helped the process. LSTs, with LCTs in sections on their decks, sailed in a steady stream to Bizerte, Oran and Arzeu. There the LCTs were unloaded, welded together, commissioned, and sent off with cargoes which had been in the very LSTs they had traveled on. Between these jobs the LCTs joined with the rest of the landing craft in practice exercises.

The last battered German and Italian regiments, hammered and harried for two months, gave up on Cape Bône in May. That meant, according to the Casablanca Agreement, that the invasion of Sicily would take place sometime in July. The High Command set the date as the 10th.

PART FIVE

The Mediterranean—Sicily, Salerno, Anzio

Chapter Twenty-six

THERE was much talk about "the soft underbelly of Europe" long before the invasion of Sicily was begun. No illusion of vulnerability dictated the thrust, however. Preparations were made for a tough and bloody course of war, with the realization that, while the disaffected Italians were sure to collapse under the blow, the Nazis would fight stubbornly and bitterly. The Italian nation was disgruntled with its own government, shaken by the reverses in Africa, unhappy with the swaggering Germans in its midst. Italy was, in short, poised for the knockout. There were other considerations, besides the desirability of knocking out the Axis' weak sister, that prompted the Anglo-American strategy. There was a good chance of trapping a substantial German army in southern Italy, besides the certainty of tying up many German divisions, both of which accomplishments would relieve the Nazi pressure on the Soviet front, and keep that many more enemy troops from the defense of occupied France. Control of Sicily would mean, also, control of the Mediterranean and insurance of the shortest supply line from Britain and the United States to India and China.

In broad terms, the attack against Sicily was to be made by two task forces. The American strength, the Western Task Force, would land on the southeast coast of the island, while the British Eastern Task Force would land on the extreme southeast tip and around on the eastern side of the island.

Once ashore, the United States Army's mission was to secure the left flank of the operation from enemy resistance, while the center and right flanks drove toward the central highlands of Sicily, which dominate the valleys and approaches. At this point, the American Army was to make contact with the British Army, which, after securing all the eastern coast and ports, was to move inland.

The plan was designed to sever the island from its mainland connections and force it to fall of its own weight.

229

Allied military intelligence reports had estimated enemy strength on Sicily at four, possibly five, first-line Italian divisions, as well as five Coastal Defense divisions. It was believed that the Germans had the equivalent of two divisions in Sicily and two more in South Italy.

The Sicilian airfields and their defenses were manned largely by German Air Force personnel, estimated at some 24,000 men. Altogether, the enemy's defense of the island rested in the hands of the Italian Sixth Army commander and 345,000 men, plus an estimated 1,200 aircraft.

The strongest concentration of defense was known to be centered in the northwest and center of Sicily. The enemy apparently did not consider that a large-scale amphibious assault could or would be attempted on the east and southeast coasts. His conclusions were based on the eminently true evidence that the prime objectives and best landing areas lay elsewhere. The assault was planned according to the cardinal principle of warfare—strike where the enemy least expects it, or, "Hit 'em where they ain't."

Vice-Admiral Henry K. Hewitt, USN, was to command the naval strength of the Western Task Force, the American portion of the over-all naval command of Admiral Cunningham. Aboard the flagship would also be Lieutenant General George S. Patton, Jr., Commander of the Western Task Force Army troops.

Under Vice-Admiral Hewitt were three main attack forces. Each force was given a code name. The one whose landing position would be on the left flank of the beach area was called the *Joss* Attack Force, under the Commander Landing Craft and Bases, Northwest African Waters, Rear Admiral Richard L. Conolly, USN. His flagship was also carrying Major General Lucien Truscott, Commander of the 3rd Division, which would land in the *Joss* area, its first objective being the port and airfield at Licata.

The group that would strike the center of the beach area, the 1st Division, was *Dime* Attack Force, under the Commander Amphibious Force, Northwest African Waters, Rear Admiral John L. Hall, Jr., USN. Aboard the *Dime* flagship was to be Major General Terry Allen, commanding the 1st Division, whose initial objective was the capture of Gela and the airfield at Ponte Olivo.

On the right flank was the *Cent* Attack Force, under the Commander Sixth Amphibious Force, Rear Admiral Alan G. Kirk, USN, whose flagship was USS ANCON (Captain Paul L. Mather, USN). The *Cent* Force would land the 45th Division troops under the command of Major General Troy H. Middleton. The objective of this force was to capture Scoglitti and the airfields of Comiso and Biscari, and extend the beachhead to join forces with the British.

In addition, there were to be minesweeping and minelaying groups, destroyer divisions and squadrons, light cruisers and destroyers for shore bombardment prior to troop landings, PT squadrons, smaller auxiliary patrol craft and landing craft, all of whose duties were to be written into the *Husky* Naval Operation Plan, which involved the employment of roughly 2,500 vessels, 4,000 aircraft and 250,000 troops.

The plan for air and surface protection of the assault forces called for a series of accelerated bombing attacks on Sicily, Sardinia and South Italy, preceding the actual landings. Complete air coverage, both en route to Sicily and while the ships were unloading, was to be furnished by Air Marshal Sir Arthur Tedder, RAF, Allied Commander for Air Forces, and Lieutenant General Carl Spaatz, Commander Northwest Air Force. Under these two directors were divisions and subdivisions of air power available for every type of mission: the Northwest African Coastal, Tactical, and Strategic Air Forces; the Gibraltar, Malta, Middle East Commands; and the Naval Co-operation Group.

On the surface there were to be two strong British forces, consisting of both capital and escort ships. Heavy ships of the Italian fleet were dispersed, and it was planned to keep them that way. The Royal Navy covering force was to be split, one group guarding the approach to Sicily from the Tyrrhenian Sea and the second group protecting the attacking forces from any possible Italian fleet movements from the Ionian Sea. It was also thought that this group of British ships on the Ionian Sea approach would deceive the enemy into thinking that perhaps an attack on western Greece was imminent. The first force consisted of: HMS NELSON, the flagship, RODNEY, FORMIDABLE, WARSPITE, VALIANT and INDOMITABLE, which were to operate in the Ionian and Mediterranean Seas. The other force: HMS KING GEORGE V and HMS HOWE were to operate south of Sardinia.

Two American battleships, USS SOUTH DAKOTA (Captain Lynde D. McCormick, USN) and USS ALABAMA (Captain Fred D. Kirtland, USN) were temporarily assigned to the British Home Fleet at Scapa Flow guarding against a sortie by the Nazi warships, to relieve HMS KING GEORGE V and HOWE for the Sardinian operations.

Cruiser Division 8, comprising USS PHILADELPHIA (Captain Paul Hendren, USN), BOISE (Captain Leo H. Thebaud, USN) and SAVANNAH (Captain Robert W. Cary, USN), and seven destroyers under Rear Admiral Lyal Davidson, USN, was to have the job of escorting and covering all the Allied ships from the North African ports to the landing beaches of Sicily. With Cruiser Division 8 would be a British screening force of two MTB (motor torpedo boat) flotillas and one MGB (motor gunboat) flotilla.

During the dark hours before the landings paratroops would be dropped behind enemy lines.

The logistical problems that had to be solved for an operation so large are beyond imagination, and, likewise, beyond condensation. Into the job went the labor of every city, town and farm in the United States. For every man put ashore on enemy soil, tons of supplies had to be landed in an unending stream of ammunition, big guns and little guns, small arms and tanks, aviation gasoline, blood plasma, food, bandages, toilet paper, trucks, bulldozers, candy, steam shovels, writing paper, hospital beds and operating tables, categories and quantities to equip a city.

On July 1, Vice-Admiral Hewitt called a meeting of all task force and group commanders at his headquarters in Algiers.

Rear Admiral Kirk's task force had arrived in Oran from Norfolk, Virginia, after a two weeks' voyage over a suddenly calm and co-operative Atlantic. The ports of Oran, Arzeu, Algiers and Bizerte were bulging with loaded transports, landing craft and warships.

All the plans that had originated in London, Washington and Algiers were now in Vice-Admiral Hewitt's headquarters. The major points of the assault were discussed, over great maps, charts and three-dimensional models of the beach area. The part that elements of the Western Task Force would play in the great converging movement against Sicily was drilled home. Hydrographic reconnaissance and the latest intelligence information was passed out. Air plan, navigation plan and communications plan were explained. In mid-June, King George VI arrived in North Africa to acquaint himself with the plans.

The large ships would go back to North Africa as soon as possible after D-day. Rear Admiral Kirk was to return to Oran; Rear Admiral Hall to Algiers or Bizerte; while Rear Admiral Conolly, with his landing craft, would remain in the Sicilian area as Senior Officer Present Afloat until otherwise directed.

In the meantime, the first phase of the air plan was in operation—the bombing of strong points along all lower Europe and particularly on Sicily. The Axis ferry service from Messina, Sicily, to the Italian mainland had been practically destroyed. Enemy air resistance had been light, and enemy reconnaissance planes had been making fewer and fewer flights over the packed North African invasion ports.

The Allies had dropped some prospective saboteurs on Sicily by parachute in June. Approximately a dozen German and Italian submarines picketed the North African coastline from Oran to Tripoli, while the British had a much larger counterpicket force placed strategically near Italian ports.

Invasion was in the air. Those enemy reconnaissance reports that did get back to Europe were broadcast over the Axis radio. Rumors of an impending invasion of Europe were monitored, and no wonder!

The flagship of the Western Task Force lay alongside one of the quays in the port of Algiers. She was flanked by other headquarters ships, cargo and attack transports, tankers, minesweepers, sub-chasers. Ships were moored two and three deep along every available dock for miles. The large warships waited passively in the outer harbor behind a protecting wall of nets. This was a picture repeated from Gibraltar to Mers-el-Kebir, Oran, Arzeu, Tunis, Bizerte, Tripoli, and on to Alexandria, Egypt.

On board all the transports, Army and Navy personnel learned how to live together. The headquarters of both Naval and Military Task Force commanders were aboard. Living quarters, office space, for both staff officers and enlisted men, had to be assigned. Full colonels were sleeping in tiers, ten, eighteen, twenty to a cabin. The War Rooms, those map-walled cubicles where the strategic and tactical plans are plotted, were bulging with internal pressure. Messing and water facilities were strained. Life was not comfortable on these one-time passenger liners heading for invasion.

Then, one by one, the ports along the African shores of the Mediterranean began to empty. Operation *Husky* was underway.

Late in the afternoon of July 6, the flagship and all the ships around her moved out of Algiers harbor and began to form their convoy pattern. Aboard the flagship, with Vice-Admiral Hewitt and Lieutenant General Patton, were war correspondents and the staff of the Anglo-American Civil Administrators, including Lieutenant Colonel Charles Poletti, former lieutenant-governor of New York.

Several things had happened that day. Word was still awaited on the damage at Bizerte of a 50-minute air raid the previous night. (Damage was later reported slight.) Latest reconnaissance photographs showed a new Italian battery in the *Joss* attack area. Another Allied intelligence report commented optimistically on the possibility of Italy's collapse if *Operation Husky* were successful.

At noon it was discovered with dismay that an officer on one of the transports had distributed maps of Sicily to officers and copies of the *Soldiers Guide to Sicily* to the troops, before the ships had left port. How many Axis agents were in on the secret, in consequence? There was further anxiety when the local French pilot, having guided the flagship out of the harbor, waved good-bye to Commander Brittain, and called: "Have a good trip to Sicily!" His joviality vanished when he stepped ashore into protective custody; he was held incommunicado until D-day to safeguard the information he possessed.

As the convoy moved out of Algiers harbor and formed, the USS CHASE, flagship of the *Dime* Attack Force, took the lead. Around the outer harbor lay most of the heavy ships of the Royal Navy that were to participate: HMS KING GEORGE V, HMS NELSON, HMS RODNEY, HMS HOWE, HMS FORMIDABLE, and HMS DIDO.

Less than an hour underway, the first air alert was sounded. Ten minutes later, the signal to "secure from general quarters" was given. The "enemy planes" turned out to be the barrage balloons of the *Cent* Attack Force convoy, steaming up from the rear.

The next day the weather was calm as the Mediterranean coastline slipped by. Early in the afternoon the great convoy of the British Eastern Task Force, which had sailed from England, was sighted. It passed, later in the day, en route to its own rendezvous point for the assault.

Word came that the British convoy from Alexandria had been spotted by the enemy as it neared Malta. This was the first sign of enemy reconnaisance.

That evening, the following orders, the first from the Allied Commander in Chief to the Force, were posted:

> We are about to engage in the second phase of the operations which began with the invasion of North Africa.
> We have defeated the enemy's forces on the south shore of the Mediterranean and captured his Army intact.

The French in North Africa, from whom the yoke of Axis domination has been lifted, are now our loyal Allies.

However, this is not enough. Our untiring pressure on the enemy must be maintained, and . . . we are about to pursue the invasion and occupation of enemy territory.

The successful conclusion of these operations will not only strike closer to the heart of the Axis, but also will remove the last threat to the free sea lanes of the Mediterranean.

Remember that this time it is indeed enemy territory which we are attacking, and as such we must expect extremely difficult fighting.

But we have learned to work smoothly alongside one another as a team, and many of you who will be in the first ranks of this force know full well the meaning of air and naval superiority.

The task is difficult but your skill, courage and devotion to duty will be successful in driving our enemies closer to disaster and leading us towards victory and the liberation of Europe and Asia.

> DWIGHT D. EISENHOWER,
> General, U.S. Army,
> Commander in Chief.

The convoys passed through the Tunisian War Channel the next day, July 8. On the approach, the ships hugged the reddish-brown African coastline, a bare two miles to starboard. Beyond Bizerte stretched a narrow channel through a minefield sown by the Germans in an early attempt to guard the Tunisian coast. It was a narrow passage, less than 90 miles from Sicily. The ships would pass through it, and continue south before turning back in the direction of Malta and Sicily.

At 0930 the flagship's convoy made a 30-degree turn as it passed Cape Bon where the War Channel curved just outside the Gulf of Tunis and followed the coastline south. Ahead was the Eastern Task Force convoy. To the rear was Rear Admiral Kirk's *Cent* Attack Force, and to the rear of that was Rear Admiral Conolly's *Joss* Attack Force. It was a parade of ships that stretched more than a mile wide for 60 miles. At 2000—eight o'clock—that night, the convoys changed course and turned up toward Malta.

On the morning of July 9, the ships' radio picked up a German broadcast announcing the presence in the Western Mediterranean of a large Anglo-American fleet and the concentration of hundreds of thousands of tons of shipping. The day was clear, but a wind was blowing

that whipped itself up to 30-knot strength out of the northwest by sundown. The cables on the barrage balloon of the USS CHASE snapped and
the silver bag went kiting off over the sea. The aerology reports were
optimistic that the wind would die by H-hour.

Meanwhile, though, it was doing anything but dropping, and by night
the sea had built up ominously. Transports were taking spray clear up to
the navigation bridge, and the smaller craft, the LCTs and LCIs carrying
troops and cargo and the PCs of the screen, were taking the seas solidly
over the bow. Aerology remained confident, but that was a feeling not
shared by the rank and file of seasick Army men. Nor was it shared by the
officers and men who would have to be lowered overside in the small
boats from the transports, and still less by the officers and crews who would
have to do the lowering.

The men who had crossed a flat, calm Atlantic with Rear Admiral
Kirk's task force were wondering whether they were in the right body of
water. Veterans of the African landings thought that probably the storm
was just a necessary concomitant of an amphibious operation. And everybody more than half expected to get a message postponing D-day, or at
least H-hour. But even as they wondered, the parachutists were taking
off from African airfields: there could be no postponements.

That morning the BOISE and the SAVANNAH joined the flagship's
formation. Just before noon the USS BROOKLYN (Captain Hubert W.
Ziroli, USN) and USS BIRMINGHAM (Captain John Wilkes, USN) were
sighted off the port quarter. Two former Belgian Channel steamers, the
PRINCE LEOPOLD and the PRINCE CHARLES, had joined the convoy as
converted LSIs.

In the afternoon the islands of Malta and Gozo were sighted gleaming
faintly gold and red in the late afternoon sun. This was "Point X-Ray,"
where all the convoys would converge and separate again for their rendezvous points off Sicily.

A signal from USS CHASE went out: "Good Luck, Gang, Do It
Again." It was signed "Terry Allen," Commanding General of the 1st
Division, Reinforced.

Aboard every ship were last-moment, tense conferences. The men were
ready. H-hour was six hours away, and the wind and sea were, if anything, worse than ever.

As the Attack Forces of the Western Task Force separated for their
rendezvous stations, three British submarines that had reached their posi-

tions much earlier, waiting quietly in the enemy waters for this moment, surfaced and guided the silent transports into their anchorage.

The clocks of the ships ran around past midnight. It was July 10, D-day.

The ships were close to shore, close enough for the men to see the fires burning from the bombs that had been dropping all day long. On every ship, battle stations were manned. Troops and boat crews were ready.

By 0030 most of the Western Task Force was anchored in its assigned positions. The shore bombardment groups of cruisers and destroyers were ready. The antisubmarine screens of destroyers and patrol craft were sweeping like silent sentries to the seaward and on the flanks.

As the ships had drawn under the lee of Sicily the wind and sea had dropped, but there was still a nasty swell running, particularly in the *Cent* area, where the land was low and the broad Acate River valley formed no barrier to the sweep of the gale.

Getting the small craft overside was risky, tricky work. Tackle parted, boats were stove in. On the FLORENCE NIGHTINGALE, for example, a 25-ton LCM broke loose as it was being hoisted outboard, and began to swing like a pendulum with the roll of the ship, banging up against the ship, now up by the bridge, now by the fantail. And every time she struck the ship's side something gave, with a booming crash that could be heard through the entire transport area. Little rocket boats were smashed and sank as soon as they hit the water. It was a nasty, dangerous business to be carried on in pitch darkness, under the guns of a waiting enemy.

But the job was done, with surprisingly few casualties. The small boats formed their circles, came alongside; the soldiers clambered down the cargo nets into the heaving, bobbing craft. And at 0215—right on time— the boats of the *Dime* and *Joss* forces headed for the beaches of Sicily. There was an hour's delay in the *Cent* area, caused by the weather, then the boats of that force, too, raced in for the assault.

Chapter Twenty-seven

A N informal war diary written by Lieutenant Douglas Fairbanks, Jr., USNR, aboard Vice-Admiral Henry K. Hewitt's flagship, gives a good picture of what *Operation Husky* looked like as the assault got under way.

"*0245—H-hour*—The first wave should be landing now. There is some machine gun and medium artillery fire from the beach to seaward. One of our support craft is firing its rockets at a shore battery and apparently finding its mark. Some destroyers, cruising slowly inshore, are attempting to knock out enemy searchlights now focusing on incoming craft. Enemy fire from the shore has increased. The searchlights go on until our guns get their range and then they snap off again. It is difficult to know if they are being shot out, deserted, or just avoiding our five inch guns. Gela and adjacent areas are silhouetted by the fires set by incendiary bombs. Our boat officers should have little difficulty in finding their proper beaches.

"Searchlights are now centering on one of our Support Boats [NOTE: Actually, this was a scout boat which had gone in well in advance of any of the other craft to identify the beach and guide the assault waves.] and an enemy battery, of approximately three inch calibre, is firing point blank at it. An airplane beacon in the Scoglitti area is, for some reason, still functioning. It affords a perfect landmark. Shore bombardment is now visible in Rear Admiral Conolly's *Joss* area.

"*0300*—Apparently the big ships have not yet been seen from the shore. There is no word of our landing troops. We are about six miles off shore, and although the land is smoking in spots, the air to seaward is clear and there are signs of battle as far as we can see. The SAVANNAH and the BOISE are combining their gunfire to put out the enemy searchlights and gun positions.

"*0325*—Malta signals that no accurate information is yet available on the landing of our paratroops inland. They were seen to pass over the

PLATE XLIX—(*upper*) Turning of the tide! These black flecks in the surf and dots on the sand are boats and men of *Operation Torch*, first major amphibious operation of the war. From this tiny French Moroccan beachhead swelled a flood of men and materiel that overwhelmed Africa, then Europe, and finally the far reaches of the Pacific and Asia. (*lower*) Vichy French confusion and stubbornness cost them heavily at Casablanca. This aerial view, taken from a USS RANGER plane, shows the harbor littered with ships sunk or damaged by United States aerial and sea forces after the French ignored surrender pleas and demands.

PLATE L—(*upper*) The JEAN BART, unfinished French battleship, at her dock in Casablanca harbor, was a sitting duck for our battleships and planes. This aerial view shows clearly the effect of the pounding she took from the big guns of the USS MASSACHUSETTS and bombers from the USS RANGER. The sheds and pier also took severe punishment. (*lower*) A close-up of some of the damage done to the JEAN BART at her pier. Despite this terrific destruction the JEAN BART fired her main turret for some time, nearly hitting the USS AUGUSTA, and at the end her 15-inch guns and her fire control station were found to be still serviceable.

PLATE LI—(*upper*) Aftermath of the strange impersonal battle between our forces and the French ships and shore batteries off French Morocco. These three French vessels, two destroyers and a light cruiser, were beached and lost near Casablanca after a futile running battle with the U. S. invasion fleet. Several other ships also were sunk. (*lower*) In addition to the extensive casualties suffered by French combat vessels, a score or more of merchant ships were damaged by American ships and planes in the Casablanca campaign. One large liner, hit by a bomb, turned over at its berth, creating a minor "Normandie" for our salvage crews. A floating drydock sat down in the center of the harbor—itself in need of salvage.

PLATE LII—(*upper*) Under the watchful eye and with the support of U. S. Navy carrier-based planes, American transports and landing barges take over the port of Safi, 130 miles south of Casablanca on Africa's French Moroccan coast. An SBD, or Douglas Scout Bomber, can be seen, upper right. Safi was captured so quickly, thanks to fast fleet and air attacks, that only 9 out of 121 landing craft used were damaged. (*lower*) While U. S. forces stormed Moroccan Atlantic beachheads, a simultaneous attack, largely British, was launched against the ports of Oran and Algiers. Here the famous English marine artist, C. E. Turner, depicts the gallant but costly attempt to ram the harbor boom at Oran by two former U. S. Coast Guard cutters, the HMS HARTLAND (ex-USCGC PONTCHARTRAIN) and the HMS WALNEY (ex-USCGC SEBAGO). Both ships were sunk with heavy loss of life, but the port was finally opened after landings were made at Arzeu and Les Andalouses. (*Coast Guard photo of a painting by C. E. Turner.*)

PLATE LIII—(*upper*) This is one of the unusual photos of the war. It shows the exact moment a German submarine torpedo hit an American transport off Fedala, "the easy beach," 14 miles northwest of Casablanca. A few minutes later the photographer's ship also was struck. Nazi undersea boats had a field day here—sinking four ships and damaging three others within 48 hours. (*lower*) Invasion troops who arrived by train! Survivors of American ships, sunk by Nazi subs off North Africa, reach Casablanca with only the clothes on their backs.

PLATE LIV—(*upper*) USS PHILADELPHIA, cruiser, which was in the thick of action throughout the North African and Italian campaigns, lays down a smoke screen to hide supply ships and transports from enemy shore artillery during a landing. (*above left*) Rear Admiral W. Monroe Kelly, USN, commander of the north attack group in the Moroccan landings, aboard the USS TEXAS; (*above right*) Rear Admiral L. A. Davidson, USN, commander of the south attack group, aboard the USS PHILADELPHIA. (*left*) An earlier PHILADELPHIA also ranged the North African coast. The artist depicts the burning of the first USS PHILADELPHIA by Lieutenant Stephen Decatur and a group of volunteers from the American ketch INTREPID, February 16, 1804. The PHILADELPHIA had run aground, been captured, and refloated by the Tripolitan pirates. Decatur's bold enterprise prevented the use of the powerful frigate by the enemy. (*Painting by Edward Moran, Naval Academy Museum.*)

PLATE LV—Eight of the "ball team" that finally brought the French in North Africa to terms, after broadcast appeals by General Eisenhower to their "sense of realism, self-interest and ideals" failed. The code signal to attack was "play ball." *Left row, top to bottom:* USS MASSACHUSETTS, battleship; USS SAVANNAH, cruiser; USS BRISTOL, destroyer; USS SHAD, submarine. *Right row, top to bottom:* USS TEXAS, battleship; USS SUWANNEE, escort carrier; USS ROE, destroyer; USS RAVEN, minesweeper.

PLATE LVI—Free French at last. General Henri Honore Giraud, following his amazing escape from Occupied France and rescue by an Allied Force under Captain Jerauld Wright, USN, in a British submarine, is greeted at Casablanca by General de Gaulle as President Roosevelt and Winston Churchill look on.

PLATE LVII—(*upper*) Notables at the Casablanca conference, January 14–24, 1943. *Standing, left to right:* Harry L. Hopkins; Lt. Gen. Henry H. Arnold, Air Forces Commander; Admiral Ernest J. King, USN, Commander in Chief U. S. Fleet; General George C. Marshall, Army Chief of Staff; Admiral of the Fleet Sir Dudley Pound; Air Chief Marshal Sir Charles Portal; General Sir Alan Brooke, Imperial General Staff Chief; Field Marshal Sir John Dill; Head of British Joint Staff Mission in Washington; Vice Admiral Lord Louis Mountbatten, Chief of Combined Operations; Lt. Gen. B. B. Somervell, Commanding General of the U. S. Services of Supply. *Seated:* President Roosevelt and Prime Minister Churchill. (*lower*) "By the dawn's early light . . ." four U. S. Navy minesweepers clear the way for a Mediterranean landing. All invasions have been preceded by this extremely dangerous and little glorified work. The YMSs, or "sweeps," generally operate close to shore, directly under the enemy's guns. Many have fallen victim to mines themselves.

PLATE LVIII—(*upper*) Night was no protection. For many months during 1942–1943 convoys along the North African coast ran the gauntlet of German bombers, whose flares lit the sea for miles, clearly revealing ships, which became "sitting ducks." Here an Allied ammunition ship goes up after receiving a direct hit. (*Coast Guard Photo.*) (*lower*) Oil-coated survivors picked up by rescue vessels after German bombers attacked an Allied convoy off North Africa, sinking two destroyer escorts. The suffocating film of oil was not only nauseating and difficult to swim in but it also posed the threat that it would take fire. (*Coast Guard Photo.*)

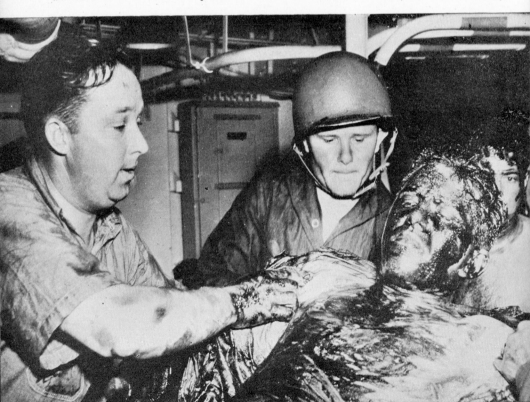

PLATE LIX—(*right*) An Army pilot heads for Africa from the deck of the USS RANGER. By using carriers, many days were saved in ferrying planes from U. S. ports to North Africa. (*above*) Rear Admiral Ernest D. McWhorter, USN, Commanding Officer of the carrier task force. (*lower*) This remarkable photo shows only a small part of the 1,000-ship force that assembled in North Africa for the invasion of Sicily, early in 1943.

PLATE LX—(*upper*) This land-based Liberator (PB4Y), over the checkerboard pattern of the peaceful English countryside, is a U. S. Navy plane returning from an antisubmarine patrol. In midsummer, 1943, Fleet Air Wing 7 took over the Bay of Biscay blockade, soon making life miserable for U-boats from Brest, St. Nazaire, L'Orient, La Rochelle, and Bordeaux, and, in turn, being harassed by long-range Junkers 88s, ME 109s and 110s and FW 190s. (*lower*) One of the triumvirate (CVE–DD–DE) that helped to bring the German U-boat to its knees. This DE, or destroyer escort, a new type of combat ship developed in this war, is on its trial runs off Miami, Florida. Smaller than a destroyer, but larger and more seaworthy than a PC, the DEs met every requirement as shepherd dogs of the convoy fleets.

PLATE LXI—(*upper*) Gibraltar was a key control point for convoys and antisubmarine patrols. Here a member of the Service Feminine de la Flotte (French Waves) gives instructions to a plane from the control tower on "The Rock." (*lower*) While the greatest armada of them all was assembling in Britain, our soldiers and sailors went on historical tours arranged by their English hosts. Here at Portsmouth a U. S. seaman, accompanied by an English Wren, inspects the HMS VICTORY, aboard which Lord Nelson broke the sea power of France at Trafalgar, a victory which cost him his life. The black ties worn by enlisted men of both the American and British navies originated as a symbol of mourning for Nelson.

PLATE LXII—Bitter weather and a ruthless enemy combined to make the "Murmansk Run" the most dangerous of World War II voyages. Here a convoy, with supplies desperately needed by retreating Russian armies, is under heavy Nazi aerial attack. Sometimes only two or three ships of large convoys ran the gauntlet safely with their supplies to Murmansk and Archangel.

Scratch one Nazi blockade runner. A few German ships, aided by bad weather and good luck, eluded Allied patrols with cargoes of rubber, tin, fats, oil, and other products needed by a blockaded Germany. But most of them met the fate of the RIO GRANDE, here bracketed by geysers of water where shells of the USS OMAHA and the USS JOUETT get the range before sending her to the bottom. Bales of rubber were found floating on the water after the sinking.

PLATE LXIII—(*upper*) Like a guardian angel, a blimp hovers over a convoy as it begins the long voyage to Europe. Lighter-than-air craft played a vital, and largely unsung, role in spotting and bombing lurking U-boats as well as such humanitarian work as locating and rescuing shipwrecked and airwrecked men. *Inset:* Rear Admiral C. E. Rosendahl, USN, Commander Fleet Air Ships, Atlantic Fleet. (*lower*) Several times the Navy moved inland to save Army and RAF flyers from jungle death. The blimps K-106 and K-11 left normal patrol duty when word came that planes were down in impenetrable South American forests, and dropped members of their own crews to assist in maneuvering a 225-foot bag into boggy Amazon clearings. The skill and daring of the blimp pilots and crews, in carrying out these unscheduled missions successfully, makes another bright chapter in the history of the Navy's lighter-than-air arm. (*Water color by Lieutenant Albert K. Murray, USNR.*)

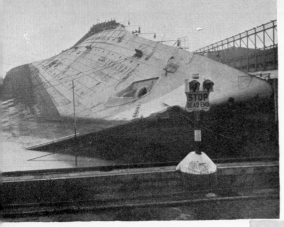

PLATE LXIV—(*upper left*) The great French luxury liner, NORMANDIE, renamed USS LAFAYETTE, on her side after the disastrous fire of February 9, 1942. A valuable Hudson river slip was blocked until two of the Navy's famous salvage experts took over the vast job of righting the 83,400-ton hulk. (*upper right*) Commander W. A. Sullivan, USN, who started the work, and (*center left*) Captain B. E. Manseau, USN, who relieved Commander Sullivan when the latter was rushed to North Africa to clear harbors blocked with sunken French ships. (*center, right*) August 9, 1943, and after nearly 18 months of effort, the USS LAFAYETTE is half way up. (*lower left*) On November 3, 1943, upright again! The largest single salvage job in history, the raising of the LAFAYETTE paid unexpected dividends by training divers, engineers and other technicians who proved invaluable in clearing African, Italian, French, German, and Far Eastern harbors.

The President of the United States takes pleasure in presenting the MEDAL OF HONOR posthumously to

ENSIGN JOHN JOSEPH PARLE
UNITED STATES NAVAL RESERVE

for service as set forth in the following

CITATION:

"For valor and courage above and beyond the call of duty as Officer-in-Charge of small boats in the U.S.S. LST 375 during the amphibious assault on the Island of Sicily, July 9-10, 1943. Realizing that a detonation of explosives would prematurely disclose to the enemy the assault about to be carried out and with full knowledge of the peril involved, Ensign Parle unhesitatingly risked his life to extinguish a smoke pot accidentally ignited in a boat carrying charges of high explosives, detonating fuses and ammunition. Undaunted by fire and blinding smoke, he entered the craft, quickly snuffed out a burning fuse and after failing in his desperate efforts to extinguish the fire pot, finally seized it with both hands and threw it over the side. Although he succumbed a week later from smoke and fumes inhaled, Ensign Parle's heroic self-sacrifice prevented grave damage to the ship and personnel and insured the security of a vital mission. He gallantly gave his life in the service of his country."

Franklin D. Roosevelt

Facsimile of the only Naval Medal of Honor awarded during the Battle of the Atlantic.

island on time, but due to wind were expected to be slightly late in the dropping area."

Actually most of the paratroops, members of the 82nd Airborne Division, in this their first operation, landed about where they were supposed to, and achieved their objectives quickly. One battalion dropped west of Gela when it should have been east, but this did not change the course of the battle.

Meanwhile, the waves of small boats churned forward under an arc of brilliance. Shells from the cruisers—they seemed to come in groups of three—drifted up and up like white balls lobbed lazily in the air, apparently never to fall at all. Fire from the destroyers was a series of red lines ruled across the sky connecting the blackness of the sea behind to the blackness of the land ahead. There was light from the shore, too. Behind the whole landing area there was the glow of bomb-set fires, and here and there sparkling streaks of antiaircraft fire. Closer at hand, the boats attacking the left flank—the *Joss* area—saw, drifting at first, speeding too fast for eye to follow as they drew nearer, the red dots that were enemy fire. Boats in the center and on the right flank saw a little less of the shore-battery shooting; there was a little less to see, and what there was was diminished to paleness by two great searchlights with beams of light so vividly blue-white they almost crackled in the air. Furthermore, over the *Cent* area, the right flank, enemy planes had dropped flares as a preliminary to making unsuccessful bombing runs on the transport JEFFERSON and the cruiser PHILADELPHIA.

With all the light, which, so far as the small-boat coxswains trying to find their own small beaches were concerned, only served "to make the darkness visible," the landings were effected with few human casualties. Equipment did not fare so well. A long, practically continuous sand bar about 75 feet offshore, turned the incoming swells into rapid, choppy little 3-foot breakers that caught the landing craft as they backed off the beach, and broached them before they could turn around and clear the bar. By noon of D-day, most of the Sicilian Assault Beaches looked as though our attack had been driven back, so thickly strewn were they with landing craft broached, abandoned and awash.

Salvage operations were begun immediately, of course, but nevertheless the loss of the small craft was great enough to pose a serious twofold problem: the transports could not get unloaded as swiftly as had been planned because there was nothing to unload them into; the few craft that were still operating had a hard time finding a clear spot to beach, and consequently tended to become fouled with craft already broached.

All this had not, however, materially slowed the landing of the troops. Strong opposition had been encountered by the men landing in the immediate vicinity of Licata and Gela when the first waves hit at 0345. But elsewhere, on beaches farther from the towns, they had met but little resistance. And over to eastward, in the area around Scoglitti, the landings, although an hour late in starting, went well once they were begun.

By sunrise—approximately 0430—the enemy began to put up a sterner show of fight. Low-flying planes in twos and threes darted out of the Acate River valley, which divided the Central and Eastern Assault Areas, roared east or west along the beach strafing and bombing, then slipped away behind the mountains which framed the whole Assault Area. Occasionally they would make a foray over the Transport Area, and in one such attack they got home on the destroyer MADDOX, screening the ships off Gela, sinking her in two minutes.

At ten o'clock an even more dangerous threat developed. Enemy tanks, part of the Hermann Goering Division, were spotted clanking down from the hills in the general direction of Gela. There appeared to be about thirty of them, and, because of the growing shortage of landing craft, the Army had not yet got ashore the antitank guns and heavy artillery with which to tackle such a thrust. At the same time, the air attacks were stepped up, and the enemy guns, which had been shooting wildly in the tricky light of the early morning, began to get better spotting and score hits.

Something had to be done quickly and only the Navy had the guns to do it with. The cruisers BOISE and SAVANNAH were ordered to move up toward Gela to silence the German batteries there. Meanwhile the British monitor HMS ABERCROMBIE had swung her great 15-inch guns on the largest troop concentrations around Comiso airport and was keeping the men there too busy to follow up the tank advance. Then, as the tanks came within range, BOISE switched her fire on them.

The tanks split up into small groups, hard to sight from the air, and kept advancing. An air spotter would see a few, and relay the co-ordinates of their position to the cruiser. His answer would come within seconds—a salvo and a broken tank. Fewer in number, but still advancing, some tanks reached the outskirts of Gela while others suddenly appeared a scant

400 yards from the mouth of the Acate, a scant 400 yards from splitting our cental and eastern beachheads.

Then the destroyers took over. Standing boldly into the shallow water some 800 yards from the shore, they took on the enemy like terriers, blasting his tanks every which way with direct fire poured in at gun-heating speed.

That was the last ground thrust the enemy made. By 1330 Gela was secure again. Vice-Admiral Hewitt had word of the capture of Scoglitti by 1440, and by 1650 Licata, the best-defended town in the American Assault Area, also had fallen.

Around the southern tip of Sicily the British on their side were making good the same progress; Augusta had fallen and Syracuse was tottering.

Meanwhile supplies and equipment were pouring in to the beach at a much better rate. LCTs, delayed by the strong head winds and heavy seas which had buffeted them villainously the night before, began to arrive around noon. As soon as they had unloaded their own cargoes, they turned back from the beach and helped unload the transports. The slight surf, which would not have bothered them anyway, had moderated; new unloading areas, clear of small craft, had been opened up along the beaches, and so the supplies flowed ashore.

Helping the LCTs were the Army DUKWs, those great 2½-ton trucks which operate with equal ease in the water and on land. These, when the small-boat scarcity had become most acute, had gamely taken up the burden and kept up at least a trickle of supplies shoreward. Now, though the strain was eased somewhat, they kept right on working. The beachhead was secure; it was up to all hands to keep it that way.

Chapter Twenty-eight

I N THE first morning light of D-plus-one the defenders again struck back viciously. From somewhere back of the sand dune hills, came enemy dive bombers and fighter bombers, converging on the *Dime* area. First the beaches were struck with machine gun spurts and bombs on the stacked equipment, then the bombers went after the ships at anchor. A near miss sprayed the flagship with water and shrapnel. The antiaircraft guns on every ship and from the entire beach opened fire, and the ships rolled and pitched in the waves made by the bomb geysers.

The raid was over as suddenly as it began, leaving two ships damaged. The transport BARNETT caught a bomb in her number 1 hatch. Her magazine was ordered flooded and the fire was under control almost as soon as the bombers were out of sight. The other transport, USS ORIZABA, could still steam, but she was crippled, six holes in her hull above the water-line, with electric and gyro leads to the bridge cut in several places. A direct hit erased the LST 158.

The strafing-bombing attack initiated a day in which no half hour was to be without enemy aircraft overhead. Allied fighter planes had scarcely cleared the sky of one determined attack when the BOISE relayed a message from its spotter reporting heavy German tank reinforcements driving along the road leading south, accompanied by other motorized equipment. The ships of the invasion fleet turned their guns on the invisible highway, riveting salvos from their 5- and 6-inch guns in support of the troops ashore in Gela. Fourteen tanks were smashed by the naval gunfire, and the balance forced to retreat.

Just before noon, Vice-Admiral Hewitt, with Major General J. P. Lucas, General Eisenhower's representative, and other Army officers boarded the fast Navy minesweeper, USS STEADY (Lieutenant Commander Frederick W. Maennle, USNR) to inspect the *Joss* area. Just as the party arrived in the area, a formation of ten dive bombers and low-level fighter-bombers came in to blast the docks and quays of Licata and the ships tied up alongside. One bomb struck the Licata breakwater and a warehouse with some stores. Another stick of bombs straddled the bow of six LSTs beached and unloading. One LST nearby was struck and started burning.

But the STEADY continued on course. Aboard the *Joss* headquarters ships Vice-Admiral Hewitt, after conferring with Rear Admiral Conolly, ordered the Minelaying Division, CHATEAU THIERRY, ORIZABA and their escorts, to move to Bizerte. The destroyer escort was to make a round trip and return to Sicily immediately.

By the time the Admiral's party left his flagship in midafternoon, there had been five more bombing attacks. As the USS STEADY steamed down the coast past *Dime* toward *Cent* area, "general quarters" was sounded. Twenty twin-engined bombers dove in to attack *Dime*.

As the STEADY passed Gela, the generals and admirals aboard saw that the pier had been partially destroyed, forcing ships to transfer their cargoes by small boat directly to the beach in front of the town. Great stacks of stores and fuel in cans lined the water's edge. The entire *Dime* beach was one long warehouse of war material, and as vulnerable as a ham sandwich at a picnic.

An hour later the attack on the inviting target opened. First came the Axis fighters, weaving through the low hills back of the beaches, roaring out over the sand at 300 miles an hour, 20 feet above the cargo-littered sand, spraying the munitions stacked the length of *Dime* beach with incendiary bullets. All the antiaircraft guns on the beach opened fire, but the low altitude of the planes caught our own people on the beach in a cross fire.

Following close behind the fighters was a formation of fifteen or twenty Focke-Wulf 200Ks and Heinkel 111s from the west, loosing a high-level shower of bombs. Most of the bombs fell wide of any target, although there were scores of damaging near misses and fires.

The ROBERT ROWAN, a new Liberty ship, loaded with ammunition, was hit. The HOPI (Lieutenant Owen W. Huff, USN), a salvage and fire boat, was ordered to go alongside and fight the fire. But the HOPI was some distance away and time was important, so the destroyer MC LANAHAN (Commander Harry R. Hummer, Jr., USN) steamed up to the rescue. It was a hopeless mission. A signal was flashed that the ROBERT ROWAN was being abandoned and that MC LANAHAN should stand by to pick up survivors.

Less than two hours later the Liberty ship blew up. A flat sheet of crimson fire in a frame of black smoke belched a thousand feet into the sky. Pieces of the twisted metal and flaming wood hissed into the water as far as a mile distant. What was left of the ship was a burning pyre roaring from the twisted hull. The MCLANAHAN fired at point-blank range to sink the ship before it became a beacon for enemy aircraft, but the hull was in shallow water and could sink no farther.

However, news arrived that somewhat offset the grimness of the immediate scene. Paratroopers sent inland to capture a German wireless transmitter reported success and two hundred prisoners. Capture of Comiso airport was followed by the fall of Ragusa airfield. Supplies were moving across the beaches and inland to the 45th Division Command Post near Victoria. A Canadian liaison officer reported that his division of the Eastern Task Force was nearing the "contact line" with our forces.

On top of these *Cent* reports came Rear Admiral Hall's news that his transports were being unloaded at top speed, that he would be ready to sail for Africa the next day, although his area had been strafed on an average of once every half hour all afternoon.

At dusk a destroyer began to lay a smoke screen to blanket the transport area, but a wind blowing seaward whipped it away as fast as it could put it down. The hull of the ROBERT ROWAN was still burning brightly, a perfect beacon for night aerial attack.

And it came: Fifteen to twenty-five bombers, adding to the burning beacon below the light of six giant magnesium flares that dropped slowly, hoveringly over the entire transport area. One by one the planes could be heard peeling off for the bombing dive, and then came the crescendo whine of the bombs above the antiaircraft fire. Four bombs straddled the BIRMINGHAM and one landed close aboard the BROOKLYN.

During the attack a message came from Admiral Cunningham announcing his arrival next day aboard the flagship of General Eisenhower. But before anybody could offer comment, a second wave of enemy planes came in again with more flares, flying close to ground and sea. Men lay low on the decks to avoid the almost level fire. The destroyer MURPHY (Lieutenant Commander Leonard W. Bailey, USN) called out a near miss from one large bomb. A piece of flying shrapnel struck one of her men, wounding him. The MCLANAHAN's stern was lifted from the water by another near miss, without damage to ship or personnel. Then the attack was over for the night.

Vice-Admiral Hewitt ordered that all transport areas be swept in case the low-flying enemy planes had dropped mines, and all ships in the area were warned again to be on the alert for Allied transport planes carrying paratroops.

D-plus-one had been a busy day and a vulnerable one.

Chapter Twenty-nine

A LITTLE after midnight on D-plus-two, July 12, 1943, the destroyer screen began its patrol, preparatory to shepherding the empty transports to the North African bases.

Aerial activity commenced with the dawn and was briskly countered by antiaircraft fire from the ships and ashore when a frenzied order was broadcast to cease firing. The aircraft were our own. Shortly after seven o'clock a tragic dispatch from General Ridgeway: Twenty-four Allied troop transports had been shot down during the night, and although simultaneously under enemy attack the majority of the planes were believed to have been downed by our own shore- and ship-based gunners. Most of the killed were British paratroopers. "Someone had blundered" in setting the air transports on a course different from the one announced.

HMS PETARD, a corvette, with General Eisenhower aboard, arrived in the area at six o'clock for his inspection tour. At noon Admiral Lord Louis Mountbatten left his destroyer, HMS LAMERTON, and boarded the flagship for a conference with Vice-Admiral Hewitt.

The day's work started early. It was urgently necessary to get the large and vulnerable transports out of the area, and on their way to Africa, by dusk. Orders went to all transports and escorts to raise steam in preparation.

The general situation on sea and land was infinitely better this D-plus-two day. Enemy air attack waned. The follow-up supply ships were standing in with additional cargo and troops, and began dropping anchor in midafternoon. The two British LSIs, HMS PRINCESS CHARLOTTE and PRINCESS ASTRID, had arrived in the *Dime* area a day ahead of schedule, discharged their troops and were awaiting instruction.

At four o'clock in the afternoon, Vice-Admiral Hewitt notified all commands that he was sailing his flagship back with the transports that night. He had shifted his flag to a destroyer and was returning to Algiers by way of Malta and Bizerte. The ANCON, Rear Admiral Kirk's flagship, also was to return with the transports, and he had shifted his flag to the destroyer EARLE (Lieutenant Commander Hamilton W. Howe, USN) for the voyage to Oran. Rear Admiral Conolly remained in Sicily as Senior Officer Present in the Western Task Force area.

The ships began their convoy forming around the transport CHASE, Rear Admiral Hall's flagship, at 1800—6 P.M. The progress out of the area was slow. A British LSI steamed slowly by, her decks packed with war prisoners. The sounds of fighting could still be heard inland as the ships crept by the island shores on the way to sea. Cruisers and destroyers were still firing at far out-of-sight targets that the Army wanted annihilated.

With few exceptions, the only ships left behind were warships and landing craft. The latter had already started their shuttle service between North Africa and Sicily. That morning twenty-eight LSTs had left for Bizerte and eight LCIs had beached at *Joss* area on their second round trip.

The last progress report of the day came from Admiral Cunningham. A diversionary force had bombarded Favignana Island on the west coast; a cruiser had shelled Marsala; the British 15th Cruiser Squadron had bombarded Modica, Mellili and Augusta. At 1600, HMS EXMOOR and the Greek destroyer KANARIS had entered Augusta harbor, and a minesweeper had captured intact an Italian submarine off that port.

The conquest of the last steppingstone to Europe was off to a good start. It would be five weeks before Sicily fell. The cruisers and destroyers moved on, to support the troops slugging their way across the island. For the cargo transports and landing craft, the glory had departed—temporarily. For them remained five weeks of steady, backbreaking drudgery, performed without the stimulus of combat, ferrying the steady flow of men and supplies from North Africa.

Rear Admiral Davidson, aboard PHILADELPHIA, directed patrolling operations conducted by Motor Torpedo Boat Squadron 15 to prevent the enemy from landing troops and supplies on Sicily's northwestern coast, especially at the protected harbor of Palermo. British warships bombarded Catania Bay behind which British Commandos and paratroopers had been landed to capture that chief eastern port city.

Army and Navy, British and American, worked together as one. The 3rd Infantry Division called for heavy guns to reduce the enemy batteries holding up capture of Porto Empedocle and Agrigento. Rear Admiral

Conolly dispatched the cruisers PHILADELPHIA and SAVANNAH with the British monitor ABERCROMBIE, which pounded the cities' defenses into unconditional surrender on July 17. One month later, to the day, Messina flew the white flag and Sicily was wholly in Allied hands. Meanwhile Fascism's founder, Il Duce Benito Mussolini, had "resigned" as Italian premier and had been clapped into prison.

Operation Husky brought much that was new to the still new amphibious warfare. It proved the theory of its flexibility. The African landings demonstrated the effectiveness of the new arm in ship-to-shore invasion; Sicily initiated the shore-to-shore invasion. The former involved the transport of an effective army over an ocean and its debarkation ready to fight, in armed craft carried on the transports with the troops. Sicily, receiving end of shore-to-shore amphibious operations, utilized all types of the new craft for the swift over-water delivery of an overwhelming ground force on enemy soil.

New craft, indeed! Some of the amphibious vessels found themselves utilized in techniques of warfare of which their designers had no conception, and of these the LST 386 stands out as the champion guinea pig of the fleet. The usese to which LST 386 was put were combined to present the vessel at the assault on Licata as a combination of floating stable, midget aircraft carrier, anchor for a floating causeway—and, incidentally, Landing Ship (Tank), which was all she started out to be.

Parenthetically, it must be noted that the Sicilian operation marked the debut in the European combat theater of the Seabees as assault units. These men of the Navy's Construction Battalions, largely recruited from the highly skilled building trades, had begun to arrive on the yonder coast of the Atlantic in May, 1943. The speed with which captured ports were made serviceable was their work, notably the 54th, 65th, 70th and 120th Battalions. Meanwhile others of that outfit and the 1006th Pontoon Detachment were put to experimenting with the use of pontoon-floated piers to be set up on assault beaches (the shadow cast before by the great artificial harbors that were to make the invasion of Normandy possible).

Most of this experimental work was performed with "USS GUINEA PIG"—LST 386. Her captain was Lieutenant Harold R. Fleck, USNR, who wore the rainbow ribbon of World War I, whose ending found him Ensign, USNR, aboard USS DRAYTON, the Navy's second oil-burning destroyer. Between wars Fleck had worked his way up to the presidency of a photographic business in New York, which he left at the age of forty-seven to join the company of "Re-treads" and to be introduced to LST 386 on the training beaches of Chesapeake Bay, little knowing she was to be the first LST to reach the Sicilian beach, and in what strange business.

One of Lieutenant Fleck's first specialized jobs (the first one, of course, being to master the handling of the new LST for which there was absolutely no rule book) was experimenting with pontoon causeways. The bulk of this work was done in the late spring and early summer of 1943 by the first Seabee units in North African bases. Both pontoons and LSTs were to be used for the first time in Sicily.

Then late in June, 1943, with the plans for *Husky* completed, there was a discussion about the desirability of taking small reconnaissance planes into the invasion beaches as artillery spotters and to use for liaison work. The problem was: How to get them there? Once there, they could use roadways or any level pasture lot to land and take off, but the problem of getting them ashore seemed to have its only answer in a ship with a flight deck. The inevitable question, with amphibious craft around, was: Why not use one of those things? Why not make a flight deck on an LST?

The proposal was placed before Rear Admiral Richard L. Conolly. LSTs had been used for almost everything else in the book, why not this? The Admiral agreed to an experiment. Since Fleck's ship had been a good guinea pig for the pontoon experiments, it was assigned to the "Cub-carrier" task.

Carpenters were called in for a rush job. Lumberyards were raided and the work started. The 40-mm. gun on the bow of the LST 386 was removed, and down the length of the deck from the bridgehouse to the bow the carpenters began hammering into shape a 20-foot-wide platform supported by heavy beams. When the platform was finished, thirty-six hours later, it was covered with the heavy metal mesh used to make temporary airfields on mud and sand. A little plane was brought down to the dock and swung aboard.

The only thing lacking was the usual bevy of official spectators. And they soon arrived. Major General Lucian K. Truscott, Jr., USA, with a group of staff officers, came aboard, and the 386 got underway, heading toward the northeast end of Lake Bizerte.

There was a mild wind blowing from the northwest. In carrier fashion, the plan was to sail into the wind for the take-off, but that's about as far as the resemblance to a regular aircraft carrier went. This was an LST, a ship designed to land on beaches and unload tanks, with a wooden platform built on her deck and a very small plane containing a dubious but devil-may-care pilot who had never made a carrier take-off before.

When the 386 turned for the take-off run, two small boats were lowered. In one was an Army doctor. In the other was a Navy pharmacist's mate, Robert Summers, USNR. There were the crash boats, in case the take-off was not successful. On the ship other preparations, in case of failure, were made. The deck on either side of the wooden platform was lined with water hoses and fire extinguishers.

Then the LST got underway, running into the wind. In one of the forward gun tubs was a sailor with a semaphore flag. He had a telephone connection with the bridgehouse, and when Lieutenant Fleck gave him the word he would drop the flag as a signal for the pilot to be on his way.

The sea was smooth. The 386's bow had been forced down with ballast so that the runway was level. She began to gain speed. A few minutes later, making all of 9 knots, Fleck picked up his phone and spoke to the man with the flag. The flag dropped, and the pilot gunned his motor. Then it was over almost before it began. The little plane raced down the platform.

"She was off like a bird leaving a tree," Fleck says.

Major General Truscott was delighted, and from a nearby LST, whose men had been watching this apparition, came a blinker signal: "I saw it, but I still can't believe it."

The problem was settled. The 386 would take planes into Licata, Sicily.

She returned to dock in Bizerte harbor and began loading for invasion. The pontoons and causeway sections were made fast to the sides of the ship. In the tank deck went heavy tanks; tied to the flight deck were four small planes. And then came—mules, thirty of them! They refused to walk up the ramp or to be led. They had to be pushed in backwards. Once aboard, they were tied under the flight-deck platform.

On the way to Sicily, the only living things not seasick in the heavy storm were the little Spanish mules, who placidly ate their salt-soaked hay and flicked their long ears.

By 0800 on D-day, the LST 386 was lying off the beach at Licata, her pontoons stretching from the bow to the shore. Two of the planes had taken off at dawn. This had presented a problem, too, since there were four planes, and each plane needed the entire length of the runway to take off. It was solved, however, by lowering the little planes nose down over the side by ropes, to clear the runway for the plane taking off. When one plane left, the next to go was hauled back on the platform.

The last two planes took off after daylight, when the 386 was anchored.

Unloading the mules proved to be just as difficult a task as loading them had been. They didn't want to come aboard, and they didn't want to leave. Brute force was able to drag them from their stalls, place them on the deck elevator and lower them to the tank deck. Once there, however, they refused to walk to shore over the pontoon causeway; they were not accustomed to such elegance. Pushed into the water, they placidly swam ashore to go to work packing ammunition for the Army.

"The LS in LST 386 must stand for 'landing-stable,'" the crew wit observed when, on her second trip to Sicily, she brought in a tank deck full of Goums, French Native African cavalry. Three French officers were with the men on this trip. The day before the ship reached Licata was July 14, Bastille Day. Lieutenant Fleck, in an effort to help the French officers celebrate this national holiday, had his cook bake a cake which the Frenchmen found on the dinner table, its white icing topped off with a brave tricolor rising from the center—a flag made by pasting up red, white and blue paper cut from the colored advertising pages of a magazine.

The planes taken in on the first trip proved their worth as artillery spotters. It was a precedent that was followed up in both the Anzio and Normandy operations.

On the way back to Bizerte after unloading, a delegation came to Lieutenant Fleck's door. They had a proposition.

"They wanted to know if our ship was eligible for flight pay!" Fleck said. "It seemed like a good idea, but we never got around to putting in for it."

There is little glamour about the LCTs (Landing Craft, Tank), homely little sisters of the LSTs. They are slow, awkward and bargelike, the work-horses of the amphibious fleet that have acquired pseudonyms that range from "Flatbottomed Fannys" to "Elsie-Tares," "Elsie" being a phonetic elision for the first two letters of the designation, and "Tare" being the Navy code word for the letter "T."

But occasionally the drudgery of these scowlike craft was lightened by a laugh, and the American bluejacket's ability to laugh is not matched even by his ability to "beef." There was the time at Sicily, before the landings were very old, when one LCT had come into the beach from a transport with a load of mixed cargo. Night found her with the cargo only partially unloaded. What remained was a stack of high-test gasoline drums and a considerable pile of Oerlikon ammunition. The LCT was ordered to halt unloading for the night and remain on the beach.

During the night came an air raid. A bomb missed the little craft, but one of its hot splinters cut through a gasoline drum and started a fire, which spread beyond control and the crew abandoned ship, as the ammunition started exploding. On the beach, the LCT captain started to count noses and found all men accounted for except one.

By daylight the fire had burned itself out, and the men went back aboard their craft to investigate. They went below and found the bulkhead in the engine room charred from the heat, the babbitt melted from the engine bearings. They opened the blistered door into the crew's quarters beyond. In the crew quarters was a bulging hammock. One of the men reached inside the hammock and a sleepy head reared. A hand rubbed puffy eyes.

This man had slept through the entire fire of flaming gasoline and exploding ammunition. When he was taken to the incredulous skipper of the LCT, the survivor's story was simple: "Well, sir, maybe I just sleep a bit heavy."

Another time, after Palermo had fallen and the port was in Allied hands, ten LCTs had been working for a week at 18- to 20-hour stretches, ferrying in supplies to the Army as it leapfrogged its way along the north coast of the island. They had done a remarkable job, and Admiral Davidson was aware of it. Six of these LCTs had labored so hard pacing the Army advance that Rear Admiral Davidson decided to honor the ugly-duckling flotilla in Navy style. Only—somebody forgot to tell the LCT boys about it.

They were barging in to the docks in their usual haphazard formation, and on the leading craft the skipper sprawled on the deckhouse in the standard LCT uniform of grease-soaked sun helmet, bleached and spotted shorts, and a coat of sunburn. He passed the stern of the flagship PHILADELPHIA and cocked a jaundiced eye at the big, trim cruiser which, he knew, had an ice-cream soda fountain, inexhaustible scuttle butts of cold water, and a galleyful of thick steaks. And blow him down if the band wasn't playing.

He looked up again, a skipper in his own right even if he did have less than half the stripes of the cruiser's captain, and what he saw made his helmet rise under the impetus of upstanding hair. There stood the Admiral and his staff at full salute in tribute to the job the LCTs had accomplished.

Somehow the astonished LCT skipper managed simultaneously to dress ship, return the salute and pass word back down the line to the craft in train. The happy-go-lucky rabble of LCTs straightened into line, the nonexistent rails manned, and as each one swept past the flagship, proud as a destroyer, each was saluted.

The Sicilian campaign also saw the Amphibious Force chalk up two other strange firsts: the peaceful conquests of Ustica by an LCI and the equally peaceful conquest of one of the Lipari Group by an LST. The ships simply sailed right up to the beaches, guns bristling—and the cheering Italians prepared a banquet.

But gradually these hod carriers of the sea began to break down under the strain. Repair facilities at Sicilian ports were not yet adequate, and so it was decided somewhere up the line that when amphibious craft deteriorated beyond salvage by local repair they were to be assembled and sent across the Mediterranean to Bizerte for major surgery, under escort of a couple of sound LCIs.

Lieutenant Craig Livingston, USNR, skipper of an escorting craft, tells in unvarnished language the adventure of one such convoy of sea casualties, twenty battered, strained and leaking LCTs, Bizerte-bound from Licata.

"It was a clear day, but at noon the breeze freshened and continued to grow more brisk as the afternoon wore on. At 1600 the outfit formed up and cleared Licata, the LCTs bucking a rough sea that was piled up by the southerly wind. I led one section of the LCTs in the LCI(L)-8, and Lieutenant Woolcott in the 39 headed the other section of them.

"I'm perfectly certain we stood still at times during the night because of the strong headwind. Right after dark the convoy became just a milling bunch of craft; try as they might, they couldn't keep station. Signaling was out of the question because we were allowed to use only small red blinkers, and the signalmen couldn't stand still enough so anyone could read what they sent. Everybody did his best to stay out of everybody else's way.

"By daylight the convoy was whittled down to 15 LCTs and the two LCI(L)s. Five LCTs had turned back to Licata, and the other two had sunk. Nothing dramatic; the skippers found they were breaking up in the heavy seas, so they had other LCTs come alongside and take them off.

"The morning sky was clear but there was a heavy ground-haze. While the wind had died down some, it was still fresh enough to pile up big seas, and the LCTs still sloshed and pounded and plowed up huge chunks of green water that cascaded back over their flat open decks. Most of them now had at least one engine out, so when they lost steerage way they had to fall off to leeward and come around 180 degrees to get back on course.

"All over the convoy you could hear the high-pitched whine of the little gasoline-driven handy-billy pumps. The skippers had to run them frequently to keep from foundering. At one point I got a frantic signal from one for gasoline. He had used all his to keep his boat pumped out. I dropped back abreast of him, rigged a line and passed him a can of gas, and in a few moments his pump was whirring again. It was particularly important that this skipper keep his pumps going, too; he had no ramp on his craft, so the seas flooded back over his deck in a continual torrent. He had a tarpaulin rigged forward; but that was like trying to dam a river with a picket fence.

"Whenever I got feeling sorry for myself I had only to look back and see these ugly ducklings, these miserable, broken-down behemoths, snailing along with the seas cascading over them, and then I realized I was pretty well off. My ship wasn't taking solid water over the main deck; my quarters weren't running six inches deep; my galley still could turn out hot coffee.

"Just after full daylight I looked around to see if I could find anything to give us a fix. Our dead-reckoning position was a joke because no one even dared to guess what speed we'd made during the night; and we couldn't get a star-fix because of the haze. Presently we saw a plume of cloud and figured it must be hanging over Pantelleria, so we changed course to bear on it. Finally we made out the outline of the island 20 miles off.

"It took nine hours to cover that 20 miles. About 1530, LCT 247 semaphored and asked if he might put in at the harbor at Pantelleria along with the one with the ramp missing; he felt he might not be able to finish the trip to Bizerte. I decided he should try and stay with the rest of us. An hour later I found I'd made a mistake; looking back, I saw the No. 247 heading through the convoy formation right for the little harbor about three miles away, his craft humped up in the middle, so that he looked like an inverted V. He was breaking in two, and my only hope now was that it would hold together till he made port. Signaling the rampless LCT to stand by the 247 until he made it in, I decided this was the time to break the voyage. As I turned the formation and headed in toward the harbor, a British air-sea rescue craft buzzed out of the harbor to tell me we could not come in; there just wasn't room. With the No. 247 and the other craft already safely inside, there was no room for any more of us.

"Well, what was I to do with these craft? I had to get them in out of weather. . . . He said he'd show me an anchorage; follow him.

"We followed him three-quarters of the way around the island to a small deep-water cove on the lee side. This took over three hours, so that it was about 2030 now; and in the fading light I had misgivings about getting them all inside this apparently tiny cove. But one by one they bumbled in and dropped their hooks.

"Next morning it was still too rough to attempt the trip. I contacted Bizerte, told them where I was and said I'd be along when the weather calmed a little. As soon as this word got around all hands swarmed ashore on holiday. Everyone spent the day gathering souvenirs and trading C-rations, cigarettes and candy to the natives for the biggest, juiciest grapes I've ever seen.

"The following morning an SC appeared. She came in and tied up alongside, and after a short chat the skipper and I decided we would start for Bizerte at noon if the weather improved. It did and we did. The SC led the formation and the two LCI(L)s acted as sort of roving escorts. Late in the afternoon the wind died down completely, but the sea still had a long, deep swell. We made better speed, entered the channel and rounded Cape Bon shortly after midnight.

"Our troubles weren't over, though. LCT 17, I noticed, had been dropping back steadily so I decided to find out why. I went alongside him and learned that he was having such engine trouble he wasn't able to keep up. I decided I'd better keep him company, and before long the rest of the convoy was over the horizon. Things got worse instead of better; finally the engines had quit completely. We lay pitching dead in the water at 0300 with the moon far enough down to make us a beautiful silhouette to seaward. After what seemed hours we had a tow rigged and got under way at the best possible speed. At about 0830 the next morning we caught the rest of the convoy—just as they were approaching the entrance to

Bizerte harbor. So without too much difficulty we finished what must be the longest passage on record between Licata and Bizerte. . . ."

At that, it should be remembered that the weather on this return passage was no worse than these same vessels had encountered, fully laden, on their way to the original assault on Sicily.

That, in very brief, is the Navy's story of Sicily. As an operation, it was—aside from the essential conquest of that giant insular blockhouse defending Italy—vital schooling in the tasks and techniques for the invasion of the European continent, secure in the grasp of a confident enemy. Panic ran epidemic through Italy, but Italy was a German province.

When Rear Admiral Kirk returned to the United States he told the representatives of the exulting American press that the war was not over by any means.

"We were damned lucky," he warned. "One of these days somebody is not going to be that lucky. They're liable to run into a real mess."

That was sound prophecy. Ahead lay Salerno and Anzio.

Chapter Thirty

T HE end of the Sicilian campaign came with the fall of Messina on August 17, 1943. The same day the islands of Lipari, 35 miles north of Messina, and Stromboli, 50 miles north, surrendered to a United States naval expedition and with them went control of the Aeolian Islands. Now the pathway to Hitler's Europe led up the long leg of Italy, with only the narrow Strait of Messina to cross.

That night the United States warships moved in to shell the Italian mainland for the first time. Cruisers and destroyers bombarded Gioia Tauro and Palmi on the toe of Italy. At the same time, British cruisers and destroyers up the coast of Italy halfway to Naples were shelling Scalea on the Gulf of Policastro. Two days later, on August 19, a United States naval force again bombarded Gioia Tauro, and American PT boats spread out in patrols from Messina harbor as far north as Vibo Valentia. (In neutral Lisbon that night representatives of Marshal Badoglio and General Eisenhower met to begin discussion of Italy's capitulation.)

On September 3, the British Eighth Army crossed the Messina Strait and landed on the mainland near Reggio di Calabria for the push north, the first of four invasions scheduled for the week. British amphibians landed in the Pizzo area on the Gulf of San Eufemia, 50 miles northeast of Reggio, and at Taranto, second only to Spezia as a naval base, with the troops striking east to Brindisi and north to the Adriatic port of Bari. Early in the morning of September 9 American troops landed on the continent, at the beaches of Salerno, just south of Naples. Part of an Anglo-American force, their objective was Naples, while the three wholly British landing forces drove north to sever the Italian boot on a line from Foggia to Salerno.

Supreme Naval Command for the Salerno operation remained in the hands of the Commander in Chief Mediterranean, Admiral of the Fleet Sir Andrew Cunningham; command of the task force working off the beaches and in the Gulf of Salerno went again to Vice-Admiral Henry K.

Hewitt. The naval task was to pound holes in Salerno's defenses, provide the landing forces with artillery support, and to maintain a rapid shuttle service system of reinforcements and supplies.

For days the ships from Salerno had been gathering, more than five hundred of them, ranging from battleships and aircraft carriers down to sturdy little tugs and the ubiquitous swarms of landing craft.

This task force was divided into a Northern Attack Force and a Southern Attack Force.

The Southern Attack Force, commanded by Rear Admiral John L. Hall, Jr., USN, with his flagship, USS SAMUEL CHASE (Captain Roger C. Heimer, USCG), had as its objective the landing of United States troops and their supplies over beaches extending eight miles from the south bank of the River Sele to Agropoli.[1]

The Northern Attack Force, whose objective was landing British troops and supplies on a 10-mile length of beach running north from the Sele River to within three miles southeast of the town of Salerno, was under Commodore G. N. Oliver, RN. Working with Commodore Oliver as a Task Group Commander was Rear Admiral Richard L. Conolly, USN.[2]

[1] Ships of the Southern Attack Force, in addition to transports and landing craft, included:

The cruisers USS PHILADELPHIA (Capt. Paul Hendren, USN), flagship of Rear Admiral Davidson; SAVANNAH (Capt. Robert Cary, USN) and BOISE (Capt. Leo H. Thebaud, USN). Capt. Charles Wellborn, Jr., USN, Commander George L. Menocal, USN, and Commander Edward R. Durgin, USN, were in command of destroyer divisions consisting of: USS PLUNKETT (Lt. Comdr. Edward J. Burke, USN); NIBLACK (Lt. Comdr. Ray R. Conner, USN); BENSON (Lt. Comdr. Ronald J. Woodaman, USN); GLEAVES (Lt. Comdr. Byron L. Gurnette, USN); MAYO (Lt. Comdr. Frederick S. Habecker, USN); WAINWRIGHT (Lt. Comdr. Robert H. Gibbs, USN); TRIPPE (Lt. Comdr. Russell C. Williams, USN); RHIND (Lt. Comdr. Otto W. Spahr, USN); ROWAN (Lt. Comdr. Robert S. Ford, USN); KNIGHT (Lt. Comdr. Joel C. Ford, Jr., USN); WOOLSEY (Lt. Comdr. Henry R. Wier, USN); LUDLOW (Lt. Comdr. Liles W. Creighton, USN); EDISON (Lt. Comdr. Hepburn A. Pearce, USN); NICHOLSON (Comdr. Lewis M. Markham, Jr., USN); BRISTOL (Comdr. John A. Glick, USN); COLE (Lt. Comdr. Briscoe Chipman, USN); BERNADOU (Lt. Comdr. Benjamin L. E. Talman, USN); DALLAS (Comdr. Anthony C. Roessler, USN). For the difficult job of sweeping the approaches to the beaches and the anchorages where the transports and bombardment units would lie were the minesweepers: USS STRIVE, SEER, SKILL, SPEED, STEADY, SUSTAIN, SYMBOL, PILOT, PREVAIL. In addition there were fifteen YMS, Yard Minesweepers, smaller craft for work in coastal waters. And two tugs: USS HOPI and MORENO. Ships of the British Navy working with the Southern Attack Force were: HMS ABERCROMBIE, ULSTER QUEEN, PALOMARES, DELHI, OAKLEY, HAMBLEDON, DERWENTDALE, EMPIRE, CHARMAIN, BOXER, BRUISER, THRUSTER.

[2] Ships of the Northern Attack Force for bombardment and other purposes included six British cruisers, 18 destroyers, 15 minesweepers, 13 minesweeping trawlers, four motor launch minesweepers, four motor minesweepers, four USN Yard sweepers,

The Air Support Group, the carriers whose planes would provide a considerable part of the fighter cover over the inshore ships and beaches during the opening phases of the Salerno landings, was commanded by Rear Admiral Sir Phillip L. Vian, RN, and consisted of three cruisers, five aircraft carriers, two destroyers of the Polish Navy, SLAZAK and KRAKOWIAK, and eight Royal Navy destroyers.

There was a Covering Force, commanded by Vice Admiral Sir Algernon U. Willis, RN, to protect the battleships, aircraft carriers and destroyers operating in the Tyrrhenian Sea. This force, with attendant destroyers, included such familiar battlewagons with resounding names as HMS NELSON, WARSPITE, ILLUSTRIOUS and FORMIDABLE, and eight more of Britain's best.

Fifth Army troops, for the south beaches, were ferried to Salerno from Bizerte, a scene of truly indescribable activity as the armies of two nations embarked for Italy.

It had been impossible to conceal preparations of such magnitude from enemy reconnaissance. On the night of September 6 the huge fleet put to sea after fighting off waves of German bombers for an hour and twenty-three minutes.

Aboard the flagship Vice-Admiral Hewitt and Lieutenant General Mark Clark of the Fifth Army had spent the thirty-six hours of the Mediterranean crossing studying an oversize map of Salerno Bay. Running down from the mountains, across the flat level land, onto the beaches and into the blue paper that marked the Tyrrhenian Sea was a heavy black line, the Sele River. As has been said, that river divided the American and British beaches. To the south, the first objective of the Americans was Paestum and the heights of Mount Soprano, which looked down on the sandy water's edge. The British to the north were to drive for Battipaglia, the most important road junction in the beachhead area.

Two sections of the task force had special assignments. One was a detachment of British Commandos and American Army Rangers, under Commander S. H. Dennis, RN, on HMS PRINCE CHARLES. After landing, these selected troops were to push on past Salerno town, to capture the two mountain passes guarding the approach to the plains of Naples. The other special section was a group of ships and men under command of

10 transports and miscellaneous ships and the Greek destroyer PINDOS. The British fleet, all told, was twice the number of United States ships employed, amphibious craft not included.

Captain Andrews aboard the destroyer USS KNIGHT, which included the gunboats SOEMBA and FLORES of the Royal Netherlands Navy. Its assignment was the occupation of the islands lying off the Gulf of Naples: Ventotene, Ponza, Procida, Ischia and the Isle of Capri.

While the landings were taking place on Salerno beaches, a little fleet within a fleet, a group of sixteen United States Navy PT boats under Lieutenant Commander Barnes, USN, was charged with patrolling the water behind and on the flanks of the task force, against surface craft and E-boats.

By sundown of Wednesday, September 8, the Salerno invasion fleet passed Cap d'Orlando, Sicily, and headed straight for the Gulf of Salerno. H-hour was 0330 on the morning of September 9.

Ahead of the invasion fleet moved the minesweepers, pathfinders of the invasion. With supreme impudence they entered Salerno Gulf an hour after midnight to begin their dangerous task of clearing the water of the extensive minefields. An hour later the transports and waiting warships received the signal that the bay was swept, the water clear. (In the northern area the sweepers swept up or exploded 20 mines during the assault and 135 in the first four days.)

The night was oppressive. Not a breeze rippled the still water. The landing craft loaded with hot, sweating men, circled while waiting for the signal to go in.

And then, fifteen minutes before H-hour, the silence was ripped to tatters as the bombardment destroyers opened fire on the beaches in concentrated salvos. With that, the waiting German artillery ashore screamed back in fiery defiance as it loosed heavy-shelled 88s over the water. The destroyers and gunboats moved in closer and stepped up their fire. Five minutes before H-hour the rocket boats flared their whistling projectiles, newest addition to modern warfare. Small craft added mortar fire. It was as if all the fires of Vesuvius had been freed. Now, a minute and half before the landing craft were due to touch beach, every craft within range doubled the fiery bedlam with small rockets, machine gun and rifle fire to clear the beaches for the seaborne troops.

On split-second timing the assault wave went in. The bows of the landing craft grated on sand, jolted and stopped. Down crashed the ramps and over them charged the first of Lieutenant General Mark Clark's Fifth Army.

To those first waves of first assault troops, the beaches seemed clear of the enemy. Some areas were not even marred by the black web of barbed wire. Mine-detecting squads felt their way ahead with their round, flat, lily-pad detectors, like humped, biped anteaters, clearing paths through the mines and marking them with white tape. In came the DUKWs, the amphibious trucks, light artillery; more landing craft grated to a stop on the steep beaches. For five minutes after the first soldier stepped ashore the landing was unopposed.

Then the Germans in their well-hidden pillboxes and gun positions opened up. They had been waiting. They weren't surprised by this invasion. They had simply been waiting for the moment when the beaches were full, when it was unnecessary to aim to find a target.

Machine guns and rifles chattered, spit and snarled from positions 150 yards behind the waterline, and, beyond these, belched 88-mm. and larger shells from German tanks and pillboxes. One shell struck a landing craft and it sank in a geyser of splinters, gray paint and water. The troops dug in, balked by the mobile artillery of the tanks. Then, instead of the blast of guns, there were louder explosions where the tanks had been wheeling and firing. Their position had been relayed to the destroyers three miles out in the bay; salvo after salvo shattered the steel monsters.

More troops came in under the covering fire of the destroyers. The beachhead widened; in some places the assault thrust inland as deep as a mile. The cruisers' guns joined the destroyer fire, reaching out ahead of the driving infantrymen.

In four hours the troops had pushed in to Paestum, behind the creeping naval barrage. They held a length of the coastal highway and were forcing the Germans into the hills of Mount Soprano. Dawn arrived, concealed by the glare of shell fire, until suddenly it was daylight, and with it the German shell fire from the heights inland began blasting the beaches. Three German tanks came within 200 yards of the foxholes into which the beach parties and shore engineers had driven and started shelling the transport area. Casualties began to mount. An urgent signal was sent to one of the other beaches for a boat to evacuate the wounded, but it was sunk by enemy fire before it could reach the beach. Seaman 1st Class Andrew Allardi, USN, took off his clothes and swam out to the shelled boat to help the wounded crew ashore.

Now the Luftwaffe appeared to make the agony supreme, sweeping in from the sea in lightning attacks to aim heavy bombloads on the ships at anchor, and blasting the beaches with loads of light fragmentation bombs that exploded a rain of needle-pointed steel on the men and the stacks of equipment that lined the beaches.

News that Italy had surrendered unconditionally seemed somehow terribly unimportant.

A hundred yards offshore an oncoming destroyer turned broadside to the beach and began moving slowly up the bay, pumping shell after shell into the German gun positions on Mount Soprano.

In a sheltered position at the foot of the mountain the American Divisional Command Post had been established, hard by the smoking steel skeletons of four Mark IV German tanks, shattered by the shells of a cruiser out in the bay.

Across the Sele River, the British beachhead was taking reverses. Battipaglia, the coastal road junction, had been taken and then lost again to a strong German counterdrive. North of the city of Salerno the American Rangers and British Commandos were digging into their mountain-pass positions to fight off a German drive which had cut them off from their beaches with only a 48-hour supply of food and ammunition.

After daylight the heavily laden LSTs came in to unload. Strapped to their sides were long pontoons and sectional causeways. Some distance from the beach was a broad sand bar, which would ground an LST. There they anchored, while the crews floated the pontoons, bolted the causeway sections together, and built a floating bridge from ship to shore, across which tanks clanked precariously, and tractors dragged field artillery.

With these heavy fighting engines once ashore, the Germans found their counterattacks becoming costly, although undetected land mines took their toll as the equipment rolled over the beaches. On one beach in the Northern Attack Force area, the Germans pushed tanks out onto the beaches. They were driven back into the wooded area behind the beaches by ship fire which lasted an hour and a half. It was impossible to see from the ships whether the tanks were knocked out, so a landing craft was sent in toward that particular beach as a test. The tanks fired again. So did the destroyers. The ship-to-shore unloading continued, after that, with no more tank trouble.

First the Commandos, then the Rangers began to vanish quickly inland; the beach battalions next, and then the Seabees, and finally the infantry. The Seabees went in with their equipment: bulldozers, trench diggers and tractors. Their first job was to arrange a beachhead and mark off spaces for the LSTs and LCIs to come in. Then they arranged to handle the traffic of the incoming ships. They had to clean up the debris and lay mats on the sand for the wheeled vehicles to drive on. By the time the Seabees had finished, what in peacetime had been a pleasant bathing beach was little short of a naval base. They had cleared spaces for storing ammunition and reserve equipment. They had cleared spaces for dressing stations, and erected lean-tos in which the wounded would be treated and sheltered until they could be taken aboard ship.

As the landing continued, German shelling increased from mobile 88s forever on the move behind the hills. Enemy fire took a terrific toll of the equipment on the beaches. The beach was strewn with dead and wounded.

"As I stepped out onto the beach," recalls Lieutenant Commander Frank C. Grismer, USNR, "an armored car was hit and started to blaze. I turned, and stumbled over a soldier. I stopped to apologize, and saw that he was dead. One could hardly move in any direction without stumbling over the American, British and German dead. Later, I went up beyond the beach by a little road that ran to a dairy farm. The farm buildings were entirely enclosed by stone walls, and leading up from the farm buildings was a lane about ten feet wide bordered on either side by a stone wall about four feet high. Along these walls our troops had dug in during the night, making foxholes about six feet apart. But at some time in the darkness, a German tank came down the lane. There was no escape for the troops. All were killed.

"In the fields the cattle had been killed, by machine-gun cross fire and by artillery. Where hand-to-hand fighting had taken place, the dead lay sprawled. Our troops in single file marched up past their dead, looking neither to right nor left, moving forward to the enemy who had taken cover in the hills."

Hottest spot of the Salerno landings was a place called Green Beach, one that had to be abandoned under weight of enemy resistance. Three LSTs, manned by the men who called themselves "Re-treads," were scheduled to make early landings here. There were Lieutenant Harold Fleck, USNR, with the 386 of Sicilian fame; Lieutenant Robert Browning, USNR, with the 388; and Lieutenant Frank Bidwell, USNR, with the 336.

On the way in to the beach, Fleck received a message, "Mines off your starboard beam." The next thing he heard was a dull explosion.

The heavy LST seemed to be riding on a roller-coaster. The warning had been accurate, if too late. Two of the massive pontoon sections were blown up on the main deck, wrecking a British ambulance and killing three soldiers, wounding nine. Pharmacist's Mate Robert Summers, USNR, and Lieutenant Willis Mitchell, USNR, of the Seabee unit carried the wounded men into the wardroom for treatment, as Fleck started in for the beach, his gyro knocked out, the rudder and one engine damaged.

Lieutenant Browning and Lieutenant Bidwell came in too. Green Beach was a place where the German 88s were heaviest, and they started to concentrate on the three LSTs. For some reason only Bidwell's ship was struck.

"She took it for all of us, I guess," said Browning. "She had eighteen direct hits."

The LSTs were ordered to retract from the beach and delay unloading. Browning and Fleck moved off, but Bidwell's radio had been shot away and he failed to get the order. His ship proceeded to unload and then the battered hulk pulled out. The men on the ships could see a gray stone wall about 100 feet from the water of Green Beach. Enemy lines were about 80 yards from the water. On the seaward side of the wall, the last thin line of British troops was pinned down, unable to move or to retreat.

Fleck's ship and Browning's were unloaded on another beach. On the next trip into Green, they saw the cargo that Bidwell had unloaded. It was still on the beach, charred and shell-torn beyond salvage.

Some beaches were abandoned, some were held. By nightfall, however, the troops had consolidated and the beachhead needed as the entering wedge to pry Naples from German hands had been seized as planned.

The diversionary force under Captain Andrews on USS KNIGHT had captured Ventotene Island, about 40 miles west of Naples. The Italian garrison had surrendered quickly, but a detachment of ninety Germans fought until overcome.

D-day had passed and the first tension of invasion was over, but all gains were doomed unless an endless chain of ships could roll in with more troops, more guns, more ammunition. None knew that better than the Nazis, who maintained persistent and concentrated air attacks. Allied carrier aircraft and Army fighter planes from bases 200 miles away in Sicily competed with German fighters and bombers from airfields only

16 miles inland, to keep that endless supply of men and machines rolling ashore.

The Germans singled out Vice-Admiral Hewitt's flagship, which also served as headquarters for Lieutenant General Clark, and in thirty-six hours made thirty attacks, in twenty-two of which the ship was tossed by near misses. But it was no better to be on the ships anchored outside, waiting to come in. Safety hatches were closed and the ventilating systems cut off to prevent sucking in the acrid smoke from smoke screens and burning ships. There was nothing to do but sweat, strangle and wait under a mad sky in which tracers wove a hideous plaid of fire. The Germans attacked in waves of thirty and more planes, losing five to eight on every attack. But still the attacks came.

They came, too, in some new forms. High-flying heavy bombers, staying out of antiaircraft range, released what first appeared to be midget airplanes. Swooping down in a long glide, these tiny winged flying machines were a poor target for gunners, because they would change from a glide to a roaring dive over their targets, the anchored ships. Thus did the long-rumored German "secret weapon," the radio-controlled bombs, forerunners of V-1 and V-2, make their entry.

It was an impressive one; the radio-bombs did a better job than their younger, but larger, brethren, the "buzz-bombs," in the destruction of purely military targets. Not until Allied aircraft could climb up to chase the spawning bomber away was the menace eliminated. For the time being, the ships in Salerno Bay had to stay and take it—cruisers, destroyers, LSTs and LCTs alike—suffering and sweating it out.

Part of the strategy of any invasion is to follow up the initial landings with a ceaseless flow of landing craft coming into the beaches with fresh men, more equipment, reinforcements to keep the momentum of invasion pushing constantly at the enemy. Sometimes this build-up phase is as dangerous as the original assault, or more so. It was so at Salerno (and, later, at Anzio) as witness the adventures of LST 352. Her captain was Lieutenant Joseph Kahrs, Jr., USNR, a lawyer in Newark, New Jersey, before the war. Kahrs and his crew tasted of war in the invasion of Sicily. He had started from the homeland with a mixed crew, more fortunate than most LST captains in that he had a bosun with twenty-three years in the Navy, and another man who was eighteen years a chief. But most of the crew was young, raw, green and scared like everyone else. Those who had not stepped out of school into the Navy had worked at jobs varying from plumbing to bookkeeping. One man had been a bartender in a San Francisco hotel, another was a professional roller skater, who had toured the vaudeville circuits with his father and mother. It was men like these who kept the Fifth Army supplied at Salerno.

The LST 352 made eleven trips to Salerno's beaches, the first on D-day, carrying British troops and 120 Indian volunteers from the state of Jodhpur. And there was the ship's dog, Oscar, bought in Brooklyn for $2.00 by the quartermaster, Eugene O. Bauman. Oscar was just a long-tailed semi-fox terrier of decided tastes. He disliked officers and loved oranges and raw onions.

The 352 was not scheduled to hit the Salerno beach until 0800 on the morning of D-day, September 9. Consequently, her position in the convoy was in the rear echelon.

It was well after dark on D-plus-one when the men on the LST saw all the signs of a naval engagement far ahead. Their first conclusion was that the invasion convoy had been attacked. Then the word was passed back, ship to ship, that Italy had surrendered and part of the Italian Fleet was under attack by German aircraft and E-boats as it tried to leave for an Allied port under the terms of the Italian capitulation.

Italy out of the war? The Axis partners shooting at each other?

It was true. "The word" was official. And immediately there was rejoicing. To many, keyed up to fine tension for landing on enemy beaches in a few hours, it spelled reprieve from one more fight. Certainly, if Italy had capitulated, then the landings would be unopposed: the Allied ships would merely sail into Naples harbor, tie up at a dock and unload over a gangplank.

But Italy was no better off than France or Norway or the Netherlands, and an enraged German army was waiting to smash the invasion, not only to preserve the Hitler domain but to demonstrate which was the master race to the Italians.

When Lieutenant Kahrs's ship came within sight of the beaches next morning, he was told to anchor and wait instructions for coming in.

There was a long wait until the 352 could go into the beach, and it was a bad wait. Enemy mines that had been swept loose were drifting out to sea. They had been painted green for camouflage and looked like ugly round-bellied sea monsters to the men on the waiting ships that maneuvered sluggishly to keep out of their paths.

In the afternoon, word was flashed to Lieutenant Kahrs to bring the

LST 352 into the beach. Then the Germans counterattacked and the order was canceled. All night the ship waited, its men standing at general quarters stations, with plenty of time to think about the drifting mines. In the morning orders came to beach at a point north of the Sele River where the German air attack had been lightest.

The ship started in. "I didn't think we were going to stop until our bow was in a group of olive trees back of the beach," Kahrs recalls. "We were going full speed when the bow touched sand. Standing at the conning station, I could see the bow rise, the deck bend and curve up a little and then we stopped. The bow doors opened, the ramp came down and the troops walked off on dry sand."

That night the 352 started back to Bizerte for another load. Arriving in Salerno the second time, the crew had their first introduction to the deadly German 88-mm. shells.

"You heard a bang first, then a low whistle. They were spotting us, getting our range, each shell falling about fifty yards closer to us than the last one. When one shell landed fifty yards from our ship we thought the next one would be right on us. But it wasn't. They lifted elevation too much and the next one passed over," Kahrs recalls.

After another quick unloading the 352 and thirteen other LSTs were ordered to Tripoli for troops and equipment. When they returned, the ships were waiting in Salerno Gulf for orders to enter the harbor. Over the radio they came, in clear English: "All LSTs close Salerno . . . All LSTs close Salerno . . ."

The fourteen LSTs pulled up their hooks and started in. Suddenly a British cruiser charged across their path and over a loud-speaker a voice screamed at the lead ship:

"The harbor's under enemy fire! You'll jolly well be shot up if you go in there!"

A Nazi ruse had almost worked. Somehow the Germans had picked up the LST's radio frequency and code. The fake order had lured the ships almost within range of the enemy guns when the alert British cruiser spoiled the Nazi game.

On the next trip to Tripoli the cargo was a load of Palestinian troops. With them was an 8-piece jazz band that they refused to leave behind in North Africa. They were especially proud of on old desert-scarred upright piano that had followed them all the way across the sands from El Alamein. And a major brought his dog along. She had ten puppies en route bringing the dog cargo of the 352 up to twelve dogs, including Oscar.

The fourth trip from Africa brought a load of the "Desert Rats," the sun-browned, hard-bitten veterans of General Montgomery's Eighth Army. One of the men had a mascot that he kept in his pocket day and night . . . it was a genuine desert rat picked up somewhere along the hard trek from Alexandria to Tripoli, and the LST boys gave the vicious little beast all the respect due a tiger. Another cargo for Salerno beaches was the first French troop contingent to fight in Italy, an assortment of French Regulars, Moroccans, and native troops of French Indo-China.

Multiply the 352's experiences by fifty, by one hundred, by five hundred, and you have the story of breaching the walls of Hitler's Europe.

On D-plus-one, Friday, September 10, the port of Salerno was taken. The unloading of ships continued, and so did the German counterattack. The shuttle system of reinforcements and supply began. As soon as an LST, LCI or LCT unloaded, it backed off the beach, swung its bow south and started for a refill.

On September 11 the German glider bombs made their startling appearance. The cruiser SAVANNAH, which was supporting the landing operations with PHILADELPHIA and BOISE, had the dubious honor of being the first ship struck and damaged. The bomb pierced the number 3 turret. In the afternoon the radio room of USS ANCON, Vice-Admiral Hewitt's ship, intercepted an enemy message describing and identifying the flagship, and ordering the German air force to sink her at all costs.

Vice-Admiral Hewitt immediately gave orders for the ship to move out of the Salerno area. Escorted by two destroyers she moved out to sea and, without air protection and in absolute radio silence, took shelter overnight in a low, heavy night haze that hid her shape from enemy planes, which obediently scoured the area in search, as those aboard the ANCON could clearly hear.

Next morning, September 12, the ANCON entered Salerno Bay and Lieutenant General Clark, with his staff, went ashore. The beachhead now extended 25 miles from Salerno south to Agropoli, and the German counterattacks, although continuous, were being repulsed with losses the enemy could not long endure. South of Sele River the bridgehead extended inland from 4 to 7 miles. To the north, the army was 2 to 4 miles inland. The British had recaptured the road junction at Battipaglia, and, once the blockade of scuttled shipping was removed from the channel of

Salerno harbor, the LSTs and LCIs were able to discharge troops, tanks and cargo direct to the city's piers.

All seemed to be going very well, after a bitterly fought beginning. Then, fresh from the Alpine garrisons, arrived the German reinforcements who hit the Allied lines like an avalanche at dusk on the evening of September 13. The thin lines of weary American troops broke, and German tanks raced through toward the junction of the Sele and Calore rivers to strike at the American left wing.

Lieutenant General Clark presided at a tense conference which decided that, at all cost, the German strength must be held in the triangle of the Battipaglia-Eboli-Altavilla area. If the Nazis could be pinned down there, the enemy would be concentrated for a combined naval and air bombardment.

The Fifth Army saved the Salerno bridgehead that night. Before dawn next morning the Allied Navy and air forces saved the Fifth Army.

The opportune hour struck. The still moonlit sky was suddenly torn by a concentrated naval and air bombardment. Corner by corner the German-held triangle was chewed to piece. By daylight the enemy was trying to break off contact and retreat.

The cruiser PHILADELPHIA, alone, fired over 1,100 rounds of shells into the German positions, and she was but one of the many supporting ships engaged in the rescue of the invasion. The ships had to be deliberately risked in mined water where they were also liable to air attack, but the risks taken were necessary and justified. The success of the invasion of Italy was in the balance, and the weight of the warships' guns tipped the scales.

The next five days of land fighting entrenched the Army in Central Italy beyond any possibility of retreat, and by September 20 the heights of Sorrento Peninsula were taken, giving the Fifth Army an artillery sweep across the entire bay of Naples, 12 miles away.

Following the capture of Ventotene Island by Captain Andrews's force on September 9, the islands of Capri, Procida and Ponza were occupied, providing a chain of bases for launching a drive against Naples itself.

Chapter Thirty-one

BLOODY Salerno had been a complete victory for the Allies; they had put troops ashore in spite of the worst the enemy could throw at them. And that alone was the measure of the achievement for the men who fought there. But Salerno, like every other Allied beachhead established in Old World waters, had a deeper, more far-reaching meaning. Successful landings at Fedala, Safi, Port Lyautey meant that the Allies could use the great harbor of Casablanca, pouring troops and supplies into it, repairing and refitting ships there. Landings at Algiers and Arzeu freed the ports of Algiers and Oran. Men and equipment poured through them into Africa to dislodge Rommel and give access to Bizerte, the most strategically located harbor of them all from which to mount invasions against Southern Europe and the Mediterranean islands. Next, the conquest of Sicily provided the ports of Syracuse, Augusta and Palermo.

Indeed, Allied military and naval progress can as easily be charted by the ports captured as by the beachheads established. Prodigies of effort and ingenuity had been demonstrated in getting armies ashore across open beaches and through tiny fishing villages, it is true, but such operations were at the mercy of the weather which seldom fought on the Allied side. Unloading in *Operation Torch* was held up by heavy seas the day after it started; weather casualties to small boats off Sicily came dangerously close to halting our drive before it had fairly begun. To put the heavy paraphernalia of war ashore ports are needed, deep-water ports with piers and cranes, railroad sidings and sheltered roadsteads.

So it was with Salerno; the landing there and the capture of the little harbor were great victories, but the real prize was the port of Naples, one of the great harbors of the world.

It took the Army, helped by naval gunfire in a bombardment witnessed by Secretary of the Navy Frank Knox, twenty-one days to capture Naples and when they did they found the harbor for which they had struggled so cruelly to be as total a wreck as the Nazi genius for destruction could make it—and the Nazis were past masters at ruining other people's property.

Every dock was blocked, every channel fouled, at least partially, by a sunken ship, and the more important berths usually had two ships, loaded with cement and extensively booby-trapped, sunk crosswise at the entrance. All dockside installations—railways, cranes—were smashed; all warehouses destroyed, all drydocks and graving docks demolished. And hidden in a thousand places amid this debris were booby traps, mines and delayed-action bombs. That was the harbor of Naples the Allies had fought so hard for, the harbor they had to use if we were going to support an army in Italy and, ultimately, send another army to Southern France. The fight to restore Naples harbor was in its way as tremendous a task as the fight to capture it.

For this mighty job the Army and the Navy had no little practice: At Casablanca, where our own bombardment had sunk ships in important channels and berths; at Bizerte, where the trapped Germans had improved the gloomy hour by blowing up everything that floated; at Palermo, where, in addition to their regular destructive tactics on departing, the Germans had returned to blast the harbor from the air. Salvaging harbors and putting them to work in short order was right down the American alley. We had had plenty of recent experience.

As a matter of fact, our training in such work antedated our entry into the war, and came as a result of what was at the time regarded as a calamity: the sinking of the French liner NORMANDIE at her pier in New York in the winter of 1941.

The NORMANDIE had barely cooled from the disastrous fire which swept her, before Commander William A. Sullivan, CEC, USN, had not only seen the possibility of refloating her, but the even more important possibility of using the very same operation to school Navy personnel in ship and underwater salvage operations. From every Navy shore station and from every ship in the Fleet, volunteers came to New York to learn the manifold tricks of the marine salvage trade.

It was an education that paid dividends—to say nothing of raising the NORMANDIE—first at Pearl Harbor, later in the ruined ports of Africa and Europe. Two months after the capture of battered Bizerte it was one of the largest ports in North Africa in tonnage handled, and together with Ferryville nearby, the leading amphibious base of Vice-Admiral Hewitt's

Eighth Fleet. (During the course of the work there, the salvage crews made one of the most ironic captures of the war—a shipload of medals for Rommel to hand out after the Germans' triumphal parade through Cairo, together with the cargo of wine and brandy to be drunk with appropriate "Hochs!" and "Heils!" on the same delightful occasion.)

Palermo went into operation as an Army and Navy supply depot and staging point almost as soon as it was captured, and by the time the fight for Salerno came up, it was not only capable of handling freight traffic but also ready to turn to as a repair station for the ships shattered off the contested beach.

In Naples, at the war's end, hulks still rest on the bottom of the harbor, masts still project forlornly above the calm waters. But the important channels and the important berths have been usable throughout the whole invasion of continental Europe. In some instances the Army engineers or the Seabees (clearing a harbor is as much a joint operation as capturing it) simply built causeways across the sunken ships; others they floated and towed away, and still others they blew apart with explosives.

Four months after the Allies took the harbor, Commander Sullivan and his salvage teams had the port of Naples leading the world in amount of tonnage received.

They needed that harbor badly, not only because of its capacity or its nearness to the fighting front but also because they had taken a nasty setback at our other big Italian port, Bari.

Chapter Thirty-two

I T WAS December 2, 1943. With luck and a lot of speed, some of the ships in the oil-slimed water that filled the harbor of Bari might be home for a late Christmas.

Some of the men thought so, anyway. Any December day before Christmas a man is likely to calculate his chances on getting home for New Year's Eve anyhow, especially when that man is at war. He thinks about it whether the chances are good or not. In this case there was a possibility. Some ships might make it if their luck held—their luck against enemy air attacks, enemy submarine attacks, or just plain sailing orders that would send them east when they wanted to go west.

But at Bari their luck ran out on December 2. For six days German reconnaissance planes had been flying over the harbor. They seemed to be waiting for something. On December 2 they saw what they wanted.

That morning a large convoy from the United States had arrived with supplies for the Eighth Army pushing up the Adriatic calf of Italy's leg. The harbor was full. Every dock was occupied, at every pier and for the length of the seawall were ships heavy with cargo.

That night sixteen ships lay bombed and sunk in the harbor, and six more were floating junk heaps.

Five of the sunken ships were American merchantmen. There was SAMUEL J. TILDEN and JOHN HARVEY, JOSEPH WHEELER and an ammunition ship, JOHN L. MOTLEY. And there was JOHN BASCOM.

The JOHN BASCOM was an ordinary merchant ship carrying "ordinary war cargo" for the Army fighting the Germans up the rocky spine of Italy, 8,000 tons of what an Army needs. But some hundreds of tons of that cargo was in 50-gallon drums of aviation gasoline, almost as choice a bomb target as the ammunition-loaded JOHN L. MOTLEY a few boat lengths away.

Although her cargo was called "ordinary," the BASCOM carried a crew of extraordinary men, among whom was the Armed Guard officer, Ensign

Kay K. Vesole, USNR, of Davenport, Iowa, whose bravery under fire and devotion to his men earned him the Navy Cross at the price of his life. Those who lived through the attack that night, from the captain of the ship through the lowest rated deck hand, will honor Vesole in their memories as long as they live as one of the most courageous of men.

The ships that entered the harbor on December 2 went to their assigned places along the docks and piers and the sea wall, for unloading. As the late afternoon light grew dim and the unloading continued, the ships blacked out, but lights were burning along the dock and sea wall for the cargo handlers.

The JOHN BASCOM was moored stern first to the sea wall. The men on the ship were going about their usual business. Those who had a watch were standing it and those who were off duty were lying at ease. Two of the Armed Guard crew, Donald L. Norton, Seaman 2/c, and William A. Rochford, Seaman 1/c, were standing by their guns. Another man, Stanley Bishop, Seaman 1/c, was below, in the messhall, writing a letter home.

Suddenly, the strident signal for general quarters squawked.

Norton and Rochford had spotted planes. They bawled the alarm as they jumped for their guns, and with that the first wave of planes dropped a shower of brilliant white flares that lighted the entire harbor area, parachute flares that hung in mid-air and concealed the planes above even as they revealed the harbor below. Blinded by the glare, unable to see the planes they were shooting at, the gunners on all ships wove a protecting tent above their vessels with tracer bullets.

At the sound of the general alarm, Stanley Bishop left his letter writing and ran up to the deck.

"The sky was full of tracers and flares and exploding shells," he said. "Then the first stick of bombs plunked down a hundred yards away, striking a ship, which exploded and sank. Then there was another heavy jar, and a wave of heat. There was explosion all around us. The ship next to us began burning."

When the alarm was sounded all the lights on the piers and in the harbor went out, except a single bright light on the tip of a shore crane, which continued to shine for a few minutes until it was shot out by one of the British Military Police. But the Germans had brought their own illumination, and burning ships eclipsed the flares in lighting the harbor.

Ensign Vesole was standing by his gunners directing their fire when the JOHN BASCOM was hit. She was struck with a stick of three bombs, falling in the number 1, 3 and 5 holds.

Men on the deck went down like pins in a bowling alley. As one man said, "When the bombs hit the BASCOM, concussion knocked men around all over. We could see hits being scored on ships on every side, and there was fire and disaster no matter where you looked."

Stanley Bishop fired 400 rounds of 20-mm. shells before his gun jammed. He fussed with the mechanism, and then the bombs struck.

"The bomb that killed the man standing next to me blew me off my feet," he recalls. "The air was full of flying splinters and stuff, and a couple of German planes were strafing us on top of it all. I was burned all over and my back and stomach were hit pretty bad. I was hit in the head by shrapnel so much that my helmet was cut all to pieces." Nevertheless, Bishop went below to help carry out the worse hurt.

That bomb concussion had knocked Ensign Vesole to the deck, too, and when the smoke cleared away his crew could see him. He scrambled to his feet, awkwardly because his right arm was broken. His clothes were scarecrow tatters, revealing a deep shrapnel wound on his right shoulder and a long, vicious slash across his chest. But Vesole kept going. He went from gun station to gun station, directing action, inquiring about the safety of his men, directing first aid for the injured and wounded.

The raid passed. Vesole called out some names: "Goldstein!" (That was Dave Goldstein, the coxswain.) "Baker! Bishop! Ainsworth!"

The scorched quartet lined up. "Let's go below and see who's hurt," Vesole said. Through the fire and the twisted wreckage of the bombed ship they led the search for wounded men, and helped to carry them to the top deck. Vesole saw that syrettes of morphine and other medical supplies were gathered together, and fell back long enough to salvage a few cartons of cigarettes to pass out to his wounded crew.

The enlisted men were equally cool. Seaman Arthur Behm, for example, volunteered to go below and flood the magazine to prevent further explosions. It was Behm who had the idea to throw overboard all buoyant objects, anything that would help a man to keep himself afloat, because only one lifeboat remained undamaged, and the ship was surely going down.

Fifteen minutes after the BASCOM was struck, the order to abandon ship was passed. It was the longest quarter hour in the lives of those who survived it.

Seamen Reginald Baker, Walter Ainsworth, Robert Boyce, Arthur Behm, Robert Kelley, Rodney Ruddiman, and Gunner's Mate 3rd Class Horace Anderson, despite their own injuries, volunteered to swim the 100 feet from ship to jetty. As the single lifeboat started to load, Ensign Vesole insisted that he, too, would swim to the jetty to make room in the boat for others whom he considered more badly wounded than he, with his broken arm and deep body wounds. His men picked him up bodily and placed him in the boat. Once seated, he insisted on rowing with his one good arm.

When the lifeboat reached the sea wall, Vesole took command of the unloading of wounded. Stretchers were improvised from oars. Wounds gaped and spurted blood as the comparatively lesser injured carried their helpless shipmates to shelter.

The flaming BASCOM stubbornly refused to sink. Her lines snapped, and she began to drift down toward the ammunition ship.

Vesole and his men, although now suffering additionally from smoke and gas fumes, labored to save those doomed by the inevitable explosion. Vesole gave his good hand to men in the water, helping three of his wounded crew out and onto the sea wall. Signalmen William Kreimer and Robert Kelley, both suffering from badly burned hands, went out to the extreme end of the sea wall with flashlights to signal to the undamaged ships, begging for small boats to come in and pick up survivors still in the oil-slick water, over which a blue flicker of flame was beginning to play, flaring into crimson here and there.

"Ain't this hell, though?" one man groaned.

"I hope you'll never see anything more like it." Vesole laughed. "Bear a hand here with this stretcher. That ammunition ship will blow any minute."

Then it did. With a bright red rush of fire.

"It seemed as if the entire world was burning," said one of the men, later. "The explosion threw the Ensign at least thirty feet, and everyone was knocked to the ground."

The force of the explosion hurled the floating oil fire over the sea wall, cutting off the escape of the men out on the end of the jetty. Escape to the shore was impossible through this flaming mass.

The two signalmen with the flashlights had been trying frantically to call for rescue boats. The oil flames were sweeping closer to the huddled group of scorched and wounded men. Some of them had been able to take advantage of a small bomb shelter on the jetty, and had suffered less from the explosion of the ammunition ship than others, but all were facing death by fire unless those boats came.

And they did come, maneuvering around the flaming oil pools. When the boats arrived, Ensign Vesole, bordering on almost complete collapse, refused to take the first boat, leaving his place for others who were injured, although none was worse wounded. He was carried into the next boat and taken ashore to the 98th General Hospital in Bari, and there he died.

In addition to the American ships sunk, there were four British, three Norwegian, two Italian, and two Polish ships destroyed. The LYMAN ABBOTT was damaged along with three British, one Dutch and one Norwegian ship.

Ensign Vesole was awarded the Navy Cross posthumously.

Bronze Star awards went to Goldstein, Anderson, Boyce, Ainsworth, Baker, Bishop, Behm, Kelley, and Ruddiman.

Chapter Thirty-three

WE bloodied our nose at Bari, and on land the Allies were finding "the soft underbelly of Europe" was actually a rock-ribbed chest.

By mid-January, 1944, the Fifth and Eighth Armies had battled a way up the Italian mainland beyond Naples to a line that ran from the mouth of the Garigliano River, on the west coast to a few miles south of Ortona on the Adriatic side.

One of the advantages of amphibious warfare, perfected to the extent that it was by the Allies in January, 1944, is the ability to move great quantities of men and fighting equipment in a surprise strike from the sea faster than the enemy can bring in his reserve ground troops overland to meet the invasion.

Such an operation was planned for execution on the early morning of January 22. The landing area selected was a stretch of coastline that ran from the Nettuno bathing beach, about 30 miles south of Rome, and north through the little port city of Anzio toward the estuary of the River Tiber. The code name for the job was *Shingle*.

Although the operations ashore after the landing were heartbreakingly slow, the assault phase in this operation was smooth and easy.

The object of the Anzio landings can be stated simply: to outflank the German Gustav and Adolf Hitler lines by effecting a landing 55 miles to their rear. The amphibious operation was timed to coincide with a general Fifth Army offensive calculated to tie up the German Tenth Army, thirteen divisions strong. At the same time, Allied air power would hit the German lines of communication around Rome and between the beachhead and the German land front.

The United States naval forces were to be under Rear Admiral Frank Jacob Lowry, USN, Commander Moroccan Sea Frontier; while Rear Admiral Thomas Troubridge, RN, who had participated in the Oran landings, would have charge of the Royal Navy ships. Working with the two admirals were French, Dutch and Greek ships.

Enemy reconnaissance discovered the Mediterranean suddenly free of the carpet of little ships that had so long been a familiar pattern on that water. The surprising absence gave the Nazis a beautiful conclusion at which to jump. German propaganda reports went out over the radio immediately that the Allied navies had withdrawn from the Mediterranean to England for the western invasion of Europe.

At dawn on the morning of January 21 the ships that were supposed to have left for England, but which had actually been concentrated around Naples, sailed north from that port.

The convoy sailed all day under cloudless skies. Three times before nightfall there was a fleet air alarm, but no enemy planes were sighted. The convoy's course was set so that the destination, if guessed, might at first appear to be the island of Corsica. Then it turned, and a reconnaissance pilot might have reported the invasion ships bound for the mouth of the Tiber River.

After dark, the ships in formation wheeled for the last time and turned in for their target—the beaches north and south of Anzio, the little town where Nero is said to have fiddled while Rome burned. Most of the men on those ships were veterans of at least one amphibious landing. They were expecting a fight and were ready for it, and didn't fidget as the night advanced and the ships of five nations went into position for H-hour. Mostly they slept. It would be a long while before they would have anything as comfortable as the bare deck to sleep upon.

H-hour was 0200—two o'clock in the morning. A pale moon hung low over Italy as Rear Admiral Lowry stood on the bridge of his flagship to watch the waves of landing craft depart.

Later, at the first press conference of his 37-year naval career, Rear Admiral Lowry said that as he counted the boats going in he waited for the sound of enemy fire to come from the beaches.

"From the moment it started until the troops were landed, I was scared to death," Rear Admiral Lowry said. "My heart was in my shoes. Any monkey wrench might have spoiled the show. But when I knew the troops were on land, I had a moment of great exaltation. The Lord held us by the right hand."

For the enemy shore received the invaders in darkness, and in silence.

The signal flashed: "Troops have landed." A machine gun chattered briefly, and was silenced.

The Admiral was not alone in his surprise. Fighting in plenty was ahead of this unit of the Fifth Army, to hold the tiny bridgehead back of the German lines, but the men in the landing craft approaching the beaches of Anzio almost felt disappointment at the absence of opposition. It was the reverse of Salerno, where the men, having heard of Italy's capitulation and expecting a peaceful landing, ran into well-planned waiting German defenses.

At dawn the men on the ships could see the beaches, strangely empty. Most of the troops had left them, gone inland, out of sight. From the ships began to trickle the stream of heavy equipment, the big guns and armored vehicles.

But at dawn the German defenders could see the beaches, too, and beyond; 88s began pumping shells at the ships in the water and the Luftwaffe made its appearance. But this time, unlike the lack of Allied air defenses at Bari, fighter planes had the advantage of short runs from fields near Naples, and the German bombers were kept under control.

The most serious obstacle encountered on the beaches was mines. The sands of the British beach area were especially heavily mined and caused some casualties.

Once, however, the German minefields saved the lives of a naval beach party, who were suddenly cut off by a German tank break-through. The first thing a shore party does when it hits the sand is to dig foxholes, so these were ready when the approaching tanks were sighted bearing down. The men dove for their holes, from which they cautiously watched the tanks advance. Abruptly they stopped. Between the foxholes and the tanks was a minefield laid by the Germans themselves. It was their own minefield that halted the tank advance across the beachhead.

The situation was described over the portable radio to the warships, but just as the position and range were being given the radio failed. The ships, unable to make contact with the men in the foxholes, assumed that the unit had been wiped out. Destroyers moved in, and began to search the approximate area with gunfire, not realizing that the Navy men were still alive. Shells began to fall within 50 feet of the foxholes. The men lying in the sand were confronted with the unhappy choice of being killed by their own guns or by the German tanks, unless a warning could be signaled to the ships. One man decided to chance it. He crawled from his foxhole, and running, creeping, worming his way, reached another unit on the beach which relayed the vital information to the gunners on the ships. The destroyers raised their sights and the men in the foxholes had thereafter box seats from which to watch the tank attack smashed.

By the afternoon of D-day the port towns of Anzio and Nettuno had been occupied. The Germans had prepared an extensive demolition system for Anzio, but so complete was their surprise that they had no time to carry out the destruction.

Why were the Germans surprised?

Probably they depended too much on the natural barriers at the invasion point. Sand bars paralleled the beaches at a distance which, in the Nazis' careful calculation, made the beaching of LCIs and LSTs impossible. But American ingenuity as usual eclipsed Teutonic logic. The sand-bar barriers were to be bridged again by pontoon causeways, those long floating bridges that could be made to extend from the opened bow of an LST on the sand bar across the deep water beyond to the shore.

In some cases, however, the pontoons were too short to bridge the gap between sand bar and shore. But here again the same ingenuity that developed the pontoon system solved this problem. One of the LSTs in this situation was the No. 352, captained by Lieutenant Joseph Kahrs, Jr., who had been through the Salerno and Sicilian landings. With Kahrs, as a passenger from Naples to Anzio, was the GI-Joe correspondent Ernie Pyle on his first ride in an LST.

The only opposition the 352 met was one machine-gun nest, shooting without tracers, which killed one man and wounded another. That, and a school of uprooted mines which cut off the LST from the other ships as they floated ponderously out to sea.

After the last mine had floated clear, a tug came in with the pontoons. And then it was discovered the causeway was too short to reach from the bow, across the sand bar, to shore. But in a few moments this dilemma was solved by the Seabees, who built and manned the causeways. One end of the pontoon was snubbed up against the ramp of the LST. The drivers were given the signal to "roll out," and from the tank deck came a stream of vehicles, driving out onto the pontoon. When the floating bridge was full, a cable was secured to the shore end of the pontoon and its free end hooked onto a bulldozer. Up the beach clanked the bulldozer, towing the pontoon bridge like a raft until it touched bottom. The ramp was lowered, the vehicles drove off onto the beach, and then a winch on the LST reeled the raft back across the water to the bow doors for another load. This impromptu floating cable railway continued in use until the LST was unloaded. The system was makeshift, but effective, and it thwarted the Nazis completely.

The emptied landing craft took aboard the wounded, who began to trickle back to the beach by midday, and shoved off for Naples for another load of munitions, and thus a shuttle system of reinforcement and supplies began. It was known as the "Anzio highway" by the men on the landing craft who made as many as five round trips to the beachhead from Naples in the five days following D-day.

Some of these trips into Anzio harbor demanded expert seamanship. The harbor entrance lay between the end of the sea wall and a sunken hulk. The Germans had moved heavy guns up to within range of the harbor and were shelling both ships and the sea wall. They were more successful in hitting the sea wall than the ships, but even this was damaging. By the time the guns were silenced, their shells had moved the sea wall 20 feet out of position. Jagged lumps of concrete and sharp rocks lay a few feet below the surface of the now even narrower harbor entrance. But the LCIs and LSTs went in. Nor were the return trips simple. The weather was generally stormy and the ships were riding light off the jagged, rocky weather shore of Italy.

Naval activity in the area as usual had a twofold mission. Besides the ships bringing in supplies and reinforcements there was the Fire Support Group, cruisers and destroyers, a seaborne artillery front in support of the ground troops that were settling down to the slow, hard fight that would last until the Fifth Army joined the Anzio beachhead for the final drive into Rome.

It was a fight made slower and harder by the weather, which turned bad on the day after the landings, and ranged from bad to rotten thereafter throughout the rest of January and all of February. The gales, storms, and squalls that stalled the armies before Cassino blew over the Anzio beachhead too, broaching small craft and wrecking and driving ashore all the Seabees' pontoon causeways. And these causeways were what had been counted on to land supplies across the offshore sand bar.

Nor were the causeways the only weather casualties—the Amphibious Force lost as many craft to the sea as they did to enemy action, usually when the craft were returning light to Naples from the beachhead.

The naval bombardment first went into action on the night of January 23, shelling the Terracina-Formia road south of Anzio to prevent German reinforcements from reaching the beachhead. As if to make up for the surprise they had suffered, the Nazis were moving heavy equipment to the Anzio area to blast that pocket off the map and prevent juncture with the stalled Fifth Army.

As the ships moved in north and south patrol, their guns were on constant call from the Army. On February 8 the USS BOISE, with destroyers and other British ships, was called in to shell a heavy German artillery emplacement that had moved in north of Anzio and was threatening the northern end of the beachhead and the unloading supply ships.

When the cruiser approached Anzio, the beach was under bombing attack. There was a ceiling of flak puffs and smoke, then the Spitfires and Warhawks arrived, and the German planes left. As the heavy ship started to fire, the destroyers laid a smoke screen around them and around the shipping in the harbor. The bombarding ships moved in "close enough for the Germans to count the rivets." Shore batteries returned the fire, but the smoke screen hid their floating targets. Geysers of white water spouted through the gray smoke. Occasionally the wind would rip a window in the murk and the men on the ships could glimpse the shore, with American tanks roaring across the fields firing upon the German mortar and artillery nests, and the Fifth Army's big guns on the beach blazing away. When the shelling had ceased, the Germans had been pounded by the heaviest bombardment of the entire Italian operation.

Next day the Germans came back with heavy-caliber railway guns from north of Anzio. Again the warships hurled tons of shells in from the sea in a duel with the German shore positions, and in fifteen minutes destroyed the target. Then four and a half hours of steady shooting followed, the Navy guns ranging from ammunition dump to artillery post, supply dump to command post. The ammunition dumps made the most satisfying target. There was no conjecture when they were hit. The gunners could check their shooting by the brilliant, orange-red explosions that lifted acres of Italy high into the sky.

It had been a destructive and bloody two days for the Germans. But twenty-four hours later they would have laid down more gun positions, piled up more ammunition dumps, and carried in thousands of new troops. Holding the Anzio beach was a day-to-day task. But, day after day, the Anzio beach held by the aid of planes and guns from the sea. It held until one day a sun-bleached, sand-encrusted beachhead fighter shook hands with a muddy, unshaved Fifth Army soldier, vanguard of the Army moving north across the Pontine Marshes and across the whole Italian peninsula. Anzio was no longer a beachhead.

Past battered Cassino, through Purple Heart Valley, with nerve-racking slowness, the Allies had inched their way northward through Italy, struggling from one German defense line to the next in battles where every yard gained was a victory. And the Navy kept pouring the supplies ashore both at Naples for the main drive and at Anzio for our pocketed troops there, while other light units stopped the enemy from supplying himself or harassing our armies by sea.

It was a full-scale bloody war, and its first notable victory after Salerno came on May 25 when the main Allied armies linked up with the Anzio troops. This was followed by the swift drive on Rome, a drive given impetus by the vast quantity of stores the Allies found waiting for them at Anzio.

On June 4 Rome fell to the Allies. That was great news. And, even as it was being broadcast, even greater news was on the way. Far north of Rome, in the gray, cold chop of the English Channel, the Allied navies were already at sea bound for their greatest adventure, the direct assault on Northern Europe.

PART SIX

The Great Assault — Normandy and Cherbourg

Chapter Thirty-four

PLANS for the invasion of Germany through France had probably begun to take shape in British minds as the last Tommy crawled off the blackened beaches of Dunkerque.

Those plans developed, certainly, through the dark days and fiery nights of the Blitz. They were accelerated when the Luftwaffe, beaten in its efforts to open up Britain for an invasion, threw its strength against the British Mediterranean life line.

Then the United States came into the war and abruptly those plans turned from grimly fantastic hope to some of the substance of reality. American troops debarked on British soil, British harbors sheltered American warships, and the Army Air Force put its strength beside the British until the airfields overlapped.

United States bases had already been established under reverse Lend-Lease in 1941 at Rosneath, Scotland, and Londonderry in Northern Ireland. Projected originally as defensive convoy supply bases, Londonderry retained only this function, but Rosneath became first a submarine base and then an amphibious and receiving base after the United States entered the war. It was from these two still-expanding establishments that the assault on Africa was partially mounted in late October, 1942. A few weeks later, in January, 1943, the Combined Chiefs of Staff agreed at the Casablanca Conference that the invasion of Western Europe was set for "as early as possible in 1944."

Even then that prognostication must have appeared to the Nazis as sheer propaganda, which, although it might cheer the stupid Americans and British, would not frighten the Germans. They held or controlled every port on the European continent, and the resources of that continent were theirs. Perhaps it is true that the Nazis were eager for the trial of arms, counting upon bleeding the Allies into impotence on Europe's fortified threshold.

The British and American commanders did not care what the victory-drunk Germans thought. They doggedly went to work to convert the plans for the invasion of Hitler's *Festung Europa* into fact.

Theirs was not optimism, such as permeated the United States at the time. It was determination. The magnitude of the job was self-evident, and most of the preliminary labor of smashing a hole in the Continent through which troops could pour to hew a bloody highway to the Rhine had to be performed literally under the enemy's eyes.

But first things first. In mid-year of 1942, Admiral Sir Bertram Ramsay, RN, naval commander in chief of the joint expeditionary forces, surveyed the perimeter of the United Kingdom for suitable ports of assembly and training for the expected United States forces and the British invasion teams. Roughly, the southwest quarter of the United Kingdom was to be the Americans' schooling ground for amphibious personnel and craft, and on December 15, 1942, the British Admiralty informed the United States Navy that accommodations would be ready by July 1, 1943.[1] That was almost a whole year before D-day.

Sites were chosen and work began on the "loading hards," concrete-

---

[1] The first U.S. Naval Advanced Amphibious Training Base established specifically to prepare for the invasion was Appledore in Devon. It was commissioned July 29, 1943; Commander Chauncey Camp, Commanding Officer. Other bases and sub-bases were commissioned as follows:

St. Mawes (sub-base of Falmouth, Cornwall—Sept. 7—Lt. Comdr. Frank A. Varney, USNR, C.O.

Falmouth, Cornwall—Sept. 25 (approx.)—Comdr. James E. Arnold, USNR.

Fowey (sub-base of Falmouth), Cornwall—Oct. 25—Lt. Comdr. John P. Beale, USNR.

Plymouth, Devon—Nov. 8—Capt. C. F. M. S. Quinby, USN.

(This was the largest U.S. Naval Amphibious and Operating Base in England, comprising repair, maintenance and training sub-bases at Calstock, Saltash, Vicarage Barracks, Queen Anne's Battery, Shapter's Field, Martin's Wharf and a Hospital at Manadon Field.)

Salcombe, Devon—Nov. 25—Lt. Comdr. Beale, USNR.

Teignmouth (later combined with Salcombe)—Dec. 3 (approx.).

Dartmouth, Devon—Dec. 28—Capt. John E. Reinberg, Jr., U.S.N.

(Dartmouth used the buildings of the Royal Naval College, the Annapolis of England.)

Milford Haven, Wales—Jan. 1, 1944 (approx.)—Comdr. William L. McDonald, USNR.

Penarth, Wales—Jan. 1, 1944 (approx.)—Comdr, Isaac R. Boothby, USNR.

Exeter, Devon—Feb. 3, 1944—Comdr. Victor F. Blakeslee, USN (Ret.).

(This was the largest U.S. Navy Supply Base in England, and comprised in addition to the main base, sub-bases at Launceston, Tiverton and Bugle.)

Deptford, London—Apr. 10—Lt. Comdr. E. G. Janeway, USNR.

Portland-Weymouth-Dorset—May 1—Capt. J. J. McGlynn, USN.

Poole-Dorset—May 1—Comdr. William L. McDonald, USNR.

Southampton-Hampshire—May 11—Lt. Comdr. Richard S. Aldrich, USNR.

surfaced beaches where the LSTs and LCTs could be loaded directly from shore. Negotiations were pressed with local property owners and municipalities for the acquisition of fields, schools, homes, hotels, piers and rights of way for the amiable invasion of the Americans.

All these installations were obtained from the British through the Admiralty on reverse Lend-Lease. Nor was this all; as Admiral Harold R. Stark, USN, reported to Admiral King, "The British are making available to us nearly all the housing, office and ship facilities we will need. . . . Also, speaking generally, the Royal Navy will supply us with about 65% of the naval stores, port machinery, boats, moorings, etc., which we will require."

Dry provisions the Navy obtained from Army stores, but fresh meat, vegetables, bread and pastries came to us on reverse Lend-Lease through the Admiralty and the Joint British Navy, Army, Air Force Supply Organization (NAAFI), as did all galley equipment, refrigerators, cutlery, stoves and the like. The United States Navy had to supply the converters and transformers to make our electrical equipment operate on English current, as well as bringing our own hospital supplies and equipment.

Over-all administrative and logistical command of this network of bases and all the ships that used them rested in Admiral Stark, who had been appointed Commander Naval Forces Europe (COMNAVEU) on March 15, 1942. This was a job for a diplomat as well as a naval officer, for COMNAVEU not only had the responsibilities of his vast command but also served as Naval Adviser to the United States Embassy and, as such, represented our Navy in all conferences having to do with naval operations in Europe.

In April, 1943, Prime Minister Churchill and his staff met in Washington with President Roosevelt and his military and naval leaders to shape the plans for finality. The code name for the invasion was *Overlord,* and its naval phase was solemnly dubbed *Neptune.* A full-size war was being fought in the Mediterranean; the U-boats were swanking around the Atlantic; in the Pacific the Navy was battering down the bastions of Japan's defenses at grim cost. In Washington the planners worked in secret on the operation that was to dwarf all of these, and then moved on to Great Britain.

"Get to know your opposite number," was Admiral Stark's order of the day to his staff, and so thoroughly was this order carried out that the entire business of securing bases, facilities and supplies, as well as establishing joint operational procedure, went through swiftly and smoothly.

On July 15, 1943, COMINCH wrote to COMNAVEU outlining the additional duties and the means of handling them which would come to the command as the time for invasion drew near. The letter said, in part:

> (2) As a first step in the build-up for operations and prior to the later appointment of a U.S. Naval Commander for future operations afloat, a new command is established, of Landing Craft and Bases, Europe. (Short title—LANCRABEU).
>
> (6) It is expected that a Captain or Commander under Commander, Landing Craft and Bases, Europe, will act as officer-in-charge of each training establishment or base with a minimum of such other officers as required.
>
> (8) It is contemplated that the Commander, Landing Craft and Bases, Europe (short title—COMLANCRABEU), will perform the following tasks:
>
> (a) Command U. S. Naval Bases for landing craft in the United Kingdom, . . .
>
> (b) Provide for the reception and effective maintenance of U. S. landing craft in the United Kingdom.
>
> (c) Establish facilities as required for use of landing craft during the training phase, mounting of any operation, and the follow-up.
>
> (d) Act in liaison with British authorities in charge of British bases used by U. S. landing craft in the care and operation of such craft.
>
> (e) Act as Commander, Amphibious Forces, Europe, until relieved.
>
> (f) During combat operations, it is not expected that Commander, Landing Craft and Bases, Europe, will have a tactical command afloat. It is considered that the development of maximum efficiency of landing craft and bases will require the full employment of his time on the tasks involved.

In accordance with this letter Rear Admiral John Wilkes, USN, reported on September 1, 1943, to take up his duties as COMLANCRABEU and, in November, Rear Admiral Alan G. Kirk, USN, who had been placed in operational command of all United States naval forces participating in the forthcoming operations as Commander Task Force 122, arrived in London. Shortly after that Rear Admiral John H. Hall, Jr., USN, arrived aboard the ANCON from the Mediterranean to act as Commander Eleventh Amphibious Force. This, then, was the operational chain of command as it was to function from that time on through Operation *Overlord-Neptune*: Commander in Chief Allied Naval Expeditionary Force (Admiral Sir Bertram Ramsay, RN, naval hero of Dunkerque), Commander Task Force 122 (Rear Admiral Kirk, who had commanded our naval forces at Sicily), Commander Eleventh Amphibious Force (Rear Admiral Hall), and Commander Landing Craft and Bases Europe. Later, the lower echelons of Task Force 122 were expanded to provide for three further task forces: Task Force O, under Rear Admiral Hall, Task Force U, under Rear Admiral Don P. Moon, USN, and the Follow-Up Force under Commodore Campbell D. Edgar, USN.

This was a more complex and weightier organization than had been first contemplated. Originally it had been intended to strike the French coast on the Atlantic and the Mediterranean simultaneously.

By deferring the southern assault and strengthening the blow against Normandy, the strategists calculated to hit the Germans harder with the initial blow and then to stagger the enemy with the assault on his rear.

With the commands set up and the bases functioning, more and more Navy ships and naval personnel poured into England until there seemed some justification for the standard American joke that the only thing that kept the Yookay up out of the Channel was the barrage balloons. As the day for the invasion drew nearer and nearer, the weight of arms, ammunition, supplies and men spread out in every field, along every lane in Southern England must have given the barrage balloons a tough struggle for the tight little isle.

One of the primary functions, as outlined in COMINCH'S letter already quoted, of COMLANCRABEU was training, and accordingly every amphibious base conducted exercises for the attached small-boat personnel. In addition, large-scale rehearsals were held from January through April off Slapton Sands in Start Bay near the old Devon town of Dartmouth. These were as realistic as the commanding officers could make them, and on one occasion the Germans took a hand, too.

At the briefing in Plymouth before Exercise *Tiger*, as the rehearsal was coded, the British officer in command of the screen said, "If Jerry doesn't have a go at us this time, he's absolutely crackers." Jerry wasn't crackers. On the second night of the maneuver three E-boats sneaked in on a convoy of LSTs, sank two of them and damaged a third. It added a grisly touch of realism to the exercise, but, ironically, the attack was better than the enemy was able to do during the actual invasion.

While preparations for the great adventure were going forward rapidly along the Channel coast of England, work of great moment was also in progress over the Continent. The RAF and the Eighth and Ninth United States Army Air Forces were taking care of the Luftwaffe and the Wehrmacht's communications, supplies and installations, as well as Germany's production and materiel centers. That left one small but highly important pre-invasion chore for the Navy; the neutralization of German sea power, which consisted effectively of submarines and light surface units like E-boats, based around the Bay of Biscay.

The RAF Coastal Command and the USAAF began the Bay of Biscay Offensive to take care of this menace early in 1942; the United States Navy did not take a hand until midsummer of 1943, when the Liberators of Fleet Air Wing 7, commanded by Captain William H. Hamilton, USN, relieved the American Army fliers.

The operating principle of the Offensive was simple: to maintain a constant patrol over the area and attack any U-boat sighted. This meant a routine well described by one of the men who went through it in the following words: "You went out there, flew for hours and hours, week in and week out, and never saw anything. Then, maybe, after months or even years, you sighted a submarine which was visible for perhaps thirty seconds."

Tedious, nerve-racking work it was, but it served its purpose. It kept the submarines submerged, cutting their effective operating time drastically—some fourteen or fifteen days, it has been estimated—which meant a reduction of from 25 to 30 per cent in the total U-boat effort. The most glowing testimony to the value of the job came from the German submarine men themselves: one Nazi U-boat skipper recommending that the Iron Cross be automatically awarded all members of crews crossing the Bay of Biscay.

The work of the Offensive was as dangerous as it was effective. A Liberator patrolling alone over the Bay of Biscay was an invitation to formations of German fighter planes swarming out to clear a path for the U-boats, and many a pilot of the wing is alive today only because he found cloud cover in time. Even that failed on occasion.

There was the case of Lieutenant (jg) Lance F. Ellis, USNR, for instance. He had twice been attacked by Junkers 88s and twice escaped by following orders and hiding in a cloud—his business was to hunt subs, not to play target for the Luftwaffe. And then, on an almost cloudless day, he was attacked again. Again he raced for the nearest cloud, making it with seconds to spare. He found, however, that this time his cloak of invisibility did not fit too well; he kept breaking into the open every time he turned. And, of course, the Germans soon discovered this and simply waited in the open for him. Then, to make matters worse, Ellis found that what little cover he had had was shrinking. His propellers were churning up and dissipating the layers of mist. Literally, he wore out the cloud! He got away finally and found himself a bigger, more permanent cloud.

Enemy planes were not the only danger, perhaps not even the worst, that the Navy fliers faced. The weather also was a deadly foe at times. The very nature of their mission called for the men on the Biscay Offensive to fly in bad weather when ceilings were so low that everything else would be grounded. It was on just such cloudy days that the U-boats were likely to take a chance and run for it on the surface to save time, fuel and batteries. That spelled good hunting for the Liberators: subs on the surface, protecting clouds overhead. It spelled grave risks and slim chances, though, when it came to finding the way home and landing safely.

One landing made by Lieutenant (jg) Robert B. Meihaus, USNR, shows what coming home from flying the Biscay Offensive could mean. One engine of his Liberator had broken down off the coast of Spain, and he flew back to England on three. His home field was closed. Diverted to another base, he found virtually no visibility there either. Circling low in this soup, Meihaus first hit some power lines and then the thatched roof of a house on a nearby hill. His landing gear was smashed, one engine caught fire and a propeller dropped off. In an attempt to shut off the burning engine, a member of the crew threw the wrong switch, cutting out one of the two remaining engines. And yet Meihaus managed to land on the runway without injury to himself or his crew.

Not all the fliers were so unlucky as Ellis, who used up his cloud, or Meihaus. By the same token, not all were so lucky, either. Casualties ran high in Fleet Air Wing 7. But the work went on; it had to.

It had its compensations, too. Sub sightings were few, but they did occur. And when they did, the Liberators roared in to the attack with devastating effect, either sinking the U-boat or crippling it for the next fellow. Perhaps the most spectacular single action of the Offensive was not against undersea craft at all, however.

Late in December of 1943, the Germans, although spotted from the air, managed to sneak some blockade runners through the bay into port, escorted by eleven destroyers. A few days later they tried it again, but this time they were not so lucky. A Czech-manned Liberator sank the blockade runner—full of crude rubber—before she met her escorts. All Allied aircraft on the Bay Offensive were then ordered to search for the destroyers. Lieutenant Stuart D. Johnson, USNR, found them. Despite heavy antiaircraft fire, despite repeated air attacks, he kept them under observation, reporting their position, until two British cruisers arrived on the scene and took the Germans under fire, sinking three. Johnson was awarded the Navy Cross for his work.

When news of the engagement was flashed to the headquarters of Wing 7, a special striking force, armed with bombs instead of depth charges, was organized and sent out in the record time of two hours. Some planes scored direct bomb hits, some near misses; all pressed home repeated strafing attacks in the face of heavy flak and all earned a warm "Well done" from the High Command.

That fight may have been the high point of Wing 7's stay in England so far as excitement was concerned, but it was not necessarily their most important job. What really counted was their work in holding down the U-boats, dull drudgery though that was to all hands, base personnel as well as fliers. By harassing the subs, they made the gigantic build-up for invasion easier. And, at the same time, developed the technique that was to protect that invasion when the time came.

The Germans did what they could to save the situation; it was not much. Admiral Doenitz called in all his undersea craft to hoard them for the day when the Allied attack across the Channel began. He equipped his subs with long breathing tubes—promptly dubbed "schnorkels" by the fliers—to draw in fresh air and expel foul air and exhaust fumes. These did, it is true, enable the U-boats to stay submerged for longer periods, but the schnorkels themselves left easily spotted wakes which the airmen soon learned to recognize and bomb.

Time was running out for the Germans. The big day was approaching for the Allies: closer and closer.

Chapter Thirty-five

D AY in, day out, and all night long the broad perimeter of Hitler's Europe was rocked and churned and torn by bombs. Far behind the frontiers to the industrial areas the Allied bombers ranged, destroying railroads, shops, factories, bridges, highways homes.

The Luftwaffe was knocked out of the sky and beaten on the ground, so that toward the end Germany would have more airplanes underground than on its airstrips.

Everybody knew invasion was coming. When? The Germans could not tell within a day or two, or yet a week; but they were ready for it, should the attempt be at Marseilles, at Bordeaux, at Brest, Antwerp, Rotterdam—Narvik even. Let the Allies bomb! Who should know better than the German Wehrmacht—yes, and the Luftwaffe itself—that you cannot conquer a country with bombs? You have to land armies; to keep the armies supplied you need deep-water ports, so they can be furnished weapons and munitions superior to the defenders'. The Germans must have laughed: They had every European port so well defended that it would take a map-changing catastrophe to dislodge them, indeed. Any force great enough to move the Germans out would so effectively destroy the place as to make it totally and forever useless. *Ja wohl!* And while you are getting yourself another beer, Fritz, take another look in the radar.

And Fritz, looking into the radar screen that night of June 5–6, 1944, first said to himself that the contraption is *kaput,* and then let out a yell that the whole island of Great Britain was moving down upon the Norman coast.

The signs that marked the mighty movements of light coastwise forces had merged into a single pulsating streak on the screen, and other blurs and blips and spots and streaks were forming, shifting, merging, until the whole scanning field was glowing like an electric grill. *Was gibt's!*

All up and down the Normandy coast fronting the Channel came like reports of ships on the move, and the sentries looked out over the choppy sea to take fresh comfort from the knowledge that every inch of the coast-line was mined, was under the noses of the greatest artillery, was, to top it all, bedeviled by bad weather and nasty tides.

The Allied bombers came over, and the sentries did not even look up. They could tell by ear: that grinding roar high, high up, those were the big bombers, and the snarling noise in mid-sky was the medium bombers. Presently the screeching buzz of the fighters catching up would be heard, and—but what was that new sound? No bomber, no fighter, ever emitted that deep, whistling drone!

Fritz hadn't heard the paratroop aerial trains before, big transport machines towing gliders laden with armed men. And that green glow in the east—that wasn't dawn. Not the natural dawn. It came from chandelier flares, by whose light the paratroopers and glider troops were finding a footing behind the coastal defenses.

Up in all that welter of winged noise imagine that a lone German reconnaissance pilot, delayed over London by unusual aerial activity, is trying to sneak home. Over his left shoulder he can see the sky brighten-ing far away—about where the Rhine is. And then flak tears holes in the darkness that is the French coast, and the green and red trails of German rockets snake up through the clouds. Bad business, this, for the pilot will have to dodge enemy planes and his own artillery to make a safe landing. He turns south toward Cherbourg for safer haven, and flies low over the Bay of the Seine. The dawn is coming upon him, the cloud cover is breaking up.

Then he sees it! He stutters over his radio. How to describe it?

"Ships—ships as far I can see. Thousands of ships. What kind? *Du lieber Herr Gott,* every kind there ever was. Battleships, cruisers, de-stroyers, transports, and things I never saw before."

The pilot sees the vastly populated sea suddenly erupt fire; the sullen shore beyond it flames into electric life—some of it is the flash of can-nonading, but most of it is the glare of bursting shells.

The pilot is trapped, now. He mechanically describes the unprec-edented sight into his radio mouthpiece.

". . . Hundreds of little boats making like merry-go-rounds—far back are the big ships—now come rockets—Ah! The little boats stop their circling and head in for the shore. And from the west come bombers, hundreds of bombers, flying steeple-high—!"

The bombers roar in as the naval gunfire ceases, to blast and blitz and strafe the final beach areas. Behind them, more bombers hurdle the beaches and bluffs to add to the devastation inland, and, behind *them*, the transport planes hauling gliders that cut loose and circle down to shellpocked fields, pastures, roads. Some of them crash; some plow into trees, into buildings, into each other, and some disintegrate in air from shellfire, but from most of them emerge men with guns, bazookas, flame throwers, mortars. The coastal defenders are under fire front and rear. To the German pilot it looks like the end of the world. It is, for him. An American fighter spots the enemy plane, and stitches a multiple row of bullet holes down its length. It is just another little noise in a world of noise, another small puff of smoke in a world of flame, another splash in a sea that is boiling with ships, shells, mines and bombs, in the turmoil of the greatest military movement in history. D-day! D is for *Dämmerung*, the twilight of the Nazi gods.

Hitler had everything—had had everything—except a navy. He claimed the world's biggest army, the best tanks, the most and best aircraft. But when he came to the water's edge he was stopped; stopped by 20 miles of sea water and the British Home Fleet. So he turned against Russia, having gone as far westward as he could. The Soviet Union, its might reinforced by guns, tanks, planes and food sent over the ocean by the maritime powers, threw back the Nazi legions. And now Germany was trapped, its outer bastions crumbling under the bombardment of plain, old-fashioned warships, while from their nightmare horde of landing craft poured the armies that had crossed the sea for the extinction of Nazidom.

Chapter Thirty-six

F OR weeks, all roads in England had led south. Before that, for months, ships had crowded British ports, pouring men and tanks and machines ashore.

From Falmouth to the Thames Estuary, Britain's chin bore a stubble of steel, a fringe of ships and boats of every kind that floats—even ancient excursion steamers from Norfolk, Virginia. Even quiet little yachting harbors like Salcombe and Poole were jammed with invasion craft.

Men who had cursed for months at being chained to desks found themselves puffing on the quays, suddenly pressed into duty as combination boss-stevedores, freight agents and traffic cops. It seemed as though England were being drained of men and machines, feet and wheels, as the Armada loaded for the invasion.

At the big United States Naval Supply Depot at Exeter a hurried call was received for extra quantities of equipment on the night of June 4. Under the leadership of Commander Victor Blakeslee, USN (Ret.), who had gone from a public relations job to be an assistant naval attaché remote from the sea in Russia before being made the commander at Exeter, the camp turned to. Barbers, yeoman, cooks and photographers became truck drivers, hauling tons of equipment over unlighted, unfamiliar roads to the waiting ships. For the last twenty-four hours before the Armada sailed, there was little sleep for anybody except the involuntary slumber of complete exhaustion. Every machine shop and repair depot worked until the last vessel pushed off, making last-minute repairs and alterations. In those final hours, black-out rules went by the board as welding arcs burned electric-blue and where, in the last minutes, if light meant speed, then let there be light and the devil take the consequences—and the watchful Germans!

Just getting ready for the invasion was a masterful job. Rear Admiral Kirk paid tribute to the way it was done in his first press conference upon his return to the United States. He said:

"Rear Admiral John Wilkes, who commanded the amphibious bases in the British Isles, did a perfectly splendid job. His percentage of readiness of the ships assigned to the operation was 99.5 per cent, and the reason it wasn't 100 per cent was because the German bombers got into Portland shortly before the battle began. They knocked out a few craft which could not be repaired in time. I could not give enough praise to Admiral Wilkes and his organization. It was splendid! Out of 2,493 ships that were supposed to sail, 2,480 actually did."

The ships were ready. The men were ready. This was it. This was the beginning of the end of the war. Shove off!

Aboard the vessels that were to do the job—and they ranged from battleships like USS TEXAS and NEVADA down to little 36-foot rocket boats —there was the quieter bustle of last-minute preparation. Officers attended briefings, drew charts from the Hydrographic Office, drew stores from the Supply Office, ammunition from the Ordnance Office, code books from the Communications Office. Crews checked, and rechecked, and then checked their gear again.

Did anybody doubt that this was the real thing? There were the large transports; the arrival of drafts of doctors; the disappearance of small craft from the western harbors (LCVPs having gone to the transports, LCMs having moved eastward nearer the beaches of the Far Shore).

Then the troops came aboard. The ships were sealed. The last mail went ashore, and with it the last lingering doubt whether or not the historic day was at hand.

A sailor at the rail of an LCT anchored in the narrow Dart River nodded at the pleasant wooded shore twenty feet distant and said to his mate, "Brother, that's an awful long ways away."

Normandy was closer, and Normandy was far away.

The Bay of the Seine, where the Allies had determined to strike, is a shallow troughlike depression in the north coast of France lying between Cap d'Antifer in the northeast and Pointe de Barfleur in the northwest. It is roughly 75 miles across the mouth of this bay on a line from Cap d'Antifer to Pointe de Barfleur. If such a line were drawn, it would never be more than 15 miles from the shore, which is another way of saying that the bay is five times as long from east to west as it is from north to south. And it is exposed to all winds north of east and west.

Operation Overlord called for the establishment of a beachhead about 50 miles long stretching westward along the southern shore of the Baie de la Seine from the mouth of the Orne River to the beach of Varreville, a little town about halfway up the Cotentin Peninsula.

To do this job the Allies assembled more than four thousand vessels, two thousand transport planes and gliders, a million men—not all of whom would land on D-day, of course, but all of whom would be either on the beach, over it, or lying off to seaward of it. There were ships and men from all the Allied nations that were, or had been, sea powers. And behind these ships that were to make the first attack there were other thousands waiting, loaded and ready, to pile reinforcements, men, armor, equipment and supplies ashore in the follow-up days of the invasion.

The English Channel all these ships would have to cross (each ship with her own peculiar characteristics of speed, draft and maneuverability) is a narrow, nasty piece of water. The tide rips through it west-to-east on the flood, east-to-west on the ebb, directly athwart the simple north-south course from England to France that looks so easy on the chart. The Baie de la Seine is a shallow unsheltered roadstead full of strange tricks of current, tide rips and eddies. At the time of the invasion—and maybe even now—there were German mines—magnetic mines, contact mines and other mines.

Back of the mines, in the shallower waters near the beaches, were erected the giant steel jackstraws and wooden stakes and long fences of tube steel—all mined so that if they didn't straightway rip the bottom out of a landing craft they would blast it out. On the beaches themselves were buried more mines. Back of the beach obstacles were the pillboxes, machine-gun emplacements, the mobile and fixed batteries of 88s, 105s, 155s, the casemated coastal defense guns and the huge railroad-mounted naval siege guns—every type of defense four years of ingenuity harnessed to unlimited slave labor could devise.

The plan of *Neptune* of necessity took each obstacle and difficulty into detailed account. *Neptune* had to put *Overlord's* armies ashore in spite of those impediments.

The first problem was the tremendously complex one of volume of traffic; more than four thousand ships had to arrive at virtually the same place and be ready to strike at virtually the same minute. They had to do it in the dark. This alone would have been a ticklish enough task, but it was further complicated by the fact, already mentioned, that this armada was composed of widely differing types of craft with widely differing tasks steaming from different ports. The heavy ships of the American

Fire Support Groups, for example, came from the north of Ireland, in time to rendezvous with transports sailing from Falmouth, Plymouth, Weymouth and Portland. These, in turn, were to arrive off the Normandy shores no earlier than the tank-laden LCTs and the rocket- and gun-carrying LCTs which would support the first infantry waves clear in to the beach.

Now, the fighting ships could go twice as fast as the transports, and the transports could go three times as fast as the LCTs; yet they all had to be at the same place at the same time. Furthermore, they had to take substantially the same routes or no air or sea screen could protect them. In any event, there were not enough minesweepers in the world to get the whole Channel clean, so the best that could be done was for all vessels to stick to the few narrow paths that could be swept.

All this would have called for the nicest type of calculation had there been only one task force to think of, but there were five; three under Admiral Sir Philip L. Vian, RN, assaulting the eastern end of the proposed beachhead, and two under Rear Admiral Alan G. Kirk, USN, attacking the western portion. And, of course, no element of one task force could get mixed up with another, without throwing the whole vast program into disastrous chaos.

The larger ships could handle their navigation problems themselves; they had the latest and best gear; they had the most experienced personnel. But what of the LCTs, whose best speed was little more than the drift of the tide, whose navigation gear was primitive, whose skippers were accustomed to sailing largely on a follow-the-leader principle? What of the little LCMs with no navigation gear at all, piloted by coxswains who would have been riding their bucking bathtubs almost twenty-four hours before dark on the night of the crossing? Multiply the problem of each ship by 4,000. Multiply the vastly more complex problem of each task force by 5. Throw in a calculation of all the possibilities, probabilities and imponderables of weather, enemy air attack and enemy sea attack. There you have a notion of what the planners of *Neptune* had to take into account in devising a way to get to the place where they would start to fight.

Part of the problem could be answered in the disposition of ships and landing craft at the time of loading. Rear Admiral Moon's task force, which was to tackle the west flank of the beachhead on the Cotentin Peninsula, gathered in the westernmost English ports—Falmouth, Ply-

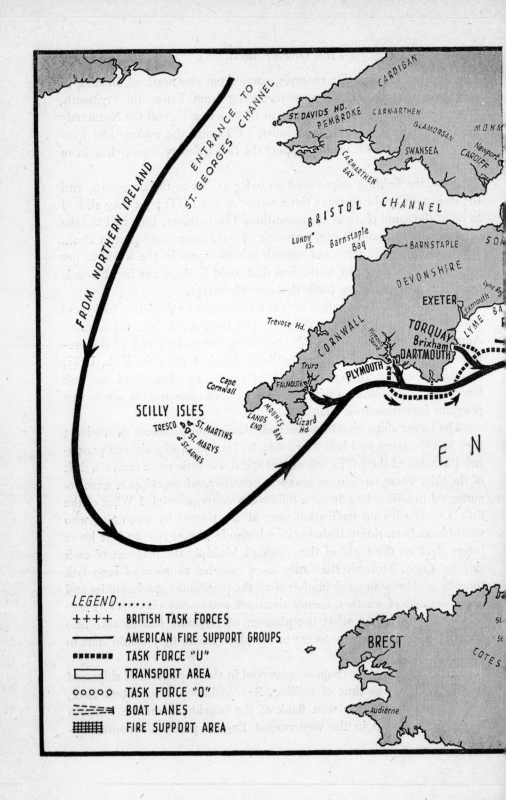

LEGEND......

++++ BRITISH TASK FORCES
——— AMERICAN FIRE SUPPORT GROUPS
▪▪▪▪▪▪▪ TASK FORCE "U"
▭ TRANSPORT AREA
ooooo TASK FORCE "O"
⊟⊟⊟ BOAT LANES
▦▦▦ FIRE SUPPORT AREA

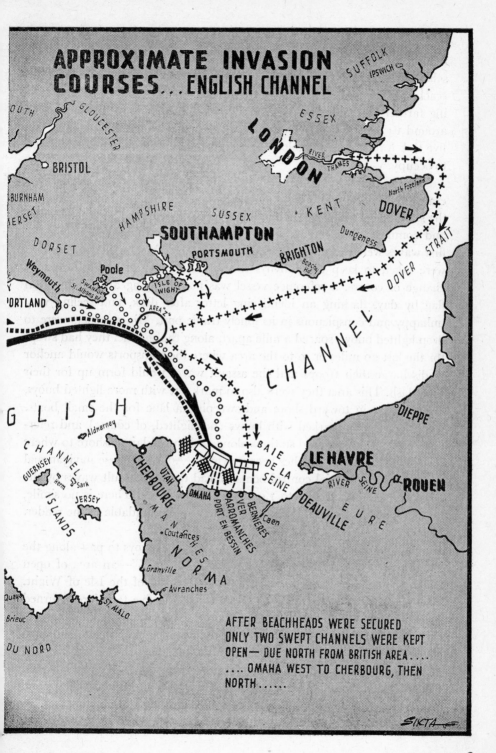

APPROXIMATE INVASION COURSES... ENGLISH CHANNEL

AFTER BEACHHEADS WERE SECURED
ONLY TWO SWEPT CHANNELS WERE KEPT
OPEN— DUE NORTH FROM BRITISH AREA....
.... OMAHA WEST TO CHERBOURG, THEN
NORTH......

FIGURE 6

mouth, Salcombe, Dartmouth and Tor Bay. Rear Admiral Hall's force, scheduled to land its troops closer to the center, was based in the wide reaches of Portland Harbor and Weymouth Bay. The British forces, landing farther east, were based from Portsmouth and Southhampton clear around to the Thames Estuary. Thus, as nearly as possible, each of the five task forces was assembled opposite the enemy shore it was scheduled to occupy.

To the twin problems of timing and navigation of the amphibious craft, the solution was to herd vessels of the same type and approximately the same speed together, shepherded by vessels equipped with navigation and communications gear. The craft that were to hit the beach in the first waves were put at the head of the columns. Two further precautions were taken to keep the convoys from getting lost: at every important change of course, a reference vessel was posted, flying an identification flag by day, flashing an identifying letter after dark, and feeling very unhappy and conspicuous in its lonely traffic post. Minesweepers were to drop lighted buoys, spaced a mile apart, along the channel they had swept for the last 20 miles or so to the area where the transports would anchor to discharge their troops and the assault waves would form up for their final dash. This area they were also to mark out with more lighted buoys, before going in toward shore and sweeping a lane for the small boats. These lanes were marked with buoys (not lighted, of course) and reference vessels were assigned stations along each swept lane inshore to where the selected invasion beaches became visible. Added to these navigational aids there were special control boats to lead the first assault waves by the hand from the transports to 1,000 yards from shore. There is no simile, no metaphor, to make this paragraph more understandable to the reader. There was never anything like it before.

Channels were swept broad enough for two convoys to pass along the English coast to a single rendezvous area—"Point Z"—an area of open water about 13 miles due south of the western tip of the Isle of Wight. This was the final control point from which the five task forces turned south to begin their run across the Channel. Five swept channels, one for each task force, led from Point Z half the distance to France; then each channel was divided into a slow lane and a fast lane, which merged again at the Transport Area. Down the former course the LCTs were to plod through the preinvasion night while the transports and the battleships and cruisers raced along the other, all to arrive on their stations together.

Those plans took care of the mechanics of crossing the Channel and arriving in amphibious battle formation. Once across, there were mine-sweepers to take care of mines, demolition teams to take care of the beach obstacles, the guns of the Fire Support Groups to take care of the enemy cannon, shallow-draft rocket craft and gunboats to blast machine-gun nests and enemy defenders on the beach itself.

Every ship in the great Armada had her job to do, had her station to maintain for every moment of the passage and the assault. The plan was clear. All that remained was to put it to work, and—it worked!

What determined the choice of D-day and H-hour? It had to be a date on which low water occurred just about daybreak. The cross-Channel approach would be safest during the dark hours; the chances of surprising the enemy greatest. The landing had to be made near low tide so that all underwater defenses would be visible to the demolition teams who had to blow passages through them. But the landing also had to be made on a rising tide, rather than a falling one, so that boats which beached early would float off easily. There was one other consideration: the assault should be made at, or near, the spring tides, when high water is highest (and low water lowest), since that would enable the Army to get its vast quantity of armor ashore at high water with a minimum of open beach to cross.

Spring tides over the selected invasion beaches rise 19 feet in about four and a half hours. Then there is a stand of about three hours during which the level of the water does not change appreciably. After that the tide ebbs swiftly for five hours, with virtually no low-water stand. The beaches have very gradual slopes, much more shallow than any in the United States; technically speaking, they have a gradient of 1 to 100, which simply means that for every foot the tide rises vertically the sea sweeps in over a hundred feet of beach. This is a fact to bear in mind when reading of the underwater demolition teams racing the onrushing tide to blast channels through the row upon row of mined obstacles that guarded the beaches.

Every such problem had to be examined from every angle, by itself and in its relation to the whole. The plan for so vast an operation had, of necessity, to be completed in detail months before its execution. By the same token, it had also to be so adjustable that last-minute delays or emergencies would not wreck the elaborate structure. That is how it was calculated that the invasion would strike the Germans in Normandy at

0600, Monday, June 5, 1944. Some of the invasion craft were already on their way toward the enemy when a 24-hour postponement had to be called.

It was like stopping a tidal wave; like ordering a hurricane to stop blowing for twenty-hour hours and then to resume course and speed. It was impossible, but it was done. And, once underway again, the seaborne invasion moved ahead with the inexorable power of freedom on the march.

The carefully worked out plan to keep the U-boats out of the English Channel was put into effect. This followed the principle of the Biscay Offensive, amplified and intensified so as to be as foolproof as possible. It meant laying on the thickest antisubmarine patrols the world has ever seen. Every square mile of the Channel and its approaches was covered by aircraft flying overhead every few minutes. Patrols of rover airplanes, which could be diverted to assist in a contact, augmented their watch. French coastal waters had been mined during the preceding weeks to make it difficult for the enemy to sneak in around the Brest Peninsula, close to the beaches. On top of all this were the important surface ship patrols, hunting submerged U-boats with their sound gear. The subs would have no easy time in the relatively shallow and cramped waters of the English Channel.

"Hold them down and they can't get in; sink them if they pop up." This was the essence of the Allied plan. And it worked.

Out came Admiral Doenitz's hoarded U-boats, large numbers of them, from Saint-Nazaire, Lorient, Bordeaux and the other submarine bases along the Bay of Biscay. Properly respectful of the Allied aerial patrols, they crept forward underwater, "schnorkels" alone showing. The only trouble with it was that our air patrols were so thick and alert that the tips of the schnorkels were sighted and the U-boats attacked. Not one got through. The convoys, fast and slow, great and small, moved across the Channel like trolley cars in the rush hour.

The first convoys to set out were, of course, those which had farthest to go and those which were slowest in speed. Remember that everything had to come together at the rendezvous, and then move along the five great lanes to its appointed place for the final assault. The pathfinders were the minesweepers, more than two hundred of them, streaming over 70 miles of wire. One, USS OSPREY (Lieutenant Commander Charles H.

Swimm, USNR), was struck by a mine just as she took station, and went down with a rush. The first mine casualty, she was by no means the last. But OSPREY was the only ship lost to mines in the crossing of the Channel, and there were no more thickly mined waters anywhere, so her destruction was, in a way, fiery accolade to the efficiency of her sisters-in-sweeping.

How it felt to be in the van of that great, mixed flotilla is described by one of the co-authors of this volume, Lieutenant Stephen L. Freeland, USNR, who was Officer in Charge of an LCC—Landing Craft Control, to the brass hats but Lily Cup Cruisers to the men who manned them. There are many stories of battle. Here is the story of prebattle, the labor and tension of making ready for the opening gun.

"LCCs—'those little spitkits with the Buck Rogers gear'—look, from a distance, like cut-down PTs. They are 56 feet long, 13 feet in beam— all steel, and if they look like PTs, they act like nothing else in the world. Designed as navigation leaders and traffic dispatches for the small boat waves, they had a great deal of heavy, space-consuming equipment, beginning with a gyro-compass, radar, and two fathometers and running on through a cargo of devices still in the secret class. In addition, they mount three radio transmitters and receivers as permanent equipment.

"We were armed with three twin-mount 50-caliber machine guns. What with ammunition for them, food and personal gear—the latter kept to a minimum, but still bulky—for 14 men and 2 officers plus a steel hoisting sling and, in the case of the 70 (my boat) and the 90, an extra gyro-compass stand and binnacle, we weighed an awkward 30 tons or more.

"Four of these craft, 60, 70, 80, 90, were assigned to Rear Admiral Moon's task force (five more were with Rear Admiral Hall), and sortied from Dartmouth into Start Bay on the afternoon of June 3rd to form Convoy U2-A-1 the LCT assault convoy for *Utah* Beach.

"We lay to for two and a half hours watching landing craft spill out of the narrow entrance of Dartmouth Harbor, between Kingswear and Dartmouth Castles—the British vessels white and light blue, the American dark gray, all of them overlaid with the greenish tan of army uniforms, army vehicles and army camouflage nets. When our convoy finally formed, LCTs strung out in two columns about ten miles long, and behind them 90 LCMs bucked and banged in four columns, with our LCCs acting as outsiders. From my station at the tail of the starboard columns, the line of ships stretched forward out of sight even then, and the convoy was not yet complete.

"We headed east with more than a full day's run ahead of us before we turned south for the final legs of our journey to the shores of Normandy. Tides run strong through the Channel, upwards of six knots in some places, and since our convoy was scheduled to proceed at five knots that meant some straining for the LCTs. Breakdowns that first night appeared to be frequent. At least, we stopped often, a tricky business for the LCMs, who'd be barreling along at top speed with a following sea, and suddenly find themselves climbing the fantails of the LCTs ahead. All night long we could hear them banging around like tin-framed bass drums.

"Soon after sundown, which came about 10 P.M., the sky became overcast, the breeze freshened, and the sea grew rougher. Occasionally the overcast would break and the moon would light up the ghost-white hull of a British LCT. Morning of the 4th was gray and gusty. We were getting thoroughly wet and well slammed about by the steep chop building up on our starboard quarter. We'd done what we could to stow all personal gear securely, but an LCC in a sea has a snappy roll with a kind of walloping wriggle tied onto it that can jar the fillings out of your teeth, and soon our small free space below-decks looked like the steerage of an old Black Ball liner—a confused litter of sleeping men and miscellaneous gear. One green-faced gunner's mate hoisted himself wearily topside explaining, 'Sleeping down there is damn rugged duty.'

"Matters were uncomfortable enough while we were underway; when we were forced to lie to, which was often, we slopped and sloshed around even more unhappily. Trying as that was physically, there was an indecisiveness, an apparent lackadaisical quality to our progress that tired us as much as the beating we were taking from the sea.

"Along about nine o'clock we were taking heavy spray over the bow. The interval between waves was just right to have us burrowing into each one. Then we got the radio signal in the clear, 'Post Mike One—Postpone D-day one day.'

"Our convoy, however, went bucketing along just as though nothing had happened. About fifteen minutes later the signal was repeated, and again fifteen minutes after that. I was a little worried, since we were still moving along our invasion course. I signaled Jim White—Lieutenant (jg)

James A. White, USNR—in the LCC 90, who was bringing up the rear of the port column, and he replied that he hadn't heard any message. That had me really bothered until we got another signal from the 90 saying that their radio hadn't been working in the first place.

"From time to time ships of the screen would come within range of our blinker, and, of course, we'd pass along the message to them. They always acknowledged, but maybe they didn't get what we said. After all, rolling, pitching and squirming as we were, our signalmen had to be a combination of chimpanzee and acrobat to flash messages anywhere near the ship he was sending to. A little more than two hours after we got the first radio signal, we got orders to accompany the LCMs back to Portland —Weymouth and take aboard fresh water and fuel.

"It was a long wet haul against wind and tide, with rain squalls to complicate matters, but eventually by six in the afternoon, we entered the delightful calm waters of the canal which forms Weymouth Harbor. There we tied up, ate and grabbed some sleep—four beautiful hours.

"At 11:30 we were awakened and given orders to rendezvous with the LCMs off the harbor mouth by one o'clock.

"It was blowing harder, but the rain had stopped, and the low scud racing across the sky opened up to give us flashes of moonlight on high white cliffs, flashes of moonlight on the frothing whitecaps. It was impressive enough for me to remember, apparently, but at the time our four LCCs were more concerned with standing by near enough the LCMs to see them, distant enough to keep out of their way.

"We must have stayed out there almost two hours before the LCM Group Commander showed up, and we all moved slowly south past Portland Bill. The wind was still from the west and we felt it as soon as we cleared the headland. After a full day of blowing, the chop had grown much heavier, longer and higher. Our radio antenna were whipping dangerously, water was coming aboard as fast as our pumps would handle it. Our generator lubrication lines parted. This put all our electrical equipment out of action, of course.

"The wind and sea were still following, so we snow-plowed along, yawing wildly, scooping up great gobs of English Channel with our bow and heaving it back into the forward cockpit where the helmsman and I drank it, inhaled it, blotted it up with our clothes and then shed the residue.

"The LCMs were having their troubles, too; we may have been

steering letter S's, but they sometimes did figure 8's. All of them had been rigged with canvas from ramp to engine room, and sometimes the wind would get under there and pop the whole thing out, leaving a sad litter of cots, bedding and gear all jumbled up exposed to the drenching spray. Men were supposed to sleep aboard the LCMs, and I've heard later that some actually managed to, but I can't see how. The LCMs didn't have the trouble we had of acting like a submarine about to crash dive, but they had a motion just as bad. A wave would pass under them about two thirds of their length, and then, instead of coasting down the hill of water, they'd simply ski-jump off and slam into the trough with a spine-shattering crash that sent spray clear over to the craft in the next columns.

"About eleven o'clock the convoy stopped, just stopped and wallowed. It looked to us as though the invasion were going to be postponed again; certainly the weather was as bad or worse than it had been the day before. I don't think anyone felt relieved or reprieved by the prospect of delay, for we knew that we'd have to do the thing sometime and, having made up our minds to that, we were anxious to get it done.

"The LCMs started to circle—a maneuver that is second nature to Amphibious coxswains since it is the only way they can keep relative station. My coxswain said, between gulps of spray, 'If any of those turkeys own cars after the war, I'll bet they have to drive around the block twenty times before they start downtown for groceries. They don't feel comfortable unless they're going round and round and round.'

"We must have spent an hour or more lying to, wondering, while the LCMs circled in their Amphibious Waltz.

"The sun came out briefly, or rather, the overcast thinned a bit, but visibility was still limited. And we certainly never saw the rainbow that seems to have cheered the convoys still in port.

"Then, finally we started up again, sorting ourselves out as we went. Our speed improved, and, better still, there were no more stops. The entire convoy seemed more purposeful somehow. The day wore on, and we slammed and slopped toward our goal.

"Shortly before six, the LCCs began to move up through the convoy so we could reach the Transport Area in time to take station before any of the assault waves we were to lead could form up. As we'd worked it out, we were to be ahead of the LCTs at the time the convoy reached mid-Channel, and swung almost due south toward our beach.

"It was a wild ride. The columns of LCTs were supposed to be two hundred yards apart, but with a heavy beam sea, that two hundred yards could shrink to a hundred before you wiped the spray out of your eyes. Naturally, we had to proceed at our best speed to get where we wanted to be before dark, but that didn't leave us any reserve for maneuver if we needed it. Probably every LCC skipper still dreams of suddenly finding himself poised on a wave directly over an ammunition-packed LCT, about to be flipped right aboard, or sees, towering over him, the broad, bulky ramp of an LCT, and feels the long minute of pause before the wave which drew them together parts them again.

"Tom Glennon—Lieutenant (jg) Thomas J. Glennon, USNR—must see all that and more than the rest of us, for Tom, trying to thread his way through a suddenly narrowed lane ran onto a buoy, dropped by the minesweepers, fouled and dragged out of position by an LCT. He hadn't a chance of missing it, and he didn't. As luck would have it, his screw fouled the buoy's anchor cable somehow, and the LCC 80 spent a black, black night, blacked out, bouncing up and down right in the middle of the convoy lane. I've seen Tom since; he doesn't talk much about that experience.

"The rest of us were luckier, getting in position before it got completely dark. It was a long haul, but impressive. Mile after mile of LCTs, slogging along, pounding and pitching and rolling and yawing, clumsy, perhaps, but purposeful. Passing them, waving at the Army to cheer them up, you got the feeling that these big banging barges were almost beautiful. They were going somewhere and they weren't going to stop.

"Last light came before sundown that night; came as a long ray of brilliance through a rift far off to starboard, making a glitter on the horizon for a moment. Then the clouds flamed red briefly; that was all.

"Just before dark the 'Motor Macs' reported that they'd fixed the generator. They'd been working at it steadily for twelve hours; twelve hours of slamming around a tiny engine room we couldn't ventilate properly (if we'd left the hatches open the Channel would have taken over the space they worked in), foul with diesel and lube oil fumes, hot from all the exposed surfaces of the main engines. They'd stopped work just once during the day. That was along about eight o'clock when we were at last steaming southward, making our way forward through our convoy. The sea was no better than it had been, and they came slipping and slithering forward, completely covered with oil, brown scum over pale greenish faces. One of them said to me, 'Y'know, sir, if we could only put in to some nice quiet port for about four hours we could get this thing fixed.' He was quite serious, much more worried about the generator than about the invasion. 'It was like trying to fix a washing machine with us on the inside of the damn thing and it running,' they told me.

"Running after dark wasn't much different from running in daytime except that the wind and sea had increased in force. We began to ship water, but there wasn't much we could do about it except try to keep a weather eye open and avoid heading right into the biggest waves. We couldn't reduce speed much for fear of being run down by an LCT thundering up astern.

"Our convoy was the first through the port, slow approach, lane to the Transport Area, consequently we had the benefit of the buoys dropped by the minesweepers—those of them that remained alight. Actually navigation at that point was about as difficult as driving down Broadway; the trouble was not in finding your way, but in keeping out of other people's.

"As we drew into the lee of the continent the wind and sea abated. High time, too, for we were getting more and more sluggish as our cockpits filled with water. Still, we were getting near our goal. There was a faint reddish flicker on the horizon—antiaircraft fire and bombing, the latter reflected from the overcast. We had more dramatic confirmation of our position soon. Quite suddenly, as I was looking for a small patrol craft I'd spotted off to starboard before, I saw something else. It was big and black, big enough to be an island. I looked again, and this time I recognized it; the lead battleship of our Fire Support Group. Another followed, and then the cruisers, all boiling along to get in position for the opening of the festivities. Battleships and cruisers look big any time. They looked bigger and deadlier, black against the blackness, that night than ever before. And then their wash hit us, and by the time we were through standing on our beam ends they had vanished. But you couldn't forget that they were out there somewhere just waiting to cut loose. It was a good feeling.

"By this time, it was clear that we would be late if we stayed with our convoy. Accordingly we pulled up alongside the convoy flagship and asked permission, which was granted, to go on about our business.

"There was plenty of firing, antiaircraft mostly, all along the horizon. Then, there was a flash of flame about two miles off. And a minute later a red and green start shell burst in the air about a quarter of a mile away and fell, still burning, into the water two hundred yards dead ahead. The water blazed red and green. Six chandelier flares drifted down through the overcast off to starboard. They had the effect of lighting the water with such a glare that it seemed flat calm. I remembered them from Sicily, and got the same feeling—'My boat a very black fly in the middle of a very white sheet and we'd be awfully easy to swat.' Only this time there were so many other flies around nobody'd think of swatting us. There was some fire toward the Transport Area; we were close to it now. A whole batch of rockets went up from shore, and a plane in the air burst into flame. And then we were passing between two transports and there was the Primary Control Vessel. We reported to him, assumed our station, and our passage was over. Sixty hours after our sortie, we had arrived at the scene of the operation and were about to go to work, dispatching the assault waves to the beach."

Chapter Thirty-seven

A T THE start of an amphibious assault, the Transport Area is the point of reference and the point of focus of all activities.

In the Transport Area the troopships anchor and lower the amphibious craft, the LCVPs or LCMs, which forthwith assemble off the quarters of the ships to be unloaded first, and circle about in a huge, spray-festooned ring-around-a-rosy until they are called alongside the transport to take on troops. Then they resume their circling.

That merry-go-round of small craft has as much meaning and purpose as any formation of troops ashore or warships at sea. It is more like the formation of airplanes leaving, or approaching, a carrier. Circling keeps them in order. The unloaded craft are summoned to the troopships by colored light signals; the troops scramble down the cargo nets into the amphibious craft, which chug off for the rendezvous circle hard by, each roundabout composed of boats that will hit the beach in the same wave. The rendezvous circling is performed, usually, off the bows of the transports on the landward side.

Marking the inshore extreme of the Transport Area are the control vessels that guide the first four or five waves of small craft through the mine-swept lanes to the beach. Five minutes before this final dash, a light gleams from each control craft. When that light goes out, the run for the beach begins. The circles straighten out into columns.

It is an orderly run; there is nothing of the cavalry charge about it. The control boats take the troop- and gun-laden craft in prearranged waves to an imaginary line known as the Line of Departure, from 1,500 to 4,000 yards off the beach target. From the Line of Departure the small craft are supposed to be able to see the beach, and to recognize from landmarks and detailed charts the spot at which they are to discharge their troops. The control boats remain on station on the Line of Departure, acting as close control of all boat traffic near the beach. In the Normandy invasion the Line of Departure was 3,000 yards off the beach, and the Transport Area was from 10 to 14 miles distant.

Until the Army signals that the beach is securely held, the Transport Area remains the heart and brain, the nerve and arterial system, of the invasion. Through it pass all troops, cargo and craft that are to hit the beach, no matter when. To it and through it pass all messages, for the Naval Task Group Commander and the Commanding General, with their respective staffs, are all there.

Flanking the Transport Area are the Fire Support Areas where the bombardment groups form, to provide the landing forces with artillery support, to blast any probing artillery fire directed at the heart of the invasion: battleships, cruisers, destroyers for closer work, and rocket ships and gunboats to charge in with the first waves of the landing craft.

Later, with the beaches secured and the invasion forces in control far enough inland to eliminate enemy shore batteries, the transports move closer in, to speed the movement of troops and supplies to the beach. When the Admiral in charge deems that safety permits, the Transport Area is expanded to a general anchorage.

Such was the pattern of amphibious invasion; evolved in 1942 on the shores of the Chesapeake, tested and emended in forty different invasions from Africa to Attu, Salamaua to Sicily in the intervening years, and now to meet its ultimate test on the shores of captive France.

In the dark hours of D-day morning the Allied forces lined up in that combat array off the coast of France. The British and Canadian invasion troopships lay off the eastern half of the beachhead area from the mouth of the Orne westward to the little fishing village of Port-en-Bessin. Supporting them were the great guns of battleships HMS WARSPITE, NELSON and RAMILLIES. There were cruisers, too: HMS BELFAST and the Canadians HMCS SIOUX and ALGONQUIN.

From Port-en-Bessin westward to Pointe de Hoe, Rear Admiral Hall's Task Force O took over. This was the beach called Omaha. Then, on the other side of the Vire Estuary, Rear Admiral Moon's Task Force U faced what was to be the right flank of the entire beachhead, Utah Beach. Supporting the two American forces (which combined as Rear Admiral Kirk's Western Task Force) were three American battleships, grand old girls of the fleet: USS TEXAS, NEVADA and ARKANSAS. There were the cruisers TUSCALOOSA, QUINCY and the AUGUSTA, from which flew the flag of Admiral Kirk. There were, too, the British cruisers, HMS BELLONA,

GLASGOW, HAWKINS, ENTERPRISE and BLACK PRINCE; the French cruisers, overhauled and modernized in American yards, MONTCALM and GEORGES LEYGUES; the Dutch gunboat SOEMBA; thirty-four United States destroyers and five destroyer escorts. All these ships formed the Fire Support Group under the command of Admiral Deyo. In the darkness they deployed along their mine-swept channels, each taking her allotted station, lining herself up to fire at her allotted target. And still what gunfire there was from the enemy shore was directed skyward, not seaward!

The transports began unloading troops into small boats, some 13 miles offshore. In Rear Admiral Hall's sector, ranged in line from east to west, at 600-yard intervals, were his flagship, USS ANCON, an amphibious veteran of Africa, Sicily and Salerno; SAMUEL CHASE, the British transports EMPIRE ANVIL and HENRICO, then USS CHARLES CARROLL and THOMAS JEFFERSON. Then seven more British troopships. Astern of these, in the same order, were USS ANNE ARUNDEL, DOROTHEA DIX, THURSTON, ten LSTs with rhino ferries (great self-propelled pontoon barges capable of carrying almost a full LST load), and a British fighter-director ship. Astern of these again was USS OCEAN WAVE, a new type of craft, a Landing Ship Dock. On both sides of this double line, and astern of it, were rendezvous areas for the LCT and LCI convoys.

Rear Admiral Moon's task force was somewhat smaller; his transports were USS BAYFIELD, his flagship BARNETT, DICKMAN and the British EMPIRE GAUNTLET. Behind these ships were ranged five LSTs with rhino barges, and around the whole, as around Admiral Hall's big ships, were the rendezvous areas of the LCTs and LCIs.

Task Force O was designed to carry the main push of the American assault, spearheaded by troops of the 1st and 29th Divisions. Theirs was to be a tough row to hoe. The intelligence section of Rear Admiral Hall's Operation Order described the terrain with brutal clarity:

"In the Omaha Beach Area the coast is a flat land rising gradually from 100 feet in height on the right to 200 on the left. On the right this plateau reaches the sea in a bold chalk cliff. On the left the cliff is topped by a rugged 200-foot bluff. The shore between is a beach approximately 7,500 yards in length backed by a shelf of an average 100-yards width. Immediately behind this shelf, a bluff rises to the plateau presenting a steep, grassy or bush-covered slope. There are four valley exits through this bluff. . . .

"Except for the extreme right (Western) end, which is backed by cliffs, the entire Omaha Beach Area is backed by a low, wavy-cut, grassy or shingle embankment, faced for parts of its length by a masonry wall. This embankment can be bull-dozed down, but will require some sort of ramp or matting. Behind the embankment, the flatland, or shelf, should have sufficient grass cover to support vehicular movement. The bluff behind this shelf will probably restrict such movement, and channel it into the four valley exits. . . .

"Since the Beach Area is dominated by bluff there is little effective cover, and much of what there is the enemy is progressively clearing."

To defend this formidable piece of terrain the Germans had wrought with their usual thoroughness. Machine-gun emplacements were dug in the face of the cliffs, pillboxes dominated every inch of the four narrow beach exits, mortars and 88s were zeroed in on each square foot of beach. Very few guns pointed seaward, and consequently very few of them were good targets from seaward. (There was a battery of 105s on Pointe de Hoe which commanded the Transport Area of Task Force O, yet Task Force O assembled in that Transport Area and the 105s never woke up until too late.)

The geography of Utah Beach differed radically from Omaha. It was not dominated by bluffs; instead, back of the beach there was about a mile of low dunes and then swamp. There were casemated big guns, strong points, pillboxes and machine-gun nests in profusion, of course, but reconnaissance had showed the intelligence officers where most of them were, and they were simply marked down as fat targets.

Of course, there was high ground to the westward running out to Pointe de Barfleur, and guns there could fire down the beach if they weren't put out of action. And the Cotentin Peninsula was supposed to hold some of the huge German railroad guns which could dominate the Transport Area and duel on even terms with a battleship. But generally it was assumed that Utah Beach would be the easier to assault. It turned out to have its own kind of deadly defense.

Chapter Thirty-eight

AT 0530, Lieutenant Arthur Newmyer, USNR, speaking over the
public address system of Rear Admiral Hall's flagship ANCON, gave
to all hands this description of the preparations against Omaha Beach:

"In a few minutes, coinciding with the first break of dawn on this
historic day, the most tremendous naval bombardment ever to blast out
against the European Continent will start.

"During the night our warships—battleships and cruisers—protected
from enemy submarines and E-boats by their screen of destroyers—went
ahead of us as we neared the Baie de la Seine.

"They took their position—ready to pour fire at the enemy gun
emplacements—as we lined up in the Transport Area.

"The ANCON, leading the transport group in Rear Admiral Hall's
Force, arrived at the transport area at 0230.

"We dropped anchor at 0251.

"We are now on the port side of the transport line in Force O.

"We are approximately 20,000 yards—10 miles—off the beach.

"The APAs [Auxiliary, Personnel, Assault—a combat-loaded trans-
port] already have lowered their LCVPs, which are milling about their
mother ships, waiting for the bombardment to open up, waiting for their
time to go in.

"Our big ships are in very close to bombard in this assault. The
TEXAS is going to fire at 12,000 yards. The ARKANSAS is going to fire at
a range of only 6,000 yards. At those ranges those fourteen-inch guns
mean business.

"Battleships—cruisers—destroyers—and monitors—are going to blast
at Hitler's Normandy defenses with rapid fire—concentrated fire—pin-
point fire—for forty minutes before the first troops hit the beach.

"We know where Hitler's guns are. They are banked in concrete.
And they will be hard to knock out. But we are going to give them an
awful wallop.

"In addition to the warship firepower I spoke about before, we have some more items to dish out. Our LCTs carry medium tanks, and these tanks will be cutting loose on the way in. They are scheduled to hit the beach at exactly H-hour—0630. Just before the tanks hit the beach, our rocket ships, carrying many banks of rockets apiece, will open up.

"The infantry, in our LCVPs, will hit one minute after our tanks hit—at H plus one minute.

"We have air bombardment helping us blast out those Nazi gun emplacements. They have been blasting for the past twenty-four hours. During the night paratroopers landed behind the enemy lines to help cut off enemy reinforcements. The paratroopers will be coming in today.

"The Armies that are going to land are part of the British Second and the U.S. First Armies. Together they are known as the Twenty-first Army Group. The First U.S. Army is commanded by Lieutenant General Omar Bradley, who was aboard the ANCON during the Sicilian invasion. He is aboard the AUGUSTA right now. Until General Bradley establishes his headquarters on the far shore, General Montgomery will command the Allied Armies, the Twenty-first Army Group.

"General Montgomery is the man who chased Rommel across the North African desert until tens of thousands of Italians and Germans surrendered in Tunisia. Reports from Germany indicate that Rommel is Hitler's choice to face General Montgomery again. If so, he hasn't long to wait.

"The naval bombardment is about to begin.

"H-hour is fast approaching.

"The Liberation of Europe is on the way!"

His tone was buoyant, his voice had a ring.

Shortly after eight o'clock that evening, he broadcast again:

"This has been a long—tough—day.

"On the whole, our naval bombardment this morning was accurate and powerful. Generally, our first waves reached their designated beach areas within five minutes of their scheduled time. But, as you know, we were faced with strong winds and choppy seas. And on the way in, in certain instances, our small landing craft capsized—and there we lost valuable equipment and precious lives.

"On some beaches the landing was successful from the start. On others the going was very hard.

"One of the principal objectives of Admiral Hall's Force was a powerful battery on Pointe de Hoe, at the westernmost end of our initial target area. At and near this point the Nazis had placed six 105-mm. guns. Even though we were 20,000 yards offshore, our transports and the ANCON were within range of those guns. Those guns were mounted in concrete and were firmly embanked on top of a rugged cliff which rose sharply, almost at the water's edge, to a height of 200 feet.

"The American Rangers really went after that Pointe de Hoe battery. They captured it amazingly quickly." (And, Lieutenant Newmyer might have added, they suffered appalling casualties when they were trapped after doing it.)

"As must be expected, however, on a beachhead as large as the one assigned Force O, in other areas, particularly towards the eastern end of our beach, it was not so easy. At first it wasn't the larger guns that bothered the invading troops—it was the steady stream of machine-gun fire that pinned down our boys as they attempted to go ashore. Added to the steady stream of machine-gun fire were the difficulties we had with certain beach obstacles in those areas.

"The choppy seas hampered our demolition units. They were unable to clear entrance channels as fast as they, and we, had hoped.

"So in some of those areas our landing craft tangled with these obstacles, many of which contained mines, and we had other losses of men, supplies and landing craft here.

"When the word of this condition reached our fire-support ships they moved in—and moved in fast.

"Destroyers—cruisers—and battleships supported those boys on the beaches. Our bombing aircraft poured in—fast and effectively. By noon, some of those troops that had been trapped were moving inland at a satisfactory pace. By early afternoon the APAs had unloaded nearly all their troops. They already have left us to start back to England. Their first mission has been accomplished.

"A few hours ago, Force B of the Western Task Force arrived. Force B is the support force, commanded by Commodore Campbell D. Edgar, USN. Commodore Edgar's Force, containing a large number of LSTs and LCI(L)s, already is unloading.

"As you know, by the steady announcements from Sky Control that 'P-47s, P-38s, Spitfires and Typhoons are overhead,' our air cover has been excellent.

"Generally, we feel we surprised Hitler and his cohorts this time. But the Germans were quick to announce that we had landed, and undoubtedly large Nazi reinforcements are on the way. Certain guns, we suspect, already have been moved up, and the going, at the moment, is again hard.

"Our aircraft, which for weeks have been pounding vital bridges and other transportation arteries, will continue to disrupt these German attempts to reinforce.

"But to really be in position to face the German counterattack, our boys on the beaches have got to get more supplies, more equipment and more men.

"That job is up to the Navy."

What had occurred between the two broadcasts? Lieutenant Commander Joseph H. Gibbons, USNR, who was in command of the Naval Combat Demolition Units, explains it in part in his report:

"The Naval Combat Demolition Units were charged with the responsibility of clearing sixteen 50-yard gaps on the beaches assigned to that force. They worked in close conjunction with the Army engineers throughout the entire operation. There was an understanding between Lieutenant Colonel O'Neil and myself that, while the initial responsibility of clearing the seaward gaps was the Navy's and the shoreward gaps was the Army's, that they would work as just American men fighting for an over-all objective. If I got stuck he was going to help me, and if he got stuck I would help him. We agreed that as soon as the seaward gaps were blown we would join in helping the Army clear the shoreward gaps if that had not been accomplished.

"After accomplishing our initial objective of sixteen 50-yard gaps we were then to proceed to clear all enemy obstacles off the beaches. It was expected that enemy gunfire would be neutralized by H-hour when we were to land. The plan called for the Navy Combat Demolition Units to land at bare minutes after H-hour. Unfortunately the gunfire was not neutralized and as we approached the beaches we were subjected to heavy enemy fire from 88-mm., 75s, 50s, machine-gun and rifle fire. In the engagement we suffered 41 per cent casualties, 20 per cent killed, 21 per cent wounded, exclusive of those wounded not evacuated from the beaches.

"The gunfire was intense, but we were successful in clearing initially six gaps 50 yards each and three semipartially cleared gaps. One entire crew was killed by a single direct hit of an 88-mm. gun. By the end of

D-day we had been successful in clearing 10 gaps completely. By D-plus-two day, 85 per cent of the enemy obstacles on the beaches had been cleared and by D-plus-four the beaches were cleared of all enemy obstacles dangerous to invasion craft.

"The job was done at heavy cost. One boatload received a direct hit by an 88 and all were killed except two men. In another case an officer was standing by to pull the fuses after the charges had been placed when rifle fire cut off his fingers and the fuse assemblies. In still another instance enemy rifle fire set off the charges which cleared the gap but unfortunately also caused casualties. One unit was wiped out with the exception of three men by enemy sniper fire. Throughout the entire operation the loyalty, bravery and devotion to duty of the men were most outstanding. All of those who were killed died with their faces toward the enemy and as they moved forward to accomplish their objectives.

"One gets rather fatalistic regarding operations of this nature.

"Three of my officers were walking down the beaches, which were strewn with mines. They were walking in the ruts of a truck. Twenty paces behind the last officer came a soldier. The three naval officers advanced by stepping in each other's footprints. The soldier, following their procedure exactly, stepped on a mine and was blown to pieces.

"In another instance, an officer was in the command post, which was a foxhole on the beach behind half a dozen stalled ammunition trucks. Another officer approached him, declaring that he thought that particular position was dangerous for the evening, inasmuch as there was a road which had been cut through the sand dunes and which would probably be subjected to enemy gunfire during the night. The officer accosted at first declined to accept the advice but subsequently informed the other that if he could find a more secure place he would be willing to move there for the night. They conversed for about five minutes, and then left in search of 'a better 'ole,' whereupon enemy gunfire opened on these trucks, setting them on fire, and they burned and exploded all night long.

"On the enemy-placed obstacles on the beaches they had also placed teller mines. These were placed on approximately 75 per cent, on the top of stakes at the apex of ramps and at the top of the elements 'C' and in some cases in the center of hedgehogs. In order to eliminate those mines, it was decided that they should be detonated at the time the obstacle was destroyed.

"To accomplish that, it was necessary to place a charge alongside the mine to assure it being detonated when the obstacle was demolished. To accomplish this men shinnied up the stakes and stood on each other's shoulders all in the face of heavy enemy gunfire."

The worst part of that kind of combat job is that one does not shoot back. As a result of the performance and the successful accomplishment of their mission, the Naval Combat Demolition Units of Force O was awarded the Presidential Unit Citation.

The teams on Utah Beach were given the Navy Unit Commendation with the following citation by Secretary Forrestal:

> For outstanding heroism in action against German forces during the landing on the Coast of Normandy, June 6, 1944. Ruggedly trained and fiercely determined to effect the gap through which would flow our whole battle effort in the assigned sector, Naval Combat Demolition Units, Assault Force U, boldly moved in toward sands raked by German mortars, machine guns and 88-mm.'s. Crowded into LCMs and LCVPs, and with minutes only in which to blow the obstacles before they were obscured by racing tides, these gallant men landed, each weighed down by forty pounds of TNT and carrying two-pound blocks around his chest, to place demolition charges on pyramids of steel, timber or concrete; on ramps, hedgehogs and other obstructions. Constantly in peril from terrific fire of hostile pillboxes and casements, they ignited their fuses and, as the tide swept in during the critical hours of D-Day, saw the line of khaki move slowly up the eastern American beach and inland through a 300-yard gap cleared of German emplacements. Individually courageous and working as a valiant team in the face of fearful destruction wrought by enemy fire, Naval Combat Demolition Units, Assault Force U, achieved a hazardous mission vital to the initiation of our land war against ruthless German aggression.

That first day on Omaha Beach was the time of which Field Marshal Montgomery spoke when he said that "the American troops held on by their eyelashes." That first day was the day on which Ernest Hemingway saw that "the first, second, third, fourth and fifth waves lay where they had fallen, looking like so many heavily laden bundles on the flat pebbly stretch between the sea and the first cover." A naval officer who saw the same thing remembered it three weeks later so vividly that all he could say for description was, "The poor bastards. From seven in the morning till four in the afternoon. From seven in the morning until four in the afternoon. The poor bastards!"

What happened at four o'clock on the afternoon of D-day was that destroyers of the Fire Support Group moved inshore until, as Rear Admiral Kirk described it in an interview, "they had their bows against the bottom." From there they simply blew a path up the beach exits for the troops. The system they employed was to blast away at the lowest pillboxes until they were knocked out, then, as the army moved forward, to start on the next higher group of pillboxes. Because the enemy was dug into the hillsides and had the valleys in a cross fire, the destroyers established a cross fire, too—the destroyer on the right of a valley firing at the enemy on the left, the destroyer on the left taking the enemy on the right.

With our troops pinned on their main assault beaches, the Germans had a magnificent opportunity to attack. Or it might have been a magnificent opportunity had it not been for one formidable fact: they couldn't get near the beach themselves to reinforce its defenders. They couldn't get away from the beach to regroup. Every move the Nazis tried to make was spotted from the air, relayed to the battleships and cruisers and then blasted to whatever kingdom come wants Nazis.

Because our Army couldn't move inshore over Omaha Beach, the naval gunfire liaison officers there couldn't do the spotting jobs that earned them fame in Africa and Sicily. Still, they managed, time after time, to call down death and destruction on strong points that were holding up the advance near the beach. Farther inland, specially trained RAF fliers, manning Spitfires, called the shots for the Navy.

And what shots they were! "Five tanks at two-nine-zero-three, two-nine-zero-three—repeat at two-nine-zero-three," calls the pilot spotting for the TEXAS. Deep down in the most protected part of the gallant old ship Lieutenant Commander Richard B. Derickson, USN, the gunnery officer, scans his map. Reading off the grid co-ordinates he sees that 2903 is a little cross-roads some nine miles behind the beach. The ship is steaming on course 315 at 10 knots, the wind is blowing so many knots from such a direction—the factors pour into the calculators as fast as they come to the mind trained for just such problems. And as each factor is entered the great guns swing. Thirty seconds after the pilot in the Spitfire has named the target there is a blanketing orange flash from the number 1 turret of the TEXAS, a flash that seems to start about three feet from the muzzles of the guns and billows swiftly into a cloud of flaming gas. There is a crack like the Rock of Gibraltar splitting and then, three miles away, a small-boat coxswain feels a mighty shudder in the air from the firing. Compressed air, cleaning the gun barrels, has blown a broad puff of brownish smoke out after the belch of flame and this smoke now diffuses about the TEXAS' sides.

Meanwhile, overhead, with the rumble of a runaway freight on a downgrade, the great projectiles are roaring toward their target. The German tanks edge slowly, tentatively forward. And then, with a shattering roar, the shells of the TEXAS hit. Earth, dust, smoke and the debris that once was tanks geyser skyward. The RAF pilot, abandoning military phraseology in his excitement, calls back to the battleship—"Oh, simply champion! Only one of the blighters left and he's running away."

Repeat that scene for every turret on the TEXAS, for every gun on every battleship, cruiser, gunboat and destroyer. Repeat it from the moment the preliminary, preinvasion bombardment of selected beach targets is lifted until darkness falls that first night. Begin it again the next morning and keep up every time a target is spotted—an ammunition dump, a truck convoy, a strong point, a gun battery, a troop concentration, anything German that could move or shoot. Keep that up for a week, day after day of steady pounding wherever and whenever the Army calls for it. There you have a picture of naval gunfire support of the Normandy landings.

Add to that aerial bombardment of every road, every bridge, every canal, every rail line from the beaches clear back to Germany and you have the reason the Nazis could not capitalize on the momentary stalling of our offensive on Omaha Beach. For stalled it was until well along into the afternoon of D-day.

By four o'clock the bundles on the beach began to move slowly forward, and upward, those that could move at all. Meanwhile lives had been lost and time, which might well mean more lives, had been lost. Because the demolitions had not gone on schedule it was impossible to land the heavy supporting weapons and equipment the Army needed; the LCTs and rhino barges that were to carry them couldn't find a clear space to beach. Of the few LCTs and LCIs that did manage to find a place to beach on D-day, fewer got off, almost none unscathed. Hemingway, in the *Collier's* article already quoted, described one vessel he saw: "Out a way, rolling in the sea, was a Landing Craft, Infantry, and as we came alongside of her I saw a ragged shellhole through the steel plates forward of her pilot-house where an 88mm German shell had punched through. Blood was dripping from the shiny edges of the hole into the sea with each roll of the LCI. Her rails and hull had been befouled by seasick men, and her dead were laid forward of her pilot-house."

And she was one of the lucky ships that had managed to hit the beach without staving in her sides against hedgehogs, without blowing a hole in her bottom on a mine. She was one of the few lucky ones that had been hit only once as she lay motionless on the beach; one of the lucky ones that had managed to get off the beach at all.

LCT 540 was bound for the beach working her way slowly through one of the channels cleared of obstacles when she took nine hits from 88s in quick succession. Her skipper was killed instantly, six soldiers were killed or wounded and seven of the Navy crew were wounded. The ramp door was blown off and the ship was crippled. Ensign William L. Wilhoit, USNR, aboard as a relief skipper, new to combat, twenty-one years old, took command, though he himself was severely wounded. He maneuvered the craft to the beach, discharged his cargo and turned the wounded Army personnel over to a beach casualty station. Then he backed his battered ship off the beach, backed her out to the Transport Area—high seas were running and he couldn't meet them head-on with no ramp. He took aboard another cargo and headed in for the beach again. Day and night for four days, the smashed LCT 540, with Ensign Wilhoit in command, crawled from the transports to the beach pumping material ashore. Ensign Wilhoit was awarded the Navy Cross.

Omaha Beach was a place for heroism. Thirty-six hours after H-hour Lieutenant Newmyer's broadcast was far from optimistic:

"The troops on some of our beaches are still having a pretty tough time.

"We are anchored, as you know, about five miles off Port-en-Bessin. Admiral Hall's Force landed, you remember, in an area that stretches about 12½ miles from here to Pointe de Hoe, to the east.

"About in the middle of that area, less than a mile from the beach, is a small French village named Saint-Laurent-sur-Mer. On the western side of Saint-Laurent-sur-Mer we landed the 116th Infantry Regiment; on the eastern side, the 16th Infantry Regiment.

"At that point—the beachhead before Saint-Laurent—the going is the hardest. The unloading area there is quite congested, with many landing craft broached or tangled with underwater obstacles. Getting rid of those underwater obstacles continues to be one of our principal problems. For because of them, in most instances in that area, we have been unable to use our rhino ferries; our larger types of landing craft have been unable to reach the beach—and unloading, generally, has been delayed. Going in, yesterday morning, in the choppy seas, the Navy demolition units and the Army engineers, who work together in getting rid of those underwater obstacles, lost much of their equipment. Steady machine-gun fire, as I mentioned during last night's talk, increased the hazard of their work. In these fast rising and fast falling tides, you don't have much time to work on underwater items, and the job just could not be done in time.

"Some more progress was made this morning—now that we control the bluffs overlooking the beaches, and the machine-gun fire is not so intense—and we are hopeful that the situation off Saint-Laurent was improved during low tide this afternoon, although complete reports are not back yet.

"In other areas on our beaches the troops are moving inland rather well. On the average, they are estimated to be about five miles inland.

"The British Second Army and the American First Army are now closing in on Port-en-Bessin. Our ships have been giving those Armies gunfire support in their drive against Port-en-Bessin during the afternoon. B-25s also pitched in.

"Port-en-Bessin has been used as a German E-boat base, and there was quite a bit of firing in the harbor area last night. It is primarily a fishing port, as are so many of these small villages on the Normandy coast. But we hope that during rising tides, once the town is ours, we will be able to get LSTs, LCI(L)s, and LCTs in there for unloading.

"Fortunately, during the brief but sharp attack on our shipping last night, the boys on the beaches were not bothered too much. Only one enemy plane bombed our beachhead positions, and that did little if any damage.

"Intelligence estimates that during last night's raid on Admiral Hall's Force, about midnight, six to eight enemy planes, mostly Ju-88s, came in. Three were shot down. So our batting average was pretty good. Gun 40-2, the ANCON's 40-mm. gun on our port side, chalked up one of those kills, and the boys topside were treated to a real thrill as the wing tore off the Ju-88 and the Nazi plunged into the sea.

"The Germans used their old trick of coming in low over the bluffs, but they did no damage whatsoever to any of our shipping.

"You will be interested to know that Supreme Headquarters announced this morning that from dawn yesterday to dawn today Allied aircraft flew 13,000—13,000—sorties.

"This morning—about four miles off our starboard—the largest ship we've lost so far in this operation hit a mine and went down. She was the SUSAN B. ANTHONY, the troopship that was with the ANCON during the Sicilian invasion and was with the ANCON convoy coming up from the Mediterranean. She was fully loaded with troops, but the rescue ships had about an hour to rush to the scene and start picking up survivors between the time of the explosion and the time the ANTHONY finally slid under at 1013, and it is believed that all except those killed in the explosion were saved and that casualties were very few.

"Another ship, a Liberty ship, hit a mine this morning in the same area, but she was taken in tow and is all right.

"The ANTHONY and the Liberty ship were part of the tremendous convoy that sailed from the Bristol Channel about the same time we sailed from Portland and arrived early this morning. Many more convoys will be coming in during the next few days. Admiral Hall has ordered that the troopships be unloaded as quickly as possible, and all available LCTs are being put to that work.

"In these days of big jobs, that's another big job. For most of these troopships don't carry their own LCVPs like the APAs that came over with us, so we must take those troops ashore in the landing craft that are available around here."

By the night of June 8, Newmyer was cheerful again:

"Today was our best day thus far, and at the moment things are going very well on the beaches.

"As we had hoped, by nightfall last night, a great many of the beach obstacles which had been delaying our landing operations, had been removed. We were able to unload many troops and much supplies and equipment late yesterday. This progress has been continuing all day today. The beaches are now relatively clear, and our unloading parties there are no longer hampered by sniper fire and shell fire."

And, from then on, Omaha Beach went well. The beachhead became what all successful beachheads become—a supply port where everyone worked until he was walking in his sleep, and then kept right on working.

Chapter Thirty-nine

THINGS went well from the start at the British and Canadian beaches. The preliminary bombardment knocked out the targets it was supposed to knock out; the aerial bombing and the landing-craft rocket fire kept the Germans cowering in their shelters until it was too late for them to man their machine guns. Then, too, because the approaches to the British beaches were rock-strewn, Admiral Vian elected to wait until the tide was higher before beginning his assault. By 8 A.M. the Eastern Task Force H-hour, the sea had abated considerably and far fewer small craft were weather casualties than on the American beaches.

The British and Canadians found the going tough soon enough around Caen and Troarn, but on the beaches they came ashore with refreshingly few losses.

Likewise Utah Beach looked good from the start for the Army. The landing went off on schedule, the demolitions proceeded according to plan, and in general Utah appeared to be an easy beach. Compared to Omaha during the first two days, it *was* easy on the Army. The Navy, however, did not fare quite so well, as the story Lieutenant Commander Rency F. Sewell, Jr., USNR, Commanding Officer of USS PC 1261, shows:

"PC 1261 was primarily a control vessel for Red Beach in the Invasion of France. The primary purpose of this vessel was to lead the assault waves into the beach, and to hit the right beach at the right time. It was early in the morning and we were all gathered at the transport area awaiting H-hour. There was some delay in proceeding to the beach due to bad weather. The initial wave was delayed about twenty minutes.

"At first there was no enemy fire experienced. This, of course, encouraged us very much for we realized that the planes had bombed their objectives. For the next twenty minutes we proceeded to the beach with very little occurring. Upon reaching a point about 5,000 yards from the beach the coastal batteries opened fire upon us; one shell seemed to hit about 30 yards off the starboard quarter. I knew immediately that they had our range and the next one would probably hit us, which it did. It hit us right in the starboard side, aft of midships. The ship immediately took a 20-degree list to starboard with the fantail under the water.

"The order was not given to abandon ship at once, for we felt that we might be able to save it. However, two minutes later the ship took a 90-degree roll and order was given to abandon ship and all hands walked over the side as one would walk over a treadmill. There was very little confusion as we walked over the side of the ship and all hands immediately tried to get to their life rafts. The water was very cold; in fact, I think that most of the men that were lost were lost by the coldness of the water. I, myself, was stiff from my shoulders down.

"We all realized it was impossible for anyone to pick us up at this time for all the waves that passed us had a specific job to do and we did not want to stop them; so actually we were cheering them to the beach as they passed by. We realized that we would eventually be picked up.

"A Coast Guard rescue vessel came in sight and began picking up the rafts. It was a small vessel and had not only to rescue the personnel of my ship, but of three others which had sunk almost simultaneously. There was quite a number of the crew in the water and we were all afraid that the Coast Guard vessel would not be large enough to pick up all the crew. However, this did not worry us as much as did the current, which was carrying our rafts towards the beach. We were afraid that we would be taken prisoner.

"The Coast Guard vessel picked us up out of the water about three hours after we had abandoned ship. It immediately carried us back to the Transport Area where we boarded a transport ship that was doing duty as a hospital evacuation ship, USS DICKMAN."

Two of the other ships mentioned by Sewell were large rocket craft, upon which much of the neutralization of machine-gun nests and beach pillboxes might well have depended. The third was an LCT carrying amphibious tanks. The belief is that these ships struck mines; despite the splendid work of the minesweepers, there were still plenty of them around. Indeed, two months after D-day three minesweepers were blown up by mines in as many days off Utah Beach. Before H-hour on June 6 they had already claimed another victim, the destroyer CORRY, Lieutenant Commander George D. Hoffman, USN, commanding.

Here is the story of his ship by one of the surviving officers:

"The CORRY was commissioned on the 18th of December, 1941, shortly after our entry into the war. At that time I was gunnery officer on board that vessel. For the first year we had the duty of escorting an aircraft carrier in a task force in the Atlantic during which time her mission was that of being on guard against sorties of any of the German fleet units from Norwegian bases.

"Then in the fall of 1943 we were attached to the British Home Fleet during which time we sortied several times. Once when the German fleet raided Spitzbergen and a later time to effect relief for the remaining garrison at Spitzbergen at which time the USS TUSCALOOSA brought in more personnel to man the base and take off the wounded. The mission of the CORRY during this time was to escort units of the British Fleet and American Fleet and interpose themselves between Spitzbergen and the German bases.

"The mission was successfully completed, the base reopened and we had one more job to do before turning home. It involved escorting the HMS ANSON with a Vice-Admiral, second in command, British Home Fleet, aboard to lie off the entrance of Alten Fjord while the first Russian convoy went north of Bear Island to Murmansk. Twenty-four hours we remained off the entrance to Alten Fjord but the SCHARNHORST at that time did not come out.

"The convoy successfully arrived in Murmansk. Our unit returned back to Scapa Flow where we were based. On the 17th of March, 1944, the CORRY, while off the Azores, sank a U-boat with the assistance of USS BRONSTEIN at which time we took forty-seven prisoners and delivered them later in the day to USS BLOCK ISLAND. Two days later, the 19th of March, planes from the BLOCK ISLAND sank a German submarine. The CORRY was dispatched at a distance of about 70 miles to go over to pick up survivors of a plane that had been shot down, and the sunken submarine's survivors. It picked up one surviving officer from the plane and two officers and six German sailors from the submarine. The CORRY had the job to carry the German prisoners back to the States. Had them aboard for eleven days and during the period we had them aboard we got them all fairly well cured of their wounds. Most of them were badly wounded from bomb fragments. We turned them over to the Army at Boston.

"The last job for the CORRY was participation in the invasion of the coast of France, June 6, 1944. Previous to this period, we had escorted a convoy across the Channel and upon arrival in the Transport Area led the first boat waves down the boat lane in company with the USS FITCH and HOBSON, destroyers of our own class. This was before H-hour. We turned off from the boat lane at about H-minus-one, and took our station at about 4,000 yards from the beach near the Îsles de Saint-Marcouf to fire at selected beach targets.

"However, before we left the boat lane, we were being fired upon by shore batteries, so the FITCH and the CORRY were about the first ships to commence firing in the invasion for purposes of self protection. After firing for fifteen to twenty minues we managed to silence the battery firing upon us, so we commenced firing at scheduled beach targets. However, fire was resumed by other batteries and we had to cease firing at the selected beach targets in order to defend ourselves. There ensued rapid continuous fire by us and rapid fire by the shore batteries because at this time our forces had laid a smoke screen which pretty well blanked out our heavier units further out to sea, so we were being concentrated upon.

"At 0633, about three minutes after H-hour, we hit a mine, which we ourselves had probably stirred up by our high-speed maneuvers in dodging the shells and throwing off the salvos by going full speed ahead, backing full, giving hard right rudder, hard left rudder. There was a fearful explosion and we seemed to jump clear of the water. The ship broke in two, almost at once. The forward fireroom, forward engine room and after fireroom flooded immediately, keel was broken, main deck was severed causing a large fissure that crossed the main deck and around through the hull. We tried to get out by calling for flank speed, but all power was lost and the ship started going in a high-speed circle, because just prior to being hit we had given right full rudder, increased speed. However, the ship gradually slowed down to a stop. We put the boats over for the purpose of towing the ship clear of the area, so we wouldn't drift ashore into enemy-held territory.

"Shortly after the boats were over, the water was up over the main deck and we gave word to prepare to abandon ship. A couple of minutes later it became obvious that the ship was going down very fast. I gave the word to abandon ship and then we got all the men over and, then, I stepped off into the water from the main deck and all this time the ship was being rather heavily shelled; in fact, probably the majority of the casualties occurred in the water, for as late as an hour and a half after the ship had been sunk the batteries continued to shell the men in the water."

Thus, before the invasion had properly started, more large ships were sunk off Utah, the "easy" beach, than all the German guns on Omaha could account for. And the toll kept rising. The executive officer of the minesweeper USS TIDE, Lieutenant Commander George Crane, USNR, operating in the Utah Area, said amazingly that ". . . we found that the forward areas had not been heavily mined . . .

"When the first landings started on the beach it was obvious that the Germans had concentrated their mining operations at that time, in a defense inshore, small obstacle mines to destroy landing craft and personnel as they came in. These were, of course, too far inshore for ships of our draft to reach and they could not have been destroyed by any sweeping by minesweepers. As the day wore on, enemy planes came over and during the afternoon of D-day and the night of D-day the waters in the areas of Utah Beach and adjacent to Utah Beach were heavily mined from the air. The Germans dropped ground mines and nothing could be done about that during the night of D-day.

"During the night of D-day the minesweepers of the AM class, including the TIDE, were moved in close inshore guarding the Carentan estuary, where we were stationed to prevent the egress of enemy E-boats based up the river. There was some flurry of activity during the night in which it was believed that E-boats had made an attempt to come down the river and had been driven back. There was some firing but there were no casualties to the ships during the night time.

"Early on the following morning, which was June 7, we received an order to go close inshore in company with the THREAT and the SWIFT, another of the AMs of our squadron, to make a clearance sweep of the area mined during the night. At that time it was believed that this area had been mined not only magnetically but with moored mines, perhaps dropped by smaller craft during the night and so quite early on the morning of June 7, we went in close inshore and made this clearance sweep for 'O'-type mines. No 'O'-type mines were encountered during the sweep and at 9: 37 we recovered our gear preparatory to leaving the area and perhaps conducting other type sweeping operations.

"The TIDE had just taken her gear aboard and had come to 6 knots speed when a tremendous explosion below decks lifted the entire ship completely out of the water. Officers and men watching from other ships stated that the ship was lifted a full five feet into the air. The force of the explosion broke the TIDE's back, blasted a tremendous hole in her bottom, and tore away all bulkheads below the waterline and when I went below to ascertain the damage done by the explosion, I found that mattresses from the forward crew's compartment were being swept into the after engine room on the flood of water which was sweeping in very rapidly. That meant that those mattresses had been carried through the forward crew's compartment, the after crew's compartment, the forward engine room, the refrigeration spaces, and into the after engine room. As soon as the damage had been ascertained below-decks, which was a matter of seconds only, I went to the bridge and found that there were practically no men of the crew able to be on their feet. All hands had been killed or wounded and the greatest percentage of them very seriously wounded, the commanding officer, Lieutenant Allen B. Heyward, USNR, being among the dead."

The flight of mine-laying aircraft mentioned by Lieutenant Commander Crane came to be a constant feature of life in the Utah Area. Regularly every night somewhere between a quarter of midnight and a quarter past, German planes would fly over, usually in three groups. First a plane dropping flares, then a small group of bombers stooging around, making quick runs at the beach, drawing all the antiaircraft fire while the minelaying planes glided in silently sowing the deadly seeds. The tidal currents along the Utah Area (indeed, throughout the Baie de la Seine) set parallel to the shore line, so that mines laid at one end of the area or the other during the darkness would drift into it by morning.

On the night of D-plus-two, the SUSAN B. ANTHONY, a troop-laden transport, veteran of earlier Mediterranean amphibious operations, struck a mine as she passed through the outer edge of Utah on her way to Omaha. All aboard were rescued, but the ANTHONY went to the bottom.

And still the list of ships sunk off the "easy" beach grew. Between 0100 and 0900 of June 8 two new destroyers and a destroyer escort struck mines off Utah. The MEREDITH, third ship of that name, second to be sunk during the war, hit at 0120. The GLENNON, engaged in a duel with enemy artillery off Quineville, struck at 0800, and the destroyer escort RICH got hers as she was proceeding to GLENNON's assistance. The GLENNON, incidentally, took a long time sinking, and her officers and men utilized that period of grace to carry on their bombardment missions, working all guns that could be brought to bear until all her remaining ammunition was expended or rendered useless by flooding. Of course, once she was dead in the water, the stricken destroyer made a fine target for enemy shore batteries, and they riddled her. But she gave back as good as she got, before she finally broke up and went under. No finer story of fighting determination has come out of this war.

Two laden LSTs were later mine victims. Nor did the shallow draft of the lesser landing craft protect them entirely. Some of them struck mines, and when they did there were no survivors to tell what happened, just a little wreckage drifting along in the tidal current.

Personnel on larger craft were more fortunate; the operation plan called for the presence of a flotilla of Coast Guard rescue cutters, and these tiny 83-foot craft saved almost four hundred and fifty men from the cold waters of the Channel on D-day alone. This was dangerous work and produced its own brand of heroism.

Carter Barber, a Coast Guard combat correspondent aboard the Coast Guard Rescue Cutter 16, told this story of his ship's duties on D-day:

"The cutter had just made a round trip to a transport standing out in the harbor mouth, to discharge some ninety casualties picked up earlier this morning when she saw a stricken LCT which was slowly capsizing as it sank, and dashed to the aid of the stranded personnel.

"On the decks of the LCT over thirty men were trapped, including a wounded man with nearly severed legs, dangling only by pieces of flesh, who was unable to leave his ship. When the rescue cutter was skilfully maneuvered under the slowly lowering side of the LCT, despite the choppy seas surrounding the craft, all the other men were safely brought aboard the smaller craft, except for the wounded sailor.

"When the sailor's plight became apparent, Arthur Burkhard, Jr., a member of the cutter's crew, jumped over the side of the rescue cutter, rushed to the wounded man's side, and helped to secure a line around him, completely disregarding the smoke that was beginning to pour from the LCT's hatches.

"'At that time I didn't know that the LCT was doubling as a small-arms ammunition ship,' said Burkhard. 'It was a good thing that I was able to get the line around the lad before that gigantic, sinking bomb blew up. However, the man helped me get the line around him.

"'He was the bravest man that we picked up,' Burkhard continued. 'He was unable to talk because of weakness, but he managed to keep a grin on his face. Even when we were cutting his clothes off him to administer morphine when we saw that his two legs were severed above the knees, he kept himself under control, and even winked at us.'

"Once the wounded sailor had the line secured about him, Burkhard unsuccessfully tried to lower him from the settling LCT to the smaller rescue cutter. The LCT's starboard side was dropping lower and lower as the whole ship began to capsize, and it was impossible for the skipper, Lieutenant (jg) R. V. McPhail, USCGR, to keep his craft under the LCT's side lest his own boat be pinned beneath it.

"The only alternative was for Burkhard to throw the wounded man off the LCT's deck into the water, where he could be pulled aboard the rescue craft.

"'I never saw anyone so game as that man,' adds Burkhard. 'I hated to throw such a badly wounded man into the water, but that was the only way I could get him to safety. But he helped himself, and pulled himself hand-over-hand up the side of our boat when our fellows had towed him to the boat's side.'

"Once his charge was aboard, Burkhard himself had to plunge into the water and make his way back to his ship. Although he couldn't swim himself, he was dragged aboard by his mates. 'I've got a brother in the Navy myself, and figured that he might be the man aboard the sinking LCT. So the fact that I couldn't swim didn't stop me,' said Burkhard.

"No more than two minutes after Burkhard and the casualties were taken aboard the rescue cutter and the boat had left the LCT, the burning ship completely turned turtle and disappeared from sight."

Chapter Forty

MINING was not the only enemy activity to harass the men working Utah Beach. Although originally the beach had not come under much artillery fire—nothing to compare with the plastering Omaha was given—along about the time that such activity in the latter area ceased, the Nazis woke up to the opportunities of bombarding Utah. Mobile 88s and 105s located on the ridges and high ground to the north and west of that beach began to shell it, whenever a concentration of landing craft unloading made the target look inviting. Because Utah was a flank beach and the Army plan called for driving straight inland, no large forces could be diverted to clean out these nuisance nests. So, for almost ten days the beach and ships near it were subjected to sporadic fire, well spotted and directed, from the hills. Amazingly few casualties resulted, but unloading operations were delayed, and exploitation of the entire length of the beach as a debarkation station was made impossible. Light units of the Fire Support Group, and fighter bombers of the Tactical Air Force did what they could to deal with this nuisance, but the German batteries were mobile and well concealed, and it was not until our ground forces had commenced their swing up the Cotentin Peninsula that the bombardment of Utah ended.

Meanwhile, despite the D-day carnage on Omaha, despite the constant hazards of mines and harassing fire on Utah, *Operation Neptune* moved inexorably from its assault phase into its build-up stage. Troopships and cargo vessels poured men and supplies into the areas, and the Navy, once the beaches were tenable at all, moved key personnel ashore to run Omaha and Utah as regular harbors.

These harbors were each run by a Naval Officer in Charge (a title shortened to NOIC in conversation as well as in dispatches). It was to him that the Army made its requests for priority in unloading ships. He was the man who assigned incoming ships their anchorages, told departing ships when they would sail and with which convoys. He established naval

339

communications, supply, mail and pay systems. In short, he kept the show running for the Army and the Navy. Captain Chauncey Camp, USNR, and Captain James E. Arnold, USNR, had these duties at Omaha and Utah, respectively. As important a function as any of NOIC was the supervision of salvage, repair and maintenance work, both on the beaches and throughout the anchorage area.

Previous landings had shown that the sooner salvage and repair work could be started, the likelier it was to be completed at all. Accordingly, each assault area had salvage groups both ashore and afloat, equipped with everything from bulldozers to welding rods for effecting immediate emergency repairs. In addition, each beach had a converted LST completely fitted out with repair shops to take care of work too complicated for the smaller units. These vessels—USS ADONIS at Omaha and USS ATLAS at Utah—and the salvage units ashore had been originally assigned with the repair of small landing craft in mind. They soon found themselves taking on jobs widely and wildly different. An excerpt from the official report of the activities of the salvage groups on Omaha Beach gives a fair idea of this:

"At break of day on D-plus-1, Group No. 2 landed its repair personnel and equipment. The situation was evident at a glance. It was plain that before naval salvage work could begin as planned, the bigger and more critical job of removing debris, booby traps and other hazards had to be undertaken. This was imperative if the Army was to get ashore and start its stream of supplies moving inland. This section of the beach seemed to be littered with everything imaginable—boats, vehicles of all types, tanks, ammunition, and stacks of dead. Still standing were most of the obstructions the enemy had put on the beach. Not being able to find the Beachmaster, Lieutenant Henri [Officer in Charge of the salvage unit. Ed.] reported to an Army colonel, stating that his men would do everything they could to help clear the beach and make it serviceable for landing. The Colonel welcomed this assistance eagerly. All Army and Seabee tractors and bulldozers which had reached shore had been sent inland with the troops to open roads, thus leaving no Army equipment to clear the beach.

"For the next three days the salvage bulldozers and tractors appeared to be the only machines of that type operating on the beach, and they were kept busy day and night. Pulling out beach obstacles was always exciting, as no one could be sure, even after Army engineers had removed all visible mines, that one underground might not be exploded by moving the superstructure. During the morning a tractor being operated under Lieutenant Henri's direction set off a mine. The tractor was wrecked, and the three men on it were injured, two seriously.

"During those few days when the landing of soldiers and their equipment was all-important, the Navy salvage force on Omaha pulled several heavy guns out of the water, located and hauled up on the beach scores of drowned-out jeeps, trucks and ambulances, and even salvaged two Piper Cub planes which the Army needed badly for gun-spotting. Frequently its men waded out in shoulder-deep water in order to swing a line aboard an LCI so that soldiers wading ashore with heavy equipment should have something to guide them through the surf. Although this work of salvaging Army vehicles continued throughout the summer— when some of the tanks or trucks hauled ashore had been in the water so long as to have barnacled!—it was only during the critical first few days that it was given top priority."

The primary function of NOIC, administered by a Port Director, was not salvage, however, but the vital one of lighterage. Much cargo arrived from England in LSTs and LCTs, and they could unload directly on the beach, of course. But Liberty ships and other merchantmen had to lie in the open roadstead and discharge their cargoes onto LCTs, LCMs, and rhino ferries. These last were a development of the famous Seabee pontoon causeway which had done such yeoman service in every invasion since Sicily. The rhinos were, in effect, self-propelled causeways, great rafts of pontoons, powered by huge outboard motors.

One of the great sights of the beaches in operation was the spectacle of one of these rhinos, piled high with freight, moving in to shore. On the topmost pinnacle of the cargo stood the officer in charge, guiding his strange craft by hand signals to the two coxswains standing at the wheels of their outboard motors quite unable to see where they were going. Each barge had a tent pitched in the back—they could hardly be said to have a bow and a stern—and from it there was usually a column of smoke rising as the Seabees, who seemed at it continuously, cooked themselves a meal or brewed up a pot of coffee.

Little coasters—British, Dutch, Norwegian—carried most of the ammunition to the beaches, and they were unloaded into DUKWs driven, for most part by men of Negro port battalions. These men, along with the small-boat crews, almost forgot the meaning of the word "rest." They worked from a little before sunrise to a little after sunset, and in those latitudes in June the sun rises early and sets late.

Occasionally a DUKW driver would be caught at sea after dark when the inevitable nuisance air raids started. On one such night, a picket boat was moving through the harbor when the skipper heard the frantic tooting of an automobile horn. After some looking, he made out the bow wave of a DUKW, and lay to until it came alongside. Except for the magnificent flash of white teeth, which the skipper swears was all he could see, the seagoing truck might have been driverless until, out of the darkness, came a plaintiff call, "Say, boss! Where at is land?" Just then a bomb hit the beach a quarter of a mile away, striking a gasoline-laden truck and sending up a great glare. The DUKW driver took a look and said matter-of-factly, "Never mind, boss! I see it now."

Chapter Forty-one

THE fighting moved away; so did the correspondents, taking their headlines with them, but the Navy stayed and made the beaches serve as harbors. They attempted to do even more; they attempted to make the harbors too. It was a mighty effort. Lieutenant Commander Hartley E. Howe, USNR, was the Naval Observer of this job at Omaha Beach and this chapter is his personal report on the operation:

The whole thing started at the Quebec conference, where Roosevelt and Churchill planned the invasion of Europe with their Joint Chiefs of Staff. The ground forces were sure they could seize an invasion beachhead. But holding it was another matter. The landing would be followed by a race between ourselves and the Germans in concentrating men and weapons at the invasion point. Our supplies would have to be carried by sea and landed on the beaches. Bad weather or even an onshore breeze would make landing impossible and break the precious life line. So the Army made one condition for the invasion: they must have some kind of port as insurance against bad weather.

They went further. They made a timetable of just what they wanted, when:

D-plus-2. Shelter for half a mile of coastline and one thousand tons of small craft.

D-plus-7. Shelters behind which coasters could unload onto ferry craft, regardless of weather.

D-plus-14. Sheltered water for seventeen coasters plus seven pierheads, plus one motor transport pier for LSTs to send their vehicles directly ashore.

Plus, as soon as possible, a harbor for large ships to discharge their cargoes into lighters.

Now there were, of course, plenty of ports in Western Europe that could fill the bill—but intelligence reports showed clearly that the Germans recognized their importance as much as we did. Each port suitable for an invasion base had been fortified so that it would take weeks or even months to capture it—weeks during which bad weather might at any time bring our offensive to a standstill. We needed a port for a prolonged invasion; we needed a prolonged invasion to seize a port.

It was to break this iron circle of frustration that Mulberry A and Mulberry B were born. The military leaders turned the problem over to the engineers and technical experts. They produced a plan that sounded deceptively simple: if you must have a port and cannot capture one, then make one—build a port on the beachhead.

Easier said than done. But the experts—adjourning to the heat of a Washington June—went on to consider scores of suggested ways to carry out the plan. In the end they combined four of them into an over-all plan for the construction of two artificial harbors—code named "Mulberry:" one each in the American and British sectors of the beachhead.

For the small-craft shelter, which had to go in right on the heels of the actual landing, they took an old idea and turned it inside out. Sunken ships had been used in the past to block ports: now it was proposed to use them to build one. Ships could go across under their own power: a line of them sunk end to end along the 15-foot line would form an excellent shelter close inshore. The ship shelters were given the code name of "Gooseberry."

For the larger harbor the experts took a half-forgotten idea and expanded it enormously. Sunken ships couldn't be used: the water where the breakwater had to go in would be so deep that they would be covered at high tide. So the engineers proposed a portable breakwater made up of sections, which could be floated over and then sunk in place. These sections were to be huge, hollow concrete caissons, in assorted sizes, the largest being 60 feet high and weighing many tons, as much as many an ocean freighter. According to the code, one of these units was a "Phoenix."

In order that the lighters might unload and the LSTs discharge their vehicles directly to the shore, piers—once more, portable—were needed. Fortunately a design for these was ready. The British War Office had developed a floating steel pier similar to a pontoon bridge in principle, known as the Loebnitz pier. This pier had a steel scow for a head, resting on an ingenious arrangement of steel stilts at the four corners so that it could rise and fall with the tide while remaining firmly fixed in place. These "spuds" could be lifted while the head was being towed, giving the scow a vague resemblance to a Mississippi River steamer. "Whales" was the code name for the pier units.

For the outermost breakwater the experts turned to a young Scot physicist in the Royal Naval Volunteer Reserve, Lieutenant Commander Robert Arthur Lockner. Lockner had been working for some time on the problem of a floating breakwater, and his latest development was accepted for Mulberry. It consisted of a series of floating steel units moored end to end in two long lines. Each unit was cruciform and 200 feet in length, three of the arms being filled with water while the air-filled fourth kept it afloat. These curious objects—their code name was "Bombardon" —were possessed of great inertia. When a wave came along they lifted so slowly that much of the energy of the swell was deflected instead of being transmitted to the waters beyond. Tests showed that this cut wave levels considerably.

Of the two artificial ports, the American harbor was to be primarily for the direct discharge of motor vehicles from LSTs over the piers to the shore: the British port would be especially adapted for the unloading of coasters. They were to handle 10,000 to 12,000 tons of supplies a day and many hundred vehicles. The twins would be very similar in appearance—a line of sunken ships close inshore forming one end of the harbor, then a connected line of caissons forming a breakwater for the piers, outside of all this rows of floating breakwaters making a roadstead for the ocean freighters.

In addition, there would be three more small-craft shelters, formed by sunken ships, outside the main harbors.

Preliminary construction of the units would be carried out by the British alone, but each country would be responsible for transporting its own Mulberry to the other side and assembling it there.

Designing the harbors was one thing; getting them built was another matter. British heavy industry was already overloaded with war production. Steel and concrete were as scarce as hens' teeth—and the caissons alone required over 30,000 long tons of steel and more than 500,000 long tons of concrete. Manpower was equally scarce—and it took some 22,000 men to build the caissons alone.

The result was constant struggle—struggle for priorities for labor and raw materials, to get drydocks, to carry out tests of the designs, which had to be checked even as the building got under way. There never was enough time for anything—time for construction, time for testing, time for training. The necessary division of the job among four distinct agencies—the British Ministry of Supply, War Office and Admiralty and the United States Navy—further slowed things up. The whole construction program, exclusive of the planning period, had to be carried out in only five months. In this time units had to be built for 10 miles of piers, 23 pierheads, 93 Bombardons, and more than a hundred Phoenixes, while eighty odd block ships had to be prepared for sinking.

No small order—and not made easier by the fact that it had to be carried out under the very nose of the Luftwaffe. The thousands of men who worked on the program further complicated the security problem. Many of them were Irishmen who returned periodically to the Free State where there was a German legation. Since it was impossible to keep them from talking, they were given something quite misleading to talk about— a "cover" story, convincing but highly inaccurate, for each unit. The men aboard the block ships, for example, were told that these were to be "port repair ships," designed to fill holes in damaged breakwaters which might be found in captured ports.

Despite all handicaps the work went on, and by late winter the first units were delivered to the men who were to handle them in the invasion. Over-all control of the project was in the hands of Admiral Tennant of the Royal Navy, but a special American Task Group, later to become Task Force 128, had been set up under Captain Augustus Dayton Clark, USN, to take over Mulberry A. Seabees of the 108th Naval Construction Battalion commanded by Commander Erwin T. Collier (CEC), USNR, a University of Florida graduate, were given the job of riding the units across the Channel and putting them into place on the Norman coast. The tug problem was given to Captain Edmund J. Moran, USNR, in civil life the head of a large New York towing company, who found himself trying to divide up the limited supply of tugs among a host of clamoring claimants, each convinced that his need was the greatest. More tugs were sent for posthaste from the United States and all the available tugs for the entire invasion—civilian, salvage, handling tugs, Army tugs, and Navy tugs, British, Allied and American tugs, were put in a pool under Captain Moran.

All spring the men trained in sinking and floating the caissons, linking up the pier units, anchoring the pierheads, handling the towing lines, maneuvering the tugs. More units of every type came dribbling in. By June 6, D-day, they were ready to go.

As it started out, TF 128 was probably the strangest task force ever to fly the American flag. Not one of its three divisions resembled the conventional idea of a task force as a glamorous group of swift cruisers and hard-hitting carriers. Captain Clark's flagship was a tiny submarine chaser. The biggest unit that set out under his immediate command from The Solent, on the South Coast of England, was a lumber vessel from the Baltic trade—her heavy lifting gear fore and aft gave her a number of ribald nicknames. There were some old side-wheelers with tender memories of picnicking excursionists along the English coasts. There were boom layers—or net tenders, according to United States Navy usage—with their strange snoutlike bows. And there were tugs.

The block ship division which sailed from Poole, to the westward, was no fancier. The ships had been taken from the dregs of the North Atlantic shipping pool, old freighters, battered by years of overwork, many of them carrying gaping wounds left by bomb, torpedo or mine. But they had no ordinary cargo—and their crews of merchant volunteers knew it. Below-decks there was only sand ballast—and high explosives, carefully planted where they would blow out the bottom at the touch of a button on the bridge. Nevertheless, the old veterans had plenty of protection as they limped out to the Channel and headed for France at a furious 5 knots. Planes and escort craft showed how highly they were valued.

Strangest of all, of course, were the Phoenixes and the Whale units. These had been gathered in shallow waters in The Solent and along the coast to the eastward. The piers had been set up on the shore and the Phoenixes sunk in place until they were needed. Now, after pumping vessels emptied them out, they looked for all the world like the biggest Noah's Arks in history. Their ends—there was no way to tell the bow from the stern—were square and barge-like. As their crews clambered onto the 3-foot ledges that were their decks, their boxlike superstructures towered into the air 40 feet above. The men climbed hand over hand up the iron ladders that clung to the sides, to the narrow wooden platforms running across the open tops. "Phoenix" was the official name—but the riding crews, who were about to spend a day and a half at sea living in concrete caves built into one end, called them a lot of things as they pried open their cold K rations.

At that, the Phoenix crews were better off than their fellow Seabees aboard the Whales. Their quarters were tents pitched on an open pier span a few feet above the water. The spans were towed across in units

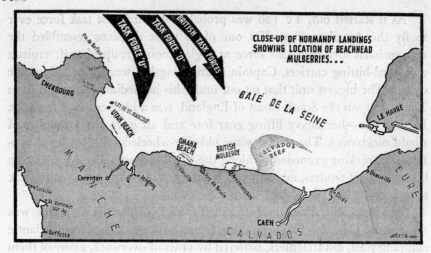

CLOSE-UP OF NORMANDY LANDINGS
SHOWING LOCATION OF BEACHHEAD
MULBERRIES...

FIGURE 7

of six and looked like nothing so much as a chain of little country bridges putting out to sea. The men aboard the pier heads were more fortunate. Their quarters in the depths of the scowlike vessels were narrow and cramped, but they were at least warm and dry.

The first units—handling tugs, net tenders, boom vessels, and so forth —arrived off the beachhead early on the morning of June 7, D-plus-one.

The area offshore was a fantastic sight. Sprawled as far as the eye could see, all the way to the horizon, were the ships of the invasion fleet— ships of every size and description, tankers, freighters, transports, landing craft, destroyers, cruisers, battleships. It was as if all the everyday shipping in New York harbor, plus half the Navy, were gathered off the French coast. Landing craft were going in to the few cleared areas on the beach. Transports were discharging men over the side onto barges and small craft. Supply ships had dropped anchor ready to discharge their cargo. And moving in and out were the fighting ships of the support force, their shells roaring overhead at unseen targets inland.

Mulberry A was to go in off Omaha Beach, near the village of Vierville. There was little advance information about this area. The coasts were little frequented by seamen and the most recent charts were based on surveys made in the nineteenth century. Aerial surveys and raiding parties had added to this dubious store of information, but even so, D-day found TF 128 depending on an on-the-spot survey for final selection of

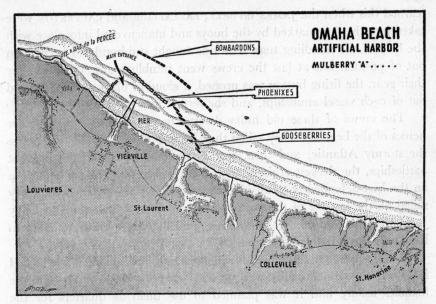

FIGURE 8

installation points. Royal Navy survey parties and American Seabee surveyors in LCCs were therefore the first to go in. They had to check previous estimates of water depths, some of which proved wrong, and mark with buoys the lines for the ships, Phoenixes and piers.

The main elements of the task force began to gather for the job during the afternoon of the 7th.

The first ships for the Gooseberry arrived at noon, coming in to the beachhead with their regular civilian crews. They were under the over-all command of Lieutenant George Hoague, USNR. Lieutenant Commander John Bassett, USNR, a veteran New York dockmaster, had the task of sinking them in position. Bassett had devoted his life to putting ships in the right place at the right time; to him this was just one more job, even though the toughest.

They found out just how tough it was as they put down the first three ships that afternoon. The tide was a bitter enemy. Throughout the area it ran parallel to the shore—eastward with the flood and westward with the ebb—and it ran from 3 to 5 knots. To hold a heavy ship or caisson against this force and at the same time drop it on the bottom exactly in line with two bobbing buoys called for the highest seamanship. They learned this when the JAMES IREDELL, BAELALIADE and GALVESTON were taken into the line marked by the buoys and maneuvered into place with the help of the handling tugs. The tide fought stubbornly to keep them out of position but at last the crews went tumbling over the side after their gear, the firing button was pressed, a cloud of black smoke billowed out of each vessel amidships, and she settled into place.

The crews of these old hulks deserve mention alongside the other heroes of the beaches. They sailed their leaking beaten-up old tubs across the stormy Atlantic, and then, just as though they were the heaviest battleships, the sleekest cruisers, took them right up to the enemy's guns on the best-defended seacoast in the world. They were told before they sailed on the last leg of the voyage that was to send their ships to Davy Jones that their mission was hazardous, and they were given a chance to back out. Not a man refused the job.

These ships were to be used for more than a breakwater. They lacked fresh water, but their cabins were a good deal more comfortable than the foxholes ashore and it was planned to use them as quarters for the Seabees.

It was a fine spring evening when they were taken in on D-plus-one to their new quarters aboard the sunken 555. Smoke from somewhere inland and the occasional boom of land mines, exploded by engineers clearing the roads, were the only signs of war. But as the men scrambled onto the deck of the 555, the gray bursts of smoke from the land mines were replaced by fountains of water, first along the edge of the beach, then walking out across the water toward the sunken ships. For the first time a preliminary whistle could be heard before the explosion. The men halfway across scrambled back on an LCI fitted out with extra communications equipment to serve as a control vessel—which had brought them in. A shell landed 50 feet off the bow, and a shower of fragments sprayed the ship. The lines were cast off in a hurry and the LCI moved out to seaward with more haste than dignity. Behind her the shells bracketed the 555. Then there was a hit in the stern. A destroyer came dashing in and opened fire at the shore. As she did so, a handling tug next to the line of block ships was hit and scurried off with a white plume from a smashed steam line trailing out behind. The destroyer found the range and the shelling suddenly stopped. Ten men had been wounded. Beautiful evening or not, this was a battlefront.

The first Phoenixes had arrived that first evening of D-plus-one, eight hours ahead of schedule, the next day saw them put down. The riding crews—dirty, tired and bewhiskered from their long trip—were taken off and put aboard the towing tug for good food, showers and sleep on the trip back to the United Kingdom, for another unit. Meanwhile the sinking crew took over.

If the ships proved tricky, the Phoenixes were more so. They had, of course, no power of their own, their box shape made them far crankier in a tide than a ship, while in any breeze their huge superstructures acted like sails. Most of the tugs were put on the down-tide side with one or two on the other flank to help guide the unwieldy unit into place. Lieutenant Commander Bassett directed the whole operation by hand signals to his boatswains from the top of the Phoenix, watching the pull of the tide, how each tug was affecting the movement of the unit, the push of the wind on the huge superstructure, the distance to the sinking-site, the angle of approach that would bring her in line with a minimum of way. When the Phoenix was lined up with the buoys, the tugs would struggle to hold her in place, the signal to sink would be given, the men stationed at the valves would turn the great wheels, and far below in the depths huge spurts of water could be seen pouring into her flat bottom. It was not easy to put her down on even keel. There had to be a constant adjustment of valves as the Phoenix would begin to list. But twenty-five or thirty minutes later the big caisson would be on the bottom.

The men soon lost all track of time as the days ran one into another. Everyone knew that the fighting men ashore must have more and more supplies—and that Mulberry A was needed to get the stuff to them. It was a race against time—and against the German ability to concentrate forces for a counterattack. The men worked from the first light of dawn until far into the gray twilight, which lasted nearly until midnight. There was the unchanging backdrop of the shore—and the endless lines of men in khaki who poured ashore. Each night there would come an air raid, and from the harbor great fountains of red tracer fire would climb up into the sky toward invisible targets. An occasional bomb would split open the seams of an unlucky landing craft. Sometimes the night raiders dropped mines. TF 128 knew too much about the mines. HMS MINSTER, a tender, was sunk off the Utah Beach with the loss of seventy-odd men, trapped below at dinner. They were bound for home and safety, their mission smartly and swiftly completed, when they met destruction.

But if the scene didn't change, the harbor did. It grew steadily. The freighters came in for the Gooseberry, and the grim old British battleship CENTURION followed them into line, her crew bidding her farewell with some ceremony. All the ships of the Gooseberry had been put down by D-plus-four—June 10—while the other American Gooseberry, a shelter off the other United States beach, was completed a day later, despite heavy fire from German batteries, under the guidance and driving leadership of Commander Alfred B. Stanford, USNR, an ocean-racing yachtsman who properly called his duty "the damnedst race I ever saw." On the 8th the first floating breakwaters had arrived off Omaha and the work of mooring them offshore began. On the 9th the first Whale spans showed up. The pierheads soon followed. There was a delay while the shoreline was cleared of mines, then the Seabees built ramps of earth faced with rubble and surfaced with netting to connect the piers with the road that ran along behind the sea wall, and soon the piers began to grow out from the shore, as small Army tugs towed the units into place. The piers had to be built out about 3,000 feet to reach water deep enough for LSTs at low tide.

Late on Saturday, June 17—D-plus-11—the piers were sufficiently far along for the first LST to come nuzzling in to unload. Four pierheads had been formed into two Ts, so that, if necessary, four LSTs could come alongside at once. An overhead ramp on the body of the Ts further speeded things up by enabling an LST to unload over the side at the same time that the cargo in the hold was pouring through the bow gates.

The 18th was fair and sunny. Although the pier system was still only partially finished—only two of the three roadways and four of the heads were installed—the Mulberry was in constant use. LST after LST came in, unloaded her cargo of men and vehicles and started back at once for another. The average unloading time ran something under an hour— a 1200 per cent saving over the twelve hours required to unload an LST on the beach, where the landing ship had to go onto the sands at high tide, discharge her cargo when the water went out, and then wait for the next high tide before she could haul off. Sunday evening saw the Mulberry waiting for new customers. Everybody felt good. The worst was over. Now it was just a matter of finishing her up.

But further work had to be postponed. The morning of D-plus-13 —June 19—dawned gray and cold with rain squalls whipping in before a rising northeast wind. The forecasts called for the best weather since D-day—so no one worried particularly. Further reassurance was to be found in the *Channel Pilot,* the seaman's bible for these tricky coastal waters. There, in a table giving the probable number of days of storm to be expected each month in the Mulberry Area, opposite the month of June stood a round, comfortable o.

But it was soon evident that the forecasts and the *Channel Pilot* were both wrong. The wind was pushing the swells down the channel at an ever-quickening tempo and the spray began to smash high over the line of caissons. It was the worst time of the month for a storm. Two days later the new moon was to bring the spring tides, and already high water was well above the normal level.

In reality, things were far worse than they looked. The worst storm in eighty years was roaring down on the invasion fleet: a storm that was to wreak havoc among the landing craft, stop the flow of supplies ashore, jeopardize the whole invasion—and leave the American Mulberry a shattered wreck. Ironically enough, the artillery of heaven was to succeed where the artillery of Hitler had failed dismally.

For the moment, it looked as though there would be merely a temporary interruption of work. As a purely precautionary measure, it was decided to evacuate the Army antiaircraft crews who had ridden the Phoenixes across the Channel and who were still living on them in corrugated-iron shelters beneath the platforms of their Bofors guns. They got them off all right, although some of the rescue craft were all but smashed against the caissons whose 3-foot ledges made approach perilous even in good weather. A few hours later, swells swept across the open tops of the Phoenixes and only the guns could be seen sticking out of the surf like lonely spindles marking hidden reefs.

Our anxiety grew by 12-hour cycles. Each six hours of rising tide was six hours of anxiety when the wind pushed the tide some 10 feet above normal, buried the caissons, hammered at the deckhouses of the sunken ships and rocked the pierheads. Then the flood would pass and all of us would feel a little better as we waited for the next tide, hoping by then the wind would drop. For three long days and three long nights we hoped, until there was nothing left to worry about.

Darkness on the 19th brought evidence of real trouble ahead. A Phoenix broke her back, sagging at the ends where sea and tide had scoured out the sand from beneath her bottom. At the same time, in the comparatively sheltered area behind the breakwater, pier spans and floats, which had been anchored near the roadway, broke loose to become drifting menaces to ships and piers alike. Repeatedly they bashed into pontoons and the mooring lines on the piers were torn away.

Tugs chugged frantically from one end of the harbor to the other, rounding up drifting units, answering appeals from the small landing craft that were beginning to drag anchor all along the line. Concrete connecting floats broke loose and smashed around like floating juggernauts. In desperation, Lieutenant William L. Freeburn, USNR, a veteran of the Merchant Service, in charge of the pier installation, put men aboard the floats to hack holes in them and sink them, so they could do no more harm. His little motor tugs corralled the drifting span lengths, towed them free and moored them, a most formidable job now that broken pontoons had dropped half the spans underwater.

Anchors and lines were at a premium. At midnight, a bearded Seabee chief went over the side of a 60-foot Army fisherman into a frail mooring skiff whose anchor had been carefully fitted so that it could be released only through the bottom. His job was to cut it loose. The skiff heaved sickeningly, water surged through the anchor well, the chief hacked away for two and a half hours before the anchor fell away through the bottom. Then he crawled back over the side, more dead than alive.

By now some of the spans lacked mooring of any sort. Somehow, the tugs got lines on them. Somehow, they managed to hold them, biting into the gale. It was nearly dawn when, exhausted, all hands who could be spared turned in. They were up again at 6 A.M.

The sun was out, but the wind had risen, and ugly, lead-colored seas raced stronger than ever down the Channel. The beach was piled with landing craft—their ground tackle having proved too light for this kind of weather—and during the night four landing ships had smashed into the eastern pier.

The tide went out, and men from the windrowed landing craft checked hulls for damage. At one spot, soldiers in masks were digging where a body lay beneath the sands. A few feet away, three shipwrecked men sat down to a beach picnic. The little packages that come in K rations were spread daintily on a battered tarpaulin serving as a cloth. Cans of pork and egg yolks were warming over a driftwood fire.

But the tide returned across the flats—and the wind held. Each span of the piers would heave up on the crest of the surf, twist to the right, slump over to the left and drop crazily into the hollow, weaving and snaking so that the roadway was impossible for even a jeep and it took an acrobat to walk ashore. Fountains of water surged up through the spans. More and more derelicts rode in the surf and pounded at the roadways. A landing ramp drifted against the eastern spans with deadly force, working its apron under a pontoon so that it banged up and down on solid cement instead of yielding water. The pierheads began to pull apart. At the same time, the cables by which the heads were hung on the supporting spuds started to snap as the scows lifted and fell with the racing swells.

The Gooseberries, those abused freighters, were catching it, too. Their main decks were now awash and the seas were tearing at their superstructures. The Seabees were taken off as the swells raced through the cabins where they had been quartered, washing away most of their personal gear. During the night the wretched CENTURION, which had gone through Jutland unscathed, broke her back just as the caissons had broken theirs, as the sands were scoured out from her uneasy bed.

The Phoenixes were taking the worst pounding of all. Several Phoenixes already had collapsed. At low water their shattered ruins were cliffs crumbling into the surf.

Chaos compounded during the night of June 20-21. Radio channels, jammed with appeals for help, told the story of ships drifting helplessly, of collisions, of founderings and of craft abandoned. LCI 414, Mulberry A's small control ship, banged ominously at her pierhead and all night long men stood by to check the strain on her great towing hawsers. An LCT came scudding around the end of the pier, out of control, barely missed LCI 414, smashed into another LCT moored nearby and knocked her off her moorings, the two drifting helplessly off into the night, headed for the beach. Shortly after 1 A.M., a coaster loaded with ammunition drifted into the eastern pier, her whistle crying piteously for help. A searchlight broke the blackout to pick her out—a dim shape in rain and spray like a Hollywood version of disaster by night. A handling tug bustled to the rescue. The coaster's frightened crew was ready to jump off, leaving ship and deadly cargo to blunder on to catastrophe. Leaning from the pilothouse of the tug, Lieutenant C. M. Barnett, USCG, cursed and argued the men into staying aboard. A line was passed and Barnett snaked her out and tied her to a Liberty ship offshore.

Morning of the third day found sea and wind unabated. Planks, personal gear, smashed small craft, empty gasoline cans—debris of all sorts littered the water. Once or twice a body bobbed by in an orange life preserver. The mass of landing craft crammed against the pier had multiplied. During the morning, the easternmost of the two pierheads parallel to the shore lifted from the bottom and drifted off, its giant spuds fractured like twigs. One pier already was severed from its head. Now the drifting head smashed in behind its mate and snapped the spans that had linked it with the shore.

The day was a repetition of the two before—seas racing endlessly, winds of 40 knots and much more in gusts, tides far above normal, splattering rain squalls alternating with lightening of the overcast to give a momentary illusion of better weather. By four in the afternoon, the last Phoenix at the western end of the front wall had half crumbled away. The 414 banged worse than ever against her pierhead, threatening to smash in her sides or dislodge the pier. Overwhelmed by discouragement at defeat by the elements, the men stared gloomily into the storm, fingering the inflation valves of their life belts, wondering if they would end up swimming for the beach.

By mid-evening, the LCI was battering the pier so heavily that she was ordered to sea. Commander Stanford, Captain Clark's deputy, and several task force staff officers boarded the pierhead to spend the night there. The rest remained aboard the LCI.

Lieutenant Erickson, skipper of the 414, was faced with a delicate problem in seamanship as he prepared to take his vessel out of the shattered harbor. He knew that if he didn't solve it on the first try, he was unlikely to have another. It meant backing around the end of the pier directly against the full force of the storm and then heading out at full speed through the gap between the remains of the front and side lines of the caissons, a maneuver carried out directly across the heavy onshore set of wind and sea. The gap was none too clearly marked. The Phoenixes on either side had crumbled, and it was hard to tell what jagged hulks lay just beneath the surface. All hands held their breath as Erickson rang for reverse, and swung her sharply out and around so that she faced the opening, snapping her last line as she did so. She made for the gap at full speed as the storm took her broadside on and tried to push her aside. In one final lunge she made it, slipped through and headed for open water.

Morning at last brought a break in the weather. It was bright and sunny. Although the seas were still running high, the wind had dropped. Men spread out soaked clothing to dry, checked over lines, overhauled guns. Others just sat around soaking up the warm sunshine while a cracked tenor from the deep South plucked at a guitar and sang "Pistol-packin' Mama." The storm was over, but too late. Mulberry A was dead.

Only the line of sunken ships, battered but still in line, could be used. They remained as a shelter for small craft: whatever could be salvaged from the remainder was sent off to Mulberry B. For this harbor, 10 miles along the coast to the eastward, had largely survived the storm. Its more sheltered position under the lee of Cap de la Hève was partly responsible for its good fortune: so was an offshore reef, which took much of the brunt of the storm. In the days ahead Mulberry B was to prove invaluable in supplying the eastern end of the beachhead.

Chapter Forty-two

THE harbor of block ships at Utah Beach had been home to the small-boat crews, those gypsies of every beachhead, and to Army antiaircraft teams. In the storm of June 19 the ships began to break up with deafening crashes as though they were being hit by artillery fire. Water rose higher and higher through them, and as the water rose, so did the rats. They were anxious enough to abandon a sinking ship; their squeals as they fought each other on the slippery ladders and up and down the swiftly flooding passages were clearly audible over the wind, the waves and the cracking of the ship's hull.

After The Storm (those who went through it will always remember it in capital letters) the beaches sorted themselves out. The salvage teams and repair ships performed prodigies of ingenuity and plain hard work. Originally they had been sent to the beaches to salvage and repair small landing craft; after the storm they found themselves handling jobs on ships up to and including a 7,000-ton British freighter.

Twice they rendered important service to the Army. During the early fighting ashore, when the guns were pounding their way into Cherbourg's strong defenses, an Army officer came aboard the repair ship ATLAS with an emergency request. It had been found that certain springs in the firing mechanism of the Long Toms—155-mms.—were wearing out under the heavy demands put upon the artillery, and that there was danger that many of them would have to cease fire. A search of the ATLAS's spare parts revealed a heavy-duty spring used in diesel engines, which, with a slight change, could be made to work in the guns. A hundred of these springs were immediately handed over to the Army, and the Long Toms continued to roar.

Again, when General Patton's Third Army staff was preparing for the final break-out from the Normandy beachhead, an appeal was made to the Navy for steel plate with which to build a big plow or shears on the front of tanks. These were designed to pierce Normandy's tough and argumentative hedgerows. Naval units ashore provided much of the steel plate, and the ATLAS contributed three-quarters of a ton of welding electrodes with which to install the shears.

The beaches began working again, taking in supplies, taking out wounded. LCMs, rhinos and LCTs hauled the freight hour after hour, day in and day out. LCVPs scooted about the areas acting as water taxis. British craft anchored inside the breakwaters to supply hot food, fuel and water to the small boats. The small-boat men slept (when they did) aboard the Liberty ships housing the offices of the Port Directors. The American beaches, even though they never became the artificial harbors their planners had hoped for, kept open for business and kept the freight rolling through, month after month, long after the original estimates had said they could be closed. At long last, the weather, which had never been good for any length of time, promised to turn worse, and on November 3 Utah Beach was closed, followed by Omaha on the 15th.

They had been dearly bought, those beaches, with the lives of men and ships. They paid us well; by the 1st of September 2,093,855 men, 440,199 vehicles and 2,480,652 tons of stores were landed by the Allies, and all but a very small portion of them had gone in over the beaches. True, by September 1 the Allies had one major port, Cherbourg, but it was not an easy port to use.

And it had not been an easy port to take. The story of its capture is an exciting one, and one in which the Navy played an important part.

Chapter Forty-three

THE beachheads held, despite the Nazis, despite the weather. They grew from beachheads to active busy harbors and for almost three weeks all the complicated fuel for the great Allied war machine was pumped ashore through them. They served their purpose well long after the time they were supposed to have served their purpose. Nevertheless, the Allies still needed a major deep-water port, with all the facilities of docks, piers and railroad sidings, if they were to apply their full strength and deploy to advantage their great superiority in men and materiel. The port of Cherbourg, lying in the middle of the north coast of the Cotentin Peninsula, was therefore an immediate objective. In two weeks' time American troops had knifed across the base of the peninsula, isolating the great seaport. And by D-plus-20, troops of the First Army were drawn in a ring about the city preparing for the final assault.

In assaulting Cherbourg from the landward side, a leaf was taken out of the Axis book; Singapore had fallen to land attack, so had Sevastopol. Cherbourg, as heavily armed against sea attack as either of them, was likewise to be taken from the rear. But the High Command amplified its plans to give play to naval bombardment.

Naval gunfire support had done its part in every amphibious operation. Not only could the Navy supply overwhelming firepower of almost every type, from the short-range rockets of the assault craft to the terrific long-distance slugging blows of the battleships' big guns, but they could also deliver it when and where the Army wanted it.

Perhaps the most sincere testimony to the Navy's shooting came from the enemy. Praise from a Nazi is no compliment, of course, but in this case it has value as evidence; Field Marshal von Rundstedt, explaining the success of the Allied landings in Normandy, said, "We naturally expected a landing attempt, but could not tell where it would come, whether in Holland, central France or southern France. So I could not put all my reserves in one place. Yet our reserves were not so dispersed and placed that I could not have met the D-day landing, even though it surprised us, except for the fact that we had no mobility, and could not bring up our reserves. Between Paris and Rouen there was not a single bridge across the Seine.

"Furthermore, your naval artillery was terrific."

Von Rundstedt's remarks, which were made in an interview after he had been captured, are testimony to the efficacy of our aerial bombardment and the preinvasion sabotage of the French underground. But they also point up what stuck in his mind as it stuck in the mind of every man who ever faced it; that naval artillery is a terrible weapon. This was the weapon with which the Allies proposed to soften up Cherbourg on June 25 for the Army waiting to enter the city the next day.

Chapter Forty-four

COMMANDER HAROLD B. SAY, USNR, one of the Navy's representatives ashore with the Army, had a view of that bombardment from the dubious vantage point of the receiving end. He describes it much as a German lucky enough to live through it might have seen it:

An official release by Supreme Headquarters Allied Expeditionary Force—dated June 26, 1944, described the bombardment of Cherbourg of Sunday, June 25, by British and United States vessels in the following paragraphs:

"At noon on June 25 this Force rendezvoused in the Channel off the Cherbourg peninsula and broke the silence of a calm bright Sunday with the first salvo from the 14-inch guns of the USS NEVADA. The other battleships quickly opened up on their assigned targets, the heavily casemated shore batteries flanking Cherbourg. The USS QUINCY and USS TUSCALOOSA followed suit with fire from their 8-inch guns, and HMS GLASGOW and HMS ENTERPRISE with their 6-inchers. Particular accuracy was required of the naval gunnery, as American troops were known to be concentrated close to the target areas.

"The enemy shore batteries lost no time in replying with heavy fire. As the Allied ships swept up and down in plain view of the French coast, their guns blazing, enemy shells fell close among them. As the fire grew more intense, destroyers laid a smoke screen, behind which the bombardment continued.

"After ninety minutes of continuous shelling, the ships were scheduled to withdraw, but Rear Admiral Deyo extended the time limit in order to remove further obstacles from the path of the Army's advance into the vital port. Brief billows of smoke and dust were seen ashore. For another two hours ships continued to pour shells into the enemy targets."

"Brief billows of smoke and dust were seen ashore." A natural and logical line, the foregoing, for that is the way it likely seemed from out at sea.

But such is not the picture as the infantrymen fighting into the city of Cherbourg saw it; nor the picture that the writer has painted away in his mind for all time.

With Lieutenant John Escher, USNR, on censorship duty with the First Army on its landing in Normandy, and two Army lieutenants, I had driven up the Valognes-Cherbourg road to a little route marker which read "Cherbourg, Two Kilometers." From experiences with German shelling while driving up the peninsula and from memories of 1918 which suddenly seemed very fresh, I suggested that the jeep be pulled off the road and not taken over the last rise in the hills above Cherbourg and upward from which was coming a continuous, thundering roar. I didn't want to walk home. From this point, one of the Army officers and I picked our way through a Frenchman's barnyard, where four fine cows of two days before, lay still and swollen with feet straight out or up, victims of mines or shell fire. The barnyard ended abruptly in a sharp slope that looked down on the white buildings of Cherbourg, some still as sound and untouched as in the days of peace, others wreathed in smoke and fire. On the edge of the crest was a concrete emplacement, still with its 88 gun, twisted and out of shape, pointed back in the direction from which the American forces had worked their way up the peninsula. Oddly, a mass of unexploded ammunition lay about it on the ground and still stacked in orderly piles in covered shelter alongside the gun. Grenades, both the potato masher and small egg type, lay around the gun and in the protected overhang of the cement emplacement. Gingerly one of the Army officers and I picked our way into the gun position and, from its shelter from sniper bullets or sudden shelling, looked down on Cherbourg below.

On a high area in what seemed more or less the fore-center of the city, great dancing balls of fire rose and fell—in a line as if someone were pressing a key, dancing the fiery blasts up and down at will. The roar was continuous, and it was all but impossible to separate any sound except that of nearby machine-gun and crackling rifle fire, much of which was coming from our immediate right, slightly to our rear, where knots of stubborn Germans, apparently by-passed, were fighting to the bitter end as our troops closed in on them.

I was with a 9.2 howitzer regiment in 1918, and have a fair idea of what a bursting shell can do; also a fair recollection of the visible effects of different caliber.

"What's the biggest guns the Army's using up here?" I asked with a general wave toward the hills and forests about us.

"Six inch—one fifty-fives," answered one of the Army officers.

"If that's the case," I told my companion, "the Navy's moved in on Cherbourg." None of us had knowledge that the Navy had suddenly moved in to help reduce Cherbourg, but the gigantic billowing red bursts that could come only from big gun shells gave evidence beyond all doubt. Without glasses we could not spot the ships from our position. Even with binoculars, it is doubtful that we could have seen the ships; for the sea was cloaked in haze which we later knew came from the stouthearted destroyers' smoke screens.

Fascinated, all of us stood watching the vast billows of red fire and smoke, which seemed to float rather than explode into being.

Unanimously, we agreed we would hate to be on or under the receiving end of the fire coming down on the German-held forts.

And when, during the course of our stay at this point of vantage, we saw a group of some 140 prisoners herded out from the defenses below us and marched up past the spot where we had parked our jeep, I think each of us felt a tinge of pity for the Germans who had this type of fire coming down on them. And some of them had taken shell fire for many days.

Even the hardest, toughest of them, I am certain, was tired and spent, and anxious to get away from this maelstrom. It took little urging to keep them moving along, hands over their head, back to the first stockade from whence they would be hauled back in trucks to the gathering compounds.

Suddenly from the direction of the sea, a Navy plane swept in over the inferno below. It traveled in an easy curve, apparently intent on only one objective—spotting for the ships laying down their fire on Cherbourg. From our right, perhaps a mile distant and slightly to our rear, a German antiaircraft battery came to life, its bursts trailing the plane across the sky. You always send up a prayer for your own aircraft; but I particularly hope that the lad in that particular plane is still sound and whole.

"Particular accuracy was required of the naval gunnery, as American troops were known to be concentrated close to the target areas."

The foregoing sentence is another from the SHAEF official release of June 26 describing the battle.

I've told you that our particular vantage point was just inside the two-kilometer signpost. With the various things that were flipping through the air not far from us, it did not seem wholly impossible that a flying hunk of one of those big shells could drop in our vicinity. And we were fully a mile and a quarter from the edge of the town below where infantrymen were edging in foot by foot. So you can know that the fire from the naval vessels was coming down with astounding accuracy. The soldiers marveled at it, and there is no doubt in my mind but that in their hearts was gratitude for the ships which steamed into the range of the German guns to make the job of the soldiers easier and more quickly accomplished.

We saw other signs of this modern accuracy in employment of naval gunnery, stories of which have been told before. Of naval shells that came raining down on German tanks on roads far in from the beach; of fire delivered on strong points holding up the advance. German equipment, blasted and twisted, lying in fields that appeared as if churned by hundreds of shells testified to the effectiveness of fire laid down from the sea. All the ships had to know was the exact spot where fire was wanted.

If you'll recall some of the motion pictures that you saw in the first two weeks after D-day, particularly those showing German prisoners being marched down the slopes to the beaches to board Tank Landing Ships and other craft that hauled them across to England, you find one quality common to virtually every prisoner's face. No matter whether he was a veteran Nazi still carrying himself tough, aloof and haughty, or whether he was a round, simple-faced peasant boy of sixteen or seventeen, the expression that was common to all as they beheld the mass of tanks, gun carriers and other equipment still piling out of the landing vessels along with the maze of shipping off the beaches—was amazement. They could not believe this power of the Allies. It was not in anything that they had read or been told that there was such a deluge as this to expect.

And a restrained expression of this same quality was in the faces of Lieutenant General von Schlieben and Rear Admiral Hennecke and lesser officers who came out of Cherbourg as prisoners when the end came. I saw two of them sitting in an Army truck near an airstrip that was only a cow pasture above one of our beachheads, disconsolately munching on a piece of bread and tinned cheese which a guard had broken out for them, while they awaited transportation to England. Close by, Army engineers were exploding land mines which had been planted by the Germans in a futile hope before D-day. They, too, while they waited, were having a close-up look of new striking power rolling ashore from the ships and landing craft. On their faces, too, was that look of disbelief at what they saw.

Writing of Cherbourg, Hanson Baldwin, the New York *Times* military and naval expert, summed up the fall of the French port in the following words:

"The capture of Cherbourg three weeks after the first landing in Normandy represents the greatest Allied strategic triumph of the war.

"It may well be written by future historians as a decisive victory, for Cherbourg's loss probably means the beginning of the end for the Germans. If anything can be forecast in war, it seems to mean—unless the enemy has 'secret weapons' of undreamed-of potentialities—that the Germans have lost their last chance for victory or even for averting defeat.

"This is not to say that the enemy has 'thrown in the sponge' or that he is likely to do so soon. In one sense the bitter, week-long defense of Cherbourg by second-rate troops and the hard, slow fighting in Normandy are disappointing. Tactically we can expect only more of the same; just as Cherbourg's capture took somewhat longer than we had hoped and expected, so future battles in France are likely to be protracted and difficult.

"Nevertheless, June 27 must go down as a red-letter day for the Allies for Cherbourg's fall means the bankruptcy of German strategy."

My specific mission and orders did not permit me to remain with the troops until the final fall of the city on Monday, but I would not trade for a great deal the privilege and experience of having seen what I did the afternoon of Sunday, June 25, when our ships and those of the British moved in from sea to slam down their flaming power to make the soldiers' job easier and its accomplishment faster.

Monday, June 26, while the Army's artillery and infantry were still smashing down the last defenses and defenders of the port, I met Commodore William Sullivan, USN, the United States Navy's salvage expert, easygoing and genial, just ashore in France from England. With him were a group of assistants. Next day, while desultory firing still continued around the city, the Commodore and his group were at work. I have a feeling that had Lieutenant General von Schlieben or Rear Admiral Hennecke seen and recognized Commodore Sullivan that Monday morning before the German guns had all been silenced, they would have

PLATE LXV—(*right*) Preceding the Sicily landings (*Operation Husky*) battleships, cruisers, and destroyers softened up shore defenses at Gela and other points along the south shore with a terrific night bombardment. H-hour was 2:45 A.M. July 10, 1943.

(*left*) A violent storm, preceding the Sicilian D-day, left the sea chopped up for days. Seabees, in action for the first time as an organized force, had a real problem on their hands when an LST grounded on a sandbar. Despite the pounding of heavy surf, and occasional enemy sniper and strafing fire, the Seabees managed to lash steel pontoon barges to the bow of the LST. Unloading proceeded on schedule.

(*right*) Enemy spotter planes, flying over the beachheads after our night landing, must have thought we were beaten, judging by the disorderly array of boats on the sand or swamped in the surf. But Navy salvage crews and Army Engineers soon had our broached and battered landing craft back on duty, ferrying urgently needed supplies from transports to every landing point along the south shore of Sicily.

PLATE LXVI—(*above*) Ensign John Joseph Parle, USNR, who gave his life to save his shipmates aboard a burning LST during the Sicilian landings. Thus he earned the only Congressional Medal of Honor awarded to a Navy man during the Battle of the Atlantic. (*left*) Swaying in the heavy ground swell, attack transports lower small boats, carrying the first wave of troops, as night operations off Sicily begin. (*Water color by Lieutenant Mitchell Jamieson, USNR.*)

(*right*) "Park it here!" A beachmaster indicates the predetermined spot where a big LST (Landing Ship, Tank) is to hit the Sicilian beach. The bow doors already are open to discharge men, tanks, and supply vehicles by the scores. In Sicily, profiting by the mistakes and shortcomings of the Casablanca and North African operations, modern amphibious landing techniques were further developed and perfected. These were the methods later used so successfully in Italy, France, and in the far Pacific.

PLATE LXVII—(*upper*) Hitting the continent of Europe for the first time, assault waves of American troops pour ashore from an LCI at Salerno, below Naples, as *Operation Avalanche* begins, September 9, 1943. Beyond, an LST has been set afire, while, at left, an LCVP heads for the beach as a German "88" shell sends up a narrow plume of smoke and water. Allied cruisers and destroyers move in to give fire support. (*Water color by Lieutenant Mitchell Jamieson, USNR.*) (*lower*) Foxholes on Green Beach, hottest spot at Salerno, contain both dead and sleeping. Toward sunset two members of a 5th Army burying detail pause briefly in their labors beside the body of a fallen comrade, covered by his army blanket. Behind him, barely discernible, another comrade, exhausted, sleeps in the aftermath of battle.

PLATE LXVIII — (*left*) During the battle for the Salerno beachhead, September 11, 1943, a Nazi radio-controlled glider bomb struck the USS SAVANNAH, penetrating the number three turret, where it exploded, causing many casualties. The cruiser, however, continued to bombard shore installations.

(*right*) Close-up of a captured German radio-controlled glider bomb, of which the USS SAVANNAH was the first victim. The bomb was launched from a plane, which controlled its movements by radio. Resembling somewhat the Japanese Baka bomb, it, however, carried no suicide pilot.

(*left*) Army nurses shared the same hardships and inconveniences as GIs. With Naples harbor a shambles this young lady, her shoes tied around her neck and her gear passed along by her shipmates, wades ashore from the ramp of a Navy LCI.

PLATE LXIX—(*right*) The Secretary of the Navy, the late Frank Knox, was an inveterate traveler, and, like his successor in office, James Forrestal, a believer in seeing things at first hand. This photograph shows Mr. Knox and the party that accompanied him on an extensive inspection of overseas bases, at Dakar, Senegal, West Africa, in 1943. The plane is a Douglas four-motor transport, operated by NATS (Naval Air Transport Service).

(*left*) Secretary Knox labored long and earnestly to cut red tape and to promote friendly relations between the United States Navy and the naval forces of our Allies. During his inspection tour of U. S. Naval facilities in Europe he spoke before a distinguished audience in the famous Painted Hall, Greenwich, London. Toastmaster (right) was A. V. Alexander, First Lord of the Admiralty. To the left sits Anthony Eden, Foreign Minister.

(*right*) These Nazi prisoners, mugging the camera, did not know that a high-ranking American cabinet member was watching them disembark near Salerno, Italy. *Left to right, in background group:* Rear Admiral F. J. Lowry, USN (in battle helmet); Secretary of the Navy Knox (sun helmet); Captain L. P. Lovette, USN, Director of Navy Public Relations; and Captain L. S. Perry, USN, Naval Aide to the Secretary.

PLATE LXX—(*upper*) While m
Allied ships assigned to the
lantic were engaged in the M
terranean, HMS MALAYA, U
SOUTH DAKOTA, and USS A
BAMA prowled the North Sea
an attempt to lure the remna
of the Nazi fleet into action.
set: Admiral Harold R. St
USN, Commander Naval For
Europe. (*above*) Rear Adm
Frank Jacob Lowry, USN, C
mander U. S. Naval Forces,
zio. (*left*) One of the most fie
ly contested landings in Eu
was *Operation Shingle*, Jan.
1944, near Anzio. Here woun
brought to Anzio by lan
craft, await transfer to hos
ships offshore.

PLATE LXXI—(*right*) "I had a little talk with the Lord." Typical of many pre-D-day services is this simple communion aboard an LCI in a sheltered English cove. The Navy chaplain again and again showed his courage under fire, sharing all risks to tend the wounded and dying, and to lead rescue parties in the face of hazards far beyond the call of duty.

(*left*) An LCT moves across the English Channel on D-day with a full load of reinforcements. To observers in other ships it seemed at times that men in the crowded landing craft must be treading water. Code name for the Normandy invasion was *Operation Overlord;* for the naval phase, *Operation Neptune.*

(*right*) Belying peaceful appearances, This was It! Barrage balloons float overhead, protecting the ships from dive bomber attacks, as the steady flow of ships of the largest task force in history moves from England to the Norman beaches. It is D-day and the "D" is for *Dämmerung,* the twilight of the Nazi gods.

(*right*) On the bridge of the USS
AUGUSTA, studying the Norman-
dy beachhead, are (*left to right*) :
Rear Admiral Alan C. Kirk, USN,
Task Force Commander ; Lt. Gen.
Omar Bradley, Commanding Gen-

eral of American Ground Forces
and Rear Admiral A. D. Struble
USN, Chief of Staff to Admiral
Kirk. (*above left*) Rear Admiral
John L. Hall, Jr., USN, Com
mander Task Force "O," Omaha
beach, Normandy landing. (*left*
"Destroyed to pieces" by the Jap
at Pearl Harbor, the USS NEVADA
shows there is plenty of life in
the old ship yet. The NEVADA
added its 14-inch broadsides to
the Navy fire support given on
Normandy D-day.

TE LXXIII—(*right*) One of the
w photographs of the moment
hen men with rifles in hand must
mp ashore and fight—man to
an. Ahead may be seen troops
ing flat; some already dead,
hers dodging German fire along
e beach. (*Coast Guard Photo.*)

(*above*) Commodore Campbell
D. Edgar, USN, Commander
Support Force, D-day landings.
(*left*) D-day-plus-1 finds the
hard-won beachhead packed with
men and materiel pouring ashore
and heading inland. (*Coast Guard
Photo.*)

ove right) Rear Admiral Don
. Moon, USN, Commander Task
orce "U," Utah beach, Nor-
nandy landings. (*right*) The first
anding craft hurried back empty
or reinforcements, but soon
very returning boat was filled
vith the grim harvest of battle.
oined in a common bond of suf-
ering, wounded Nazi prisoners
f war lie side by side with Allied
asualties in the bottom of an
CVP (Landing Craft, Vehicle,
ersonnel). American paratroop-
rs are among the casualties.

PLATE LXXIV—The Nazis concentrated their defenses in and around Europe's harbors. They hoped to make the invasion supply problem so difficult and costly that Allied troops could soon be forced back into the sea. But Allied strategists decided as early as the Quebec conference that, if you cannot capture a good harbor, build one—and in a spot where the enemy least expects it. Two elaborate artificial harbors (Mulberry A and B) were planned, to be created along a bleak section of the Norman coast. Three types of breakwater for the Mulberry are shown above. (*top*) A row of sunken ships close inshore, known as "Gooseberry." (*center*) Hollow concrete caissons, called "Phoenixes," built in England, and towed to a predetermined site and sunk. (*bottom*) Floating steel units, moored end to end, whose purpose was to diffuse and enervate waves as they reached the outer limits of the Mulberry. Their code name was "Bombardon." The Bombardons, however, were dispersed by the storm and never given a chance to prove their worth.

PLATE LXXV—(*right*) Because of the 16- to 18-foot range of the tide it was necessary to construct a pierhead, well out from shore, that would rise and fall with unloading ships. The Loebnitz pier (code name

"Whale") was the answer: steel stilts rested on the bottom and held the floating pierhead in place. Pontoons formed roadways to shore. (*above*) Captain A. D. Clark, USN, Commander, Task Force 128 (American Mulberry Operation).

(*left*) Almost overnight the two Mulberrys became the busiest ports in all Europe. The first LST unloaded at the American harbor June 17—D-day-plus-11. At the pierhead an LST could unload in an hour as against twelve hours on the beach.

right) The sites of Mulberrys were dearly bought, but they paid us well: by September 1 more than 2,000,000 men, 440,000 vehicles and 2,480,-000 tons of stores were landed by the Allies, all but a small part of which had gone in through the artificial harbors. Parts of these beachheads were used as late as November 15, 1944.

caissons, battered the sunken ships and broke the causeways leading to the pierheads. For three days and nights it raged, recalling the tempest that dispersed the Spanish Armada. (*above*) Rear Admiral Morton L. Deyo, USN, Commander, U. S. Navy squadron bombarding Cherbourg.

(*right*) When The Storm finally blew itself out, the American Mulberry was a mass of tangled wreckage, usable only as a shelter for small boats. Whatever could be salvaged was sent off to Mulberry B, the British harbor, where an offshore reef took the brunt of the storm.

(*left*) Germans, at last, sailing *nach England!* These D-day prisoners, however, were in no mood to sing their once-popular marching song. Thousands were brought back to England whenever ships were not needed for the transportation of wounded. In the foreground a stream of casualties boards an LST.

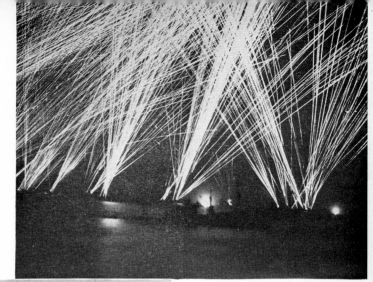

ATE LXXVII—(*right*) Bitterly the Nazis resisted the Allied siege of Cherbourg. Even after the Allies had closed in on the French port from the land and from the sea, Nazi planes kept up repeated night attacks. This tapestry of flame was thrown up by Allied land and naval guns. In the foreground an American ship sinks, mortally wounded by a bomb hit. (*Coast Guard Photo.*) (*above*) Rear Admiral Carleton F. Bryant, USN, aboard the USS TEXAS, Commander of a bombardment squadron, Cherbourg.

(*left*) Nazi harbor mine lets go, harmlessly, as the grim work of sweeping the anchorage goes on. Minesweeping and harbor survey were under British control, but Army Engineers, Navy Seabees, and the Coast Guard Port Director's office also assisted. Four weeks after its capture, Cherbourg was handling more freight than it had in peacetime.

(*right*) This is all that is left of one of Cherbourg's bombproof U-boat pens. How much of the damage was done by flyers, and how much by Nazi demolition squads, however, may never be known. Cherbourg, owing to its strategic location near the English Channel convoy lanes, was one of the most active German submarine bases.

Hewitt, USN (to Secretary's left), over-all commander of *Operation Anvil*. (*above*) Rear Admiral Calvin T. Durgin, USN, aboard the USS TULAGI, Commander of U. S. Carriers, Tactical Air Support.

(*right*) Although the Southern France assault, August 15, 1944, was called "the worst kept secret of the war," casualties were comparatively light. Many German gun positions were unmanned. Naval flyers from the USS TULAGI, finding nothing better to do, ranged far inland to destroy railroad trains and nearly 500 motor vehicles of the fleeing Wehrmacht.

(*left*) Part of the reinforcemer landing on the Riviera fro was a contingent of America Red Cross workers. (*Coc Guard Photo.*) (*above*) Re Admiral Theodore E. Chan ler, USN, commander of a fi support group.

PLATE LXXIX—(*upper*) The Atlantic was proving ground for all the "first team" battleships that helped to blast the Japanese Navy into impotence. Here the mighty USS MISSOURI fires her two forward turrets during a trial run. The photographer, on an accompanying destroyer, managed to catch six one-ton projectiles in flight (upper right). It was aboard this great ship that the Japanese signed the surrender terms, September 2, 1945, ending the war. (*lower*) En route to the historic Yalta conference, President Roosevelt traveled as far as Malta aboard the USS QUINCY, which replaced the cruiser of the same name lost in the Solomons, August 8, 1942. Here the late President confers with Prime Minister Churchill at much-bombed Valetta, as the President's daughter, Mrs. Anna Boettiger, and the Prime Minister's daughter, Sarah Oliver, listen. The President rejoined the QUINCY at Suez to receive aboard the Kings of Egypt and Saudi Arabia, and the Emperor of Ethiopia.

(*right*) The U–858 was the
first German submarine to
surrender to the U. S.
Navy in accordance with
the V-E armistice terms.
Flying a black flag (a crew
member's blanket) as re-
quired, the Nazi raider was
taken into custody off Cape
May, New Jersey, May 14,
1945.

(*left*) End of an era. The Amer
ican flag, flying proudly from
the U–858, seems to symboliz
the triumph of Allied nava
forces over the great Germar
underseas fleet—the secon
such victory within a genera
tion. Overhead a helicopte
looks down on the last chapte
of the Battle of the Atlantic

been a bit amazed by such accurate timing of his arrival. So ends Commander Say's report.

Had the German officers remained in the area long enough to watch the Commodore perform his usual short-order miracle of restoration on the harbors, they would have been more than merely amazed.

Chapter Forty-five

THE naval bombardment, terrific though it was, did not entirely eliminate resistance in Cherbourg; there were some pockets that guns from the sea couldn't get at, some strong points and bunkers too deep for even a 15-inch shell to penetrate. And, the fire from the sea was not unopposed. At Cherbourg, for the first time since the assault on Casablanca, the Navy was going up against guns of the same range and weight as its own. It had its casualties. The TEXAS, steaming within 8,000 yards of one of the principal forts on Cherbourg's outer breakwater, took at least ten hits—one square on the conning tower—and suffered losses in dead and wounded. The destroyer O'BRIEN, making smoke for the heavier ships, also took a pasting, a direct hit from an 8-inch shell killing ten and wounding eleven more.

At three in the afternoon of June 25, after three hours of intense shelling, Rear Admiral Deyo signaled for his ships to retire.[1] Their work was done. Even though some of the forts held out until days later, the heavy guns in those forts had been put out of commission. Cherbourg harbor, except for the inevitable minefields, lay open to Allied shipping. All that remained was to put it to work.

The first step, of course, was to clear out the dug-in Nazis, and here,

[1] The following United States and British ships took part in the bombardment of Cherbourg: USS TUSCALOOSA (Capt. J. B. W. Waller, USN), flying the flag of Rear Admiral Morton Lyndhold Deyo, USN; USS TEXAS (Capt. C. A. Baker, USN), flying the flag of Rear Admiral Carleton Fanton Bryant, USN; USS NEVADA (Capt. P. M. Rhea, USN); USS ARKANSAS (Capt. F. G. Richards, USN); USS QUINCY (Capt. Elliot M. Senn, USN); HMS GLASGOW (Capt. C. P. Clarke, DSO, RN); HMS ENTERPRISE (Capt. H. T. W. Grant, DSO, RCN). Among the destroyers that took part in the operation were: HMS ONSLOW (Capt. J. A. McCoy, DSO, RN); HMS OFFA (Lt. Comdr. R. F. Leonard, RN); HMS MELBREAK (Lt. G. J. Kirkby, DSC, RN); USS O'BRIEN (Comdr. W. W. Outerbridge, USN); USS MURPHY (Comdr. R. A. Wolverton, USN); USS RODMAN (Comdr. J. F. Foley, USN); USS EMMONS (Comdr. E. B. Billingsley, USN). The minesweeping forces consisted of British and United States flotillas of fleet sweepers, the three senior officers being: Comdr. R. W. D. Thomson, RN, Comdr. Henry Plander, USN, Lt. Comdr. S. E. Davies, DSC, RNR. Units of the 5th Minesweeping M/L Flotilla also were engaged in the operation.

too, the Navy took a hand. Navy officers and men, part of the original contingent assigned the task of putting Cherbourg in operation as a harbor, armed with submachine guns, carbines and hand grenades, had marched and fought with the Army from the American beachheads in Normandy to Cherbourg to carry out their mission of surveying the huge harbor for naval occupation. Hours before the city fell, the Navy men had penetrated into the waterfront area, where the fighting during the last stages of the battle was fiercest.

During that time, these Navy footsloggers accounted for the capture of two large forts in the harbor area and participated in the capture of the ranking German general and admiral in Normandy.

Lieutenant Commander Quentin R. Walsh, a wiry, 32-year-old Coast Guardsman, and Lieutenant Frank Lauer, USNR, a 53-year-old Seabee officer, forced the surrender of Fort du Homet, one of the Nazi strongholds in the harbor area, taking three hundred marine soldiers and liberating about fifty American paratroopers who had been held prisoner since D-day.

The two officers entered the fort knowing that it had not surrendered and when within shouting distance of the stronghold told the Nazis that all resistance had ceased. The Germans did not believe the naval officers, but later were convinced after accepting an invitation to view the situation in the city.

"We're supposed to be crazy guys," one grinning paratrooper said to their liberators, "but you're the ones who are nuts!" The paratroopers revealed that the Germans had machine guns leveled on the two Navy men, but held their fire because they thought a large patrol was following them.

A few hours after this fantastic adventure a party of four Navy men, headed by Lieutenant (jg) Harrison G. Shearon, USNR, was sent on a mission to Fort de Querqueville, another of the German harbor bastions.

When the Navy men started toward the fort French civilians told them that about thirty Germans still were holding out in the bastion. Shearon then borrowed the services of four Army enlisted men from a nearby unit. The eight men jumped into a single jeep and headed for the fort.

"We thought eight men would be enough to take care of thirty Jerries," the bewhiskered lieutenant explained.

En route to the fort the party encountered a United States Army Air

Corps captain and his driver in another jeep. They wanted to survey an airfield which the Americans had captured in the area, so they joined the Navy party.

While driving up to fort the men noticed innumerable Nazi trenches and pillboxes, but did not see a single German. But when they dismounted to reconnoiter, Germans to their rear opened up with machine-gun and small-arms fire, isolating them on the breakwater road leading to the fort. The Nazi fire was so intense that the ten Americans were pinned to the ground and were virtually unable to use the small arms they carried.

They scattered in tall grass alongside the fort area and popped up occasionally for a pot shot at the Germans. Some of the men found a large supply of German hand grenades which they used to rout the Jerries from nearby pillboxes and trenches.

For five hours the men were under intense fire. The Germans used 3-inch guns, hand grenades and machine guns, as well as small arms, on the patrol. Just as the Americans were losing all hope of escape, the German hoisted a white flag and marched out of their entrenchments with hands upraised.

"We were so damned surprised," Lieutenant Shearon reported, "that you could have knocked us over with a mortar."

Another naval officer distinguished himself on the march to Cherbourg when, through location of a key entrance to Villa Maurice on the outskirts of the city, he brought about the capture of General von Schlieben and Admiral Hennecke, German army and navy leaders in Normandy.

The two military leaders were in a huge underground stronghold defended by about a thousand men. Capture of the Nazi leaders was facilitated by Lieutenant John Lambie, Jr., USNR, an intelligence officer. While checking up on the entrance he was wounded by a Nazi machine gunner, whose bullet ripped through Lambie's right cheek. Despite his wound Lieutenant Lambie contacted an Army unit and directed them to the entrance. He then had his wound dressed and continued his trek to Cherbourg.

Even while German snipers were still taking toll of incautious personnel, while land mines and booby traps were still a constant danger, Cherbourg assumed its status as a United States naval base. Rear Admiral Wilkes, relieved of his duties as Commander Landing Craft and

Bases, Europe, assumed command of United States Ports and Bases, France, and hoisted his flag in the French city. His deputy was Captain Willis M. Percifield, USN; his chief of staff, Captain A. D. Clark, USN. His command was divided into two sections: Captured Ports under Captain N. S. Ives (incorporating United States Naval Advanced Amphibious Base, Cherbourg) and Port Director, Cherbourg, Captain William H. Barton, USCG.

These officers had command of groups which had been formed back in the United States, long before the invasion, with the specific job in mind of running Cherbourg. The men in these units wasted no time learning their way around the city or their way around their individual jobs; they had studied nothing else for months in advance.

Minesweeping and harbor survey were under British command, though the Army engineers, the Seabees and the Port Director also did some survey work for their own immediate purposes. Mines were thick in the harbor, and demolitions were extensive to all shore installations— the great French naval bases were wrecked with combined German thoroughness and ruthlessness—but despite these handicaps, four weeks after its capture, Cherbourg was handling more freight than it had in its palmiest days as a peacetime port.

With the British and American beaches going full blast, with Cherbourg exceeding all estimates of its capacity—a trans-Channel pipeline for diesel oil and gasoline was part of the miracle—the tenacity of the Germans in holding Brest, Saint-Nazaire, Lorient and Bordeaux became a gesture rather than an operation of military significance. The counter-invaders could afford to by-pass them. Then, too, eyes were fixed on even greater ports: Toulon, Cannes and Marseilles were objectives clearly outlined on the horizon.

PART SEVEN

The Mediterranean — Final Phase

Chapter Forty-six

BEFORE the port of Cherbourg had come under Allied control, preliminaries for the invasion of Southern France were under way. On June 17, United States and British craft put picked French Commandos and Bataillon de Choc troops ashore on the rocky little isle of Elba. This island, once scene of Napoleon's temporary exile. lies across a 10-mile strip of water from the Italian mainland, opposite Cape Piambino. With the Fifth Army moving rapidly up Italy's west coast, there seemed little likelihood that resistance on Elba, which had already been partially flanked by the French capture of Corsica, would be strong. Intelligence reports seemed to indicate that the Germans had been evacuating the place, and the entire Elba operation was designed as a brisk cutting-out affair that would be a small-scale rehearsal for the bigger show coming up. There was to be a rocket barrage on the main landing beaches—the southwest portion of the island; British sailors in small boats were to come alongside and board a German flak lighter, while Commandos, who had sneaked ashore earlier, were to take out important dominating gun positions. With the lighter and the gun positions taken care of, the rest of the landing was to be a breeze.

No one thought it would be much more as they sailed from Corsica the day before. The French troops (Senegalese and Moroccans for the most part) cheerfully sharpened their knives and bayonets as they lolled on the decks of the LSTs transporting them. The American small-boat crews who were to take them ashore, having enjoyed a good swim before shoving off, went over their beach identification charts again. The British patrol craft and destroyers of the screen slipped quietly through the flat calm sea.

H-hour for the main assault was 0400, the Commandos having been scheduled to land at 0100, and presumed to have cleaned out the gun emplacements by 0345. The whole operation was to be a surprise attack; one quick rush overwhelming the defenders.

375

It did not work out that way. The Commandos were discovered shortly after they landed, and although they did succeed in handling their assignment, they also succeeded in alerting the defenders. And there were a surprising number of them, all willing to fight. As the Bataillons de Choc swept into the narrow, covelike Golfo di Campo in their American LCVPs, the whole area lit up like a carnival of death, with a murderous cross fire from shore batteries of all calibers. Coxswains who had been through bloody Salerno found themselves in something worse.

For three hours, as the darkness drained from the sky, it was uncertain whether full light would show a firm Allied beachhead or a bitter shambles. But after the toughest kind of fighting in the dark, dawn saw the French Colonials ashore in force. By June 19 the French controlled the island.

Naval action in the Mediterranean was never entirely a matter of making invasions and carrying freight, although it is too easy to think of it that way. From the first moment at which they could turn their attention from protecting their own convoys, the United Nations fleets engaged in harassing and destroying the enemy seaborne traffic. And there was plenty of it to destroy. The Air Force had done so well with disrupting land communications that the Germans were forced more and more to depend on water transport to keep their Italian front supplied. This made happy hunting for the light task forces of the Allies, consisting of British MLs (120-foot patrol boats), LCGs (LCTs mounting two 4.5-inch guns plus six twin-mount Oerlikons) and American PT Squadron 15. The PTs were commanded by Lieutenant Commander S. M. Barnes, USN, who has been awarded the Navy Cross for his share in destroying enemy communications and trade routes through the Ligurian and Tyrrhenian seas. Barnes repeatedly went out on missions himself to put in practice the tactics he had taught so often in those briefings his squadron irreverently called "wardroom sinkings."

Starting operations from Africa in April of 1943, Squadron 15 fought its way north until, by July of 1944, they were operating out of Corsica making things uncomfortably hot for the enemy every mile of the voyage.

Operating at night, when the Axis convoys were attempting to sneak along the coast of Italy undetected from the air, the PTs of Squadron 15, working with the heavier British units, made that the most hazardous stretch of water in the world. All types of hostile craft were grist to their mill, from large tankers to small speedy German E-boats—armed and armored cutters and Italian MASs—torpedo boats.

It was a matter of teamwork, like every other Allied operation in the theater. American PTs would flush the enemy convoys, single out targets suitable for torpedo attack, and then harry the rest until the British gunboats could get to the scene with their heavier armament and finish off the enemy. It wasn't all as easy as that; fighting at sea never is. The Allied units sustained their losses, too, as Nazi craft after Nazi craft flamed briefly in the night and then sought the bottom.

Occasionally the enemy sent out destroyers, which he could ill spare, to escort particularly valuable convoys, but for the most part the Nazis relied on flak lighters. These craft were the Nazi equivalent of the Allied landing craft. Originally they had been designed to ferry Hitler's Wehrmacht across the Channel to conquer England. Somehow, they never got around to that chore and they were, instead, converted into formidable floating gun platforms mounting two of the famous 88s in addition to a large number of standard antiaircraft guns. Extremely shallow in draft, these flak boats could work in shoal water where they were safe from everything but their Allied counterpart, the LCG. In their "invasion" fleet the Nazis had actually succeeded in constructing a fairly effective form of mobile harbor defense and slow coastal convoy escort vessel.

One night in March of 1944, well before the capture of Elba, a combined Allied scouting force encountered a convoy of six flak boats with two destroyers in company, outward-bound from Leghorn and headed, perhaps, for some French port where they would pick up cargo vessels to escort. The PTs boldly attacked the two destroyers, darting out of their own smoke screen to make their torpedo run. As the heavier ships occupied themselves in trying to avoid torpedoes and at the same time to destroy their attackers, the rest of the Allied force fell on the flak ships. The result, after an hour of brisk fighting, was one German destroyer hit by a torpedo and probably sunk, all six German flak ships certainly sunk. Two men were injured aboard one of the PTs.

Mussolini's Mare Nostrum, the Mediterranean, had become an Allied pond. Far to the north, Patton's Third Army had broken out of Normandy and was sweeping through France, heading, under a cloak of censorship, for Paris in a great arc. The German Seventh Army, ground powder-fine, was trickling as best it could through the Falaise Gap. The war in the west was matched by the war in the east as the Russian Army rolled implacably forward all along its widespread front. The time was ripe for the next great blow. The invasion of Southern France got under way.

Newspaper correspondents have called the Southern France assault "the worst-kept secret of the war." They bolster the claim with incidents: Italian civilians who blurted out the exact date and place of the invasion days ahead of time, GIs who did the same thing, one Italian paper which ran a page-one story on the coming attack, French civilians in far-off Brittany who seemed strikingly well informed of the Allied plans. Indeed, it seemed inconceivable that the enemy himself did not know just when and where it had been planned to strike. If he did, however, he gave little indication of acting on the knowledge.

The secret was an almost impossible one to keep, in any case. Southern France was the obvious place to attack if the Allies were to support and build up their drive in the north—and it was clear that the Battle of France had been chosen by the Germans as the Battle of Europe against the Western powers. Furthermore, the assault had to come somewhere within swift striking distance of the great ports of Toulon and Marseilles and, even more important, somewhere near the great Rhône Valley route through which to effect a junction with the northern Army groups nearing Germany. Only the time of the attack could be a matter of doubt. There again, Allied intentions were, of necessity, pretty clear: While the Germans held the port of Leghorn (Livorno) and clung to their Pisa-Rimini line, there could be no release of the battle-wise, invasion-learned divisions like the American 45th, 36th and 3rd. Furthermore, until it was certain that all was going well in Northern France there could be no relaxation of the weight of sea power brought to bear in that area; heavy ships like the TEXAS and NEVADA could not be spared.

Then, too, the Nazi observers, comfortable in their posts on the high cliffs of neutral Spain and Spanish Morocco bordering the Strait of Gibraltar, had had ample opportunity to learn what an invasion in the making looked like. Receiving their reports, the German High Command could get a fair idea that the hour for another big attack was rapidly approaching.

Operations against Genoa and intensified air attacks, plus a concentration of war shipping in the Gulf of Taranto and across the Mediterranean at Alexandria, may have helped to keep the enemy off balance somewhat. He can have had no doubt, however, that big things were in store for him. Oran, Algiers, Bizerte, Tunis and Alexandria on the

North African shore bulged with shipping, while closer to the point of attack, Palermo, Naples and the little ports of Corsica and Sardinia, were packed with landing craft, LSTs, LCTs and LCIs all awaiting Vice-Admiral Henry K. Hewitt's signal.

The assault was to be a four-pronged drive, a great claw of men and steel to seize the vital French-Mediterranean portal. Three of the talons were to strike from the sea, against the leverage exerted by a vast force of British and American paratroopers and glider-borne infantry put down from 10 to 15 miles inland.

Clawing in from the sea, amphibious forces of the 3rd Division under Major General J. W. O'Daniel were to attack just east of the Rade de Hyères with the task force of Rear Admiral Bertram J. Rodgers, USN. This was the left flank of the assault. In the center, a task force under Rear Admiral Frank J. Lowry, USN, was to put ashore units of Major General W. W. Eagles's 45th, or "Thunderbird," Division near Cape Nègre on Bougnon Bay. The right, or east, flank was to be composed of the 36th Division under Major General J. E. Dahlquist, in the task force placed under the command, a fortnight earlier, of Rear Admiral Spencer S. Lewis, USN.

Operational commands—Navy, Army and Air—Vice-Admiral Hewitt, Major General Alexander M. Patch and Brigadier General Gordon P. Saville—had had the advantage of working out their plans under a single roof, and this close meshing of all the gears in the intricate amphibious machine paid off handsomely when the time came to put it to work.

As in the invasion of Normandy, the first great problem was one of timing; fire-support ships from far-off Oran and Alexandria had to arrive off the beaches through the same swept channels at the same time as lumbering LCTs from Corsica. Convoys of LSTs threading their way from Naples through the narrow Strait of Bonifacio had to join smoothly with speedier LCIs coming out of Ajaccio. And inevitably the whole armada, some eight hundred ships of all types, had to be compressed into narrower waters as it neared the assault beaches.

The invaders had some advantages they could count on: deep water close to the beaches, making mining and the laying of extensive under-water obstacles difficult; an absence of reefs and sand bars; sheltered landing areas; and very slight tidal currents. They had, also, the expectation of good weather. Of course, every other assault had been begun with that last expectation but, for once, it came true. Prime Minister Churchill aboard HMS KIMBERLEY and Secretary of the Navy Forrestal aboard Vice-Admiral Hewitt's flagship had a fine smooth ride under a broken sky, over calm seas, to the scene of the attack.

The shores of the French Riviera, the playground of the world, are picturesque; steep beaches of shining sand run up from the blue waters of the Mediterranean to low pine-clad cliffs, and back of these rise the hills with their great resort hotels, and their exclusive villas commanding a view of sea and beach. Ideal country for a vacation; ideal, too, for a determined defender who wants good observation posts and strong gun positions covering every possible sea approach. In terrain, the country resembled Salerno, and there was not a member of the attacking forces who did not think of that bloody battleground as he neared the coast of France.

The landings were scheduled for eight o'clock on the morning of August 15. Hours earlier, in the darkness, thousands of paratroopers, British and American—more than had ever before been employed in a single day of operation—had whirled overhead, and made their drops inland about 15 miles, where the single good military road from Cannes to Toulon and Marseilles ran. These troops seized their objectives— strong points, crossroads, bridges—and set up their guns. One outfit, how- ever, was dropped out of place. Instead of being some 10 miles inland in a little valley, they found themselves right on the coast, conveniently near the delightful resort town of Saint Tropez. Being paratroopers, they were a resourceful lot when it came to finding a fight and finishing it. "Okay, gang! Let's go!" was the word. And with no more ado they captured the town of Saint Tropez, and had the situation there well in hand by the time the assault waves were leaving their rendezvous circles and heading for the beach.

There were other operations in advance of H-hour. Westward of all the invasion points, off the beach of La Ciotat, lying midway between Toulon and Marseilles, and a likely place for a landing, a diversionary raid was staged. Under the over-all command of Captain Henry Johnson, USN, from Rear Admiral Lyal A. Davidson's staff, raiding parties com- manded by Lieutenant Commander Douglas Fairbanks, Jr., USNR, in special PT boats, roared landward in simulated assault. They were backed up by HMS APHIS and SCARAB, British gunboats, and by the American destroyer ENDICOTT, commanded by Commander John D. Bulkeley, USN, of PT boat fame. The German defenders were promptly alerted, as it was hoped they would be. And doubtless the Nazi area commandant was properly harried by howls for help from that region.

The raiders after an hour or two of highly diverting shenanigans in and around the bay, during which they drew the wildest kind of inaccurate fire, retired. Not until the next night did Bulkeley get the action he seems to attract no matter what ocean he is in. Then PTs and British gunboats made contact with two German corvettes trying to sneak out of Toulon. For such light craft, that type of contact was like getting hold of a couple of bears by the tail. This time, however, they were fortunate in having Bulkeley as an experienced bear tamer to rush to the rescue. In a rapid-fire, slam-bang engagement, the ENDICOTT roared in to the attack and blasted both Nazis to the bottom in a running duel lasting just under an hour.

There was other surface action on the night of the assault itself before H-hour. The USS SOMERS (Commander W. C. Hughes, Jr., USN), moving in to her shore bombardment station off Camoscio around five o'clock in the morning of D-day, sighted two unidentified craft. They refused to reply to her challenge, so the SOMERS promptly opened fire on them and, just as promptly, sank them both. Survivors were picked up who identified the sunken vessels as a German auxiliary craft and her escort. At about the same time, the minesweepers working in toward the beaches of Saint Tropez were met by five Nazi harbor patrol craft starting their routine search. They finished it at the bottom of the Mediterranean.

Meanwhile, American Rangers had gone ashore on two of the rocky little islets in the bay of Hyères, Ile de Levant and Port Cros. These small islands were actually strong gun positions, covering not only the entire range of the western assault beaches, but also the approaches to Toulon. Knocking them out was a necessary preliminary to a successful invasion. The Rangers went ashore at 12:30 the morning of the 15th, almost four hours before the main attack, and the enemy guns were spiked, the Rangers overwhelming the gun crews in the rapid, silent rush they have made their trademark.

Daybreak found all in readiness for the assault: The big transports anchored, the LSTs, LCTs and LCIs coming up astern of them, the small boats loaded and on their way in to the beach. In the fire-support areas, no fewer than seven separate bombardment groups—almost a hundred ships in all—were awaiting the word to fire. There was Rear Admiral Lyal A. Davidson, USN, on the USS AUGUSTA (Captain Edward H.

Jones, USN), Rear Admiral Carleton F. Bryant, USN, on the TEXAS (Captain Charles A. Baker, USN), Rear Admiral Morton L. Deyo, USN, on the TUSCALOOSA (Captain John B. Waller, USN), Rear Admiral Theodore E. Chandler, USN, aboard the OMAHA (Captain Elwood M. Tillson, USN), Rear Admiral J. M. Mansfield, RN, with his flag on HMS ORION. The French Navy, too, participated, and participated gloriously: There were fire-support groups under Rear Admiral Philippe Aubonyeau on the MONTCALM and Rear Admiral Robert Joujard aboard the ÉMILE BERTIN, all part of the French naval forces under the command of Admiral André Le Monnier, flying his flag from the GIRUNDIA.[1]

The moment for firing arrived. The beach shuddered and jumped as the shells smashed in. A great cloud of dust began to cover the area. Smoke mixed with it as ammunition and fuel dumps were hit. It was a calm day, bright blue, and the huge billowing column of gloom marked off the invasion area clearly for the bombers rapidly approaching to give the beach its final blasting before H-hour.

These low-level bombers represented something new in the amphibious team as it worked in Europe. They were ship-based. Taking a cue from the Pacific commanders, and his own success in the North African invasion, Vice-Admiral Hewitt relied on carriers for his tactical air support. Seafires from the seven British carriers,[2] Grumman Hellcats from the USS KASAAN BAY (Captain Bradford E. Grow, USN) and TULAGI (Captain Joseph C. Cronin, USN) were the medium bomber and fighter elements in Brigadier General Saville's air force. The carriers themselves were under the over-all command of Rear Admiral Thomas Troubridge, RN, with the American flat-tops commanded by Rear Admiral Calvin T. Durgin, USN, who had commanded the RANGER in her action during the North African landings.

Once they finished their brisk pummeling of the beaches, the Navy planes were diverted to other duties: some acted as spotters for the naval artillery; others were sent ranging far afield, covering all of Southern France west of the Rhône, as protection to the exposed flank of the inva-

---

[1] The French heavy units participating in the assault on Southern France were: the battleship LORRAINE; the cruisers GEORGES LEYGUES, ÉMILE BERTIN, MONTCALM, GLOIRE, DUGUAY-TROUIN; and the destroyers LE MALIN, LA FORTUNE, BASQUE.

[2] The British carriers—all CVEs—were: KHEDIVE, PURSUER, EMPEROR, SEARCHER, ATTACKER, HUNTER, STALKER. Other British heavy units were battleship RAMILLIES, cruisers ORION, ROYALIST, AURORA, DIDO, ARGONAUT, BLACK PRINCE, SIRIUS. All told some 300 ships of the Royal Navy participated.

sion (the Alps guarded the landings to eastward). Then, when it became apparent that the Germans were not going to attempt any serious stand, the flying sailors had themselves a field day shooting up the fleeing Wehrmacht. One squadron from the TULAGI alone turned in a record of 487 motor vehicles destroyed, from staff cars to tanks, and damaged 114 more. Other squadrons found fat targets in railroad trains jammed with men and material scurrying pell-mell northward. So effectively did the Navy fliers operate in front of the Army that Brigadier General Saville wrote to Vice-Admiral Hewitt:

"I would like to express my appreciation for the outstanding work they have done and for their perfect co-operation. I consider the relationship and co-operation of this force to be a model of perfection and a severe standard for future operations. Today I personally counted 202 destroyed enemy vehicles from four miles west of Saint-Maximin to two miles east of LeDuc. Well done and thanks."

But first the naval air power went in slashing at the beaches just in advance of the first landing waves. Then the rocket ships opened up with their barrage, blackening the landing areas with explosives. Finally, at two minutes past eight on the morning of August 15 (just two minutes late), the first assault craft touched the beaches. Down went the ramps and the troops rushed ashore.

The first wave made it unopposed—well, so it had at Salerno. Then the second; still almost no enemy fire. A machine gun stuttered here and there and there was sporadic shooting from small arms, but nothing serious.

Then the third wave hit the beach—it was the third and subsequent waves that caught it at Salerno. No fire—even the machine-gunning was slacking off as the troops of the first two waves wiped out the nests. And on and on the invasion rolled. Offshore the waters were relatively free of mines and so were the sands of the beaches, so were the roads inland. The onrushing troops passed strong point after strong point, batteries of 88s and 105s, well concealed—but unmanned; heavier caliber guns strongly casemated—but unmanned. So it went all day long. Whether the attack had been a secret well kept or an open secret did not seem to matter. No enemy met the boats and troops where they would be most vulnerable—on the beaches.

Actually, it is possible that tactical surprise was achieved. Herr Goebbels's propaganda merchants, who had been prompt to announce the invasion of Normandy, were over ten hours late getting out the news of the attack on Southern France. And even when they did release their stories, they appeared confused as to just where and in what strength the assault had been made.

There was one hitch in the orderly shoreward parade: over on the eastern flank of the invasion near the little town of Saint-Raphael one of Rear Admiral Lewis's assault teams, scheduled to go ashore at two in the afternoon, in a little cove known for operational purposes as Red Beach, met intense fire as they neared the beach. It was actually a "wall of fire," so often described, so seldom seen. The first wave was turned back. Rear Admiral Lewis ordered another going over of the area by guns of his Fire Support Group. Then the assault waves tried again. Still no chance. So Rear Admiral Lewis, failing in his line buck, ordered an end run; the troops slated to hit Red Beach were simply directed around a little cape to Green Beach, five miles away to eastward, where earlier landings had been effected without serious opposition. This decision was not an easy one. In an amphibious operation naval responsibility is clearly outlined; the Navy must put the Army ashore, where and when the Army has decided. An alteration in that rule may send the whole Army operation completely awry. On the other hand, in the case of Saint Raphael-Red Beach, scheduled landings could have been made only at the cost of extremely heavy casualties. Major General J. E. Dahlquist, commanding general of the troops assaulting that area, had already gone ashore, so the decision rested entirely with Rear Admiral Lewis. He made his choice, and informed Vice-Admiral Hewitt of the change in plan. Vice-Admiral Hewitt approved and signaled permission to go ahead with the altered program. Secretary of the Navy Forrestal and Vice-Admiral Hewitt came aboard the USS BAYFIELD, Admiral Lewis's flagship later that afternoon and were there when a message came from Major General Dahlquist addressed to Rear Admiral Lewis:

"I appreciate your prompt action changing plan when obstacles could not be breached. Expect to take Red Beach tonight, no matter how late. Opposition irritating but not too tough so far."

By the evening of D-day the operation was going so well that objectives scheduled for D-plus-two had already been taken. Some pessimists may have remembered Anzio—everything went very well there, too, at the start. But Southern France was to prove no Anzio. Bombers of the Fifteenth Air Force had effectively isolated the invasion area from reinforcements and supplies; bad news from Northern France had under-mined German morale, and the Luftwaffe had changed from a force of fighting pilots to a crew of buzz-bomb launchers. There was a single flurry of air activity on the evening of D-day. A flight of Dornier bombers with a fighter escort made a pass at the Saint Raphael beachhead, releasing glider bombs, the same radio-controlled bombs which had wreaked such havoc on shipping off Salerno and Anzio. They scored one hit—on LST 282, which was heavily laden with ammunition. His ship in flames, ammu-nition exploding all around him, the skipper, Lieutenant Lawrence E. Gilbert, USNR, still managed to beach the vessel. And then, amid the fire and bursting explosives, although seriously injured himself, Gilbert assisted in the rescue of two wounded men. For all this, Gilbert was awarded the Navy Cross, which was presented to him by Vice-Admiral Hewitt.

The 282 represented the sole Allied ship casualty of D-day. To Vice-Admiral Hewitt and all his invasion-wise subordinates, who had worked and fought the joint naval war in the Mediterranean since its very begin-ning, the easy assault on Southern France must have seemed like a glori-ously happy anticlimax. To the battle-toughened veterans of the army, to whom D-days were becoming an old story, their unhampered progress must have seemed like a pleasant interlude, one with more fighting to follow inevitably, sooner or later.

To one vast segment of the Allied armed might, however, that calm bright August day was epoch-making. This was the French Expeditionary Corps—the first fully equipped French Army, led by French officers once again fighting the detested Boche on the free soil of France. (True, certain French units participated in the Normandy fighting, but they operated with British or American armies under British or American com-mand.) This Expeditionary Force, commanded by fiery General Jean de Lattre de Tassigny, comprised some 300,000 men, the forerunners of a reborn French national army. Landing on the afternoon of D-day and the morning of D-plus-one, the troops leapfrogged across the American and British lines and roared up the road to Toulon and Marseilles. General Sir Henry Maitland Wilson, over-all Allied commander of the Mediter-ranean Area at that time, hailed their advent with a ringing greeting which concluded: "Victory is certain. Remember 1918!" Simultaneously, General de Gaulle's National Committee of Liberation called upon all French Forces of the Interior—whose gallant underground struggle against the Germans had made history for four years—to break out in open revolt. "The last blow is about to be struck!" the Committee declared in a radio broadcast appeal.

Certainly the FFI needed no urging. By their hundreds and thousands, some armed with World War I rifles, others with the latest weapons dropped secretly by Allied planes, they joined their uniformed countrymen and stormed Toulon and Marseilles.

Those two great ports, however, were tough nuts to crack. As in Brest, Lorient and other Channel ports, the German garrisons had been trapped by rapid knifelike thrusts of the swiftly moving American Army. And, once trapped, they made a virtue of necessity by fighting a strenuous defensive operation, prompted to desperation by the common German terror of surrendering to any wrathful people who had experienced German occupation. Toulon, in particular, was well defended, and the Allied fleets were called on to clear their own way into its vital harbor.

Principal defense of the Port of Toulon, once the greatest naval base in France, was the Island of Saint Mandrier, where two turrets, each mounting 340-mm. naval guns in pairs, were situated. These giant rifles had been removed from the PROVENCE, a sister ship of the very LORRAINE which was the first vessel to exchange fire with them. The formidable weapons, with a range of almost 22 miles, were housed in heavy armor plate bedded deep in the rocky sides of the island itself. Beneath them, around them and behind them was a labyrinth of underground passages connecting supporting gun positions, bomb- and shellproof magazines, living quarters complete with their own kitchens, light plants and other facilities. This fortress, constructed by the French, commanded every approach to Toulon and, until it was demolished, not even a battleship could get close enough to the port to engage the other guns on the high ground ringing the city.

The battle with "Big Willie," as all the Saint Mandrier long-range guns were jointly called, began on the 19th, when the French battleship LORRAINE together with the venerable USS NEVADA (Captain Powell N. Rhea, USN) and the American cruisers AUGUSTA (Captain Edward H. Jones, USN) and QUINCY (Captain Elliott M. Senn, USN) steamed past the fortress. The LORRAINE probed at Big Willie without drawing a reply. Encouraged, the QUINCY worked a little closer in and let go. That woke the giant up and evidence of his reply could be seen in the great geysers spouting astern of the cruiser as she slid back into the smoke screen diligently provided by escorting destroyers. She darted out again for a few 'more rounds, then it was the turn of the other ships. One by one they slammed away at the fortress. The engagement was inconclusive. Big Willie had scored no hits, but he was still belching his defiance as the Allied ships steamed away for bombardment operations farther up the coast in immediate support of ground troops.

Almost every day thereafter the guns of Saint Mandrier drew the attention of one or more heavy Allied warships from the bombardment group under Rear Admiral Davidson's command. Occasionally, to vary the program, flights of low-level bombers would make a pass at the fortress.

Eventually the strain began to tell on Big Willie, and he started coming apart at the seams, like a boxer who has been taking too much punishment around the midsection. The round most damaging to Big Willie was fought on August 23, when for six and a half hours he slugged it out with a bombardment force headed by the NEVADA. All told, the American battleship fired some 354 salvos, each shot flinging almost a ton of steel and explosive at the shore installation. Next day, the cruisers HMS AURORA and USS QUINCY took their turn at bat, and, the day after, on August 25, Toulon fell. But the fort at Saint-Mandrier held out three days more. Big Willie's last shot was fired at the LORRAINE.

Not until three weeks later was the harbor of Toulon ready to receive shipping. First all the ghastly garbage of war had to be removed—the wreckage and the mines, ashore and in the harbor waters, to be cleaned up. Commander Thomas L. Davey (CEC), USN, and Commander Harvey Anderson, USN, deputy miracle workers for Commodore Sullivan in salvage and restoration work, were rushed to the harbor with their teams of experts, and set to work at once getting the place in shape to handle ships.

On land, with support from the big guns at sea, the fighting had swept swiftly westward until Marseilles, second city of France and her first seaport, was surrounded. This city offered far less in the way of natural opportunities for defense, but it, too, was guarded by island forts: Ratoneau, Pomègue and Château d'If (the famous prison fortress built in 1524 where Edmond Dantes was imprisoned before he escaped to become the Count of Monte Cristo in Dumas's novel).

As at Cherbourg and Toulon, Marseilles was taken by ground fighting in which naval artillery assisted. When, on August 29, the city garrison surrendered to the French troops, the troops on the island forts offered to surrender—but not to the French. The Nazis were terrified at becoming the prisoners of those they had so long enslaved. Accordingly, to get the fighting over with and the port in operation as soon as possible, Rear Admiral Davidson authorized Captain Walter Ansel, USN, commanding officer of USS PHILADELPHIA, to accept the surrender of the islands.

Marine detachments from PHILADELPHIA and AUGUSTA were dispatched to the islands to read and enforce the terms of capitulation and to guard the prisoners, some 750 dejected, apprehensive Nazis.

This "action" by the Marines was not their first in the battles for the Atlantic and Mediterranean. The 1st Provisional Brigade had served in defense of Iceland from the autumn of 1941 until the spring of 1942. Marines took over the defense of all the Lend-Lease bases we acquired from Great Britain, until the Army could relieve them—in some such places they are still serving as guards for naval installations. When the United States first established bases in Scotland and North Ireland, Marines were sent to guard them. And it was from the battalion stationed at Londonderry, where Colonel Lucian W. Burnham, USMC, was commanding officer, that the small detachment of Marines under command of Major Louis C. Plain, USMC, was sent to participate in the North African landings. Six of these men were assigned to HMS HARTLAND on her daring mission of crashing the boom at Oran harbor, while the remainder, after landing at Arzeu, proceeded overland and captured the principal harbor fort at Mers-el-Kebir. During the assault on Normandy, too, Marines had played a part, manning lookouts, armed with rifles (in the ancient Marine manner), to detect and shoot up floating mines.

With the capture and occupation of the islands of Marseilles by the Marines, the large-scale naval war in the Mediterranean came to a close. There remained, of course, the dirty, mean—and dangerous—chores: patrol and shore bombardment activities along the north coast of Italy, carried out by destroyers of the United States Navy to make the Germans unhappy. There were the antimine and antisubmarine patrols by the lighter-than-air ships of Blimpron 14,[1] which had flown six blimps across the Atlantic early in the summer of 1944. These airships, which had a long and worthy history with the Atlantic Patrol, were first based at Port

---

[1] The following ships composed Blimp Squadron 14—K-101, K-109, K-112, K-123, K-130, K-134.

Lyautey, after an historic ocean crossing under their own power, and did yeoman service on antisubmarine patrol in the Gibraltar approach areas under the command of Commander E. J. Sullivan, USN.

As soon as the Cuers-Pierrefeu airdrome near Toulon (built just after World War I by the French as a lighter-than-air base) was captured and cleared of land mines, two blimps were dispatched there to act as antimine scouts. And in performance of that duty they proved themselves invaluable, hovering over minefields and guiding the sweepers until every lethal underwater explosive was cleared away.

With the seas swept clear of mines, with German waterborne traffic at a standstill, with Allied destroyers making the entire Ligurian coast a hot spot for von Kesselring, it appeared that so far as the Navy's war in the Mediterranean was concerned it was all over but the shouting.

The shouting came with the return of the French Fleet to Toulon, September 13, and culminated in a gala celebration and parade through a city gone wild on September 16. The French sailors, of course, were the heroes of the occasion as they swept through streets lined with cheering throngs, gay as only the resilient Frenchmen of Provence can be. But there were cheers, too, for the British Marines from the cruiser HMS sirius and for "les Américains," the Marines from USS philadelphia.

Toulon was given over to the holiday. The important guests, Admiral Sir John Cunningham, RN, Commander in Chief Allied Naval Forces, Mediterranean, Vice-Admiral Henry K. Hewitt, Commander United States Eighth Fleet, leader of every invasion that had made possible such celebration in Toulon, were suitably feted. But, understandably enough, the loudest cheering was for the French sailors, led by gallant Admiral André Le Monnier, Naval Chief of Staff of the French General Staff. For them it was a homecoming, and after four years there was not a man there, French, British or American, who begrudged them their welcome home.

And home, for all the Navy across the Atlantic, was becoming more and more an immediate prospect. Deep in his heart every sailor, each in his own terms, was singing the searching song "Going Home." For most of the naval personnel this theme rang true. For others, however, another spiritual came nearer the mark: "There's One More River to Cross."

The Allied armies were racing toward the Rhine. The Navy had to be there to help them across when the time came.

PART EIGHT

The Crossing of The Rhine

Chapter Forty-seven

NOW three great fissures had been blasted in Hitler's Fortress Europe by the fleets of the United States and Great Britain, and through them poured the seaborne armies of the United Nations.

The Battle of the Atlantic was won. The Battle of Europe was being won.

It seemed, even in the Navy Department in Washington and the Admiralty in London, that the fleets had accomplished their mission in the war against Hitler. They had beaten his submarines; they had battered down the sea walls of his continent and put their armies ashore, and now there remained only the humdrum labor of maintaining unending delivery of more troops, more munitions, to the portals of battle.

Meanwhile, there was Japan. Britain began polishing her battle-grimed warships for the war in the Pacific, where the bulk of United States naval power had been concentrated as it was amassed, and had, by itself, driven the Japanese off the ocean to hide behind the farthermost islands.

There were still submarines to be hunted in the Atlantic, and all convoys had to be guarded against the U-boats that snapped like vicious curs at the fringes of the great herds of ships, occasionally dragging down a solitary straggler. But, so far as the war in Europe was a concern to the American bluejacket, he chanted happily the old preinvasion war cry, "It won't be long now."

But—a big "but"—the was one more river to cross, one more battle to win. From the Army of the United States, preparing for the final overwhelming assault on the Nazi Fatherland, came an appeal to the United States Navy.

The mighty Rhine, sacred to the Germans since Caesar's day, stood in the Army's way.

"Fest steht und treu die Wacht am Rhein." Would the Navy bear a hand in blasting it loose? Would it!

The call came in October, 1944. The Rhine was still a long way ahead of the Army, but General Eisenhower knew where he was going, and pretty close to when he would get there. The Reich itself was still intact, save for the loss of Aachen to the Americans and a few nibbles which the Soviet forces had chewed into East Prussia.

Vice-Admiral Alan G. Kirk, USN, commander of United States naval forces in France (COMNAVFORFRANCE), who led the amphibious assault on Normandy, was given general command of the Navy's strangest assignment.

The craft chosen for the Navy's use in the heart of Europe were LCVPs and some LCMs. The Army was familiar with both. They were "the damn little water bugs" that had landed the Army wherever it went to fight in Africa or Europe.

From the official summary it is learned that "Numerous tests of equipment under varying climatic conditions were made, while technical problems arising from the boats' operation in fresh, rather than salt, water had to be solved. It was necessary, too, to test the capacity of the equipment to perform the tasks required."

The Rhine units were organized and assembled in England; seasoned personnel, veterans of many a landing on hostile shores, were chosen for the Navy's fresh-water expeditionary force. Selected to command the forward units when they went into battle was Commander William J. Whiteside, USN, who had led a group of LSTs with the British task forces at Normandy. He was attached to the staff of the Commanding General, Twelfth Army Group.

Three LCVP units were assembled by November 15, and moved from England to training sites on the Meuse and Moselle rivers in Belgium and France. Two others were organized, one to be kept at Le Havre as a replacement and spare-parts unit, and one in reserve in England. The basic organization of each unit was 13 officers, 205 enlisted men, and 24 LCVPs.

The first thing the small-boat men had to learn was to look and act like soldiers. Lieutenant Loring C. Merwin, USNR, a press relations officer of COMNAVEU assigned to the first unit, writes:

"The sailors worked and lived exactly like soldiers. To camouflage themselves as much as possible, officers and men wore Army field uniforms and helmets, covering or discarding all naval insignia. I am sure it was the hardest part of the training for them to take. The picture of disconsolation is a young Navy petty officer who has worked hard for years to earn his rating badge and then has no opportunity to show it off.

"The boats were more difficult to disguise but even they took on a GI appearance. Blue hulls which proudly wore the USN gave way to olive drab under Army sprayguns. They were brought to their training sites as unobtrusively as possible, moving mostly at night. Where possible they came by water, through the North Sea and down through the waterways of Belgium and France. Those with the Third Army came all the way by land from Le Havre, a journey of 300 miles. They arrived festooned with treetops, telephone wires and bits of buildings from the French villages through which they had passed like not-too-silent ghosts in the night."

Training came easy to these veterans, most of whom had yet to reach voting age. The difficulties were with craft designed for salt water now placed in river operations; mud and silt and ice brought complications, and tricky river currents added more.

"Mainly they fought mud," Lieutenant Merwin reports. "Mud which bogged down their cranes and launching equipment, mud which mired their trucks and oozed about their ankles. . . .

"Then came the German break-through. The men prepared to destroy their boats if necessary. The unit with the First Army was moved six times. Men lived wherever they could find a spot to lie down. . . . By the time the Germans were repulsed and our lines formed for the great spring push, this inland Navy was as much a part of the Army as its infantry or its tanks."

But let the skipper of Unit No. 1, Lieutenant Wilton Wenker, USNR, tell his own story:

"We were attached to the 1120th group of the XII Corps, First Army, October 18, 1944. The boats were brought up to this area [Andenne, Belgium] on 40-foot flat bed trailers and dumped on the little secondary road completely covered with camouflage, to be painted olive drab for security reasons.

"Within a week six of the boats were taken down to Cheratte, Belgium, along with 298th Battalion, Combat Engineers to find a successful method, or methods, of launching the craft in a river similar to the Rhine. One week later a second training site was opened at Liége, Belgium, with the 297th Battalion, Combat Engineers.

"The Cheratte base was moved back to Andenne after the experiments for launching had been worked out and three successful methods had been decided upon. The training site at Andenne was used as a combined training site, the boats being used to assist the engineers in the construction of various bridges across the Meuse River.

"This training program went on for six weeks and was stopped only because of the November offensive that the 1st Army was going ahead with. However, this offensive did not go forward and all but six boat crews of the unit were then moved up to Aachen, Germany, until the Andennes break-through. General Collins of the XII Corps released our unit to be taken back 100 miles out of the danger area. The personnel and craft had to be moved hurriedly and were taken to Waremme, Belgium. The six boat crews under Lieutenant (jg) F. B. Eby, USNR, the Executive Officer, at Andenne were at this time in a very dangerous position, with the Germans only 11 miles away."

However, the German tide was again reversed, and with the advancing Army went the Navy. On March 8, Lieutenant Wenker recalls, they reached the Rhine, near Remagen.

Remagen, it will be remembered, was where the First Army came up so suddenly the Germans did not have a chance to blow up the bridge, and so for ten days the Americans had the use of the span—such use as could be made under continuous bombardment.

"While these first U.S. Naval units were being placed in the water," the official summary related, "Army Engineers erected a heavy 1,200-foot pontoon bridge about 100 yards above the boat-launching point. Two-thirds of the river had already been spanned, but the remaining third proved difficult because of the 6-knot current on the east bank of the river."

So the first LCVP in the water took some pontoons in tow and chugged over to the enemy side of the river to enable the engineers to complete their bridge. But the current pushed the pontoon bridge into an arc, and the anchorages became weakened. Two of the LCVPs put their blunt noses against the bulge of the bridge and shoved upstream; when the bridge had been straightened out, the LCVPs just stayed there, pushing six knots' worth south to offset the river's six-knot thrust north. It was funny business to be in, but not boringly so. The Germans did their best with bomb and shell to get the Navy out of there. After two days the engineers had their bridge buttoned down tight, and the LCVPs went about their calculated business of hauling troops and guns and gasoline across the river.

"The punishment those youngsters took during those first days at Remagen Bridge belongs in the history book," Lieutenant Merwin writes.

But Lieutenant Wenker merely recalls that "besides the assistance given to the engineers in the construction of their bridges, the craft were used to evacuate casualties and to carry personnel across. We took the personnel of the 1st, 2nd and 69th divisions across the river.

"It is interesting to note that some of the boat crews of this unit had taken members of the 1st Division in at Normandy!"

Lieutenant (jg) Eby, who was in such danger of capture at Andenne, has some interesting sidelights on the Navy's chore at the Rhine.

"At the upstream end of the bridgehead our unit ran a patrol during the day and also at night," Lieutenant Eby recalls. "On the night patrol we had one boat whose sole purpose was to drop depth charges at intervals of about two minutes, just to combat swimmers who were attempting to destroy the bridges which had been built by the First Army. We were twice successful in bringing swimmers—so-called human torpedoes—to the surface, and forcing them ashore to the Army custody.

"When the Ludendorff Bridge finally collapsed, after serving its purpose for five or six days, the boats which were downstream of this bridge were used to collect debris and divert it away from the other bridges under construction. This operation saved at least one of the bridges from being carried away or seriously damaged.

"Again, one of the heavy pontoon bridges started to carry away in the swift current, because the anchors were not heavy or strong enough to hold the bridge. Three of our boats went out to the bridge. Putting their bows against the bridge and going at full speed, they were able to hold the bridge in place for eighteen hours until heavier anchors were secured."

Chapter Forty-eight

NAVAL UNIT No. 2, under Lieutenant Commander William Leide, USNR, was attached to General Patton's Third Army, and as might be expected from no more introduction than that, Commander Leide has an interesting yarn to relate:

"The eight officers and LCVP crews ordered to U.S. Naval Unit 2 came from eight different LSTs. A staff with a yeoman, cooks, stewards' mates, and miscellaneous rates, which we laughingly called a house-keeping unit, was also furnished. On November 10, we left the United Kingdom, embarked in an LSD.

"On November 11, we reached Le Havre and set out under our own power for the port where we were to be embarked on heavy pontoon trailers and be taken to our ultimate destination near the headquarters of the Third United States Army. But, upon arriving at Le Havre, an ammunition ship struck a mine and our small boats participated in the rescue work. After three days in Le Havre a U.S. Army liaison officer, representing the Third U.S. Army, arrived to direct us to our destination which was Toul, France.

"On November 15, we reached Toul, France, and tried to get estab-lished on land as quickly as possible. We were ducks in a desert. We had come equipped with everything from pyramidal tents to special cots so that we could compete with the Army on land.

"Our unit became attached to the 1134th Combat Engineers, com-manded by Colonel James Fitch. We were shown a bombed-out cavalry school. I was impressed with the bombing but the Colonel said, 'Don't laugh, this is your new home.' No windows, doors, water or lights were available. The name of the place was the Adolf Hitler Kaserne and one of the sailors immediately renamed it the USS BLOOD AND GUTS.

"In less than a week we had a creditable mess organized and intensive training had been begun since the assault itself was scheduled in December. It was bitter cold and rained continuously. In fact, all weather records for the past hundred years were broken.

"Day and night maneuvers ensued. The river on which we practiced was the Moselle, and as far as the Navy craft were concerned the river itself was no obstacle whatsoever, and the coxswains easily proved themselves quite adept at managing the LCVP in a river. The Moselle at this time, as a result of the heavy rains, was in flood and with a very fast current.

"On Thanksgiving Day the Moselle River had by then reached proportions that were staggering. The river had risen to a point where the craft themselves were actually on a country road. That afternoon, Thanksgiving afternoon, an alarm was sounded that the Navy craft had broken their moorings. An officer and his entire boat division had been placed on day-and-night duty in order to forestall any such events. The river fell rapidly and this officer, Ensign W. H. Klein, USNR, and his enlisted men, in an endeavor to secure the craft, started them down the river and they eventually got away.

"Twenty of the twenty-four craft went over the falls as did Ensign Klein. He did this without a barrel. In fact Ensign Klein as he approached the falls jumped out of his boat but failed to make shore. He was saved by two Frenchmen and by midnight of that night the craft had been retrieved with no damage done except to seven. The river had fallen so fast that seven LCVPs were high and dry in a meadow. It was a strange sight to see cows and goats grazing under the bow of a Navy assault boat.

"Under the auspices of Colonel Fitch every type experiment loading and unloading LCVPs was practiced. Every type gun that would fit an LCVP was loaded on and taken off. The LCVP was fitted as litter-bearing craft, fittings permitting the carrying of 14 casualties at one time. We even went so far as to put on a bulldozer weighing nine and half tons, and although the freeboard was negligible with this tremendous load, the LCVP showed that it could manage this load in a stream. Command cars, jeeps, trailers of every shape and description were loaded on and off our craft in a series of interminable practice experiments. Later this stood us in good stead.

"On the 10th of December, we were ordered to Nancy, then the headquarters of the United States Third Army, for a briefing on the actual assault. Places were selected on the Rhine and the assault was to be on a two-corps front similar to Omaha Beach. Therefore, my executive officer and I divided the unit into two parts and we practiced alternate assaults with one half of U.S. Naval Unit 2 serving as one complete self-sufficient unit.

"On December 17, a fellow by the name of von Rundstedt upset all our plans. The United States Third Army left the Saar, evacuated Dillingen and turned practically northwest to hammer at von Rundstedt's flank in the famous bulge. Our practice sessions ceased. Thought was given to the safety of our boats and instead of practicing assaults we practiced demolition. Thermite grenades were obtained and in the event of a breakthrough it was decided to destroy the boats and attempt to make a getaway ourselves.

"Early in January 15 LCMs arrived to swell our unit. We were then about 250 strong in enlisted men and had a total of 18 officers. This included a small Seabee detachment of six enlisted men and one officer whose job was to instruct the Army in the assembly of NL pontoons. The NL pontoons were to be used in carrying pile-driving equipment so that permanent bridges could be installed when, as and if the assault took place.

"In early March Lieutenant General Patton's forces broke through northwest of Koblenz and we were alerted. Someone decided that Lieutenant General Patton was not to cross the Rhine at this time, so the alert was off. This was not particularly good for our morale. After five months with the Army we were ready for some naval activity. The men had done everything from loading barbed wire on railroad trains to painting over 15,000 directional signs.

"A couple of weeks later, at Third Army headquarters at Luxembourg, I was informed by Brigadier General Conklin, head of the Engineers, that we were alerted. He told me that the unit was to be loaded and leave the following afternoon through a blazing Germany which had not yet been mopped up. I was informed that the road through which we were to pass was still in German hands but would be captured by the following morning.

"On the 21st of March we were under way for Worrstadt, which was some 20 miles from Oppenheim, Germany, where the Third U.S. Army was all set for the assault. My executive officer and I reached the offices of XII Corps and were informed that a reconnaissance of the Rhine River had yet to be made. Lieutenant (jg) D. L. Spaulding, USNR, and I then played cops and robbers on the river front selecting embarkation and debarkation points. We were then briefed and introduced to the Commanding General of the 5th United States Infantry Division. This famous division was charged with the mission of establishing and securing a bridgehead. Imagine our consternation when we were told that the jump-off time was 2200 the same night. Our boats were still en route.

" 'Far Shore' was established at 1305 with Lieutenant (jg) H. S. Szalach, USNR, as the far shore control officer. Ensign O. Miller, USNR, was the near shore control officer and farther downstream, Ensign R. D. Carter, USNR, took his post. Lieutenant (jg) Spaulding, my executive officer, crossed the river and directed these operations. As soon as the preponderance of the boats were launched and dawn was breaking we were heavily shelled by enemy artillery. The shelling was inaccurate and did no damage.

"The launching of the boats was not a signal for intense activity. In fact my executive officer and I had to solicit business from the infantry Joes who were still paddling across the river. By 0700 a full-scale business was under way, contacts had been made with traffic control officers and an endless stream of infantrymen and light combat division vehicles was crossing the river.

"The turn-around was speedier than anticipated. Crews were reduced by one-half and a German hotel requisitioned so the men could be housed. A six-hour on, six-hour off watch was instituted, but the officers stayed on continuously.

"With the advent of daylight we were subjected to more artillery fire which again was very inaccurate. The vaunted German accuracy with the 88-mm. was not in evidence. We were strafed four times during the day and casualties were light. The Germans were merely indulging in nuisance raids and accomplishing nothing as far as slowing down of traffic was concerned.

"Three of the LCVPs were employed in the building of bridges, laying of nets and booms, and one of them pushed what is known as a heavy pontoon ferry bringing across seventy tank destroyers and tanks in less than thirty hours. The number of infantry crossed in forty-eight hours was in excess of 15,000 men. This does not take cognizance of the tremendous loads of prisoners and wounded which the craft were bringing from the far shore.

"At 1700 that evening I was notified that the VIII Corps was to make an assault using our other 12 LCVPs. We were notified that the 15 LCMs left at Toul, France, were en route, their destination unknown. This again changed the plans, since we had anticipated making a crossing with

XX Corps, a crossing with VIII Corps had not been contemplated and was not in our plan.

"Lieutenant (jg) Spaulding and I set out by command car for Simmern, Germany, the headquarters of the VIII Corps, Third United States Army. As we left German planes were overhead and we did a quick abandon ship. I tried to dig a foxhole in asphalt with my bare hands, but was highly unsuccessful; so was the strafing. We reached Simmern at 2230 the same night. The Corps Colonel, named Keller, advised us that the assault would not take place that night. We were grateful. After seventy-two hours on our feet we were completely out. The following morning we were briefed and told that the assault would be on a two-infantry division front, with one taking place at Boppard between two tremendous cliffs, headed up by the 87th Infantry Division, and the next would be at St. Goar in the vicinity of the famed Lorelei (rock) with the 89th Division, again another change.

"Six LCVPs were to be used in each of these assaults and LCMs if they arrived, and they did.

"Our six LCVPs were launched the morning of the 24th and immediately did a full-scale business which exceeded the fondest expectations. The value of the craft proved themselves in the first forty-eight hours. However, it was decided that it was too dangerous to bring the LCMs down these mountain passes and the LCMs stayed on the hillside helping nobody.

"This experience did not help us the following night, since the 89th Infantry made the assault at St. Goar and the only help they had was ten DUKWs furnished by the Army.

"By the afternoon of the 26th, when the St. Goar bridgehead was not very successful, the orders were given to bring the Navy craft to the water with our LCMs. Before 2 A.M., we were going to town. We transported an entire infantry division and all their attendant vehicles in less than forty-eight hours. The results were spectacular.

"The evening of the 27th of March, scuttlebutt reached us that the decision had been for the XX Corps to make an assault in the vicinity of Mainz, Germany. My executive officer and I were totally unfamiliar with the roads, but again reported to Colonel Keller of the VIII Corps who confirmed this fact: the craft to be used were to be taken from the Oppenheim area and supplemented with six LCMs so that XX Corps could be carried across.

"Sniping and small-arms fire was terrific from the outset. Zero hour was 0100 the morning of the 28th. Lieutenant (jg) Spaulding and I reached Mainz, Germany, one hour before H-hour and were completely unsuccessful in finding the craft. Staying on the riverbanks was too dangerous and we were accomplishing nothing. We dug in with two MPs and waited until dawn. At dawn the craft were found.

"At 0420 artillery fire was quite heavy but had not located the launching site. Coxswain Johnny Farah volunteered to take his boat to the river in order to draw enemy fire. He was quite successful. He then returned to the lagoon and took the first boat of infantrymen across. An island in the middle of the Rhine, which was heavily fortified, had not been neutralized. Small-arms fire was quite heavy. Although some six hundred infantrymen had reached the far shore the bridgehead was not established. In three hours the naval craft transported more than thirty-five hundred men. The spectacular work of the naval craft was again in evidence.

"At roughly 0700 German artillery fire came down heavily while Lieutenant (jg) Spaulding and I were on the far shore. This error in not finding the launching site at once probably saved our lives. This time the German artillery was very accurate. They scored a direct hit on our bulldozer, demolished several of our trucks and Lieutenant (jg) Vincent Avallone, USNR, was killed. Minor shrapnel wounds were incurred by others.

"The work of this section of the unit continued unabated in the regular pattern—six hours on, six hours off, three days of no respite and then practically nothing to do. Bridge maintenance, assisting in the building of bridges, pushing of pontoon ferries, laying nets, patrol, launching of depth charges to force suicide swimmers to the surface, was the familiar pattern engaged in by U.S. Naval Unit 2 after all the assaults.

"We all felt that a good job had been done."

So, evidently, did General Patton, who wrote to Lieutenant Commander Leide this letter:

THE HEADQUARTERS THIRD UNITED STATES ARMY
Office of the Commanding General
23 April 1945

Subject: Commendation.
To: Commanding Officer, U.S. Naval Unit Number Two.
    1. Please accept for yourself and pass on to the officers and men of your command the sincere appreciation and admiration of all

the elements of The Third U.S. Army for the superior work accomplished by your unit in Third Army assault crossings of the Rhine River.

2. During the period from 19 March to 31 March, 1945, U.S. Naval Unit Number Two assisted in four assault crossings of the Rhine River by Third Army. The first crossing was made on 22 March, 1945 by the XII Corps at Oppenheim, where craft of Naval Unit Number Two in the first 72-hour period transported over 15,000 troops and over 1200 vehicles. The second crossing by the VIII Corps at Boppard was made 24 March 1945, and here during the first 24-hour period Naval Unit Number Two transported approximately 5000 men and 200 vehicles. The third crossing was made at Oberwesel on 26 March, 1945, where very nearly an entire division with its supporting vehicles was crossed in 48 hours. The fourth crossing was made by the XX Corps at Mainz on 28 March 1945, and here in the first three hours, Naval Unit Number Two transported 3,500 men to the far shore in spite of intensive artillery fire. Each and every officer and man of U. S. Naval Unit Number Two is hereby commended for the superior manner in which his task was performed.

Signed G. S. Patton, Jr.,
General, U.S. Army,
Commanding.

Chapter Forty-nine

THE third unit, under Lieutenant Commander W. T. Patrick, USNR, assisted Lieutenant General William H. Simpson's Ninth Army to cross the Rhine, very nearly simultaneously with the Third Army's crossing. Unit No. 3 had the toughest going; it suffered the most casualties —thirteen out of the fifteen total—but it helped smash the gateway of the Ruhr.

As reported by Lieutenant Merwin:

WITH UNITED STATES NAVAL FORCES ON THE RHINE.—(March 26, Delayed.)—This is being written in a tiny village near Duisburg, Germany. The Ninth United States Army crossed the Rhine here yesterday morning, assisted by the American Navy.

I said that I was confident that this would be the last naval D-day before the collapse of Hitler's armies. Even Army D-days, I believe, are numbered now. Not that I think there will be immediate surrender— I saw too much in Brittany last summer of the kind of fighting the German army can do against hopeless odds—but I am confident that with the Ruhr in Allied hands and Silesia in those of Russia, the Nazi means of making war will soon be gone. For the first time I am willing to think of the end of the European war in terms of weeks rather than many months.

The crossing of Lieutenant General William H. Simpson's forces here yesterday was the real power play among Allied breachings of the Rhine. For this is the critical and most heavily fortified point of the river defenses. It is the gateway which leads up the broad valley of the Ruhr to the heart of the industrial Reich. Our high command has known that it must eventually strike here and Hitler has known it too. Both sides have been girding their loins for many weeks.

The attack was co-ordinated with the British thrust downriver to the north and with airborne landings to the northeast. It was carried out by more soldiers, both infantry and armor, than have ever before been assembled behind a narrow front. They were supported by the heaviest concentration of artillery yet brought to bear on such a target.

Lieutenant General Simpson felt confident that his artillery could soften up the far bank efficiently for his assault troops to get ashore. At that point the critical stage of the crossing would come. These troops must be supplied with the reinforcements and weapons to fight their way quickly inland while the enemy was still off balance. Three-fifths of the secret of success in modern war is the ability to "build up" powerfully and rapidly.

That is where the Navy was to come in. Our small-boat men in their husky landing craft were to rush tanks, guns and ammunition across—and more soldiers to reinforce the flying wedge. They were to fill that all important time gap before heavy ferries could be put into operation and temporary bridges erected.

H-hour was set for three o'clock in the morning of March 24 and the artillery barrage was to commence at two. About eight o'clock in the previous evening our boats were ordered to move up from the woods in which they had been hidden to points close to their launching sites at the west edge of the river.

There was a complete blackout of the assault area but a half moon in a cloudless sky was enough to light up the endless lines of men and vehicles making their way through every back road and lane to the points of rendezvous. It etched out the immense silhouettes of the boats as they rocked along at treetop levels on their huge carriers.

Since we had hours to wait, some of the crews tried to sleep on the open decks of their boats. At least they rolled up in their blankets and closed their eyes. To my amazement, I saw one boy carefully wind a small alarm clock and place it on the deck beside him. It was set for 2 A.M.

If that alarm clock ever went off I am sure nobody heard it. For precisely at 2 A.M. every gun of that mighty array behind us began to fire. We knew that we were in front of the artillery but we didn't know that the guns were going to fire directly through our ears—for so it seemed. Their blasts made the thick steel boat hulls shiver and dance like tuning forks and we had the feeling that our nerve endings were dancing with them.

German batteries held their fire until well after the barrage began, attempting to locate our guns by their muzzle flash. Then the Nazi shells started coming in, probing for the source of our salvos.

The German guns found few of ours and that terrific barrage had its calculated effect. At three o'clock the first assault troops started going over and found a shoreline so softened that some battalions did not lose a single man. Half an hour later the Navy boats were in the water and a steady stream of tanks, mobile guns and reinforcement troops was on its way into the bridgehead.

At daylight the real opposition on the beach area began. With the river in clear sight, the Germans hammered it with every gun and mortar at their command in a desperate effort to stop the traffic flowing across. But they couldn't stop it and only a few of our boats were hit. Battle-wise coxswains who had learned how to avoid enemy fire by twisting and swinging their craft in ocean surf, were equally nimble here. Their skill —and the luck which skill always brings—carried them through.

Today there is no more doubt. The bridgehead is assured. Spearheads are two miles inland and enough reinforcements are across so that they can no longer hope to push us back. This greatest breaching of the Rhine has been accomplished.

Ten hours later Lieutenant Commander Patrick and his equally exhausted and grimy executive officer, Lieutenant R. S. Kennedy, USNR, thought there was nothing on earth that could ever excite them again.

And then up came Lieutenant General Simpson with General Omar Bradley, and Field Marshal Sir Alan Brooke and Field Marshal Sir Bernard Montgomery, himself, with a man who looked enough like Prime Minister Churchill to be "Winny" himself. And so it was, with the stink of battle still in the air and the noise of it plain in one's ears.

Mr. Churchill wanted to cross the river in a United States naval craft. And across he went, with his whole party; across the Rhine. It must have been a moment of triumph, an experience of great exaltation, to the Prime Minister.

"What did he say?" the coxswain, 19-year-old Hyman Bloom of Brooklyn, New York, was asked, after the party had debarked and left.

"Hell, sir," said Hyman, "he didn't say anything in particular. He just took that big black cigar out of his mouth and spit in the Rhine."

THE END

Appendix A

TRAINING PROGRAM OF NAVY

FOR many years the supply of naval officers and enlisted men of the "Regular Navy" had been augmented by the Naval Reserve, men whose interest in the sea and in the national defense took the practical expression of study, drill and short cruises. In 1926 units of the Naval Reserve Officers Training Corps were established at six universities, for the purpose of providing for the Navy basically well-educated, partly trained young naval and Marine Corps reserve officers, as an emergency pool of leadership for an expanded Navy. In 1938 two more units were established, and one in 1939. In 1940 and 1941, with war on all sides, the number was tripled by addition of eighteen more NROTC university units, enrolling in all 7,200 students.

Upon the presidential announcement of national emergency, these young reserve officers were ordered to active duty as billets opened for them in the fleet and ashore. At the war's end hundreds of them commanded their own ships; in fact, the majority of commands afloat were men who sign "USNR" to their names.

When the United States became a belligerent, it was quickly apparent that the dearth of junior officers would have to be solved by means much quicker than four years at the Naval Academy or an ROTC course could provide.

Referring to Fleet Admiral King's report of March, 1944, one sees how the situation was met:

"In February, 1942, therefore, offices of Naval Officer Procurement were established in key cities throughout the country. Hundreds of thousands of officer candidates went to these offices and there presented their qualifications. With the requirements of health, character, personality and education duly considered, the applications of those who appeared qualified were forwarded to the Navy Department for final consideration.

Under this procedure some 72,000 officers were commissioned in the Navy directly from civilian life, to meet immediate needs.

Meanwhile, educational programs designed to produce commissioned officers had been established in numerous colleges throughout the country. Included were the aviation cadet program (V-5) principally for physically qualified high school graduates and college students, and later the Navy college program (V-12) which absorbed undergraduate students of the accredited college program (V-1, the naval ROTC) and of the reserve midshipman program (V-7)." At the time of the report there were 66,815 members of the V-12 program in some 241 different colleges.

Another fertile source of high-grade officer personnel was the body of enlisted men. In 1943 alone over twenty thousand men left the ranks to put on the officers' gold braid, and figures for our other war years correspond.

While the Navy was drawing on its enlisted personnel for officers, it had also the problem of increasing that same enlisted personnel rapidly and logically. The news of the attack on Pearl Harbor was all the recruiting poster the Navy needed for a while; December and January saw enlistments hit forty thousand a month. Then, as might be expected, the spate slackened, and the Navy had to go to the recruits instead of waiting for them to come to it. A field recruiting force was organized and, by the fall of 1942, each month saw a total enrollment equivalent to the Navy's peacetime strength, not including the women of the Naval Reserve whose admission to the Navy was authorized by Congress in July.

But even this was not enough. On December 5 the Navy announced that, as of February 1, 1943, it would take men through the Selective Service System.[1] This was a break with a tradition as old as the Navy; a proud, honest boast that every man in blue was a volunteer. Only overwhelming need prompted the change. It was a change, incidentally, that meant a slight lowering in the physical standards for acceptance into the Navy since both Army and Navy had to draw from the same manpower pools on the same basis.

Once in the Navy, officers and men alike had to be trained. Here, again, the report of the Commander in Chief United States Fleet is particularly enlightening:

[1] The total number of personnel inducted into the Navy through Selective Service up to March 1, 1945, was 1,432,339, out of a total enrollment of 3,269,670. The average monthly input by induction for 1943–1944 was 20,983; by vountary enlistment, 57,299.

"When we entered the war we experienced a dilution in trained men in new ships because of the urgency of keeping trained men where fighting was in progress, and initial delays in getting under way with the huge expansion and training program had to be accepted. As the war progressed, and as the enemy offensive was checked, we were able to assign larger numbers of our trained men to train other men. Our ability to expand and train during active operations reflects the soundness of our peacetime training and organization. With that as a foundation on which to build and with the tempo of all training stepped up [The course at the Naval Academy was cut a whole year, while the standard six to eight months' preliminary, or "boot," schooling for enlisted men was hacked to three and sometimes two months. Ed.] adequate facilities, standardized curricula, proper channeling of aptitude, full use of previous related knowledge, lucid instructions and top physical condition became criteria for wartime training.

"Generally speaking, the first stage in the training of any new member of the Navy is to teach him what every member of the Navy must know, such as his relationship with others, the wearing of the uniform, the customs of the service, and how to take care of himself on board ship. The second stage involves his being taught a specialty and being thoroughly grounded in the fundamentals of that specialty. The third stage is to fit him into the organization and teach him to use his ability to the best advantage."

For officers, except for two groups, the first stage was taken care of by the V-12 program coupled with the Naval Reserve Midshipman Program, V-7.

This training worked out in three main ways for officers. The V-12 program, which, in effect, took selected young men direct from high school or from the ranks of enlisted personnel, gave them in concentrated form a general college background coupled with naval indoctrination. This was followed by specialized training, and, when the whole course was completed (usually a matter of six semesters), the man was commissioned. The second type of training was the V-7 program whereby college graduates—or men about to complete their college training—were accepted by the Navy as apprentice seamen, sent to one of the six reserve midshipman schools—Columbia University, Notre Dame, Northwestern, the Naval Academy, Cornell, Plattsburg—where they served a month as seamen and then were appointed midshipmen. As midshipmen they received three months' naval indoctrination and were then granted commissions as ensigns, following which they were either sent direct to the Fleet or to one of the numerous special advanced schools for their final training. The third type of training was the two-month naval indoctrination course for officers commissioned directly from civilian life. Here, again, the officers were assigned to specialized training following their indoctrination, except in cases where their Navy assignments paralleled their peacetime occupation.

The advanced training took two forms. There were schools, for example, like the Communications School at Harvard, where the course consisted of six months' intensive classroom work. And then there were the training bases like the MTBSTC (Motor Torpedo Boat Squadron Training Center) at Melville, Rhode Island, the ATBs (Amphibious Training Bases) along the Chesapeake and at Fort Pierce, Florida, where theoretical and practical schooling went hand in hand.

Training of enlisted men followed the same general pattern—an overall indoctrination in one of the regular training stations: Newport, Rhode Island; Norfolk, Virginia; Great Lakes, Illinois; San Diego, California, and, later, Bainbridge, Maryland; Sampson, New York; and Farragut, Idaho. Following basic training at these "boot camps" sailors were assigned to other schools or advanced training bases as their abilities and interests and the needs of the Navy dictated.

And, of course, officers and men alike were taken from the Fleet and sent to special service schools if they showed special talents the Navy could use.

The Naval Aviation Training program was the same in essence except that specialization began as soon as a cadet entered the service and was assigned to one of the preflight schools. In general, too, the aviation training period was longer and more intensive since the candidates had to be fully trained before they took to the air in operations.

Another exception to the regular course of Navy training was made in the case of what has become one of the Navy's most famous groups, the Seabees.

It was apparent as soon as war started that the Navy was going to have to do a lot of base building and other construction work in combat zones. It was also apparent that this work could not be done, as it had been, by civilian personnel. Accordingly, in January of 1942 the Navy began to recruit civilian personnel qualified in all aspects of construction work, from riggers to divers, into Construction Battalions under command of Rear Admiral Ben Moreell, USN, Chief of the Bureau of Yards and Docks. Rates and commissions were assigned on the basis of civilian experience, and age and physical standards maintained throughout the rest of the Navy were relaxed for the Seabees, so great was the need for their services.

Originally the plan had been to form twelve companies of 226 men each to do the Navy's construction work—2,712 men. Today there are in the neighborhood of 240,000 Seabees in the Navy.

At first the construction men received a brisk and brief indoctrination in Navy ways at seven National Youth Administration work centers in the East. Later the great CB centers at Camp Peary, near Williamsburg, Virginia, and at Port Hueneme in California were established as the flourishing training centers of all the Seabees.

Even with this extensive training program, the United States Navy faced acute personnel needs to man a tremendously expanding fleet. Too many officers and men were tied to shore jobs—and shore establishments would naturally be greater in number and larger in size to support the largest Navy in United States history.

To supplement manpower, the Navy called for womanpower to take over administrative and desk work, offering the same rank, rates and pay scale as given men in the service. On July 30, 1942, the Women's Reserve of the United States Naval Reserve was created by law. Mildred H. McAfee, president of Wellesley College, was made Director of the WAVES and the first woman lieutenant commander in the Navy.

By November 23 of the same year, President Roosevelt had signed a similar bill creating the Coast Guard Women's Reserve. Shortly afterward, on February 13, 1943, the Women's Reserve of the Marine Corps came into being.

Dorothy C. Stratton, then a lieutenant in the WAVES, and in civilian life Dean of Women and Professor of Psychology at Purdue University, became director and ranking officer (lieutenant commander) for the Coast Guard "SPARS."

Ruth C. Streeter, a woman active in civic and welfare work in New Jersey and a flier holding a commercial pilot's license, was made a major and director of the Women Marines.

All three women's services were designed to release men for combat duty by taking over noncombatant, shore-based jobs.

By 1945, the total number of women in the Navy, Coast Guard and Marines had reached 112,000—with approximately 83,000 WAVES, 19,000 Women Marines and 10,000 SPARS. Official listings of their respective Directors were: Captain Mildred H. McAfee, USNR; Captain Dorothy C. Stratton, USCGR; and Colonel Ruth C. Streeter, USMCR.

Lieutenant Rhoda L. Luray, USNR, contributes the following detailed account of the training and work of women in all branches of the Navy:

A traditional "FOR MEN ONLY" sign hung over the door of every United States Naval Recruiting Office for years. Had an American woman dared disregard that unseen barrier to announce, "I want to enlist," a Navy man probably would have shouted for a strait jacket. Or politely ushered her out the door, muttering to himself that "women are always bad luck aboard a ship."

But, by the spring of 1942, wartime manpower needs focused observing eyes on the work of women in Allied navies. Several of our naval officers, during visits to the British Isles, were well impressed with the fine record of the Women's Reserve of the Royal Navy. If Englishwomen could accept military responsibility successfully, why couldn't the women of the United States?

No one person in our Navy, however, is credited with asking that question. Perhaps many did. As Vice-Admiral Randall Jacobs, USN, Chief of Naval Personnel, admitted, years afterward: "Some of us favored this revolutionary move, some of us did not. There were a number of traditionalists whose enthusiasm was kept well under control."

Human nature being what it is, today many a Navy man is eager to claim he was the first to speak up and say: "Look here—we need more trained men to man all these ships we're building. If we enlist women for shore-based work, the men tied to desks will be available for combat duty."

Whoever made that initial suggestion, Vice-Admiral Jacobs approved. The Bureau of Naval Personnel undertook a preliminary survey to determine how many billets in various continental commands could be taken over by women.

An Advisory Committee, composed of twenty or thirty representatives from colleges throughout the nation, met at the request of the Secretary of the Navy. An Advisory Educational Council evolved later, with eight nationally known women planning possible training for women in the

Navy. Mildred H. McAfee, president of Wellesley College, was a member-at-large on that Council.

In the summer of 1942, Congressional halls reverberated with heated pro and con arguments concerning the bill authorizing the formation of a Women's Reserve, United States Naval Reserve. Estimated goal was 1,000 officers and 10,000 enlisted women to volunteer to serve the "duration and six months."

The 11,000 Yeomanettes of World War I provided some precedent for this bill. In 1917 the Navy's shortage of clerical help inspired investigation of the regulations governing the enlistment of yeomen. Josephus Daniels, then Secretary of the Navy, is quoted as asking: "Is there any law that says a yeoman must be a *man*?" It was found that the law did not specifically state any such thing—but heretofore only men had been enlisted.

Through this loophole in the law, the Navy promptly recruited women in the Naval Coast Defense Reserve. They were classified as Yeomen (F) and served as enlisted women only. In addition to performing purely clerical duties, other Yeomen (F) served as translators, fingerprint experts, draftsmen, camouflage designers and recruiters. Five of them served with Navy hospital units in France. Yeomen (F) were stationed in Guam, Puerto Rico, the Panama Canal Zone and Hawaii, in addition to the continental United States and France. About 300 Marinettes were on duty as enlisted personnel of the Marine Corps.

Some of the daughters of Yeomanettes are WAVES today, and a number of the former Yeomen (F) of the last war have become officers in World War II. Among the latter is Commander Joy Bright Hancock, USNR, who serves in the Navy Department as Assistant for the Women's Reserve in DCNO for Air.

Another ex-yeomanette is now Major Helen O'Neill, USMCR, with the title of Departmental Director, Marine Corps Women's Reserve, with the Department of the Pacific.

The Women's Reserve of World War II, however, were to have unquestioned legal status and were not to be an auxiliary corps. By Congressional law women were in and of the Navy, with the same responsibilities and subject to the same military discipline and regulations. Educational and health requirements were high. Women with children under eighteen were disqualified for enlistment. Navy women were expressly forbidden to serve at sea or outside the continental limits of the United

States. (The continental limitation irked the members of the Women's Reserve not a little. They were destined to remain annoyed for more than two years, before partial removal of this restriction.)

While Congressional action still pended, Mildred H. McAfee was unofficially requested as director. Obtaining a year's leave of absence as president of Wellesley College, she came to Washington as a civilian early in July of 1942. President Roosevelt signed the bill creating the Women's Reserve on July 28, 1942; and on August 3 Miss McAfee was sworn in by Secretary of the Navy Frank Knox—the first woman lieutenant commander in United States Naval history.

The American press blossomed with colorful remarks. Headlines busily thought up names to paste on the Navy women, including: "Ladies-o'-War," "Jill Tars," "Distaff Navy," "Sailorettes," and "Gobs of Gentle Gender." A southern newspaper, tongue in newsprint cheek, suggested that the pacifist song of this war might be: "I didn't raise my girl to be a yeoman, nor even for a Lady Marine . . ." (The latter was prophetic—with Women Marines scheduled to make their debut less than a year later.)

A group of naval officers put their heads together. If the Women's Reserve was to be nicknamed, the Navy itself would decide which nickname. "WAVES" was selected as appropriate, and the words, "Women Accepted for Volunteer Emergency Service" would explain the letters.

On August 28, approximately a hundred women began indoctrination as officers, at the United States Naval Reserve Midshipmen's School (WR) at Northampton, Massachusetts. Captain Herbert W. Underwood, USN (Ret.), was commanding officer.

First official class of future officers arrived at Northampton on October 6, 1942; and a few days later three schools for enlisted women opened. The beginning needs of the Navy determined the type of training: radio communications at Madison, Wisconsin; storekeeper training at Bloomington, Indiana; and yeoman training at Stillwater, Oklahoma.

Officers and enlisted women of the Women's Reserve completed training and reported for active duty in naval shore establishments throughout the country on November 6.

Those who followed these proud pioneer enlistees in the WAVES could not reminisce of days when the only furniture in a training schoolroom was a double-decker bunk—or when Navy men assigned to WAVES schools hid the fact from their friends, and defensively announced at the beginning of each lecture: "I certainly never *asked* for this duty!" But later-day WAVES compensated by pioneering new fields of work for women in the Navy.

The number of WAVES did not stop at 11,000 but was steadily increased to 83,000 in 1944. The officer who, in the early days, greeted a Bureau of Aeronautics request for "22,000 women" as "too fantastic to take seriously" may have laughed at himself when two years later the number of WAVES exceeded the entire personnel strength of the 1916 Navy.

Peak of enlistment and training came in the spring and summer of 1944, with more than a thousand women enlisted every month and fifty-one training schools established—some for WAVES only, others at which women received advanced training along with Navy men. Members of the Women's Reserve were on duty in five hundred shore establishments within the continental United States, including air stations, hospitals, supply depots, naval operating bases, district offices, ammunition depots and navy yards.

Beginning with service in only three ratings, WAVES were eventually requested in 38 ratings, representing approximately 250 different types of work. The number of women holding yeoman and storekeeper ratings remains the largest; but those in the Hospital Corps and holding aviation ratings run second and third in number.

Navy women are now aviation machinists' mates, metalsmiths, aerographers, flight orderlies, parachute riggers, control tower operators and Link Trainer instructors on air stations. They teach gunnery and instrument flying to men gunners and pilots. Women officers serve as Air Navigation instructors, in the Supply Corps, Medical Corps, in Ordnance, Aerology, Air Combat Intelligence, and a variety of other fields. The individual work of WAVES would make a lengthy list. Forty-five different jobs are classified under the general title of "seaman."

Largest concentration of WAVES is in Washington, D.C., where 52 per cent of all naval personnel on duty in the Navy Department are members of the Women's Reserve. The real purpose of enlisting women is being fulfilled. In the first year alone, enough men were replaced and released from shore duty to man a battleship, two large aircraft carriers, two heavy cruisers, four light cruisers and fifteen destroyers.

In the meantime, a Coast Guard Women's Reserve was formed on November 23, 1942. Dorothy C. Stratton, a lieutenant in the WAVES, was selected as ranking officer. Transferring to the Coast Guard, she became a lieutenant commander and director of the new women's service. The name "SPARS" she coined herself, taking the first letters of the Coast Guard's fighting motto with its English translation: "Semper Paratus—Always Ready."

To speed the program for SPARS, a sufficient percentage of WAVES in training at that time volunteered to transfer from the Navy to the Coast Guard. In this way, the SPARS obtained a nucleus who could report for duty simultaneously with the WAVES.

For many months, Coast Guard women continued to receive basic training with the WAVES at the largest boot camp—the U.S. Naval Training School on the uptown campus of Hunter College, the Bronx, New York. Later, all SPAR recruit and specialist training was conducted at the Coast Guard Training Station, Palm Beach, Florida. Today all their training centers in Manhattan Beach, Brooklyn, New York.

Requirements for enlistment, duties and regulations for SPARS are similar to those for WAVES. Uniforms are also the same, with the exception of the Coast Guard shield replacing WAVES insignia on collar and sleeve, and Coast Guard lettering on the hat.

Establishment of the Marine Corps Women's Reserve on February 13, 1943, ended the rash of official nicknames. The Commandant's decision was clear: "These women will be Marines, doing the work of Marines. I can think of no coined word that means more." The women in "forestry green," therefore, were known simply as "Women Marines." Major Ruth C. Streeter became director.

Until the summer of 1943, Women Marines also were trained with WAVES, at the officers' school at Mt. Holyoke (near Northampton), and at the enlisted school at Hunter. In June, all training was shifted to Camp LeJeune, North Carolina—both Marine boot camp and the Officer Candidate School.

Fifty per cent of the 19,000 Women Marines went into aviation. They serve on ground crews—going along as mechanics and radiomen on continental flights—and perform clerical work on the air stations. One woman Marine actually became Operations Officer for an air station. An enlisted girl trained as a stevedore. Another woman officer completed a grueling 45-hour combat training course with the men in lifesaving, abandoning ship and handling rafts, and ended up as a combat instructor.

Largest numbers of Women Marines are clerical workers, truck drivers, supply clerks, aircraft assembly and repair workers, and radio operators. Changing tires on bombers, acting as plumbers, painters, sheet-metal workers—and 125 other types of work—they assert with cocky good humor that "the hip pocket of a pair of dungarees is a dandy place to keep a lipstick."

Women of the Navy, Coast Guard and Marine Corps are a familiar sight throughout the nation. Public interest has necessitated thorough explanation of work performed by women in taking over men's jobs. As a result, the average American is increasingly familiar with the Navy's shore establishments—the eight-ninths of the iceberg that usually doesn't show.

Many changes have taken place in the Women's Reserve program since its inception. Women in service may now marry at the completion of recruit training or indoctrination period, without restrictions as to difference in rank, rating or military service of the men. Women are promoted in rank or advanced in rating on the same basis as men, and receive the same benefits and allowances (with the exception that husbands of enlisted women may not be considered "dependents"). Negro women were admitted in December, 1944, and are on duty as officers, seamen and hospital corpsmen.

An Act of Congress of September 27, 1944, permits women in the Navy to serve in the American area and the Territories of Hawaii and Alaska on a volunteer basis. By midsummer of 1945, estimated strength of the WAVES in Hawaii was 3,000; Women Marines, 1,250; SPARS, 200—with 300 SPARS in Alaska.

Navy women received an enthusiastic welcome overseas. A station newspaper went all out, commenting: "It was truly an event in Navy history for the Hawaiian Islands, when the WAVES stepped down the gangway and landed in Oahu. Their record of work well done and spirit of service will make us proud." Rumor had it that the Seabees voluntarily worked late into the night for weeks to have the WAVES Quonset hut quarters in complete readiness. The job was finished far in advance of their actual arrival.

Surveying the Hawaiian area prior to shipping a unit of Navy women overseas, a group of women officers were amused and flattered to see a wishful sign: "To WAVES Quarters—We Hope!"

On May 15, 1945, recruiting in the WAVES was changed from the replacement policy of many months. Two thousand women a month were

needed—to fill seamen billets in various commands—and to enter the
Hospital Corps. It is estimated that 10,000 additional WAVES are needed
in the Hospital Corps alone, due to the increase in Pacific battle casualties.

But no statement of facts and figures can completely describe the
effect on the American scene of these women in uniform. Certainly, the
grimness of war was somewhat alleviated by the turnabout humor of husbands who bake cookies and send them to wives in naval training schools.

The Navy itself faced new situations with the admission of women.
Ships' service stores and Marine post exchanges now stock bobby pins and
lipstick, as well as shaving cream and razor blades. Naval custom under-
went an abrupt change in one notable instance, in the matter of addressing
enlisted personnel by last name only. The enlisted woman's name was
"Darling!"

Prior to the entrance of women into the ranks, the Navy never found
reason to rule whether or not two members of the same service could
marry each other. When the final ultimatum in April, 1943, was "yes,"
a midwestern station newspaper published a "New Wedding Ceremony
for Bluejackets and WAVES." This facetious ceremonial ended with these
words: "Subject to the latest Bureau of Personnel Bulletin concerning
matrimony, you are now man and wife, by direction of the Commanding
Officer."

Because women in uniform were something new, civilians tended to
regard them at first as an entirely different and strange breed. Women's
barracks often rock with laughter as odd civilian remarks are repeated.
For example: one WAVES officer was shaken by the hand by an obviously frightened gentleman who informed her she was the first WAVE
he'd ever met. He shook his head for several moments, puzzled. Then
announced, obviously believing he was being complimentary: "Why
IT'S human, isn't IT?"

Equally disconcerting are two other common civilian misconceptions.
One, that women in uniform do nothing in the Navy but drill, ad
infinitum. And, two, that every servicewoman is "the great American
heroine, following in the footsteps of her heroic great-grandmother who
'fit the Indians.' "

To the women themselves, it is self-explanatory. They are the same
women who worked as secretaries, schoolteachers, business executives,
newspaper reporters, college girls and fashion models before the war.
They, too, have husbands, fiancés, brothers and friends in the service.
Being somewhat above average in health, the right age and unencum-

bered by dependents, this cross section of American women enlisted when the Navy needed them.

For the majority of Navy women, being in uniform represents a long but necessary hiatus in the ordinary business of living. In this, they are no different than millions of men in the Reserve. Many of them have learned new skills and hope to use them in similar civilian work. Others hope to return to interrupted careers. Large numbers expect to be homemakers as well as workers when the war is over. In preparation for such postwar careers, the SPARS in New York City attend optional homemaking courses in their free evenings. They heartily applaud a group of civilian experts who teach them cooking, sewing, how to budget and run a home.

As veterans and peacetime citizens, it is predicted by some that the servicewoman's firsthand knowledge of service life will influence her, heighten her interest in questions of national and international import.

At present, WAVES, SPARS and Marines will continue to serve in shore establishments here and abroad until demobilization is completed, and their job is done.

Citizens of this country have gradually realized that without these volunteers, 112,000 additional men—older and possibly fathers—would have reported for induction. The least that can be said, therefore, of the Women's Reserve organizations is that these women accepted their responsibility as citizens. In so doing, they live in their own generation, doing what must be done—because this, too, is their time in history.

That, in bare outline, is the story of naval procurement and training. It does less than justice to the magnitude of the task which the Bureau of Naval Personnel, under Vice-Admiral Randall Jacobs, USN, undertook and carried out. It was a complex task, for it involved, as one sees, not only the mere mechanics of getting men and teaching them but also the infinitely more delicate business of selecting the right men, deciding what to teach, how to teach it, when to teach it, in a war where changes were constant and rapid, where training had to be geared to situations that altered as one looked at them. It was a job that called for constant training of the very men entrusted with the training of others; courses of instruction had to be standardized for ease and continuity of instruction; at the same time they had to be susceptible of instant change to meet altered circumstances. And, ultimately, dramatic or not, it was a job that had to be done and done well. If it had not been, there would have been no United States Navy and, perhaps, no United States!

Appendix B

Appendix B

ALPHABETICAL LIST OF UNITED STATES NAVAL VESSELS
ANNOUNCED LOST IN THE ATLANTIC-MEDITERRANEAN
THEATER, DECEMBER 7, 1941–MAY 31, 1945, WITH PERTI-
NENT DETAILS

USCGC ACACIA, Coast Guard cutter
    Was shelled and sunk presumably by an enemy submarine in the
    Caribbean area in March, 1942. She was a small unarmed ship of
    the tender class.

USCGC ALEXANDER HAMILTON, Coast Guard cutter
    Torpedoed by an enemy submarine off Iceland. While being towed
    into port, capsized and had to be sunk by gunfire.

USS BEATTY, DD 640, destroyer
    Sunk as the result of enemy aircraft action in the Mediterranean on
    November 6, 1943.

USCGC BEDLOE, Coast Guard patrol craft
    Sunk at sea in Atlantic hurricane.

USS BLOCK ISLAND, CVE 21, aircraft carrier escort
    Sunk by a German U-boat in the Atlantic, May 29, 1944. She was the
    only United States aircraft carrier lost in the Atlantic.

USS BORIE, DD 215, destroyer
    While engaged in patrol in the Atlantic, encountered a submarine,
    which she sank with depth bombs. Encountering a second submarine
    a short time later, she rammed and sank this enemy vessel also. The
    force of the ramming, however, opened holes in BORIE's hull below the
    waterline. Although BORIE managed to rejoin the task force to which
    she was assigned, the extent of her damage was so great that it was
    necessary for her personnel to abandon ship, after which she was sunk
    by bombs from her own group's planes.

USS BRISTOL, DD 453, destroyer
  Sunk in the Mediterranean on October 13, 1943, as the result of underwater explosion.
USS BUCK, DD 420, destroyer
  Sunk off Salerno on October 9, 1943, as the result of an underwater explosion.
USS CORRY, DD 463, destroyer
  Lost due to enemy action in Allied operations for Europe's liberation.
USS CYTHERA, PY 26, small patrol vessel
  Overdue in Atlantic area since May, 1942, and presumed to be lost.
USS EDWARD RUTLEDGE, AP 52, transport
  Sunk off Casablanca during the early part of November, 1942, as a result of enemy submarine torpedoes during the occupation of North Africa by Allied forces.
USCGC ESCANABA, Coast Guard cutter
  Reported lost while engaged in convoy duty in the North Atlantic.
USS FECHTELER, DE 157, destroyer escort
  Sunk in the Mediterranean during the month of May, 1944, as the result of enemy action.
USS FISKE, DE 143, destroyer escort
  Sunk in the Atlantic by a submarine torpedo.
USS FREDERICK C. DAVIS, DE 136, destroyer escort
  Sunk in the Atlantic by an enemy submarine.
USS GANNET, AVP 8, tug
  Torpedoed and sunk in the Atlantic area.
USS GLENNON, DD 620, destroyer
  Lost due to enemy action in Allied operations for Europe's liberation.
USS HUGH L. SCOTT, AP 43, transport
  Sunk off Casablanca during the early part of November, 1942, as a result of enemy submarine torpedoes during the occupation of North Africa by Allied forces.
USS INGRAHAM, DD 444, destroyer
  Sunk as a result of a collision in a fog in the Atlantic.
USCGC JACKSON, Coast Guard patrol vessel
  Sunk at sea in Atlantic hurricane.
USS JACOB JONES, DD 130, destroyer
  Sunk by an enemy submarine off Cape May, New Jersey, just before dawn on February 28, 1942.

USS JOSEPH HEWES, AP 50, transport

Sunk off Rabat during the early part of November, 1942, as a result of enemy submarine torpedoes during the occupation of North Africa by Allied forces.

USS LANSDALE, DD 426, destroyer

Sunk in the Mediterranean as the result of attack by enemy aircraft on April 20, 1944.

USS LCI(L) 20, landing craft, infantry (large)

Lost as the result of operations in the Mediterranean Theater during the period January 22 to March 31, 1944.

USS LCI(L) 32, landing craft, infantry (large)

Lost as the result of operations in the Mediterranean Theater during the period January 22 to March 31, 1944.

USS LCI(L) 85, landing ship, infantry (large)

Lost as the result of enemy action or the perils of the sea during the Allied operations for the liberation of Northern France.

USS LCI(L) 91, landing craft, infantry (large)

Lost as the result of enemy action or the perils of the sea during the Allied operations for the liberation of Northern France.

USS LCI(L) 92, landing craft, infantry (large)

Lost as the result of enemy action or the perils of the sea during the Allied operations for the liberation of Northern France.

USS LCI(L) 93, landing craft, infantry (large)

Lost as the result of enemy action or the perils of the sea during the Allied operations for the liberation of Northern France.

USS LCI(L) 219, landing craft, infantry (large)

Lost as the result of enemy action or the perils of the sea during the Allied operations for the liberation of Northern France.

USS LCI(L) 232, landing craft, infantry (large)

Lost as the result of enemy action or the perils of the sea during the Allied operations for the liberation of Northern France.

USS LCT(5) 26, landing craft, tank

Lost as the result of operations in the Mediterranean Theater during the period January 22 to March 31, 1944.

USS LCT(5) 35, landing craft, tank

Lost as the result of operations in the Mediterranean Theater during the period January 22 to March 31, 1944.

USS LCT(5) 36, landing craft, tank

Lost as the result of operations in the Mediterranean Theater during the period January 22 to March 31, 1944.

USS LCT(5) 340, landing craft, tank

Lost as the result of operations in the Mediterranean Theater during the period January 22 to March 31, 1944.

USS LEARY, DD 158, destroyer

Torpedoed and sunk in the Atlantic on December 24, 1943.

USS LEEDSTOWN, AP 73, transport

Sunk off Algiers during the early part of November, 1942, as a result of enemy submarine torpedoes during the occupation of North Africa by Allied forces.

USS LEOPOLD, DE 319, destroyer escort

Sunk on March 10, 1944, as a result of an underwater explosion while on escort duty in the Atlantic.

USS LST 282, landing ship, tank

Sunk during operations in the Mediterranean as the result of enemy action.

USS LST 314, landing ship, tank

Lost as the result of enemy action or the perils of the sea during the Allied operations for the liberation of Northern France.

USS LST 348, landing ship, tank

Lost as the result of operations in the Mediterranean Theater during the period January 22 to March 31, 1944.

USS LST 359, landing ship, tank

Lost in the Atlantic as the result of enemy action.

USS LST 376, landing ship, tank

Lost as the result of enemy action or the perils of the sea during the Allied operations for the liberation of Northern France.

USS LST 496, landing ship, tank

Lost as the result of enemy action or the perils of the sea during the Allied operations for the liberation of Northern France.

USS LST 499, landing ship, tank

Lost as the result of enemy action or the perils of the sea during the Allied operations for the liberation of Northern France.

USS LST 523, landing ship, tank

Lost as the result of enemy action or the perils of the sea during the Allied operations for the liberation of France.

USS LST 921, landing ship, tank
Lost as the result of enemy action or the perils of the sea during the Allied operations for the liberation of Northern France.

USS MADDOX, DD 622, destroyer
Sunk July 10, 1943, by aircraft off Sicily.

USS MEREDITH, DD 726, destroyer
Lost due to enemy action in Allied operations for Europe's liberation.

USS MIANTONOMAH, CM 10, minelayer
Lost as the result of enemy action or the perils of the sea during the Allied operations for the liberation of Northern France.

USS MOONSTONE, PYc-9, patrol craft
Sunk in the Atlantic on the night of October 15–16, 1943, as the result of a collision.

USCGC MUSKEGET, Coast Guard cutter
Overdue in the Atlantic and must be presumed to be lost.

USCGC NATSEK, Coast Guard cutter
Overdue in the North Atlantic and must be presumed to be lost.

USS NAUSET, AT 89, tug
Sunk as the result of enemy action in the Mediterranean on September 9, 1943.

USS OSPREY, AM 56, minsweeper
Lost due to enemy action while participating in the Allied operations for Europe's liberation.

USS PARTRIDGE, ATO 138, fleet tug
Lost due to enemy action in Allied operations for Europe's liberation.

USS PC 496, submarine chaser
Sunk June 4, 1943, as result of underwater explosion in the Mediterranean area.

USS PC 558, submarine chaser
Sunk as a result of enemy action in the Mediterranean on May 9, 1944.

USS PC 1261, submarine chaser
Lost due to enemy action while participating in the Allied operations for Europe's liberation.

USS PE 56, patrol boat
Sunk as the result of an explosion three miles off Cape Elizabeth, Maine.

USS PLYMOUTH, PG 57, gunboat
  Sunk a short distance off the North Carolina coast on August 5, 1943, as result of underwater explosion.

USS POLLUX, AKA 2, cargo ship
  Ran aground in foul weather off the coast of Newfoundland and was lost.

USS PORTENT, AM 106, minesweeper
  Lost as the result of operations in the Mediterranean Theater during the period January 22 to March 31, 1944.

USS PT 202, motor torpedo boat
  Sunk during operations in the Mediterranean as the result of enemy action.

USS PT 218, motor torpedo boat
  Sunk during operations in the Mediterranean as the result of enemy action.

USS PT 311, motor torpedo boat
  Lost in the Mediterranean area as the result of enemy action.

USS PT 509, motor torpedo boat
  Lost as the result of enemy action or the perils of the sea during the Allied operations for the liberation of Northern France.

USS PT 555, motor torpedo boat
  Sunk during recent operations in the Mediterranean as the result of enemy action.

USS R 12, submarine
  Lost while engaged in training exercises off the east coast of the United States.

USS REDWING, ARS 4, submarine rescue vessel
  Sunk June 29, 1943, as the result of underwater explosion in the Mediterranean area.

USS RICH, DE 695, destroyer escort
  Lost due to enemy action in Allied operations for Europe's liberation.

USS ROWAN, DD 405, destroyer
  Sunk as the result of an underwater explosion in Italian waters on September 11, 1943.

USS S 26, submarine
  Sunk in a collision with another United States naval vessel on the night of January 24, 1942, off Panama. The collision occurred while the submarine was operating on the surface.

USS ST. AUGUSTINE, PG 54, gunboat
Sunk January 6, 1944, in a collision with a merchant vessel off Cape May, New Jersey.

USS SC 694, submarine chaser
Sunk on August 23, 1943, as a result of enemy bombing in the Mediterranean area.

USS SC 696, submarine chaser
Sunk on August 23, 1943, as a result of enemy bombing in the Mediterranean area.

USS SENTINEL, AM 113, minesweeper.
Sunk July 11, 1943, in landing operation off Sicily.

USS SKILL, AM 115, minelayer
Sunk on the morning of September 25, 1943, as the result of an underwater explosion in the Gulf of Salerno.

USS STURTEVANT, DD 240, destroyer
Sunk off the coast of Florida by an underwater explosion.

USS SUSAN B. ANTHONY, AP 72, transport
Lost on June 7, 1944, due to enemy action in Allied operations for Europe's liberation.

USS SWERVE, AM 121, mine vessel-minesweeper
Sunk in the Mediterranean as the result of enemy action.

USS TASKER H. BLISS, AP 42, transport
Sunk off Casablanca during the early part of November, 1942, as a result of enemy submarine torpedoes during the occupation of North Africa by Allied forces.

USS TIDE, AM 125, mine vessel-minesweeper
Lost due to enemy action in Allied operations for Europe's liberation.

USS TRUXTUN, DD 229, destroyer
Ran aground in foul weather off the coast of Newfoundland and broke up almost immediately after grounding.

USS TURNER, DD 648, destroyer
Exploded and sank six miles off Sandy Hook, New Jersey, on January 3, 1944.

VINEYARD SOUND, Coast Guard lightship
Missing from her position off the tip of Cuttyhunk Island in Vineyard Sound, Massachusetts, and is presumed to have been lost in a hurricane.

USS WARRINGTON, DD 383, destroyer
Sunk at sea in Atlantic hurricane.

USCGC WILCOX, Coast Guard patrol craft
Foundered in a storm off the Atlantic coast on September 30, 1943, and was lost.

USS YMS 21, motor minesweeper
Sunk in the Mediterranean as the result of enemy action.

USS YMS 24, motor minesweeper
Sunk in the Mediterranean as the result of enemy action.

USS YMS 30, motor minesweeper
Lost as the result of operations in the Mediterranean Theater during the period January 22 to March 31, 1944.

USS YMS 304, minesweeper
Lost as the result of enemy action or the perils of the sea during the Allied operations for the liberation of Northern France.

USS YMS 350, minesweeper
Lost as the result of enemy action or the perils of the sea during the Allied operations for the liberation of Northern France.

USS YMS 378, minesweeper
Lost as the result of enemy action or the perils of the sea during the Allied operations for the liberation of Northern France.

USS YP 389, fishing craft
Sunk by gunfire in the Atlantic area. She was a small fishing craft that had been taken over by the Navy and armed for antisubmarine patrol duty.

USS YT 198, harbor tug
Lost in the Mediterranean Theater during the period January 22 to March 31, 1944.

Appendix C

Listed below are the transports which took part in amphibious operations and naval transport service in the Atlantic and Mediterranean, and the men who commanded them. These vessels, with their cargoes of assault troops and supplies, were the real battle line of invasion. Without armor, without much armament—their main batteries were the soldiers they carried—the transports stood in under enemy guns, and discharged their cargoes in narrow, shallow, mined waters, fighting off air attacks that were always aimed straight at them. These vessels, as much as any battleships, were men-of-war in the thick of the fight.

ACHERNAR, AKA 53	Commander Harold R. Stevens, USN
ALGORAB, AKA 8	Commander J. R. Lannom, USN
ALMAACK, AKA 10	Commander Thomas R. Cooley, USN
	Commander Chester L. Nichols, USN
ANCON, AGC 4 (Ex AP 66)	Captain Paul L. Mather, USN
	Commander M. S. Pearson, USN
ANDROMEDA, AKA 15	Commander W. A. Fly, USN
ANNE ARUNDEL, AP 76	Captain Lunsford Y. Mason, Jr., USN
	Captain William S. Campbell, USN
ARCTURUS, AKA 1	Commander John R. McKinney, USN
	Lt. Comdr. Attilio A. Vischio, USN
	Commander Charles R. Woodson, USN
BARNETT, APA 5	Captain C. A. Bailey, USN
	Commander George E. Maynard, USN
	Commander Stuart S. Reynolds, USN
BAYFIELD, APA 33	Captain Lyndon Spencer, USCG
BETELGEUSE, AKA 11	Commander John F. Grube, USN
CEPHUS, AKA 18	Captain Rae B. Hall, USCG
	Commander R. C. Sarratt, USCG
CHARLES CARROLL, APA 28	Commander Harold Biesemeier, USN
	Commander William W. Whitaker, USN
DOROTHEA L. DIX, AP 67	Captain Leo B. Schulten, USN
	Commander William I. Leahy, USN

EDWARD RUTLEDGE, AP 52	Captain Myron W. Hutchinson, USN
ELECTRA, AKA 4	Commander James J. Hughes, USN
	Lt. Comdr. C. S. Beightler, USN
ELIZABETH C. STANTON, AP 69	Captain Ross A. Dierdorff, USN
	Captain Gerald L. Schetky, USN
	Commander Wilbur A. Wiedman, USN
FLORENCE NIGHTINGALE, AP 70	Captain Edwin D. Graves, Jr., USN
	Commander Joseph W. McColl, Jr., USN
	Commander Frederick J. Nelson, USN
FREDERICK FUNSTON, APA 89	Commander John E. Murphy, USN
	Captain Charles C. Anderson, USN
GEMINI, AP 75	Lt. Comdr. Woody L. Cain, USN
GENERAL A. E. ANDERSON,	Captain William E. Miller, USN
AP 111	Captain George W. Meade, Jr., USN
GENERAL G. M. RANDALL, AP 115	Captain Carl C. von Paulson, USCG
GENERAL G. O. SQUIER, AP 130	Captain A. E. Uehlinger, USN
	Captain Robert D. Threshie, USN
GENERAL H. W. BUTNER, AP 113	Captain Andrew P. Lawton, USN
	Captain Clayton S. Isgrig, USN
GENERAL J. C. BRECKINRIDGE, AP 176	
GENERAL J. R. BROOKE, AP 132	Captain D. L. Nutter, USN
	Captain William Wakefield, USN
	Captain Charles J. Nager, USN
GENERAL JOHN POPE, AP 110	Captain George D. Lyon, USN
	Commander Charles R. Khoury, USN
GENERAL M. C. MEIGS, AP 116	Captain George W. McKean, USCG
GENERAL T. H. BLISS, AP 131	Captain Burton Davis, USN
	Captain B. S. Mansfield, USN
GENERAL W. A. MANN, AP 112	Commander R. H. Smith, USN
	Commander P. S. Maguire, USN
GENERAL W. H. GORDON, AP 117	Captain Russell E. Wood, USCG
GENERAL W. M. BLACK, AP 135	Captain J. P. Murray, USCG
	Captain D. G. Jacobs, USCG
GENERAL W. P. RICHARDSON, AP 118	Captain J. S. Rosenthal, USN
GENERAL WILLIAM MITCHELL, AP 114	Captain Henry Coyle, USCG
	Captain John Roundtree, USCG
GENERAL WILLIAM WEIGEL, AP 119	Captain Thomas Y. Awalt, USCG
GEORGE CLYMER, APA 27	Captain Arthur T. Moen, USN
HARRIS, APA 2	Captain Otto M. Forster, USN
HARRY LEE, APA 10	Captain James W. Whitfield, USN
	Captain Donald W. Loomis, USN
	Commander Joseph G. Pomeroy, USN

HENRICO, APA 45	Commander John H. Willis, USN
HENRY T. ALLEN, AP 30	Captain Paul Augustus Stevens, USN
HERMITAGE, AP 54	Captain D. F. Patterson, USN
	Captain A. D. Douglas, USN
	Captain Rockwell J. Townsend, USN
	Captain Joseph T. Talbert, USN
HUGH L. SCOTT, AP 136	Captain Harold J. Wright, USN
JAMES O'HARA, APA 90	Commander C. Allen, USN
JOHN PENN, APA 23	Captain Harry W. Need, USN
JOSEPH HEWES, AP 50	Captain William P. O. Clarke, USN
	Captain Robert McL. Smith, USN
JOSEPH T. DICKMAN, APA 13	Captain Charles W. Harwood, USCG
	Captain Raymond J. Mauerman, USCG
	Captain F. A. Leamy, USCG
LAKEHURST	Commander Harold J. McNulty, USN
LEEDSTOWN, AP	Lt. Comdr. Duncan Cook, USN
(first ship of name)	
LEJEUNE, AP 74	Captain Laurence E. Kelly, USN
	Captain Frank W. McDonald, USN
LEONARD WOOD, APA 12	Commander Harold G. Bradbury, USCG
	Commander Ephraim Zoole, USCG
	Commander Merlin O'Neill, USCG
LYON, AP 71	Captain Martin J. Gillan, Jr., USN
	Captain Thor C. Sorenson, USN
MONROVIA, APA 31	Captain Charles D. Leffler, USN
	Captain Thomas B. Brittain, USN
MONTICELLO, APA 61	Captain Bayard H. Colyear, USN
	Captain Berwick B. Lanier, USN
	Captain Leonard Frisco, USN
MOUNT VERNON, AP 22	Captain Emory P. Eldridge, USN
MUNARGO, AP 20	Commander R. G. Pennoyer, USN
	Commander H. F. Ely, USN
	Commander R. C. Moureau, USN
OBERON, AKA 14	Commander Ion Pursell, USN
	Commander David G. Greenlee, USN
	Lt. Comdr. Harold T. Cameron, USN
ORIZABA, AP 24	Captain Clarence Gulbranson, USN
	Captain Laurence E. Kelly, USN
	Captain J. P. Conover, Jr., USN
PROCYON, AKA 2	Commander Lemuel F. Padgett, Jr., USN
	Commander Beverly A. Hartt, USN
	Commander Thomas O. Cullins, USN
SAMUEL CHASE, APA 26	Commander Roger C. Heimer, USCG
	Captain Edward H. Fritzsche, USCG

STRATFORD, AP 41	Commander C. C. Anderson, USN
	Commander Chester Claude Farmer, USN
	Lt. Comdr. Aloysius Elb, USN
	Lt. Comdr. Nathan McKenzie, USN
SUSAN B. ANTHONY, AP 72	Captain Henry Hartley, USN
	Commander Thomas L. Gray, USN
TASKER H. BLISS, AP 42	Captain Gerald L. Schetky, USN
THOMAS JEFFERSON, APA 30	Commander Chauncey R. Crutcher, USN
	Captain P. P. Welch, USN
	Commander Joseph R. Barbaro, USN
THOMAS STONE, AP 59	Captain Orton R. Bennehoff, USN
THURSTON, AP 77	Captain Jack E. Huff, USN
	Commander Roland B. Vanasse, USN
TITANIA, AKA 13	Commander Victor C. Barringer, USN
U. S. GRANT, AP 29	Captain H. R. Hein, USN
	Captain Charles L. Hutton, USN
WAKEFIELD, AP 21	Captain R. L. Raney, USCG
WEST POINT, AP 23	Captain Frank H. Kelley, USN
	Captain Robert A. Dyer, USN
	Captain Webb C. Hayes, USN
WILLIAM P. BIDDLE, APA 8	Captain Campbell D. Edgar, USN
	Commander Paul R. Glutting, USN

Awards and Citations

MEMORANDUM *

For: Rear Admiral Harold B. Miller, U.S. Navy
The Director of Public Information

1. In accordance with instructions from the Director of Public Relations, January 12, 1945, the attached compilation has been made for inclusion in Battle Report II. It contains lists of naval decorations awarded members of the Naval Service, for action in the Atlantic, European, Caribbean, Mediterranean and North African Theaters of World War II. Several awards from the Army to Naval personnel and from the Navy to Army personnel are included. Attached also are Presidential Unit Citations awarded to U.S. Naval Vessels for action in these theaters.

2. But this compilation is not all-inclusive as the records of some spot awards made in the fleet are not yet available in the Navy Department.

3. This compilation contains over 3,500 names of persons who received awards for the above named theaters of war. Data on approximately 1,000 were received from the Bureau of Naval Personnel. Information on the remainder was obtained from other sources:—Navy Department Press Releases, District Press Releases and Reports. All have been cleared with the Security Section, OOR-E-1.

Respectfully,
HELENE PHILIBERT

AWARDS INCLUDE

Medal of Honor
Gallantry and intrepidity at the risk of his life above and beyond the call of duty.

Navy Cross
Extraordinary heroism in connection with military operations against an armed enemy.

Distinguished Service Medal
Exceptionally meritorious service to the Government in a duty of great responsibility.

Legion of Merit
Exceptionally meritorious conduct in the performance of outstanding services.

* Credit is due Captain Harry G. Patrick, USN (Retired), Member and Recorder of the Navy Board of Awards and Decorations, and to Mrs. Maude Crawford of the Bureau of Naval Personnel for their valuable assistance in preparing this work.

Silver Star Medal

Gallantry and intrepidity in action, such gallantry and service not being sufficient to justify the award of a Medal of Honor or a Navy Cross.

Distinguished Flying Cross

Heroism or extraordinary achievement while participating in aerial flight.

Navy and Marine Corps Medal

Heroism not involving actual conflict with an enemy.

Air Medal

Meritorious achievement while participating in an aerial flight.

Bronze Star Medal

Heroic or meritorious achievement or service, not involving participation in aerial flight, in connection with military or naval operations against an enemy.

Presidential Unit Citation

Outstanding performance in action.

Navy Unit Commendation

Heroism in action with the enemy but not sufficient to justify award of the Presdential Unit Citation.

ATLANTIC *

Navy Cross

COPE, Cdr. Harley F., USN

As Commanding Officer of the USS SALINAS, in handling his ship and crew, when that vessel was torpedoed on October 30, 1941, and in bringing his ship safely to port, under most difficult circumstances, after it had sustained severe damage in an engagement with an enemy submarine.

DANIS, Cdr. Anthony Leo, USN

As Commanding Officer of the USS KEARNY, in bringing his ship safely to port, under most difficult circumstances, after that vessel was torpedoed on October 17, 1941.

GAINARD, Cdr. Joseph Aloysius, USNR

As master of the steamer CITY OF FLINT, at the time of its seizure upon the high seas and during its detention by armed forces of a belligerent European power. His skill, fine judgment and devotion to duty were of the highest order and in accordance with the best tradition of the Naval Service.

HIRSHFIELD, Cdr. James A., USCG

As Commanding Officer of the USCG CAMPBELL during action against an en-

emy submarine on February 22, 1943. Surprising the hostile undersea craft on the surface during escort operations, Commander Hirshfield, in a quick attempt to ram, collided with the vessel and destroyed it in a fierce attack by depth charges and point-blank fire. Although painfully wounded by flying shell splinters, he gallantly remained in command throughout the action and during the subsequent period while the CAMPBELL was towed safely into port with several prisoners from the sunken submarine.

MONCY, Cdr. Peter N., USN

As Commanding Officer of the USS LARAMIE, in handling his ship and crew when that vessel was torpedoed on August 28, 1942, and in bringing his ship safely to port, under most difficult circumstances, after it had sustained severe damage in an action with an enemy submarine. When Commander Moncy observed that a submarine attack was imminent he promptly ordered all hands to battle stations. As a result of this prompt action numerous casualties were prevented when the LARAMIE was torpedoed.

NORTON, Cdr. Stanley Cook, USN

As Commander Destroyer Division FIFTY-FOUR when the flagship of his divi-

* Names starred indicate that the award is being received for the second, third or fourth time.

sion, the USS ROPER, made a successful attack upon the German submarine U-85, on the night of April 13-14, 1942, causing complete destruction of that enemy vessel without injury to his flagship or its personnel.

ABEL, Lt. Cdr. Brent M., USNR

As Commanding Officer of the USS BUCKLEY in offensive action against a German submarine during the early morning of May 6, 1944.

ESSLINGER, Lt. Cdr. Robert John, USN

For extraordinary heroism as Engineer Officer of the USS KEARNY during the torpedoing of that vessel by an enemy submarine on October 17, 1941. After a quick and accurate analysis of the situation, Lieutenant Commander Esslinger, working under extremely hazardous and difficult conditions, coolly and skillfully surmounted all obstacles and kept the engines operative, permitting the KEARNY to proceed out of the dangerous submarine area and make port.

HOWE, Lt. Cdr. Hamilton W., USN

For distinguished service in the line of his profession as Commanding Officer of the USS ROPER, when on the night of April 13-14, 1942, Lieutenant Commander Howe with an offensive singleness of purpose tracked, attacked and completely destroyed the German U-85 without injury to his vessel or its personnel.

HUTCHINS, Lt. Cdr. Charles H., USNR

For extraordinary heroism as Commanding Officer of the USS BORIE during action against two enemy submarines in the Atlantic on the night of October 31, 1943.

SMITH, Lt. Cdr. Ashton B., USN

For extraordinary heroism, as executive officer of the USS SALINAS, in operating the carbon dioxide fire extinguishing system after the first torpedo struck the ship, and, after being injured by the explosion of the second torpedo, in giving the necessary orders to the crew of that vessel to keep her afloat and at the same time open fire on the attacking submarine.

BROWN, Lt. Morrison R., USNR

For extraordinary heroism as Engineer Officer of the USS BORIE when that vessel attacked and sank an enemy submarine on the morning of November 1, 1943. To keep the engines of the BORIE operative to complete her mission, despite serious damage sustained during the prolonged battle, Lieutenant Brown remained steadfastly at his post, buffeted by debris in the heavy rolling of the vessel and with water pouring into the forward engine room. As the flooding increased and the compartment became untenable, he calmly ordered his men to safety while he stayed below, standing neck-deep in water at the throttle until the BORIE had completely destroyed the submarine.

DAVID, Lt. Albert Leroy, USN

For heroism and intrepidity in boarding an abandoned German submarine running on the surface off the Coast of French West Africa in June 1944. Leading a prize crew aboard after the German crew had been driven overboard by gunfire from a Task Group, he courageously plunged through the conning tower hatch, facing the uncertain dangers of lurking enemy resistance, imminent detonation of demolition bombs or sudden sinking of the ship from bilging sustained in action, and he remained below directing salvage operations so that the ship remained afloat and could be towed across the Atlantic Ocean to an Allied Naval Base, thus delivering a valuable enemy weapon for intelligence study.

GRANT, Lt. James Dorr, USN

On the morning of April 16, 1942, the USS R-1 was conducting a patrol submerged when the Officer of the Deck sighted an enemy submarine on the surface. Lieutenant Grant, as soon as this report was made to him, immediately ordered his crew to battle stations, and pressed home a torpedo attack. He executed this expeditious attack with such splendid judgment and outstanding skill that a torpedo hit was scored and the enemy submarine was sunk 8 minutes after it was sighted.

HEIM, Lt. Elbert S., USNR

For extraordinary heroism as Pilot of a United States Navy Fighter Plane in action against enemy submarine in the Atlantic on October 4, 1943. Flying to the support of a bomber which was in contact with four surfaced hostile submarines, Lieutenant (then Lieutenant junior grade) Heim commenced firing at a range of two thousand feet and came in through a barrage of deadly cross-fire from the enemy vessels, strafing the largest and most heavily armed submarine until he was within fifty feet of his target. After a skillful second run in which the enemy's anti-aircraft battery was silenced, he vigorously strafed two of the surfaced U-boats, making them easy targets for unopposed bombing attacks which resulted in the probable destruction of one of the hostile vessels.

JERMANN, Lt. Theodore L., USNR

For extraordinary heroism, as Engineer Officer of the USS SALINAS, in inspecting the engineering spaces after the first torpedo struck the ship, and in securing overboard valves and ruptured lines when the second torpedo struck and the ship opened fire on the attacking submarine. His coolness and courage in taking that action, under the circumstances described, contributed materially in making it possible for the SALINAS to reach port under her own power.

JESTER, Lt. Maurice D., USCGR

For distinguished service in the line of his profession as Commanding Officer of the United States Coast Guard Cutter ICARUS during a successful action on May 9, 1942, with an enemy German submarine.

MITCHEL, Lt. Ormsby M., Jr., USNR

For heroism and outstanding performance of duty as Commanding Officer of USS PLYMOUTH during and after the sinking through enemy action of USS PLYMOUTH on August 5, 1943. Lieutenant Mitchel was on the bridge at the time of the submarine attack. He had just completed evaluation of sound contact as a possible submarine, had given the "stations" order, had increased speed to 12 knots, and had started turning the ship on the attack course when a torpedo, unseen by the lookouts, crashed into the port side, amidships, and exploded. Flames immediately broke out from the engine room level to the bridge, trapping and killing many in the forward part of the ship. Lieutenant Mitchel, thrown violently against a bulkhead by the explosion sustained serious injuries including dislocation of the left knee. Nevertheless, he remained at his post during the three remaining minutes before the ship sank. When driven from the bridge by the enveloping flames, Lieutenant Mitchel was forced to jump from the bridge to the well-deck because ladders had been carried away by the initial explosion. In spite of this painful leap Lieutenant Mitchel insisted on being supported so that he could continue to give orders for abandoning ship. Several life rafts were cut away, all depth charges were set on "safe," and numerous officers and men who had been on the upper decks went over the side. Lieutenant Mitchel remained aboard his ship until it sank. He went down with his ship; then was able to reach the surface. When a raft was brought alongside Lieutenant Mitchel in the water, he pointed to other men in greater need of assistance, and refused to be taken aboard the raft until those about him had been rescued. Once aboard USCGC CALYPSO, Lieutenant Mitchel immediately insisted that he be supported on deck until he was assured that all rescue operations were completed or nearing completion. Subsequently he was treated for multiple burns on both hands, extending over his forearm, first and second degree burns of the face, the right leg and foot, the left leg and ankle. Even after Lieutenant Mitchel had been given first aid, he continued to show primary interest for the condition of those officers and crew who had been rescued. His condition remained critical for several days after the disaster, and within a week, it was found necessary to amputate his left leg above the knee.

STEARNS, Lt. Robert Lloyd, USNR

For extraordinary heroism and courageous devotion to duty as Pilot of a Navy Torpedo Bomber in action against an enemy submarine on July 23, 1943. Although rain and light mist necessitated frequent instrument flying, Lieutenant (then Lieutenant, junior grade) Stearns launched an immediate attack when the hostile undersea craft was sighted in the waters below. Skillfully maneuvering his plane for maximum striking power despite intense enemy anti-aircraft fire, he accurately released several depth bombs which exploded at the stern of the submarines, causing fatal detonation aboard the hostile ship.

Gold Star in Lieu of a Second Navy Cross

For extraordinary heroism as Pilot of a United States Navy Torpedo Bomber in action against enemy submarines on October 4, 1943. Sighting a concentration of four surfaced enemy undersea craft while on an antisubmarine patrol flight, Lieutenant (then Lieutenant, junior grade) Stearns immediately closed in for a bombing attack, simultaneously making a contact report to his carrier. After launching an expert and daring run in the face of withering anti-aircraft fire from the surfaced U-boats, he courageously remained in hazardous contact with the enemy to direct relief planes to the area and, skillfully coordinating the supporting craft in a concerted effort, fought his bomber valiantly, scoring devastating hits and probably destroying one of the hostile submarines as it attempted to crash dive.

WILLIAMS, Lt. Robert Pershing, USNR

For extraordinary heroism as Pilot of a United States Navy Torpedo Bomber during an attack on an enemy German submarine in the Atlantic Area on July 14, 1943. An aggressive and valiant fighter, alert to every attack opportunity, Lieutenant Williams immediately went into action upon sighting the periscope of a German submarine. Launching a vigorous bombing run as the hostile vessel commenced surfacing, he released four depth charges, one of which exploded close aboard the port bow and caused the submarine to submerge slowly on an even keel.

CROSS, Lt. (jg) Frederick C., Jr., USNR

For extraordinary heroism and courageous devotion to duty while serving with Bombing Squadron ONE TWENTY-EIGHT, Fleet Air Wing NINE, United States Atlantic Fleet, as Pilot of a Navy PV-1 plane during an engagement with an enemy submarine, August 7, 1943. Although he sustained mortal wounds and his aircraft's starboard engine was shattred by a direct hit during the approach to a hostile submarine, Lieutenant (junior grade) Cross, undeterred by his extremely painful injuries and the hazards of concentrated enemy gunfire, pressed home an aggressive attack, dropping his depth bombs in a stick across the ship's bow and possibly damaging the undersea craft. After struggling in vain to maintain flight, he succeeded in effecting a perfect water landing, thus enabling his co-pilot and radio operator to survive and subsequently to attain safety.

DOWTY, Lt. (jg) Norman Taylor, USNR

For extraordinary heroism as Pilot of a Torpedo Bomber in action against an enemy submarine in the Atlantic Ocean on March 19, 1944. Sighting the hostile ship while participating with an accompanying fighter plane in a search flight, Lieutenant (junior grade) Dowty unhesitatingly went into action and, skillfully maneuvering his craft into position for a powerful strike, pressed home his daring, aggressive attacks at perilously low altitude in the face of intense, persistent anti-aircraft fire and accurately released depth bombs which exploded on the deck of the submarine and completely destroyed the enemy vessel.

HOPGOOD, Lt. (jg) Robert B., USN

For distinguished service in action and in the line of his profession while participating in an aerial flight as Senior Pilot of a Navy Patrol Plane on August 20, 1942, when an enemy submarine was engaged and so severely damaged that it was abandoned and sunk. The enemy submarine was sighted on the surface while the Navy Patrol Plane was on a regular air coverage flight over a convoy. Lieutenant (junior grade) Hopgood maneuvered his plane skillfully and accurately dropped five depth charges which straddled the submarine and exploded close aboard on each side just abaft the conning tower. In the face of the enemy's anti-air-craft fire Lieutenant (junior grade) Hopgood proceeded to maneuver his plane over the submarine and strafe it with machine gun fire; he then led a destroyer from the convoy to the scene. As the destroyer was approaching, the enemy abandoned the sinking submarine. A large number of prisoners were taken by the destroyer. The action described above in which the initiative and resourcefulness of Lieutenant (junior grade) Hopgood, in the face of enemy anti-aircraft fire and undesirable weather conditions, resulted in the certain destruction of the enemy submarine and capture of many survivors, reflects great credit and honor to the Naval Service.

KINASZCZUK, Lt. (jg) Thomas, USNR

For extraordinary heroism and oustanding courage as Pilot of a United States Navy Bombing Plane in offensive action against an enemy submarine on 27 April 1943. Lieutenant (junior grade) Thomas Kinaszczuk was on a convoy coverage flight when he sighted a surfaced enemy submarine approaching the convoy on an intercepting course at high speed. Immediately increasing speed, he began his approach for an immediate attack. When the range had closed to about one and one half miles, the submarine commenced a very accurate and heavy anti-aircraft fire which it maintained throughout the attack. With complete disregard for the accuracy of the enemy's fire and the damage which several hits caused to the plane's starboard wing and aileron, the pilot pressed home his attack. Finally, from an altitude of only twenty-five feet, he released his depth bombs. Of the four depth bombs released, three were observed to have exploded beneath the submarine. Shortly after the attack, the submarine broke surface at an extreme angle and soon thereafter sank, stern first, in a nearly perpendicular attitude.

PUCKETT, Lt. (jg) David O., USNR

For extraordinary heroism and outstanding courage as Pilot of a United States Navy Fighter Plane in offensive action against enemy submarines on 4 October 1943. Lieutenant (junior grade),

David O. Puckett was flying to the support of another plane which had surprised, attacked, and was maintaining contact on a group of enemy submarines. Immediately on reaching the concentration of U-boats, he followed closely on the attack of a companion fighter by strafing the largest, most heavily armed submarine of the group. Opening fire at a range of fifteen hundred feet, in spite of the heavy barrage put up by his target, the crossfire from other U-boats, and damage incurred to his plane by several shrapnel bits, he persisted in his attack until he had materially reduced the volume of fire from his target. An attack on a second submarine was pressed home with equal determination, effectively silencing its anti-aircraft battery and enabling a bomber to attack unopposed. A total of three more attacks were made on the remaining submarines, one in the face of equally heavy anti-aircraft fire which had characterized the first attack, the remaining two unopposed.

SALLENGER, Lt. (jg) Asbury H., USNR

For extraordinary heroism and outstanding courage as Pilot of a United States Navy Torpedo Bomber Plane during an attack on two enemy submarines on 7 August 1943. Lieutenant (junior grade) Asbury H. Sallenger, though unaided by support from other aircraft and while under intense anti-aircraft fire from both surfaced enemy submarines which he had sighted, made an exceptionally accurate depth-bombing attack, leaving one submarine badly damaged and smoking heavily. After making his first attack, Lieutenant (junior grade) Sallenger remained in the vicinity of the submarines to direct relief planes to the scene. As the one undamaged U-boat began to submerge, Lieutenant (junior grade) Sallenger immediately made a second attack which necessitated an approach at reduced speed close aboard to and through the heavy screen of anti-aircraft fire put up by the damaged submarine. Despite the difficulty of his approach, Lieutenant (junior grade) Sallenger reached a favorable release point and attacked the now submerged second submarine. On completion of this second attack, with all depth bombs expended,

Lieutenant (junior grade) Sallenger remained in close proximity to the damaged submarine until relief planes arrived and completed its destruction.

STEIGER, Lt. (jg) Earl Henry, USNR

1500 July 13, 1943, a United States Navy Fighter Plane piloted by Lieutenant (junior grade) Earl H. Steiger, USNR, strafed a German submarine which had been caught on the surface. Lieutenant Steiger had made two strafing attacks under continuous anti-aircraft fire, clearing the submarine's decks sufficiently to permit a TBF plane to make a depth-charge run which resulted in disabling of the submarine. On the third attack, with ammunition in one gun only, Lieutenant Steiger's plane was seen to fall off the left wing and disappear into the water. Search of area failed to locate body or wreckage of plane.

ARNOLD, Ens. John S., II, USNR

For extraordinary heroism as Commanding Officer of the United States Navy Armed Guard aboard the SS ESSO GETTYSBURG following an attack upon that vessel by an enemy submarine on June 10, 1943. When two torpedoes ripped into the port side of the tanker and set fire to the oil-covered deck, Ensign Arnold, his own clothing ignited by the explosive blast, sustained severe burns about the upper body before he could smother the blaze. Although suffering acute pain and menaced by the spreading inferno which swept across the topsides, he calmly ordered the forward gun manned and, with the stricken ship fast settling beneath him, fired one round of ammunition to deter a possible surfacing of the submarine. The last man to go over the side as the vessel began to capsize, he remained in the water several hours before he was finally picked up by other survivors who had salvaged a charred lifeboat.

KELTCH, Ens. Rubin, USNR

For extraordinary heroism while serving aboard the USS PLYMOUTH during and after the sinking of that vessel through enemy action on August 5, 1943. When an enemy torpedo crashed into the port side amidships and exploded, causing spreading fires, Ensign Keltch unhesitatingly risked his life to assist several survivors to safety.

BISHEIMER, Alexander Joseph, S1/c, USN

For extraordinary heroism in action, on March 10, 1943, when as a member of the boarding party from the USS EBERLE, he boarded an intercepted Blockade Runner. Bisheimer boarded the Blockade Runner in company with the boarding officer and assisted in an energetic and determined effort to salvage the ship and to obtain information regarding the enemy. He remained on board the Blockade Runner until several explosions rocked her and forced him to dive overboard into the water from whence he was recovered.

KNIGHT, Frank LeRoy, T1/c, USN

For meritorious conduct, extraordinary courage and devotion to duty while serving on the USS STACK on the occasion of a collision of that vessel with a large aircraft carrier on March 17, 1942, when, as a result of the collision, No. 1 fireroom of the STACK was flooded, the lighting circuits out and the ship was heeled over at a dangerous angle and being carried across the bow of the aircraft carrier. Despite the pending danger of the depth charges being dislodged by further contact with the carrier, Knight made his way aft in the darkened vessel and, wading waist deep, set all the depth charges on safe.

McGINTY, Franklin A., SoM3/c, USNR

For extraordinary heroism while serving aboard the USS PLYMOUTH during and after the sinking of that vessel through enemy action on August 5, 1943. When an enemy torpedo crashed into the PLYMOUTH amidships, causing devastating fires and extensive damage, McGinty unhesitatingly risked his life in behalf of his endangered shipmates. In a courageous attempt to rescue a man known to be trapped in the ship's flaming armory, McGinty entered the compartment and was himself trapped.

McDANIEL, Aucie, CMoM, USN

For extraordinary heroism as Chief machinist's mate in charge of the forward engine room, USS KEARNY, when that vessel was torpedoed on October 17, 1941.

McIntyre, Francis H., CMoM, USN

For extraordinary heroism, in assisting the engineer officer of the USS SALINAS in his inspection of the engineering spaces after the first torpedo struck, and in securing overboard valves and ruptured lines when the second torpedo struck and the ship opened fire on the attacking submarine.

Saum, Irving Randolph Jr., MM1/c, USNR

For extraordinary heroism while serving aboard the USS BORIE in combat against an enemy German submarine in Atlantic waters on November 1, 1943. When the forward engine room was severely holed by enemy action, resulting in rapid flooding to the vessel's water line, Saum unhesitatingly volunteered to enter the damaged compartment in order to close the secondary drain suction, enabling all available pumps to be placed on the suction of the after engine room and prevent its flooding. At great risk to his own life, he courageously descended ten feet below the surface of the debris-filled water and, despite heavy rolling of the ship, succeeded in accomplishing the hazardous task.

Wilson, Rual S. MoM1/c, USN

For extraordinary heroism in assisting the engineer officer of the USS SALINAS in his inspection of the engineering spaces after the first torpedo struck, and in securing overboard valves and ruptured lines when the second torpedo struck and the ship opened fire on the attacking submarine.

Distinguished Service Medal

Ingersoll, Adm. Royal E., USN

For exceptionally meritorious service to the government of the United States in a duty of great responsibility as Commander in Chief, United States Atlantic Fleet. A forceful and resolute leader under the critical conditions existing throughout a period of approximately three years, Admiral Ingersoll conducted a sustained offensive against enemy submarines in this vital combat area and, as a result of his unfailing judgment, resourcefulness and initiative, maintained an uninterrupted flow of United States troops and their supplies across the Atlantic.

Andrews, Vice Adm. Adolphus, USN

For exceptionally meritorious and distinguished service to the Government of the United States in a position of great responsibility as Commander Eastern Sea Frontier. During a period of intense enemy submarine activities, Vice Admiral Andrews displayed the highest qualities of leadership, judgment, and planning, and initiated and put into effect the antisubmarine organization of this Sea Frontier which proved to be highly effective in driving German submarines from our coastal waters and which became the model for the antisubmarine organizations of the other sea frontiers.

Bellinger, Vice Adm. Patrick Neison Lynch, USN

For exceptionally meritorious service to the Government of the United States in a duty of great responsibility as Commander Air Force, Atlantic Fleet, from March 1943 to November 1944. A resourceful and aggressive administrator, Vice Admiral Bellinger exercised keen foresight and sound judgment in organizing the Air Force of the Atlantic Fleet and subsequently in directing its expansion, development and operations and, by his superior knowledge of aeronautical and naval problems and his thorough comprehension of the tasks assigned him, discharged his myriad duties expeditiously and effectively, contributing in large measure to the protection of Allied shipping in the Atlantic.

Sharp, Vice Adm. Alexander, USN

For exceptionally meritorious service to the Government of the United States, as Commander of a Battleship Division, Commander Battleships, Atlantic Fleet, as an Atlantic Fleet Major Task Force Commander and as Commander Service Force, Atlantic Fleet, during the period from November 1941 to October 1944. A brilliant administrator and tactician, Vice Admiral Sharp discharged the multiple responsibilities of his command with splendid success, consistently maintaining his forces in a high state of combat efficiency. Confronted, as Commander Service Force, with a task of great magnitude in supplying and supporting the widespread operations of the Atlantic Fleet, Vice Admiral Sharp brought to this duty a knowledge and resourcefulness based on wide experience. Handling these complex problems with marked ability, he also furnished effective logistic support for Naval Forces afloat in the Mediterranean and the Eastern Atlantic and for outlying bases in the Atlantic and European Theaters.

BEARY, Rear Adm. Donald Bradford, USN

For exceptionally meritorious service to the Government of the United States in a duty of great responsibility as Commander, Fleet Operational Training Command, Atlantic Fleet, from March 1943 to November 1944. A resourceful and aggressive administrator, Rear Admiral Beary organized and expeditiously developed this vital command, skillfully formulating comprehensive plans to meet the tremendous task of the initial training and, by his thorough understanding of the many and varied problems involved, capably effected their efficient and speedy solution.

DAUBIN, Rear Adm. Freeland Allan, USN

For exceptionally meritorious service to the Government of the United States in a duty of great responsibility as Commander Submarines under the Commander in Chief, Atlantic Fleet, from March 1942 to November 1944. By his capable and dynamic leadership, Rear Admiral Daubin was largely responsible for the excellent training techniques and procedures formulated and carried out for the intensive schooling of officers and crews for many of the Fleet submarines. Through his wide knowledge of undersea operations and his initiative and outstanding professional skill in the development of new and the perfection of old procedures and weapons, he has contributed to the splendid results of our submarine operations

against the enemy and to the brilliant success of our naval forces.

SMITH, Rear Adm. Edward H., USCG

For exceptionally meritorious service to the Government of the United States in a duty of great responsibility as Commander of the Greenland Patrol and later as Commander of a Task Force in the Atlantic Fleet from December 1941 to November 1944. During the critical years of 1942 and 1943, Rear Admiral Smith planned, built, organized and efficiently administered the naval bases and stations in Greenland and in the Arctic for the support of the Army in those areas and the Naval control of the North Atlantic.

VAN HOOK, Rear Adm. Clifford E., USN

For exceptionally meritorious and distinguished service in a position of great responsibility as Commandant of the 15th Naval District and Commanding Officer of the Panama Sea Frontier, during the period from 15 April, 1942 to 14 October 1943. The outbreak of the present war created many difficult and intricate problems in connection with the expansion of the Naval forces and their activities in defense of the western approaches to the vital waterway of the Panama Canal.

SMITH, Maj. Gen. Holland, USMC

For exceptionally meritorious service to the Government of the United States in a position of great responsibility as Commanding General of the Amphibious Corps, Atlantic Fleet, and later as Commanding General, Fleet Marine Force, San Diego Area, and Commanding General of the Amphibious Corps, Pacific Fleet.

GALLERY, Capt. Daniel V., USN

For exceptionally meritorious and distinguished service to the Government of the United States in a duty of great responsibility as Commander of an Atlantic Fleet Antisubmarine Task Group from January 4 to June 22, 1944. By his judicious planning and sound tactical judgment in selecting the most strategic localities for his task force searches during this period of restricted submarine activity, Captain Gallery enabled his highly efficient, expertly trained command to achieve unparalleled success against the enemy

ISBELL, Capt. Arnold J., USN

For exceptionally meritorious and distinguished service to the Government of the United States in a position of great responsibility as Commanding Officer of the USS CARD and as Antisubmarine Task Group Commander from July 27 to November 9, 1943. Operating in the Central Atlantic convoy route, the planes and escort destroyers under Captain Isbell's intrepid leadership, developed into a powerful combat force, seeking out the enemy with relentless determination and striking with superbly coordinated action in a sustained drive.

Legion of Merit

MUNROE, Vice Adm. William R., USN

Commandant Third Naval District, March 25 to November 1, 1944.

TARRANT, Vice Adm. William Theodore, USN (Ret.)

Operating in the vitally important area of the First Naval District from the time of our entry into the current war until August 1, 1942, Vice Admiral Tarrant devised sound and comprehensive measures in combating enemy encroachment in that territory.

ALLEN, Rear Adm. William H., USN (Ret.)

Commandant Sixth Naval District and Task Group Commander of the Eastern Sea Frontier Forces.

BADGER, Rear Adm. Oscar Charles, USN

Assistant Chief of Naval Operations for Logistics Plans and Director, Logistics Plans Division, during the period from December 1942 to January 1944.

BARBEY, Rear Adm. Daniel E., USN

Chief of Staff, Commander Service Force, Atlantic Fleet, during the period January 1941 to July 1942.

BENNETT, Rear Adm. Andrew C., USN

Organized and trained an Advance Base, United States Naval Unit, for duty

with the Center Task Force, from September 1942 to January 1943.

BUCK, Rear Adm. Walter Albert (SC), USN

Force Supply Officer on the Staff of Commander Support Force, Atlantic Fleet, March 5, 1941 to February 10, 1942.

DURGIN, Rear Adm. Calvin T., USN

Commander Fleet Air, Quonset Point, March 1943 to June 1944.

HUSTVEDT, Rear Adm. Olaf M., USN

Chief of Staff to the Commander in Chief, Atlantic Fleet, October 25, 1941 to May 4, 1943.

*JONES, Rear Adm. J. Cary, USN

Commander Destroyers, United States Atlantic Fleet, during the period from January 1944 until September 1944.

KAUFFMAN, Rear Adm. James L., USN

Commandant Seventh Naval District and Commander Gulf Sea Frontier.

KILPATRICK, Rear Adm. Walter Kenneth, USN

Chief of Staff and Aide to the Commander in Chief, Atlantic Fleet, May 1943 to November 1944.

*ROCKWELL, Rear Adm. Francis Warren, USN

Commander of the Amphibious Training Command of the Atlantic Fleet from March to November 1944.

SIMONS, Rear Adm. Manley H., USN

Commander Chesapeake Task Group, Eastern Sea Frontier, operating in the vitally important area of the Fifth Naval District from the time of our entry into the current war until May 31, 1943.

VAN HOOK, Rear Adm. Clifford Evans, USN

Commandant Fifteenth Naval District and Commander Panama Sea Frontier from 15 April 1942, to 14 October 1943.

WATSON, Rear Adm. Adolphus E., USN (Ret.)

Operating in the vitally important area of the Fourth Naval District from the time of our entry into the current war until September 4, 1942.

YOUNG, Rear Adm. William B. (SC), USN

Fleet Supply Officer, Atlantic Fleet, April 1941 to May 1942.

JOHNSON, Commodore Lee P., USN

Commander Rear Echelon, Amphibious Force, and Commander Amphibious Training Command, Atlantic Fleet, April 1943 to April 1944.

ASHBROOK, Capt. Allan W., USN

Commanding Officer of the Naval Mine Warfare School, Yorktown, Virginia, December 31, 1940 to November 25, 1944.

BARCHET, Capt. Stephen George, USN

Operations Officer on the staff of Commander Submarines, United States Atlantic Fleet, from July 1943 until August 1944.

*BOYLE, Capt. James D. (SC), USN

Member of the staff of Commander Service Force, United States Atlantic Fleet, from May 1942 until September 1944.

BUSBEY, Capt. Leroy W., USN

Operations Officer on the staff of Commander Service Force, United States Atlantic Fleet, from July 1942 to August 1943.

CHADWICK, Capt. James H., USN

Fleet Material Officer on the staff of the Commander in Chief, United States Atlantic Fleet, during the period of December 1940 to November 1944.

CLARK, Capt. Sherman R., USN

Commanding Officer, USS HILARY P. JONES, performed arduous escort duties in the North Atlantic.

*CLARKE, Capt. William Price Oliver, USN

Commanding Landing Craft Group of the Amphibious Force, Atlantic Fleet.

CLEXTON, Capt. Edward W., USN

Staff of Commander Air Force, Atlantic Fleet, March 1941 to July 1944.

CONNOR, Capt. John, USN

Antisubmarine Warfare Officer on the Staff of Commander Destroyers, Atlantic Fleet, and as Commander of an Atlantic Fleet Task Group, March 1942 to January 1944.

CRAWFORD, Capt. George Clifford, USN

Chief of Staff and War Plans Officer on the staff of Commander Submarines, United States Atlantic Fleet, from June 1943 to 1944.

DENEBRINK, Capt. Francis C., USN

Chief of Staff to the Commander, Fleet Operational Training Command, Atlantic Fleet, February 1943 to March 1944.

DUNN, Capt. Joseph C., USN

Executive Officer and later as Commanding Officer of the USS BOGUE, October 1942 to April 1944.

GREER, Capt. Marshall R., USN

Task Group Commander, Atlantic Fleet, May 1943 to October 1943.

*HARTLEY, Capt. Henry, USN

Commander, Auxiliary Vessels Shakedown Group, Fleet Operational Training Command, United States Atlantic Fleet, from August 1943 until June 1944.

HARTUNG, Capt. Richard R., USN

Commander Mine Squadron Six and Service Squadron Five, Service Force, Atlantic Fleet.

HOSKINS, Capt. John M., USN

Chief of Staff, Commander Fleet Air, Quonset, R. I., June 1943 to September 1944.

HUGHES, Capt. Francis M., USN

Commanding Officer of the USS BLOCK ISLAND, March 10, 1944 to May 29, 1944, and an Atlantic Fleet Antisubmarine Task Group.

*JOHNSON, Capt. George W., USN

Commander Destroyer Division Sixtyone and as an Escort Unit Commander in operation and administrative capacities in the United States Atlantic Fleet from November 1941 until August 1944.

KIEHL, Capt. Elmer, USN

Gunnery Officer on the Staff of the Commander in Chief, Atlantic Fleet, from May 1943 to August 1944.

LEWIS, Capt. Thomas L., USN

Commanding Officer of an Antisubmarine Warfare Unit, Atlantic Fleet, March 1942 to May 1943.

*MADEIRA, Capt. Dashiell L., USN

Commander Destroyer, Destroyer Escort Shakedown Group, Fleet Operational Training Command, Atlantic Fleet, November 1943 to September 1944.

McCLURE, Capt. Jesse S., USN

Assistant Chief of Staff and Planning Officer, Staff, Commander Air Force, Atlantic Fleet.

McCORKLE, Capt. Francis D., USN

Operations Officer on the Staff of Commander Destroyers, Atlantic Fleet, September 1943 to January 1945.

McCOWN, Capt. Henry Y., USN

Operations Officer on the Staff of Commander in Chief, United States Atlantic Fleet, in the period August 1943 to November 1944.

MENDENHALL, Capt. William Kavanaugh, Jr., USN

Commanding Officer, Atlantic Fleet Antisubmarine Warfare Unit and while on special duty under the Commander in Chief, Atlantic Fleet, from April to November 1944.

MILLS, Capt. Donald L., USN

Operations Officer on the Staff of Commander Air Force, Atlantic Fleet, January 1943 to February 1944.

MOSES, Capt. William M., USN

Gunnery Officer on the Staff of the Commander in Chief, Atlantic Fleet, September 21, 1941 to June 1, 1943.

PIERCE, Capt. Edward H., USN

Assistant Operations Officer on the Staff of Commander in Chief, United States Atlantic Fleet, from May 1942 until June 1944.

PORTER, Capt. Robert L., Jr., USN

Chief of Staff, Commander Destroyers, Atlantic Fleet, June 1942 to April 1944.

RIDDLE, Capt. Frederick Leavenworth, USN

Assistant Operations Officer on the Staff of Commander in Chief, Atlantic Fleet, January 1942 to March 1944.

SEILLER, Capt. Henry A., USN

Planning Officer and as Production Officer of the Navy Yard, Philadelphia, Pa., July 8, 1940 to September 23, 1944.

SHORT, Capt. Giles E., USN

Antisubmarine Task Group Commander, Atlantic Fleet, April 1943 to June 1943.

VEST, Capt. John Pinckney Wheeler, USN

Commander of an Antisubmarine Task Group, Atlantic Fleet, November 1943 to November 1944.

VOSSELLER, Capt. Aurelius Bartlett, USN

Commander Antisubmarine Development Detachment, Atlantic Fleet, April 1943 to March 1944.

Gold Star in Lieu of a Second Legion of Merit

Commander of an Antisubmarine Task Group during the seven months, directed the operations of the fighting forces under his command so as to involve the sinking of an outstanding number of enemy submarines.

WOOD, Capt. John Enos (SC), USN

Supply Officer on the Staff of Commander Air Force, Atlantic Fleet, January 1943 to July 1944.

BERDINE, Cdr. Harold Sloop, USCG

Commanding Officer of the USCGC SPENCER when that ship engaged and sank a German submarine on 17 April 1943.

BOWLING, Cdr. Jack F., Jr., USN

Commander of a United States Atlantic Fleet Antisubmarine Task Group.

CORBUS, Cdr. John, USN

Commanding Officer of the USS HER-RING in combat against an enemy German submarine, March 20, 1943.

DIMMICK, Cdr. John B, USN

Gunnery Officer on the Staff of the Commander Destroyers, Atlantic Fleet, May 20 to December 18, 1943.

FRENCH, Cdr. Reginald H., USCG

Commander of a United States Atlantic Fleet Antisubmarine Task Group while engaged in offensive action against the enemy.

GIAMBATTISTA, Cdr. Frank D., USN

Commander Escort Division Thirteen while engaged in extensive operations and actions against enemy submarines during the period from 24 March 1944 until 15 July 1944.

HARRIS, Cdr. Morgan H., USNR

Commanding Officer of the USS AHRENS engaged in enemy submarine action on 29 May 1944.

HUMMER, Cdr. Harry R., Jr., USN

Commanding Officer of the USS MC-LANAHAN.

LANK, Cdr. Theodore Small, USN

Officer in Tactical Command during an antisubmarine action by air and surface units on 13 March 1944.

MARSHALL, Cdr. James G., USN

Commanding Officer, USS DUPONT, while engaged in action against an enemy submarine during 12–13 December 1943.

MURDAUGH, Cdr. Albert C., USN

Commanding Officer of the USS EDISON and also Commanding Task Unit, escorting convoy, Task Force TWENTY-FOUR, February 21–24, 1942.

RICHARDS, Cdr. Gilbert H., Jr., USN

Commanding Officer, USS MOFFETT, against an enemy submarine the night of 3–4 August 1943.

SARSFIELD, Cdr. Eugene S., USN

Commanding Officer of the USS MAD-DOX during an attack against an enemy German submarine in the Atlantic Area.

SHAFFER, Cdr. John J., III, USN

Commanding Officer USS CHAMPLIN during action against an enemy German submarine in the Atlantic area April 7, 1944.

SISSON, Cdr. Thomas Upton, USN

. Aviation Officer on the Staff of Commander in Chief Atlantic Fleet, May 22, 1942 to September 11, 1943.

SMEDBERG, Cdr. William R., III, USN

Commanding Officer of the USS LANS-DOWNE during action against an enemy submarine on July 3, 1942.

Gold Star in Lieu of a Second Legion of Merit

Commanding Officer of the USS LANS-DOWNE during action against an enemy submarine on July 13, 1942.

SPECHT, Cdr. William C., USN

Commanding Officer, Motor Torpedo Boat Squadron Training Center, Melville, Rhode Island, from March 16, 1942 to August 30, 1943.

TAYLOR, Cdr. Alfred H., USN

Fleet Communication Officer on the Staff of Commander in Chief, United States Atlantic Fleet, from December 31, 1941 to January 3, 1944.

TROSINO, Cdr. Earl, USNR

In charge of boarding parties sent by the GUADALCANAL to reinforce the original boarding party from the PILLSBURY in connection with the capture of the German Submarine U-505 on 4 June 1944 off Cape Blanco in French West Africa.

WAIT, Cdr. Delos E., USN

Executive Officer of the USS BLOCK ISLAND when that vessel was sunk by enemy action on May 29, 1944.

WALSH, Cdr. David J., USNR

Commanding Officer, Motor Torpedo Boat Squadrons Training Center, Fleet Operational Training Command, United States Atlantic Fleet, and as Squadron Commander of vessels assigned to that activity, and as Commanding Officer of the Motor Torpedo Boat Repair Unit Training Center.

WEEKS, Cdr. Robert H., USN

Assistant Fleet Communication Officer to the Commander in Chief, United States Atlantic Fleet, from June 1941 until June 1944.

YANCEY, Cdr. Evan W., USN

Screen Commander of a United States Atlantic Fleet Antisubmarine Task Group.

AVERY, Lt. Cdr. Howard M., USN

Commanding Officer of Composite Squadron NINE during the period from 24 September 1943 until 10 November 1943.

BREWER, Lt. Cdr. Charles W., USN

Commanding Officer of an aircraft squadron during the period March 1943 to December 1943.

CONKEY, Lt. Cdr. George L., USN

Commanding Officer of the USS EUGENE E. ELMORE engaged in action against an enemy submarine on 29 May 1944.

ELLIS, Lt. Cdr. Lee A., USN

Radio Officer on the Staff of Commander Destroyers, Atlantic Fleet, during the period June 6 to December 14, 1942.

FELDMAN, Lt. Cdr. Herbert, USCGR

Commanding Officer, USS LOWE, on 18 March 1945, in an attack against an enemy submarine.

FOLEY, Lt. Cdr. James L., USN

Commanding Officer of the USS CHATELAIN while conducting offensive operations against an enemy submarine on 9 April 1944.

HEADLAND, Lt. Cdr. Edwin H., Jr., USN

Commanding Officer of the USS POPE while conducting offensive action against an enemy submarine on 9 April 1944.

HILL, Lt. Cdr. Herbert D., USNR

Commanding Officer USS BARRY from July 27, 1943 until 9 November 1943.

HOFFMAN, Lt. Cdr. George D., USN

Commanding Officer of the USS CORRY during a successful action against an enemy submarine in March 1944.

HOFFMAN, Lt. Cdr. Norman C., USNR

Commanding Officer of the USS BAKER while engaged in action against an enemy submarine on 5 July 1944.

HUEY, Lt. Cdr. Fred, USNR

Commanding Officer of an Atlantic Fleet Destroyer Escort.

IRVINE, Lt. Cdr. James M., USNR.

Commanding Officer of an Atlantic Fleet Destroyer Escort while engaged in offensive action against an enemy submarine.

JONES, Lt. Cdr. Carl Eugene, USNR

Commanding Officer of Squadron VC-1 from May to September 1943.

KELLOGG, Lt. Cdr. David M., USNR

Commanding Officer of the USS THOMAS while engaged in action against an enemy submarine.

*KINNEY, Lt. Cdr. Sheldon H., USN

Commanding Officer of the USS BRONSTEIN in offensive action against an enemy submarine during the night of 29 February–March 1, 1944.

LOGSDON, Lt. Cdr. Earl W., USN

Commanding Officer, USS SCHENCK, during engagements with enemy submarines during the night of 23–24 December 1943.

LOVELAND, Lt. Cdr. Kenneth, USN

Commanding Officer of the USS HOBSON during an antisubmarine action on 13 March 1944.

MATHEWS, Lt. Cdr. Jerry A., USNR

Commanding Officer of the USS HAVERFIELD during antisubmarine action on 13 March 1944.

McCORMICK, Lt. Cdr. Nelson C., USCG

On 13 June 1942, USCGC THETIS made an attack on an enemy submarine in position Latitude 24-13 N. Longitude 82-03 W. This attack designated by Incident #853 was assessed "B" (probably sunk) by the Committee on Assessment of Damage to Enemy Submarines.

McWHORTER, Lt. Cdr. John H., USNR

Commanding Officer of the USS FROST while engaged in action against an enemy submarine on 11–12 June 1944.

Gold Star in Lieu of a Second Legion of Merit

Commanding Officer of USS FROST while engaged in action against an enemy submarine on 3 July 1944.

MILLER, Lt. Cdr. Roger Farrington, USNR

Commanding Officer of the USS OSMOND INGRAM in action against an enemy submarine in the Atlantic Area on December, 12–13, 1943.

MYHRE, Lt. Cdr. Leonard A., USNR

Commanding Officer of a United States Atlantic Fleet destroyer escort while engaged in offensive action against an enemy submarine.

PETERSON, Lt. Cdr. Carl U., USCG

Commanding Officer of the USCGC ESCANABA while that vessel was engaged in rescue operation in behalf of survivors of a United States transport which was torpedoed and sunk on February 3, 1943.

PRESSEY, Lt. Cdr. George W., USN

Aide, Flag Lieutenant and Fleet Navigator on the Staff of the Commander in Chief, United States Atlantic Fleet, December 31, 1942 to September 18, 1943.

SESSIONS, Lt. Cdr. William A., USNR

Commanding Officer of the USS CANDY while engaged in offensive action against an enemy submarine on April 16, 1944.

SMITH, Lt. Cdr. Hinton I., USNR

Commanding Officer of the USS GOFF during the period from 27 July 1943 until 9 November 1943.

STANLEY, Lt. Cdr. John Theodore, USCG

Munitions Officer, Port Security Command, Third Naval District, during firefighting aboard the SS ELESTERO, loaded with a cargo of explosives in New York Harbor, N. Y., on April 24, 1943.

SYNON, Lt. Cdr. George D., USCG

On 22 May 1943, USCGC NIKE made an attack on enemy submarine in position Latitude 27-11 N. Longitude 79-56 W. This attack was assessed "B" by Committee on Assessment of Damage to Enemy Submarines.

*TUFTS, Lt. Cdr. David A., USNR

Commanding Officer, USS INCH, while engaged in action against an enemy submarine on 3 July 1944.

WANLESS, Lt. Cdr. Robert Hume, USNR

Commanding Officer of the USS HUSE in action against an enemy submarine on April 7, 1944.

WILCOX, Lt. Cdr. Robert, USCG

Commanding Officer, USS JOYCE, in offensive action against an enemy submarine on 16 April 1944.

BROWN, Lt. Philip Bosche, USNR

Executive Officer of the USS BORIE from June until November 1943.

FLYNN, Lt. Walter T., USNR

Commanding Officer of the USS PC-565 during an attack against an enemy German submarine in the Atlantic on June 2, 1943.

GARLAND, Lt. John D., USN

Commanding Officer of the USS CHOCTAW during the period from 7 March until 30 March 1944.

HAMPTON, Lt. Deward E., USNR

In charge of one of the boarding parties sent by the GUADALCANAL to reinforce the original boarding party from the PILLSBURY and second senior officer aboard the submarine during the salvage operations of the capture of the German Submarine U-505 on 4 June 1944 off Cape Blanco, French West Africa.

HIGGINS, Lt. Edward M., USNR

Commanding Officer of the USS GEORGE E. BADGER while engaged in action against an enemy submarine during 12–13 December 1943.

HOUSTON, Lt. Lewis C., USCGR

On July 8, 1942, USCGC NEMESIS made an attack on an enemy submarine in position Latitude 22-51 N. Longitude 84-42 W. This attack designated by Incident #1055 was assessed "B" (probably sunk) by the Committee on Assessment of Damage to Enemy Submarines.

MORAN, Lt. William F., USNR

Commanding Officer of the USS CLEMSON while engaged in action against an enemy submarine on 13 December 1943.

ROSS, Lt. Clayton, Jr., USN

Engineer Officer of the USS HAMBLETON from November 11, 1942 to June 15, 1943.

DIVER, Lt. (jg) William Greenlaw, USNR

Antisubmarine Warfare Officer of the USS FROST while participating in actions against enemy submarines during the period from late April until early July 1944.

BURR, Robert P., Gunner, USNR

For service on the USS GUADALCANAL.

CULLEN, John C., BM2/c, USCG

Patrol at Long Island, New York, on the night of June 13, 1942, when several Nazi saboteurs bearing boxes of TNT and other destructive apparatus landed on the beach at Amagansett.

DUCKWORTH, Clifton M., CCM, USCG

Serving aboard the USCGC CAMPBELL following the sinking of an enemy submarine by that vessel on February 22, 1943.

PILLARD, Edmond E., CBM, USCG

Senior deck petty officer aboard the USCGC CAMPBELL during and following the sinking of an enemy submarine by that vessel on February 22, 1943.

SCHRUM, Howard A., CPhM, USN

Attached to a vessel engaged in picking up survivors from torpedoed vessels on January 9, 1943, performing outstanding medical services.

STELMASCZYK, Benjamin, CRM, USCG

Chief radioman while attached to the USCGC CAMPBELL on February 22, 1943, when an enemy submarine was severely damaged and sunk, and during the ensuing period when the USCGC CAMPBELL, which was damaged in the engagement, was towed safely into port.

Silver Star Medal

CAUFIELD, Cdr. Cecil T., USN
COWART, Cdr. Kenneth K., USCG
BRALLIER, Lt. Cdr. Bret H., USCG
FOWLER, Lt. Wilma Sim, USNR
ROGERS, Lt. Richard Spalding, USN
VANOUS, Lt. William W., USN
BALLIETT, Lt. (jg) Leston S., USNR
CHAMBERLAIN, Lt. (jg) William F., USNR
LaFLEUR, Lt. (jg) Wallace A., USNR
PERABO, Lt. (jg) Phil, USNR
ROUNTREE, Lt. (jg) Frederick Manning, USNR
SALLENGER, Lt. (jg) Asbury H., USNR
VANVRANKEN, Lt. (jg) Edward, USNR
ANDERSON, Ens. Jack Darrell, USNR
SPRAGUE, Ens. John F., USNR
STEWART, Ens. Jack Howard, USNR
STONE, Ens. Merrill R., Jr., USNR
TEBO, Ens. Kenneth MacLean, USN
ALBRIGHT, William H., Cox., USN
BEAVER, Ernest J., S1/c, USN
BUCKLEY, Dennis Joseph, F1/c, USN
BURKE, Rayner C., CQM, USCG
BURLEIGH, Alvin Richard, S1/c, USNR
DAVIS, Wilbur Gaylord, S2/c, USNR
DIACHENKO, Alex Maxwell, WT2/c, USN
DOLL, Louis James, S2/c, USNR
GREEN, William J., CMM, USNR
GUNTHER, Alvin, CMM, USCG
HAINRIHAR, Anton J., CWT, USCG
HARRISON, Benjamin F., CMM, USCG
HEYMAN, Harry, Cox., USN
JENKINS, Robert R., MoMM3/c, USNR
JENNINGS, Damon, CMM, USCG
JONES, William Jay, F1/c, USN
METIVIER, Joseph Erene Henry, Cox., USN
MEYERS, John, Jr., S2/c, USNR
MYERS, Merton Bennell, MM1/c, USN
PAGNOTTA, James Mario, MM2/c, USNR
SHOCKLEY, Robert Merrill, CM1/c, USN
WHITE, John Hardin, CTM, USN
TINSMAN, Carl Welby, S2/c, USNR
THRUSHEIM, Philip N., Cox., USNR

Distinguished Flying Cross

BURKE, Cdr. Richard L., USCG
COPE, Cdr. Alfred L., USN
RUDDY, Cdr. Joseph Aloysius, USN
WESTHOFEN, Cdr. Charles Louis, USN
AVERY, Lt. Cdr. Howard M., USN
*BREWER, Lt. Cdr. Charles Walter, USN
KLINSMANN, Lt. Cdr. George Otto, USN
TAYLOR, Lt. Cdr. David Wooster, USN
TAYLOR, Lt. Cdr. Jesse D., USNR
AUSLANDER, Lt. Stanley Ernest, USNR
BOLT, Lt. Stewart Baldwin, USNR
BRADFORD, Lt. Gerard, Jr., USNR
CROWLEY, Lt. R. J., USNR
DAVIS, Lt. H. S., USNR
GOULD, Lt. Richard T., USN
HANCE, Lt. K. P., USN
*HODSON, Lt. Norman Douglas, USN
HOERNER, Lt. Helmuth E., USNR
HOLT, Lt. Stewart B., USNR
JAAP, Lt. Joseph Abraham, USN
LAIR, Lt. Carl E., Jr., USNR
LONG, Lt. Ralph W., USNR
LYONS, Lt. Wilbert Alan, USNR
MATUSKI, Lt. A. R., USNR
MAYO, Lt. Robert C., USNR
MILLARD, Lt. Robert C., USN
MURRAY, Lt. Franklin M., USNR
PARISH, Lt. William Wells, USNR
PARSONS, Lt. Samuel G., USNR
PEARCE, Lt. Robert Edward, USNR
**WILLIAMS, Lt. Robert Pershing, USNR
ROBERTS, Lt. H. S., USN
ROBERTS, Lt. Wolffe W., USNR
ROGERS, Lt. Richard S., USN
SCHRADER, Lt. Richard E., USNR
STAPLER, Lt. Charles Ramsey, USN
AUSLANDER, Lt. (jg) S. E., USNR
AYLWARD, Lt. (jg) Thomas James, Jr., USNR
PALLANTINE, Lt. (jg) John H., USNR
BALLIET, Lt. (jg) L. S., USNR
BARTON, Lt. (jg) Claude N., USNR
BRADSHAW, Lt. (jg) S. G., USN
BROKAS, Lt. (jg) Alex X., USNR
BROWNSTEIN, Lt. (jg) Julius Rueben, USNR
CAREY, Lt. (jg) H. C., USN
CHAMBERLAIN, Lt. (jg) W. F., USNR
COCKROFT, Lt. (jg) I. G., USNR
COX, Lt. (jg) Clifford C., USN
CROSS, Lt. (jg) Frederick C., USNR
DAVIS, Lt. (jg) Lowell L., USNR
FELTER, Lt. (jg) William A., USNR

*FORNERY, Lt. (jg) Junior Clyde, USNR
*FOWLER, Lt. (jg) Wilma S., USNR
FRYATT, Lt. (jg) Harry E., USNR
GORDON, Lt. (jg) William D., USNR
HAYMAN, Lt. (jg) Robert W., USNR
HEIM, Lt. (jg) Elbert S., USNR
HEWITT, Lt. (jg) Charles G., U3NR
*HOGAN, Lt. (jg) Gerald Griffin, USNR
HOLMES, Lt. (jg) Theodore M., USNR
JACKSON, Lt. (jg) Ernest Emerson, USNR
JOHNSON, Lt. (jg) Robert J., USNR
McAUSLAN, Lt. (jg) Alexander Cubie, USNR
MOORE, Lt. (jg) Frederick Lee, Jr., USNR
O'NEILL, Lt. (jg) M. G., USNR
PINHOLSTER, Lt. (jg) David C., USNR
RICHMOND, Lt. (jg) R. F., USNR
ROBERTSON, Lt. (jg) Thurmond E., USN
SCHOBY, Lt. (jg) James Frank, USNR
SELLARS, Lt. (jg) Jimmie J., USNR
SORENSON, Lt. (jg) Paul, USNR
STEARNS, Lt. (jg) Robert L., USNR
TENNANT, Lt. (jg) Raymond J., USNR
CADLE, Ens. John W., USNR
GOODWIN, Ens. G. C., USN
HANDSHUH, Ens. Harold L., USNR
HORN, Ens. Joseph D., USNR
HUDSON, Ens. Bert "J," USNR
McLANE, Ens. William M., USNR
PINTER, Ens. Francis E., USNR
SMOLSNIK, Ens. Hubert, USN
STEWART, Ens. Jack Howard, USNR
TEPUNI, Ens. William, USNR
GRINSTEAD, Morris C., ARM1/c, USN
*MASON, Donald Francis, ACMM, USN
THOMPSON, L. H., ACMM, USN

Navy and Marine Corps Medal

DENEBRINK, Capt. Francis C., USN
DUKE, Cdr. Irving, USN
TWOMEY, Cdr. John J., USN
JOHNSON, Lt. Cdr. Lloyd M., USNR
PFISTER, Lt. Cdr. Arthur F., USCGR
ANDERSON, Lt. Langford, USCGR
CONE, Lt. Burtis P., USCGR
DRAKE, Lt. James P., USN
FREEMAN, Lt. James Stewart, USCG
GASTON, Lt. John G., II, USNR
GEE, Lt. Roy P., USN
MACK, Lt. Lawrence John, USNR
MANSFIELD, Lt. Richard D., USNR
MILLER, Lt. Herbert John, USNR
PAYNE, Lt. Ernest W., USCG

PFEIFFER, Lt. Arthur, USCG
PHILIP, Lt. Clifford Duncan, USNR
POST, Lt. Henry A. V., USNR
PRAUSE, Lt. Robert H., USCG
QUINN, Lt. Robert James, USNR
SCANLON, Lt. Emmet E., USN
SILBERSTEIN, Lt. David, USNR
STARKS, Lt. Roger N., USN
WETZEL, Lt. J. L., USNR
CARTER, Lt. (jg) Sydney Gregory, USNR
CONNERY, Lt. (jg) John J., USNR
CROWE, Lt. (jg) Guthrie F., USNR
DALE, Lt. (jg) Carlos K., USCGR
GARNAUS, Lt. (jg) Russel J., USNR
GOODWIN, Lt. (jg) Frederick D., Jr., USNR
GOUKER, Lt. (jg) Roy E., USCGR
HARPER, Lt. (jg) Rufus Cecil, USN
HERZOG, Lt. (jg) William R., USNR
HUTCHINS, Lt. (jg) Roy M., USCG
LEOVY, Lt. (jg) Thomas M., Jr., USNR
McCARTHY, Lt. (jg) Arthur J. F., USN
MILLER, Lt. (jg) Harvey J., USCG
RYND, Lt. (jg) Robert W., USN
SCHROEDER, Lt. (jg) Martin H., USN
SWANSON, Lt. (jg) Leslie Oscar, USNR
VAN METER, Lt. (jg) Herbert E., ChC, USNR
WALKER, Lt. (jg) Woodrow T., USN
ANDERSON, Ens. Robert W., USCGR
ARRIGHI, Ens. Richard A., USCGR
DERING, Ens. Philip R., USNR
GRAY, Ens. W. T., USCG
GUJA, Ens. Arthur T., USNR
HAMMER, Ens. Robert, USNR
HUFFMAN, Ens. Robert Earl, USNR
MIDDAUGH, Ens. Fred L., USN
REHBERT, Ens. Earl James, USNR
ROWAN, Ens. John Egerton, USNR
SEYMOUR, Ens. William Oren, Jr., USNR
SMITH, Ens. C. W., USNR
SPARKS, Ens. Ben, Jr., USNR
ANDERSON, Frank Arnold, GM1/c, USNR
BAILEY, Clarence M., Chief Carp., USN
BACKER, Arthur E., Jr., BM1/c, USCG
BALAS, Andrew Ambrose, S2/c, USNR
BELL, Woodrow C., B2/c, USN
BENFIELD, James A., Cox., USN
BENNETT, Warren, CMM, USCG
BILLOS, Harry P., EM2/c, USCG
BRADSHAW, Odell I., MoMM1/c, USCGR
BRENNAN, Vincent Roy, S1/c, USNR
BILLOS, Harry P., EM2/c, USCG
BRIGHT, Thomas J., S1/c, USNR
BULLARD, James D., ACMM1/c, USN

CAMPBELL, Leonard W., CBM, USCG
CARIENS, Richard J., MM1/c, USCGR
CARROZZA, A. D., Y2/c, USCG
CHANDLER, R. E. L., Jr., AOM3/c, USNR
CLARK, Hal A., PFC, USMC
COASKLEY, Thomas Joseph, ACOM, USNR
CONGER, Claude, CGM, USN
COOPER, Charles E., Cox., USN
COPLIN, Jesse Homer, AMM3/c, USNR
COULTAS, William F., S1/c, USCG
COWLE, Rolland Francis, Jr., MM2/c, USN
CRAMER, Louis J., CBM, USCG
CREGGER, James L., SF1/c, USN
CUNNINGHAM, F. F., SoM2/c, USCG
DAISEY, John R., AMM2/c, USNR
DAVID, Charles W., Jr., StM1/c, USCG
DEROSA, William A., Bkr3/c, USNR
DEYAMPERT, Warren T., StM3/c, USCG
DUDLEY, R. L., Cox., USCG
DULCOS, Edward Francis, CM1/c, USN
DUPUY, Alfred M., SK3/c, USNR
ERBSLAND, George J., S2/c, USNR
ESHELMAN, Walter George, BM1/c, USN
FARRAR, M. J., Jr., S1/c, USCGR
FLOYD, Harold D., CMM, USN
FORD, Byron Russell, SM2/c, USNR
FOSTER, Charles Wilson, ARM1/c, USN
FRANK, David, QM3/c, USNR
GAMBLE, Robert James, S1/c, USN
GARDNER, John N., AS, USCGR
GARGIULO, Louis, SF1/c, USNR
GOLDMAN, Claude Ceremelian, TM2/c, USN
GOULD, James R., AS, USCGR
HARLAND, George J., S1/c, USCGR
HARRISON, John P., Cox., USCG
HENDRIX, John T., CEM, USCG
HENDRICKSON, Lavon R., RM2/c, USN
HIGGINS, Harold James, AMM1/c, USN
IZZI, Basil Dominic, S1/c, USNR
JAILLET, R. R. J., CBM, USN
KECK, M. C., SK1/c, USN
KILLEBREW, Clyde J., QM2/c, USNR
KOROWICKI, Stanley, S1/c, USCGR
KRAM, Herman H., GM3/c, USCGR
KRINSKY, Jacob M., S1/c, USNR
KUBRAN, William J., ChM, USNR
KUPAC, Wendel J., S1/c, USCGR
LEWANDOWSKI, Edward P., RM3/c, USCGR
LITTLE, Joseph F., GM3/c, USNR
LOGAR, H. J., QM3/c, USCG
LYSAGHT, M., CBM, USCG

McArdle, Arthur T., ACMM, USN
McGrath, Charles J., SoM2/c, USCG
McIntire, R. W., MM2/c, USNR
McLaughlin, Bruce Emerson, S1/c, USNR
McManus, Edward J., RM3/c, USCGR
McPhee, J. D., SC3/c, USN
Martin, Henry, Jr., S2/c, USCGR
Meeberg, U. I., S1/c, USCG
Miller, Ralph McCoy, EM3/c, USNR
Miller, Eugene Richard, EM3/c, USNR
Mitchell, William G., SK1/c, USCGR
Mueller, William H., BM1/c, USCG
Mulligan, Maurice B., Jr., HA1/c, USNR
Netterville, LeRoy T., ARM3/c, USNR
Nickerson, Arthur, CM1/c, USCGR
Norris, Calvin E., S1/c, USNR
O'Brien, Frank Leo, SF3/c, USNR
O'Donnell, Harry Smith, CM3/c, USN
O'Malley, Donald J., Corp., USMC
Paternoster, Raymond Chester, S1/c, USNR
Peckham, James R., Cox., USNR
Pelletier, Lionel Frederick, ARM1/c, USN
Petrenko, J., Jr., MoMM2/c, USCGR
Power, John Bell, SoM3/c, USNR
Read, Jerome T., CBM, USN
Rednour, Forrest C., SC2/c, USCG
Redwine, Maurice Earl, WT3/c, USNR
Rogers, Charles Daniel, Sp1/c, USCGR
Ruff, J. O., S1/c, USCGR
Scaffe, Charles P., CBM, USN
Scaffe, Norman Bryan, EM3/c, USN
Sirmons, Robert Wycliffe, S1/c, USN
Smith, Hoke, MM1/c, USNR
Smith, Richard Marshall, S1/c, USN
Sparks, R. T., Cox., USN
Sweeney, John Paul, S1/c, USNR
Terrien, Ross H., AMM1/c, USCG
Thomas, Horace Leslie, CEM, USCGR
Tillinghast, Ernest B., S2/c, USN
Uzzel, Ollie Lee, WT1/c, USN
Venker, F. H., MM3/c, USNR
Viens, Marcel V., Cox., USNR
Viera, Joseph CM1/c, USNR
Vile, Robert G., F1/c, USCGR
Warren, William Jackson, ACMM, USN
Washburn, Carl Raymond, ACMM, USN
Watts, Edwin Bruce, BM2/c, USN
Wells, E., BM1/c, USN
Wells, James Darius, F3/c, USN
Werlia, C. V., CPhoM, USNR

West, Milton O., Jr., S1/c, USCGR
Whitten, Madison Neal, S2/c, USN
Wiegand, C. E., BM2/c, USCG
Wolfgram, John Ohman, BM2/c, USNR
Wood, Clayton Albert, SM3/c, USN
Wright, J., Jr., BM1/c, USNR
Zimmerman, Philip Edward, Jr., BM2/c, USNR

Air Medal

Erdmann, Capt. William L., USN
*Hollister, Cdr. William W., USN
Brewer, Lt. Cdr. Charles W., USN
Gannon, Lt. Cdr. John W., USN
Estabrook, Lt. Cdr. William T., USNR
Greer, Lt. Cdr. Julian D., USN
Moore, Lt. Cdr. Charles Leighton, USN
Slagle, Lt. Cdr. Robert J., USN
Bass, Lt. Harry B., USN
Bly, Lt. Homer B., USNR
Gibson, Lt. Ben W., Jr., USNR
Griggs, Lt. Paul C., USN
Hoerner, Lt. Helmuth E., USNR
*Irish, Lt. Arthur S., USNR
Lawrence, Lt. Harry B., USNR
Mayhew, Lt. Boyd Nelson, USNR
Pettingell, Lt. Winslow L., USNR
Reviere, Lt. John P., USNR
Reynolds, Lt. Frank G., USN
Stagle, Lt. Robert J., USN
Steffen, Lt. Ernest W., Jr., USNR
Sutherlin, Lt. Robert J., USNR
*Tepuni, Lt. William, USNR
Watson, Lt. John B., USNR
Weeks, Lt. Cyrus Foss, USNR
Williams, Lt. Robert P., USN
Bomar, Lt. (jg) R. E., USNR
*Bradshaw, Lt. (jg) Harold G., USN
Brooks, Lt. (jg) Douglas W., USNR
Burstad, Lt. (jg) Marshall E., USNR
Davis, Lt. (jg) Sumner Robertson, USNR
Devore, Lt. (jg) Harry E., USNR
Dill, Lt. (jg) William Edward, USNR
Dowty, Lt. (jg) Norman Taylor, USNR
Fogde, Lt. (jg) F. D., USNR
Goldstein, Lt. (jg) Richard W., USNR
Gordon, Lt. (jg) Prince Hodgson, USNR
Hamrick, Lt. (jg) Lawrence Lee, USNR
Hardesty, Lt. (jg) Charles D., USNR
Kersey, Lt. (jg) Robert L., Jr., USNR
Mabry, Lt. (jg) George C., USNR
McFord, Lt. (jg) Leonard L., USN
Ogle, Lt. (jg) James E., III, USNR

O'Neill, Lt. (jg) M. G., USNR
Pattison, Lt. (jg) William F., USNR
Porter, Lt. (jg) W. S., USNR
Prewitt, Lt. (jg) E. K., USNR
Reeder, Lt. (jg) Louis P., USNR
Richmond, Lt. (jg) Robert F., USNR
Russell, Lt. (jg) Edward B., USNR
Ryan, Lt. (jg) William H., USN
Seeley, Lt. (jg) D. Willis, USNR
Sherbring, Lt. (jg) Milton J., USNR
Shevlin, Lt. (jg) W. A., USNR
Sissler, Lt. (jg) Bernard C., USNR
***Smith, Lt. (jg) G. S., USNR
Sulton, Lt. (jg) John, Jr., USNR
Tompkins, Lt. (jg) John Erwin, Jr., USNR
Tucker, Lt. (jg) Clyde Adair, Jr., USNR
Wallace, Lt. (jg) Eugene E., USNR
Abrams, Ens. Earle B., USNR
Blalock, Ens. William R., USNR
Doty, Ens. Stewart Edward, USNR
Field, Ens. Richard P., USNR
Gierisch, Ens. Jack K., USN
Hodgson, Ens. Edward Ralph, USNR
Jenkins, Ens. Thomas E., USNR
Koos, Ens. Edwin M., USNR
Lovell, Ens. C. O., USN
*Mason, Ens. Donald F., USN
*Maulding, Ens. Everett M., USNR
*Miller, Ens. William B., USNR
Oster, Ens. Jonathan, USNR
Pierce, Ens. Wallace I., USNR
Reeves, Ens. James O., USNR
Ruth, Ens. Robert Frederick, USNR
Sharkey, Ens. William, USNR
Shea, Ens. John J., USNR
Shella, Ens. Barton Cecil, USNR
Smolsnik, Ens. Hubert, USN
Taylor, Ens. Ellis R., USNR
Taylor, Ens. W. R., USNR
Thomas, Ens. Gerald Waylett, USNR
Volm, Ens. Bernard Henry, Jr., USNR
Aleshkowtch, John William, RM3/c, USNR
*Alford, Frank AMM1/c, USN
Baldwin, Algia M., AMM1/c, USN
Benecke, Joe Freeman, ACMM, USN
Bentrod, W. J., AP1/c, USN
Berg, Robert W., ARM3/c, USNR
Blazer, David W., ACRM, USN
Bosserman, James William, ARM3/c, USNR
Boyce, Chester R., ARM3/c, USNR
Boyland, Ralph H., AMM2/c, USN
Brown, G. J., ACRM, USN

Bucholtz, Harold Eugene, AMM1/c, USN
Burger, Curtis E., AMM1/c, USN
Burnham, Willis Lee, AMM3/c, USN
Burton, Edgar W., ARM1/c, USN
Cannady, Stephen Joel, RM2/c, USN
Carthen, R. B., ARM2/c, USNR
Chapman, Barney Lee, ARM1/c, USNR
Coombs, Harry B., AMM3/c, USNR
Copple, Hal E., AMM1/c, USN
*Copple, James H., AMM1/c, USN
Dittmer, Frank Weyman, AOM2/c, USN
*Day, Edward W., AMM3/c, USN
Docteur, Mark Francis, AMM1/c, USNR
Dodd, Kenneth G., AOM2/c, USN
*Downes, John David, ACRM, USNR
Easterly, Paul D., ARM2/c, USN
Edwards, W. E., AP1/c, USN
Eichhorn, N. C., AMM/2c, USN
Erickson, Richard M., AOM3/c, USNR
Ermer, Herbert August, ARM1/c, USN
Evans, William Henry, AMM3/c, USNR
Fallin, George Louis, AOM1/c, USN
Falwell, Claude Donald, AMM1/c, USN
Fisher, C., S2/c, USNR
Fisher, Herbert Raymond, ARM2/c, USNR
*Fisher, Joseph Richard, AMM3/c, USN
*Garner, William Dudley, RM1/c, USN
Goodman, Billy, AMM2/c, USN
Graves, Robert Louis, AOM3/c, USN
Greenfield, William E., ARM3/c, USNR
Gregory, Robert I., AOM2/c, USNR
Griffin, Lloyd Eugene, RM3/c, USN
Gunderson, Knute Oscar, AMM1/c, USN
Gunther,, Alvin F., CMM, USCG
Harris, William Perin, AMM2/c, USN
*Hawley, Truett Smith, AMM1/c, USN
Haywood, F. E., ARM3/c, USNR
Heffner, Marlin V., ARM1/c, USN
*Hodde, Werner William Henry, AMM2/c, USN
Holland, Mark O., ARM1/c, USN
Holt, Joseph A., AMM3/c, USNR
Horacek, Raymond J., ARM3/c, USNR
Howard, Turner J., ARM2/c, USN
Hutchinson, William Issac, AMM3/c, USNR
Iwanicki, Henry Walter, ARM3/c, USNR
Jones, A. W., ACMM, USN
Jones, Morgan R., AOM3/c, USN

KING, Paul Alfred, AOM2/c, USN
KRAMER, Virgil E., AMM1/c, USN
LA PORTE, Thaddeus L., ACMM, USN
LOVE, Earl M., AP1/c, USN
LUFF, Clifton Floyd, RM2/c, USN
McCONNELL, Robert W., ARM1/c, USN
McDONNELL, John B., CAP, USN
McGUIRE, J. J., S2/c, USNR
McKEE, Foch Clinton, ARM2/c, USNR
McLEMORE, Aubrey A., AMM3/c, USN
MacCABLE, Gordon, AMM2/c, USN
MATTINGLY, K. A., AMM3/c, USNR
MEDLER, Clement Daniel, ACRM, USN
MEDLEY, Doc Stough, ARM3/c, USNR
*MELLINGER, Charles Darwin, ACRM, USN
MIDDLETON, Russell C., AOM3/c, USNR
*MILES, Leslie, AOM2/c, USNR
MINNEHAN, Burr Joeph, RM3/c, USN
MYERS, Elton Leroy, AOM3/c, USN
MYLES, A. L., AP1/c, USN
NEALE, L. M., ARM1/c, USN
*NEHRBAS, Thomas Charles, RM3/c, USN
*NEIDERT, Charles George, ACMM, USN
*O'HAGAN, James H., Jr., AMM2/c, USNR
OTWAY, Robert John, RM3/c, USN
PADEN, Melvin H., AMM2/c, USN
PAINTER, William D., ARM2/c, USNR
PARIS, Charles E., AMM2/c, USNR
PARKER, Ralph Lloyd, RM3/c, USN
PETERSON, Willard Leo, RM2/c, USN
*PFEIFER, Casper Joseph, ARM3/c, USN
POTTER, Wellington Harned, ARM2/c, USN
RAKES, Charles Edward, AMM3/c, USNR
REGAN, Maurice F., AMM3/c, USNR
RICHOZ, Eugene L., AP1/c, USN
ROBERTS, Franklin O'Brien, AMM3/c, USN
RODDY, Alfred Joseph, Jr., AOM3/c, USNR
SARNA, Russell Edgar, AMM1/c, USN
SAULTZ, Vernon, AMM1/c, USN
SCHULTZ, Wilbert H., AMM3/c, USNR
SCHWAHN, Peter, AOM1/c, USNR
SCOTT, Albert James, AMM2/c, USN
SHIELL, Willis Reid, AMM2/c, USNR
SHIRLEY, Henry Ray, ARM2/c, USNR
SHOCKLEY, Donald F., ARM3/c, USNR
SLAYTON, William Avery, AMM2/c, USN
SMITH, Robert Lee, RM3/c, USN
STAMPS, Robert Baker, AMM1/c, USNR

STEPNOWSKI, Leon Adam, RM2/c, USN
TARSILLIA, Enoch P., AMM2/c, USN
TKAC, Michael, RM1/c, USN
TORRES, Anthony C., ARM2/c, USN
TRAUB, Egon F., ARM2/c, USNR
VANDELIST, Clarence H., Jr., ARM3/c, USN
VASU, J., AMM2/c, USN
VAUGHN, Charles Albert, Jr., ARM2/c, USNR
VICKERS, Wrencie, ARM3/c, USN
VON SPREECKEN, Raymond E., AOM2/c, USNR
WELCH, James Arlidge, ARM1/c, USNR
WEIDE, Herman Henry William, AMM2/c, USN
WELLS, John Clay, Jr., AMM2/c, USN
WHITLOCK, Edward A., ART1/c, USN
WOJCIK, C. J., ARM2/c, USN
WOODSON, Richard T., ACRM, USN
ZINK, Albert James, AMM2/c, USN

Bronze Star Medal

BANNERMAN, Capt. Graeme, USN
CROMBE, Capt. Charles Edwin, Jr., USN
EDWARDS, Capt. Raymond D., USN
FICK, Capt. Harold F., USN
HARRISON, Capt. Beverley R., Jr., USN
HAVEN, Capt. Hugh E., USN
HOLT, Capt. Walter Coler, USN
McINTOSH, Capt. Howard D., USN
MENTZ, Capt. George F., USN
OLCH, Capt. Isaiah, USN
RAMSEY, Capt. Logan C., USN
ROONEY, Capt. John B., USN
VOSSELLER, Capt. Aurelius B., USN
WORTHINGTON, Capt. Joseph Muse, USN
BARRETT, Cdr. Russell S., USNR (Ret.)
BRYAN, Cdr. Louis A., USN
CAMERA, Cdr. Robert S., USN
CORDINER, Cdr. Douglas Lee Liscomb, USN
CORLISS, Cdr. Warren George, USN
CUSTER, Cdr. Jasper L., (MC), USNR
DORNIN, Cdr. Marshall E., USN
DURBORG, Cdr. Christian H., USN
GROVERMAN, Cdr. William Heald, Jr., USN
HALL, Cdr. Frederick S., USN
HATCHER, Cdr. Julian S., USN
JOHNSON, Cdr. Jesse Gearing, USN
LIND, Cdr. Alfred L., USNR
LOOMIS, Cdr. Almon E., USN

MABLEY, Cdr. Louis C., USNR
NATION, Cdr. Milton A., USN
PARKINSON, Cdr. George A., USNR
PARRISH, Cdr. Lloyd W., USN
QUINN, Cdr. Charles H., USN
SEAY, Cdr. George C., USN
SIMMERS, Cdr. Clayton Rogers, USN
SULLIVAN, Cdr. Emmett John, USN
TITUS, Cdr. Jack Clarence, USN
WEV, Cdr. Bosquet N., USN
CASSLEMAN, Lt. Cdr. George W., USNR
CHURCH, Lt. Cdr. John H., Jr., USNR
DRANE, Lt. Cdr. William M., USN
GRONVOLD, Lt. Cdr. George R., USNR
GUGGENHIME, Lt. Cdr. Richard E., USNR
HUNTER, Lt. Cdr. Edward N. W., USNR
JOHANSEN, Lt. Cdr. John E., USNR
JOHNSTON, Lt. Cdr. Means, Jr., USN
KELLOGG, Lt. Cdr. David M., USNR
KINNEY, Lt. Cdr. Sheldon H., USN
KNOWLES, Lt. Cdr. Robert S., USNR
KREMER, Lt. Cdr. Sandor (SC) USNR
LOUTREL, Lt. Cdr. Louis F., Jr., USNR
LOVE, Lt. Cdr. Henry H., USNR
McWHORTER, Lt. Cdr. John H., USNR
MARTIN, Lt. Cdr. Frederick H., USNR
MONTGOMERY, Lt. Cdr. Richard J., USNR
MOORE, Lt. Cdr. Winford O., USN
ROLLINS, Lt. Cdr. G. L., USCG
RYDEEN, Lt. Cdr. Francis Clyde, USN
STAGGS, Lt. Cdr. William R., USN
STEWART, Lt. Cdr. Claude W., USN
STREET, Lt. Cdr. Gordon M., USNR
BATCHELLER, Lt. James H., Jr., USN
BAUGHAM, Lt. Robert L., USN
BENDER, Lt. John L., USCGR
BLANC, Lt. Joseph William, USNR
BYRD, Lt. Thomas H., USNR
COE, Lt. Robert Campbell, USNR
EVE, Lt. Henry P., USNR
FELTER, Lt. John Francis, USNR
GILL, Lt. Calvert Burke, USN
HAYES, Lt. Byron C., USNR
HILDITCH, Lt. Frank D., USCG
HURD, Lt. John Gavin, USNR
HODSON, Lt. Norman Douglas, USN
KILLEEN, Lt. Thomas A., Jr., USNR
LOZIER, Lt. Edwin R., USNR
MICHELS, Lt. John H., USCGR
OVERMYER, Lt. Irvin Alfred, USNR
RISER, Lt. Frederick F., USNR
RODI, Lt. Merton P., USNR
WILMER, Lt. John Wittingham, USNR
DAVIS, Lt. (jg) John Jackson, USN

KEYES, Lt. (jg) Edward Joseph, Jr., USNR
KRAMER, Lt. (jg) Boris B., USNR
SETZER, Lt. (jg) Gene W., USNR
SNYDER, Lt. (jg) Elwood, USNR
THUM, Lt. (jg) Cleo, USN
WALDRON, Lt. (jg) John A., USCGR
SHERIDAN, Ens. William John, USN
TILLMAN, Ens. William N., USCGR
WEITZ, Ens. Herman Louis, USN
COLIHAN, John Patrick, Boat., USNR
ALLEN, Nelson W., SoM2/c, USCGR
COBURN, Winston T., SoM3/c, USCGR
CULBERSON, Alexander, AMM2/c, USNR
HEYWOOD, Clayne Frederick, BM1/c, USNR
JOHNSON, Leonard L., AMM3/c, USNR
McGHGHY, Harmon D., ABM3/c, USNR
MUZA, Earl V., S2/c, USNR
PRICE, Arthur, CBM, USNR
SCHNEIDER, Albert Martin, CCM, USNR
TAYLOR, Don A., AMM2/c, USNR

Army Soldier's Medal

ECKLEY, William G., CMM, USN
GUYERMELLI, Joseph E., S2/c
HOLTMEYER, William L., CM3/c, USNR
IRVING, Wallace J., EM2/c, USNR
McINERNEY, Michael A., CM2/c, USNR
OLSON, Einar C., CM1/c, USNR
SWINEHART, Harley N., MM2/c, USNR
WEBSTER, Cleveland A., EM1/c, USNR

PRESIDENTIAL UNIT CITATIONS
ANTISUBMARINE TASK GROUPS

Which Operated with the USS BOGUE
As Flagship

United States Ships BOGUE, LEA, GREENE, BELKNAP, OSMOND INGRAM, GEORGE E. BADGER, and VC-9, from April 20 to June 20, 1943.

United States Ships BOGUE, OSMOND INGRAM, GEORGE E. BADGER, CLEMSON, and VC-9, from July 12 to August 23, 1943.

United States Ships BOGUE, OSMOND INGRAM, GEORGE E. BADGER, CLEMSON, DUPONT, and VC-19, from November 14 to December 29, 1943.

United States Ships BOGUE, HAVER-FIELD, SWENNING, WILLIS, HOBSON (until March 25), JANSSEN (until April 7), and VC-95, from February 26 to April 19, 1944.

United States Ships BOGUE, HAVER-FIELD, SWENNING, WILLIS, JANSSEN, F. M. ROBINSON, and VC-69, from May 4 to July 3, 1944.

United States Ships BOGUE, HAVER-FIELD, SWENNING, WILLIS JANSSEN, WIL-HOITE and VC-42, from August 1 to 24, 1944.

For extraordinary heroism in action against enemy submarines in the Atlantic Area from April 20, 1943 to August 24, 1944. Carrying out powerful and sustained offensive action during a period of heavy German undersea concentrations threatening our uninterrupted flow of supplies to the European Theater of Operations, these six Antisubmarine Task Groups tracked the enemy packs relentlessly and, by the unwavering vigilance and persistent aggressiveness of all units involved, sank a notable number of hostile U-boats. The gallantry and superb teamwork of the officers and men who fought the embarked planes and who manned the BOGUE and her escort vessels were largely instrumental in forcing the complete withdrawal of enemy submarines from supply routes essential to the maintenance of our established military supremacy.

TASK UNIT TWENTY-ONE FOURTEEN

Consisting of the

USS CARD, USS BARRY, USS BORIE, USS GOFF and VC Squadrons ONE and NINE

For outstanding performance during antisubmarine operations in mid-Atlantic from July 27, 1943. At a time when continual flow of supplies along the United States–North Africa convoy route was essential to the maintenance of our established military supremacy and to the accumulations of reserves, the CARD, her embarked aircraft and her escorts pressed home a vigorous offensive which was largely responsible for the complete withdrawal of hostile U-boats from this vital supply area. Later, when submarines returned with deadlier weapons and augmented anti-aircraft defenses, this heroic Task Unit, by striking damaging blows at the onset of renewed campaigns, wrested the initiative from the enemy before actual inception of projected large-scale attacks. Its distinctive fulfillment of difficult and hazardous missions contributed materially to victorious achievements by our land forces.

North Atlantic

Navy Cross

KYES, Cdr. James E., USN

For extraordinary heroism as Commanding Officer of the USS LEARY during action against a concentrated force of hostile submarines in the North Atlantic on the night of December 23, 1943. As Commander Kyes boldly maneuvered to close the range on four of the hostile pack, the enemy struck, mortally damaging the LEARY with three torpedo hits and causing her to start sinking rapidly. After giving the order to abandon ship, Commander Kyes coolly and courageously made a personal inspection in order to assure himself that none of his men remained aboard. Preparing to abandon the stricken vessel and observing one of his crew whose life jacket was torn and useless, Commander Kyes gallantly removed his own, gave it to the man and then calmly went over the side.

Distinguished Service Medal

BRISTOL, Vice Adm. Arthur L., Jr., USN

For exceptionally meritorious service as Commander Task Force TWENTY-FOUR, United States Atlantic Fleet. While in that position of great responsibility he directed North Atlantic escort operations for more than sixty convoys, totaling twenty-four hundred ships, with a total loss of eight ships. This was accomplished from small beginnings and under the arduous circumstances prevailing in the North Atlantic during the winter of 1941–1942.

BRAINARD, Vice Adm. Roland M., USN

For exceptionally meritorious service to the Government of the United States in a duty of great responsibility as Commander Task Force TWENTY-FOUR, United States Atlantic Fleet, during the period from April 20, 1942 to April 30, 1943. Despite the extremely rigorous climate of the northern portion of the Western Atlantic Area and the constant menace of preying submarines, Vice Admiral Brainard directed the escort-of-trade-convoy operations with such skill and sound judgment, that out of more than one hundred and ninety-three convoys, only one hundred and eighty-six ships were lost of the seven thousand seven hundred and twenty involved.

CARNEY, Capt. Robert B., USN

For exceptionally meritorious service in a duty of great responsibility as Operations Officer and later as Chief of Staff, Support Force, Task Force TWENTY-FOUR of the United States Atlantic Fleet, during the period March 3, 1941 to April 17, 1942. With remarkable and distinctive skill, Captain Carney prepared all operational plans preceding and during belligerent operations of the Force. In this connection, he made important contributions to the escort-of-convoy instructions which resulted in the notable record of the safe escort of over two thousand ships with a loss of only eight ships, and the development of escort tactics which have proved highly effective in combating the submarine menace.

WOOLDRIDGE, Capt. Edmund T., USN

For exceptionally meritorious and distinguished service to the Government of the United States in a position of great responsibility as Operations Officer and later as Chief of Staff of Task Force TWENTY-FOUR, United States Atlantic Fleet, from April 20, 1942 to April 30, 1943. During this period of intensive anti-submarine activities, Captain Wooldridge, with brilliant initiative and excellent judgment, prepared and supervised the operational plans, which included the strategic employment of the United Nations Forces and highly successful coordination of air and surface units engaged in the protection of shipping in the Northwest Atlantic.

Legion of Merit

DENFIELD, Rear Adm. Louis E., USN

Chief of Staff, Task Force TWENTY-FOUR, United States Atlantic Fleet, during the period April 7 to December 26, 1941.

COHEN, Capt. Marion Y., USN

Commander of Escort Units with North Atlantic trade convoys during the period September 16, 1941 to March 10, 1942.

HEFFERNAN, Capt. John B., USN

Commander Task Unit, escorting convoy, Task Force TWENTY-FOUR, April 5–17, 1942.

HUNGERFORD, Capt. Ralph W., USN

Commander of Escort Units with North Atlantic trade convoys during the period September 16, 1941 to April 17, 1942.

INGERSOLL, Capt. Stuart H., USN

Assistant Operations Officer and later as Operations Officer, Staff, Commander Task Force TWENTY-FOUR, United States Atlantic Fleet, from April 20 to December 1, 1942.

JOHNSON, Capt. Charles Reid, (CEC), USN

Public Works Officer and Officer-in-Charge of Construction at the United States Naval Base in Iceland from February 16, 1942 to September 8, 1943.

JOHNSON, Capt. George William, USN

Commander Task Unit, escorting convoy, Task Force TWENTY-FOUR, October 27–31, 1941.

McKEE, Capt. Logan, USN

Material Officer of the Staff of Commander Task Force TWENTY-FOUR, United States Atlantic Fleet, from April 20, 1942 to April 30, 1943.

MILLER, Capt. Harold B., USN

Aide and Flag Secretary on the Staff of the Commander Task Force TWENTY-FOUR, United States Atlantic Fleet, from March 3, 1941 to February 22, 1942.

OREM, Capt. Howard E., USN

Senior Liaison between United States and British Naval Forces in Icelandic, British, and North Sea waters during the period August 1941 to August 1942.

THOMAS, Capt. Charles W., USCG

Commander of a Greenland Patrol Task Unit and as Commanding Officer of a Coast Guard ice breaker during the fall of 1944.

WENTWORTH, Capt. Ralph S., USN

Commandant of the United States Naval Operating Base, Iceland, from 10 May 1943 to 14 July 1944.

WOOLDRIDGE, Capt. Edmund T., USN

Assistant Operations Officer and later as Operations Officer, Staff, Commander Support Force, Task Force TWENTY-FOUR, United States Atlantic Fleet, from March 3, 1941 to April 17, 1942.

CURRY, Cdr. Ralph R., USCG

Commanding Officer of the USCGC CO-MANCHE during the rescue of survivors from the SS DORCHESTER when that vessel was torpedoed and sunk in North Atlantic waters on February 3, 1943.

FREDERICK, Cdr. Theodore R., USN

Pilot during the initial selection and survey of United States Army and Navy Bases in Newfoundland in September 1940.

GRAVES, Cdr. Van A., USCG

Commanding Officer of the Ice Information Detachment and of the Canadian Arctic Task Unit, and later as Chief of Staff, Commander Greenland Patrol.

HEINEMAN, Capt. Paul R., USN

Commander of Escort Units with North Atlantic trade convoys during the period February 12 to April 17, 1942.

Gold Star in Lieu of a Second Legion of Merit

Commander of an escort unit engaged in the protection of North Atlantic trade convoys from April 20, 1942 to April 30, 1943.

Second Gold Star in Lieu of a Third Legion of Merit

HEINEMAN, Cdr. Paul R., USN

Commanding Officer of the Antisubmarine Warfare Unit, Fleet Operational Training Command, United States Atlantic Fleet, from July 1943 until August 1944.

KAPLAN, Cdr. Leonard, USN

Naval Architect and Technical Advisor to the War Shipping Administration representative at the Naval Operating Base, Iceland, during the year 1942.

TIBBETS, Cdr. Joseph B., USN

Commander of Patrol Plane Squadron NINETY-FOUR in action against enemy forces in North Atlantic waters from January 14 to November 12, 1943.

WOOD, Cdr. Chester C., USN

Operations Officer from September 29, 1942 to April 30, 1943 and since then as Chief of Staff responsible for the protection of the Atlantic trade convoys.

POLLARD, Lt. Cdr. Francis C., USCG (Ret.)

Commanding Officer of the USCGC NORTHLAND during attacks on an enemy submarine in the North Atlantic, June 18, 1942.

Silver Star Medal

ANDERSON, Lt. (jg) Alfred W., USNR
FREDERICKS, Harry C., Cox., USN
HARRISON, Woodrow W., S2/c, USNR

Distinguished Flying Cross

DUNLOP, Lt. Cdr. Bernard W., USN
PARUNAK, Lt. Aram Y., USN
PRITCHARD, Lt. John A., Jr., USCG
SMITH, Lt. Leonard B., USN
WATERS, Lt. (jg) Nathan F., USNR
SNYDER, Ens. John C., USNR
BOTTOMS, Benjamin A., RM1/c, USCG

Navy and Marine Corps Medal

HAMAN, Cdr. Claude W., USN
POLLARD, Lt. Cdr. Francis C., USCG
NEWMAN, Lt. A. L., USN
PRITCHARD, Lt. John A., USCG

SANDS, Lt. James, USNR
DUNN, Lt. (jg) George W., USN
FULLER, Ens. Richard L., USCG
TAYLOR, Ens. H. W., USNR
BLOOMINGDALE, Lloyd H., Ptr2/c, USNR
BROWN, Walter W., SM1/c, USN
CHASTAIN, Weldron B., S1/c, USN
COPELAND, Rex E., GM3/c, USN
FRIEND, Charles, MoMM2/c, USCGR
GREENE, Eugene C., S1/c, USCGR
HARRIS, Elmer, GM1/c, USCG
IRWIN, Patrick B., BM2/c, USCG
McGINNIS, Bill M., S2/c, USNR
NELSON, Roy C., MoMM1/c, USCG
OLSEN, Bjarne O., S2/c, USCGR
SCHAFFER, George V., CEM, USNR
SHORDT, Peter Henry, MM2/c, USN
SMITH, Wilbur R., EM1/c, USCGR
SMITH, William E., S2/c, USCGR
VANN, George D., S1/c, USCGR
YOUNG, J. E., QM2/c, USCG

Air Medal

FREDERICK, Capt. Theodore R., USN
ISBELL, Capt. Arnold J., USN
MOYNAHAN, Lt. Cdr. B. J., USN
MUNSON, Lt. Cdr. William Harvey, USN
SEABORN, Lt. Cdr. E. L., USNR
TOUART, Lt. Cdr. R. G., USN
BANKHARDT, Lt. P. F., USN
BEACH, Lt. J. W., USNR
BENSON, Lt. Delbert Howard, USNR
*BROOKS, Lt. Douglas Wayne, USNR
CAIN, Lt. E. B., USNR
CAMPBELL, Lt. James B., USNR
CARLEEN, Lt. Forrest J., USNR
COLE, Lt. William, USN
COWART, Lt. A. H., USNR
DITTRICK, Lt. R. W., USNR
GULICK, Lt. Raymond L., USN
*HOERNER, Lt. Helmuth Ernest, USNR
KRANTZ, Lt. Carl D., USN
LEONARD, Lt. Robert W., USNR
MERKT, Lt. E. W., USNR
MERTZ, Lt. C. F., USN
MORRIS, Lt. Van Horne, USNR
NEFF, Lt. H. L., USNR
PARSONS, Lt. Samuel Garrett, USNR
PUETT, Lt. Nelson, USN
SHEPARD, Lt. Robert W., USNR
SHEVLIN, Lt. W. A., USNR
SMITH, Lt. G. S., USNR
SMITH, Lt. Russell H., USNR
SNYDER, Lt. John C., Jr., USNR

THOMPSON, Lt. Alfred Ronald, USNR
TOMLIN, Lt. Hollier G., USN
*WALLACE, Lt. Eugene Edward, USNR
WALSH, Lt. J. J., USNR
WOOD, Lt. E. W., USNR
ABRAMS, Lt. (jg) E. B., USNR
ALLEN, Lt. (jg) E. T., USNR
BEDSOLE, Lt. (jg) Donald S., USNR
BLAIR, Lt. (jg) Alfred L., USNR
BODINET, Lt. (jg) P. A., USNR
BORDELON, Lt. (jg) Robert E., USNR
CHATHAM, Lt. (jg) George E., USNR
deSTWOLINSKI, Lt. (jg) L. C., USNR
GUECK, Lt. (jg) Edwin J., USNR
*HARDESTY, Lt. (jg) Charles D., USNR
HENDERSON, Lt. (jg) Frank J., USN
HERSEY, Lt. (jg) Paul F., USCG
JENKINS, Lt. (jg) Henry C., USN
LAZAR, Lt. (jg) Victor A., USN
LOUGHRAN, Lt. (jg) James M., USNR
ORCUTT, Lt. (jg) Harry D., USNR
POSTON, Lt. (jg) Robert B., USN
RETTIG, Lt. (jg) Charles E., USNR
SMITH, Lt. (jg) R. N., USN
TURNER, Lt. (jg) R., USNR
WADE, Lt. (jg) Ralph J., USNR
WELCH, Lt. (jg) Gordon R., USNR
BOOKOUT, Ens. Roderick E., USN
HENDERSON, Ens. Frank J., USN
McCORMICK, Ens. Joseph T., USCG
SCHNEIDER, Ens. Daniel Anthony, USNR
ADAMS, George Knowles, AOM2/c, USNR
ARMSTRONG, J. E., AMM1/c, USN
*BOYCE, Chester Russell, ARM2/c, USNR
BROWN, Earle E., ACMM, USN
CASPER, Lawrence Freeman, ARM2/c, USNR
DE MENNO, Francis Anthony, ARM2/c, USNR
*GREGORY, Robert Irvington, AOM2/c, USNR
HEFFNER, Marlin V., ARM1/c, USN
JOHNSTON, Robert Phillips, AMM2/c, USNR
LARSON, Harold A., ACRM, USNR
*MIDDLETON, Russell Carter, AOM2/c, USNR
MOORHEAD, Alexander Ralph, ARM1/c, USNR
OBERMAN, Sam, ARM3/c, USNR
POOLE, Ridgeway Kendall, CAP, USN
SABO, Alex, AMM1/c, USN
SHERRILL, James Vernon, ARM1/c, USN
*SHOCKLEY, Donald Frederick, ARM2/c, USNR

STAPP, Blair Edgar, AOM 1/c, USNR
STEWARD, Albert Eugene, AOM2/c,
 USNR
STONE, Leland Frank, AOM1/c, USNR
TRINKLE, Robert Lee, AOM1/c, USNR
*VON SPREECKEN, Raymond Eugene,
 AOM1/c, USNR
WOJCIKI, Alfred W., ARM1/c, USCG

Bronze Star Medal

FITZ, Capt. Harold Carlton, USN
GALLERY, Capt. Daniel V., USN
SOULE, Cdr. Floyd M., USCGR
McMULLAN, Lt. Cdr. Albert L., USNR
PEDERSEN, Lt. Arne C., USCG
STARR, Lt. (jg) John, USCG

South Atlantic

Navy Cross

AVERY, Lt. Cdr., Howard Malcolm, USN

For outstanding courage, heroism, and leadership as pilot of a United States torpedo bomber, and as Officer in Tactical Command in offensive action against an enemy submarine which was destroyed on June 15, 1944. Lieutenant Commander Avery was on an antisubmarine flight in search for possible squadron survivors in the area of a known enemy submarine, when the vessel, fully surfaced, was sighted a few minutes before sunset. Lieutenant Commander Avery immediately made a contact report, circled the submarine and maintained contact despite anti-aircraft gun fire. He coolly analyzed the situation and realized that a single plane would have little chance of sinking the hostile vessel. He kept the enemy occupied until assistance arrived. He then calmly directed the attack on the enemy submarine which resulted in its destruction. During the action Lieutenant Commander Avery, with great skill and courage, personally made two strafing runs against the enemy in the face of heavy anti-aircraft fire. The aggressiveness, determination, coolness, courage, and leadership shown by Lieutenant Commander Avery in attacking and coordinating the well-planned action with the supporting aircraft are all in keeping with the highest traditions of the United States Navy.

EDWARDS, Lt. Frederick L., Jr., USNR

For extraordinary heroism as the Boarding Officer of the USS EBERLE when an enemy blockade runner was intercepted and destroyed on March 10, 1943. When the EBERLE was ordered to put a boarding party on the hostile ship, Lieutenant Edwards courageously led his party to the runner and was the first to board her. In the face of grave danger from the rapidly spreading fires and explosion of demolition charges, he made an energetic and determined effort to salvage the ship and to obtain information of the enemy. Only after several explosions had rocked the vessel and she began to sink did he dive over the stern into the sea, from which he was later rescued.

JOHNSON, Lt. Robert T., USNR

For outstanding and courageous conduct above and beyond the call of duty while participating in an aerial flight as the Commander of a United States Navy bombing plane on January 2, 1944, when an enemy blockade runner was apprehended and subsequently attacked. Lieutenant Johnson was on a barrier sweep when he was ordered to a position where a suspicious ship had been sighted. He immediately proceeded to the position and remained on the scene to home in other air surface craft. The plane encountered heavy anti-aircraft fire from the ship and was hit almost immediately. Although the plane was damaged, Lieutenant Johnson elected to remain in the area to make absolutely certain that the relief plane reached the scene. Engine trouble developed on his return and the plane crashed at sea and was lost with all hands.

WILLETT, Lt. (jg) Kenneth M., USNR

For extraordinary heroism and conspicuous courage as Commanding Officer of the United States Navy Armed Guard aboard the SS STEPHEN HOPKINS during action with unidentified enemy forces while enroute from Capetown to Paramaribo, September 27, 1942. In an attack launched by the enemy, and with no friendly ship in sight, Lieutenant (junior grade) Willett promptly manned his station at the 4-inch gun as the first shell struck, and opened fire on the most heavily armed of the two enemy raiders. Although seriously wounded in the stomach almost immediately, he kept up a sustained and rapid fire at close range, hitting his target along the water line with most of the 35 shells fired. Because of his great personal valor and gallant spirit of self-sacrifice, he was able to maintain a determined and heroic defense of his ship until forced by a magazine explosion to cease his fire. Still refusing to give up, Lieutenant (junior grade) Willett, obviously weakened and suffering, went down on deck and was last seen helping to cast loose the life rafts in a desperate effort to save the lives of others. The STEPHEN HOPKINS was shelled repeatedly from stem to stern, but before she plunged stern first, wrecked and blazing into the sea, her guns had inflicted serious damage on both enemy raiders and caused the probable destruction of one of them.

PATTISON, William J., SM3/c, USN

For extraordinary heroism while attached to the USS EBERLE in action against enemy forces on March 10, 1943. When a hostile blockade runner was intercepted and attacked, Pattison, as a member of a boarding party attempting to salvage the vessel, was the second man to reach her deck. Despite grave danger from threatening flames and the powerful explosions of demolition charges, he courageously assisted in conducting a determined effort to execute salvage operations, and by his skillful use of semaphore flags kept his own ship accurately informed of the situation, remaining at his post until the runner began to sink.

Distinguished Service Medal

INGRAM, Vice Adm. Jonas H., USN

For exceptionally meritorious and distinguished service to the Government of the United States in a duty of great responsibility while serving successively as Commander Task Force, and Commander Fourth Fleet and South Atlantic Forces

of the United States Atlantic Fleet from July 1941 to January 1944. Formulating comprehensive and painstaking plans to meet the needs of rapidly changing conditions during his critical period of service as Task Force Commander, Vice Admiral Ingram overcame tremendous difficulties involving lengthy and exposed supply lines, inadequate facilities and limited equipment, supplies and personnel, enabling the forces under his command to defeat enemy thrusts against Allied commerce in the highly vulnerable South Atlantic Area. Later, under his forceful and inspiring leadership as Commander Fourth Fleet and South Atlantic Forces, the entire area was quickly and decisively developed into a powerful war front from which rapidly expanding sea and air forces of the United Nations combined to strike with devastating results at enemy submarines and surface ships.

Gold Star in Lieu of a Second Distinguished Service Medal

For exceptionally meritorious service to the Government of the United States in a duty of great responsibility as Commander Fourth Fleet and South Atlantic Forces of the United States Atlantic Fleet from January to November 1944. Frequently faced with inadequate facilities, limited supplies and personnel and long exposed supply lines, Admiral Ingram skillfully utilized the resources and facilities available in the direction of the war against enemy surface forces operating in the South Atlantic Area.

Legion of Merit

BEAUREGARD, Rear Adm. Augustin T., USN (Ret.)

Chief of our Naval Mission to Brazil and Commandant of the Naval Operating Base in Rio de Janeiro from December 1, 1942 to May 8, 1943.

READ, Rear Adm. Oliver M., USN

Commander of a Task Group operating against the enemy in the South Atlantic Area.

BRADY, Capt. Edmund E., Jr., USN

United States Naval Attache and United States Naval Attache for Air, Rio de Janeiro, Brazil, from November 14, 1941 to September 28, 1942.

CONVESE, Capt. Adelbert F., USN

Commander of an antisubmarine hunting group which located and destroyed an enemy submarine off Cape Santa Pola, Spain, on 17 May 1944.

KINNEY, Capt. Philip R., USN

Communications Officer, South Atlantic Force of the United States Atlantic Fleet.

LEFFLER, Capt. Charles D., USN

Commanding Officer of the USS OMAHA during action against enemy German blockade runners in the South Atlantic Area.

MACAULAY, Capt. Walter S., USN

Chief of the United States Naval Mission to Brazil, he has been directly under the Brazilian Minister of Marine, but also had collateral duty as an important ex-officio member of the Staff, Commander Fourth Fleet.

SENN, Capt. Elliot M., USN

Commanding Officer of a unit of the South Atlantic Force and as a Task Group Commander during the period from May 1942 to October 21, 1943.

FITZGIBBON, Cdr. John E., USN

Flag Secretary to the Commander South Atlantic Force.

GENTNER, Cdr. William E., Jr., USN

Operations Officer of Fleet Air Wing Sixteen from July 7, 1943 until April 18, 1944 and Squadron Commander of Bombing Squadron 127 from May 14 to July 7, 1943, the first PV Squadron to be attached to this command.

HUGHES, Cdr. William C., Jr., USN

Commanding Officer of the USS SOMERS during an extensive campaign against enemy blockade runners and raiders in the South Atlantic Area.

PARHAM, Cdr. John C., USN

Commanding Officer of the USS JOUETT during action against German blockade runners in the South Atlantic Area.

RISSER, Cdr. Francis B., USN

Supply Officer of the advanced base and also Area Petroleum Officer, contributed to accomplishments of the Atlantic Force.

RUCKER, Cdr. Colby G., USN

Commanding Officer of the USS OWL during the period April 18–20, 1942.

SNYDER, Cdr. Rony, USN

Commanding Officer of the USS MELVILLE in the South Atlantic Area from February 5 to September 23, 1943.

WEAKLEY, Cdr. Charles E., USN

Commander Destroyer Division 67— GOFF, BORIE, and BARRY—which unit later distinguished itself in action against the enemy and received the Presidential Citation, as former Commanding Officer, USS GOFF, and as Commander of two Task Groups engaged in escort of convoy operations in the South Atlantic Area.

WILLIAMS, Cdr. Lowell W., USN

Commander Headquarters Squadron, Fleet Air Wing 16, from February, 1943 to June 6, 1944, effected the establishment and subsequent maintenance of air bases in Brazil under difficult circumstances.

KRAUSE, Lt. Cdr. John M., USNR

A Naval Member of the United States Military Mission in Cayenne, French Guiana.

PRUEHER, Lt. Cdr. Bertram J., USN

Executive Officer and later as Commanding Officer of Patrol Squadron 83, United States Fourth Fleet, during the period April 1, 1942 to August 16, 1943.

TOTH, Lt. Cdr. Joseph C., USN

Commanding Officer of a Patrol Plane Squadron in combat against enemy German submarines in the South Atlantic Area, February 1, 1943.

TURNER, Lt. Cdr. Renfro, USN

Commander of Bombing Squadron 107, during the period from August 12, 1943 to February 20, 1944.

Silver Star Medal

BENNETT, Jennings J., Cox., USN

Distinguished Flying Cross

PRUEHER, Lt. Cdr. Bertram Joseph, USN
BALDWIN, Lt. Charles A., USNR
BURTON, Lt. John Thomas, USNR
**FORD, Lt. William R., USNR
KRUG, Lt. Edward Arthur, Jr., USNR
TAYLOR, Lt. Samuel K., USNR
*CHAMBERLAIN, Lt. (jg) William Francis, USNR
DAWKINS, Lt. (jg) M. Vance, Jr., USNR
HANNEVER Lt. (jg) Grover Cleveland, USNR
HARE, Lt. (jg) Frank Fisher, USNR
SMITH, Lt. (jg) Walter F., USN
SWAN, Lt. (jg) Robert S., USNR
WAUGH, Lt. (jg) Goree E., USNR
WEIGLE, Lt. (jg) Donald Ellsworth, USNR
WHITCOMB, Lt. (jg) Roy Seldon, USN
YOUNG, Lt. (jg) Walter Chappell, USNR
CLARK, Ens. Harland C., USNR
COUPE, Ens. Eugene Louis, USNR
EDWARDS, Ens. George Ernest., Jr., USNR
EIDE, Ens. Marvell E., USNR
McMAHON, Ens. Richard Eugene, USNR
SPEAR, Ens. Moncrieff Johnston, USNR
TEHAN, Ens. Robert, USNR
WADSWORTH, Ens. Thomas Johnston, USNR
WIMPEY, Ens. George A., USN
BRANDON, Howard Clifton, ACRM, USN
GARDNER, Donald Wayne, ARM2/c, USNR
GODDELL, Billie, AMM3/c, USN
MERRICK, Gordon Granville, AOM1/c, USNR
MILHALSKY, Joseph, S2/c, USN
SMITH, Clyde Adelbert, ACMM, USN
VAN HORN, John Roy, AMM1/c, USNR

Navy and Marine Corps Medal

THORNTON, Capt. William N., USN
JACOBS, Lt. (jg) Howard A., USNR
LUCKETT, Lt. (jg) Harvey Boyce, USNR
BURR, Ens. William A., USNR
GREGONIS, Ens. Peter J., USN
MULCANY, Ens. Donald V., USNR
SCOTT, Ens. James W., USNR
CAPONIO, Sam, S1/c, USNR

MULCARE, William E., S1/c, USN
MURPHY, John James, PhM2/c, USNR
NAY, Merrill G., AMM1/c, USNR
ROONEY, Donald R., S1/c, USNR
TILLER, Hugh D., F1/c, USN
TINSMAN, Carl W., S2/c, USNR
WATTERS, Charles F., ARM2/c, USNR

Air Medal

GARDNER, Capt. Fellows D., USMCR
AYERS, Lt. Cdr. Louis McClellan, USNR
CALDER, Lt. Cdr. William E., III, USNR
ANDRETTA, Lt. Fred C., Jr., USNR
BAXLEY, Lt. William M., USNR
BROWN, Lt. Stanley V., USN
*BURTON, Lt. John T., USNR
COLLINS, Lt. Jorden Busby, USNR
DAVIS, Lt. James N., USNR
FORD, Lt. William R., USNR
*HILL, Lt. William E., USNR
LAURATIS, Lt. Lawrence A., USNR
POWERS, Lt. Robert A., USNR
TAYLOR, Lt. Mearl G., USNR
TOBIN, Lt. Joshua S., USNR
TOMPKINS, Lt. John Erwin, USNR
BOFENKAMP, Lt. (jg) William, USNR
DAVIS, Lt. (jg) David, USNR
DEUTSCH, Lt. (jg) Morton Marcus, USNR
FITZGERALD, Lt. (jg) Paul D., USN
HANNEVER, Lt. (jg) Grover Cleveland, USNR
GROTTS, Lt. (jg) Claude Franklin, USNR
HOUCHIN, Lt. (jg) George A., USNR
MARATI, Lt. (jg) Dino, USNR
OLSEN, Lt. (jg) Harold G., USNR
PARKER, Lt. (jg) Lloyd G., USNR
RILEY, Lt. (jg) Robert Amory, USNR
SPARKS, Lt. (jg) Robert Merritt, USNR
SWAN, Lt. (jg) Robert S., USNR
WALKER, Lt. (jg) William N., USN
ARNOLD, Ens. Leonard H., USNR
BESMEHN, Ens. Donald R., USNR
BUTLER, Ens. Norman, USNR
DAWKINS, Ens. Marion V., USNR
DUGAN, Ens. William, USNR
FECKOURY, Ens. Nicholas, USNR
GALLAGHER, Ens. Pete William, USNR
GRIMM, Ens. Wayne A., USNR
HELFENBEIN, Ens. George Henry, USNR
KIEFNER, Ens. Jim C., USNR
MAIERHOFER, Ens. William G., USNR
McCOY, Ens. Boyce Sample, USNR
MORRISON, Ens. Eugene Colley, USNR

RALEIGH, Ens. William T., Jr., USNR
*RIGGS, Ens. Richard M., USNR
SCHOLAR, Ens. Williby, USNR
SHANNON, Ens. George M., USNR
STERLING, Ens. Calhoun, USNR
VALENTINE, Ens. George H., Jr., USNR
WHYTE, Ens. Edward G., USNR
BAMBER, Jesse W., Mach., USN
DESMOND, John F., Boat., USN
BENNETT, James Frederick, AMM2/c, USNR
BERGSTROM, Lee Maurice, ACRM, USN
BLAIR, John A., AOM2/c, USNR
BOHON, Raymond L., S1/c, USN
BROWNLEE, George, Jr., AMM1/c, USNR
BURGGRAFF, Arnold Peter, S2/c, USNR
CHAPMAN, Edward L., ACRM, USN
CHIRDON, John Martin, AOM2/c, USNR
COWDERY, Thomas Wilson, ARM1/c, USNR
*DAMIANO, Rodney Louis, AMM1/c, USN
*DICKINSON, Wallace J., AMM1/c, USN
DONAHUE, Francis Leonel, ACMM, USN
*DUPREE, Daniel William, ARM3/c, USNR
*EDWARDS, John D., AMM2/c, USN
ELLIS, William E., ARM3/c, USNR
*ERNST, George, AMM2/c, USNR
FORD, Daniel J., AMM2/c, USNR
GEER, Roy E., AMM3/c, USNR
GILPIN, Richard D., AOM3/c, USNR
GORSKI, William Joseph, ARM2/c, USNR
*GREENBERG, Solomon, ACRM, USN
HALE, Sydney Brown, AMM2/c, USN
HAMILTON, William Titus, AMM1/c, USNR
HAMMER, Thomas S., AMM2/c, USN
HENNICK, Richard Galen, AMM2/c, USNR
HILGEMAN, Charles William, ARM2/c, USNR
HUNT, Everett Marks, S2/c, USN
JENKINS, Jack Veitch, ARM1/c, USN
JOHNSTON, Marvin Emery, RT1/c, USNR
*JORGENSEN, Murray I., ARM3/c, USN
*KLOSS, Earl Joseph, S2/c, USNR
KUCZINSKI, Frank, Jr., AMM2/c, USN
LAURY, John Anthony, Jr., AOM2/c, USN
LAUX, Douglas Melvin R., AMM2/c, USNR
LUCK, Earl Weathers, ARM1/c, USN
MACLATCHIE, Donald W., S2/c, USNR
MANGANO, Guy Benito, S1/c, USNR
McPHERSON, Clifton Forest, AOM3/c,
*MEYER, George Edgar, ARM2/c, USNR

MOSHER, William Howard, AOM2/c, USNR
NICPON, Edmund Albert, AMM2/c, USNR
NIX, Samuel Eugene, AM2/c, USN
PACYNA, Albert Donald, ARM2/c, USNR
PALMER, Luther Adam, Jr., AMM3/c, USN
PETACCIO, Anthony J., ARM2/c, USNR
PITTMAN, John Wesley, Jr., AM2/c, USN
POLLARD, Calvin Arthur, ARM3/c, USN
RACKLEY, Floyd Jones, AOM3/c, USNR
RATKA, Lawrence G., ARM3/c, USNR
RENDA, Francisco S., AMM2/c, USNR
RESNER, Floyd Edward, AMM3/c, USNR
RICHARDS, Charles Walter, AMM1/c, USN
RICHTER, Paul G., ARM1/c, USN
ROBERG, Carl Verner, ARM1/c, USNR
*SCHNEIDER, Harry Adolph, ARM1/c, USN
SCHOOLFIELD, James E., AMM2/c, USNR
SCOTT, Ray M., S2/c, USNR
SEIDEL, Walter G., ARM3/c, USNR
SEYMOUR, Sterling F., AMM2/c, USN
SLUSHER, Henry Lee, Jr., AMM2/c, USN
STARK, Joseph, ARM3/c, USN
*STERN, Fred W., S2/c, USNR
*STRIANO, Martin, AOM2/c, USNR
TAYLOR, Clark Burnaby, AOM2/c, USNR
VERITY, Arnold Howell, ARM3c, USNR
VON BURKIRK, Carl N., Jr., AMM3/c, USN
WILSON, Richard Allen, ARM3/c, USNR
ZUKIEWICZ, George J., AOM3/c, USN

Bronze Star Medal

TAYLOR, Capt. Howard William, USN
THORNTON, Capt. William Nelson, USN
WILL, Capt. Charles Raymond, USN
WERTS, Cdr. Charles Luther, USN
WHITESIDE, Cdr. William Joseph, USN
BRENNAN, Lt. Joseph Cantwell, USNR
MORTON, Lt. William Benjamin, USN
ALTON, Lt. (jg) Abner Lonnie, USN
FOURNIER, Lt. (jg) Paul Eugene, USN
HAWKINS, Lt. (jg) Gordon Stuart, USN
TAYLOR, Lt. (jg) Robert Leonard, USN
WALTRIP, Lt. (jg) Fruman Dorwin, USN
CLAYTON, William Robert, ACMM, USNR
LEFTWICH, James Milton, AMM1/c, USN
GALLAGHER, Joseph Patrick, AMM1/c, USN

Caribbean

Navy Cross

BINNING, Lt. (jg) Edward G., USNR

For distinguished service in the line of his profession as Patrol Plane Commander, operating in the Caribbean Area, while conducting antisubmarine patrol on the night of May 26, 1942.

FEENEY, Lt. (jg) Joseph, USNR

For extraordinary heroism and outstanding devotion to duty while serving as Commander of the Armed Guard Crew aboard the tanker SS CITIES SERVICE MISSOURI when that ship was torpedoed and sunk in the Caribbean Sea on the night of March 12, 1943. Proceeding aft to take his station with the gun crew after the first torpedo had struck the vessel, Lieutenant (junior grade) Feeney was suddenly hurled into the air by the force of a second torpedo hit and was severely injured. Despite the incapacitating effect of this injury, and with heroic courage, Lieutenant (junior grade) Feeney dragged himself to the bridge, where he manned the phones to the battery and continued directing the fire of the gun until the crew reported that the ammunition had been rendered ineffectual by water, and the order to abandon ship was given.

MUIR, Ens. Kenneth H., USNR

For extraordinary heroism as Officer in Charge of the United States Navy Armed Guard on board the SS NATHANIEL HAWTHORNE, destroyed in the Caribbean Sea by enemy torpedoes November 6, 1942. In the glow of salt water flares that lighted up the stern of the sinking ship, Ensign Muir, disregarding his own severe injuries and great suffering, ordered the three men near him to leap clear of the ship and then rushed back to help more of his men to escape.

Distinguished Service Medal

COOK, Vice Adm. Arthur B., USN

For exceptionally meritorious and distinguished service to the Government of the United States in a position of great responsibility as Commander Caribbean Sea Frontier and Commandant Tenth Naval District.

HOOVER, Vice Adm. John H., USN

For exceptionally meritorious and distinguished service to the Government of the United States in a position of great responsibility as Commander Caribbean Sea Frontier and Commandant Tenth Naval District.

OLDENDORF, Rear Adm. Jesse B., USN

For exceptionally meritorious service to the Government of the United States in a duty of great responsibility as Commander All Forces Aruba-Curacao Area from March 2 to July 2, 1942, and as Commander Trinidad Sector, Caribbean Sea Frontier, and Commandant of Naval Operating Base, Trinidad, from July 2, 1942 to April 19, 1943.

HOUSE, Maj. Gen. Edwin J., AC, USA

Commander of the Antilles Air Task Force in the Caribbean Sea Frontier during the period December 7, 1941 to June 10, 1943. Carrying on his assigned task with marked zeal and tireless energy, Major General House personally supervised and inspected air installations, personnel and equipment, throughout this important area, and, under his fine leadership, marked progress was made in developing tactics and improving technique necessary to combat hostile submarines.

Legion of Merit

CHANDLER, Rear Adm. Theodore E., USN

Commander All Forces, Aruba-Curacao, Netherlands West Indies, from April 27, 1943 to July 25, 1944.

JAMES, Rear Adm. Jules, USN

Commandant Naval Operating Base and Commander Combined Local Defense Forces, Bermuda, from April 7, 1941 to March 24, 1943.

ROBINSON, Rear Adm. Arthur G., USN

Commander All Forces, Aruba-Curacao Area from June 6, 1942 to April 28, 1943, and subsequently as Commander Trinidad Sector, Caribbean Sea Frontier and Commandant of Naval Operating Base, Trinidad.

SOWELL, Rear Adm. Ingram Cecil, USN

Commandant Naval Operating Base, Bermuda, from April 1943 until September 1944.

VAN HOOK, Rear Adm. Clifford E., USN

Commandant Fifteenth Naval District and Commander Panama Sea Frontier from April 15, 1942 to October 14, 1943.

WEYLER, Rear Adm. George L., USN

Commandant of the Naval Station, Guantanamo Bay, Cuba, from September 1, 1940 to April 6, 1944.

BORN, Brig. Gen. Charles F., AC, USA

Air Operations Officer on the Staff of Commandant, Naval Operating Base, Trinidad, British West Indies, during the period July 2, 1942 to July 1, 1943.

COMPO, Capt. George L., USN

Army Legion of Merit

Commander of Fleet Air Wing 3 from 21 June 1942 to date, operating under Army command in conjunction with Army Air Force units, he was engaged continuously in antisubmarine operations in the Atlantic Sector and offshore patrol operations in the Pacific Sector of the Panama Coastal Frontier.

DEWEESE, Capt. Wade, USN

Port Director, Port au Spain, Trinidad, B.W.I., Captain Wade DeWeese made important contributions to the antisubmarine campaign by his skillful routing of shipping, limited as he was by inadequate aircraft for coverage and surface vessels for escort.

HICKEY, Capt. Andrew S., USN (Ret.)

Naval Observer at Fort de France, Martinique, since November 22, 1942.

HOLLOWAY, Capt. James L., Jr., USN

Commander of the DD-DE Shakedown Group at Bermuda, British West Indies, from March to November 1943.

MATTHEWS, Capt. Mitchell D., USN

Commanding Officer on the USS BLAKELEY during and following an enemy torpedo attack on that vessel, May 25, 1942.

TOMLINSON, Capt. William G., USN

Commander United States Naval Forces, Azores, from January 1944 to December 1944.

RATTAN, Col. William V., USA

Commanding Officer, Ground Forces, Aruba-Curacao, and Commanding Officer, Force Curacao, from July 29, 1942, to November 24, 1943.

MONK, Lt. Cdr. Ivan, USNR

Engineer Officer of the USS BLAKELEY during a surprise torpedo attack on that vessel off Fort de France, Martinique, French West Indies, May 25, 1942.

MULLANY, Lt. Cdr. Roger V., USNR

Executive Officer, USS BLAKELEY during and following an enemy torpedo attack on that vessel May 25, 1942.

BRACKEN, Lt. John P., USNR

On staff of the Commander All Forces Aruba-Curacao during the period from July 9, 1942 to May 6, 1943.

BREWSTER, Hubert A., CWT, USN

In general charge of firerooms, serving on board the USS BLAKELEY during and following an enemy torpedo attack on that vessel, May 25, 1942.

SAVAGE, Leo Martin, WT1/c, USN

On board the USS BLAKELEY when that ship was torpedoed May 25, 1942.

VICTOR, Anthony Paul, WT1/c, USNR

On board the USS BLAKELEY when that ship was torpedoed May 25, 1942.

Silver Star Medal

MACK, Capt. Andrew R., USN
SWEENEY, Lt. Cdr. Daniel J., USN
MARSHALL, Ens. Hunter, II, USNR
ABASTA, Frank Patrick, AS, USN
DAY, Troy W., GM2/c, USN
SKALING, Howard D., GM3/c, USNR
WALLER, John J., S2/c, USNR

Distinguished Flying Cross

CROCKETT, Lt. Lewis D., USNR
FISS, Lt. Gordon R., USN
CHRISTIAN, Lt. (jg) Oren R., USNR
DRESBACH, Lt. (jg) John William, USNR
DRYDEN, Lt. (jg) J. E., USN
GIERISCH, Lt. (jg) Jack K., USN

Navy and Marine Corps Medal

GAUGHAN, Lt. Edward J., USNR
KURTA, Lt. (jg) Stanley B., USCGR
BURKE, F. P., Sp1/c, USN
BROWN, M. R., CSp, USN
CREIDER, Anthony S., Mach., USN
DILORENZO, Edmond, S2/c, USCG
GLAUER, Arthur W., CGM, USNR
GORUM, B. G., Sp2/c, USN
HAMLIN, H. E., Sp1/c, USNR
HAMMOND, R., Sp1/c, USNR
HYATT, Elmo Jewett, AS, USNR
KECK, G. A., CSP, USNR
KEELEY, Bartley G., Sp1/c, USNR
KLEIN, Jacob, Jr., S1/c, USCGR
O'NEILL, Edward F., SP1/c, USNR
PECK, Leighton F., SP1/c, USNR
ROBERTI, Joseph, CQM, USNR

Air Medal

CLEARY, Capt. J. M., USN
BEAL, Lt. (jg) S. C., USN
SLATER, Lt. (jg) F. G., USN
CALHOUN, Ens. W. B., USN
*GIERISCH, Ens. Jack K., USN
HOOKER, Ens. Gerald, USN
ALBERT, A., S1/c, USN
BROOKS, H., ARM3/c, USN
CONNELLY, J. F., AMM3/c, USN
JACKSON, W. H., ACMM, USN
LAND, W. F., ARM2/c, USN
LEGROS, R. T., AMM3/c, USN
MACE, G. J., ARM2/c, USN
MADRAS, M., AMM2/c, USN
MINIE, F. C., S1/c, USN
PORTER, H. E., AMM2/c, USN
RANEY, W. C., AMM3/c, USN
RISTER, G. W., AMM3/c, USN
VARGAS, I. A., AMM3/c, USN
WALKER, O. P., AMM3/c, USN
WARD, D. T., AP2/c, USN

Bronze Star

RULE, Capt. Adrian O., USN

NORTH AFRICA

French Morocco

Navy Cross

BOOTH, Lt. Cdr. Charles T., II, USN

For extraordinary heroism as Commanding Officer of Fighting Squadron FORTY-ONE, attached to the USS RANGER, during the assault on and occupation of French Morocco, November 8-11, 1942. Attacked by sixteen hostile fighters while raiding the Cazes airdrome, Lieutenant Commander Booth and his flight of eighteen planes shot nine of the interceptors out of the sky, damaged another, and destroyed fourteen aircraft on the ground. In addition to subsequent strafing raids which silenced enemy shore batteries near Port Lyautey and El Hank, he led a flight of eleven planes through a bursting hail of anti-aircraft fire to bombard two surfaced submarines and a light cruiser off Casablanca. Later, Lieutenant Commander Booth led four additional flights in successful attacks against hostile troops, planes in the air, and tank and truck columns.

BRADDY, Lt. Cdr. Robert E., Jr., USN

For extraordinary heroism and courage as Commanding Officer of the USS BERNADOU in leading the assault against hostile forces during the occupation of the harbor of Safi, French Morocco, November 8, 1942. In a remarkable demonstration of seamanship and resourcefulness, Lieutenant Commander Braddy navigated the BERNADOU by a difficult and hazardous approach through unknown waters into the crowded harbor where she was beached to allow the immediate landing of troops. This exceptional feat was accomplished in almost total darkness while the ship was under the crossfire of three enemy coast defense batteries and several machine guns mounted on the harbor jetties without loss of embarked personnel and with only slight damage to the ship's hull.

BRODIE, Lt. Cdr. Robert, Jr., USN

For extraordinary heroism and courage as Commanding Officer of the USS DALLAS in action against hostile forces during the occupation of Port Lyautey, French Morocco, November 10, 1942. In a remarkable demonstration of seamanship and resourcefulness, Lieutenant Commander Brodie, proceeding with a detachment of raider troops across a treacherous bar through heavy surf, entered the shallow Sebou River and by breaking a steel cable boom with the bow of his ship, forced his way, often literally ploughing through mud, ten miles up the river where he landed the raider troops at Port Lyautey airfield.

CARVER, Lt. Cdr. Lamar P., USN

For extraordinary heroism as Squadron Commander and pilot of a plane of Scouting Squadron FORTY-ONE, attached to the USS RANGER, during the assault on and occupation of French Morocco from November 8 to 11, 1942. In the early morning of November 8, Lieutenant Commander Carver, leading a division of planes on an offensive mission over Casablanca harbor, sighted a nest of hostile submarines. Despite intense anti-aircraft fire, he skillfully maneuvered his division into position and executed an accurate dive-bombing attack, personally making one of the two direct hits which resulted in the sinking of two undersea craft. Again the same day, he led another dive-bombing attack on a group of hostile surface vessels which were being engaged bv our ships and, in the face of heavy anti-aircraft fire, several near-misses were scored by his command. His outstanding leadership and fearless devotion to duty were in keeping with the highest traditions of the United States Naval Service.

NATION, Lt. Cdr. Milton A., USN

For extraordinary heroism as Flight Leader of Escort Scouting Squadron TWENTY-SEVEN attached to the USS SUWANEE, during the assault on and occupation of French Morocco, November 8–11, 1942. On November 8, undaunted by withering anti-aircraft fire, Lieutenant Commander Nation, leading a seven-plane group, courageously attacked and successfully bombed three submarines and a battleship and, later the same day, in a four-plane raid, scored direct hits on a cruiser and a destroyer. Steadfast and untiring in his performance of duty, he again, on November 10, led four planes in shattering attacks on enemy coastal defense anti-aircraft installations and, on the morning of November 11, launched a forceful depth-charge attack on a hostile submarine, probably sinking that vessel.

PALMER, Lt. Cdr., George G., USN

For extraordinary heroism and courage as Commanding Officer of the USS COLE while leading the first wave of assault boats against enemy forces during the occupation of the harbor of Safi, French Morocco, November 8, 1942. In a remarkable demonstration of seamanship and resourcefulness, Lieutenant Commander Palmer navigated the COLE by a difficult and hazardous approach through unknown waters into the crowded harbor where she landed all troops alongside a dock. This exceptional feat was accomplished in almost total darkness while the ship was under the crossfire of three enemy coast defense batteries and several machine guns mounted on the harbor jetties, without loss of embarked personnel or material damage.

RABY, Lt. Cdr. John, USN

For extraordinary heroism as Commanding Officer of Fighting Squadron NINE, attached to the USS RANGER, during the occupation of French Morocco, November 8–11, 1942. Leading a flight of eight planes into combat against sixteen hostile fighters, Lieutenant Commander Raby, persistently striking at the foe until he himself shot down two planes, contributed materially to the aggressive fighting spirit which enabled his command to destroy a total of five enemy aircraft and probably two more. On previous and subsequent raids, pressed home under relentless fire, he led his squadron in effective bombing and strafing attacks against hostile airdromes, shore batteries, machine-gun nests, and flying and grounded aircraft.

RUDDY, Lt. Cdr. Joseph A., Jr., USN

For extraordinary heroism as pilot of an airplane in Escort Scouting Squadron TWENTY-NINE, attached to the USS SAN-TEE, during the occupation of French Morocco, November 8–11, 1942. In order to obtain accurate and vital information concerning hostile operations at the Marrakech airdrome, Lieutenant Commander Ruddy, with utter disregard for his own personal safety, set out upon a hazardous reconnaissance flight over the area at an extremely low altitude. Although his plane was hit during a fierce concentration of gunfire, he made a second approach on the airdrome and scored a direct bomb hit on the hangar. Later, when enemy troops lay in ambush ahead of advancing United States forces, he searched for and led an effective aerial attack against their threatening positions.

DARROCH, Lt. James W., USNR

For extraordinary heroism as member of a demolition party attached to the USS BRANT during the assault on and occupation of French Morocco from November 8 to 11, 1942. Assigned the extremely dangerous task of cutting through an enemy obstruction in order that the USS DALLAS could navigate up the Sebou River, Lieutenant Darroch and his crew, on the night of November 9, proceeded with grim determination toward their objective. Despite the treacherous surf, he and his shipmates skillfully and courageously accomplished their hazardous mission of cutting the cables at the mouth of the river, just as guns from the French fort opened fire. Countering the enemy's attack until out of range, Lieutenant Darroch dauntlessly started back and, in spite of enormous breakers which battered his boat and washed one of his machine guns overboard, brought her and her courageous crew back to safety.

DeVANE, Lt. John M., Jr., USN

For extraordinary heroism as Flight Officer of Scouting Squadron FORTY-ONE, attached to the USS RANGER, during the occupation of French Morocco, November 8–11, 1942. Participating in four dive-bombing and strafing raids, Lieutenant DeVane, under a bursting hail of anti-aircraft shells, pressed home vigorous and persistent attacks against hostile airfields, light vessels, gun emplacements, tanks and trucks.

EMBREE, Lt. Ralph A., USN

For extraordinary heroism as Acting Squadron Commander of Scouting Squadron FORTY-ONE, attached to the USS RANGER, during the occupation of French Morocco, November 8–11, 1942. Leading five flights of planes in vigorous dive-bombing raids against hostile warships and coastal defense batteries, Lieutenant Embree, courageously pressing home his attacks in the face of tremendous anti-aircraft fire and fierce fighter opposition, aided greatly in the infliction of severe damage upon the enemy.

ERSHLER, Lt. Arthur M., USN

For extraordinary heroism as pilot of an airplane in Escort Scouting Squadron TWENTY-NINE, attached to the USS SAN-TEE, during the occupation of French Morocco, November 8–11, 1942. When his plane was badly damaged by gunfire during a raid upon a convoy of hostile trucks, Lieutenant Ershler, although severely nauseated by escaping gasoline fumes, gamely continued his flight to an enemy airdrome where he damaged several planes by strafing and scored a direct bomb hit on a hangar.

FERGUSON, Lt. John N., Jr., USN

For extraordinary heroism and distinguished service as Executive Officer and Navigator of the USS DALLAS during the assault on and occupation of French Morocco from November 8–11, 1942. While under fire of hostile artillery, Lieutenant Ferguson coolly and efficiently navigated the DALLAS across a treacherous bar through heavy surf and mud into the shallow Sebou River where our Army raider troops, supported by gunfire from the ship, captured the Port Lyautey airfield.

FURNEY, Lt. Maynard M., USNR

For extraordinary heroism as a Section Leader of Fighting Squadron FORTY-ONE, attached to the USS RANGER, during the assault on and occupation of French Morocco, November 8–11, 1942. Through intense enemy anti-aircraft fire, Lieutenant Furney, on November 8, led a section of an eighteen-plane flight in a destructive attack on the Cazes airdrome. With courage and skill he provided cover for other units of the flight and, when our planes were attacked, he unhesitatingly engaged the hostile fighter craft, outmaneuvering and sending two down in flames. In the subsequent six flights in which he participated during the following two days, Lieutenant Furney, in addition to bombing and strafing shore batteries at El Hank, also led his four-plane section in strafing two submarines and patrolling over the RANGER and transports at Fedala.

JOHNSON, Lt. Cecil V., USN

For extraordinary heroism as pilot of an airplane in Scouting Squadron FORTY-ONE, attached to the USS RANGER, during the occupation of French Morocco, November 8–11, 1942. Leading a section of planes in repeated dive-bombing raids, Lieutenant Johnson, under a bursting hail of anti-aircraft shells, pressed home vigorous and persistent attacks against hostile warships, coastal defense batteries, and anti-aircraft gun emplacements in the vicinity of Casablanca.

JONES, Lt. Ralph Meldrim, USNR

For extraordinary heroism as a pilot of Escort Scouting Squadron TWENTY-SIX, attached to the USS SANGAMON, during the assault on and occupation of French Morocco, November 8–11, 1942. While leading a section of airplanes in the initial attack on Port Lyautey, Lieutenant Jones, suddenly aware that one of his comrades was being attacked by a hostile fighter, courageously maneuvered to challenge the assailant and succeeded, with only a .30 caliber machine gun, in forcing the enemy craft to withdraw, thereby extricating his comrade from a perilous situation. Later, upon discovering that an enemy anti-aircraft battery was menacing our forces, Lieutenant Jones, flying at dangerously low altitude, sought out and vigorously attacked the gun positions. Despite the serious damage which his plane had received, he displayed superb airmanship in maintaining control until a safe landing was made aboard the carrier.

McELROY, Lt. Rhodam Y., Jr., USN

For extraordinary heroism as Tactical Leader of Escort Scouting Squadron TWENTY-SIX, attached to the USS SANGAMON, during the assault on and occupation of French Morocco, November 8–11, 1942. While leading his squadron on a mission to locate camouflaged enemy tanks, Lieutenant McElroy, on the afternoon of November 10, deliberately subjected his plane to withering anti-aircraft fire by flying at low altitude in order to ascertain the exact location of the tanks. Although his plane was hit many times, he courageously and resolutely persevered in his task, making repeated attacks which resulted in a complete rout of enemy tank forces. On two other occasions, Lieutenant McElroy led his squadron in perfectly timed and well executed attacks against hostile gun positions and an enemy airdrome.

MICKA, Lt. Edward, USN

For extraordinary heroism as pilot of an airplane in Fighting Squadron NINE, attached to the USS RANGER during the occupation of French Morocco, November 8–11, 1942. Leading a section of four planes in vigorous raids against hostile airdromes at Rabat-Sale and Port Lyautey, Lieutenant Micka, grimly pressing home his attacks in the face of relentless fire, contributed materially to the destruction of seventeen enemy planes on the ground and the silencing of three machine gun emplacements. Later, he participated in a series of hazardous, low-altitude strafing runs on the airdrome at Mediouna, persistently striking at his target through bursting shells of anti-aircraft fire until, on his fifth run, he was finally shot down.

PALMER, Lt. Fitzhugh L., Jr., USN

For extraordinary heroism as Tactical Leader of Escort Fighting Squadron TWENTY-SIX, attached to the USS SANGAMON, during the assault on and occupation of French Morocco, November 8–11, 1942. Pressing home audacious low-altitude attacks in the face of intense anti-aircraft fire, Lieutenant Palmer, on the morning of November 8, led his squadron in daring raids against enemy anti-aircraft installations and hostile aircraft both on the ground and in the air and, by his courage and skill, personally sent one bomber down in flames. Later, while attacking hostile ground forces, his plane was hit and severely damaged by enemy fire, but, despite the consequent operational difficulties, he persevered in maintaining control of the aircraft until a safe landing had been made on board his carrier.

STAGGS, Lt. William R., USNR

For extraordinary heroism as pilot of an airplane in Escort Scouting Squadron TWENTY-NINE, attached to the USS SANTEE, during the occupation of French Morocco, November 8–11, 1942. Upon sighting a hostile submarine on the surface, Lieutenant Staggs, in a quick dive to attack, struck the conning tower of the vessel with armor-piercing bullets from his 50-caliber machine guns and set off a depth charge in immediate proximity to its hull. Shortly thereafter, he led a group of seven scout bombers and three fighters in persistent raids against enemy troop convoys and intense aerial bombardment of the airdrome at Marrakech. Although flying through a continuous hail of anti-aircraft fire, this attacking flight, under Lieutenant Staggs' brilliant and inspiring leadership, succeeded in destroying twelve aircraft on the ground, demolishing three hangars, and immobilizing approximately twenty units of motor transports.

STARKWEATHER, Lt. Mark W., USNR

For extraordinary heroism as Officer in Charge of a demolition party attached to the USS CHEROKEE during the assault on and occupation of French Morocco from November 8 to 11, 1942. Assigned the extremely dangerous task of cutting through an enemy obstruction in order that the USS DALLAS could navigate up the Sebou River, Lieutenant Starkweather and his crew, on the night of November 9, proceeded with grim determination toward their objective. Despite the treacherous surf, he and his shipmates skillfully and courageously accomplished their hazard-

ous mission of cutting the cables at the mouth of the river, as guns from the French fort opened fire. Countering the enemy's attack, Lieutenant Starkweather dauntlessly started back and, in spite of enormous breakers which battered his boat, brought her and her courageous crew back to safety.

WORDELL, Lt. Malcolm T., USN

For extraordinary heroism as section leader in Fighting Squadron FORTY-ONE, attached to the USS RANGER, during the occupation of French Morocco, November 8–11, 1942. When a force of hostile cruisers and destroyers was observed bearing down upon our transports at Fedala, Lieutenant Wordell led a flight of sixteen planes through terrific anti-aircraft fire to intercept their attack. Pressing home vigorous and persistent strafing raids in support of a furious bombardment from our own surface ships, he contributed materially to the relentless fighting spirit which enabled our forces to set fire to three of the enemy vessels and drive off the others. No longer able to carry on because of severe wounds, he successfully extricated himself from a precarious situation by bringing down his badly damaged plane in a skillful forced landing.

EATON, Lt. (jg) Maxwell A., USNR

For extraordinary heroism as Pilot of an airplane in Scouting Squadron FORTY-ONE, attached to the USS RANGER during the occupation of French Morocco, November 8–11, 1942. Launching a vigorous dive-bombing raid on hostile surface units in the vicinity of Casablanca, Lieutenant (junior grade) Eaton, under a bursting hail of anti-aircraft shells, scored a direct 500-pound bomb hit on a light cruiser. On another flight, he voluntarily pressed home a daring attack which silenced an enemy shore battery in the face of terrific fire.

MAYHEW, Lt. (jg) Boyd N., USNR

For extraordinary heroism as Pilot of an airplane in Fighting Squadron FORTY-ONE, attached to the USS RANGER, during the occupation of French Morocco, November 8–11, 1942. Attacked by sixteen hostile fighters while raiding the Cazes airdrome, Lieutenant (junior grade) Mayhew and his flight of eighteen planes shot nine of the interceptors out of the sky and destroyed fourteen aircraft on the ground. In addition to subsequent strafing raids which silenced enemy shore batteries near Port Lyautey and El Hank, he fought his way through a bursting hail of anti-aircraft fire to bombard two surface submarines and a light cruiser off Casablanca.

SMITH, Lt. (jg) Norman Clark, USNR

For extraordinary heroism and distinguished service as Engineer Officer of the USS DALLAS during the assault on and occupation of French Morocco from November 8–11, 1942. Proceeding under heavy fire of hostile artillery up the shallow Sebou River to the Port Lyautey airfield, Lieutenant (junior grade) Smith successfully kept the engineering plant of the DALLAS in full operation while crossing over a treacherous bar through heavy surf and mud for miles up the river. Prior to this action, Lieutenant (junior grade) Smith had brought the engineering plant of the ship to a high degree of readiness and during the engagement at the Port Lyautey airfield, he coolly and efficiently kept the plant operating, regardless of his own personal safety.

BELL, Ens. John Julius, USNR

For extraordinary heroism while serving as Officer in Charge of a scout boat from the USS HARRIS during the assault on and occupation of French Morocco from November 8 to 11, 1942. Preceding the assault on Safi on November 8, Ensign Bell skillfully maneuvered his boat in complete darkness from the transport area eight miles off the coast into position near the main jetty of the harbor. Despite enemy fire, he steadfastly maintained his station and continued to signal directions to the USS BERNADOU, the USS COLE, and the leading assault waves, in order to guide them to the harbor entrance and to the nearby beaches.

O'TOOLE, Ens. John A., USNR

For extraordinary heroism and fearless devotion to duty as Commander of a boat wave from the USS JOSEPH HEWES during the assault on and occupation of French Morocco from November 8 to November 11, 1942. During intense naval and shore bombardment, Ensign O'Toole skillfully organized and led his boat wave toward the beach in the face of devastating and concentrated artillery fire of hostile forces which threatened annihilation of troops before they could debark. With no thought of his own danger, he then stood at the wheel of his boat calmly directing the unloading of both personnel and equipment and the saving of as many of the Navy craft as possible. After directing a squad of machine gunners to safety through the barrage, Ensign O'Toole attempted to withdraw from the beach but was killed by enemy fire.

TRIPSON, Ens. John R., USNR

For extraordinary heroism while in charge of a scout boat from the Northern Attack Group during the assault on and occupation of French Morocco from November 8 to 11, 1942. Preceding the assault on Mehdia on November 8, Ensign Tripson, who was then a Chief Specialist, skillfully maneuvered his craft in complete darkness from the transport area seven miles off the coast toward the mouth of the Sebou River in order to locate and mark this locality for the assault battalions of the Northern Attack Group. After locating his position, he guided incoming boat waves of troops by prescribed signals to their proper destination. Although under fire from hostile forces, Ensign Tripson gallantly maintained his station until his mission was accomplished, thereby contributing to the successful landing of our troops.

ARSENAULT, Frederick L., SF2/c, USNR

For extraordinary heroism as member of a demolition party attached to the USS BRANT during the assault on and occupation of French Morocco from November 8 to 11, 1942. Assigned the extremely dangerous task of cutting through an enemy obstruction in order that the USS DALLAS could navigate up the Sebou River, Arsenault and his shipmates, on the night of November 9, proceeded with grim determination toward their objective. Despite the treacherous surf, he and his comrades skillfully and courageously accomplished their hazardous mission of cutting the cables at the mouth of the river, just as guns from the French fort opened fire. Countering the enemy's attack until out of range, Arsenault and the other members of his party, in spite of enormous breakers which battered their boat and washed one of the machine guns overboard, finally brought her back to safety.

BYROM, Jack A., Chief Specialist, USNR

For extraordinary heroism while in charge of a scout boat from the USS JOSEPH T. DICKMAN during the assault on and occupation of French Morocco from November 8 to 11, 1942. Preceding the assault on Fedala on November 8, Byrom skillfully maneuvered his craft in complete darkness from the transport area six miles off the coast toward the landing beach designated for the assault battalion of the JOSEPH T. DICKMAN. Despite a dangerous rock reef at the end of the beach and enemy batteries menacing the shore, he located his position and by prescribed signals guided incoming boat waves of troops. Although under fire from hostile forces, Byrom gallantly maintained his station until his mission was accomplished, thereby contributing to the successful landing of our troops.

CLARK, Paul Leaman, F1/c, USCG

For extraordinary heroism while serving as engineer of a landing boat attached to USS JOSEPH T. DICKMAN during the assault on and occupation of French Morocco from November 8 to 11, 1942. When a hostile plane strafed his boat with machine gun fire, mortally wounding the bowman and severely injuring the coxswain, Clark, with quick initiative, immediately withdrew from the beach. Speeding toward the USS PALMER, he placed the wounded men aboard and, although his craft was riddled by enemy bullets, courageously returned to his station at the beach.

DONNELL, John G., Chief Specialist, USNR

For extraordinary heroism while in charge of a scout boat from the USS THOMAS JEFFERSON during the assault on and occupation of French Morocco from November 8 to 11, 1942. Preceding the assault on Fedala on November 8, Donnell skillfully maneuvered his craft in complete darkness from the transport area six miles off the coast toward the landing beach designated for the assault battalion of the THOMAS JEFFERSON. Despite a dangerous rock reef at the end of the beach and enemy batteries menacing the shore, he located his position and by prescribed signals guided incoming boat waves of troops. Although under fire from hostile forces, Donnell gallantly maintained his station until his mission was accomplished, thereby contributing to the successful landing of our troops.

DOWLING, Roy B., CBM, USNR

For extraordinary heroism as member of a demolition party attached to the USS CHEROKEE during the assault on and occupation of French Morocco from November 8 to 11, 1942. Assigned the extremely dangerous task of cutting through an enemy obstruction in order that the USS DALLAS could navigate up the Sebou River, Dowling and his shipmates, on the night of November 9, proceeded with grim determination toward their objective. Despite the treacherous surf, he and his comrades skillfully and courageously accomplished their hazardous mission of cutting the cables at the mouth of the river, as guns from the French fort opened fire. Countering the enemy's attack until out of range, Dowling and the other members of his party, in spite of the enormous breakers which battered their boat, brought her back to safety.

FREEMAN, William R., GM1/c, USNR

For extraordinary heroism as member of a demolition party attached to the USS CHEROKEE during the assault on and occupation of French Morocco from November 8 to 11, 1942. Assigned the extremely dangerous task of cutting through an enemy obstruction in order that the USS DALLAS could navigate up the Sebou River, Freeman and his shipmates, on the night of November 9, proceeded with grim determination toward their objective. Despite the treacherous surf, he and his comrades skillfully and courageously accomplished their hazardous mission of cutting the cables at the mouth of the river, as guns from the French fort opened fire. Countering the enemy's attack until out of range, Freeman and the other members of his party, in spite of the enormous breakers which battered their boat, brought her back to safety.

GENTILE, Ernest J., MM1/c, USNR

For extraordinary heroism as member of a demolition party attached to the USS CHEROKEE during the assault on and occupation of French Morocco from November 8 to 11, 1942. Assigned the extremely dangerous task of cutting through an enemy obstruction in order that the USS DALLAS could navigate up the Sebou River, Gentile and his shipmates, on the night of November 9, proceeded with grim determination toward their objective. Despite the treacherous surf, he and his comrades skillfully and courageously accomplished their hazardous mission of cutting the cables at the mouth of the river, as guns from the French fort opened fire. Countering the enemy's attack until out of range, Gentile and the other members of his party, in spite of the enormous breakers which battered their boat, brought her back to safety.

GREELY, Joseph, MM1/c, USNR

For extraordinary heroism as member of a demolition party attached to the USS BRANT during the assault on and occupation of French Morocco from November 8 to 11, 1942. Assigned the extremely dangerous task of cutting through an enemy obstruction in order that the USS DALLAS could navigate up the Sebou River, Greely and his shipmates, on the night of November 9, proceeded with grim determination toward their objective. Despite the treacherous surf, he and his comrades skillfully and courageously accomplished their hazardous mission of cutting the cables at the mouth of the river, just as guns from the French fort opened fire. Countering the enemy's attack until out of range, Greely and the other members of his party, in spite of enormous breakers which battered their boat and washed one of the machine guns overboard, finally brought her back to safety.

HALPERIN, Robert, Chief Specialist, USNR

For extraordinary heroism while in charge of a scout boat from the Northern Attack Group during the assault on and occupation of French Morocco from November 8 to 11, 1942. Preceding the assault on Mehdia on November 8, Halperin skillfully maneuvered his boat in complete darkness from the transport area seven miles off the coast into a position to locate and mark landing beaches on the hostile shore. Landing an Army scout party at the prescribed beach, he then, at great risk of his life and despite the strafing of enemy planes, steadfastly maintained a position off shore and guided incoming waves of assault troops to their proper destination. When all had landed, he assisted the shore party in locating points of egress from the beach and connecting roads inland, and personally captured two enemy officers.

HERRICK, Robert F., Chief Specialist, USNR

For extraordinary heroism while in charge of a scout boat from the USS DOROTHEA L. DIX during the assault on and occupation of French Morocco from November 8 to 11, 1942. Preceding the assault on Safi on November 8, Herrick skillfully maneuvered his boat in complete darkness from the transport area eight miles off the coast into position near a landing beach, from which he guided incoming waves of assault troops by prescribed signals to their proper destination. Despite the delay in arrival of the initial boat waves, the imminent danger of attack from hostile craft, and fire from other enemy forces, Herrick gallantly held his position for nine perilous hours until his mission was completed.

HOUSE, Andrew J., BM2/c, USN

For extraordinary heroism as member of a demolition party attached to the USS BRANT during the assault on and occupation of French Morocco from November 8 to 11, 1942. Assigned the extremely dangerous task of cutting through an enemy obstruction in order that the USS DALLAS could navigate up the Sebou River, House and his shipmates, on the night of November 9, proceeded with grim determination toward their objective. Despite the treacherous surf, he and his comrades skillfully and courageously accomplished their hazardous mission of cutting the cables at the mouth of the river, just as guns from the French fort opened fire. Countering the enemy's attack until out of range, House and the other members of his party, in spite of enormous breakers which battered their boat and washed one of the machine guns overboard, finally brought her back to safety.

Howe, Kenneth E., Chief Specialist, USNR

For extraordinary heroism while in charge of a scout boat from the USS LEONARD WOOD during the assault on and occupation of French Morocco from November 8 to 11, 1942. Preceding the assault on Fedala on November 8, Howe skillfully maneuvered his craft in complete darkness from the transport area off the coast toward the landing beach designated for the assault battalion of the LEONARD WOOD. Despite a dangerous rock reef at the end of the beach and enemy batteries menacing the shore, he located his position and by prescribed signals guided incoming boat waves of troops. Although under fire from hostile forces, Howe gallantly maintained his station until his mission was accomplished, thereby contributing to the successful landing of our troops.

Johnson, John Waldon, Chief Specialist, USNR

For extraordinary heroism while in charge of a scout boat from the USS CHARLES CARROLL during the assault on and occupation of French Morocco from November 8 to 11, 1942. Preceding the assault on Fedala on November 8, Johnson skillfully maneuvered his craft in complete darkness from the transport area six miles off the coast toward the landing beach designated for the assault battalion of the CHARLES CARROLL. Despite a dangerous rock reef at the end of the beach and enemy batteries menacing the shore, he located his position and by prescribed signals guided incoming boat waves of troops. Although under fire from hostile forces,

Johnson gallantly maintained his station until his mission was accomplished; thereby contributing to the successful landing of our troops.

Johnson, Raymond E., SF3/c, USNR

For extraordinary heroism as member of a demolition party attached to the USS CHEROKEE during the assault on and occupation of French Morocco from November 8 to 11, 1942. Assigned the extremely dangerous task of cutting through an enemy obstruction in order that the USS DALLAS could navigate up the Sebou River, Johnson and his shipmates, on the night of November 9, proceeded with grim determination toward their objective. Despite the treacherous surf, he and his comrades skillfully and courageously accomplished their hazardous mission of cutting the cables at the mouth of the river, as guns from the French fort opened fire. Countering the enemy's attack until out of range, Johnson and the other members of his party, in spite of the enormous breakers which battered their boat, brought her back to safety.

Joyce, Richard W., SF1/c, USNR

For extraordinary heroism as member of a demolition party attached to the USS CHEROKEE during the assault on and occupation of French Morocco from November 8 to 11, 1942. Assigned the extremely dangerous task of cutting through an enemy obstruction in order that the USS DALLAS could navigate up the Sebou River, Joyce and his shipmates, on the night of November 9, proceeded with grim determination toward their objective. Despite the treacherous surf, he and his comrades skillfully and courageously accomplished their hazardous mission of cutting the cables at the mouth of the river, as guns from the French fort opened fire. Countering the enemy's attack until out of range, Joyce and the other members of his party, in spite of the enormous breakers which battered their boat, brought her back to safety.

Music, William A., Jr., EM2/c, USN

For extraordinary heroism as member of a demolition party attached to the USS CHEROKEE during the assault on and occupation of French Morocco from November 8 to 11, 1942. Assigned the extremely dangerous task of cutting through an enemy obstruction in order that the USS DALLAS could navigate up the Sebou River, Music and his shipmates, on the night of November 9, proceeded with grim determination toward their objective. Despite the treacherous surf, he and his comrades skillfully and courageously accomplished their hazardous mission of cutting the cables at the mouth of the river, as guns from the French fort opened fire. Countering the enemy's attack until out of range, Music and the other members of his party, in spite of the enormous breakers which battered their boat, brought her back to safety.

PERRY, Lucas J., GM1/c, USN

For extraordinary heroism as member of a demolition party attached to the USS BRANT during the assault on and occupation of French Morocco from November 8 to 11, 1942. Assigned the extremely dangerous task of cutting through an enemy obstruction in order that the USS DALLAS could navigate up the Sebou River, Perry and his shipmates, on the night of November 9, proceeded with grim determination toward their objective. Despite the treacherous surf, he and his comrades skillfully and courageously accomplished their hazardous mission of cutting the cables at the mouth of the river, just as guns from the French fort opened fire. Countering the enemy's attack until out of range, Perry and the other members of his party, in spite of enormous breakers which battered their boat and washed one of the machine guns overboard, finally brought her back to safety.

SHELLEY, Richard G., BM1/c, USNR

For extraordinary heroism as member of a demolition party attached to the USS BRANT during the assault on and occupation of French Morocco from November 8 to 11, 1942. Assigned the extremely dangerous task of cutting through an enemy obstruction in order that the USS DALLAS could navigate up the Sebou River, Shelley and his shipmates, on the night of November 9, proceeded with grim determination toward their objective. Despite the treacherous surf, he and his comrades skillfully and courageously accomplished their hazardous mission of cutting the cables at the mouth of the river, just as guns from the French fort opened fire. Countering the enemy's attack until out of range, Shelley and the other members of his party, in spite of enormous breakers which battered their boat and washed one of the machine guns overboard, finally brought her back to safety.

SPERRY, Edwin, BM1/c, USNR

For extraordinary heroism as member of a demolition party attached to the USS CHEROKEE during the assault on and occupation of French Morocco from November 8 to 11, 1942. Assigned the extremely dangerous task of cutting through an enemy obstruction in order that the USS DALLAS could navigate up the Sebou River, Sperry and his shipmates, on the night of November 9, proceeded with grim determination toward their objective. Despite the treacherous surf, he and his comrades skillfully and courageously accomplished their hazardous mission of cutting the cables at the mouth of the river, as guns from the French fort opened fire. Countering the enemy's attack until out of range, Sperry and the other members of his party, in spite of the enormous breakers which battered their boat, brought her back to safety.

WAGNER, Arthur, CBM, USNR

For extraordinary heroism as member of a demolition party attached to the USS CHEROKEE during the assault on and occupation of French Morocco from November 8 to 11, 1942. Assigned the extremely dangerous task of cutting through an enemy obstruction in order that the USS DALLAS could navigate up the Sebou River, Wagner and his shipmates, on the night of November 9, proceeded with grim determination toward their objective. Despite the treacherous surf, he and his comrades skillfully and courageously accomplished their hazardous mission of cutting the cables at the mouth of the river, as guns from the French fort opened fire. Countering the enemy's attack until out of range, Wagner and the other members of his party, in spite of the enormous breakers which battered their boat, brought her back to safety.

WISNIEWSKI, Edward L., S1/c, USNR

For extraordinary heroism as member of a demolition party attached to the USS CHEROKEE during the assault on and occupation of French Morocco from November 8 to 11, 1942. Assigned the extremely dangerous task of cutting through an enemy obstruction in order that the USS DALLAS could navigate the Sebou River, Wisniewski and his shipmates, on the night of November 9, proceeded with grim determination toward their objective. Despite the treacherous surf, he and his comrades skillfully and courageously accomplished their hazardous mission of cutting the cables at the mouth of the river, as guns from the French fort opened fire. Countering the enemy's attack until out of range, Wisniewski and the other members of his party, in spite of the enormous breakers which battered their boat, brought her back to safety.

ZYMROZ, Czeslaw, MM1/c, USN

For extraordinary heroism as member of a demolition party attached to the USS CHEROKEE during the assault on and occupation of French Morocco from November 8 to 11, 1942. Assigned the extremely dangerous task of cutting through an enemy obstruction in order that the USS DALLAS could navigate up the Sebou River, Zymroz and his shipmates, on the night of November 9, proceeded with grim determination toward their objective. Despite the treacherous surf, he and his comrades skillfully and courageously accomplished their hazardous mission of cutting the cables at the mouth of the river, as guns from the French fort opened fire. Countering the enemy's attack until out of range, Zymroz and the other members of his party, in spite of the enormous breakers which battered their boat, brought her back to safety.

Distinguished Service Medal

*GLASSFORD, Vice Adm. William A., USN

For exceptionally meritorious service to the Government of the United States in a position of great responsibility as head of a mission of grave importance at Dakar, French West Africa. By his intelligent and tactful direction of negotiations with the representatives of France, Vice Admiral Glassford was able to pave the way for close and effective operations at sea in that important area. His profound understanding and judicious conduct of an undertaking of far-reaching significance were decisive factors in the successful accomplishment of a strategic mission.

HEWITT, Vice Adm. Henry K., USN

Commander of the United States Naval Forces which escorted and supported the United States Army Forces in successful landings and occupation of certain objectives in French Morocco from November 7 to November 15, 1942.

Army Distinguished Service Medal

Commander of the Amphibious Force, Atlantic Fleet, and of the Western Naval Task Force No. 34 with the highest type of skill and leadership, conducted his large fleet from the United States to the shores of French Morocco, through waters infested with hostile submarines, without loss. Through his care, foresight, and leadership, the forces he transported were landed 8 November 1942, on a hostile and unknown shore, during hours of darkness, in a heavy sea, at the proper time and places. In subsequent tactical action he handled his forces so as to prevent interference by hostile naval units with the landing of our forces as planned. His services contributed in marked degree to the success of the enterprise.

DAVIDSON, Rear Adm. Lyal A., USN

Commander of the Southern Attack Group of the Western Naval Task Force during the occupation of French Morocco on November 7–8, 1942. Faced with the task of occupying the port of Safi preparatory to further operations against Casablanca, Rear Admiral Davidson, exercising brilliant judgment and superb seamanship in total darkness, conducted the ships under his command in a successful approach to their stations for the attack.

GIFFEN, Rear Adm. Robert C., USN

Commander of the Covering Group of the Western Naval Task Force in the occupation of French Morocco, November 8 through November 11, 1942.

HALL, Rear Adm. John Lesslie, Jr., USN

Acting Chief of Staff of the Commander Western Naval Task Force and as Commander of the West African Sea Frontier Force and Commandant Naval Operating Base at Casablanca. Although continuing to perform his duties as Chief of Staff, Rear Admiral Hall, during the period of November 8 to 20, 1942, organized, established and assumed command of the Sea Frontier Forces. In addition to preventing sabotage during the occupation of Casablanca, Safi, Fedala and Port Lyautey, he effectively re-established the services of these ports, removed merchant ships which were blocking the harbors, salvaged United States vessels which had been damaged during the operations and cleared the way for Western Task Force units and the convoy which followed them.

KELLY, Rear Adm. Monroe, USN

Commander of the Northern Attack Group of the Western Naval Task Force in the occupation of French Morocco from November 7–11, 1942. Assigned the task of occupying the town of Port Lyautey, French Morocco, and certain airdromes in the vicinity, preparatory to further operations against Casablanca.

McWHORTER, Rear Adm. Ernest D., USN

Commander of the Air Group of the Western Naval Task Force, prior to and during the attack phase of the occupation of French Morocco, terminating on November 11, 1942.

EDGAR, Capt. Campbell D., USN

Army Distinguished Service Medal

Captain Edgar's seamanship and skill in handling the Transport Division enabled Combat Team 39 to land men and equipment in rough seas in the face of heavy enemy air and submarine attacks, thus contributing greatly to the success of the operation which resulted in the capture of the city and port of Algiers.

WRIGHT, Capt. Jerauld, USN

A duty of great responsibility immediately before the occupation of French

North Africa by the United States Army Forces. As a member of the advance party which effected a successful night landing along the northern coast of the continent and kept a secret rendezvous prior to the outbreak of hostilities, Captain Wright participated in vital conferences preliminary to the invasion of Morocco and Algeria.

Legion of Merit

*BACHMAN, Capt. Leo A., USN

Intelligence Officer on the Staff of an Amphibious Force Commander during the landings in French Morocco.

BRIGGS, Capt. Josephus Asa, USN

Commander of a Fleet Air Wing and as Commanding Officer of the Naval Air Station at Port Lyautey, French Morocco, during November and December 1942.

*BROOKMAN, Capt. Harold Robert, USNR

Material Officer on the Staff of an Amphibious Force Commander during the landings in French Morocco.

COOK, Capt. Albert G., Jr., USN

Commander of Mine Squadron Seven and Mine Division Nineteen during the assault on and occupation of French Morocco from November 8–11, 1942.

CUMMINGS, Col. Gale T., USMC

Fleet Marine Officer on the Staff of Commander in Chief, United States Atlantic Fleet, from 23 April, 1942, to 1 January, 1944, and was of great assistance in planning the Algeria-Morocco occupation in 1942.

*ENGLISH, Capt. Robert A. J., USN

Assistant Operations Officer on the Staff of an Amphibious Force Commander during the landings in French Morocco.

*EVANS, Capt. Donald S., USN

Communications Officer on the Staff of an Amphibious Force Commander during the invasion of French Morocco.

HUBER, Capt. Vernon, USN

Commanding Officer USS LIVERMORE, performed arduous escort duties in the

North Atlantic and participated in the assault on and the invasion of Mehdia, Morocco.

HUTCHINS, Capt. Gordon, USN

Army Legion of Merit

Commander of the USS AUGUSTA, flagship in the operations of the Western Task Force from the time of embarkation, October, 1942, until the debarkation, November, 1942.

JOHNSTON, Col. Edward S., USA

Deputy Chief of Staff to an Amphibious Force Commander prior to and during the invasion of French Morocco.

LAIRD, Capt. Horace C., USN (Ret.)

Commanding Officer of the Naval Landing Force Equipment Depot, Norfolk, Virginia, prior to and during landing operations in French Morocco on November 8, 1942.

*MITCHELL, Capt. Edward A., USN

Operations Officer on the Staff of an Amphibious Force Commander prior to and during landing operations in French Morocco on November 8, 1942.

PUPEK, Capt. Bernard S., (MC), USN

Medical Officer on the Staff of Commander Amphibious Force, United States Atlantic Fleet, and later on the Staff of a Major Task Force Commander during the landings in French Morocco.

SHEPARD, Capt. Andrew G., USN

Assisted in planning the Algeria-Morocco Occupation in 1942.

SICKEL, Capt. Horatio G., IV, USN

A position of great responsibility during the assault on and occupation of French Morocco in November 1942.

WOODS, Capt. Ralph W. D., USN

Aviation Officer on the Staff of an Amphibious Force Commander prior to and during landing operations in French Morocco on November 8, 1942.

BOIT, Cdr. Julian M., USNR

Flag Secretary on the Staff of Commander Amphibious Force, U.S. Atlantic Fleet, and on the staff of Commander U.S. Naval Forces, Northwest African Waters, during the invasions of French Morocco, Sicily and Italy.

HEYWARD, Cdr. Alexander S., Jr., USN

Commanding Officer of Patrol Squadron SEVENTY-THREE transferred from Iceland to French Morocco in November 1942.

HUTCHINGS, Cdr. Curtis Howell, USN

Commander Patrol Squadron SIXTY-THREE engaged in antisubmarine operations in the Moroccan Sea Frontier from September 22, 1943, to May 31, 1944.

HYATT, Cdr. Roger Clair, USNR

Served on the Staff of Commander Moroccan Sea Frontier Forces subsequent to the occupation of French Morocco on November 8, 1942.

MORENO, Cdr. John A., USN

Leader of a Patrol Squadron during occupation of the airport at Port Lyautey, French Morocco and the establishment of an antisubmarine patrol in adjacent waters in November and December, 1942.

RAGSDALE, Cdr. Edmund M., USN

Repair Officer at the U.S. Naval Operating Base, Casablanca, subsequent to landings in French Morocco on November 8, 1942 and at the U.S. Naval Operating Base in Palermo during the occupation of Sicily.

STEERE, Cdr. Richard C., USN

Aerological Officer on the Staff of Commander Amphibious Force, Atlantic Fleet, and on the Staff of Commander United States Naval Forces, Northwest African Waters, during the amphibious invasions of French Morocco, Sicily and Italy.

DROUIN, Lt. Cdr. Paul L., USNR

Attached to the USS SUSAN B. ANTHONY during the assault on and occupation of French Morocco, November 8–11, 1942.

O'CONNOR, Lt. Cdr. Desmond K., USNR

Executive Officer of the USS COLE during the assault on and occupation of

French Morocco from November 8 to 11, 1942.

WROTEN, Lt. Cdr. Wiley L., USNR

Officer in Charge of Salvage Operations at Casablanca subsequent to the invasion of French Morocco, November 1942.

BENNETT, Lt. Harvey S., USNR

Naval Gunfire Liaison Officer during the assault on and occupation of French Morocco from November 8 to 11, 1942.

CASSADY, Lt. Harold A., (MC), USNR

Medical Officer of the beach party from the USS GEORGE CLYMER during the assault on and occupation of French Morocco from November 8 to 11, 1942.

COGLEY, Lt. William T., Jr., USNR

Naval Gunfire Liaison Officer with Commander Landing Force and in charge of all Shore Fire Control Parties at Safi during the assault on and occupation of French Morocco from November 8 to 11, 1942.

HINES, Lt. Edward C., USN

Navigator of the USS COLE during the assault on and occupation of French Morocco from November 8 to 11, 1942.

MATTOX, Lt. Don M., (MC), USNR

Medical Officer of the beach party from the USS CHARLES CARROLL during the assault on and occupation of French Morocco, November 8–11, 1942.

SOUTHWORTH, Lt. Robert A., USNR

Naval Gunfire Liaison Officer with Commander Landing Force, during the assault on and occupation of French Morocco from November 8 to 11, 1942.

HORES, Lt. (jg) Edward F., USNR

Commander of a boat wave of assault troops from the USS CHARLES CARROLL in the initial action at Fedala during the assault on and occupation of French Morocco, November 8–11, 1942.

KREUTZER, Lt. (jg) Richard, Jr., USNR

A beachmaster attached to the USS GEORGE CLYMER during the assault on and occupation of French Morocco from November 8 to 11, 1942.

SMYTHE, Lt. (jg) Henry B., USNR

Pilot for three prize craft attached to the USS TILLMAN during the assault on and occupation of French Morocco, November 8–11, 1942.

SWENSON, Lt. (jg) Caydar E., USN

Commander of the leading boat wave of assault troops from the USS CHARLES CARROLL in the initial action at Fedala, during the assault on and occupation of French Morocco, November 8–11, 1942.

BALDOCK, Ens. Charles W., USN

Navigator of the scout boat preceding a boat wave of assault troops from the USS CHARLES CARROLL, during the assault on and occupation of French Morocco, November 8–11, 1942.

ALVIS, Fred, BM2/c, USN

Coxswain of a landing boat of the USS CHARLES CARROLL during the assault on and occupation of French Morocco, November 8–11, 1942.

BLACKETER, Jimmie W., S2/c, USN

A member of the crew of a tank lighter attached to the USS FLORENCE NIGHTINGALE during the assault on and occupation of French Morocco from November 8 to 11, 1942.

CAMP, Cecil W., F1/c, USN

Attached to the USS EDWARD RUTLEDGE when that vessel was torpedoed and sunk off Fedala, French Morocco, on November 12, 1942.

COLLINS, James D., S1/c, USNR

Attached to the USS CHARLES CARROLL during the assault on and occupation of French Morocco, November 8–11, 1942.

COOTS, Jack W., CPhM, USN

Attached to the USS EDWARD RUTLEDGE as senior hospital corpsman of the beach party organized when that ship was torpedoed and sunk off Fedala, French Morocco, on November 12, 1942.

DEAL, John A., CQM, USN

Attached to the USS TILLMAN during the assault on and occupation of French Morocco, November 8–11, 1942.

DURGIN, Willard L., MoMM1/c, USCG

Engineer of a landing boat from the USS CHARLES CARROLL during the assault on and occupation of French Morocco, November 8–11, 1942.

EASTMAN, Elton M., GM1/c, USN

Gun Captain of Gun Number One of the USS COLE during the assault on and occupation of French Morocco from November 8 to 11, 1942.

GAGER, Frank B., MM1/c, USNR

Attached to the USS WICHITA during the assault on and occupation of French Morocco, November 8–11, 1942.

GAJDOSTIK, Joseph A., CPhM, USN

In charge of the accessory operation room and troop sick bay attached to the USS EDWARD RUTLEDGE when that vessel was torpedoed and sunk off Fedala, French Morocco, on November 12, 1942.

GARRETT, William A., Cox., USNR

Attached to the USS FLORENCE NIGHTINGALE during the assault on and occupation of French Morocco from November 8 to 11, 1942.

GOLENIECKI, John V., BM1/c, USCG

Attached to the USS CHARLES CARROLL during the assault on and occupation of French Morocco, November 8–11, 1942.

HAISLIP, Bobby L., Cox., USN

A member of the crew of a tank lighter attached to the USS FLORENCE NIGHTINGALE during the assault on and occupation of French Morocco from November 8 to 11, 1942.

HOLMES, Kenneth O., CM1/c, USNR

A member of the repair party aboard the USS MURPHY during the assault on and occupation of French Morocco, November 8 to 11, 1942.

HORVAT, Stephen J., MoMM2/c, USN

Engineer of a tank lighter of the USS CHARLES CARROLL in the initial action at Fedala, during the assault on and occupation of French Morocco, November 8–11, 1942.

KEENAN, Charles S., CSM, USN

Attached to the USS TASKER H. BLISS when that ship was torpedoed and sunk off Fedala, French Morocco, on November 12, 1942.

LIMES, Jack E., SM3/c, USN

Attached to the USS TILLMAN during the assault on and occupation of French Morocco, November 8–11, 1942.

NUNES, Frederick, CGM, USN

Directed the supply of ammunition to the after guns aboard the USS MURPHY during the assault on and occupation of French Morocco, November 8 to 11, 1942.

PAINE, Howard H., CGM, USN

Attached to the USS BERNADOU in the assault on and occupation of French Morocco from November 8 to 11, 1942.

RABAK, Edward, PhM3/c, USNR

Attached to the USS EDWARD RUTLEDGE during the assault on and occupation of French Morocco from November 8 to 11 and when that ship was torpedoed and sunk on November 12, 1942.

SPENCER, Charles H., Jr., BM1/c, USN

Attached to the USS JOHN PENN during the assault on and occupation of French Morocco from November 8 to 11, 1942.

WANDRIE, Otto B., Jr., PhM3/c, USN

Attached to the USS EDWARD RUTLEDGE during the assault on and occupation of French Morocco from November 8 to 11 and when that ship was torpedoed and sunk on November 12, 1942.

ZINTER, Donald G., PhM3/c, USNR

Attached to the USS EDWARD RUTLEDGE during the assault on and occupation of French Morocco from November 8 to 11 and when that ship was torpedoed and sunk on November 12, 1942.

Silver Star Medal

SMITH, Capt. Robert McLanahan, USN
CARTER, Lt. Cdr. George H., USN
CURTIS, Lt. Cdr. Robert W., USN
HAISCH, Lt. Cdr. Howard B., USN

HUFFMAN, Lt. Cdr. Moore P., USNR
ROGERS, Maj. Francis M., USMC
WINTERS, Lt. Cdr. Theodore H., Jr., USN
BOYD, Lt. Randall T., Jr., USN
CHILDERS, Lt. Kenan C., Jr., USN
EDER, Lt. Willard E., USN
GRELL, Lt. Theodore A., USN
HAMMOND, Lt. Keene G., USN
HIGLEY, Lt. Robert H., USN
HOWELL, Lt. Willard Y., USN
MOORE, Lt. Theophilus H., USNR
MOORE, Lt. Waller C., USN
ONSTOTT, Lt. Jacob W., USN
PATTIE, Lt. Donald A., USNR
POPE, Lt. David H., USN
ROBERTS, Lt. Charles P., (MC), USNR
RODEEN, Lt. Donald C., USNR
WHITE, Lt. Horace R., USNR
WOOD, Lt. Ernest W., Jr., USN
AUGUST, Lt. (jg) Charles V., USNR
AUSTIN, Lt. (jg) William Randolph, USNR
BREWSTER, Lt. (jg) William R., Jr., USN
CONNER, Lt. (jg) Andrew B., Jr., USNR
DEIBLER, Lt. (jg) William H., Jr., USN
FRANGER, Lt. (jg) Marvin J., USNR
HADDEN, Lt. (jg) Mayo A., Jr., USNR
HARRIS, Lt. (jg) George M., Jr., USNR
HILL, Lt. (jg) Donald R., USNR
McREYNOLDS, Lt. (jg) John G., Jr., USNR
MENARD, Lt. (jg) Louis A., Jr., USNR
MIKRONIS, Lt. (jg) Christos E., USNR
NICKS, Lt. (jg) Carney B., USNR
PERRY, Lt. (jg) John E., USNR
RENT, Lt. (jg) William S., USNR
ROBBINS, Lt. (jg) Spencer E., USN
SHIELDS, Lt. (jg) Charles A., USNR
TUCKER, Lt. (jg) Clyde A., Jr., USNR
TWIDDY, Lt. (jg) Clarence A., Jr., USNP
VITA, Lt. (jg) Harold E., USNR
DUFFY, Ens. Charles J., USNR
JAQUES, Ens. Bruce D., USNR
O'NEIL, Ens. Robert Edward, USNR
TAYLOR, Ens. Will W., USNR
WILHOITE, Ens. Thomas M., USNR
BEAHM, Andrew J., CMM, USNR
BERRY, Kenneth P., CQM, USN
BURDGE, Floyd W., Sgt., USMC
CLARK, James Albert, S1/c, USNR
CURRY, Charles C., Jr., PhM2/c, USNR
DONAVAN, Samuel H., Platoon Sgt. USMC
FLYNN, Elmer J., Jr., Sk1/c, USN
GONIA, Loury B., CGM, USN

HINKLEY, George S., AOM2/c, USN
HOTTENDORF, Leonard M., S2/c, USNR
JARRELL, Arley P., CQM, USN
KAGEY, Clarence C., MM1/c, USNR
KALINOWSKI, Joseph T., F3/c, USNR
KUJAWINSKI, Anthony E., Cpl., USMCR
McMAHAN, Y. J., CBM, USN
MEERMAN, Robert, CPhM, USN
NIERLE, Joseph M., Jr., S1/c, USNR
PATTERSON, Aubra T., ARM3/c, USN
POOR, Lawrence F., CBM, USN
POPPA, Clyde W., BM1/c, USN
RICK, Robert J., PhM3/c, USNR
ROOKS, Ervil L., S1/c, USN
SHEPHERD, Daniel H., CMM, USN
STEWART, Marion E., RM3/c, USN
TAYLOR, Robert, CBM, USN
YOUNG, Wilson M., QM1/c, USN

Distinguished Flying Cross

MADDEN, Lt. Walter F., USNR
FRNKA, Fred Richard, AMM2/c, USNR
GIBSON, Earl James, ARM3/c, USNR
MACKEY, Harry Edward, Jr., AMM2/c, USNR

Navy and Marine Corps Medal

BARRETT, Cdr. John P. B., USN
HUGHES, Cdr. James J., USN
MURPHY, Cdr. John E., USN
RUCKER, Cdr. Colby G., USN
RYAN, Cdr. William D., USNR
JAMES, Lt. William Francis, USNR
LOGAN, Ens. Robert K., USNR
BENOIST, Peter E., MoMM2/c, USNR
DECKER, Harold S., PhM1/c, USN
HARDEN, Robert W., S2/c, USNR
HOLDER, Lee A., F1/c, USN
HOUSE, Charles R., S1/c, USN
JACOBS, Edwin M., F2/c, USNR
KULCZAK, Henry B., Cox., USNR
LORCH, William, M1/c, USN
LUDWIG, Herman R., ARM2/c, USNR
MEEKER, Rex G., F1/c, USCG
MURCH, Douglass A., CSM, USN
PETERSCHMIDT, Leo F., S2/c, USN
PIERCE, Julian O'Neal, AOM1/c, USNR
RAGAN, Oran D., BM2/c, USCG
TURCOTTE, Armand G., S2/c, USNR
WILLERT, Elmer C., PhM3/c, USN
YOUNG, Charles Edward, MM2/c, USNR
YOUNG, Joseph F., Boat., USN

Air Medal

SMITH, Lt. Cdr. Donald Emanuel, USN
MALMSTROM, Lt. Carl R. N., USNR
BURNS, Lt. (jg) Ralph W., USNR
CAPANO, Lt. (jg) Patsy, USNR
CHESLEY, Lt. (jg) Franklin R., Jr., USNR
COUGHLIN, Lt. (jg) Paul E., USNR
HOLLINGSWORTH, Lt. (jg) Lloyd D., Jr., USNR
PEGLOW, Lt. (jg) Gilbert F., USNR
TURNER, Lt. (jg) William Anson, USNR
ABATSIS, George C., AMM1/c, USN
ANDERSON, Arthur C., AOM1/c, USNR
CARTER, Jack, AOM3/c, USNR
DRUMMOND, Ray G., Mach., USNR
GORKA, Walter S., AOM3/c, USNR
GRIFFITH, Thomas R., ACMM, USN
HOFINGER, Ralph, AOM1/c, USNR
JANNUZZI, Henry J., AMM1/c, USN
JONES, William Thomas, ARM1/c, USNR
KENNEDY, Whitney H., ARM1/c, USNR
MATTOCKS, Louis S., CCM, USN
MORTON, William H., Jr., AOM1/c, USN
OJEDA, Ernest E., AMM2/c, USNR
SIEBEL, Nathan V. L., ARM3/c, USNR
STEADMAN, Robert "C," ARM1/c, USNR
STEARNS, George R., Y1/c, USNR
WEBER, Clyde L., ARM1/c, USNR
ZEPHT, Eugene W., AMM1/c, USN

Bronze Star Medal

PATTERSON, Lt. Eugene F., USNR
LAURIE, William E., GM2/c, USN

PRESIDENTIAL UNIT CITATIONS

UNITED STATES SHIP BERNADOU

For outstanding performance in leading the attack on Safi, French Morocco, November 8, 1942. Under crossfire from three enemy coast defense batteries and machine guns mounted on harbor jetties, the BERNADOU, proceeding through unknown waters in total darkness, effectively countered hostile opposition with only slight damage to her hull, beached at Petite Jetee, and disembarked a company of U.S. Army assault troops without personnel casualty or loss of life. Her distinctive fulfillment of a difficult and hazardous mission contributed materially to the victorious achievement of the Southern Attack Group.

UNITED STATES SHIP COLE

For outstanding performance as guide for the first wave of landing boats in tne attack on Safi, French Morocco, November 8, 1942. Under crossfire from enemy coast defense batteries and machinegun emplacements, the COLE, proceeding through a narrow harbor entrance in total darkness, effectively countered hostile opposition, disembarked a company of U.S. Army assault troops, and supported their attack by accurate fire from her main battery. Her distinctive fulfillment of a difficult and hazardous mission contributed materially to the victorious achievement of the Southern Attack Group.

UNITED STATES SHIP DALLAS

For outstanding participation in the capture of Port Lyautey Airfield, French Morocco, November 10, 1942. With a U.S. Army raider detachment embarked, the DALLAS, crossing a treacherous bar against heavy surf in order to reach the mouth of Sebou River, broke through a steel cable boom obstructing the channel, forced her course ten miles upstream under hostile fire, and successfully landed troops without material damage or loss of life. Her distinctive fulfillment of a difficult and hazardous mission contributed materially to the victorious achievement of the Northern Attack Group.

EUROPE

Navy Cross

KENNEDY, Lt. Joseph P., Jr., USNR

For extraordinary heroism and courage in aerial flight as Pilot of a United States Navy Liberator Bomber on August 12, 1944. Well knowing the extreme dangers involved and totally unconcerned for his own safety, Lieutenant Kennedy unhesitatingly volunteered to conduct an exceptionally hazardous and special operational mission. Intrepid and daring in his tactics and with unwavering confidence in the vital importance of his task, he willingly risked his life in the supreme measure of service, and, by his great personal valor and fortitude in carrying out a perilous undertaking, sustained and enhanced the finest traditions of the United States Naval Service.

SPALDING, Lt. Ralph D., Jr., USNR

As Commander of a patrol plane of Patrol Bombing Squadron 110, volunteered for and completed with excellent results a particularly hazardous mission of vital importance.

WILLY, Lt. Wilford J., USN

As co-pilot of a United States Liberator Bomber, volunteered to participate in an exceptionally hazardous and special operational mission on August 12, 1944.

ALEXANDER, Lt. (jg), James H., Jr., USNR

For extraordinary heroism as Pilot of a PBY Patrol Bomber during action against enemy German forces over the Bay of Biscay on September 4, 1943. While conducting a highly dangerous antisubmarine patrol, Lieutenant (junior grade) Alexander, under a vicious attack by six twin-engined fighters, maneuvered the bomber with such precisive skill that his gunners were able to shoot down one hostile craft and cripple three others. Although his own plane was set afire in the vigorous air battle, her flying instruments rendered inoperative and her four engines badly damaged, he nevertheless carried on, despite a painful head wound, until he had evaded the remainder of the enemy and effected a safe landing at sea. Successfully abandoning the big flying boat, he and his crew rode out a severe storm in a rubber life raft before reaching land two days later.

ORTIZ, Maj. Peter J., USMCR

For extraordinary heroism in connection with military operations against an armed enemy, in enemy-occupied territory, from January 8, 1944, to May 20, 1944. During this period, Major Ortiz, together with two other officers of an Inter-Allied Mission, after having been dropped from an airplane, in civilian clothes, reorganized existing Maquis groups and organized additional groups in the region of the Rhone in a highly successful manner. By his tact, initiative, resourcefulness, and leadership, he was largely instrumental in the acceptance of the mission by the local resistance leaders and in effecting the organization of parachute operations for the delivery of arms, ammunition, and equipment for the Maquis in his region. When four Royal Air Force officers were shot down in his region, Major Ortiz, although his identity had become known to the Gestapo with the resultant increase in his personal hazard, voluntarily conducted them to the Spanish border, after which he returned and fearlessly resumed his duties until he was directed to return to the British Isles. Throughout the period of this assignment, Major Ortiz repeatedly led successful raids against enemy forces greatly superior in number, inflicting heavy casualties with small losses to his own forces. His courageous leadership and the astuteness with which these forays were planned and executed were an inspiration to his subordinates. As these duties were performed in civilian clothes, Major Ortiz was at all times subject to execution as a spy in the event of his capture.

Distinguished Service Medal

STANDLEY, Adm. William Harrison, USN (Ret.)

For exceptionally meritorious service to the Government of the United States in duties of great responsibility during his distinguished career as an Officer of the Navy.

FRANKEL, Cdr. Samuel B., USN

For exceptionally meritorious service in a duty of great responsibility as Assistant Naval Attaché in Murmansk and Archangel, USSR, during the period from November 1941 to September 1942. Under adverse conditions, Commander Frankel displayed extraordinary initiative and tireless energy in the direction of repairs to damaged United States vessels, in the salvaging of stranded and abandoned vessels, and in the supervision, rescue, hospitalization and repatriation of survivors of sunken vessels. As a result of his courage and resourcefulness, certain vessels which would otherwise have been lost have been saved for future service in the war effort.

Legion of Merit

LOGAN, Commodore James A., USN

Commandant of the U.S. Naval Operating Base at Londonderry, Northern Ireland, from March 15 to September 4, 1943.

CAMPBELL, Brig. Gen. Harold D., USMC

USMC Aviation Officer on the Staff of the Chief of Combined Operations, from 16 June 1942 until 26 April 1943.

ARNOLD, Capt. James E., USNR

Commanding Officer of the United States Naval Advanced Amphibious Base, Falmouth, Cornwall.

DIETRICH, Capt. Neil K., USN

Head of the Logistical Plans Section on the Staff of the Commander, U. S. Naval Forces in Europe, prior to and during the invasion of the continent of Europe, June 1944.

FORSYTH, Capt. Edward C., USN

Maintenance Officer on the Staff of Commander, Landing Craft and Bases, Eleventh Amphibious Force.

HUNT, Capt. Ralph B., USN

Logistics Officer of the Staff of Commander, Landing Craft and Bases, Eleventh Amphibious Force, during the invasion of Europe, June 6, 1944.

KORNS, Capt. Virgil Eben, USN

Chief of Staff to Commander, Landing Craft and Bases, Eleventh Amphibious Force.

*LEPPERT, Capt. John Henry, USN

Communication Officer on the Staff of the Commander U. S. Naval Forces in Europe, prior to and during the invasion of the continent of Europe, June, 1944.

*NELSON, Capt. Roger E., USN

Operations Officer on the staff of Commander, Landing Craft and Bases, Eleventh Amphibious Force, during the assault

on the continent of Europe on June 6, 1944.

PERCIFIELD, Capt. Willis M., USN

Chief of Staff for the Far Shore Organization of the Staff of Commander, Landing Craft and Bases, Eleventh Amphibious Force.

QUINBY, Capt. Charles Fenton Mercer Spotswood, USN

Commanding Officer of a U.S. Naval Advanced Amphibious Base in the United Kingdom.

REINBURG, Capt. John E., Jr., USN

Commanding Officer of the United States Naval Advanced Amphibious Base, Dartmouth, Devon.

*WELLINGS, Capt. Timothy F., USN

Training and Gunnery Officer of the Western Naval Task Force during the assault landing on the coast of Normandy in Northern France on 6 June 1944.

BLAKESLEE, Cdr. Victor F., USN (Ret.)

Commanding Officer of the United States Naval Amphibious Supply Base, Exeter, England.

EASTON, Cdr. William Thomas, USN

Chief Staff Officer and Operations Officer of a Patrol Wing during the Bay of Biscay Offensive and during the invasion of occupied France.

McGREGOR, Cdr. Clifford James, USNR

Aerologist on the Staff of a Patrol Wing engaged in antisubmarine warfare during a period of concentrated action in the Bay of Biscay and the English Channel.

WILLIAMS, Cdr. Chauncey C. (SC), USNR

Supply Officer of the United States Naval Amphibious Supply Base, Exeter.

HARRIS, Lt. Cdr. Eugene P. (MC), USN

Medical Officer on the Far Shore Staff of Commander, Landing Craft and Bases, Eleventh Amphibious Force.

LASSITER, Lt. Cdr. Frederic H., USNR

Flag Secretary on the Staff of Commander, Landing Craft and Bases, Eleventh Amphibious Force.

LECKIE, Lt. Cdr. William Irvine, USNR

Personnel Officer for Logistics on the Staff of the Commander, U. S. Naval Forces in Europe, prior to and during the invasion of the continent of Europe, June, 1944.

MICHAUX, Lt. Cdr. Frank Watkins, USNR

Serving on the Staff of Commander U.S. Naval Forces in Europe as Planning Officer for Fuel Logistics, Lieutenant Commander Michaux, in connection with the logistical support of task forces, skillfully devised a supply and distribution plan for all fuel products that insured the proper support for all U.S. naval units concerned.

HOAGUE, Lt. George, Jr., USNR

Officer in charge of Gooseberry One and Two, coordinating the establishment of artificial harbors of refuge for small craft off the assault beaches during the invasion of France, June 1944.

McGINNIS, John, CSClk, USN

Assistant Naval Attaché stationed North Russia in the early part of 1942.

Silver Star Medal

LETTS, Cdr. Kenneth P., USN
PARHAM, Cdr. John C., Jr., USN
ZAHN, Cdr. John C., USN
POWELL, Lt. Cdr. Edgar S., Jr., USN
TUTT, Lt. Cdr. Alvin H., USN
WILMERDING, Lt. Cdr. Henry A., Jr., USNR
METTLER, Lt. Harry A., USNR
STONE, Lt. Richard M., USNR
BOUCHER, Lt. (jg) Ralph Emerson, USNR
BROWN, Lt. (jg) Willard W., USNR
CARTER, Lt. (jg) William A., USNR
LAIRD, Lt. (jg) John Landers, USNR
LENNING, Lt. (jg) George B., USNR
MARKS, Lt. (jg) Louis D., USNR
RICKS, Lt. (jg) Robert Byron, USNR
WOLFSON, Lt. (jg) Morton E., USNR
BILLINGS, Ens. Roy M., USNR
BRINN, Ens. Rufus T., USNR
COLLINS, Ens. Wilbur P., USNR
KROETZ, Ens. Rudolph H., USNR
MADDALENA, Ens. Arthur D., Jr., USNR
MAHONEY, Ens. Jeremiah Ehret, USNR
MAYNARD, Ens. Albert, USNR

ROOKER, Ens. Daniel J., USNR
SCHAEFER, Ens. Regis J., USNR
ULRICH, Ens. Charles M., USNR
WELCH, Ens. Brian C., USNR
ARTERBERRY, Winifred L., MoMM3/c, USNR
CHANDLER, James William, GM2/c, USN
DECOTTES, Eaton P., BM1/c, USNR
DIXON, Thomas J., GM3/c, USNR
DOLE, Charles E., BM2/c, USN
FARMER, Arthur Latney, Cox., USNR
GEMMER, Ward Laverne, Cox., USN
HOBAN, Edward C., GM3/c, USN
LAMBERT, George F., GM2/c, USNR
LEAHY, Joseph Donald, RM2/c, USNR
McLEOD, John Nelson, Jr., GM3/c, USN
NORTON, George J., GM3/c, USN
O'SAVAGE, Joseph, BM2/c, USNR
RICHARDS, Floyd Eugene, SM1/c, USN
SCHILBE, William A., GM3/c, USNR
SCHILL, Gustav W., Jr., GM3/c, USNR
WEEKS, Lloyd Richard, AS, USNR
WRIGHT, Hugh Patrick, S2/c, USNR
WOHLERS, Albert Franklin, AS, USNR
ZOLPER, Ira G., GM3/c, USNR

Distinguished Flying Cross

DENTON, Lt. Cdr. William, Jr., USN
ENLOE, Lt. George Albert, USNR
HARMON, Lt. Leonard E., USN
NORTH, Lt. Raymond Lewis, Jr., USNR
TANNER, Lt. William P., Jr., USNR
BEDELL, Lt. (jg) Robert I., USNR
DELHOM, Lt. (jg) James Joseph, USNR
GOODRICH, Lt. (jg) John Emerson, USNR
KINNEY, Lt. (jg) Paul Bruce, USNR
ROBERTSON, Lt. (jg) Billy England, USNR
WRIGHT, Lt. (jg) Kenneth Leon, USNR
JOHNSON, Ens. Roy Walter, USNR
POHLING, Ens. Emrick, USNR
ALLEN, Ralph LeRoy, ARM2/c, USNR
CARTER, Roy Alexander, AMM3/c, USNR
DEAN, Francis Earl, AOM2/c, USNR
JONES, Dallas Harding, ACOM, USN
LEMARR, Clifton Marion, ARM1/c, USN
LETOURNEAU, Ralph Joseph, AMM1/c, USNR
RITTEL, Arthur A., AP1/c, USN
TONER, Joseph Bernard, AOM3/c, USNR
VAN DOREN, Elliott Watson, ARM3/c, USNR

Navy and Marine Corps Medal

CROWLEY, Lt. Leo E. (CEC), USNR
MCCLUNG, Lt. Norvel M., USNR
OLSEN, Lt. Richard Frank, USNR
SNELLING, Lt. William M., USNR
ASPER, Lt. (jg) William L., USNR
ELLICOTT, Lt. (jg) Joseph R., USNR
PALADING, Lt. (jg) John Lincoln, MC, USNR
BAKER, Wayne, GM2/c, USN
BERRY, H. P., SM2/c, USNR
BISHOP, Philip L., CBM, USNR
BRENNAN, Henry T., CY, USNR
CAFFEY, Chester S., Cox., USNR
CAYER, Paul Eugene, S1/c, USNR
DAVIS, John, S1/c, USNR
DEBAUN, Garnett Cury, S2/c, USNR
DENNEHY, Robert E., BM1/c, USNR
DOWNER, John W., Cox., USNR
DURANTI, Louis, PhM1/c, USNR
EBRIGHT, Richard C., GM3/c, USN
ELLIS, Robert Earl, PhM2/c, USNR
EMERY, Wilfred H., Jr., CEM, USNR
FOEHNER, George Allen, RM2/c, USN
GARDNER, Ralph, SM2/c, USNR
HAINES, Gerald R. L., F1/c, USNR
HAWKINS, John Bell, St3/c, USNR
HEACOCK, Luther Joe, S2/c, USNR
HUPERTZ, L. A., MoMM1/c, USNR
KEITH, Cleatus M., MoMM3/c, USN
MADDEN, Richard B., CSK, USNR
MITSCHA, Max E., QM3/c, USN
O'BRIEN, John F., BM2/c, USNR
PEDEN, Charles Oliver, BM1/c, USNR
RATZ, Charles, S2/c, USN
SEREY, William C., MM2/c, USNR
SPILLER, Frank Arthur, Cox., USNR
STEVENS, Everett D., S2/c, USNR
TYCER, Forster Commaigera, CMM, USN
TENGELSEN, Arnold W., S1/c, USNR
VANDIVER, Donald Lee, AS, USNR
WHITTEN, Aubrey D., QM2/c, USNR
WOOD, Joseph L., MM1/c, USNR

Air Medal

PURVIS, Capt. Robert S., USN
KLINSMAN, Lt. Cdr. George O., USN
ARMSTEAD, Lt. M. E., USNR
ENLOE, Lt. George Albert, USNR
KRAUSE, Lt. William Bruno, USNR
ELLIS, Lt. (jg) Lance "F", Jr., USNR
KEMPER, Lt. (jg) Kenneth George, Jr., USNR

KESSEL, Lt. (jg) Jack Cooper, USNR
KINNEY, Lt. (jg) Paul Bruce, USNR
THUESON, Lt. (jg) Theodore Stanley, USN
ANDERSON, Ens. Philip Randolph, USNR
BALLARD, Ens. Donald Harrison, USNR
COLYER, Ens. Cecil Raymond, USNR
D'HARLINGUE, Ens. Victor, Jr., USNR
HOLLORAN, Ens. Robert Emmett, USNR
LANE, Ens. Robert Wylie, USNR
LOVELACE, Ens. Roger William, Jr., USNR
MEYER, Ens. Carl Theodore, USNR
MILLER, Ens. Clair LeVaughan, USNR
MILTON, Ens. George Pendroy, USNR
*O'MARA, Ens. Brendan, USNR
PETERSEN, Ens. Lawrence Merritt, USNR
*POHLING, Ens. Emrick, USNR
SCHWAN, Ens. Theodore Carl, USNR
*ALLEN, Ralph LeRoy, ARM2/c, USNR
BEANE, Edwin Albert, Jr., AMM2/c, USNR
BEARD, Thomas Stone, AOM3/c, USNR
BENSON, John Francis, ARM3/c, USNR
BRIGGS, Donald Ray, AOM1/c, USN
BROWN, Owen Clayton, AMM1/c, USNR
BROWN, Walter Franklin, ARM1/c, USN
BULLOCK, Andrew Franklin, Jr., AMM1/c, USNR
CAMERON, John Mark, AOM2/c, USNR
CARMACK, David R., AMM2/c, USN
*CARTER, Roy Alexander, AMM3/c, USNR
CLARK, Dewey Matthew, AOM3/c, USNR
CLAYTON, William, Jr., S2/c, USNR
COUNTS, Harold Lewis, AMM1/c, USN
CROSSMAN, James Arthur, CAP, USN
CURLEY, James Stephen, AOM3/c, USNR
CURRAN, Philip Joseph, AMM1/c, USNR
DAVENPORT, Leo Merrill, ARM2/c, USNR
*DEAN, Francis Earl, AOM2/c, USNR
EDWARDS, Levy Mono, AMM2/c, USN
ERDMAN, Robert Charles, ARM3/c, USNR
FAUBION, Bennie, AOM3/c, USNR
FEATHERSTON, Jack Lyndon, ARM1/c, USN
*FINCH, Thomas Harlan, ARM3/c, USNR
GARLOFF, Edward Franklin, Jr., ARM3/c, USNR
GOLDER, William H., ACMM, USN
HARVEY, Harry Henry, AOM2/c, USNR
HODGE, Carl Leslie, CAP, USN
HONSAKER, Herschel Melvin, ACMM, USN
HUBBELL, Milford Myron, AMM1/c, USN

Huff, Frank Charles, AOM3/c, USNR
Hush, George Nelson, AOM2/c, USN
Jardine, Donald Clarence, AMM3/c, USNR
*Jones, Dallas Harding, ACOM, USN
Klaus, Max "K", AOM3/c, USNR
Klaus, Sylvain Wolff, AOM3/c, USNR
*Klein, Robert George, AMM1/c, USN
Knauff, Charles Scott, ACOM, USN
Lamb, Russell Daniel, AMM2/c, USNR
Law, Robert Bonar, AMM3/c, USNR
*Lemarr, Clifton Marion, ARM1/c, USN
Letourneau, Ralph Joseph, AMM1/c, USNR
Levering, Walter Orville, AMM2/c, USNR
Lillie, Carleton Fenn, Jr., AOM3/c, USNR
McClendon, John Gillis, ARM3/c, USN
McDaniel, Richard Calvert, AMM3/c, USNR
McKinney, Albert Leo, Jr., AMM3/c, USNR
Malounek, Frank G., Jr., AMM2/c, USNR
*Masters, Clay McKellar, ARM3/c, USNR
Meekins, Cecil Lewis, AOM3/c, USNR
Middleton, William Emmett, AMM1/c, USN
Millard, Russell Benton, AMM2/c, USNR
Mills, John W., AOM3/c, USNR
Moore, E. K., CAP, USN
Nash, Dwight Everett, AMM3/c, USNR
Olson, Warren Walter, AOM2/c, USNR
*Paterson, Douglas C., AOM3/c, USNR
*Pendleton, William Wade, AMM3/c, USNR
Peterson, Douglas Stewart, ACRM, USNR
Purdy, Warren Elton, AOM3/c, USNR
Quinn, Robert Eugene, AMM3/c, USNR
Redd, John Alexander, Jr., S1/c, USNR
Reynard, Charles Allen, AMM3/c, USNR
Robinson, Arthur Edward, AOM2/c, USNR
Rude, Werdin O., ARM2/c, USN
Ryan, Thomas Edwin, ARM3/c, USNR
Sauer, Jack Murray, AMM2/c, USN
Sayers, Robert Allen, AMM3/c, USN
Scott, Raymond Carl, ACRM, USNR

Shaffer, John Edwin, AMM2/c, USN
Shope, Leonard Sidney, ARM1/c, USNR
Smith, William Elmer, F2/c, USNR
Stork, Arthur James, AMM2/c, USNR
Taylor, James Wallace, ARM2/c, USNR
*Tittle, Murrel Estus, ARM2/c, USNR
*Toner, Joseph Bernard, AOM3/c, USNR
Van Benschoten, John R., AMM2/c, USNR
*Van Doren, Elliott Watson, ARM3/c, USNR
Vidrine, Theodore Hilaire, AMM2/c, USNR
Waldron, Frederick Joseph, Jr., ARM2/c, USNR
*Young, Jack, AMM1/c, USN

Bronze Star Medal

Baughman, Commodore Cortlandt C., USN
Camp, Capt. Chauncy, USNR
Lyons, Capt. George M. (MC), USNR
McGlynn, Capt. James Joseph, USN
Kerr, Col. James Edwin, USMC
Anderson, Cdr. Robert Palmer, USCGR
Bell, Cdr. Luther G. (MC), USN
Borstelmann, Cdr. Louis John, USNR
Damon, Cdr. Newcomb Lincoln, USN
Elliott, Cdr. Richard English, USN
Henszey, Cdr. William H., USNR (Ret.)
Lowrie, Cdr. Noble Wayne, USN
Simpson, Cdr. John Hammond, USN
Snell, Cdr. Lawrence Wordsworth, USNR
Bingham, Lt. Cdr. George Barry, USNR
Carreiro, Lt. Cdr. George Francis, USNR
Courtney, Lt. Cdr. Raymond Finley, USNR
Crockett, Lt. Cdr. Philip Dyer, USNR
Gay, Lt. Cdr. Donald, Jr., USN
Haggerty, Lt. Cdr. Robert Foy, USNR
Leiser, Lt. Cdr. Harry Wesley, USNR
Luke, Lt. Cdr. Raymond Henry, USNR
Mann, Lt. Cdr. Stanley Alexander, USN
Middlebrooks, Lt. Cdr. James L., USNR
Montgomery, Lt. Cdr. Henry, Jr., USNR
Murrell, Lt. Cdr. Drue L., USNR
O'Connell, Lt. Cdr. George A., Jr., USN
Paige, Lt. Cdr. Clayton W., USNR
Pierce, Lt. Cdr. Charles L., USNR
Pullman, Lt. Cdr. William Allen Pinkerton, USNR

ROBBINS, Lt. Cdr. Orme C., USN
ROBINSON, Lt. Cdr. Kenneth George, USN
BROWN, Lt. Ralph, USN
CARR, Lt. Colwell W., USNR
CHAMBERLIN, Lt. Douglas Franklin, USNR
COWAN, Lt. Stuart D., Jr., USNR
DANIEL, Lt. Jaquelin J., USNR
DePALMA, Lt. Anthony Guy, USNR
HARRIS, Lt. Allen H., USNR
HILSABECK, Lt. Lawrence Everett, USNR
HOWARD, Lt. Nelson F., USNR
KINNEBREW, Lt. Lee, USNR
LARKIN, Lt. Leo J., USNR
MASON, Lt. Appleton A., Jr., USNR
MORGAN, Lt. Sam Patterson, USN
MOSS, Lt. Peyton H., USNR
SNELLING, Lt. William M., USNR
SWARTZ, Lt. James S., USNR
TWADDELL, Lt. C. E., USNR
AUSTIN, Lt. (jg) John P., USNR
FREEMAN, Lt. (jg) Harold D., USNR
HOFFMAN, Lt. (jg) Bruce B., USNR
KRAMER, Lt. (jg) Irving, USNR
LIEBENOW, Lt. (jg) William F., USNR
PINKERTON, Lt. (jg) Lessley G., USN
RHODE, Lt. (jg) Donald A., USNR
SHERWOOD, Lt. (jg) Harold B., Jr., USNR
STERN, Lt. (jg) Henry R., USNR
WHORTON, Lt. (jg) Calvin R., USNR

FAUX, Ens. Donald Eugene, USNR
MARSHALL, Ens. Richard F., USNR
NELSON, Ens. Sigfred A., USNR
SEVER, Ens. John W., USNR
STURDEVANT, Ens. Stephan Allen, USNR
BARTLETT, Samuel, M1/c, USNR
BROGAN, Joseph E., MoMM3/c, USNR
BRUMBACK, T. B., SF1/c, USNR
CHEEK, William J., MoMM1/c, USN
CRONIN, Robert E., TM2/c, USNR
CUNNINGHAM, M. J., GM3/c, USNR
EDMONDS, George E., MoMM2/c, USNR
GARTEN, Charles W., GM3/c, USNR
HAWRYS, Walter J., GM3/c, USNR
JACKSON, Morris, StM3/c, USNR
KEITH, Cleatus M., MoMM3/c, USNR
LOHE, William Constantin, S2/c, USNR
LUCAS, Edward Pete, MoMM2/c, USNR
MATTHEWS, Wallace R., Cox., USNR
McCALLUM, Angus, CMM, USN
McCARTHY, John Fenten, MoMM2/c, USN
MILLER, Thomas Edward, GM3/c, USNR
MOFFETT, William R., MoMM2/c, USNR
MULLINIX, William J., ARM2/c, USNR
NEW, Edward Ralph, Cox., USNR
PAQUETTE, William L., TM3/c, USNR
PERMENTER, J. W., GM3/c, USNR
SULLIVAN, Charles E., TM2/c, USNR
THILL, John Leonard, BM1/c, USNR
WAGNER, W. E., F1/c, USN
ZAGROCKI, J. A., TM3/c, USNR

Mediterranean

Medal of Honor

The President of the United States takes pleasure in presenting the *Medal of Honor* posthumously to

Ensign JOHN JOSEPH PARLE, USNR for service as set forth in the following citation:

"For valor and courage above and beyond the call of duty as Officer in Charge of small boats in the USS LST 375 during the amphibious assault on the Island of Sicily, July 9–10, 1943. Realizing that a detonation of explosives would prematurely disclose to the enemy the assault about to be carried out and with full knowledge of the peril involved, Ensign Parle unhesitatingly risked his life to extinguish a smoke pot accidentally ignited in a boat carrying charges of high explosives, detonating fuses and ammunition. Undaunted by fire and blinding smoke, he entered the craft, quickly snuffed out a burning fuse and after failing in his desperate efforts to extinguish the fire pot, finally seized it with both hands and threw it over the side. Although he succumbed a week later from smoke and fumes inhaled, Ensign Parle's heroic self-sacrifice prevented grave damage to the ship and personnel and insured the security of a vital mission. He gallantly gave his life in the service of his country."

/s/ FRANKLIN D. ROOSEVELT

Navy Cross

EUBANK, Cdr. James V., Jr., USNR

For extraordinary heroism as Commander of a Naval Beach Battalion during the amphibious assault on the West Coast of Italy in September 1943. During the first phases of the assault, Commander (then Lieutenant Commander) Eubank successfully established the battalion under his command on the beaches in the Gulf of Salerno and, skillfully organizing divisional beach activities, made complete and meticulous preparations for the expeditious disembarkation of the assault troops. Fearlessly directing beach operations under fierce enemy aerial and ground attack, he provided a steady flow of urgent supplies and equipment in support of our invasion forces during the critical maintenance period.

MESSMER, Cdr. William L., USN

For extraordinary heroism as Commander of a Minesweeper Group of thirteen vessels in action against enemy forces off Porto Empedocle, Sicily. Assigned the extremely hazardous mission of clearing a channel through an active hostile minefield, Commander Messmer directed the operations of his command with expert tactical ability and brilliant initiative, aggressively returning the continuous fire of enemy shore batteries without retarding the progress of his forces. When another ship of the formation was mined, he skillfully supervised difficult rescue activities and the subsequent towing of the severely damaged vessel into port. By his superior technical knowledge he was largely responsible for successfully opening an unloading harbor vital to the support of our assault troops.

RICHARDS, Cdr. Alfred Humphreys, USN

For extraordinary heroism as Commander of a Minesweeper Group during the amphibious assault at Anzio, Italy, on January 22, 1944. Although in ill health from his strenuous duties, Commander Richards skillfully trained and supervised the activities of personnel and maintained the equipment of twenty-three minesweepers and escorts during landing operations in this vital area. Hampered by darkness and intermittent gunfire attacks from hostile shore batteries, he fearlessly led his group into heavily mined enemy waters and, by expert control and navigation, quickly cleared approach channels for transportation and gunfire support ships.

BARNES, Lt. Cdr. Stanley M., USN

For extraordinary heroism as Commander Motor Torpedo Boat Squadron FIFTEEN during the Tunisian and Sicilian Campaigns. Displaying expert administrative ability, Commander (then Lieutenant Commander) Barnes trained and operated his squadron during the enemy's evacuation of Tunisia and also during the preparatory phase, assault and final operations leading to the occupation of the island of Sicily. On many occasions he personally commanded his squadron and with brilliant tactical skill and fearless devotion to duty enabled his men to carry out patrol and reconnaissance missions of inestimable value to our forces, as well as daring raids on hostile shipping which seriously disrupted the enemy's sea communications. From August 1 to 20, 1943, he directed offensive sweeps along the north coast of Sicily, resulting in the capture of the Eolie Islands and stoppage of hostile seaborne traffic which contributed materially to the rapid advance of the Seventh Army toward Messina.

COLEMAN, Lt. Cdr. Robert Louis, USNR

For extraordinary heroism as Commanding Officer of the USS LST 311 during the amphibious assault on Sicily, July 10, 1943. When another landing ship was struck by an aerial bomb off the beach near Gela, Lieutenant Commander Coleman, observing the ignition of a cargo of ammunition loaded on trucks, unhesitatingly brought his own vessel close aboard and fought desperately to help control the rapid spread of the flames. Forced to withdraw when his own ship became imperiled by exploding shells and realizing that the fire was inextinguishable, he returned shortly afterward, placed the bow of the LST 311 alongside the stern of the stricken vessel and rescued forty men who otherwise might have been lost.

KLEIN, Lt. Cdr. Millard J., USN

For extraordinary heroism as Commanding Officer of the USS BUCK during an attack on an enemy submarine while on convoy escort off the Island of Pantelleria, August 3, 1943. Contacting the hostile vessel which was preparing to attack the convoy, Lieutenant Commander Klein skillfully maneuvered for vigorous and aggressive action, depth charging the submarine and forcing her to the surface where the guns of the BUCK completed her destruction.

PHILLIPS, Lt. Cdr. George Lincoln, USNR

For extraordinary heroism as Commanding Officer of the USS SENTINEL in action against enemy forces during the assault on the Island of Sicily. Although his ship was severely damaged by one hostile dive-bombing strike, Lieutenant Commander Phillips gallantly and aggressively directed the performance of the vessel throughout four ensuing raids, driving off two attacks and scoring hits on two of the enemy bombers before being forced to abandon ship. By his expert seamanship and brilliant initiative he was largely responsible for the success of subsequent difficult rescue activities, carrying out these hazardous operations with a minimum loss of life.

SARSFIELD, Lt. Cdr. Eugene S., USN

For extraordinary heroism as Commanding Officer of the USS MADDOX during the amphibious invasion of Sicily on July 10, 1943. While his ship was effectively supporting the assault at Gela, Lieutenant Commander Sarsfield, in the face of terrific aerial bombardment, maintained alert and accurate direction of gunfire until the MADDOX was gravely damaged by one direct hit and two near misses. Grimly standing by to supervise abandonment of the rapidly sinking vessel, he was responsible for saving the lives of nine officers and sixty-five men out of a total of two hundred and eighty-four on board.

ALEXANDER, Lt. Samuel Hugh, USNR

For extraordinary heroism as Commanding Officer of the USS LST 313 during the amphibious assault on the Island of Sicily, July 10, 1943. After beaching his ship at the assigned point near Gela, Lieutenant Alexander was disembarking assault troops and vehicles when enemy aircraft bombed his vessel, setting fire to the cargo of ammunition, land mines, and other inflammable material loaded in trucks. With great courage, he skillfully directed the fighting of the blaze and the rescue and transfer of all survivors, many of whom had been severely burned and injured from the terrific explosion. By his prompt and gallant action, Lieutenant Alexander temporarily checked the spreading of the fire and saved the lives of many of the embarked personnel who otherwise might have been lost.

CRAIG, Lt. D. M., USNR

For extraordinary heroism in action as Commander of a division of motor torpedo boats engaged in operations against the enemy convoys off the West Coast of Italy and the South Coast of France in June and July 1944. Lieutenant Craig led his group on six missions against enemy convoys attempting to maintain supply lines to Axis armies in Northern Italy. He skillfully and with the utmost courage and determination disposed his forces on these operations to seek out the enemy and intercept and destroy his shipping. On all occasions he patrolled well within enemy coastal waters and conducted his attacks with great daring and effectiveness with minimum damage to his own forces. In the final success of these operations, he accounted for the sinking of one corvette, one coaster and three F lighters and the severe damaging of one small ammunition ship, two MAS boats and one or more F lighters, thereby seriously cutting off enemy reinforcements of supplies and other essential materials to the front lines.

DuBOSE, Lt. Edwin A., USNR

For extraordinary heroism in action as Commander of a division of motor torpedo boats engaged in operations against enemy coastal traffic off the West Coast of Italy in March and April 1944. Lieutenant DuBose in cooperation with British Coastal Forces led his units on several night missions against enemy convoys attempting to maintain supply lines to Axis armies in the Rome, Italy area. He skillfully and with the utmost courage and determination disposed his forces on these operations to seek out the enemy and screen the main attack group from destroyer and E-boat attack. These tasks he accomplished with complete success, enabling the main force to destroy several convoys carrying vital war materials to the front lines. On all occasions he attacked with great daring and drove off all hostile forces which threatened the main body, escaping with minimum damage to himself. In the final success of the operations, he was in large measure responsible for the decisiveness of the action which resulted in the sinking of fifteen F lighters, one corvette, a tug, and the severe damaging of two destroyers.

KENDALL, Lt. John G., USNR

For extraordinary heroism in action as Commanding Officer of the USS LCL (L) 212 during an enemy air raid on the Harbor of Palermo, Sicily, on August 1, 1943. When hostile bombs straddled his ship and set fire to gasoline drums stored on the dock and to ammunition loaded on a nearby merchant vessel, Lieutenant Kendall immediately recognized the imminent threat to his own craft and three others moored alongside and, directing the cutting of all lines to the blazing dock, successfully got underway with the four ships. Supervising the operations with cool efficiency, he skillfully maneuvered the group to a position of safety, thereby saving all vessels from possible loss.

KIRWIN, Lt. John J., USN

For extraordinary heroism as a Turret Officer aboard the USS SAVANNAH while that vessel was stationed in the Gulf of Salerno supporting our landings during the amphibious invasion of Italy on September 11, 1943. When the detonation of an enemy bomb inflicted heavy casualties, set off numerous fires and filled the turret with dense smoke and toxic gases, Lieutenant Kirwin promptly ordered the area abandoned and, despite the imminent danger of magazine explosion, stood by his station in the turret booth. With full knowledge of the serious hazards involved and with complete disregard for his own personal safety, he calmly supervised evacuation and deliberately remained behind to aid in saving the lives of as many of his command as possible when he might easily have escaped.

MITCHELL, Lt. William French, USNR

For extraordinary heroism as Commanding Officer of the USS SC 676 during the amphibious invasion of Sicily on July 10, 1943. Despite terrific enemy crossfire, Lieutenant Mitchell skillfully maneuvered his ship to a point within five hundred yards of the hostile shore line in order to conduct various assault waves to their designated beaches and, by effective gunfire, provided excellent support throughout the landing operations.

MORRIS, Lt. George Kenneth, USNR

For extraordinary heroism in aerial flight as Patrol Plane Commander during an attack against an enemy submarine off the West Coast of Africa on July 6, 1943. Sighting a surfaced hostile submarine fifteen miles ahead of a convoy while flying protective cover, Lieutenant (then Lieutenant, junior grade) Morris promptly maneuvered to favorable attack position and, diving to perilously low altitude in bold defiance of the enemy's withering antiaircraft fire, relentlessly pressed home an effective bombing and strafing attack. With his craft seriously damaged by the fierce barrage and all but one of his crew wounded, he steadfastly remained in the area and, although suffering intense pain from his own wounds, protected the convoy from further attack until relief arrived more than two hours later, then skillfully flew his crippled plane back to base.

MULLER, Lt. Julian P., USNR

For extraordinary heroism while serving as Turret Officer aboard the USS SAVANNAH during the invasion of Italy on September 11, 1943. When his vessel received a direct hit from an enemy aerial bomb which pierced the top of a turret, exploded deep within the ship and filled the forward turrets with smoke and toxic gases, Lieutenant (then Lieutenant, junior grade) Muller coolly and courageously directed the abandoning of the area. Discovering that two of his crew were not accounted for, he re-entered the turret and, despite the extreme danger, searched until he found the missing men. After getting them to safety, he went into an adjacent turret which was badly damaged and skillfully assisted in the rescue of personnel trapped inside.

ORLECK, Lt. Joseph, USN

For extraordinary heroism in action as Commanding Officer, USS NAUSET during the amphibious invasion of Italy on 9 September 1943. During the approach to the assault area in the Gulf of Salerno, the convoy in which the USS NAUSET was proceeding was attacked by enemy aircraft and this ship struck by several aerial bombs which caused extensive damage, numerous casualties, and ignited fires which completely enveloped the boat deck. Lieutenant Orleck coolly and courageously directed the fire-fighting activities, the control of flooding to correct a dangerous list which immediately developed and the transfer of all survivors to the rescue ships. With complete disregard for his own safety, he remained on board the stricken ship to attempt beaching and prevent total loss, but, while engaged in this operation, he lost his life as the ship struck an enemy mine and sank. His persistent and gallant efforts to save his ship were an inspiring example to all and contributed materially to minimizing the loss of life incurred by the initial attack.

ROBISON, Lt. Carl F., USNR

For extraordinary heroism as Commanding Officer of the USS LCI (L) 1 in action against enemy forces during the amphibious assault on the Island of Sicily, July 1943. Although his ship broached under pounding by the heavy surf while attempting an extremely hazardous landing on Caffi Beach in the face of tremendous opposition from hostile shore batteries, Lieutenant Robison returned the enemy fire with cool courage and tenacious determination, relenting only when his supply of ammunition became exhausted. Through his gallant efforts, maintained despite imminent personal danger, he enabled the embarked attack troops to effect a successful landing.

ALLEN, Lt. (jg) Augustus T., Jr., USNR

For extraordinary heroism as Naval Gunfire Liaison Officer, Amphibious Force, Atlantic Fleet, during the attack on the Island of Sicily, July 10–13, 1943. In command of a shore fire control party of the 45th Infantry Division, United States Army, Lieutenant (junior grade) Allen (then Ensign) landed with the initial assault waves and, despite terrific opposition, courageously maintained position in the front lines and directed supporting gunfire upon enemy machine guns and troop concentrations, frequently advancing beyond friendly front lines in order to observe enemy positions. When hostile tanks threatened to encircle his battalion, he controlled the fire of his guns with devastating accuracy, scoring four direct hits and repulsing the attack. By his outstanding ability and excellent judgment, he assisted materially in overcoming enemy resistance and in capturing the town of Biscari with its strategic airfield.

GILL, Lt. (jg) Warren Calavan, USCGR

For extraordinary heroism in action as Officer in Charge of small boats for the amphibious assault at Salerno, Italy. Lieutenant (junior grade) Gill, while directing the lowering of small boats from USS LST 357, which was under enemy fire, was seriously wounded. Despite his wounds he continued with utmost intrepidity to efficiently carry on his duty as commander of the assault flotillas, giving last-minute instructions to the officers and crews. He then collapsed and his injuries were found to be so severe that many months of hospitalization will be required for recovery. Lieutenant (junior grade) Gill's heroism was an inspiration to all officers and men of the flotilla. Because of this and the patient and thorough instruction he had carried out in the landing technique throughout the training periods and the landings in Algeria and Sicily, the performance of this boat was in the assault was most admirable.

RANDALL, Lt. (jg) John W., USNR

For extraordinary heroism as Assistant Boat Group Commander during participation in the amphibious assault on the southeast coast of Sicily, July 10, 1943. Setting out in a small landing craft, Lieutenant (junior grade) Randall led the last four waves of boats through total darkness and dangerously rough sea to the line of departure, and from there to the center of the designated beach. After the landing had been successfully effected, he returned to his ship and voluntarily led a salvage party back to the beach where, in a courageous attempt to recover broached and foundered boats, he was swept offshore by the turbulent surf and lost at sea.

BUCKLEW, Ens. Phil H., USNR

For extraordinary heroism while in charge of a scout boat in action against enemy forces during the amphibious assault on the Island of Sicily, July 1943. Achieving a high degree of success in his capable and resourceful training of scout boat crews for the entire attack force, Lieutenant (junior grade) (then Ensign) Bucklew participated in the actual invasion with outstanding courage. Undeterred by glaring searchlight illumination and withering blasts of hostile weapons, he proceeded through hazardous waters, located the designated beach and directed the assault boat wave. Utterly disregarding shore battery and machine-gun fire which repeatedly struck his vessel, Lieutenant (junior grade) Bucklew persevered in guiding subsequent waves to the proper beach.

CAVALLARO, Ens. Salvatore J., USNR

For extraordinary heroism while in charge of a scout boat attached to the USS LYON during the amphibious assault on the Island of Sicily. Undeterred by glaring enemy searchlights and gunfire, and by the prevailing adverse weather conditions, Ensign Cavallaro skillfully directed the first assault boat wave ashore and, with complete disregard for his own personal safety in the continuous fire from enemy shore batteries, carried on throughout the night and the early daylight hours in order to direct succeeding boat waves to the proper beaches.

HOMER, Ens. William N. P., USNR

For extraordinary heroism as Officer in Charge of the Fire and Rescue Party from the USS BISCAYNE during action against enemy forces while participating in the amphibious assault on Sicily, July 10-12, 1943. Although flames spread rapidly on the bombed USS LST 158, igniting her deck cargo and causing continuous gasoline and ammunition explosions, Ensign Homer courageously boarded the blazing vessel during a severe hostile aircraft attack and remained despite imminent personal danger from fire and suffocation until he succeeded in removing a seriously wounded Army officer to safety. Through his unswerving devotion to duty and gallant spirit of self-sacrifice, he undoubtedly saved the life of a man who otherwise might have perished.

VESOLE, Ens. Kay K., USNR

For extraordinary heroism as Commanding Officer of the United States Navy Armed Guard aboard the SS JOHN BASCOM when that vessel was bombed and sunk by enemy aircraft in the harbor of Bari, Italy, on the night of December 2, 1943. Weakened by loss of blood from an extensive wound over his heart and with his right arm helpless, Ensign Vesole valiantly remained in action, calmly proceeding from gun to gun, directing his crew and giving aid and encouragement to the injured. With the JOHN BASCOM fiercely ablaze and sinking, he conducted a party of his men below decks and supervised the evacuation of wounded comrades to the only undamaged lifeboat, persistently manning an oar with his uninjured arm after being forced to occupy a seat in the boat, and upon reaching the seawall, immediately assisted in disembarking the men. Heroically disregarding his own desperate plight as wind and tide whipped the blaze along the jetty, he constantly risked his life to pull the wounded out of flaming oil-covered waters and, although nearly overcome by smoke and fumes, assisted in the removal of casualties to a bomb shelter before the terrific explosion of a nearby ammunition ship inflicted injuries which later proved fatal.

ZACEK, Ens. Edward C., USNR

For extraordinary heroism as Boat Wave Commander during the amphibious assault at Salerno, Italy, September 9,

1943. Undeterred by fierce opposition, Ensign Zacek courageously proceeded through heavy enemy gunfire off the assault beaches and while leading a wave of tank lighters to designated landing position was seriously wounded in the head and hip. Disregarding his own grave condition, he persisted with the landing operations and ordered the unloading to be continued and boats retracted for return to the ship before he would receive first aid.

DAUGHERTY, James William, CWT, USNR

For extraordinary heroism while serving aboard the USS SHUBRICK during the Sicilian Campaign on August 4, 1943. Hearing the cries of men who were trapped in the after fireroom when an enemy bomb inflicted severe damage on his ship, Daugherty disregarded imminent peril to himself and promptly went to the rescue of his helpless comrades. To facilitate escape, he cut away a blackout device, then entered the fast-flooding, steam-filled compartment and assisted the imprisoned crew members to safety.

FLETCHER, Charles Binford, Y2/c, USNR

For extraordinary heroism in action against enemy forces while attached to the LCI (L) 5 during the amphibious assault on the Island of Sicily, July 1943. Determining the depth over sand bars by swimming toward the beach within hazardous range of hostile guns ashore, Fletcher located a suitable beaching point for disembarking our attack troops. Upon completing this dangerous task and observing several soldiers perilously close to drowning, he risked his life under an unrelenting shower of deadly machine-gun bullets to swim through extremely heavy surf and bring the helpless men to safety. Through his courageous efforts and heroic endurance in the face of withering fire, he was able to accomplish the successful rescue of the soldiers who otherwise might have perished.

MOORE, Edward Charles, GM2/c, USNR

For extraordinary heroism during action against enemy forces as Gunner on board the LCI (L) 1 while participating in the amphibious assault on the Island of Sicily, July 1943. Although his ship broached under pounding by the heavy surf while effecting an extremely hazardous landing on Caffi Beach, Moore operated his gun with such outstanding skill and accuracy, despite perilous exposure to a deadly hailstorm of bullets, that he succeeded in silencing at least one and possibly two enemy machine-gun nests. Firing tenaciously on the hostile positions until his ammunition was exhausted, he contributed immeasurably to the safe disembarkation of troops from his and other beached landing craft.

PILEWSKI, George S., HA1/c, USNR

For extraordinary heroism aboard the USS SAVANNAH while that vessel was stationed in the Gulf of Salerno supporting our landings during the amphibious invasion of Italy on September 11, 1943. When the detonation of an enemy bomb inflicted heavy casualties, set off numerous fires and filled the turrets with dense smoke and toxic gases, Pilewski unhesitatingly risked his life to enter one of the turrets and, unmindful of the imminent danger of magazine explosions, coolly evacuated personnel who had been overcome, continuing his unselfish service until he himself was overcome while administering artificial respiration to one of the men he had rescued.

SHARP, Stanley J., Jr., QM2/c, USN

For extraordinary heroism while serving aboard the USS LCI (L) 212 during an enemy air raid on the harbor of Palermo, Sicily, August 1, 1943. When hostile bombs closely straddled his ship, setting fire to gasoline stored on the dock to which she was moored, and to ammunition loaded in a nearby merchant vessel, Sharp was seriously wounded by flying bomb fragments. Although in great pain and bleeding profusely, he manned the helm and engine room telegraphs and courageously remained at his station over an hour without revealing the extent of his injuries until his ship was anchored in a safer berth.

Distinguished Service Medal

*Hewitt, Vice Adm. Henry K., USN

Commander of the EIGHTH FLEET. Operating jointly with the forces of the United States Army, the forces under Vice Admiral Hewitt's command executed a successful landing on hostile shores with the meticulous planning and sound tactical knowledge which were essential in the accomplishment of a particularly strategic mission.

British Distinguished Service Cross

Durgin, Cdr. Edward R., USN

For daring and inspiring leadership as Commander of a Landing Craft Convoy and of a Gunfire Support Unit in the operations which led to the capture of Sicily by the Allied Forces.

Barnes, Lt. Cdr. Stanley M., USN

For daring and inspiring leadership as Commander Motor Torpedo Squadron Fifteen in the operations which led to the capture of Sicily by Allied Forces.

Legion of Merit

Conolly, Rear Adm. Richard L., USN

Commander of a Major Task Group and later as Commander of a Task Force during the amphibious invasion of Italy. In the assault his aggressive and exemplary leadership enabled this Task Group to successfully land troops, supplies and mechanized equipment over the beaches in the Gulf of Salerno.

Gold Star in Lieu of a Second Legion of Merit

Commander of a Major Task Group and later as Commander of a Task Force during the amphibious assault on Italy. Volunteering to serve under an Allied Commander who was his junior, Rear Admiral Conolly tactfully and with expert professional skill supervised and coordinated the formulation of the highly complex plans for the Attack Group assigned to his command.

Davidson, Rear Adm. Lyal A., USN

Commander of transports and fire support ships during the landing attack on the coast of Sicily, July 10–12, 1943.

Gold Star in Lieu of a Second Legion of Merit

Commander of a Task Force during the invasion of Italy.

DuBose, Rear Adm. Laurance T., USN

Commander of a Support Group during the landing attack on the coast of Sicily, July 10–12, 1943.

Hall, Rear Adm. John L., Jr., USN

Commander of a Task Force during the amphibious invasion of Sicily.

Gold Star in Lieu of a Second Legion of Merit

Commander of a Naval Task Force prior to and during the amphibious invasion of Italy.

Kirk, Rear Adm. Alan G., USN

Commander of a Task Force during the amphibious invasion of Sicily.

*Lewis, Rear Adm. Spencer S., USN

Chief of Staff to the Commander Western Naval Task Force during the amphibious assault on the Island of Sicily in July, 1943.

Second Gold Star in Lieu of a Third Legion of Merit

Chief of Staff to a Naval Task Force Commander prior to and during the amphibious invasion of Italy, September 1943.

Lowry, Rear Adm. Frank J., USN

Commander Moroccan Sea Frontier Forces and as Commander of a Task Force during the invasion of Italy.

Gold Star in Lieu of a Second Legion of Merit

Commander of a Naval Task force prior to and during the amphibious landings in the Anzio-Nettuno area, Italy, on 22 January 1944.

THEBAUD, Rear Adm. Leo H., USN

Commanding Officer of the USS BOISE during the amphibious assault on the Island of Sicily, July 10–12, 1943.

Gold Star in Lieu of a Second Legion of Merit

Commanding Officer of the USS BOISE during the amphibious assault on the West Coast of Italy, September 12 to 16, 1943.

Army Oak-Leaf Cluster in Lieu of a Third Legion of Merit

Commanding Officer of the USS BOISE during United States Navy operations in support of the United States Seventh Army from 8 August to 14 August 1943.

WILKES, Rear Adm. John, USN

Commanding Officer of the USS BIRMINGHAM during the assault on Sicily, July 10, 1943.

*WRIGHT, Rear Adm. Jerauld, USN

Assistant Chief of Staff of the Commander United States Naval Forces, Northwest African Waters, prior to and during the landing of forces in Sicily and Italy.

DOUGHTY, Commodore Leonard, Jr., USN (Ret.)

Commander, Naval Advanced Bases, prior to and during the invasion of the Island of Sicily, July, 1943.

EDGAR, Commodore Campbell D., USN

Commander of transports of a Task Force during the invasion of the Island of Sicily.

Gold Star in Lieu of a Second Legion of Merit

Commander of transports of a major Task Force during the Allied invasion of Italy, September and October 1943.

JOHNSON, Commodore Lee P., USN

Commander of training activities of the Amphibious Force, United States Atlantic Fleet. Executed this exacting assignment during the vitally important period prior to the invasion of Sicily in July 1943.

OWEN, Commodore George T., USN

Commander Fleet Air Wing FIFTEEN, while engaged in antisubmarine operations in the Moroccan Sea Frontier and special aircraft operations in the Mediterranean area from 7 March 1944 to 11 September 1944.

PHILLIPS, Commodore Wallace B., USN

Commander of transports of a Naval Task Force during the invasion of the Island of Sicily.

SULLIVAN, Commodore William A., USN

Commander Salvage Force, North African Waters, Sicily and Southern Italy.

YATES, Commodore Charles M., USN

Commandant, Naval Operating Base, Oran, Algeria, prior to and during the amphibious invasion of the Island of Sicily in July, and the Italian mainland in September 1943.

ZIROLI, Commodore Humbert W., USN

Commanding Officer of the USS BROOKLYN during the Sicilian Campaign.

ADAMS, Capt. Francis McKee, USN

Commander of a Landing Craft Group during the invasion of the Italian mainland in the Gulf of Salerno, September 9, 1943.

ALLEN, Capt. Charles, USN

Commanding Officer of the USS JAMES O'HARA during the amphibious invasion of Italy in July 1943.

Gold Star in Lieu of a Second Legion of Merit

Commanding Officer of the USS JAMES O'HARA during the amphibious assault on Sicily.

ANDREWS, Capt. Charles L., Jr., USN

Assisted in towing the SS SAMUEL GRIFFIN from the harbor of Oran, Algeria, when that harbor was bombed on the night of May 19, 1943.

ANSEL, Capt. Walter C., USN

Operations Officer on the Staff of the Commander of an Amphibious Task Force during the invasion of the Island of Sicily in July 1943.

BACHMAN, Capt. Leo A., USN

Intelligence Officer on the Staff of the Commander United States Naval Forces, Northwest African Waters, during the initial invasion of the Island of Sicily in July 1943.

Gold Star in Lieu of a Second Legion of Merit

Intelligence Officer on the Staff of a Naval Task Force Commander prior to and during the amphibious invasion of Italy.

BAILEY, Capt. Watson O., USN

Commander Transport Division FIVE during the amphibious invasion of the Island of Sicily in July 1943.

Gold Star in Lieu of a Second Legion of Merit

Commander of a Task Unit during the amphibious invasion of Italy.

BAUERNSCHMIDT, Capt. George W. (SC), USN

Supply Officer in Command of the Naval Supply Depot, United States Naval Operating Base, Oran, Algeria, prior to and during the amphibious invasion of the Island of Sicily in July 1943, and the Italian mainland in September 1943.

BELL, Capt. Robert C., USN

Officer in Charge of Ships Repair Forces at the United States Naval Operating Base, Oran, Algeria, prior to and during the amphibious invasion of the Island of Sicily in July, and the Italian mainland in September 1943.

BRITTAIN, Capt. Thomas B., USN

Commanding Officer of the USS MON-ROVIA while that vessel was serving as headquarters ship during the amphibious assault on Sicily, July 10–12, 1943.

BROOKMAN, Capt. Harold R., USN

Material Officer on the Staff of the Commander United States Naval Forces, Northwest African Waters, in the initial invasion of the Island of Sicily in July 1943.

Second Gold Star in Lieu of a Third Legion of Merit

Material Officer on the Staff of a Naval Task Force Commander prior to and during the amphibious invasion of Italy, September 1943.

CARY, Capt. Robert W., USN

Commanding Officer of the USS SA-VANNAH during the amphibious assault on the Island of Sicily, July 10 to 12, 1943.

Gold Star in Lieu of a Second Legion of Merit

Commanding Officer of the USS SA-VANNAH during the amphibious invasion of Italy in September 1943.

Army Oak-Leaf Cluster in Lieu of a Third Legion of Merit

Commanding Officer of the USS SA-VANNAH in support of the U. S. Seventh Army during the amphibious invasion of Sicily, 2 August to 9 August 1943.

Second Gold Star in Lieu of a Fourth Legion of Merit

Commander of a gunfire support group during the amphibious invasion at Anzio, Italy on January 22, 1944.

CATER, Capt. Charles J., USN

Aide and Flag Secretary of the Commander-in-Chief Atlantic Fleet in the occupation of Morocco and Sicily during the period from February 3 to October 1, 1943.

Gold Star in Lieu of a Second Legion of Merit

Commander of a Destroyer Squadron during advanced operations in support of the Allied armies in Italy throughout the period from 15 May to 5 August 1944.

CLAY, Capt. James P., USN

Commander Escort Group during the advanced landings in the Anzio-Nettuno area, Italy in January 1944.

CROSBY, Capt. Gordon J., USN

Executive Officer of the USS PHILA-DELPHIA prior to and during the amphibious assault on the Island of Sicily in July 1943 and the amphibious invasion of the Italian mainland in September 1943.

DAVIS, Capt. Ransom K., USN

Chief of Staff to a Naval Task Force Commander during the invasion of the Island of Sicily, August 8 to 11, 1943.

DIERDORFF, Capt. Ross A., USN

Commander of a Naval Task Group and also as Commanding Officer of the USS ELIZABETH C. STANTON during the amphibious assault on Sicily, July 10, 1943.

Gold Star in Lieu of a Second Legion of Merit

Commander of a Task Unit and Commanding Officer of the USS ELIZABETH C. STANTON during the amphibious invasion of Italy.

DYER, Capt. George C., USN

Chief of Staff to the Commander of an Amphibious Task Force preparatory to the invasion of Sicily on July 10, 1943.

Gold Star in Lieu of a Second Legion of Merit

Chief of Staff to Commander Landing Craft and Bases, Northwest African Waters, prior to and during the amphibious assault on Italy, September 1943.

EARLY, Capt. Alexander R., USN

Chief of Staff to Commander Amphibious Force, United States Atlantic Fleet, during the amphibious invasion of the Island of Sicily.

EDSON, Capt. Stephen R. (SC), USN

Supply Officer on the Staff of Commander United States Naval Forces, Northwest African Waters during the Sicilian and Italian Campaigns.

ELLSBERG, Capt. Edward, USNR

Rehabilitated the Massawa Naval Base Ships, Eritrea, from January 8, 1942 to April 5, 1943, and made possible extensive drydocking operations for the benefit of all types of Allied shipping.

ENGLISH, Capt. Robert A. J., USN

War Plans Officer on the Staff of the Commander United States Naval Forces, Northwest African Waters, in connection with the amphibious invasion of the Island of Sicily in July 1943.

Gold Star in Lieu of a Second Legion of Merit

War Plans Officer on the Staff of a Naval Task Force Commander prior to and during the amphibious invasion of Italy, September 1943.

EVANS, Capt. Donald S., USN

Communications Officer on the Staff of the Commander United States Naval Forces, Northwest African Waters, in both the planning and execution phases of the invasion of the Island of Sicily in July 1943.

Gold Star in Lieu of a Second Legion of Merit

Communications Officer on the staff of a Naval Task Force Commander prior to and during the amphibious invasion of Italy September 1943.

FINES, Capt. Clifford A., USN

Operations Officer at the United States Naval Operating Base, Oran, Algeria, prior to and during the amphibious invasions of the Island of Sicily in July 1943, and the Italian mainland in September 1943.

GLUTTING, Capt. Paul R., USN

Commanding Officer of the USS WILLIAM P. BIDDLE during the amphibious invasion of the Island of Sicily.

HARTLEY, Capt. Henry, USN

Commanding Officer of the USS SUSAN B. ANTHONY during the amphibious invasion of the Island of Sicily.

HARTMAN, Capt. Charles C., USN

Commander Destroyer Squadron FIF-TEEN in the attack on the Island of Sicily from July 10 to 12, 1943.

Gold Star in Lieu of a Second Legion of Merit

Escort Commander of a Troop Convoy during an attack by enemy aircraft off the coast of Algeria on November 6, 1943.

HARWOOD, Capt. Charles W., USCG

Commanding Officer of the USS JO-SEPH T. DICKMAN, Captain Harwood commanded the Naval Task Group which landed assault battalions directly on the beaches fronting Gela, Sicily.

HEADLEE, Capt. Colin D., USN

Commanding Officer of the repair ship USS DELTA during the amphibious invasions of Sicily and Italy in July and September 1943.

HEIMER, Capt. Roger C., USCG

Commanding Officer of the USS SAMUEL CHASE during the amphibious assault on the Island of Sicily, July 10–12, 1943.

Gold Star in Lieu of a Second Legion of Merit

Commanding Officer of USS SAMUEL CHASE during the amphibious assault on Italy.

HENDREN, Capt. Paul, USN

Commanding Officer of the USS PHIL-ADELPHIA in the assault on the Island of Sicily, June 10 to 12, 1943.

Gold Star in Lieu of a Second Legion of Merit

Commanding Officer of the USS PHIL-ADELPHIA during the amphibious assault on the West Coast of Italy, September 9 to 18, 1943.

Army Oak-Leaf Cluster in Lieu of a Third Legion of Merit

Commanding Officer of the USS PHIL-ADELPHIA in support of the United States Seventh Army in Sicily from 31 July to 15 August 1943.

HITCHCOCK, Capt. Norman R., USN

Air and Operations Officer of the Moroccan Sea Frontier Forces from 26 June 1943 to 31 March 1944.

HURFF, Capt. Jack E., USN

Commanding Officer of the USS THURSTON during the amphibious assault on Sicily, July 10–12, 1943.

IMLAY, Capt. Miles Hopkins, USCG

Commander of the Reserve Attack Group of an attack force during the campaign for the capture of the Island of Sicily.

Gold Star in Lieu of a Second Legion of Merit

Commander of the LST Convoy of a Major Task Force during the amphibious assault upon Italy in September 1943.

JALBERT, Capt. Horace Homer, USNR

Commanding Officer, Advanced Amphibious Training Base, Bizerte, Tunisia, prior to and during the amphibious landings at Anzio, Italy, in January 1944.

JOHNSON, Capt. Henry C., USN

Operations Officer on the Staff of a Naval Task Group Commander during the Sicilian Campaign and as Deputy Chief of Staff to a Naval Task Group Commander during the amphibious assault on the West Coast of Italy.

LEPPERT, Capt. John H., USN

Commander of a Landing Craft Flotilla during the amphibious invasion of the Island of Sicily.

LEWIS, Capt. Mays L., USN

Chief of Staff of an Amphibious Task Force during the invasion of the Island of Sicily.

Gold Star in Lieu of a Second Legion of Merit

Naval Liaison Officer with the Commanding General, United States Fifth Army prior to and during the amphibious invasion at Salerno, Italy in September

1943, and the advanced landings at Anzio, Italy in January 1944.

LITTLE, Capt. Marion N., USN

Operations Officer on the Staff of Commander Eighth Amphibious Force prior to and during the amphibious invasion of the Italian mainland on September 9, 1943.

LOHMANN, Capt. Philip D., USN

Executive Officer of the USS SAVANNAH during the amphibious assaults on Sicily in July 1943, and on the Italian mainland in September 1943.

LOOMIS, Capt. Donald W., USN

Commander of Transport Division SEVEN during the amphibious assault on the Island of Sicily in July 1943.

McCOLL, Capt. Joseph W., USN

Commanding Officer of the USS FLORENCE NIGHTINGALE during the amphibious invasion of the Island of Sicily.

McGURL, Capt. Daniel N., USN

Commanding Officer of the USS ALCYONE during the amphibious invasion of the Island of Sicily.

MADEIRA, Capt. Dashiell L., USN

Commander Destroyer Squadron SEVENTEEN during the invasion of the Island of Sicily in July 1943.

MASON, Capt. Lunsford Y., Jr., USN

Commander of the USS ANNE ARUNDEL during the amphibious invasion of the Island of Sicily, July 10–12, 1943.

MATHER, Capt. Paul L., USN

Commanding Officer of the USS ANCON during the amphibious invasion of the Island of Sicily in July 1943.

MAUERMAN, Capt. Raymond J., USCG

Commanding Officer of the USS JOSEPH T. DICKMAN during the amphibious invasion of Italy.

MAYNARD, Capt. George E., USN

Commanding Officer of the USS BARNETT during the amphibious assault on the Island of Sicily, July 10–12, 1943.

Gold Star in Lieu of a Second Legion of Merit

Commanding Officer of the USS BARNETT during the amphibious invasion of Italy.

MENOCAL, Capt. George L., USN

Commander Destroyer Squadron SEVEN during the invasion of Sicily, August 5–18, 1943.

Gold Star in Lieu of a Second Legion of Merit

Commander of a Screen Unit during the amphibious assault on Italy in the Gulf of Salerno, September 9, 1943.

MENTZ, Capt. George F., USN

Commander of a Task Group of Mine Layers during the amphibious assault on the Island of Sicily in July 1943.

MESSMER, Capt. William L., USN

Commander of a Minesweeping Unit during the amphibious invasion of Italy in September 1943.

MITCHELL, Capt. Edward A., USN

Operations Officer of the Amphibious Force, Atlantic Fleet, prior to and during the landing operations on the Island of Sicily July 10–14, 1943.

MORRIS, Capt. Robert Melvin, USN

Commander of an Attack Group during the assault upon the Island of Sicily.

MURPHY, Capt. John E., USN

Commander of the USS FREDERICK FUNSTON during the amphibious assault upon the Island of Sicily from July 10 to July 12, 1943.

Gold Star in Lieu of a Second Legion of Merit

Commanding Officer of the USS FREDERICK FUNSTON during the amphibious invasion of Italy.

NELSON, Capt. Roger Eastman, USN

Commander of an Attack Group during the assault on the Island of Sicily.

OLD, Capt. Francis P., USN

On the Staff of the Commander of a Naval Task Force prior to and during the amphibious invasion of Italy in September 1943.

Gold Star in Lieu of a Second Legion of Merit

On the Staff of the Naval Commander of the Amphibious Forces which seized a bridgehead in the Anzio-Nettuno area on January 22, 1944.

O'NEILL, Capt. Merlin, USCG

Commanding Officer of the USS LEONARD WOOD during the amphibious invasion of the Island of Sicily.

RAGSDALE, Capt. Edmund M., USN

Repair Officer of the U.S. Naval Operating Base, Palermo, Sicily, during a period of continual offensive operations against the enemy in the Central Mediterranean from August 1943 through September 1944.

REED, Capt. Kendall S., USN

Commander of a Task Group during the amphibious assault on the Island of Sicily, July 10, and as Joint Loading Control Officer of a Major Task Force during the invasion of Italy, September 9–21, 1943.

RICHARDS, Capt. Alfred H., USN

Commander of a Minesweeper Group during the amphibious invasion of Italy on September 9, 1943.

RITCHIE, Capt. Oliver H., USNR

Commander of the USS BELLATRIX during the amphibious invasion of the Island of Sicily, July 10–12, 1943.

ROONEY, Capt. John B., USN

Commander Destroyer Division THIRTYFOUR during the invasion of the Island of Sicily, from August 1 to 6, 1943.

SABIN, Capt. Lorenzo S., Jr., USN

Commander of an Attack Group during the assault on Sicily and as Commander of all Naval Units at Licata during follow-up operations, July 1943.

SANDERS, Capt. Harry, USN

Commander of an Antisubmarine Attack Group during the sinking of an enemy vessel off Cape Falcon, Algeria, on December 16, 1943.

SCHULTEN, Capt. Leo B., USN

Commanding Officer of the USS DOROTHEA L. DIX during the amphibious invasion of the Island of Sicily.

SNARE, Capt. Elmer D., USN

Maintenance Officer on the Staff of a Naval Task Group Commander during the amphibious invasions of Sicily and Italy.

SPELLMAN, Capt. Francis T., USN

Assumed command of the towing of the SS SAMUEL GRIFFIN from the harbor of Oran, Algeria when that vessel was bombed on the night of May 19, 1943.

TAYLOR, Capt. Thomas H., USN (Ret.)

Commodore of a United States Convoy operating in the Mediterranean Sea on 11 May 1944.

THACKREY, Capt. Lyman A., USN

Commander of the USS CALVERT, Flagship of Commander Transport Division SEVEN, during the amphibious invasion of the Island of Sicily, July 10–12, 1943.

TUGGLE, Capt. Richard B., USN

Electrical Officer of the USS SAVANNAH during amphibious invasion operations in the Gulf of Salerno, Italy, on September 11, 1943.

VON HEIMBURG, Capt. Ernest H., USN

Chief of Staff to the Commander Eighth Amphibious Force preparatory to and during the assault in the Gulf of Salerno, September 9, 1943.

WATTLES, Capt. Thomas L., USN

Commander Destroyer Squadron SIXTEEN in the attack on the Island of Sicily from July 10 to 12, 1943.

WELCH, Capt. Philip P., USN

Commanding Officer of the USS THOMAS JEFFERSON in the amphibious invasion of the Island of Sicily, July 1943.

Gold Star in Lieu of a Second Legion of Merit

Commanding Officer of the USS THOMAS JEFFERSON during the amphibious invasion of Italy.

WELLBORN, Capt. Charles, Jr., USN

Commander Destroyer Squadron EIGHT during the amphibious invasion of the Island of Sicily in July and August 1943.

Gold Star in Lieu of a Second Legion of Merit

Commander of three United States Destroyer Squadrons during the amphibious assault on Italy, September 9, 1943.

WELLINGS, Capt. Timothy F., USN

Gunnery Officer of the Amphibious Force, Atlantic Fleet, during the assault on the Island of Sicily in July 1943.

WRIGHT, Capt. Jerauld, USN

Commander of a Landing Craft Flotilla during the amphibious invasion of the Island of Sicily in July 1943.

Gold Star in Lieu of a Second Legion of Merit

Assistant Chief of Staff of the Commander United States Naval Forces, Northwest African Waters, prior to and during the landing of forces in Sicily and Italy.

ZIMMERLI, Capt. Rupert M., USN

Commander of Advanced Bases and Training Group, Tunisia, and as Commander of the Joint Loading Control for all ships in an Amphibious Task Force during the period May 12 to July 19, 1943.

Gold Star in Lieu of a Second Legion of Merit

Commander of the Assault Section of a Major Task Force during the amphibious assault on Italy in September 1943.

BARKER, Cdr. Nathaniel C., USN

Gunnery Officer of the USS PHILADELPHIA prior to and during the amphibious assault on the Island of Sicily in July 1943 and the amphibious invasion of the Italian mainland in September 1943.

BAYS, Cdr. John W., USN

Commanding Officer of the USS PARKER while performing convoy escort duty in the Central Mediterranean in November 1943.

BIESEMEIER, Cdr. Harold, USN

Commanding Officer of the USS CHARLES CARROLL in the amphibious invasion of the Island of Sicily, July 1943.

Gold Star in Lieu of a Second Legion of Merit

Commanding Officer of the USS CHARLES CARROLL during the amphibious assault in Italy.

BROWER, Lt. Col. James H., USMC

Training Officer and Loading Control Officer on the Staff of a Naval Task Group Commander prior to and during the assault on the mainland of Italy.

BUCHANAN, Cdr. Charles A., USN

Operations Officer of an Amphibious Task Force in planning and coordinating the joint activities of the Navy with those of the Army preliminary to the invasion of Sicily on July 10, 1943.

BURKE, Cdr. Edward J., USN

Commanding Officer of the USS PLUNKETT during the amphibious invasion of Italy, September 9 to 18, 1943.

CHIPMAN, Cdr. Briscoe, USN

Commander of the Beach Identification Group of a Major Task Force during the amphibious assault on the mainland of Italy at the Gulf of Salerno on September 9, 1943.

CONNER, Cdr. Ray R., USN

Commanding Officer of the USS NIBLACK while engaged in operations off Nettuno Beach, Italy in January 1944.

Gold Star in Lieu of a Second Legion of Merit

Commanding Officer of the USS NIBLACK while participating as a unit of an antisubmarine hunting group in the search for and final destruction of an enemy submarine off Oran, Algeria on 19 May 1944.

CREIGHTON, Cdr. Liles W., USN

Commanding Officer of the USS LUD-LOW operating off the North Coast of Sicily from August 1 to 18, 1943.

Gold Star in Lieu of a Second Legion of Merit

Commander of the USS LUDLOW during amphibious operations on the 9th and 10th of September 1943, in the Gulf of Salerno, Italy.

CURRY, Cdr. Ralph R., USCG

Gold Star in Lieu of a Second Legion of Merit

Commanding Officer of the USS PRIDE during an attack on an enemy submarine off the Algerian Coast on 4 May 1944.

DAVEY, Cdr. Thomas L. (CEC), USN

Base Construction Officer during the establishment of the Advanced Amphibious Training Bases in North Africa in preparation for the capture of Sicily.

DICKEY, Cdr. George D., USN

Supply and Maintenance Officer and Navigator on the Staff of Commander EIGHTH Amphibious Force in preparation for and during the amphibious assault on the Island of Sicily, July 10, 1943, and the Gulf of Salerno, September 9, 1943.

DUFEK, Cdr. George J., USN

Aviation Officer on the Staff of a Naval Task Force Commander during the amphibious assault on the Island of Sicily, July 1943, and the amphibious invasion of Italy, September 1943

DURGIN, Cdr. Edward R., USN

Commander Destroyer Squadron THIRTEEN prior to and throughout the initial assault on Sicily, July 1943.

Gold Star in Lieu of a Second Legion of Merit

Commander of a United States Destroyer Squadron during the amphibious assault in the Gulf of Salerno, Italy, September 9, 1943.

ECKELMYER, Cdr. Edward H., Jr., USN

Commanding Officer of the USS BISCAYNE during the amphibious invasion of Salerno, Italy, in September 1943.

EDERER, Cdr. Joseph E., USNR

Engineer Officer of the USS BISCAYNE during the amphibious assaults on Sicily in July, and Italy in September 1943.

*FLY, Cdr. William A., USN

Commanding Officer of the USS ANDROMEDA prior to and during the amphibious invasion of Italy.

Second Gold Star in Lieu of a Third Legion of Merit

FLOYD, Cdr. William Orrin, USN

Commander of an Attack Group during the assault on the Island of Sicily. In charge of the largest single group of ships in the assault forces.

FORD, Cdr. Robert Stevens, USN

Commanding Officer of the USS ROWAN during the Sicilian Campaign, July 26 to August 20, 1943.

GARDINER, Cdr. Josef M., USN

Air Group Commander Advance Base Number One, Fleet Air Wing FIFTEEN, from 21 February 1944 to 10 September 1944, while engaged in antisubmarine operations in the Moroccan Sea Frontier area.

GESEN, Cdr. Carl G., USNR

Navigator of the USS PHILADELPHIA during the amphibious assault on the Island of Sicily in July 1943 and the amphibious invasion of the Italian mainland in September 1943.

GIBBS, Cdr. Robert Henry, USN

Commanding Officer of the USS WAINWRIGHT during the Sicilian Campaign, July 26 to August 20, 1943.

GLEIM, Cdr. Fritz, USN

Communications Officer for an attack force during the assault on Sicily, and as Communications Officer for Commander Landing Craft and Bases, Northwest African Waters.

GLICK, Cdr. John A., USN

Commanding Officer of the USS BRISTOL during the Sicilian Campaign, August 1–18, 1943.

Gold Star in Lieu of a Second Legion of Merit

Commanding Officer of the USS BRISTOL during the amphibious operations in the Gulf of Salerno, Italy, on September 9 and 10, 1943.

GREGOR, Cdr. Orville F., USN

Commander of a task group prior to and during the amphibious landings in the Anzio-Nettuno area, Italy, in January 1944.

GRUBE, Cdr. John F., USN

Commanding Officer of the USS BETELGEUSE during the amphibious invasion of Sicily, July 10, 1943.

GULLETT, Cdr. William M., USN

Executive Officer and Navigator of the USS BISCAYNE during the amphibious invasions of Sicily in July 1943 and of the Italian mainland in September 1943.

GURNETTE, Cdr. Byron L., USN

Commanding Officer of the USS GLEAVES from May 1943 to January 1944.

HABECKER, Cdr. Frederic S., USN

Commanding Officer of the USS MAYO during the amphibious invasion of Italy, September 9 to 18, 1943.

HARTT, Cdr. Beverly A., USN

Commanding Officer of the USS PROCYON in the amphibious invasion of the Island of Sicily, July 1943.

Gold Star in Lieu of a Second Legion of Merit

Commanding Officer of the USS PROCYON during the amphibious invasion of Italy.

HELEN, Cdr. Robert R., USNR

Salvage Officer during the amphibious invasion of Sicily, July and August 1943.

JOHNSON, Cdr. Craig B. (MC), USN

Medical Officer on the Staff of a Naval Task Group Commander prior to and during the amphibious assault on the mainland of Italy.

McKINNY, Cdr. John R., USN

Commanding Officer of the USS ARCTURUS during the amphibious invasion of the Island of Sicily.

MORTON, Cdr. Frank P., USNR

Intelligence Officer on the Staff of a Naval Task Group Commander prior to and during the amphibious assaults on Sicily and the mainland of Italy.

MOSES, Cdr. Charles W., USN

Gunnery Officer on the Staff of a Naval Task Force Commander prior to and during the amphibious assault on the Island of Sicily, July 1943, and the amphibious invasion of Italy, September 1943.

POMEROY, Cdr. Joseph G., USN

Commanding Officer of the USS HARRY LEE during the amphibious invasion of the Island of Sicily.

PURSELL, Cdr. Ion, USN

Commanding Officer of the USS OBERON during the amphibious assault on the Island of Sicily, July 10–12, 1943.

Gold Star in Lieu of a Second Legion of Merit

Commanding Officer of USS OBERON during the amphibious assault on Italy.

SCHMIDT, Cdr. John W., USN

Commanding Officer of the USS GHERARDI during the Sicilian Campaign from August 1 to 6, 1943.

SORENSEN, Cdr. Thor C., USNR

Commanding Officer of the USS LYON during the amphibious assault on the Island of Sicily, July 10–12, 1943.

Gold Star in Lieu of a Second Legion of Merit

Commanding Officer of USS LYON during the amphibious assault on Italy.

SOWELL, Cdr. Jesse C., USN

Commander of an escort for a large United States Convoy in the Mediterranean 11 May 1944.

STANDLEY, Cdr. William H., Jr., USN

Training Officer on the Staff of Commander Landing Craft and Bases, Amphibious Force, Northwest African Waters, prior to and during the amphibious invasion of Italy in September 1943.

STROHBEHNM, Cdr. Walter William, USN

Commanding Officer of the USS WAINWRIGHT during an attack on an enemy submarine off the Algerian coast on December 13, 1943.

SULLIVAN, Cdr. Emmett J., USN

Commanding Officer of Blimp Squadron FOURTEEN and Commander Lighter-than-Air Group, Fleet Air Wing FIFTEEN during antisubmarine and mine-spotting operations in the Central and Western Mediterranean from 2 June 1944 to 10 March 1945.

SWIGART, Cdr. Oral R., USN

Commanding Officer of the USS NEVILLE, an assault transport of the Western Naval Task Force, during the amphibious invasion of the Island of Sicily, July 10–12, 1943.

TALLIAFERRO, Cdr. Henry B., USNR

Commander of a Landing Craft Group prior to and during the amphibious assault on the West Coast of Italy.

TUTTLE, Cdr. Magruder H., USN

Commander Headquarters Squadron, Fleet Air Wing FIFTEEN, from 15 January 1944 to 15 August 1944 while engaged in the maintenance and support of all aircraft assigned to Fleet Air Wing FIFTEEN in the Moroccan Sea Frontier and outlying detachments in the Mediterranean Theatre of Operations.

VIOLETT, Cdr. Guentell, USNR

Officer in Charge Naval Petroleum Unit during the occupation of the Island of Sicily in July 1943.

WALSH, Cdr. James E., USNR

Commanding Officer of a Beach Battalion during the preparation for and the assault on the Italian mainland in September and October 1943.

WILLIAMS, Cdr. Russell Champion, USN

Commanding Officer of the USS TRIPPE operating off the North Coast of Sicily from July 26 to August 20, 1943.

Gold Star in Lieu of a Second Legion of Merit

Commanding Officer of the USS TRIPPE during action against an enemy submarine off Cape Falcon, Algeria, December 16, 1943.

WRIGHT, Cdr. William D., USN

Commander of a Landing Craft Flotilla during the amphibious invasion of the Island of Sicily in July 1943.

ABBOTT, Lt. Cdr. Paul A., USNR

Commander of the Loading Control Group during the advanced landings in the Anzio-Nettuno area, Italy, in January 1944.

ANDERSON, Lt. Cdr. Harvey M., USN

Salvage officer at Gela, Sicily, during the amphibious invasion of Sicily in July 1943.

ANKERS, Lt. Cdr. George M., USNR

Salvage Officer at Bizerte, Tunisia, during the month of May 1943.

BUCK, Lt. Cdr. Winthrop P., USNR

Commanding Officer of the USS HOLDER while engaged in escorting a convoy in the Central Mediterranean on the night of 11 April 1944.

BURNS, Lt. Cdr. John D., USNR

Directed a fire-fighting unit during a raid by hostile bombing planes on the Harbor of Oran, Algeria, on the night of May 19, 1943.

Gold Star in Lieu of a Second Legion of Merit

Officer in charge of fire fighting during the amphibious assault on the island of Sicily, July 1943, and during the invasion of Italy, September 1943.

CLIFFORD, Maj. Robert Lanning, USA

Military Intelligence Officer on the Staff of a Task Force Commander during the campaign for the capture of the Island of Sicily.

DARROCH, Lt. Cdr. James W., USNR

Salvage Officer, participating with Naval Forces in the invasions of North Africa, Sicily and Italy.

DAUNIS, Lt. Cdr. Stanley S., USN

Commanding Officer of Motor Torpedo Boat Squadron 29 during a period in which the Squadron undertook many offensive operations against the enemy in the Ligurian Sea from ‘ May through August 1944.

FERGUSON, Maj. James W., USMC

Assistant Training Officer on the Staff of Commander Landing Craft and Bases, Amphibious Force, Northwest African Waters prior to and during two major amphibious operations.

FREESE, Lt. Cdr. John B., USNR

Commander LCT Flotilla during the campaign for the capture of Sicily.

GRISWOLD, Lt. Cdr. Benjamin H., III, USN

Aide and Flag Lieutenant to Commander Western Naval Task Force during the invasion of the Island of Sicily in July 1943.

HARRIS, Lt. Cdr. M. H., USNR

Commander of a Minesweeper Group during the invasion of the Island of Sicily.

HAYS, Lt. Cdr. Alphord, USN

Commander of a Minesweeping Group the amphibious assault on the Island of Sicily, July 1943.

LA BELLE, Lt. Cdr. James William, USNR

Commander of Assault Boat Waves from the USS ELIZABETH C. STANTON and the USS THURSTON during the amphibious invasion of Sicily, July 10–12, 1943.

LAMBERT, Lt. Cdr. George S., USN

Executive Officer of the USS BUCK during an attack on an enemy submarine while on convoy escort off the Island of Pantelleria, August 3, 1943.

LOWTHER, Lt. Cdr. Robert D., USNR

Commander of the Control Group of a Task Force during the invasion of the Island of Sicily on July 10 and 11, 1943.

Gold Star in Lieu of a Second Legion of Merit

Commanding Officer of the USS PC 624 and as Commander of the Control Group in the amphibious invasion of Italy, September 1943.

MALONEY, Lt. Cdr. John L., USNR

Commanding Officer of the USS STRIVE during the Sicilian Campaign on July 26, 1943.

MUZZY, Lt. Cdr. James S., USCG

Commanding Officer of the USS MILLS on 1 April 1944 in the Mediterranean Sea.

NEWBEGIN, Lt. Cdr. Robert George, III, USNR

Commander LCI (L) Group FIVE and as a Wave Commander of Landing Craft during the campaign for the capture of Sicily.

NOLAN, Lt. Cdr. James E., USN

Established Advanced Naval Bases during the invasion of the Island of Sicily in July 1943.

PARISH, Maj. George S., USA

For exceptionally meritorious conduct in the performance of outstanding services while serving on the staff of a Naval Task Force Commander prior to and during the amphibious invasions of Sicily in July 1943 and Italy in September 1943.

PEARCE, Lt. Cdr. Hepburn A., USN

Commanding Officer of the USS EDISON during amphibious operations in the Gulf of Salerno, Italy, on September 9 and 10, 1943.

ROBBINS, Lt. Cdr. R. C., USNR

Commanding Officer of a Destroyer Escort during the advanced landings in the Anzio-Nettuno area, Italy, in January 1944.

ROBERTS, Lt. Cdr. Lawrence D., USNR

Commanding Officer of the Advanced Amphibious Training Base at La Goulette, Tunisia, in preparation for the capture of Sicily and during the invasion of the island, July 1943.

SCOTT, Lt. Cdr. David D., USN

Gunnery Officer of the USS SAVANNAH during the amphibious invasion of the Island of Sicily in July 1943.

SOULE, Lt. Cdr. Rufus Albertson, III, USNR

Commanding Officer of a Destroyer Escort during the advanced landings in the Anzio-Nettuno area, Italy, in January 1944.

SPAHR, Lt. Cdr. Otto William, Jr., USN

Commanding Officer USS RHIND during the Sicilian campaign.

SPEER, Lt. Cdr. John O., USN

First Lieutenant and Damage Control Officer of the USS SAVANNAH preceding and during the amphibious invasion of Italy on September 11, 1943.

TAYLOR, Lt. Cdr. Crittenden Battelle, USNR

Commander of a Minesweeper Group in the assault on the Island of Sicily.

Gold Star in Lieu of a Second Legion of Merit

Commander of the United States Minesweepers attached to a Major Task Force during the amphibious invasion of Italy in September 1943.

THOMPSON, Lt. Cdr. Edward C., Jr., USCG

Commanding Officer of Patrol Craft during operations of the United States Navy in support of the Army, in the latter phase of the Campaign in Sicily.

VARDAMAN, Lt. Cdr. James Kimble, USNR

Chief of Staff Officer to Commander Advanced Naval Bases during the invasion of the Island of Sicily.

VISCHIO, Lt. Cdr. Attilio A., USNR

Commanding Officer of the USS ARCTURUS during the amphibious invasion of Italy.

WALCOTT, Lt. Cdr. Carver G. (MC), USNR

Medical Officer attached to the USS BISCAYNE during the amphibious assault on Italy in the Gulf of Salerno, September 9 to 15, 1943.

WETMORE, Lt. Cdr. Sherman B., USNR

Commanding Officer of the USS PILOT during the amphibious invasion of Italy on September 9, 1943.

WILSON, Lt. Cdr. Edward Webster, USNR

Commander LCI (L) Group FOUR and as a Wave Commander of Landing Craft during the campaign for the capture of Sicily.

ALFIERI, Lt. Paul A., USNR

Combat Intelligence Officer during the amphibious invasion of the Island of Sicily July 1943.

ANNITTO, Lt. John E., USNR

Medical Officer assigned to an attack group during the amphibious assault on the West Coast of Italy.

BISSINGER, Lt. Paul A., USNR

On the staff of a Naval Task Force Commander during the amphibious invasions of Sicily and Italy in July and September 1943, and the advance landings at Anzio, Italy in January 1944.

CAIN, Lt. John R., USNR

Commanding Officer of the USS PC 559 during the amphibious invasion of Italy in September 1943.

CALDWELL, Lt. George M. (MC), USNR

Medical Officer aboard the USS SHUBRICK during the Sicilian Campaign in August 1943.

DAVIDSON, Lt. Wilbur S., USNR

Flag Lieutenant and Aide to a Naval Task Force Commander prior to and during the Sicilian campaign in July 1943, and the amphibious invasion of Italy in September 1943.

DOWNEY, Lt. Wallace K., USNR

Officer in Charge of a Landing Craft Repair Unit during a period of almost continual offensive operations in the Central Mediterranean from March 1943 to August 1944.

GEZON, Lt. Horace M. (MC), USNR

Officer in charge of the Epidemiology Unit of United States Naval Forces, Northwest African Waters, during a typhus epidemic in Naples, Italy, in January 1944.

GRANT, Lt. William James, USNR

On board the USS OBERON during the amphibious assault on the West Coast of Italy in September 1943.

HASLUP, Lt. Charles L., USN

Commanding Officer of the USS LST 312 on July 9, 1943 during the amphibious invasion of the Island of Sicily.

HERBERT, Lt. John Robert, USNR

Officer in Charge of a Pontoon Causeway Platoon, serving with the 579th U. S. Naval Construction Battalion and Maintenance Unit during the advance landings in the Anzio-Nettuno area, Italy, January 1944.

JACOBS, Lt. Joshua, USNR

Officer in Charge of the USS LCT 220 during the advance landings behind enemy lines in the Anzio-Nettuno area, Italy, in January and February 1944.

JAMES, Lt. Harrie A., USNR

Assistant Intelligence Officer on the Staff of a Naval Task Force Commander from March to October 1943 in the Mediterranean Theatre.

JOHNSON, Lt. Louis G., USNR

Commanding Officer of the USS LCT 125 during the amphibious assault at Salerno, Italy, on September 9, 1943.

KERR, Lt. Robert B., USNR

Assistant Radio Officer on the Staff of a Naval Task Force Commander prior to and during the amphibious invasion of Sicily in July 1943 and of the Italian mainland in September 1943.

KYLLBERG, Lt. V. H., USN

Commanding Officer of the USS MORENO during the amphibious assault on Italy in September and October 1943.

MANRY, Lt. John T., III, USNR

Attached to the USS BISCAYNE at Salerno Bay during the amphibious invasion of Italy, September 12, 1943.

MILLARD, Lt. Lyman C., USNR

Radio Material Officer on the Staff of a Naval Task Force Commander prior to and during the occupation of French Morocco in November 1942 and the amphibious invasions of Sicily and Italy in July and September 1943.

MOYES, Lt. Cecil L., USNR

Officer in Charge of a Pontoon Causeway Platoon, serving with the 579th U. S. Naval Construction Battalion and Maintenance Unit during the advance landings in the Anzio-Nettuno area, Italy, in January and February, 1944.

MUTTY, Lt. John B., USN

Executive Officer of Motor Torpedo Boat Squadron FIFTEEN during offensive operations against the enemy in the Central Mediterranean from June 1943 to February 1944.

Gold Star in Lieu of a Second Legion of Merit

Executive Officer of Motor Torpedo Boat Squadron 15 and of Boat Squadrons, Eighth Fleet, during the conduct of continual offensive operations against the enemy in the Mediterranean from April 1944 to September 1944.

NYLUND, Lt. Harvey R., USN

Served aboard the USS SAVANNAH during the invasion of Italy on September 11, 1943.

PEAVEY, Lt. William B., USNR

Commanding Officer of the USS sc 690 while engaged in operations off Anzio, Italy, on 15 February 1944.

PHILP, Lt. Byron W., USNR

Commander LCT Group 27 prior to and during the advance landings in the Anzio-Nettuno area, Italy, in January and February 1944.

RAYMOND, Lt. Gordon, USNR

Commander LCT Flotilla ELEVEN during the campaign for the capture of Sicily.

REDDEN, Lt. Clarence R., USNR

Officer in Charge of Mobile Explosives Investigation Unit Number TWO during a period of almost continual offensive operations against the enemy in the Central and Western Mediterranean from April to December 1944.

SALISTEAN, Lt. John T., USN

Commanding Officer of the USS LST 379 during the amphibious attack on Sicily, July 1943.

SCHEIDEMANTEL, Lt. Clyde A., USNR

Engineering Officer aboard a large landing craft during the amphibious assault on the Island of Sicily in July 1943.

SHORT, Lt. James Woodleigh, USN

Gunnery Officer of the USS NIBLACK during the amphibious landings at Anzio, Italy, from January 22 to 29, 1944.

STEEL, Lt. William D., USNR

Commander of a Group of Assault Landing Boats during the amphibious invasion of the mainland of Italy.

STOKES, Lt. Harold James, Jr., USNR

Aide and Flag Lieutenant to Commander Eighth Amphibious Force prior to and during the assault on the Island of Sicily, July 10, 1943, and the Gulf of Salerno, September 9, 1943.

STRATTON, Lt. Darrell A., USN

Commanding Officer of the USS LST 338 during the amphibious invasion of the Island of Sicily on July 10, 1943.

VINES, Lt. Wesley Carpenter, USNR

Commander of Small Boat Flotillas while preparing for the campaign against Sicily and during the amphibious invasion of that island, July 1943.

Gold Star in Lieu of a Second Legion of Merit

Commander Boat Flotilla prior to and during advance landings in the Anzio-Nettuno area, Italy, January 1944.

BANNER, Lt. (jg) Roger H., USCG

Officer in Charge of a Support Boat attached to the USS SAMUEL CHASE during the amphibious invasion of Italy on 9 September 1943.

BEARSE, Lt. (jg) Thurlow B., USNR

Commander of a boat transporting supplies to French troops assisting our forces during the advance against the enemy on the coast of Tunisia on May 5, 1943.

BORCYCKOWSKI, Lt. (jg) Francis Martin, USN

Attached to the USS SHUBRICK during the Sicilian Campaign in August 1943.

DAVIDSON, Lt. (jg) R. R., USNR

Participated in the invasion of Sicily.

ESBENSEN, Lt. (jg) Robert E., USNR

Officer in Charge of the USS LCT 35 during the advance landings behind enemy lines in the Anzio-Nettuno area, Italy in January and February 1944.

FILE, Lt. (jg) William H., Jr., USN

Commander of a Support Boat Squadron during the amphibious assault on the Island of Sicily, July 9–10, 1943.

FREY, Lt. (jg) Robert Davis, USNR

Attached to the USS MAYRANT during an enemy air raid on the Harbor of Palermo, Sicily, on August 1, 1943.

GILL, Lt. (jg) Warren Calavan, USCGR

Commander of an Assault Force during the assault on the Island of Sicily and for outstanding service in the pre-assault training of officers and men for small boat operations.

HARVEY, Lt. (jg) Edward B., USNR

Commanding Officer USS PC 626 while on patrol off Anzio, Italy on 21 April and again on 24 April 1944.

HOLMES, Lt. (jg) Burton C., USNR

Officer in Charge of the USS LCT 217 during the advance landing behind enemy lines in the Anzio-Nettuno area, Italy in January and February 1944.

HUGHES, Lt. (jg) Hugh B., USN

Assistant to the Force Supply Officer attached to the Staff of a Major Naval Task Force Commander during the campaigns against French Morocco, Sicily and Italy.

HUMM, Lt. (jg) George A., USNR

Officer in Charge of the USS LCT 32 during the advance landings behind enemy lines in the Anzio-Nettuno area, Italy, in January and February 1944.

JACKSON, Lt. (jg) Thomas H., USNR

Operations Officer of the Escort Sweeper Group, Eighth Fleet, during a period of almost continual offensive operations against the enemy in the Central Mediterranean from January to October 1944.

LAESSLE, Lt. (jg) Frank W., USNR

Attached to the USS MORENO during the amphibious assault on Italy in September and October, 1943.

MANNING, Lt. (jg) Herbert C., USNR

Naval Gunfire Support Officer prior to and during the advance landings in the Anzio-Nettuno area, Italy, in January 1944.

MARGETTS, Lt. (jg) Richard K., USN

Squadron Commander of Support Boats during the amphibious assault upon the Island of Sicily.

McCLUSKEY, Lt. (jg) Robert A., USNR

Fire Control Watch Officer aboard the USS THOMAS JEFFERSON during the amphibious assault upon the Island of Sicily.

OSBORNE, Lt. (jg) Robert G., USNR

Naval Gunfire Liaison Officer assigned to the 36th United States Infantry Division during the amphibious invasion of Italy on September 9, 1943.

PINKERTON, Lt. (jg) Lessley C., USNR

Naval Gunfire Liaison Officer of the 36th United States Infantry Division during the amphibious invasion of Italy on September 9, 1943.

RILEY, Lt. (jg) Andrew J., USNR

Officer in Charge of a Pontoon Causeway Platoon, serving with the 579th U. S. Naval Construction Battalion and Maintenance Unit during the advanced landings in the Anzio-Nettuno area, Italy, in January and February, 1944.

SHERVEY, Lt. (jg) William D., USNR

Officer in Charge of the USS LCT 140 during the advanced landings behind enemy lines in the Anzio-Nettuno area, Italy, in January and February 1944.

TODD, Lt. (jg) Thomas D., USNR

Executive Officer of USS PC 559 during a period of offensive operations against the enemy in the Central Mediterranean from July 1943 to February 1944.

TUGGLE, Lt. (jg) Arthur J., USN

Electrical Officer of the USS SAVANNAH during amphibious invasion operations in the Gulf of Salerno, Italy, on September 11, 1943.

TYLER, Robert L., 1st Lt., USA

For exceptionally meritorious conduct in the performance of outstanding services while officer in charge of the U. S. Army fighter director group attached to the staff of a task force commander during the amphibious assault on the Island of Sicily.

VOLKART, Lt. (jg) Edmund H., USNR

Officer in Charge of the USS LCT 277 while participating in the amphibious assault on Sicily, July 1943.

AMMONS, Ens. Frank, USNR

Commanding Officer of the USS LCT 452 on July 11, 1943, during the amphibious invasion of the Island of Sicily.

CULVER, Ens. L. L., Jr., USNR

Officer in Charge of a Scout Boat Unit during the amphibious assault on the Island of Sicily in July 1943 and the advanced landings at Anzio, Italy, in January 1944.

SEIDLER, Ens. William D., USNR

Officer in Charge of a small, heavily armed scout boat, while participating in the amphibious assault upon the Island of Sicily on July 10, 1943.

ALLISON, Alfred F., CBM, USNR

Senior platoon petty officer of his Pontoon Causeway Group, serving with the 579th U.S. Naval Construction Battalion and Maintenance Unit during the advanced landings in the Anzio-Nettuno area, Italy, in January 1944.

AVIDANO, Fred Aldo, CPhM, USNR

Attached to the USS SEER on the occasion of the sinking of the USS SKILL off the Gulf of Salerno, Italy, September 25, 1943.

BARNARD, Philip E., BM1/c, USCG

In charge of a heavy landing craft loaded with vehicles and assault troops attached to the USS JOSEPH T. DICKMAN during the amphibious assault at Salerno, Italy, September 9, 1943.

BETHUNE, George G., Carp. (CEC), USNR

Attached to the USS LST 333, assisted in rescuing survivors when that vessel was torpedoed in the Mediterranean Sea.

BURKHART, Peter Joseph, AOM1/c, USNR

Participated in the invasion of Sicily.

COAKLEY, Thomas L., Cox., USNR

Member of a Pontoon Causeway Crew in rescuing survivors of the LST 158 when that vessel was bombed by the enemy during the amphibious assault on the Island of Sicily, July 1943.

EATON, Charles F., PhM1/c, USN

Attached to the USS LST 333 when that vessel was torpedoed by an enemy submarine in the Mediterranean Sea.

JONES, John H., S1/c, USNR

Machine-gunner stationed in Boat TWELVE of the USS THOMAS JEFFERSON during the amphibious assault on Sicily, July 10, 1943.

KOON, Robert Lee, PhM1/c, USN

Attached to the USS SPEED during rescue operations in the Gulf of Salerno off the coast of Italy on September 25, 1943.

LIGHTNER, Fay McLaren, Chief Gunner, USN

Battery Control Officer and Rangekeeper Operator aboard the USS MAYRANT off Palermo, Sicily, on July 26, 1943.

MINER, Edward Sullivan, CBM, USN

Coxswain of a landing boat in the first assault wave during the amphibious assault on the Island of Sicily, July 10 to 12, 1943.

PARRISH, William K., S2/c, USNR

Member of a Pontoon Causeway Crew in rescuing survivors of the LST 158 when that vessel was bombed by the enemy during the amphibious assault on the Island of Sicily, July 1943.

SELF, Robert L., Boat, USN

Commanding Officer of the USS INTENT during the amphibious assault on Sicily, July 1943.

TRUE, Donald E., SM3/c, USNR

Attached to the USS THOMAS JEFFERSON during the amphibious assault upon the Island of Sicily in July 1943.

UNKENHOLZ, Albert F., CCM, USNR

Member of a Pontoon Causeway Crew in rescuing survivors of the LST 158 when that vessel was bombed by the enemy during the amphibious assault on the Island of Sicily, July 1943.

WOODMANCY, Charles W., CM2/c, USNR

Member of a Pontoon Causeway Crew in rescuing survivors of the LST 158 when that vessel was bombed by the enemy during the amphibious assault on the Island of Sicily, July 1943.

Silver Star Medal

HUTCHINS, Cdr. Charles Slack, USN
WILLIAMS, Cdr. Jack B., USN
BERLISS, Lt. Cdr. Arthur D., Jr., USNR
DuBOIS, Lt. Cdr. Thomas H., USN
FAIRBANKS, Lt. Cdr. Douglas E., Jr., USNR

HUNT, Lt. Cdr. James S., USCG
KREMER, Lt. Cdr. John, USNR
MAHONEY, Capt. Cornelius A. (MC), USA
SCALAN, Lt. Cdr. Bernard Edward, USCG
SHAHEEN, Lt. Cdr. John M., USNR
SWIFT, Lt. Cdr. Douglas M., USN
THOMPSON, Lt. Cdr. Edward Carter, USCG
ARBUCKLE, Lt. Ernest C., USNR
BELKNAP, Lt. Robert E., USNR
BUTLER, Lt. Roy E., USN
CAIN, Lt. John Russel, USNR
CALDWELL, Lt. Richard Wayland, USNR
CLARK, Lt. Robert Smith, USNR
COGLEY, Lt. William T., USNR
DETWILER, Lt. J. W., USNR
DUBOSE, Lt. Edwin A., USNR
ESTES, Lt. Otto Pendleton, Jr., USNR
FLECK, Lt. Harold R., USNR
HUSSEY, Lt. C. W., USNR
KEENAN, Lt. Francis J., (ChC), USNR
MARGETTS, Lt. Richard K., USN
McFADZEAN, Lt. John, USNR
McILWAINE, Lt. R. H., USNR
MILLER, Lt. Wesley Norton, USNR
NAZRO, Lt. Thomas W., USNR
*O'BRIEN, Lt. Richard H., USN
POTTER, Lt. Charles S., USNR
READE, Lt. Robert B., USNR
ROOSEVELT, Lt. Franklin D., Jr., USNR
SALISTEAN, Lt. John Theodore, USN
VAN BUSKIRK, Lt. Bruce P., USNR
VINES, Lt. Wesley C., USNR
BERRIEN, Lt. (jg) Price, USNR
BURKE, Lt. (jg) E. M., USNR
CHASE, Lt. (jg) James B., USNR
CLIFFORD, Lt. (jg) Eugene S. A., USNR
CLOUGH, Lt. (jg) Walter R., Jr., USNR
CRAGGS, Lt. (jg) Donald Edgar, USNR
FIDLER, Lt. (jg) Paul F., USNR
FITZGERALD, Lt. (jg) Magnes C., USNR
GALLOWAY, Lt. (jg) Grady R., USCGR
GROEBECKER, Lt. (jg) Alan J., USNR
GROVES, Lt. (jg) Russell Robert, USNR
GRUNDY, Lt. (jg) Thaddeus, USNR
HAINES, Lt. (jg) George Eddison, USNR
HOGG, Lt. (jg) Morris B., USNR
MANRY, Lt. (jg) John T., III, USNR
NOEL, Lt. (jg) Henry Will, USNR
NORTH, Lt. (jg) Henry Ringling, USNR
O'BRIEN, Lt. (jg) Richard H., USNR
OGILBY, Lt. (jg) John D., USNR
OSBORNE, Lt. (jg) Robert, USNR
PERRY, Lt. (jg) John E., USNR

PRESSLY, Lt. (jg) Francis Y., USNR
REED, Lt. (jg) G. L., USNR
SAVADKIN, Lt. (jg) Lawrence, USNR
SCHLANGER, Lt. (jg) Nathan, USNR
SILVERSTEIN, Lt. (jg) Marvin William, USNR
SINCLAIR, Lt. (jg) Thomas L., USNR
SWENSON, Lt. (jg) C. E., USN
TOLAND, Lt. (jg) Clyde H., USN
UMSTEAD, Lt. (jg) John, Jr., USNR
ZIEGLER, Lt. (jg) Harold Herbert, USNR
AMENDOLARA, Ens. Joseph V., USNR
BILLHEIMER, Ens. Lester B., USNR
BJORKLUND, Ens. Raymond, USNR
BOOTH, Ens. Buford A., USNR
BUCKLEW, Ens. Phil H., USNR
CAVANAUGH, Ens. Joseph V., USNR
CHRISCHILLES, Ens. T. R., USNR
CLARK, Ens. James W., USNR
CLARKSON, Ens. Ferman L., USNR
CLAYBAUGH, Ens. Harry W., USNR
DELANEY, Ens. Franklyn L., USNR
DIFORIO, Ens. James P., USNR
DONNELL, Ens. John G., USNR
ELMER, Ens. Robert E. P., USCGR
FAGERLAND, Ens. John L., Jr., USNR
FINK, Ens. Frederick S., USNR
FINLAY, Ens. Robert J., USNR
FREELAND, Ens. Stephen L., USNR
FREYENSEE, Ens. Howard, USNR
GLENNON, Ens. Thomas J., USNR
GOLSON, Ens. George A., USNR
GUTHE, Ens. Alfred K., USNR
HIRSCHBERG, Ens. Simon, USNR
HOWE, Ens. Kenneth E., USNR
HULTEN, Ens. George A., USNR
JOHNSON, Ens. John W., USNR
KAHAN, Ens. Edward, USNR
KASHMER, Ens. Paul J., USNR
LAGERLOF, Ens. Clarence S., USNR
LORIA, Ens. George E., USNR
McNABB, Ens. Henry D., USNR
NEWMAN, Ens. John T., USNR
NICHOLS, Ens. Robert R., USNR
PETERSON, Ens. Raymond K., USNR
POELTLER, Ens. George J., USNR
POPPE, Ens. John D., USNR
PIRRO, Ens. Carmon F., USNR
RAFTIS, Ens. Daniel J., USNR
SEIBERT, Ens. Robert M., USNR
SEIDLER, Ens. William D., USNR
SEMPLE, Ens. Alistair, USNR
SHERWIN, Ens. Robert W., USNR
SMITH, Ens. Fred Baker, USNR
STEPHENS, Ens. Norman E., USNR

TEETER, Ens. Ransom, USNR
TURNER, Ens. Robert E., USNR
WOODMORE, Ens. George R., USNR
ANDERSON, Alvin K., Cox., USCG
ARNOLD, Arthur A., S1/c, USCGR
BAILEY, Harry Morris, SC1/c, USNR
BAMBRICK, Eugene R., SF1/c, USNR
BARNHILL, Clifford Bailey, CM1/c, USN
BARRINGER, Russell Benton, SF1/c, USN
BARTS, W. C., Cox., USNR
BEALS, George L., S2/c, USN
BEATY, Thomas C., GM3/c, USNR
BEAUSOLEIL, Henry R., S2/c, USNR
BERTHIAUME, Earle M., S1/c, USNR
BINGAMAN, Fred N., SM2/c, USN
BLUE, Herman F., S2/c, USN
BOWERS, Norman Leo, S2/c, USNR
BRIDGES, James Cecil, BM2/c, USN
BRODEUR, Robert A., CM2/c, USNR
BROWN, William J., S1/c, USNR
BULLARD, Herman Andrew, BM2/c, USNR
BYAM, Earl H., Cox., USNR
CAPEWELL, John W., MM2/c, USNR
CAPRON, Robert Harlo, S2/c, USN
CARPENTER, Francis, S1/c, USNR
CHAPMAN, Clifford Lester, BM2/c, USNR
CHEZIK, Thomas C., CBM, USNR
CHICTASSO, Edward M., CBM, USN
COLE, Edwin William, S1/c, USNR
CONVERSE, Theodore Joseph, MM1/c, USN
DANNISON, Bryon G., BM1/c, USCG
DEMARCO, Alfonse L., S1/c, USNR
DENNISON, John Joseph, CWT, USN
DODD, Joseph Edwin, MoMM2/c, USNR
DONAHOO, John F., F2/c, USN
DUGGAN, J. F., CM1/c, USN
EARHEART, James E., Jr., PFC, USMC
EDEL, George J., S1/c, USNR
EDWARDS, Robert H., CBM, USN
ELDNER, David Andrew, CSM, USN
EPPS, Edward Wells, CSM, USN
FARRIS, John Leo, MoMM1/c, USNR
FITZGERALD, Desmond P., EM3/c, USNR
FORREST, A. F., S2/c, USNR
GARDINER, Adrain P., Jr., S1/c, USN
GARNER, Ralph J., Cox., USN
GARNIER, Joseph E., S2/c, USNR
GIGER, Charles William, Cox, USN
GRIFFIN, Raymond H., SF2/c, USNR
GROOTE, Kent R., Boat., USN
HABECKER, Ralph H., Boat., USN
HANSTEIN, William J., S2/c, USNR
HOPPINS, William V., S1/c, USNR

HUFF, Newton, S2/c, USN
HUNTER, Warren, S1/c, USNR
JACKSON, Edward Joseph, Cox., USN
JACKSON, Willie James, StM1/c, USN
JANSEN, Robert E., S1/c, USNR
JEFFERSON, David W., StM2/c, USNR
JOHNSON, Willard J., PhM2/c, USNR
KARKKIANEN, Eino, CWT, USNR
KAUFMAN, Burd J., GM3/c, USN
KING, D. T., BM2/c, USN
KING, Ray Bristol, BM2/c, USN
KLINE, Stanley F., EM1/c, USNR
KLINGNER, Carl E., SF1/c, USN
KNIGHT, Cyril E., Cox., USNR
KOHN, John E., SF2/c, USN
LaCHAMBRE, Leo Charles, S2/c, USNR
LAWRENCE, William C., CBM, USCG
LENCZEWSKI, Clement John, F3/c, USN
LESPERANCE, Edgar P., EM2/c, USNR
LEWIS, Paul H., SF1/c, USN
LIGHT, Davis F., Cox., USN
LILLY, C. B., Cox., USCGR
MALONEY, C. S., MoMM1/c, USNR
MARSHALL, William Thomas, CM1/c, USN
MAYNOR, Julian Arthur, S2/c, USNR
McLEAN, Robert L., SK3/c, USNR
MERCER, Lynwood E., S1/c, USNR
MIKRUT, Joseph, GM3/c, USNR
MILLER, Ira Lee, Cox., USN
MILLER, Jack N., Cox., USCGR
MOORE, P. R., MoMM1/c, USNR
O'MALLEY, Thomas J., EM3/c, USNR
NIEDZIALEK, Anthony Stanley, S1/c, USNR
OSBORNE, Kermit K., Cox., USN
PAGE, R. V., QM2/c, USNR
PALMER, Lamar Curtis, Cox., USN
PALMER, Joseph L., Boat., USNR
PEMBERTON, Warren William, MM1/c, USN
PENNICK, Ronald J., CPh, USNR
PETERSON, R. H., MoMM2/c, USNR
PFEIFLE, Charles, F1/c, USN
PINEAULT, Eugene Alfred, AS, USNR
PORTER, Marion Anthony, ST3/c, USNR
RAIL, Robert L., SF1/c, USN
REED, Everett B., CM1/c, USNR
RICE, Samuel, F2/c, USNR
ROGERS, Roy Cinclair, S1/c, USNR
SCHEUERMAN, John C., S1/c, USCGR
SHIPLEY, Francis M., Jr., BM2/c, USN
SIRACUSA, J. J., S2/c, USNR
SMALL, Carlton Caldwell, Cox., USNR
STANFORD, William L., CSF, USNR

STEEVES, Harold Morton, CMM, USN
STINEMAN, Harold William, F1/c, USN
SWIGON, John V., SF3/c, USNR
SUMMERS, Ray O., GM3/c, USNR
TILLEY, Leon S., MoMM1/c, USNR
TRYCE, Everett Benjamin, BM2/c, USNR
UNDERHILL, George H., Cox., USN
VOGEL, John J., Mach., USN
WHITEHEAD, Harold Francis, BM2/c, USN
WILSON, Jack Carlos, Cox., USNR
YOUNTS, Jack, EM3/c, USNR
ZGIOBIS, Addie, S1/c, USNR
ZIELINSKI, John A., F1/c, USNR

Distinguished Flying Cross

STEPHENSON, Lt. Cdr. Richard Davids, USN
ANDERSON, Lt. Charles A., USN
DREW, Lt. John Walter, USNR
KENNEDY, Lt. Leland E., USNR
LEWIS, Lt. Cyril G., USNR
LIANE, Lt. Delwin A., USN
MISHANEC, Lt. John E., USNR
PATTERSON, Lt. Leo D., USNR
SPEARS, Lt. Ralph C., USNR
AIKENS, Lt. (jg) Charles Carroll, USNR
AUSTIN, Lt. (jg) William R., USNR
BAKER, Lt. (jg) Howard J., USN
BOURGEAULT, Lt. (jg) Edward, USNR
COUGHLIN, Lt. (jg) Paul E., USNR
FIERSTEIN, Lt. (jg) Stanley C., USNR
FRAZIER, Lt. (jg) John J., USNR
HARDING, Lt. (jg) William T., USNR
KNIGHT, Lt. (jg) Gilbert L., USNR
LAWRY, Lt. (jg) Edward H., USNR
LINGLE, Lt. (jg) Van A. T., USNR
McGUINNESS, Lt. (jg) Joseph Henry, III, USNR
MARLEY, Lt. (jg) Eugene Henry, USNR
MOSS, Lt. (jg) Elmo L., USNR
MOTE, Lt. (jg) Harold, USNR
OSBORN, Lt. (jg) John G., USNR
PINTO, Lt. (jg) George J., USNR
VOPATEK, Lt. (jg) Matthias J., USNR
WEAVER, Lt. (jg) David Forsythe, USNR
WILKES, Lt. (jg) Roy, USNR
WOOLLEY, Lt. (jg) T. Russell, USNR
PICKARD, Ens. Morris Glenn, USNR
ROHER, Ens. Kalb, USNR
ADAMS, Carl Eugene, AOM1/c, USN
ALLEN, R. S., ARM3/c, USN
DESJARDINS, Edward N., AMM2/c, USN
FEINBERG, Irving B., PhoM2/c, USN

GIBSON, Frederick L., ARM2/c, USN
HALE, L. M., ARM2/c, USN
HOBAN, William Joseph, ARM3/c, USN
HOGG, Anthony F., ARM3/c, USN
JOHNSON, Edward, ARM2/c, USNR
MAPLES, Robert H., ARM1/c, USN
MARKS, George L., AMM2/c, USNR
ORSI, Americo, AMM2/c, USN
PARRANT, James Delmas, ARM3/c, USNR
PIERSON, Douglas Whitney, ARM2/c, USNR
PRUTILPAC, Mackey M., AOM2/c, USN
RAMSAY, Shirley, ARM3/c, USN
RYAN, William H., ARM3/c, USN
SCHRADLE, Joseph Leslie, ARM2/c, USN
SHAFER, Richard, ARM2/c, USN
SMITH, Ralph John, ARM2/c, USN
STAHL, B. R., ARM1/c, USN
SWAN, Joseph Alvin, ARM1/c, USN
TAVERNIER, Claude E., ARM3/c, USNR
TRUE, Edward James, ACRM, USN
WALL, John Shairt, ARM3/c, USN
YATES, Paul E., ARM2/c, USN

Navy and Marine Corps Medal

BROWN, Lt. Leo Rolland, USN
ERWIN, Lt. A. E., USNR
GOUDIE, Lt. Gavin M., USNR
ISENBERG, Lt. Lester P., USNR
NEAL, Lt. William B. (MC), USNR
REDDEN, Lt. Clarence Rudolph, USNR
SCHERRER, Lt. Carl L., USNR
WALKER, Lt. Bayard, USNR
ARTHUR, Lt. (jg) Marcus Wilson, USNR
BROWN, Lt. (jg) Gordon Summers, USNR
CONROY, Lt. (jg) Bernard J., USNR
HEISTAND, Lt. (jg) H. E., USNR
McGUIRE, Lt. (jg) H. L., USNR
O'HAYRE, Lt. (jg) J., USCGR
PIERCE, Lt. (jg) James Murphy, USNR
WORTHAM, Lt. (jg) C. F., USN
DUGAN, Ens. John Joseph, USNR
HARLIN, Ens. Sylvester T., USN
HOUGH, Ens. George A., III, USNR
KOLCHIN, Ens. J. J., USNR
WALILKO, Ens. Julian John, USNR
ADAMS, Pearson B., Jr., MoMM2/c, USNR
AMOS, James Melvin, F1/c, USNR
ANTHONY, Joseph Albert, BM1/c, USNR
ASHCRAFT, John T., SP1/c, USNR
BAMFORD, Leo A., MoMM1/c, USNR
BARNHILL, Clifford Bailey, CM1/c, USN
BARTON, Everett, F1/c, USNR

BENDER, Ervin W., S1/c, USN
BENTON, Dewitt Shilling, Jr., QM2/c, USN
BONE, William M., M1/c, USN
BOURGEOIS, Alonzo J., SF1/c, USNR
BOWLING, John S., F1/c, USNR
BRACKEN, Donald James, SK1/c, USN
BRADLEY, Ronald C., MoMM2/c, USNR
BRADY, John W., Sp(F)1/c, USNR
BRANDT, Fredrick Harold, MoMM3/c, USNR
BROTHERTON, Donald E., CBM, USN
BURKE, John J., SF1/c, USNR
BUSH, Francis W., Sp1/c, USNR
CARUSO, Joseph H., Sp(F)2/c, USNR
CAUDILL, Millard V., CMM, USN
CHAPMAN, Charles Bement, WT1/c, USN
CHRISTEL, Charles, S1/c, USN
CHRISTENSEN, Svend S., MoMM1/c, USNR
CIPRARI, Louis John, CM2/c, USNR
CLAPP, Albert J., BM2/c, USNR
CLARK, Charles J., Jr., RM3/c, USNR
CLARKE, Harry K., MoMM2/c, USNR
COCHRAN, Carl E., BM2/c, USNR
COSTA, Joseph, RM3/c, USNR
COZART, Lowry D., Jr., S1/c, USNR
CULPEPPER, Jack Warren, Cox., USNR
DEMPSTER, William J., MoMM1/c, USNR
DINGEE, James, Sp2/c, USNR
DOUGLASS, Stacy A., Jr., Y1/c, USNR
DRESSER, Gordon K., SM3/c, USNR
DRUMMOND, James O., SP1/c, USNR
DUNLAP, John J., F1/c, USNR
DURAN, Melvin Joseph, CQM, USNR
DYKES, Orlo "W," SC3/c, USN
DYORICH, Mike, GM3/c, USN
EIKMEIER, Henry N., GM3/c, USNR
ELLISON, Robert, WT3/c, USN
EVANISKO, Stephen, MM2/c, USNR
FAZION, Nathan R., Y1/c, USNR
FERGUSON, Perry, Jr., S1/c, USN
FIORELLINI, Anthony Earl, MoMM2/c, USNR
FLYNN, John E., CEM, USN
FOBERT, Vincent F., SM3/c, USNR
FORD, William Welbourn, WT1/c, USN
FROST, Jack Walter, Cox., USNR
FULTON, Arch, EM2/c, USNR
GARMUSCHSKY, Robert J., RM1/c, USNR
GARMY, Robert James, RT1/c, USNR
GARRIGUES, Floyd F., SF2/c, USNR
GIORDANELLA, Matthew Phillip, Cox., USNR

GLINDEMAN, Harold L., SM1/c, USN
GOINS, Haskell Lear, SoM2/c, USN
GOODRICH, Earl W., B1/c, USNR
GREENBERG, Walter, Sp3/c, USNR
GREENE, Frank, Jr., S1/c, USNR
GRIFFEE, James R., SF3/c, USNR
HAFFEY, Frank George, Jr., MoMM2/c, USNR
HALSTEIN, John G., SoM2/c, USNR
HANWAY, John E., Jr., SoM1/c, USNR
HARRIS, E. B., PMK1/c, USNR
HART, Charles R., MM3/c, USNR
HAY, Arthur C., QM3/c, USNR
HAYDE, William, Sp3/c, USNR
HEAPS, Thomas Q., QM2/c, USN
HINCH, Marvin O., CM1/c, USNR
HOFF, William N., MoMM2/c, USNR
HOLDER, Ralph J., CM2/c, USNR
HOLDGRUN, Henry A., GM2/c, USNR
HOXIE, Alton Shaw, Sc2/c, USN
HUGHES, Clyde P., S1/c, USNR
JASIONOWIEZ, Joseph, S1/c, USN
JOHNS, Robert W., BM2/c, USNR
JOHNS, William, Sp3/c, USNR
JOHNSON, Jerry, MoMM2/c, USNR
JONES, Loften "L," SP1/c, USNR
JURKOVICH, Lawrence Steve, BM2/c, USNR
KELLY, Frank J., GM1/c, USNR
KIRBY, Howard Joseph, RT1/c, USN
KITTRELL, Robert C., RM2/c, USNR
KLAIBER, Charles C., Jr., GM3/c, USNR
KNUDSON, Frank J., S1/c, USN
KOCH, William Hardy, BM1/c, USNR
KOHLBECK, Norvert A., S1/c, USNR
KOMAY, Peter, S1/c, USNR
KRAFKA, George A., Sp1/c, USNR
KRAMER, Robert W., Jr., Cox., USNR
KULL, Walter E., SF1/c, USN
LANGDON, John E., EM1/c, USNR
LAMBERT, Maurice J., EM1/c, USN
LE HOULIER, R., CM1/c, USNR
LEWIS, Elbert J., MM3/c, USNR
LILES, James, SM2/c, USN
LINKSWILER, Charles F., F1/c, USNR
LOVELACE, Leonard Davis, BM2/c, USNR
LOWES, James H., S1/c, USNR
LUPIEN, Raymond G., EM2/c, USNR
LUTTRELL, Robert E., S1/c, USNR
MACDONALD, John A., CM1/c, USNR
MARCEY, Joseph Theodore, Cox., USN
MARRA, John, SM3/c, USNR
McCAULEY, Daniel D., GM2/c, USNR
McHENRY, Roger, MoMM2/c, USNR
McINNIS, Joseph T., BM2/c, USNR

MICKELSON, Carl R., GM3/c, USNR
MILLER, Murray M., MM1/c, USNR
MOLLET, Oliver, CMM, USN
MONROE, Joseph E., GM3/c, USNR
MONTGOMERY, Richard W., F1/c, USNR
MONTGOMERY, Robert J., Cox., USNR
MORTENSON, D. W., SF1/c, USN
MULVEHILL, Paul Joseph, PhM1/c, USN
MURPHY, J., SF2/c, USNR
MYERS, H. A., S1/c, USN
NEUMANN, William A. B., Sp3/c, USNR
ORSILLO, Lawrence T., F1/c, USNR
PALMER, J. A., SF3/c, USNR
PAPI, Lawrence A., M3/c, USN
PATTERSON, Clyde, S2/c, USNR
PAZ, Ralph Barletta, SK3/c, USNR
PELTIER, Arthur, S3/c, USNR
PERRY, Wallace Richard, S1/c, USNR
PFEIFLE, C., F2/c, USN
PHILLIPS, Samuel M., Jr., S1/c, USNR
PRICE, Harry C., Mach., USNR
REDFERN, Edwin R., S1/c, USN
RIZZI, Anthony John, RM3/c, USNR
ROBERSON, E. O., S1/c, USN
ROBERTS, John H., MM3/c, USNR
ROOP, Roy Raines, BM2/c, USN
ROYER, Howard K., S2/c, USN
SANDERS, Anthony, Cox., USN
SANTORO, John Carmine, S1/c, USNR
SARICH, Paul, MM3/c, USNR
SEYMOUR, James Edward, GM3/c, USNR
SHENE, Howard A., SM2/c, USNR
SIMMONS, J. M., S2/c, USN
SMITH, Francis L., PhM3/c, USNR
SMITH, John L., 3rd Asst. Eng., USMM
SMITH, William Richard, F1/c, USN
STANISH, Dewey, MoMM1/c, USNR
STECK, Harmon C., Cox., USNR
STEPHENS, William Francis, GM3/c, USN
STEWART, Paul Robert, F1/c, USNR
STUDLEY, E. W., GM3/c, USNR
STUMPF, George Christopher, Sp(F)1/c, USNR
TAYLOR, Walter, S1/c, USN
TERRY, D. W., S2/c, USN
THOMAS, Herman H., GM3/c, USN
TOMANSZEWSKI, S., S2/c, USN
TOZIER, Ralph Hood, MoMM2/c, USNR
TRAFFLEY, John W., CMM, USN
URQUHART, John, CMM, USN
VARLAS, Sam, GM3/c, USNR
WALLACE, Ralph E., CCM, USNR
WARD, C. M., F1/c, USNR

WATKINS, G. A., Cox., USN
WATSON, W. T., SF2/c, USNR
WEBB, J. W., MoMM2/c, USNR
WHITE, Robert J., HA1/c, USNR
WILLIAMS, Marvin I., Cox., USNR
WOLF, Elmer C., S1/c, USNR
WOODALL, Marley Adams, MM1/c, USN
ZAJAC, Stanley S., F1/c, USNR

Air Medal

FIREY, Lt. Milton J., USNR
HOFMANN, Lt. William C., USNR
ANDRUS, Lt. (jg) William S., USNR
BRUSH, Lt. (jg) Roderick M., USNR
HARTNETT, Lt. (jg) E. T. J., USNR
KELLOGG, Lt. (jg) Edward W., USNR
SCHLATER, Lt. (jg) Donald Lawrence, USNR
ABRAM, Ens. William H., USNR
BOWEN, Ens. Frank B., USN
GILLESPIE, Ens. Hoyt O., USNR
HEATH, Ens. William W., USN
McCARTY, Ens. Richard D. J., USNR
McSHARRY, Ens. William F., USN
MacDOUGALL, Ens. James E., USNR
PETERSON, Ens. Kenneth C., USNR
ZINGER, Ens. Edward W., USNR
BERGE, William R., Jr., AMM2/c, USNR
BOLSINGER, Harry M., AOM1/c, USN
*BONANNO, Placido A., ARM2/c, USNR
CHAISSON, Adam J., ARM2/c, USNR
CHIAPULIS, Joseph P., AOM1/c, USN
CLAUSEN, Ehler F., ACMM, USN
COKER, Lester M., AOM2/c, USNR
COMSTOCK, Thomas A., AOM1/c, USNR
CRIDER, Marlin, ARM1/c, USN
CUMMINS, Melvin B., AMM1/c, USN
CUNNINGHAM, James A., Jr., ARM2/c, USNR
FRANKLIN, William N., AMM2/c, USNR
GRAVEL, Charles L., ARM2/c, USN
GREEN, Kenneth E., AMM3/c, USN
*HARRIS, Leo P., ACRM, USN
HENDERSON, Bobby G., AMM1/c, USN
HUDSON, Robert G., ARM3/c, USNR
JELLISON, Joseph V., AOM2/c, USNR
McKINNEY, William A., AMM3/c, USN
McLEAN, Robert Lewis, SK2/c, USNR
MARTIN, Billy F., AMM2/c, USN
MAUCH, John V., ARM2/c, USNR
MAYHEW, Delbert I., AMM2/c, USN
MURREN, Walter H., AMM2/c, USNR
OLENSKY, Stanley, AOM3/c, USNR
PAVAO, Vasco A., AMM3/c, USNR

PAWELEK, Walter J., ARM2/c, USN
PEARSON, Francis R., AMM2/c, USN
*SOCHA, Michael F., AMM2/c, USNR
STEWART, Charles E., ACMM, USN
TANNEBERG, Karl H., AMM1/c, USNR
TAYLOR, Wetherel W., AOM3/c, USNR
WARE, Paul F., AMM1/c, USN
WHALEN, Robert H., AP1/c, USN
WHITE, Ernest D., AMM1/c, USN
WILLENBORG, Edward J., Jr., ARM1/c, USN
WILLIAMSON, Algur K., AMM2/c, USNR

Bronze Star Medal

HUME, Brig. Gen. Edgar E., USA
EVANS, Capt. Donald S., USN
GILLAM, Capt. Edwin J., USN (Ret.)
HILBERT, Capt. William E., USN
WHITE, Capt. Robert J., (ChC), USNR
D'AVI, Cdr. Joseph A., USNR
BRENNAN, Cdr. Leo, USNR
FIELD, Cdr. Benjamin P., USN
FLYNN, Cdr. John F., USN
LEGWEN, Cdr. Glenn W., Jr., USN
MILLS, Cdr. Ralph E., USNR
REVILL, Cdr. Milton K., USN
SMILEY, Cdr. Clare B., USN
WILLIAMS, Cdr. Henry G., USN
ARTHUR, Lt. Cdr. Charles, USN
BORNE, Lt. Cdr. Herbert C., (SC), USN
CARTER, Lt. Cdr. Ulysses B., USN
CHURCH, Lt. Cdr. Al C., (CEC), USNR
DUKE, Lt. Cdr. Virgil D., USN
FITZGERALD, Lt. Cdr. Gerald S., USNR
FLECK, Lt. Cdr. Francis E., Jr., USN
FOLDS, Lt. Cdr. Charles W., (SC), USNR
FOWKES, Lt. Cdr. Luther F., USNR
FREEMAN, Lt. Cdr. Clark W., USNR
GEZON, Lt. Cdr. Horace M., (MC), USNR
HILL, Lt. Cdr. Hamilton D., USNR
HOFFMAN, Lt. Cdr. George, USNR
HULL, Lt. Cdr. Frank G., USNR
HULTMAN, Lt. Cdr. John M., USNR
JANNEY, Lt. Cdr. Samuel A., USNR
LENNOX, Lt. Cdr. Frank H., USNR
McCLELLAN, Lt. Cdr. Hubert M., USNR
MILLER, Lt. Cdr. Roger F., USNR
SCARFE, Lt. Cdr. George O., USNR
STEVENS, Lt. Cdr. John D., USN
ALLEN, Lt. Jesse D., USNR
ANDRIST, Lt. Ralph K., USNR
ANKERS, Lt. George M., USNR
BARTLETT, Lt. Russell D., USNR

BELKNAP, Lt. Robert E., Jr., USNR
BROWNELL, Lt. George G., USNR
EATON, Lt. Frank C., USN
ELLIS, Lt. Charles H., USNR
GLASS, Lt. Russell G., USNR
GREENBERG, Lt. Mack K., USNR
HUDSON, Lt. Edward H., Jr., USNR
HUTCHINSON, Lt. Leslie Luther, USNR
JENKINS, Lt. Robert P., USNR
LAURIE, Lt. Robert G., USN
LIANE, Lt. Delwin A., USN
MORLEY, Lt. Frank H., Jr., USNR
NAZRO, Lt. Thomas Wibird, USNR
NICKELS, Lt. Walter E., USNR
OAKES, Lt. Harry L., USNR
ORME, Lt. Samuel T., USNR
PATTERSON, Lt. Donald H., USNR
PATTERSON, Lt. Eugene F., USNR
PIERSON, Lt. William H., Jr., USNR
POPE, Lt. Ralph L., Jr., USNR
RUSTEEN, Lt. Milton A., USNR
ST. PIERRE, Lt. A. Stowell, USNR
SCHUH, Lt. Charles J., Jr., USNR
*SHIFFER, Lt. Kenneth F., USN
STERN, Lt. Bernard B., USNR
STOTZER, Lt. Stevens S., USNR
TELLING, Lt. William P., USNR
BARR, Lt. (jg) Joseph W., USNR
BARBER, Lt. (jg) Cornelius H., USNR
BLACK, Lt. (jg) Walter E., USNR
CHAPMAN, Lt. (jg) Charles H., USNR
DECKER, Lt. (jg) Joe F., USNR
DELHOMME, Lt. (jg) George A., Jr., USNR
GAGE, Lt. (jg) Hugh F., USNR
HICKMAN, Lt. (jg) Norman G., USNR
KWILECKI, Lt. (jg) Julian G., Jr., USNR
LEBER, Lt. (jg) Edward C., USNR
LEWIS, Lt. (jg) Richard E., USNR
MAKI, Lt. (jg) Edward A., USNR
MANCHESTER, Lt. (jg) D. J., USNR
POITEVENT, Lt. (jg) Eades, USNR
RILEY, Lt. (jg) Andrew J., USNR
SCHADEWALD, Lt. (jg) Melvin A., USNR
STEINMETZ, Lt. (jg) Kenneth R., USNR
WALDRON, Lt. (jg) John C., USNR
WOLFMAN, Lt. (jg) William A., (MC), USNR
HARLAN, Ens. Derrill E., USNR
MORGAN, Ens. Harry E., USNR
PEERY, Ens. George G., USN
PREBLE, Ens. Earl Casmer, USN
AINSWORTH, Walter J., S1/c, USNR
ANDERL, Arnold R., CY, USNR
ANDERSON, Horace W., GM3/c, USNR

AVERY, Claude Lowell, F1/c, USNR
BAKER, Reginald J., S1/c, USNR
BARRATT, James F., SF2/c, USN
BEHM, Arthur A., S1/c, USN
BISHOP, Stanley, S1/c, USNR
BOTICA, Florian John, GM3/c, USNR
BOYCE, Robert L., S1/c, USNR
D'ANDREA, Frank, AOM1/c, USNR
DAVENPORT, Joseph R., Chief Gunner, USN
FAIRBANKS, Arthur E., Y1/c, USNR
GOLDSTEIN, David, Cox., USNR
GROSSMAN, Joseph Frank, MoMM2/c, USNR
KARKKIANAN, Eino, CWT, USNR
KELLY, Robert T., SM3/c, USNR
KRASJECK, Stephen, MM1/c, USNR
MASTERS, Howard Arthur, RM2/c, USNR
NELSEN, Dale Junior, CPhM, USN
OGWDOWCZYK, Bernard, M2/c, USNR
PERRY, Patrick Philip, EM2/c, USNR
REYNARD, Henry, MoMM2/c, USN
SCHIMPF, Paul, GM3/c, USNR
SCHONFELD, George C., SF2/c, USNR
WYMAN, Henry Dibble, QM1/c, USN

NAVY UNIT COMMENDATION
UNITED STATES LCI (L) 1

For outstanding performance as a unit in a Task Force during the initial landings on Sicily in July, 1943. Moving in under a fierce barrage of hostile fire, the USS LCI (L) 1 suffered vital casualties which ruptured her communications and seriously wounded her helmsman and winchman. Thus, deprived of mechanical control, she broached and lay on the beach, raked by hostile artillery and machine-gun fire but still fighting gallantly and silencing several enemy guns ashore despite her helpless position. Repeatedly attacked from the air, her officers and crew remained steadfastly with their ship throughout the four-day period until she was again afloat and salvaged for further active duty.

Northern France

Navy Cross

BISHOP, Lt. Cdr. Claude U., USNR

For extraordinary heroism and conspicuous gallantry as a member of the United States Naval Advanced Reconnaissance Party attacked by superior and overwhelming enemy ground forces between Pontorsen and Dol, France, on August 2, 1944. Lieutenant Commander Bishop skillfully deployed and directed his men, who were untrained in infantry tactics, so as to prevent the encircling of the Reconnaissance Party and hold off the enemy until reinforcements arrived several hours later to cover the retreat of the party. After the death or injury of the Senior Officers, Lieutenant Commander Bishop assumed command of the party, contributing immeasurably towards saving the lives of the great majority of the naval and military personnel involved. Throughout the action, Lieutenant Commander Bishop did not fail to appreciate the superiority of the opposition and the relative inexperience of his own force and its lack of proper munitions. The orders he gave were clear and well conceived, and he made sure that every possible officer and man received them. While directing the defense of the party and organizing the withdrawal to safe ground, he remained in dangerously exposed positions, and his gallant action and leadership inspired confidence in those under his command. By displaying such courage and resourcefulness he succeeded in withdrawing the Reconnaissance Party with the minimum of casualties, notwithstanding the overwhelming superiority of the opposition.

MICHEL, Lt. Cdr. Edward A., Jr., USN

For extraordinary heroism and devotion to duty as Commanding Officer of the USS RICH on June 8, 1944. Lieutenant Commander Michel when directed to assist the USS GLENNON which was known to have struck an enemy mine, proceeded in his vessel with utmost dispatch with disregard of the danger from enemy gunfire and possible mines and stood by close aboard the stricken ship to render assistance. While attempting to assist that ship his own vessel struck and was destroyed by the explosion of two enemy mines. Lieutenant Commander Michel, despite severe injuries, including a broken leg, steadfastly refused to leave his ship and directed and assisted in the removal of all possible survivors until his ship sank beneath him. By his action and example, all able-bodied survivors on board were inspired to remain with the ship and assist in the rescue of the greatest possible number of men.

BLACK, Lt. Clarence H., USNR

For distinguishing himself by extraordinary heroism while attached to Assault Force "U" engaged in the assault upon the coast of France, 6 June 1944. Although his beach was under incessant enemy artillery fire, his executive officer killed and all personnel ordered to take cover, Lieutenant Black fearlessly exposed himself in order to direct the incoming assault waves to successful landings. By his courageous actions he made possible the beaching of twenty-seven waves of assault craft.

HALL, Lt. Frank Martin, (MC), USNR

For extraordinary heroism as Medical Officer in Charge of a Naval Beach Party Medical Team during the invasion of the Coast of France on June 6, 1944. Forced to swim three miles to shore when his own landing craft was sunk during the initial assault, Lieutenant (then Lieutenant, junior grade) Hall gallantly carried on his mission with such meager supplies as he was able to salvage from the dead and wounded. Completely unmindful of his own danger, he labored with untiring zeal under the terrific fire of the enemy, resolutely assuming command of all medical work on an additional beach when it was determined that the officer in charge was missing in action and, despite the extreme hazards and the grueling strain, skillfully covered two beaches without relief until the afternoon of D-plus-two day.

MORRIS, Lt. Robert A., USNR

For extraordinary heroism and courage as Commander of a Landing Craft Flotilla which spearheaded the assault on the beaches of France, on June 6, 1944. Lieutenant Morris fearlessly led his wave into the beach under intense fire from enemy guns of all calibres through uncleared obstacles. Although the craft in which he was stationed was hit repeatedly by 88mm shells and machine-gun fire and several of the personnel on board were killed he pressed his attack relentlessly.

POTTER, Lt. Charles S., USNR

For distinguishing himself by extracrdinary heroism against the enemy while coordinating beach activities under intense enemy shellfire during the assault on France, June 6, 1944. Lieutenant Potter, wounded by enemy shellfire, refused to be hospitalized and when all personnel had been ordered to take cover, he fearlessly exposed himself in order to direct incoming assault waves to successful landings.

ANDREASEN, Lt. (jg) Grant G., USNR

For conspicuous bravery in the performance of outstanding services as Scout Boat Officer during the amphibious assault on the coast of France, June 6, 1944. Lieutenant (junior grade) Andreasen embarked in one of the first craft to approach the strongly defended Normandy coast and succeeded in the highly important mission of locating the beaches to be assaulted. Despite heavy surf and harassing enemy fire, he went in close to the beach to act as a guide for the approaching wave of DD tanks. While he was in this advanced position he fired the rockets from his craft at target objectives, moved in closer to the beach, and rendered close fire support to the infantry assault waves. In addition to his assigned duties, without regard for his own personal safety and under heavy enemy fire he rescued wounded personnel from burning landing craft and carried them to safety.

BRANDEL, Lt. (jg) Stuart L., USNR

For conspicuous heroism and exceptionally meritorious performance of duty as Naval Gunfire Liaison Officer in the assault on the coast of Normandy, France, June 6, 1944. Lieutenant (junior grade) Brandel was attached to the Sixteenth Regimental Combat Team and was scheduled to land in the second wave. The boat in which he was embarked was twice driven off in attempting to land, and half of Lieutenant (junior grade) Brandel's party was killed or wounded. Quickly grasping the situation, he set up his radio in the boat and established communications with a supporting cruiser. He was able to fire several very effective missions at a most critical juncture. Later he landed and finding his forward observer seriously wounded, reorganized his party and took over the duties of forward observer in addition to his own. Although under heavy enemy gunfire he continued to call for and adjust fire which was of marked effect on enemy positions and aided materially in the advance of the army units to which he was attached.

*BUCKLEW, Lt. (jg) Phil Hinkle, USNR

For extraordinary heroism as Scout Boat Officer during the amphibious assault on the Normandy Coast of France, June 6, 1944. Embarked in one of the first craft to approach the strongly defended coast, Lieutenant (junior grade) Bucklew successfully accomplished his highly important mission of locating the designated beaches and, despite rough surf and continuous, harassing enemy fire, skillfully led the first wave of DD tanks, going in close to the beach and taking his station as guide. Firing his boat's rockets over the tanks at target objectives in support of the landings, he moved in closer to direct his guns at suspected hostile machine-gun nests in houses along the beach and subsequently, in the face of heavy enemy opposition, rescued wounded personnel from burning landing craft and regulated the flow of traffic throughout the morning and afternoon of D-Day.

JENKINS, Lt. (jg) William Maxwell, USNR

For extraordinary heroism while serving as Officer in Charge of Naval Combat Demolition Unit 43 during the amphibious assault on the Normandy Coast of France, June 6, 1944. Although the LCT to which he was attached sank prior to H-Hour, Lieutenant (junior grade) Jenkins salvaged his vital equipment and, directing his crew skillfully and with aggressive determination despite intense hostile gunfire, successfully accomplished the extremely difficult mission of blowing a fifty-yard gap through the enemy seaward band of beach obstacles. When one of his men was killed while preparing a demolition charge, he unhesitatingly completed the task himself and personally placed a number of charges, subsequently supervising his crew in helping other groups to clear the inward band of obstacles.

NORTON, Lt. (jg) Kenneth S., USNR

For extraordinary heroism and exceptionally meritorious performance of duty as Naval Gunfire Liaison Officer in the assault on Normandy, France, on June 6 and 7, 1944. Lieutenant Junior Grade Norton landed with the first wave of Rangers at the base of Pointe Du Hoe. He was one of the first up the cliff. When the Second Rangers were surrounded by enemy troops in superior numbers, Lieutenant (junior grade) Norton called for and adjusted fire in great volume and with marked accuracy and effect throughout the day. Without this accurate fire it is probable that the Rangers could not have survived. On the evening of D-Day, Lieutenant (junior grade) Norton's forward observer was killed and Lieutenant (junior grade) Norton was wounded. He nevertheless continued his efforts, organized an emergency shore fire control net and successfully directed several additional fire-support missions. After being evacuated and treated on the USS TEXAS he returned to the battlefield to take up his regular duties.

PARROTT, Lt. (jg) John Oliver, USNR

For extraordinary heroism in combat against the enemy while serving as First Lieutenant in the USS CORRY near St. Vaast, coast of France, on June 6, 1944. After the word had been given to abandon ship, and while the ship was sinking under the gunfire of shore batteries, Lieutenant (junior grade) Parrott went down into the forward fireroom of the ship to rescue a Water Tender third class trapped under the grating of the upper level, who was swimming in fuel oil and water. The atmosphere of the fireroom was filled with live steam. At extreme risk to his own life, Lieutenant (junior grade) Parrott went under the grating and pulled the enlisted man to safety.

ROCK, Lt. (jg) John R., USNR

For extraordinary heroism and outstanding devotion to duty while engaged in action against the enemy during the initial landings on the coast of France June 6, 1944. Lieutenant (junior grade) Rock, observing that the LCT(5) was in sinking condition, with the Officer in Charge severely wounded, directed the evacuation of the stricken officer and leaving his own ship in command of his assistant, boarded the sinking craft to successfully beach it, and discharge its load. He further displayed courage and heroism when after the craft was hit and completely disabled by enemy shells, he swam ashore for medical assistance, despite the handicap of a broken arm sustained as a result of the concussion from enemy fire.

ROCKWELL, Lt. (jg) Dean L., USNR

For extraordinary skill and courageous devotion to duty as Group Commander of LCT's carrying tanks to the beaches June 6, 1944, Lieutenant (junior grade) Rockwell in the face of very heavy enemy fire, conducted the LCT's to the beach and discharged the tanks on the ground. By quick and sound decision he was able to land all these tanks at the correct spot and, by skillful handling, incurred only a minimum of damage to his ships.

KARNOWSKI, Ens. L. J., USNR

For extraordinary heroism in operations against the enemy as Officer in Charge of a Naval Combat Demolition Unit participating in the invasion of France on June 6, 1944. Ensign Karnowski although under heavy artillery and rifle fire succeeded in clearing a fifty yard gap through the enemy beach obstacles. He exposed himself to enemy fire to rescue a wounded member of his crew in danger of drowning in the rising tide and time after time returned alone to place charges to widen the gap when the rest of his crew had been killed or wounded. When tidal conditions made further demolition impossible, he tended wounded along the beach and assisted in the evacuation of casualties in the absence of sufficient medical personnel.

WILHOIT, Ens. William L., USNR

For extraordinary heroism as Relief Officer on board the USS LCT 540 during landing and support operations on the Normandy Coast of France beginning June 6, 1944. Severely wounded during the first moments of the assault when nine shattering blasts from German 88-mm. cannon crippled his ship, killed his Officer in Charge, killed or wounded six Army personnel and injured seven crewmen, Ensign Wilhoit unhesitatingly assumed command and despite his extreme youth and lack of combat experience maneuvered the now unwieldy craft toward the beach through German-emplaced obstacles and mines. Intrepid in the face of continued punishing gunfire and unwavering under the gruelling day and night duty of the ensuing four days, Ensign Wilhoit faithfully carried on his mission and, by his own great valor, inspired his loyal crew to supreme effort in the repeated landing of equipment, supplies and troops vital to assault operations.

BARBOUR, Loran E., ACOM, USNR

For extraordinary heroism in combat while in command of a Naval Demolition Unit engaged in the invasion of France, June 6, 1944. Barbour facing heavy machine gun and artillery fire showed exceptional bravery, leadership and initiative in the placing of charges and the blowing of a fifty yard gap in enemy beach obstacles. Although severely wounded, he calmly directed marking of the gap through which troops could be landed, and directed his men after completion of their mission to assist in aiding the wounded and evacuating casualties.

BASS, Robert Willis, GM2/c, USNR

For extraordinary heroism in combat while serving as a member of a Naval Combat Demolition Unit participating in the assault on France on 6 June 1944. Bass and his crew although subjected to heavy artillery, machine gun and rifle fire succeeded in blowing a fifty yard gap through the beach obstacles. As a result of enemy fire seven of the twelve-man crew were killed or wounded and a large share of the extra work fell on Bass, who performed the duties coolly and capably without regard to personal safety. Upon completion of the mission Bass further exposed himself to enemy fire and was wounded while carrying injured crew mates to safety.

BRIDGES, Robert Arthur, BM2/c, USNR

For extraordinary heroism and outstanding devotion to duty in action against the enemy during the assault phase of the invasion of France on June 6, 1944. Bridges, with disregard for his own safety, worked tirelessly in an effort to unload vehicles and personnel from a United States Landing Craft Tank, exposing himself in so doing to heavy machine gun and artillery fire. He further displayed heroism when, after assisting in the evacuation of the wounded from his own ship, he boarded another Landing Craft Tank and manned a 20 mm. gun to engage an enemy machine gun nest, enabling soldiers to move forward on the beach without opposition from this emplacement.

BRYAN, Brady Lawson, CMM, USN

For extraordinary heroism and outstanding devotion to duty in saving the lives of four injured men by carrying them out of a totally dark, shattered and flooded engineroom under hazardous conditions on 8 June, 1944, when the USS MEREDITH struck an enemy mine while engaged in supporting the assault on France. Bryan was in charge of the watch in the after engineroom when the ship struck a mine. Although dazed, he made his way out of the engineroom, but upon learning that the twelve men of his watch were still below, he, with total disregard for his own safety, and realizing that the room was flooded to within four feet of the overhead, went below and succeeded in rescuing four badly injured members of the crew who otherwise would have gone down with the ship.

LINE, John H., GM2/c, USNR

For extraordinary heroism under fire as a member of Naval Combat Demolition Unit 22 which participated in the assault on the coast of France on June 6, 1944. Line was a member of Naval Combat Demolition Unit 22 whose mission it was to land on the beach at H/3 minutes and blow a fifty yard gap in the enemy placed obstacles on the beach. Although half of the crew were killed before their mission was completed, Line with surviving members carried on and successfully completed their mission in the face of heavy enemy gunfire. After successfully completing this mission, Line directed incoming craft through the gap which had been blown. He exposed himself on numerous occasions while administering to and removing wounded personnel to places of safety.

McKEE, Augustus Bernard, HA1/c, USNR

For distinguishing himself by gallantry and intrepidity in action as a member of a naval beach party medical team landing with assault forces on the beaches of the Normandy coast of France, June 6, 1944. McKee, Hospital Apprentice First Class, cut off from the remainder of his unit and working under intense enemy fire with utter disregard for his own safety attended the wounded with such skill and devotion to duty as unquestionably to have resulted in the saving of many lives. His own landing craft having been sunk at sea, he had lost all of his medical supplies before reaching the beach. Working with such meager supplies as he was able to salvage from the dead and wounded, and all the while working under intense machine gun and sniper fire, McKee attended the wounded and comforted the dying with utter disregard for his own safety until help reached him several hours later.

MARKHAM, J. N., WT1/c, USNR

For extraordinary heroism in combat as a member of a Naval Combat Demolition Unit participating in the assault on France, June 6, 1944. When the Officer in Charge of his unit was killed on landing, Markham assumed command of the remainder of his unit and blew a partial gap in the enemy beach obstacles. After leading injured members of his crew to safety, he assisted other units in demolition, succeeded in saving three men buried as a result of a cavein caused by a shell explosion, and for forty-eight hours directed his men in the clearance of beach obstacles with commandeered equipment after explosives for the purpose had been expended.

SHIELDS, Arthur Virgil, EM1/c, USNR

For heroism above and beyond the call of duty in unhesitatingly plunging to the aid of two drowning soldiers in water under enemy shellfire on the Omaha beach, 6 June 1944. Although tired from swimming ashore with grapnel and line to test the depth of the water before disembarking troops, and although he had voluntarily made the trip once through shrapnel-splashed water, Shields did not hesitate to jump in once more when he saw the two soldiers in dire need of aid. Through his efforts, the lives of these men were saved and they were carried through the deep water to the shore. Later, he went aboard the USS LCI(L) 416 disabled on the beach because of mines and shellfire. In helping to carry a wounded member of the crew of that ship along the beach, Shields was killed by shrapnel.

TEETER, Herman Joseph, S1/c, USNR

For extraordinary heroism and outstanding devotion to duty while serving as senior petty officer aboard a landing craft which struck a mine and subsequently sank during the direct assault on France, June 6, 1944. Teeter as a result of the explosion was thrown clear of the ship; after landing in the water he swam back to the ship, climbed aboard, cut off the float nets, and directed the abandonment of the craft, all of the officers aboard having been thrown clear or being so sorely wounded as to be incapable of commanding the crew. Under his supervision, members of the crew took off various shipmates who had been wounded and aided the wounded men in the water clinging to the nets and rafts until help arrived.

Army Distinguished Service Medal

STARK, Adm. Harold R., USN

Commander of the United States Naval Forces in Europe. Admiral Stark was responsible for the planning, preparation and coordination of the United States naval aspects of the launching of the campaign for the liberation of Europe. Through keen foresight and exceptional administrative ability, Admiral Stark was able to plan for and meet the necessary personnel and materiel requirements for this enormous operation. Only through his untiring efforts was the accomplishment of this successful invasion completed.

KIRK, Vice Adm. Alan G., USN

Vice Admiral Kirk directed the planning for and execution of the naval phases of the landings in the United States Zone in France on June 6, 1944. He coordinated the operations of the assault and support forces, including the establishment of the naval part of the beach organization and the direct support of ground operations by gun fire up to and including the capture of Cherbourg on June 27, 1944.

HALL, Rear Adm. John L., Jr., USN

Commander of Assault Force "O" in the amphibious invasion of the coast of Normandy, commencing on June 6, 1944. Rear Admiral Hall conducted his assault against enemy opposition on the coast of Normandy with great skill and determination. He landed the V Corps, United States Army, on selected beaches against determined opposition.

MOON, Rear Adm. Don Pardee, USN

Commander of Assault Force "U" in the amphibious invasion of the coast of Normandy, commencing on June 6, 1944. Rear Admiral Moon operated his forces during the assault period of the invasion against enemy opposition and successfully landed the VII Corps, United States Army, on the selected beaches in the Madeleine area.

WILKES, Rear Adm. John, USN

Commander of the United States Naval Landing Craft and Bases in Europe. Admiral Wilkes was charged with the responsibility for the naval aspects of training all United States Navy and Army personnel in amphibious operations and preparing all landing ships and craft to be used in the assault.

Legion of Merit

BRYANT, Rear Adm. Carleton Fanton, USN

Commander of the Gunfire Support Group of Assault Force "O" during the amphibious invasion of the enemy German-held coast of Normandy, June 6, 1944.

DEYO, Rear Adm. Morton Lyndholm, USN

Commander of the Gunfire Support Group of Assault Force "U" during the amphibious invasion of the enemy German-held coast of Normandy, June 6, 1944.

STRUBLE, Rear Adm. Arthur D., USN

Chief of Staff of the Western Naval Task Force previous to and during the amphibious assault on the enemy German-held coast of Normandy, June 6, 1944.

EDGAR, Commodore Campbell D., USN

Commander of Follow-Up Force "B" during the planning, training and assault on the enemy German-held coast of Normandy, June 6, 1944.

FLANIGAN, Commodore Howard Adams, USN (Ret.)

Deputy Chief of Staff of Commander, TWELFTH FLEET, prior to and during the amphibious invasion of the European continent in June, 1944.

MORAN, Commodore Edmond Joseph, USNR

Coordinated the movement of the tugs of the different services and Allied nations and directed a unique and extremely hazardous operation.

BATCHELDER, Capt. Robert F., USN

Force Supply Officer, Western Naval Task Force, planned for and provided for the necessary supplies during the planning and operational phases of the amphibious assault landing on the coast of Normandy, France.

CLARK, Capt. Augustus D., USN

In charge of the planning for the cross-channel movement, installation and operation of the artificial port established off St. Laurent, Normandy, France.

**CONVERSE, Capt. Adelbert F., USN

Commander of Screening Destroyers during the invasion of Normandy, France, June 6 to 15, 1944, and during the engagement with enemy coastal batteries in the area of the Port of Cherbourg, France, June 25, 1944.

FRESEMAN, Capt. William L., USN

Commander Destroyer Squadron SIXTY during the assault on Normandy, France June 6, 1944, and the bombardment of enemy installations at Cherbourg on June 25, 1944.

FRITZCHE, Capt. E. H., USCG

Commander of an Assault Group both in the preparation and execution of the amphibious assault on the coast of France June 6, 1944.

HEATH, Capt. John P., USN

Force Aviator of the Western Naval Task Force for the invasion of Normandy in Northern France, June 6, 1944.

JACKSON, Capt. Milton "C", USNR

Shipping Officer of the Twelfth Fleet, Captain Jackson was responsible for the conduct of the Port Offices in the United Kingdom, the movement of vessels carrying U. S. Naval supplies to the U.K. and the preparation and loading of vessels carrying U. S. naval supplies for the assault on France.

JESCHKE, Col. Richard H., USMC

Force Marine Officer and as assistant planning officer during the planning and training phases, and as a joint operations officer Western Naval Task Force, during the amphibious assault landing and subsequent operations in Normandy, France, from 1 June to 1 July 1944.

JOHANNESEN, Capt. John R., USN

Commander of a major subdivision of Task Force 126.

*LITTLE, Capt. Marion N., USN

Planning Officer and Assistant Chief of Staff for Commander Eleventh Amphibious Force during the preparation and execution of the assault on the coast of France, June 6, 1944.

McSHANE, Capt. Ralph E., USN

Logistics Officer of the Western Naval Task Force, coordinated all matters of maintenance and supply during the planning and preparation for the allied invasion of Normandy in Northern France, commencing on June 6, 1944, and administered these services during the assault landing, the follow-up and the build-up.

**Maynard, Capt. George E., USN

Commander Transport Division FIVE under Commander Assault Force "U". This U.S. Navy Assault Force successfully landed the Seventh Corps, U. S. Army on the Cherbourg Peninsula of France against well prepared defenses and strong opposition on 6 June 1944.

*Mitchell, Capt. Edward A., USN

Force Planning Officer and Assistant Chief of Staff of the Western Naval Task Force, planned and executed the allied assault landing, commencing on 6 June 1944, and the follow-up and build-up for the Normandy campaign in Northern France.

*Murdaugh, Capt. Albert C., USN

Deputy Commander of the Area Screen during sustained operations against the enemy in the Bay of the Seine, Normandy, France, from June 6 to June 29, 1944.

Ragonnet, Capt. Lucien, USN

Force Intelligence Officer of the Western Naval Task Force did by his professional skill coordinate all intelligence activities of this force, collect and disseminate much accurate and valuable data for the successful invasion of Normandy, France, on June 6, 1944.

Richardson, Capt. Myron T., USN

Plans and Operations Officer on the Staff of Commander Assault Force "U". This U.S. Navy Assault Force successfully landed the Seventh Corps, U. S. Army on the Cherbourg peninsula of France during the period 6 June to 24 June 1944.

*Sabin, Capt. Lorenzo S., Jr., USN

Commander Gunfire Support Craft during the amphibious attack on the coast of France, June 6, 1944.

Shaw, Capt. John Drake, USN

In command of a main group of assault forces during the preparation and execution of the amphibious assault on the coast of Normandy, France, launched 6 June 1944.

*Shulten, Capt. Leo B., USN

Commander of an Assault Group prior to and during the amphibious assault on the coast of France, June 6, 1944.

Spencer, Capt. Lyndon, USCG

Commanding Officer USS BAYFIELD, the Flagship of Rear Admiral Don P. Moon, USN, Commander Task Force "U."

*Tompkins, Capt. Rutledge B., USN

Chief of Staff to Commander Assault Force "U" during the period 6 June to 24 June 1944.

*Von Heimburg, Capt. Ernest H., USN

Chief of Staff for Commander, Eleventh Amphibious Force during the preparation and execution of the assault on the coast of France, June 6, 1944.

*Bays, Cdr. John W., USN

Commander Bays, Force Operations, Western Naval Task Force, during the planning and training phases and during the amphibious assault landing of the First U. S. Army from June 6, 1944 to June 30, 1944, contributed to success of Normandy Campaign.

Benson, Cdr. William Lewis, USN

Division Commander of Destroyer Division THIRTY FOUR, in the Bay of the Seine, Normandy, France, June 6, to July 4, 1944.

Cameron, Cdr. Thomas Stevenson, USN

Commander of a convoy consisting of thirteen LCI (L)'s and escorts, Commander Cameron was charged with the coordination and execution of plans for organizing his convoy, sailing it to the Bay of the Seine through difficult swept channels, and discharging the embarked troops in the face of considerable enemy artillery fire on the beaches at that time.

Caruthers, Cdr. William R., USN

Communications Officer (U.S. Section) attached to the Staff of Allied Naval Commander-in-Chief, Expeditionary Force, planning and operational phases of the assault on Normandy, France.

GREENAWALT, Cdr. William P., USNR

Officer-in-Charge of the Eighty-first Naval Construction Battalion, during the period of preparation for, and participation in the invasion of Normandy, France, June 1944.

GREENE, Cdr. Terance Warner, USN

Commander of a major subdivision of Task Force 126 charged with the coordination and execution of the plans for organizing his convoy, sailing it to the Bay of the Seine through difficult swept channels and discharging the embarked troops and equipment in spite of repeated enemy air attacks.

JARDINE, Cdr. Douglas C., USNR

Officer in Charge of the One Hundred Eleventh U.S. Naval Construction Battalion during the period of preparation for and participation in the invasion of Normandy.

KIME, Cdr. Frederick D., USN

Force Communications Officer of the Western Naval Task Force during the amphibious landing in Normandy, France, commencing on June 6, 1944.

MILLER, Cdr. Charles H. K., USN

Operations Officer on the Staff of Commander, Eleventh Amphibious Force, in the preparation and execution of the amphibious assault on the coast of France, June 6, 1944.

NEWTON, Cdr. Frank Herbert, Jr., USN

Commander of a group of LST's during the invasion of France in June 1944.

STALLINGS, Cdr. G. B. H., USN

Staff operations and gunnery officer of Commander Battleship Division FIVE during the assault phase of the invasion of France.

STANFORD, Cdr. A. B., USNR

Coordinated the units of the U. S. Navy, U. S. Army, the British Army, and the Royal Navy for the preparation of the invasion of France, June 1943.

BOATWRIGHT, Lt. Cdr. Victor T., Jr., USNR

Gunnery Officer attached to the Staff of Commander Eleventh Amphibious Force, both in the preparation and execution of the amphibious assault on the coast of France, June 6, 1944.

BULKELEY, Lt. Cdr. John D., USN

Command of motor torpedo boat squadrons which participated in the operations in the Bay of the Seine, France from June 6, to July 14, 1944 during the invasion of Normandy.

O'NEIL, Lt. Cdr. Frank, USN

Commander LST Division and Commanding Officer of the USS LST 7 prior to and during the amphibious invasion of France, June, 1944.

AMONDOLARO, Lt. (jg) Joseph V., USNR

Naval Gunfire Liaison Officer attached to the Commanding General Twenty-ninth Division Artillery during the assault on the coast of Normandy, France, June 6 through June 30, 1944.

Silver Star Medal

IMLAY, Capt. Miles H., USCG
RHEA, Capt. Powell McClellan, USN
RICHARDS, Capt. Frederick G., USN
SENN, Capt. Elliott M., USN
WALLER, Capt. John Beresford Wynn, USN
WRIGHT, Capt. W. D., Jr., USN
*BECTON, Cdr. Frederick J., USN
BEER, Cdr. Robert O., USN
BILLINGSLEY, Cdr. Edward B., USN
CALLAHAN, Cdr. Joseph W., USN
CARUSI, Cdr. Eugene C., USNR
CURTIN, Cdr. Neale R., USN
DUNN, Cdr. William A., USN
FOLEY, Cdr. Joseph F., USN
HUGHES, Cdr. William C., Jr., USN
JOHNSON, Cdr. Clifford A., USN
LEEVER, Cdr. Lawrence C., USNR
LONGTON, Cdr. Ernest W., USN
MARSHALL, Cdr. James Gilbert, USN
MARSHALL, Cdr. William J., USN

MATHEWS, Cdr. Mitchell D., USN
MOORE, Cdr. Granville A., USN
NILON, Cdr. Leo William, USN
OUTERBRIDGE, Cdr. William W., USN
OUTERSON, Cdr. William, USN
*PALMER, Cdr. George G., USN
PLANDER, Cdr. Henry, USN
RENKEN, Cdr. Henry A., USN
STUART, Cdr. Daniel A., USN
UNGER, Cdr. Aden C., USCG
WALPOLE, Cdr. Kinloch C., USN
WOLVERTON, Cdr. Royal A., USN
BLENMAN, Lt. Cdr. William, USN
BROWN, Lt. Cdr. Harold V., USNR
GEBELIN, Lt. Cdr. Albert Louis, USN
GIBBONS, Lt. Cdr. Joseph H., USNR
HAYS, Lt. Cdr. Alphord, USN
HOFFMAN, Lt. Cdr. George D., USN
KLEE, Lt. Cdr. William M., USN
LEACH, Lt. Cdr. Robert W., USN
LEIDE, Lt. Cdr. William, USNR
LOVELAND, Lt. Cdr. Kenneth, USN
McGRATH, Lt. Cdr. Thomas D., USN
MURRAY, Lt. Cdr. Hugh Q., USN
PRUITT, Lt. Cdr. Lanceferd B., USNR
RAMEY, Lt. Cdr. Ralph L., USN
REID, Lt. Cdr. James G., USNR
*SEMMES, Lt. Cdr. James L., USN
SEWELL, Lt. Cdr. Rancy F., USNR
WESTERBERG, Lt. Cdr. Hjalmar Enoch, USNR
WILSON, Lt. Cdr. "JC" G., USN
ALLISON, Lt. Sam, USCG
BERGER, Lt. Bennie, USNR
CORSI, Lt. Albert J., USNR
FOX, Lt. Lyman Bernard, USNR
GISLASON, Lt. Gene R., USCGR
LAMBIE, Lt. John E., Jr., USNR
LEAVITT, Lt. Edward J., USNR
RICHARDS, Lt. Floyd E., USN
SALMON, Lt. Robert E., USCGR
SCHUH, Lt. Charles J., USNR
SMITH, Lt. Robert C. (CEC), USNR
WAKEFIELD, Lt. Griffith C., USNR
BERRY, Lt. (jg) Roy F., Jr., USNR
*CLARK, Lt. (jg) James W., USNR
COKER, Lt. (jg) Coit M., USNR
HENDLEY, Lt. (jg) Coit T., USCGR
HUTCHINSON, Lt. (jg) George F., Jr., USNR
KALMER, Lt. (jg) Louis, USNR
KOREN, Lt. (jg) Paul H. (MC), USNR
LOVELL, Lt. (jg) Stewart F., USNR
McCLELLAN, Lt. (jg) John William, USNR

PEASE, Lt. (jg) Everett W., USNR
VYN, Lt. (jg) Arend, Jr., USCGR
ALLEN, Ens. J. C. (CEC), USNR
BENEDETTI, Ens. Gene M., USNR
CANNASTRA, Ens. Frederick J., USNR
FEHLIG, Ens. Eugene A., USNR
GILBERT, Ens. R. B., USNR
MOSES, Ens. Frederick Nye, Jr., USNR
MURPHY, Ens. J. Carter, USNR
PELLEGRINI, Ens. A. J., USNR
SUOZZO, Ens. Joseph M., USNR
BERGAN, Louis Clifford, CM1/c, USNR
BERNSON, Elmer Rudolph, F1/c, USNR
BLACKMAN, James Horace, F1/c, USNR
BUCK, Clarence, S1/c, USNR
BUFFINGTON, E., MM2/c, USNR
DELLAPIANO, S. J., S2/c, USNR
DEVER, Jerold Donald, S1/c, USN
DOLAN, J. N., S2/c, USNR
DYER, James Albert, S2/c, USNR
FARMER, Hansen Eugene, Cox., USNR
FILTON, F. M., S1/c, USNR
HALL, C. T., GM2/c, USNR
JACOBSON, J. A., CBM, USNR
JOHNAKIN, Edward K., BM1/c, USN
JONES, Arthur, StM1/c, USNR
JONES, L. J., Jr., Cox., USNR
LA CROIX, Abraham, PhM1/c, USNR
MAGUIRE, A. C., MM2/c, USNR
MALONEY, Edward Lynch, GM2/c, USNR
MARQUARD, Carl F., Jr., Sp1/c(p), USNR
MARVEL, J. S., Cox., USN
MEYERS, Lester J., MM2/c, USNR
MOOBERRY, Merril Quentin, BM2/c, USNR
OXLEY, Gene E., S1/c, USCGR
RAYMER, N. E., Carp. (CEC), USNR
ROBERTS, Harvey J., SC3/c, USNR
SCHMIDT, Frederick R., MM1/c, USNR
STEGMEIER, Francis H., Cox., USNR
TRUMP, William F., MoMM1/c, USCGR
VERDON, Ernest P., PhM2/c, USN
WARD, Robert G., S1/c, USCGR
WEATHERFORD, Milton P., GM2/c, USNR

Distinguished Flying Cross

BARCLEY, Lt. Richard M., USNR
CAHILL, Lt. Francis A., USNR
HILL, Lt. Palmer G., USNR
SMITH, Lt. Alexander A., USNR
LATHROP, Lt. (jg) W. P., USNR
ZINN, Lt. (jg) Charles S., USNR
ADAMS, Ens. R. J., USNR
CRAWFORD, Ens. L. K., USNR

Navy and Marine Corps Medal

SCHERRER, Lt. Carl L., USNR
BUFFUM, Lt. (jg) Thomas B., Jr., USNR
KIBBEY, Lt. (jg) Mead B., USNR
McPHAIL, Lt. (jg) Richard V., USCGR
WHITTLE, Ens. Alexander A., USNR
ADAMS, Lloyd L., Jr., MoMM2/c, USNR
ALEXANDER, Ronald M., Y1/c, USNR
BALCOM, Charles E., S2/c, USNR
BANKS, George I., SC2/c, USCG
BARBER, Carter, Sp1/c, USCG
BETZ, George E., S1/c, USCGR
BLOOM, Melvin Joseph, S2/c, USNR
BOYETTE, James, S1/c, USCG
BREWER, Charles Erastus, CMM, USN
BREWER, James S., PhM3/c, USNR
BURKHARD, Arthur H., Jr., Cox., USCG
CANTWELL, John F., F1/c, USCGR
CARR, D. C., GM2/c, USNR
CHEEVER, William A., CBM, USCG
DARE, R. C., MM3/c, USNR
DODD, Neal D., SoM3/c, USCG
DOUGHERTY, Ellis C., SF2/c, USNR
ESCLAVON, Joseph Henry, MoMM1/c, USNR
EVERSFIELD, William, S1/c, USCG
FINGER, Helmuth C., GM2/c, USNR
HANNIGAN, John F., BM2/c, USCG
HANSON, Charles Oscar, SC3/c, USNR
HARRIS, Sherwood L., S1/c, USNR
HARRIS, Stanley T., S1/c, USN
HUMPHREYS, Frederick G., CMoMM, USNR
IVY, Charles B., MoMM1/c, USCG
JOHANNESEN, Robert C., QM3/c, USNR
KASHINSKAS, Jerome F., MoMM1/c, USCG
EIRSCHMAN, Henry Manheim, USNR
KLAIBER, Charles C., Jr., CM3/c, USNR
KLIMACEK, Samuel, MoMM3/c, USNR
KOZUB, Paul, MoMM1/c, USNR
LOFTON, John Hale, S1/c, USCGR
LORENZO, Joseph, F2/c, USNR
McMILLAN, William M., BM1/c, USCG
MESQUITA, William, SM2/c, USNR
MORROW, Robert L., GM1/c, USN
MUELLER, Elmer H., EM3/c, USNR
NEWMAN, Thomas, CM3/c, USNR
NORTH, James B., BM2/c, USCG
OVERDIER, Harley Andrew, MoMM3/c, USNR
PERKINS, William Amster, S1/c, USNR
PETERMANN, Lester L., CPhM, USN
POE, Thurman W., HA2/c, USNR

RIGGLEMAN, Eugene Martin, CM2/c, USNR
ROBY, Carl Lewis, SM3/c, USNR
SHORT, Willie, S1/c, USNR
STINE, Richard D., MoMM1/c, USNR
SUTINEN, Wesley M., BM2/c, USCG
SWEENEY, William F., GM3/c, USCG
SWIERG, Michael J., MoMM2/c, USCG
TALTON, Douglas H., RM3/c, USNR
VAUGHN, E. W., S1/c, USNR
VAUGHN, Wendell Marvin, S1/c, USNR
WEISS, Rudolph, MoMM2/c, USNR

Bronze Star Medal

MANNING, Rear Adm. John J., USN
WILSON, Rear Adm. George B., USN
BAKER, Capt. Charles A., USN
BERG, Capt. W. M., USMM
BROWN, Capt. Clarence J. (MC), USN
CAMPBELL, Capt. William S., USN
CHAMBERS, Capt. John H. (MC), USN
GOFF, Capt. H. L. (MC), USN
HALME, Capt. W. H., USMM
HAYMAN, Capt. D. W., USMM
HUGHES, Capt. F. J., USMM
JESSEY, Capt. H., USMM
LIVINGSTON, Capt. S. E., USMM
MILLIS, Capt. William B., USN
NOWELL, Capt. R. S., USMM
PARKIN, Capt C. I., USMM
PUBLICOVER, Capt. W. J., USMM
SHELLEY, Capt. Tully, USN
AITKENS, Cdr. Lloyd John, USN
ARD, Cdr. Lignon B., USNR
BAKER, Cdr. Robert de Coursey, USN
BARBARO, Cdr. Joseph R., USN
BIESEMEIER, Cdr. Harold, USN
BUHR, Cdr. Victor W. (CEC), USNR
DICKEY, Cdr. George Deane, USN
DUFFILL, Cdr. Monroe B., USN
EDWARDS, Cdr. John A., USN
HUIE, Cdr. Byron S., Jr., USNR
GILLIAM, Cdr. Charles R., USN
LEAHY, Cdr. William I., USN
LOWE, Cdr. Edward S. (MC), USN
McCARLEY, Cdr. Henry Harris, USN
MELLING, Cdr. R. E., USN
PEARSON, Cdr. Mead S., USN
PRYCE, Cdr. Roland F., USN
REITER, Cdr. Harry L., Jr., USN
ROBINSON, Cdr. Allan M., USNR
SARGENT, Cdr. Walter S., USNR
SINGLETON, Cdr. Charles Tod, Jr., USN
WARBURTON, Cdr. Audley L., USN

WILSON, Cdr. Edward W., USNR
YEAGER, Cdr. Howard Austin, USN
CAMPBELL, Lt. Col. Fred P., USA
ASHLER, Lt. Cdr. Philip Frederic, USN
BAINES, Lt. Cdr. Jack B., USNR
BALLINGER, Lt. Cdr. Richard H., USNR
BARRY, Lt. Cdr. Richard P., Jr., USN
BASSETT, Lt. Cdr. J. A., USNR
BERGER, Lt. Cdr. Nels L. A., USNR
BOLTZ, Lt. Cdr. Philip M., USN
BUCKLEY, Lt. Cdr. Walter John, USNR
CARDEZA, Lt. Cdr. Carlos Martinez, USNR
CASSEL, Lt. Cdr. Charles M., USN
COCKEY, Lt. Cdr. R. K., USNR
COOK, Lt. Cdr. Allen Pearcy, USN
CRAGG, Lt. Cdr. Eugene E., USNR
CRAGG, Lt. Cdr. Richard T., USNR
DIMMICK, Lt. Cdr. William Howard, USN
DREYER, Lt. Cdr. J. Frederick (MC), USNR
ELDER, Lt. Cdr. Robert Duncan, Jr., USNR
ELLIS, Lt. Cdr. R. A. L., USNR
EVANS, Lt. Cdr. C. B., USNR
FERRILL, Lt. Cdr. Homer Edwin, USNR
FOSS, Lt. Cdr. Eugene N., USNR
HURLEY, Lt. Cdr. Michael J., USN
JACINTO, Lt. Cdr. Francis M., USNR
GRANT, Lt. Cdr. Walter H., USN
HART, Lt. Cdr. Lewis E., Jr., USNR
HECK, Lt. Cdr. Mary M. (NC), USN
LESLIE, Lt. Cdr. A. V., USNR
LIEBSCHNER, Lt. Cdr. Orville O., USN
LUNDGREN, Lt. Cdr. O. D., USNR
LYNN, Lt. Cdr. Vernon R. Y., USNR
McLAREN, Lt. Cdr. William F., USN
MARKHAM, Lt. Cdr. James B., USN
MUNSON, Lt. Cdr. Curtis B., USNR
O'NEILL, Lt. Cdr. George T., USNR
PARKER, Lt. Cdr. Ralph C., Jr., USN
PATTIE, Lt. Cdr. S. H., USN
PRATT, Lt. Cdr. H. Irving, USNR
RAMAGE, Lt. Cdr. Donald Brewster, USN
RIGGINS, Lt. Cdr. Leslie E., USNR
SHIFFLETTE, Lt. Cdr. William M., USN
SMITH, Lt. Cdr. Edward Raymond, USNR
SOLIER, Lt. Cdr. Robert H., USN
STEVENS, Lt. Cdr. Ralph S., Jr., USNR
STRADFORD, Lt. Cdr. Harry T. (MC), USN
SUNDERLAND, Lt. Cdr. Morton, USN
TAYLOR, Lt. Cdr. Jerry Hampton, Jr. (SC), USN
TRAVIS, Lt. Cdr. Charles William, USN

WHETSTONE, Lt. Cdr. LeRoy M., USNR
WHITE, Lt. Cdr. James Wilber, USN
BRANIGAN, Capt. James E., USA
BUNDY, Capt. George, USA
AHLERS, Lt. Harold N., USNR
ALFKE, Lt. Charles J., Jr., USNR
ALLEN, Lt. William D., USNR
BARNES, Lt. Arthur N., USNR
BARROWS, Lt. Wilbur R. (CEC), USNR
BEATIE, Lt. Walter C., Jr., USNR
BERGHULT, Lt. Carl Rudolf, USNR
BLANCO, Lt. Ralph, USN
BOLON, Lt. Logan A., USNR
BRANDT, Lt. W. V. C., Jr., USNR
BRANTLEY, Lt. D. L., USNR
BYRD, Lt. Samuel A., USNR
COX, Lt. Robert C., USNR
CREACY, Lt. Thomas Nelson, USNR
DANZIG, Lt. Jerome A., USNR
DERKACH, Lt. Stephan F. (MC), USNR
DICKERHOFF, Lt. Edward Carl, USNR
EWING, Lt. James M., USNR
FOLEY, Lt. Joseph M. (MC), USNR
GEVALT, Lt. F. G. (MC), USNR
GIBSON, Lt. Robert G., USN
GRANT, Lt. John Thomas, USNR
GREENE, Lt. James B., USNR
HALPERIN, Lt. Robert, USNR
HAMILTON, Lt. Thomas M., USNR
HANWAY, Lt. William Claude, Jr., USNR
HATCH, Lt. Sidney S., USNR
JOHNSON, Lt. Barcley Giddings, USNR
KAYE, Lt. Henry A., USNR
KIESEL, Lt. Harold M., USNR
KOENIG, Lt. Victor M. L., USNR
KUYKENDALL, Lt. William Olvier, USN
LANE, Lt. Harry L., USN
LAUER, Lt. Frank, USNR
LA VALLEE, Lt. George A., USNR
*LEAKE, Lt. Kenneth, USNR
LEE, Lt. H., Jr., USNR
McCONVILLE, Lt. Lawrence E., USNR
McCUEN, Lt. Robert P., USNR
MARGETTS, Lt. Richard K., USN
MARSH, Lt. Seabury N., USNR
MELLER, Lt. Irwin I., USNR
MILLER, Lt. Edward G., USN
NAPIER, Lt. J. H., USNR
NETTERSTROM, Lt. Ralph W., USNR
NICKS, Lt. Carney B., USNR
OLSEN, Lt. Edward B., USNR
PALMER, Lt. Howard V. R., Jr., USNR
PIERCE, Lt. Frank E., Jr., USNR
PIETZ, Lt. Wesley C. (CEC), USNR

PLUMER, Lt. Richard B., USNR
POOLE, Lt. Thornton B., USNR
RANDOLPH, Lt. Homer V., USN
READ, Lt. Robert R., USNR
REED, Lt. John Farley, USNR
REYNOLDS, Lt. Ernest V. (MC), USNR
RIGG, Lt. Henry I., USCGR
RUSSELL, Lt. Edwin F., USNR
SHEPPARD, Lt. Charles P., USNR
SHIFFER, Lt. Kenneth F., USN
SMITH, Lt. Robert M. (MC), USNR
STACKPOLE, Lt. Harvey D., USNR
STETSON, Lt. William, Jr., USNR
STEVENSON, Lt. Wallace E., USNR
STRAUCH, Lt. William D., Jr., USCGR
SWEENEY, Lt. Edward Joseph, USNR
SWIMM, Lt. Charles H., USNR
TURQUETTE, Lt. A. D., USNR
TUTTLE, Lt. Samuel D., USN
WADE, Lt. William L., USNR
WALZ, Lt. Allen W., USNR
WHELPLEY, Lt. Robert M., USN
WHITE, Lt. James C., USNR
WILKINSON, Lt. H. E., Jr., USNR
ALLEN, Lt. (jg) A. T., USNR
ANDERSEN, Lt. (jg) Howard Arne (MC), USN
ANTO, Lt. (jg) John, USN
BLANK, Lt. (jg) J. S., USN
BRAGG, Lt. (jg) Nelson Ray, USNR
BUCKLEY, Lt. (jg) Rex G., USNR
BUETTNER, Lt. (jg) Willis E., USNR
BUSHNELL, Lt. (jg) Douglas F., USNR
CAVANAGH, Lt. (jg) Joseph V., USNR
CLARKSON, Lt. (jg) Ferman L., USNR
CLUSTER, Lt. (jg) Herbert R., USNR
COOPER, Lt. (jg) Walter, USNR
CURRAN, Lt. (jg) Charles T., USNR
DEMONTIER, Lt. (jg) Leon Roger, USNR
DRAPER, Lt. (jg) Daniel Clay, USNR
DRISLER, Lt. (jg) William A., Jr., USNR
DYROFF, Lt. (jg) George Valentine, USNR
ELLICOTT, Lt. (jg) Joseph R., USNR
FAIRCHILD, Lt. (jg) Benjamin T., USNR
FARRAR, Lt. (jg) Arthur, USCGR
FOWLER, Lt. (jg) George E., USNR
FULLER, Lt. (jg) Jack D., USNR
GARAY, Lt. (jg) Paul Nicholas, USNR
HAMMOND, Lt. (jg) Glenn N., USN
HARLIN, Lt. (jg) Sylvester J., USN
HEIDEMAN, Lt. (jg) Lawrence L., USNR
HENDRICKSON, Lt. (jg) Chester Edward, USNR

HERDER, Lt. (jg) Loren P., USNR
HOFFMAN, Lt. (jg) Robert C., USN
HUFFMAN, Lt. (jg) Robert Eugene, USNR
JACKSON, Lt. (jg) Donald, USNR
JENKINS, Lt. (jg) Luther B., USNR
JONES, Lt. (jg) Alonzo A., USNR
LEWANDOWSKI, Lt. (jg) Stanley John, USN
LITTLEFIELD, Lt. (jg) D. F., USNR
LUBKER, Lt. (jg) Robert H. (CEC), USNR
McFALL, Lt. (jg) Henry S., USNR
McMEEKIN, Lt. (jg) Malcomb Bowman, USNR
MacKENZIE, Lt. (jg) Edward P. (MC), USN
MacSWAN, Lt. (jg) Elliot B., USNR
MILLER, Lt. (jg) Samuel C., USNR
NICHOLS, Lt. (jg) Robert R., USNR
PALMER, Lt. (jg) Chester L., USNR
PERRY, Lt. (jg) Gilbert E., USN
PINSON, Lt. (jg) Theo W., USNR
REDDER, Lt. (jg) Henry H., USNR
RICKER, Lt. (jg) John B., Jr., USNR
RILEY, Lt. (jg) Francis X., USCG
SANDIE, Lt. (jg) Donald H., USNR
SHERWIN, Lt. (jg) Robert W., USNR
SHERWOOD, Lt. (jg) Charles G., USN
SMITH, Lt. (jg) Robert L., USNR
STEPHENS, Lt. (jg) Norman E., USNR
STODGHILL, Lt. (jg) Jesse E., USNR
SUMMER, Lt. (jg) John Francis, USCGR
THARP, Lt. (jg) Edward R., USCG
TURNER, Lt. (jg) Robert E., USNR
WALSH, Lt. (jg) Frederick W., USNR
WEBB, Lt. (jg) Leslie R., Jr. (MC), USNR
WIGGINS, Lt. (jg) John R., USNR
WRIGHT, Lt. (jg) Charles W., USNR
ADAMS, Ens. Hamilton, USNR
CARTER, Ens. William R., USNR
FARRELL, Ens. James L., USNR
HART, Ens. Harry David, USNR
JULIAN, Ens. William Dan, USNR
MILLIKEN, Ens. Forbes Travis, USNR
MOORE, Ens. Aubrey Lee, USNR
NORBECK, Ens. Curtis C., USNR
OAKES, Ens. Albert J., USNR
OIST, Ens. Elmer J., USNR
O'MALLEY, Ens. John D., Jr., USNR
PEER, Ens. Richard S., USCG
REYNOLDS, Ens. Thomas, USNR
RIDEOUT, Ens. Linwood B., USNR

TAYLOR, Ens. John Craven, USNR
VAGHI, Ens. Joseph P., Jr., USNR
ZAREMBA, Ens. Joseph J., USNR
BACON, William G., CY, USNR
BARBER, Ira Lee, Jr., RM2/c, USN
BAXTER, William R., MoMM2/c, USN
BEACH, Ralph E., SM2/c, USNR
BEEZER, Earl F., Jr., BM1/c, USCGR
BELLAMY, Dave C., BM2/c, USNR
BEMISS, W. H., S1/c, USN
BLACK, Clanton Chandler, Sr., CCM, USNR
BLACK, William George, CM3/c, USNR
BORDEN, Richard Winstead, HA2/c, USNR
BRAUNER, Richard Dale, MoMM1/c, USNR
BRESTICKER, Saul, CPhM, USNR
BRUCE, George A., CGM, USN
CARINO, Albert J., PhM2/c, USNR
COLE, Vernon, S1/c, USCGR
COLEMAN, James W., MoMM2/c, USNR
CONNER, Thomas H., MoMM1/c, USCGR
CONTI, Edward P., Cox., USCGR
CRAWFORD, George L., MoMM3/c, USNR
CRUMLEY, J. D., CBM, USNR
D'ANDREA, Frank, AOM1/c, USNR
DEWING, John E., SM1/c, USN
EDWARDS, E. A., S/2c, USN
EITEL, G. F., S/1c, USNR
FREEMAN, Frank W., MoMM2/c, USCG
FREEMAN, Wade Hamp, S1/c, USNR
HOPE, John Frederick, SM2/c, USNR
HRVOL, Mike, S1/c, USNR
HUNT, Frank, MoMM1/c, USNR
IRVIN, Kenneth, S1/c, USNR
JACOBS, Gordon M., PhM3/c, USNR
JAGGARS, Robert Gilbert, Cox., USNR
GARSIDE, Robert, MM3/c, USNR
GILMER, Lester Kellie, BM2/c, USNR
GUZIK, Raymond R., MoMM2/c, USCG
HARRIS, Roland T., S1/c, USNR
KENFIELD, Eugene Francis, CBM, USNR
KING, Ray B., BM1/c, USN
KNOPP, Norbert John, CGM, USNR
KNUTSON, Wayne Russell, S1/c, USNR
LADEFIAN, Leo, BM2/c, USNR
LEONARD, W. W., MoMM1/c, USNR
L'HEUREUX, Louis P., BM1/c, USN
MARTIN, Leland, SM2/c, USNR
MEADOWS, Clifford LeRoy, CM3/c, USNR
MELANGON, Leo, EM1/c, USN
MILLER, Quentin Geil, CMoMM, USNR

MILLER, Robert M., CEM, USNR
MILLICAN, Robert I., PhM3/c, USNR
MOATES, Thomas Henry, Jr., CGM, USNR
MODESETT, J. W., GM1/c, USNR
MOLDENHAUER, Fritz P., Cox., USN
MOULDS, James J., F2/c, USNR
MUNDEN, Newton Cary, S1/c, USNR
O'BRIEN, Austin, PhM2/c, USCGR
PAWLOWSKI, Joseph, Cox., USNR
POWERS, James A., S2/c, USCGR
PREWIT, L. A., CEM, USNR
PUCKETT, Marvin Burkley, GM3/c, USNR
REGAN, John J., MoMM1/c, USNR
RHOADS, David Shaubach, S1/c, USNR
ROBERTSON, H. E., S1/c, USNR
ROSS, Harold R., CM3/c, USNR
RYAN, Thomas Joseph, SM3/c, USNR
SETTANI, Daniel X., SC1/c, USNR
SMITH, Irving F., PhM1/c, USNR
SMITH, Louis B., PhM1/c, USNR
SOUTHARD, J. F., MoMM3/c, USNR
STEVENS, Lester F., AOM1/c, USNR
STONE, Elmer, MoMM2/c, USNR
THOMAS, John Primon, SM2/c, USNR
TOUSSAINT, Raymond Sylvio, MoMM2/c, USNR
VANNET, Maynard, CBM, USNR
WEAR, Willie Guy, Carp., USNR
WILBER, R. G., Cox., USN
WILBUR, Charles Earl, Boat., USN
WIRWOHN, H. E., CMM, USNR
WOODCOCK, Raymond, Cox., USNR
WOOTEN, William R., Carp., USNR
WRENN, Harold Dean, CEM, USNR

PRESIDENTIAL UNIT CITATION
NAVY COMBAT DEMOLITION
UNIT OF FORCE "O"

For outstanding performance in combat during the invasion of Normandy, June 6, 1944. Determined and zealous in the fulfillment of an extremely hazardous mission, the Navy Combat Demolition Unit of Force "O" landed on the "Omaha Beach" with the first wave under devastating enemy artillery, machine gun and sniper fire. With practically all explosives lost and with their force seriously depleted by heavy casualties, the remaining officers and men carried on gallantly, salvaging explosives as they were swept ashore and in some instances commandeering bulldozers to remove obstacles. In spite of these grave handicaps, the Demolition Crews succeeded initially in blasting five gaps through enemy obstacles for the passage of assault forces to the Normandy shore and within two days had sapped over eighty-five percent of the "Omaha Beach" area of German-placed traps. Valiant in the face of grave danger and persistently aggressive against fierce resistance, the Navy Combat Demolition Unit rendered daring and self-sacrificing service in the performance of a vital mission, thereby sustaining the high traditions of the United States Naval Service.

NAVY UNIT COMMENDATION

NAVAL COMBAT DEMOLITION UNITS, ASSAULT FORCE "U"

For outstanding heroism in action against enemy German forces during the landing on the coast of Normandy, June 6, 1944. Ruggedly trained and fiercely determined to effect the gap through which would flow our whole battle effort in the assigned sector, Naval Combat Demolition Units, Assault Force "U" boldly moved in toward sands raked by German mortars, machine guns and 88-mms. Crowded into LCM's and LCVP's, and with minutes only in which to blow the obstacles before they were obscured by racing tides, these gallant men landed, each weighed down by forty pounds of TNT and carrying two-pound blocks around his chest, to place demolition charges on pyramids of steel, timber or concrete; on ramps, hedgehogs and other obstructions. Constantly in peril from terrific fire of hostile pillboxes and casemates, they ignited their fuses and, as the tide swept in during the critical hours of D-Day, saw the line of khaki move slowly up the eastern American beach and inland through a 300-yard gap cleared of German emplacements. Individually courageous and working as a valiant team in the face of fearful destruction wrought by enemy fire, Naval Combat Demolition Units, Assault Force "U," achieved a hazardous mission vital to the initiation of our land war against ruthless German aggression.

PRESIDENTIAL UNIT CITATION

UNITED STATES LCT (5) 30

For outstanding performance and heroic service in combat during the assault on the coast of Normandy, France, launched on June 6, 1944. Defying the terrific artillery and machine gun fire of the enemy, the U.S. LCT 30 daringly advanced through mined and unswept waters, ramming and breaching enemy-emplaced obstacles at full speed to clear a channel for the assault waves standing off shore and previously repulsed by the ferocity of the German fire. With guns ablaze in answer to point-blank fire from hostile positions, LCT 30 boldly fought it out with the enemy as she went in, silencing his guns and, by her gallant example of resolute and indomitable purpose, inspired the remaining craft to follow with their vehicles and men so vital to the assault operations. Unwavering in response to an urgent need for swift action and splendid in her leadership, the LCT 30 initiated the forward movement of ships by a feat of exceptional bravery, indicative of the determination, the valor and the tenacious fighting spirit of the officers and men who determined her course.

PRESIDENTIAL UNIT CITATION

UNITED STATES LCT 540

For outstanding performance and distinguished service in combat during the assault on the coast of Normandy, France, launched June 6, 1944. Rocked by the blasts of German 88-mm. cannon during the approach, her gun turrets wrecked, fires blazing aboard, her Officer in Charge killed and eight of her men casualties, the U.S. LCT 540 hit the beach on schedule under the heaviest concentration of enemy fire. In gallant response to the urgency of her task, she operated twenty-four hours a day until June 9, beaching her cargo while still under fire and returning repeatedly to place ashore the equipment, supplies and troops vital to the success and the very life of our assault forces. Crippled, but undaunted, the LCT pursued her course unwaveringly despite German-emplaced underwater obstacles and terrific gunfire opposition, supplementing the valor and fortitude of her inexperienced officer and men by her own steadfastness in the fulfillment of a perilous mission.

Southern France

Navy Cross

STEISBURG, Cdr. Frederick M., USN

For extraordinary heroism in action against the enemy as Commanding Officer, USS HILARY P. JONES while operating in support of the Allied ground forces on the coast of the Franco-Italian Riviera in September 1944. On the night of 7–8 September 1944, when attacked by enemy explosive boats, Commander Steisburg, exercising alert and decisive action, avoided the first which exploded in the wake of his ship and forthwith engaged two others which were in all probability destroyed by his accurate and vigorous gunfire. On 10 September 1944, he displayed extreme initiative and skill in an attack on, and almost positive destruction of, two enemy human torpedoes attempting to attain a favorable firing position. At San Remo, on 18 September 1944, in the space of an hour and a half while under severe fire of hostile shore artillery, by his able cunning, intelligent use of information and expert fire control, the gunfire of the USS HILARY P. JONES destroyed an anti-aircraft battery, a fuel dump, and ammunition dump and about twelve enemy vessels in the harbor area. Subsequently, he returned to conduct additional bombardment at Port Maurizio and his gallant execution of this firing mission resulted in the destruction of enemy shipping and supply dumps and the silencing of several heavy coastal batteries. His overall accomplishments in these actions assisted materially in the advance of the Allied ground forces in clearing enemy-held territory and contributed to his ultimate defeat.

BRINGLE, Lt. Cdr. William F., USN

For distinguishing himself by extraordinary heroism in action against the enemy as Commanding Officer of Observation Fighter Squadron ONE during the Allied invasion of Southern France in August 1944. On 20 August 1944, Lieutenant Commander Bringle, as leader of an eight plane fighter bomber mission against an enemy motorized concentration near Carcassone, France, executed a series of determined and persistent attacks through intense ground fire which caused complete disruption of the enemy movement and the destruction and damaging of seventy-five motor vehicles. Later in the same day, he led a similar mission against six heavily armed trawler type vessels in the Marseilles area and carried out the attacks with such vigor and intrepidity that four vessels were beached and the other two stopped, badly damaged, alongside a breakwater. On 25 August 1944 while spotting for naval gunfire, he exposed himself fearlessly to anti-aircraft fire in order to relay the results of close observation of the fall of shot in the vicinity of three important coastal defense batteries and his accurate adjustments contributed materially to the neutralization of these positions. In the execution of this mission his plane was repeatedly hit by anti-aircraft fire and was required to make a forced landing at sea. During thirteen days of operation, Lieutenant Commander Bringle flew twenty-one sorties while conducting the most difficult and hazardous missions, inflicting severe damage on enemy positions and greatly assisting the advance of our ground forces.

BASORE, Lt. Harry H., USN

For distinguishing himself by extraordinary heroism in action against the enemy as acting Commanding Officer of Fighting Squadron SEVENTY-FOUR during the Allied invasion of Southern France in August 1944. In the period 15 August 1944 until 30 August 1944, Lieutenant Basore led with great skill and courage ten offensive missions against enemy strongpoints, motorized concentrations and lines of communications. These flights were made in the face of intense, accurate gunfire from the ground but, nevertheless, were successful in causing large damage and creating much confusion among the enemy. While the leader of an eight plane flight up the Rhone River on 27 August 1944, Lieutenant Basore made a solo reconnoitering run through heavy gunfire in the vicinity of Montelimar at an extremely low altitude in order to obtain needed information on the identity and movements of a heavy concentration of enemy motor transports in that area. This information could not be obtained from a safe altitude and he, refusing to endanger the pilots under his command, voluntarily directed them to remain aloft while he dove his plane at high speed through intense fire to a low altitude. Although his plane was hit by anti-aircraft fire, Lieutenant Basore obtained and accurately reported by radio, the desired information and subsequently returned safely with his flight to his carrier. As a direct result of his heroism and exceptional airmanship valuable information concerning the movements of enemy ground forces was promptly reported.

GILBERT, Lt. Lawrence Edwin, USNR

For extraordinary heroism as Commanding Officer of the USS LST 282 when that vessel was subjected to an enemy aerial attack and completely destroyed during the amphibious invasion of Southern France on August 15, 1944. Seriously injured and momentarily stunned when thrown to the bridge deck from his conning station by the blast of an enemy glider bomb, Lieutenant Gilbert unhesitatingly struggled through exploding ammunition and heavy black smoke from fires ignited in the cargo of motor trucks loaded aboard to carry a severely wounded signalman below, adjusting the man's life preserver and helping him over the side. Gallantly disregarding the grave danger to himself, he continued his valiant efforts by assisting a helpless officer into the water and, after securing him by a life belt to the rudder post, risked his life amid fire and explosions to search for help, remaining in the water for two hours until both men were recovered in an unconscious condition by rescue craft.

Cox, Lt. (jg) John R., USNR

For extraordinary heroism in action as Executive Officer of the USS YMS 24 during the amphibious invastion of Southern France on 16 August 1944. During mine-sweeping operations to clear the heavily mine-infested waters of the Gulf of Frejus for the landing of reinforcements and vital supplies in support of the Allied Armies in Southern France, the USS YMS 24 struck an enemy mine which blew off the bow causing her subsequent sinking, the loss in action of her Commanding Officer, and other casualties. Lieutenant (junior grade) Cox, exercising prompt, fearless and deliberate action, instituted all possible, though futile, measures to save the ship from sinking and later to remove the wounded to the care and safety of rescue vessels which had come alongside. He entered every compartment in search of missing or trapped men. Following a second mine explosion under the stern of one of the rescue vessels alongside, with complete disregard for his own safety, he unhesitatingly jumped into the water between the two foundering craft and recovered a critically injured man who had been dropped during the transfer of the wounded and was in immediate danger of drowning. His gallant, self-sacrificing and untiring efforts contributed materially to the prompt care of the wounded and to the probable saving of many lives.

MURPHY, Lt. (jg) Henry F., USNR

For distinguishing himself by extraordinary heroism in action against the enemy while leading an assault boat group during the amphibious invasion of Southern France on 15 August 1944. When the assault boat in which he was leading the initial boat waves to the designated beach struck and was demolished by an enemy mine which killed or wounded three-quarters of the embarked personnel, Lieutenant (junior grade) Murphy although in a shocked and dazed condition, swam to another assault boat and with fearless energy directed the recovery of survivors and the clearing of incoming waves from the heavily mined waters. By this action in which he displayed keen alertness, great fortitude and complete disregard of imminent danger, the lives of many assault troops and boat crews were undoubtedly saved as succeeding traffic was diverted from the dangerous areas. His prompt and courageous efforts in controlling the beaching of this assault unit contributed materially to the successful establishment of the beachhead.

HULLAND, Ens. Charles W. S., USNR

For distinguishing himself by extraordinary heroism in action against the enemy as Pilot of a U.S. Navy fighter bomber aircraft during the Allied invasion of Southern France in August 1944. On 20 August 1944, Ensign Hulland participated as one of six pilots on an armed reconnaissance mission deep into enemy held territory in the southwestern part of France. Southeast of Montpellier he followed his flight leader without hesitation and with an outstanding display of airmanship in a series of strafing attacks against a convoy of trucks and tank trucks. The attacks by the flight accounted for the destruction of four tank trucks, fifteen troop carriers loaded with troops and one command car, despite intense fire from the ground which resulted in the loss of one plane from the attacking force and in such severe damage to two others that they were ordered to return directly to base. Ensign Hulland and the other two remaining pilots continued westward on the assigned mission and in the city of Villefranche, near Toulouse, attacked another truck convoy. Once again with disregard for the risks involved and with a high degree of skill and precision Ensign Hulland made a series of strafing attacks which destroyed twelve to fourteen enemy trucks. Enemy fire during the last of these runs hit Ensign Hulland's plane, and although he strove to maintain it in flight he was finally forced to bail out over enemy territory near the Spanish border. He was seen to land safely, hide his parachute and make for cover. Information has since been received that he safely reached Allied authorities.

Distinguished Service Medal

*HEWITT, Vice Adm. Henry Kent, USN

Navy Commander, Western Naval Task Force, from August 13 to September 27, 1944. Admiral Hewitt was responsible for all Naval activities in connection with the invasion of Southern France.

*DAVIDSON, Rear Adm. Lyal A., USN

For exceptionally meritorious service to the Government of the United States in a duty of great responsibility as a Naval Task Force Commander during the amphibious invasion of Southern France in August 1944. Exercising sound judgment and expert tactical ability, Rear Admiral Davidson skillfully disposed his forces of British, French and United States combatant ships to execute and cover the preassault landings of special service troops who brought about the early capitulation of strategic coastal islands.

*LEWIS, Rear Adm. Spencer S., USN

For exceptionally meritorious service to the Government of the United States in a duty of great responsibility as Commander of a Naval Task Force prior to and during the amphibious invasion of Southern France in August 1944.

LOWRY, Rear Adm. Frank J., USN

For exceptionally meritorious service to the Government of the United States in a duty of great responsibility as Commander of a Naval Task Force prior to and during the amphibious invasion of Southern France in August 1944.

RODGERS, Rear Adm. Bertram J., USN

For exceptionally meritorious service to the Government of the United States in a duty of great responsibility as Commander of a Naval Task Force prior to and during the amphibious invasion of Southern France in August 1944.

OLD, Capt. Francis P., USN
Army Distinguished Service Medal

For exceptionally meritorious and distinguished service in the performance of duties of great responsibility as Chief of Staff, Western Naval Task Force, from August 13 to September 27, 1944. As United States Naval representative at the combined planning staff he displayed marked organizing ability, effecting coordination with the various Allied Staffs. His executive ability was of inestimable value in the formulation of important plans for the invasion of Southern France. His judgment, tenacious fidelity and courageous advice greatly contributed to the success of the combined operations and reflect great credit on himself and the Armed Forces of the United States.

Legion of Merit

*BRYANT, Rear Adm. Carleton F., USN

Commander of the Center Support Group of the Western Naval Task Force during the amphibious invasion of Southern France in August 1944.

*CHANDLER, Rear Adm. Theodore E., USN

Commander of an Assault Group of the Western Naval Task Force prior to and during the amphibious invasion of Southern France in August 1944.

*DEYO, Rear Adm. Morton L., USN

Commander of a Support Group of the Western Naval Task Force during the amphibious invasion of Southern France in August 1944.

*DURGIN, Rear Adm. Calvin T., USN

Major Task Group Commander during the amphibious invasion of Southern France in August 1944.

MOON, Rear Adm. Don P., USN

Commander of a Naval Task Force prior to the amphibious invasion of Southern France in August 1944.

***EDGAR, Commondore Campbell D., USN

Commander Transports and Commander of a Beach Assault Group during the amphibious invasion of Southern France in August 1944.

*ANSEL, Capt. Walter C., USN

Commanding Officer of the USS PHILADELPHIA during the amphibious invasion of Southern France in August 1944.

***BACHMAN, Capt. Leo A., USN

Directing the collection and correlation of important material for dissemination to all the various units comprising the assault forces on the Coast of Southern France.

**BAILEY, Capt. Watson O., USN

Commander of a Transport Division and Commander of a Beach Assault Group during the amphibious invasion of Southern France in August 1944.

CAMPBELL, Capt. William S., USN

Commanding Officer of the USS ANNE ARUNDEL prior to and during the amphibious invasion of Southern France on 15 August 1944.

**CATER, Capt. Charles J., USN

Commander of a Destroyer Squadron and of a gunfire support unit prior to and during the amphibious invasion of Southern France in August 1944.

*CLAY, Capt. James P., USN

Commander of the Antisubmarine and Convoy Control Group of the Western Naval Task Force during the amphibious invasion of Southern France in August, 1944.

CRONIN, Capt. Joseph C., USN

Commanding Officer, USS TULAGI during the amphibious invasion of Southern France in August 1944.

*DAVIS, Capt. Ransom K., USN

Chief of Staff of a Naval Task Force Commander prior to and during the amphibious invasion of Southern France in August 1944.

**DIERDORFF, Capt. Ross A., USN

Commander of a Transport Division and Commander of a Beach Assault Group during the amphibious invasion of Southern France in August 1944.

DODDS, Capt. Sidney B., USNR

Commander Beach Battalions prior to and during the amphibious invasion of Southern France in August 1944.

*DUFEK, Capt. George J., USN

Aviation Officer on the Staff of a major Naval Task Force Commander prior to and during the amphibious invasion of Southern France in August 1944.

*EDSON, Capt. Stephen R. (SC), USN

Coordination of Logistic and Supply matters with the U. S. Army authorities and agencies of Allied Services contributed materially to the advancing Allied Armies in Southern France.

FIELDING, Capt. Charles F., USN

Communication Officer on the staff of a major Naval Task Force Commander prior to and during the amphibious invasion of Southern France in August 1944.

*FLOYD, Capt. William O., USN

Commander of a Beach Assault Group prior to and during the amphibious invasion of Southern France in August 1944.

*FRITZSCHE, Capt. Edward H., USCG

Commanding Officer of the USS SAMUEL CHASE prior to and during the amphibious invasion of Southern France on August 15, 1944.

*GREGOR, Capt. Orville F., USN

Commander of all Landing Craft and of a Beach Assault Group of the Western Naval Task Force during the amphibious invasion of Southern France in August 1944.

GROW, Capt. Bradford E., USN

Commanding Officer, USS KASAAN BAY during the amphibious invasion of Southern France in August 1944.

*JOHNSON, Capt. Henry C., USN

Commander of a Special Operations Group of the Western Naval Task Force during the amphibious invasion of Southern France in August 1944.

KRAKER, Capt. George P., USN

Commanding Officer of the USS MARBLEHEAD and Commander of a Gunfire Support Unit prior to and during the amphibious invasion of Southern France in August 1944.

*MAUERMAN, Capt. Raymond J., USCG

Commanding Officer of the USS JOSEPH T. DICKMAN prior to and during the amphibious invasion of Southern France on 15 August 1944.

**MESSMER, Capt. William L., USN

Commander of the Minesweeping Group of the Western Naval Task Force during the amphibious invasion of Southern France in August 1944.

*MOSES, Capt. Charles W., USN

Coordination of the Allied Naval, Army and Air Forces to support the forces establishing the initial beachhead and to assist the advance to the vital ports of Toulon and Marseilles.

MORSE, Capt. Richard S., USN

Operations and Planning Officer on the Staff of a Naval Task Force Commander prior to and during the amphibious invasion of Southern France in August 1944.

*MORRIS, Capt. Robert, USN

Commander of a Beach Assault Group prior to and during the amphibious invasion of Southern France in August 1944.

*NICHOLS, Capt. Chester L., USN

Commandant, U.S. Naval Operating Base, Palermo, Sicily, prior to and during the amphibious invasion of Southern France in August 1944.

OPIE, Capt. John N., III, USN

Chief of Staff to a Naval Task Force Commander prior to and during the amphibious invasion of Southern France in August 1944.

PARKER, Capt. Harold E., USN

Commander of a Beach Assault Group prior to and during the amphibious invasion of Southern France in August 1944.

PLANDER, Capt. Henry, USN

Commander of a Mine Squadron during the amphibious invasion of Southern France and the subsequent operations in August 1944.

RICHARDSON, Capt. Myron T., USN

Plans and Operations Officer on the staff of a Naval Task Force Commander prior to and during the amphibious invasion of Southern France in August 1944.

RUTT, Capt. Burnice L., USN

Commander of a Beach Assault Unit during the amphibious invasion of Southern France in August 1944.

*Sanders, Capt. Harry, USN

Commander Destroyer Squadron EIGHT-EEN embarked in the USS FRANFORD, flagship, during the amphibious invasion of Southern France in August 1944.

*Shulten, Capt. Leo B., USN

Commander of a Beach Assault Group prior to and during the amphibious invasion of Southern France in August 1944.

**Sorensen, Captain Thor C., USNR

Commanding Officer of the USS LYON prior to and during the amphibious invasion of Southern France on 15 August, 1944.

Tompkins, Capt. Rutledge B., USN

Chief of Staff to a Naval Task Force Commander prior to and during the amphibious invasion of Southern France in August 1944.

Wright, Capt. George C., USN

Senior Staff Officer to a Naval Task Group Commander during the amphibious invasion of Southern France August 1944.

**Zimmerli, Capt. Rupert M., USN

Chief of Staff to a Naval Task Force Commander prior to and during the amphibious invasion of Southern France in August 1944

*Andersen, Cdr. Harvey M., USN

Commander of the Salvage Group of the Western Naval Task Force prior to and during the amphibious invasion of Southern France in August 1944.

Blair, Cdr. William S., USNR

Commander of a Beach Assault Group during the amphibious invasion of Southern France in August 1944.

***Brookman, Cdr. Harold R., USNR

Material Officer on the staff of a major Naval Task Force Commander prior to and during the amphibious invasion of Southern France in August 1944.

Clarke, Cdr. Paul W., (SC), USN

Supply Officer of the Advanced Amphibious Training Base, Bizerte, Tunisia prior to and during the Allied Invasion of Southern France in August 1944.

Cullins, Cdr. Thomas O., Jr., USN

Commanding Officer of the USS PRO-CYON prior to and during the amphibious invasion of Southern France on 15 August 1944.

**Fly, Cdr. William A., USN

Commanding Officer of the USS AN-DROMEDA prior to and during the amphibious invasion of Southern France on 15 August 1944.

Fritschmann, Cdr. George, USN

War Plans Officer on the Staff of a Naval Task Force Commander prior to and during the amphibious invasion of Southern France in August 1944.

Guillot, Cdr. James C., USN

Commander of a Landing Craft Flotilla prior to and during the amphibious invasion of Southern France in August 1944.

Havard, Cdr. Valery, Jr., USN

Commander Destroyer Division FOUR-TEEN, embarked in the USS CHARLES F. HUGHES, flagship, during the amphibious invasion of Southern France in August 1944.

*Helen, Cdr. Robert R., USNR

Commander Harbor Clearance Units of the Salvage Group, United States EIGHTH Fleet prior to and during the amphibious invasion of Southern France in the period from August to November 1944.

Herring, Cdr. Lee R., USN

Commander of a Beach Assault Group prior to and during the amphibious invasion of Southern France in August 1944.

Higgins, Cdr. Ronald D., USNR

Commander of a Beach Assault Group prior to and during the amphibious invasion of Southern France in August 1944.

Nation, Cdr. Milton A., USN

Chief of Staff to the Commander of a Carrier Task Group prior to and during the amphibious invasion of Southern France in August 1944.

REYNOLDS, Cdr. Stewart S., USN

Commanding Officer of the USS BARNETT prior to and during the amphibious invasion of Southern France on 15 August 1944.

RUTH, Cdr. Ernst A., Jr., USNR

Commander of a Minesweeping Group of the Western Naval Task Force prior to and during the amphibious invasion of Southern France in August 1944.

SODERGREN, Cdr. Albin R., USN

Commander of a Beach Assault Group during the amphibious invasion of Southern France in August 1944.

TUTHILL, Cdr. Frederick R. L., USNR

Assistant Communications Officer on the staff of a Naval Task Force Commander prior to and during the amphibious invasion of Southern France in August 1944.

VANASSE, Cdr. Roland B., USN

Commanding Officer of the USS THURSTON prior to and during the amphibious invasion of Southern France, August 1944.

*VIOLETT, Cdr. Quentell, USNR

Commanding Officer Petroleum Division ONE and as a Task Group Commander prior to and during the amphibious invasion of Southern France in August 1944.

*WALLIS, Cdr. Adelbert V., USNR

Commander of a Minesweeping Group of the Western Naval Task Force during the amphibious invasion of Southern France in August 1944.

*WALSH, Cdr. James E., USNR

Commanding Officer of the Fourth Beach Battalion during the amphibious invasion of Southern France in August 1944.

WARBURTON, Cdr. Audley L., USN

Commander of an assault convoy and of a Divisional Reserve Assault Group during the amphibious invasion of Southern France in August 1944.

WESTHOFEN, Cdr. Charles L., USN

Operations and Chief Staff Officer, Fleet Air Wing FIFTEEN, from 21 February 1944 to 10 September 1944, while engaged in antisubmarine operations in the Moroccan Sea Frontier and as the Air Officer of a United States Naval Assault Group during the invasion of Southern France in August 1944.

WIEDMAN, Cdr. Wilbur A., USNR

Commanding Officer of the USS E. STANTON prior to and during the amphibious invasion of Southern France on 15 August 1944.

WILLIAMS, Cdr. George K., USN

Gunnery Officer on the staff of a Naval Task Force Commander prior to and during the amphibious invasion of Southern France in August 1944.

WILLIS, Cdr. John H., USN

Commanding Officer of the USS HENRICO prior to and during the amphibious invasion of Southern France on 15 August 1944.

WOODSON, Cdr. Charles R., USN

Commanding Officer of the USS ARCTURUS prior to and during the amphibious invasion of Southern France on 15 August 1944.

BARNES, Lt. Cdr. Stanley M., USN

Commander of a Screening Group of the Western Naval Task Force during the amphibious invasion of Southern France in August 1944.

CAMERON, Lt. Cdr. Harold T., USNR

Commanding Officer of the USS OBERON prior to and during the amphibious invasion of Southern France, 15 August 1944.

FAIRBANKS, Lt. Cdr. Douglas E., Jr., USNR

Special Operations Planning Officer on the Staff of a Major Naval Task Force Commander and as Commander of a Naval Task Force Unit prior to and during the amphibious invasion of Southern France in August, 1944.

FERREOLA, Lt. Cdr. James A., USN

LST Group Commander and Commander of a Beach Assault Unit prior to and during the amphibious invasion of Southern France in August 1944.

*GRISWOLD, Lt. Cdr. Benjamin H., III, USNR

Aide and Flag Lieutenant to a Major Naval Task Force Commander prior to and during the amphibious invasion of Southern France in August 1944.

HARDY, Lt. Cdr. James D., USNR

Mine Officer on the staff of a Major Naval Task Force Commander prior to and during the amphibious invasion of Southern France in August 1944.

HOLMSHAW, Lt. Cdr. Harry F., USN

Commander LST Flotilla ONE and as Commander of a Beach Assault Unit prior to and during the amphibious invasion of Southern France in August 1944.

KIRSTINE, Lt. Cdr. Lance J., USCG

Commander of Landing Craft assigned to the Western Naval Task Force prior to and during the amphibious invasion of Southern France in August 1944.

*SCOTT, Lt. Cdr. David D., USN

Assistant Gunnery Officer on the staff of a Major Naval Task Force Commander during the amphibious invasion of Southern France in August 1944.

WAGSTAFF, Lt. Cdr. Ruben E., USN

Planning Officer on the staff of a Naval Task Force Commander prior to and during the amphibious invasion of the Southern Coast of France in August 1944.

WOOD, Lt. Cdr. Philo, USNR

Communications Officer on the staff of a Naval Task Force Commander prior to and during the amphibious invasion of Southern France in August 1944.

AMBRON, Lt. Raymond H., USNR

LST Group Commander and Commander of a Beach Assault Unit prior to and during the amphibious invasion of Southern France in August 1944.

BREKKE, Lt. Marshall L., USNR

Officer in Charge of a Combat Demolition Unit prior to and during the am-

phibious invasion of Southern France in August 1944.

ELLIOTT, Lt. Orlo J., USNR

Executive Officer of the First Beach Battalion prior to and during the amphibious invasion of Southern France in August 1944.

EVANS, Lt. Carnot W., USNR

Commander Small Boat Flotillas prior to and during the amphibious invasion of Southern France in August 1944.

*JAMES, Lt. Harrie A., USNR

Intelligence Officer on the staff of a Major Task Force Commander prior to and during the invasion of Southern France in August 1944.

JORDAN, Lt. Fenton G., USNR

Assistant Intelligence Officer on the Staff of a Major Naval Task Force Commander prior to and during the amphibious invasion of Southern France in August 1944.

*KERR, Lt. Robert B., USNR

Radio and Radar Officer attached to the staff of a Major Naval Task Force Commander prior to and during the amphibious invasion of Southern France in August 1944.

SHERMAN, Lt. Edwin F., USNR

Commander of a Minesweeping Unit during the amphibious invasion of Southern France from 15–19 August 1944.

Silver Star Medal

CONVERSE, Capt. Adelbert F., USN
JONES, Capt. Edward H., USN
*RHEA, Capt. Powell M., USN
*SENN, Capt. Elliot M., USN
TILLSON, Capt. Elwood M., USN
FIELD, Cdr. Benjamin P., USN
*HUGHES, Cdr. William C., USN
MELSON, Cdr. Charles L., USN
PALMER, Cdr. G. G., USN
*PEARCE, Cdr. Hepburn A., USN
STUART, Cdr. Daniel A, USN
WIER, Cdr. Henry R., USN

BARNES, Lt. Cdr. William R., USN
BROWN, Lt. Cdr. Harold V., USNR
BULKELEY, Lt. Cdr. John D., USN
FLECK, Lt. Cdr. Francis E., Jr., USN
KLEE, Lt. Cdr. William M., USN
MEYER, Lt. Cdr. Bernard H., USN
SEMMES, Lt. Cdr. J. L., USN
WILSON, Lt. Cdr. "JC" G., USN
HAMBLEN, Lt. James C., USNR
LIVINGSTON, Lt. Stanley, USNR
SCHUH, Lt. Charles J., USNR
GILRAY, Lt. (jg) John A., Jr., USNR
HUNT, Lt. (jg) John C., USNR
NORTH, Lt. (jg) John C., USNR
MAGILL, Ens. Clark, (CEC), USNR
PETERSON, Ens. William A. (CEC), USNR
THORNBER, Ens. George H., USNR
BURRIS, Henry E., GM2/c, USNR
GROSS, John S., S2/c, USN
HODGE, Cecil, S1/c, USNR
SIMPSON, Lowell E., S2/c, USNR
YOUNG, Franket A., EM2/c, USNR

Distinguished Flying Cross

BASS, Lt. Cdr. H. Brinkley, USN
SANDOR, Lt. Cdr. John H., USN
*AUSTIN, Lt. William R., USNR
CROCKETT, Lt. David S., USNR
DE VITO, Lt. Raymond J., USNR
*FIERSTEIN, Lt. Stanley C., USNR
**HOGAN, Lt. Gerald G., USNR
LONGINO, Lt. Charles S., Jr., USNR
*MOSS, Lt. Elmo L., USNR
PAUCEL, Lt. Rene E., USNR
ROUNTREE, Lt. Frederick M., USN
SCHAUFFLER, Lt. Frederick, USNR
SHROFF, Lt. John H., USNR
STRATTON, Lt. Henry T., USNR
THOMAS, Lt. John M., USNR
ARBUCKLE, Lt. (jg) William N., USN
CASTANEDO, Lt. (jg) Edwin W., USNR
COE, Lt. (jg) George E., USNR
DEWEES, Lt. (jg) Mason L., USNR
ECKARDT, Lt. (jg) Harold J., USNR
JOLLIFFE, Lt. (jg) Robert N., USNR
KENDRICK, Lt. (jg) Thomas F., USNR
OLSZNSKI, Lt. (jg) Edward W., USNR
*PICKARD, Lt. (jg) Morris G., USNR
SIKES, Lt. (jg) Richard A., USNR
*STEWART, Lt. (jg) Jack H., USNR
BECKETT, Ens. Merlin R., USNR
MARKEY, Ens. Francis H., USNR
ROBINSON, Ens. David E., USNR

SMIEGOCKI, Ens. Robert, USNR
WOOD, Ens. Alfred R., USNR
YENTZER, Ens. Richard V., USNR

Navy and Marine Corps Medal

JAVA, Lt. Frank J., USNR
DUVAL, Lt. (jg) Hugh F., USNR
NOBLE, Lt. (jg) Richard L., USNR
BOWEN, Billie D., S1/c, USN
COPPAGE, Paul H., CBM, USNR
LEE, Marion J., S1/c, USN
LUPA, Anthony A., PhM1/c, USNR
MERRIL, Leslie C., CBM, USN
PORSLEY, Roy G., CBM, USN
REED, Leroy E., EM1/c, USNR
ROMERO, John C., MoM3/c, USN
SCOCCHIO, Sam, Cox., USNR

Air Medal

ALSTON, Lt. James M., USNR
BACH, Lt. Haskon A., USNR
BROWN, Lt. Harold E., USNR
BARTLEY, Lt. John G., USNR
CAHILL, Lt. Francis A., USNR
CALLAND, Lt. Robert W., USNR
FORNEY, Lt. Junior C., USNR
HILL, Lt. Palmer G., USNR
HORACEK, Lt. Leo, Jr., USNR
JOHNSON, Lt. Robert J., USNR
LAWRY, Lt. Edward H., USNR
McLINN, Lt. Frank M., USNR
ROBERTS, Lt. Barclay M., USNR
ROBERTS, Lt. Francis R., USNR
SMITH, Lt. Alexander A., USNR
CANDLER, Lt. (jg) William R., USNR
CASE, Lt. (jg) Clifford E., USNR
DOYLE, Lt. (jg) Robert E., USNR
FINNIE, Lt. (jg) Robert J., USNR
FOX, Lt. (jg) Noel R., USNR
FRANK, Lt. (jg) John D., USNR
LATHROP, Lt. (jg) Walter P., USNR
MOKRY, Lt. (jg) Leslie E., USNR
PAULSON, Lt. (jg) Arne S., USNR
ROBINSON, Lt. (jg) John O., USNR
WITT, Lt. (jg) Ivan H., USNR
ZINN, Lt. (jg) Charles S., USNR
ADAMS, Ens. John E., USNR
ADAMS, Ens. Robert J., USNR
BAUMGARDNER, Ens. Neal G., USNR
BETHEA, Ens. William H., USNR
CLANCY, Ens. Edward, USNR
COMMELLA, Ens. Samuel E., USNR
DE MASTERS, Ens. Marion F., USNR

DENISON, Ens. John M., USNR
DIETERICH, Ens. Dale N., USNR
FENZEL, Ens. Fred W., USN
FOLEY, Ens. Walter A., USNR
GARRISON, Ens. Charles D., USNR
GELDART, Ens. Robert J., USNR
HALES, Ens. Max B., USNR
JAYNES, Ens. Sutton "L," USNR
KLINGERMAN, Ens. Raymond F., USNR
LAHEY, Ens. Walter J., USNR
LIDER, Ens. Edward W., USNR
McKEEVER, Ens. William C., USNR
McMANUS, Ens. Thomas H., USNR
MINAR, Ens. George, USNR
MOONEY, Ens. John A., USNR
MURPHY, Ens. Thomas L., USNR
ORTEIG, Ens. Jules, USNR
PAVLOVICH, Ens. Paul, USNR
RATLIFF, Ens. Clarence P., USNR
RYAN, Ens. Thomas S., USNR
SKELLY, Ens. Charles P., USNR
STAKELY, Ens. Charles P., USNR
STANTON, Ens. William E., USNR
THOMPSON, Ens. Lawrence W., USNR
TIFFANY, Ens. Albert R., USNR
ZACHMAN, Ens. George W., USNR
DUNCAN, Robert B., RM3/c, USNR
GIBSON, Frederick L., ARM1/c, USN
HOBAN, William J., ARM1/c, USN
HOGG, Anthony F., ARM2/c, USN
LAZARITES, William R., ARM3/c, USN
PARRENT, James D., ARM1/c, USNR
PERKINS, Rufus C., ARM3/c, USN
RYAN, William H., ARM2/c, USN
SHAFER, Richard, ARM1/c, USN
SWAN, Joseph A., ACRM, USN
WALL, John S., ARM2/c, USN

Bronze Star Medal

McCANDLISH, Commodore Benjamin V,
    USN
BAKER, Capt. Charles A., USN
COMP, Capt. Charles O., USN
DODGE, Capt. Frank R., USN
ERSKINE, Capt. William E. G., USN
    (Ret.)
*GREAVES, Capt. Frederick C., Jr., (MC),
    USN
MAYNARD, Capt. George E., USN
MURDAUGH, Capt. Albert C., USN
RICHARDS, Capt. Frederick G., USN
SCHLESINGER, Capt. Francis R., USMC
SIMPSON, Capt. Eugene P. A., USNR
WALLER, Capt. John B. W., USN

BOIT, Cdr. Julian M., USNR
BOYD, Cdr. Alston M., USN
BOYER, Cdr. Randolph B., USN
DAVEY, Cdr. Thomas L., (CEC), USN
ECKELMEYER, Cdr. Edward H., Jr., USN
*ELLIS, Cdr. Robert B., USN
*FLYNN, Cdr. John F., USN
FORD, Cdr. Henry W., USNR
**HECKEY, Cdr. Albert R., USN
JALBERT, Cdr. Horace H., USNR
*McKAY, Cdr. Baxter M., USN
MOORE, Cdr. Harold C., USCG
MORTON, Cdr. Frank P., USNR
MURPHY, Cdr. John W., USN
RIGLER, Cdr. Frank V., USN (Ret.)
RITTENHOUSE, Cdr. Basil N., USN
SNARE, Cdr. Elmer D., USN
SWANSON, Cdr. Clarence F., USN
VANASSE, Cdr. Roland B., USN
WINTERHALER, Cdr. Emile R., USN
ABBOTT, Lt. Cdr. Paul, USN
BATES, Lt. Cdr. Richard H., USNR
BERG, Lt. Cdr. Martin D., USCGR
CARR, Lt. Cdr. Roy E., USNR
EDWARDS, Lt. Cdr. Lyman M., USNR
EMMONS, Lt. Cdr. Kintzing B., USNR
*FITZGERALD, Lt. Cdr. Gerald S., USNR
FREITAG, Lt. Cdr. George M., USNR
GOERING, Lt. Cdr. Walter E., USNR
GRAHAM, Lt. Cdr. Selwyn H., USN
HANLIN, Lt. Cdr. Paul W., USN
HUBBARD, Lt. Cdr. Arthur L., USNR
*JANNEY, Lt. Cdr. Samuel A., USNR
KAIGLER, Lt. Cdr. David, USNR
*McLELLAN, Lt. Cdr. Hubert M., USNR
PETERSON, Lt. Cdr. Alvin A., USNR
POWERS, Lt. Cdr. Edgar C., USNR
RAMEY, Lt. Cdr. Ralph L., USN
STANFORD, Lt. Cdr. Arthur G., USNR
THAYER, Lt. Cdr. R. H., USNR
WILLIAMS, Lt. Cdr. Artie L., USNR
ZENS, Lt. Cdr. Robert V., USNR
ALLEN, Lt. Ray H., USNR
BEARDSLEY, Lt. Phillip A., USNR
CONNALLY, Lt. Walter B., USNR
DAVIDSON, Lt. Wilbur S., USNR
DILLON, Lt. James J., USNR
EMLEM, Lt. Samuel, III, USNR
ESKESEN, Lt. Bennet H., USNR
FARRIS, Lt. Marvin E., USNR
GIBSON, Lt. Robert G., USN
HAMILTON, Lt. Thomas M., USNR
HARMON, Lt. Leo D., Jr., USNR
HERON, Lt. Richard D., USNR
JACOBS, Lt. Charles S., USNR

*Jenkins, Lt. Robert P., USNR
Jeter, Lt. Max Albert, USNR
Johnson, Lt. Louis E., USNR
Johnson, Lt. R. C., USNR
Joseph, Lt. John M., USCG
Joy, Lt. Richard P., Jr., USNR
Lavin, Lt. Charles C., USNR
Lawson, Lt. Frank B., USNR
Lehan, Lt. John P., USNR
Manning, Lt. Herbert C., USNR
*Osborne, Lt. Carl B., USNR
*Patterson, Lt. Eugene F., USNR
Potts, Lt. Galen L., USNR
Pruett, Lt. Samuel R., USNR
Richardson, Lt. Gerard, USNR
Seaman, Lt. William R., USNR
Spangler, Lt. Wayne E., USNR
Talton, Lt. Wade T., USNR
Tatum, Lt. Thomas Z., USNR
Taylor, Lt. Andrew K., USNR
Watson, Lt. David P. H., USNR
Williams, Lt. Guy R., USNR
Woodriff, Lt. John I., USNR
Babyak, Lt. (jg) Joseph H., USN
Berlin, Lt. (jg) Gerald A., USNR
Brown, Lt. (jg) Edward A., USNR
Connolly, Lt. (jg) Walter Briggs, USNR
Covey, Lt. (jg) Preston K., USNR
Culver, Lt. (jg) L. L., USNR
Davis, Lt. (jg) Thomas M., USNR
Gerson, Lt. (jg) Irving B., USNR
Giles, Lt. (jg) Stuart, USNR
Groesbeck, Lt. (jg) James D., USNR
Jensen, Lt. (jg) Paul A., USNR
Jeter, Lt. (jg) Max A., USNR
Kean, Lt. (jg) Donald T., USNR
McConnell, Lt. (jg) George G., USNR
Mason, Lt. (jg) Edwin L., USNR
New, Lt. (jg) James R., USNR
Noel, Lt. (jg) Henry W., USNR
Padgett, Lt. (jg) Joseph L., USNR
Reilly, Lt. (jg) James J., Jr., USNR
Robinson, Lt. (jg) Charles W., USNR
Rosengarten, Lt. (jg) Richard A., USNR
Sandox, Lt. (jg) Edward, USNR
Shutt, Lt. (jg) J. L., USNR
Sleeper, Lt. (jg) Allan R., USNR

Taylor, Lt. (jg) Henry H., USNR
Abbott, Ens. Harold W., USNR
Barngrover, Ens. Robert G., USNR
Bynum, Ens. Albert A., USNR
Caro, Ens. Harold G., USNR
Esser, Ens. Carl F., USNR
Hon, Ens. Frederick T., USNR
Hurdle, Ens. Willard C., USNR
Klopman, Ens. M. A., USNR
Mullins, Ens. Thomas J. (CEC), USNR
Schaper, Ens. David H., USNR
Scheifley, Ens. Ralph A., USNR
Smith, Ens. John W., Jr., USNR
Sutton, Ens. Robert M., USNR
Adams, Robert H., SM2/c, USNR
Augustin, James H., SF2/c, USNR
Bartels, Walter Otto, Cox., USNR
Bontempo, Emil L., SC3/c, USNR
Bliss, William P., F1/c, USNR
Coolidge, Clinton A., S1/c, USNR
Estes, John C, SF2/c, USNR
Fountain, Glen A., S1/c, USNR
Frazier, Billy J., S1/c, USNR
Gaffney, Lewis K., S1/c, USN
Grant, Charles E., SC1/c, USNR
Henry, George T., S1/c, USNR
Johnson, Donald A., PhM1/c, USNR
Kelly, Joseph G., BM2/c, USN
Kuhn, Joseph H., CY, USNR
Lambert, Robert Lee, S1/c, USNR
Leonoudakis, Nicholas C., MoMM2/c, USNR
Loeffler, Ira J., BM2/c, USNR
McWilliams, Walter C., MoMM1/c, USNR
Moore, Robert J., S1/c, USNR
Murphy, Thomas A., PhM2/c, USNR
Noyes, C. R., Carp., USNR
Oliver, Robert J., QM3/c, USNR
O'Reilly, David, F1/c, USNR
Peterson, Raymond N., S1/c, USNR
Scurlock, Stanley A., SM2/c, USN
Simmons, Claude C., S1/c, USNR
Smith, George W. E., S1/c, USNR
Spalletta, Charles, Cox., USNR
Steinbruegge, Arthur W., EM2/c, USNR
Strausbauch, Lee E., CPhM, USN
Tibbetts, Austin B., PhM1/c, USN

KEY TO ABBREVIATIONS
United States Navy (USN)

	CHIEF	FIRST CLASS	SECOND CLASS	THIRD CLASS
Aerographer's Mate	CAerM	AerM1/c	AerM2/c	AerM3/c
Airship Rigger	CAR	AR1/c	AR2/c	AR2/c
Aviation Machinist's Mate	ACMM	AMM1/c	AMM2/c	AMM3/c
Aviation Metalsmith	ACM	AM1/c	AM2/c	AM3/c
Aviation Ordnanceman	ACOM	AOM1/c	AOM2/c	AOM3/c
Aviation Pilot	CAP	AP1/c	AP2/c	AP3/c
Aviation Radioman	ACRM	ARM1/c	ARM2/c	ARM3/c
Baker		Bkr1/c	Bkr2/c	Bkr3/c
Boatswain's Mate	CBM	BM1/c	BM2/c	BM3/c
Boilermaker	CB	B1/c	B2/c	B3/c
Buglemaster	CBgmstr	Bgmstr1/c	Bgmstr2/c	Bgmstr3/c
Carpenter's Mate	CCM	CM1/c	CM2/c	CM3/c
Chief Commissary Steward	CCStd			
Electrician's Mate	CEM	EM1/c	EM2/c	EM3/c
Fire Controlman	CFC	FC1/c	FC2/c	FC3/c
Gunner's Mate	CGM	GM1/c	GM2/c	GM3/c
Machinist's Mate	CMM	MM1/c	MM2/c	MM3/c
Metalsmith	CM	M1/c	M2/c	M3/c
Mineman	CMN	MN1/c	MN2/c	MN3/c
Molder	CML	ML1/c	ML2/c	ML3/c
Motor Machinist's Mate	CMoMM	MoMM1/c	MoMM2/c	MoMM3/c
Musician	CMus	Mus1/c	Mus2/c	Mus3/c
Officers' Cook	OCC	OC1/c	OC2/c	OC3/c
Officers' Steward	OCS	OS1/c	OS2/c	OS3/c
Painter	CPtr	Ptr1/c	Ptr2/c	Ptr3/c
Parachute Rigger	CPR	PR1/c	PR2/c	PR3/c
Patternmaker	CPM	PM1/c	PM2/c	PM3c
Pharmacist's Mate	CPhM	PhM1/c	PhM2/c	PhM3/c
Photographer's Mate	CPhoM	PhoM1/c	PhoM2/c	PhoM3/c
Printer	CPrtr	Prtr1/c	Prtr2/c	Prtr3/c
Quartermaster	CQM	QM1/c	QM2/c	QM3/c
Radarman	CRdM	RdM1/c	RdM2/c	RdM3/c
Radioman	CRM	RM1/c	RM2/c.	RM3/c
Radio Technician	CRT	RT1/c	RT2/c	RT3/c
Shipfitter	CSF	SF1/c	SF2/c	SF3/c
Ship's Cook		SC1/c	SC2/c	SC3/c
Ship's Service Man	CSSM	SSM1/c	SSM2/c	SSM3/c
Signalman	CSM	SM1/c	SM2/c	SM3/c
Sonarman	CSoM	SoM1/c	SoM2/c	SoM3/c
Special Artificer	CSA	SA1/c	SA2/c	SA3/c
Specialist	CSp	Sp1/c	Sp2/c	Sp3/c
Storekeeper	CSK	SK1/c	SK2/c	SK3/c
Telegrapher	CT	T1/c	T2/c	T3/c

(*Continued on page 546*)

	CHIEF	FIRST CLASS	SECOND CLASS	THIRD CLASS
Torpedoman's Mate	CTM	TM1/c	TM2/c	TM3/c
Turret Captain	CTC	TC1/c		
Water Tender	CWT	WT1/c	WT2/c	WT3/c
Yeoman	CY	Y1/c	Y2/c	Y3/c
Boatswain	Boat.			
Chief Boatswain	Chief Boat.			
Chief Carpenter	Chief Carp.			
Coxswain	Cox.			
Electrician	Elect.			
Machinist	Mach.			
Naval Air Pilot	NAP			
Torpedoman	Torp.			
Acting Appointment	AA			
Chaplain Corps	ChC			
Civil Engineer Corps	CEC			
Dental Corps	DC			
Medical Corps	MC			
Nurse Corps	NC			
Supply Corps	SC			

NON-RATED MEN	FIRST CLASS	SECOND CLASS	THIRD CLASS
Hospital Apprentice	HA1/c,	HA2/c	
Fireman	F1/c	F2/c	F3/c
Bugler	Bug1/c	Bug2/c	
Mess Attendant	MA1/c	MA2/c	MA3/c
Seaman	S1/c	S2/c	AS

United States Marine Corp (USMC)

Staff Sergeant	S/Sgt.
Technical Sergeant	Tech. Sgt.
Sergeant	Sgt.
Corporal	Corp.
Private, First Class	PFC
Private	Pvt.

Index

547